THE
IRONY
of
DEMOCRACY

*An Uncommon Introduction
to American Politics*

MILLENNIAL EDITION

THE
IRONY
of
DEMOCRACY

*An Uncommon Introduction
to American Politics*

MILLENNIAL EDITION

THOMAS R. DYE

HARMON ZEIGLER

HARCOURT BRACE COLLEGE PUBLISHERS

Fort Worth   Philadelphia   San Diego   New York   Orlando   Austin   San Antonio
Toronto   Montreal   London   Sydney   Tokyo

Publisher	EARL MCPEEK
Executive Editor	DAVID C. TATOM
Market Strategist	STEVE DRUMMOND
Project Editor	JOYCE FINK
Art Director	BURL SLOAN
Production Manager	LINDA MCMILLAN

ISBN: 0-15-505800-2
Library of Congress Catalog Card Number: 98-89811

Portions of this work were published in previous editions.

Address for Domestic Orders
Harcourt Brace College Publishers, 6277 Sea Harbor Drive, Orlando, FL 32887-6777
800-782-4479

Address for International Orders
International Customer Service
Harcourt Brace & Company, 6277 Sea Harbor Drive, Orlando, FL 32887-6777
407-345-3800
(fax) 407-345-4060
(e-mail) hbintl@harcourtbrace.com

Address for Editorial Correspondence
Harcourt Brace College Publishers, 301 Commerce Street, Suite 3700, Fort Worth, TX 76102

Web Site Address
http://www.hbcollege.com

Harcourt Brace College Publishers will provide complimentary supplements or supplement packages to
those adopters qualified under our adoption policy. Please contact your sales representative to learn how
you qualify. If as an adopter or potential user you receive supplements you do not need, please return them
to your sales representative or send them to: Attn:
Returns Department, Troy Warehouse, 465 South Lincoln Drive, Troy, MO 63379.

Printed in the United States of America

0 1 2 3 4 5 6 7 8   016   9 8 7 6 5 4 3

Harcourt Brace College Publishers

CONTENTS

TO THE STUDENT

In asking you to read this book, your instructor wants to do more than teach about "the nuts and bolts" of American government. This book has a theme: only a tiny handful of people make decisions that shape the lives of all of us and, despite the elaborate rituals of parties, elections, and interest group activity, we have little direct influence over these decisions. This theme is widely known as *elitism.* Your instructor may not believe completely in this theory but may instead believe that many groups of people share power in the United States, that competition is widespread, that we have checks against the abuse of power, and that the individual citizen can personally affect the course of national events by voting, supporting political parties, and joining interest groups. This theory, widely known as *pluralism,* characterizes virtually every American government textbook now in print—except this one. Your instructor, whether personally agreeing with the elitist or with the pluralist perspective, is challenging you to confront our arguments. Rather, he or she wants you to deal thoughtfully with some troubling questions about democracy in the United States.

It is far easier to teach "the nuts and bolts" of American government—the constitutional powers of the president, Congress, and courts; the function of parties and interest groups; the key cases decided by the Supreme Court; and so on—than to tackle the question, "How democratic is American society?" It is easier to teach the "facts" of American government than to search for their explanations. Although this book does not ignore such facts, its primary purpose is to interpret them—to help you understand why our government works as it does.

The Irony of Democracy is not necessarily "antiestablishment." This book challenges the prevailing pluralistic view of democracy in the United States, but it neither condemns nor endorses American political life. Governance of the United States by a small, homogeneous elite is subject to favorable or unfavorable interpretation, according to one's personal values. Each reader is free to decide whether we as a society should preserve, reform, or restructure the political system described in these pages.

The Irony of Democracy is neither a conservative nor a liberal textbook. It does not apologize for elite rule or seek to defend American institutions or leaders. On the contrary, we are very critical of politicians, bureaucrats, corporate chieftains, media moguls, lawyers, lobbyists, and special interests. But we do not advocate fruitless liberal nostrums promising to bring "power to the people," or "citizen movements" that are themselves led by elites with their own self-interests.

The Irony of Democracy is indeed an endorsement of democratic values—individual dignity, limited government, freedom of expression and dissent, equality of opportunity, private property, and due process of law. Our elitist theory of democracy is not an attack on democratic government, but rather an effort to understand the realities of politics in a democracy.

TO THE INSTRUCTOR

The Millennial Edition of *The Irony of Democracy* continues its classic theme—elitism in a democratic society. Despite the near-universal acceptance of pluralist ideology in American political science and American government textbooks, we remain unrepentant. *The Irony of Democracy* remains an *elitist* introduction to American government.

This is a textbook that will challenge your students to rethink everything they have been taught about American democracy—it is a book of ideas, not just facts.

Elite theory is contrasted to democratic theory and to modern pluralist political theory throughout the book, in examining the U.S. Constitution, American political history, power structures, public opinion, mass media, elections, parties, interest groups, the presidency, Congress, the bureaucracy, the courts, federalism, protest movements, and public policy.

Elite theory is employed as an analytic model for understanding and explaining American politics; it is *not* presented as a recommendation or prescription for America.

Is the government "run for the benefit of all of the people" or "by a few big interests looking out for the themselves"? Thirty years ago, when *The Irony of Democracy* was first written, a majority of Americans believed that their government was being run for the benefit of all; the elitist view was expressed by relatively few people. Today an astounding 80 percent of Americans believe that their government is run "by a few big interests looking out for themselves." The elitist perspective, which we developed as an analytic model of American politics, has now become part of the popular political culture!

Elites have only themselves to blame for mass distrust and cynicism. We take no great pleasure in observing that the mass public has come to share our view of the American political system.

On the contrary, we have become increasingly disenchanted over the years with narrow, self-serving elite behavior. Our elitist theory of democracy has always recognized the potential for danger in mass movements led by extremist and intolerant demagogues. But over the years we have become convinced that the principal threat to democracy in the United States today arises from irresponsible elites seeking relative advantage at the expense of shared societal values. We have always been critical of governmental, corporate, media, and interest group elites; however, we now believe that shortsighted and self-serving elite behavior has become so endemic that it threatens the fabric of the American economy and polity.

This Millennial Edition of *The Irony of Democracy* is the most extensive revision of the text since its first publication in 1969. This revision reflects, first of all, our *increasing distress over current elite distemper*—corporate greed, media arrogance, interest group gluttony, big money political influence, and, above all, the self-serving and shortsighted behavior of today's governmental leaders. And this revision also reflects a new emphasis on *teaching students to think critically about politics and public affairs.*

The Millennial Edition is more critical of America's elite, more "anti-establishment," than earlier editions, and for good reason. We have rewritten Chapter 4 "Elites in America" to describe the increasingly voracious and predatory nature of global corporations, the growing arrogance of the rich and powerful, and the increasing isolation of elites from the concerns and troubles of the masses of Americans. We provide special Focus features on such topics as "Corporate Merger Mania," "Greed in the Boardroom," "Elite Disregard of Mass Opinion," "The Hollywood Liberals," "The Business Roundtable," "The Clinton Money Chase," "Bureaucratic Maneuvers," "Is 'Congressional Ethics' an Oxymoron?," and "Presidential Sex, Lies, and Impeachment." Yet we continue in the elitist tradition to be skeptical of mass governance.

We have rewritten Chapter 5 "Masses in America" to describe the decline in real wages of working Americans, the widening gap between rich and poor, and the resulting disaffection of the masses from democratic politics. The masses in America are increasingly distrustful, cynical, and disengaged from public affairs; they view governmental and corporate elites alike as uncaring, unresponsive, and unaccountable. Yet even if the masses were to shed their ignorance and apathy and turn to political action, we believe the result would be intolerance rather than compassion, racism rather than brotherhood, authoritarianism rather than democracy.

The Millennial Edition is also more critical of the current functioning of our political institutions. A rewritten Chapter 8 "Elections, Money, and the Myths of Democracy" argues that elections are designed primarily to convince the masses that government is legitimate; that, in fact, voters have little real impact on the direction of public policy; and that big money drives the electoral system. The American two-party system is described in

Chapter 7 as "A System In Decay," and the interest group system is described in Chapter 9 as biased, distorted, and unrepresentative of the interests of most individual Americans.

The institutions of American government—Congress, the presidency, the bureaucracy, and courts—are even more critically scrutinized in this Millennial Edition. It is not only the sordid tale of "Presidential Sex, Lies, and Impeachment" on which we base our critical assessment, or even the "Ambition and Ambivalence" of the Clinton presidency. It is also the sanctimonious, self-serving, and arrogant behavior of members of Congress, federal bureaucrats, and federal judges.

Finally, the Millennial Edition includes a larger number of timely and relevant Focus features designed to stimulate students' interest and discussion. These features are deliberately provocative, opinionated, and controversial. We want to challenge "The Unpolitics of College Students" by inviting them to argue over such topics as "Mass Distrust of America's Elite," "Elite Disregard of Mass Opinion," "What If the People Voted on National Issues?," "Mass Perceptions of the Parties," "Bill Clinton, Creating a Winning Image," "Evaluating Presidential Character," "Mass Attitudes toward Washington Bureaucracies," "Regulation—Hiding the Costs of Government," "Senate Confirmation as Sleazy Spectacle," "The Supreme Court and Abortion," "Elites, Masses, and Sexual Harassment," and "The Elite Think Tanks."

Moreover, throughout the text we have attempted to simplify our descriptions of elitism, pluralism, and democracy. We do so not by "dumbing down" our discussions, but by clarifying our theoretical premises, especially in Chapter 1, where we provide a diagram contrasting the theories of elitism and pluralism. Our Epilogue is directed at students. It does not offer platitudinous clichés about citizenship, but rather realistic advice about what young people might do to help preserve democratic values in an elitist system.

Thomas R. Dye
Harmon Zeigler

ACKNOWLEDGMENTS

We offer our thanks to the people who reviewed the book in preparation for this Millennial Edition:

Stephanie L. Bressler	King's College
John Buckley	Orange Coast College
Gerald R. Farrington	Fresno City College
Ted Radke	Contra Costa College
Gregory H. Tilles	Diablo Valley College
John Whitney	Lincoln Land Community College

DEDICATION

Harmon Zeigler acknowledges the friendship and inspiration of Phillip M. Phibbs, Thomas R. Dye, Bob Gormley and Father Mike O'Neil.

1

The Irony of Democracy

Government is always government by the few,
whether in the name of the few, the one, or the many.
—HAROLD LASSWELL

Elites—not masses—govern the United States. Life in a democracy, as in all societies, is shaped by a handful of people. Major political, economic, and social decisions are made by tiny minorities, not the masses of people.

Elites are the few who have power; the *masses* are the many who do not. Power is deciding who gets what, when, and how; it is participation in the decisions that shape our lives; the masses are the many whose lives are shaped by institutions, events, and leaders over which they have little direct control. Political scientist Harold Lasswell writes, "The division of society into elite and mass is universal," and even in a democracy "a few exercise a relatively great weight of power, and the many exercise comparatively little."[1]

Democracy is government "by the people," but the survival of democracy rests on the shoulders of elites. This is the irony of democracy: elites must govern wisely if government "by the people" is to survive. The masses do not lead; they follow. They respond to the attitudes, proposals, and behavior of elites.

This book, *The Irony of Democracy,* explains American political life using elite theory. It presents the evidence of U.S. political history and contemporary political science to describe and explain how elites function in a modern democratic society. But before we examine American politics we must understand more about *elitism, democracy,* and *pluralism.*

THE MEANING OF ELITISM

The central idea of elitism is that all societies are divided into two classes: the few who govern and the many who are governed. The Italian political scientist Gaetano Mosca expressed this basic concept as follows:

> *In all societies—from societies that are very underdeveloped and have largely attained the dawnings of civilization, down to the most advanced and powerful societies—two classes of people appear—a class that rules and a class that is ruled. The first class, always the less numerous, performs all of the political functions, monopolizes power, and enjoys the advantages that power brings, whereas the second, the more numerous class, is directed and controlled by the first, in a manner that is now more or less legal, now more or less arbitrary and violent.*[2]

Elites, not masses, govern *all* societies. Elites are not a product of capitalism or socialism or industrialization or technological development. All societies—socialist and capitalist, agricultural and industrial, traditional and advanced—are governed by elites. All societies require leaders, and leaders acquire a stake in preserving the organization and their position in it. This motive gives leaders a perspective different from that of the organization's members. An elite, then, is inevitable in any social organization. As French political scientist Roberto Michels put it nearly a century ago, "He who says organization, says oligarchy."[3] The same is true for societies as a whole. According to the distinguished American political scientist Harold Lasswell, "The discovery that in all large-scale societies the decisions at any given time are typically in the hands of a small number of people" confirms a basic fact: "Government is always government by the few, whether in the name of the few, the one, or the many."[4]

Elitism also asserts that the few who govern are not typical of the masses who are governed. Elites control resources: power, wealth, education, prestige, status, skills of leadership, information, knowledge of political processes, ability to communicate, and organization. Elites in the United States are drawn disproportionately from wealthy, educated, prestigiously employed, socially prominent, white, Anglo-Saxon, and Protestant groups in society. They come from society's upper classes, those who own or control a disproportionate share of the societal institutions: industry, commerce, finance, education, the military, communications, civic organizations, and law.

Elitism, however, does not necessarily bar individuals of the lower classes from rising to the top. In fact, a certain amount of "circulation of elites" (upward mobility) is essential for the stability of the elite system. Openness in the system siphons off potentially revolutionary leadership from the lower classes; moreover, an elite system is strengthened when talented and ambitious individuals from the masses enter governing circles. However, social stability requires that movement from nonelite to elite positions be a slow, continuous assimilation rather than a rapid or revolutionary change. Only those nonelites who have demonstrated their commitment to the elite system itself and to the system's political and economic values can be admitted to the ruling class.

Elites share a general consensus about the fundamental norms of the social system. They agree on the basic rules of the game, as well as on the importance of preserving the social system. The stability of the system, and even its survival, depends on this consensus. Political scientist David Truman writes, "Being more influential, they [the elites] are privileged; and being privileged, they have, with very few exceptions, a special stake in the continuation of the system in which their privileges rest."[5] However, elite consensus does not prevent elite members from disagreeing or competing with each other for preeminence. But this competition takes place within a very narrow range of issues; elites agree on more matters than they disagree on. Disagreement usually occurs over *means* rather than *ends*.

In the United States, the bases of elite consensus are the sanctity of private property, limited government, and individual liberty. Political historian Richard Hofstadter writes about American elite struggles:

> *The fierceness of political struggles has often been misleading; for the range of vision embodied by the primary contestants in the major parties has always been bounded by the horizons of property and enterprise. However much at odds on specific issues, the major political traditions have shared a belief in the rights of property, the philosophy of economic individualism, the value of competition; they have accepted the economic virtues of capitalist culture as necessary qualities of man.*[6]

Elitism implies that public policy does not reflect demands of "the people" so much as it reflects the interests and values of elites. Changes and innovations in public policy come about when elites redefine their own values. However, the general conservatism of elites—that is, their interest in preserving the system—means that changes in public policy will be *incremental* rather than revolutionary. Public policies are often modified but seldom replaced.

Elites may act out of narrow self-serving interests or enlightened, "public-regarding" motives. Occasionally elites abuse their powers and position and undermine mass confidence in their leadership. At other times, elites initiate reforms designed to preserve the system and restore mass support. Elitism does not necessarily mean that the masses are exploited or repressed, although these abuses are not uncommon. Elitism means only that the responsibility for mass welfare rests with elites, not with masses.

Finally, elitism assumes that the masses are largely passive, apathetic, and ill informed. Mass sentiments are manipulated by elites more often than elite values are influenced by the sentiments of the masses. Most communication between elites and masses flows downward. Masses seldom make decisions about governmental policies through elections or through evaluation of political parties' policy alternatives. For the most part, these "democratic" institutions—elections and parties—have only symbolic value: they help tie the masses to the political system by giving them a role to play on election day. Elitism contends that the masses have at best only an indirect influence over the decision-making behavior of elites.

In brief, elite theory may be summarized as follows:

★ Society is divided into the few who have power and the many who do not.

★ The few who govern are not typical of the masses who are governed. Elites are drawn disproportionately from the upper socioeconomic strata of society.

★ The movement of nonelites to elite positions must be slow and continuous to maintain stability and avoid revolution. Only nonelites who have accepted the basic elite consensus enter governing circles.

★ Elites share a consensus on the basic values of the social system and the preservation of the system. They disagree only on a narrow range of issues.

★ Public policy does not reflect the demands of masses but the prevailing values of the elite. Changes in public policy will be incremental rather than revolutionary.

★ Elites may act out of narrow self-serving motives and risk undermining mass support, or they may initiate reforms, curb abuse, and undertake public-regarding programs to preserve the system and their place in it.

★ Active elites are subject to relatively little direct influence from the apathetic masses. Elites influence masses more than masses influence elites.

THE MEANING OF DEMOCRACY

Ideally, *democracy* means individual participation in the decisions that affect one's life. Traditional democratic theory has valued popular participation as an opportunity for individual self-development: responsibility for governing one's own conduct develops one's character, self-reliance, intelligence, and moral judgment—in short, one's dignity. The classic democrat would reject even a benevolent despot who could govern in the interest of the masses. As the English political philosopher J. S. Mill asked, "What development can either their thinking or active faculties attain under it?" Thus the argument for citizen participation in public affairs depends not on its policy outcomes but on the belief that such involvement is essential to the full development of human capacities. Mill argued that people can know truth only by discovering it for themselves.[7]

Procedurally, in the democratic model, a society achieves popular participation through majority rule and respect for the rights of minorities. Self-development presumes self-government, and self-government comes about only by encouraging each individual to contribute to the development of public policy and by resolving conflicts over public policy through majority rule. Minorities who have had the opportunity to influence policy but whose views have not won majority support accept the decisions of majorities. In return, majorities permit minorities to attempt openly to win majority support for their views. Freedom of speech and press, freedom to dissent, and freedom to form opposition parties and organizations are essential to ensure meaningful individual participation. This freedom of expression is also critical in ascertaining the majority's real views.

The underlying value of democracy is individual dignity. Human beings, by virtue of their existence, are entitled to life, liberty, and property. A "natural law," or moral tenet, guarantees every person liberty and the right to property, and this natural law is morally superior to human law. John Locke, the English political philosopher whose writings most influenced America's founding elites, argued that even in a "state of nature"—that is, a world of no governments—an individual possesses inalienable rights to life, liberty, and property. Locke meant that these rights are independent of government;

governments do not give them to individuals, and no government may legitimately take them away.[8]

Locke believed that a government's purpose is to protect individual liberty. People form a "social contract" with one another to establish a government to help protect their rights; they tacitly agree to accept government authority to protect life, liberty, and property. Implicit in the social contract and the democratic notion of freedom is the belief that governmental authority and social control over the individual must be minimal. This belief calls for removing as many external restrictions, controls, and regulations on the individual as possible without violating the freedom of other citizens.

Another vital aspect of classical democracy is a belief in the equality of all people. The Declaration of Independence states that "all men are created equal." Even the Founding Fathers believed in equality for all persons *before the law,* regardless of their personal circumstances. A democratic society cannot judge a person by social position, economic class, creed, or race. Many early democrats also believed in *political equality:* equal opportunity of individuals to influence public policy. Political equality is expressed in the concept of "one person, one vote."

Over time, the notion of equality has also come to include *equality of opportunity* in all aspects of American life: social, educational, and economic, as well as political. Each person should have an equal opportunity to develop his or her capacities to the fullest potential. There should be no artificial barriers to success in life. All persons should have the opportunity to make of themselves what they can, to develop their talents and abilities to their fullest, and to be rewarded for their skills, knowledge, initiative, and hard work. However, the traditional democratic creed has always stressed *equality of opportunity*, not *absolute equality.* Thomas Jefferson recognized a "natural aristocracy" of talent, ambition, and industry, and liberal democrats since Jefferson have always accepted inequalities that arise from individual merit and hard work. Absolute equality, or "leveling," is not part of liberal democratic theory.

In summary, democratic thinking reflects the following ideas:

★ Popular participation in the decisions that shape the lives of individuals in a society.

★ Government by majority rule, with recognition of the rights of minorities to try to become majorities. These rights include the freedom of speech, press, assembly, and petition and the freedom to dissent, to form opposition parties, and to run for public office.

★ A commitment to individual dignity and the preservation of the liberal values of life, liberty, and property.

★ A commitment to equal opportunity for all individuals to develop their capacities.

ELITISM IN A DEMOCRACY

Democracy requires popular participation in government. (The Greek root of the word *democracy* means "rule by the many.") But popular participation in government can have different meanings. To our nation's Founders, who were quite ambivalent about the wisdom of democracy, it meant that the people would be given representation in government. The Founders believed that government rests ultimately on the *consent* of the governed. But their notion of republicanism envisioned decision making by *representatives* of the people, rather than direct decision making by the people themselves. The Founders were profoundly skeptical of direct democracy, in which the people initiate and decide policy questions by popular vote. They had read about direct democracy in the ancient Greek city-state of Athens, and they were fearful of the "follies" of democracy. James Madison wrote,

> *Such democracies have ever been spectacles of turbulence and contention; have ever been found incompatible with personal security of the rights of property and have in general been as short in their lives as they have been violent in their deaths.*[9]

The Fear of Direct Democracy

The Founders were most fearful that unrestrained *majorities* would threaten liberty and property and abuse minorities and individuals, "the weaker party and the obnoxious individual." They recognized the potential contradiction in democratic theory—government by majority rule can threaten the life, liberty, and property of minorities and individuals.

Thus, *the U.S. Constitution has no provision for national referenda.* It was not until 100 years after the Constitution was written that political support developed in some states for more direct involvement of citizens in policy making. The beginning of the twentieth century, populists in the farm states of the Midwest and the mining states of the West introduced the initiative and referendum.

FOCUS

Mass Distrust of America's Elite

How much trust do the masses have in America's leadership? Is a "crisis of authority" confronting America's elite?

Elites have always been concerned about the possibility of mass disaffection and the opportunities that such disaffection might present for demagogues and revolutionaries. The Constitutional Convention of 1787 was inspired in part by Shays' Rebellion and the concern that the Revolutionary War had unleashed mass hostility toward established authority. John Adams worried about a general crisis in authority following the revolt against the British Crown:

> We have been told that our struggle has loosened the bonds of government everywhere, that children and apprentices were disobedient, that schools and college were grown turbulent, that Indians slighted their guardians, and negroes grew insolent to their masters. . . . [Now we have the] intimation that another tribe [women], more numerous and powerful than all the rest, were grown discontent.[a]

A major concern of the nation's elite throughout the 1960s and 1970s was the decline of mass trust in national leadership. Public opinion polls showed that fewer and fewer people were willing to "trust the government in Washington to do what is right" (see the figure).

Defeat and humiliation in war always and everywhere undermines mass support for a nation's leadership. Perhaps the most important negative influence on mass confidence in America's elite was the experience of the Vietnam War. This tragic war was followed immediately by the Watergate scandal and the first forced resignation of a president. President Carter did little to reverse the decline in mass confidence; America's humiliation by Iranian revolutionaries who took U.S. embassy personnel as hostages produced the nadir of confidence in 1980.

The long-term effect of negative media reporting—of world events and of political, military, and business leadership—is to increase social distrust and political cynicism (see Chapter 6). Television in particular has lowered general levels of trust and confidence. Because the strongest bias in network news reporting is toward conflict and controversy, scandal and corruption—bad news drives out the good news—it is unlikely in the media age that mass confidence in American institutions and leadership can ever be restored to previous high levels.

Yet clearly mass trust can be increased. No doubt the relative peace and prosperity of the 1980s made improvement possible. But the personality of Ronald Reagan and his calculated efforts to restore optimism, pride, and patriotism had a profound effect on Americans. It is somewhat ironic that Ronald Reagan, a conservative critic of big government, helped to partially restore public confidence in "the government in Washington." But the spurt proved to be transient. Although the Gulf War in early 1991 produced the usual "rally 'round the flag" effect, mass trust in government declined again as economic recession settled over the nation.

Public trust in government has risen slightly in recent years, probably as a result of improved economic conditions. Yet mass trust remains low by historic standards.

What does it matter whether the masses trust their political leaders? It is likely that mass distrust and cynicism toward politics and government contributes to a weakening of political party affiliations (see Chapter 7), low voter turnouts, opposition to taxation, and the prevalence of anti-Washington themes in political campaigns (see Chapter 8). But perhaps more importantly, mass disaffection from national leadership underlies much of the political immobility, or "gridlock," confronting the national government—its inability to deal effectively with pressing national issues. When trust in leadership is high, leaders have greater flexibility in dealing with national issues. They enjoy a reserve of mass

Mass support for American government

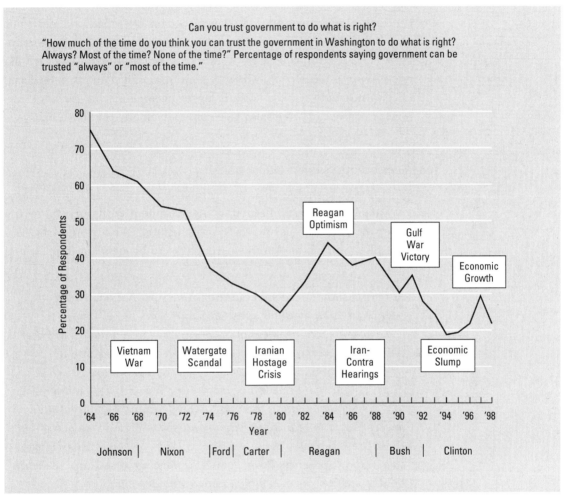

Can you trust government to do what is right?

"How much of the time do you think you can trust the government in Washington to do what is right? Always? Most of the time? None of the time?" Percentage of respondents saying government can be trusted "always" or "most of the time."

Source: Prepared by the authors from National Election Surveys, University of Michigan, data. 1994 figure from *Time*/CNN poll reported in *Time* (September 26, 1994): 49.

confidence, enabling them to call upon citizens to make short-term sacrifices in pursuit of long-term national goals. But when trust is low, leaders are pressured to make shortsighted decisions, seeking immediate mass gratification, often at the expense of the nation's future well-being.

[a]Charles Francis Adams, ed., *Letters of John Adams*, vol. 1 (Boston: Charles C. L. Little and James Brown, 1841), pp. 96–97; cited in Seymour Martin Lipset and William Schneider, *The Confidence Gap* (New York: Free Press, 1988).

Today only voters in the *states* can express their frustrations with elite governance directly. The *initiative* is a device whereby a specific number or percent of voters, through the use of a petition, may have a proposed state constitutional amendment or a state law placed on the ballot for adoption or rejection by the electorate of a state. This process bypasses the legislature and allows citizens to propose both laws and constitutional amendments. The *referendum* is a device by which the electorate must approve decisions of the legislature before these become law or become part of the state constitution, or approve of proposals placed on the ballot by popular initiative.[10]

The Impracticality of Direct Democracy

Yet even if it were desirable, mass government is not really feasible in a large society. Lincoln's rhetorical flourish—"a government of the people, by the people, for the people"—has no real-world meaning. What would "the people" look like if all of the American people were brought together in one place?

> *Standing shoulder to shoulder in military formation, they would occupy an area of about sixty-six square miles.*
>
> *The logistical problem of bringing 250 million bodies together is trivial, however, compared with the task of bringing about a meeting of 250 million minds. Merely to shake hands with that many people would take a century. How much discussion would it take to form a common opinion? A single round of five-minute speeches would require five thousand years. If only one percent of those present spoke, the assembly would be forced to listen to over two million speeches. People could be born, grow old and die while they waited for the assembly to make one decision.*
>
> *In other words, an all-American town meeting would be the largest, longest, and most boring and frustrating meeting imaginable. What could such a meeting produce? Total paralysis. What could it do? Nothing.[11]*

Representative Democracy and the Inevitability of Elites

The solution to the practical problem of popular government is the development of institutions of representation—elections, parties, organized interest

Reprinted with special permission of North America Syndicate.

groups—as bridges between individuals and their government. *But this solution leads inevitably to elitism, not democracy.*

Individuals in all societies, including democracies, confront the iron law of oligarchy. As organizations and institutions develop in society, power is concentrated in the hands of the leadership. Society becomes "a minority of directors and a majority of directed." Individuals are no match for the power of large institutions.

Power is the ability to influence people and events by granting or withholding valuable resources. To exercise power, one must control valuable resources. Resources are defined broadly to include not only wealth, but also position, status, celebrity, comfort, safety, and power itself. Most of the nation's resources are concentrated in large organizations and institutions—in corporations, banks, and financial institutions; in television networks, newspapers, and publishing empires; in organized interest groups, lobbies, and law firms; in foundations and think tanks; in civic and cultural organizations; and, most important, in government. The government is the most powerful of all these organizations, not only because it has accumulated great economic resources, but because it has a monopoly on physical coercion. Only government can legitimately imprison and execute people.

Elite Competition as the Basis of Democracy

In a democratic society, unlike a totalitarian one, multiple elites exist. A defining characteristic of Western democratic nations is the *relative autonomy* of various elites—governmental, economic, media, civic, cultural, and so on.[12] In contrast, a defining characteristic of totalitarian societies is the forced imposition of unity on elites. Fascism asserted the unity of the state in Hitler's words: "Ein Volk, Ein Reich, Ein Fuhrer" (one people, one state, one leader). Socialism asserts the government's control of economic as well as political resources, and communism extols "the dictatorship of the proletariat" and assigns the Communist party the exclusive right to speak for the proletariat.

But in Western democracies, elites have *multiple institutional bases* of power. Not all power is lodged in government, nor is all power derived from wealth. Democracies legitimize the existence of opposition parties as well as of organized interest groups. The power and independence of a media elite is a distinctive feature of U.S. democracy. Even within U.S. government, relatively autonomous multiple elites have emerged—in the Congress; in the judiciary; in the executive; and even within the executive, in a variety of bureaucratic domains. But it is really the power and autonomy of nongovernmental elites, and their recognized legitimacy, that distinguishes the elite structures of democratic nations from those of totalitarian states.

THE MEANING OF PLURALISM

No scholar or commentator, however optimistic about life in the United States, would assert that the U.S. political system has fully realized all the goals of democracy. No one contends that citizens participate in all decisions shaping their lives or that majority preferences always prevail. Nor does anyone argue that the system always protects the rights of minorities, always preserves the values of life, liberty, and property, or provides every American with an equal opportunity to influence public policy.

However, *pluralism* seeks to affirm that American society is neverthe-less democratic by asserting that:

★ Society is divided into numerous groups, all of which make demands upon government and none of which dominates decision making.

★ Although citizens do not directly participate in decision making, their many leaders make decisions through a process of bargaining, accommodation, and compromise.

★ Competition among leadership groups helps protect individuals' interests. Countervailing centers of power—for example, competition among business leaders, labor leaders, and government leaders—can check one another and keep each interest from abusing its power and oppressing the individual.

★ Although individuals do not participate directly in decision making, they can exert influence through participating in organized groups, as well as parties and elections.

★ Leadership groups are open; new groups can form and gain access to the political system.

★ Although political influence in society is unequally distributed, power is widely dispersed. Access to decision making is often determined by how much interest people have in a particular decision. Because leadership is fluid and mobile, power depends on one's interest in public affairs, skills in leadership, information about issues, knowledge of democratic processes, and skill in organization and public relations.

★ Multiple leadership groups operate within society. Those who exercise power in one kind of decision do not necessarily exercise power in others. No single elite dominates decision making in all issues.

★ Public policy does not necessarily reflect majority preference but is an equilibrium of interest interaction—that is, competing interest group influences are more or less balanced, and the resulting policy is therefore a reasonable approximation of society's preferences.

Pluralism, then, is the belief that democratic values can be preserved in a system where multiple, competing elites determine public policy through bargaining and compromise, voters exercise meaningful choices in elections, and new elites can gain access to power.

HOW ELITISM AND PLURALISM DIFFER

Elite theory differs from the prevailing pluralist vision of democracy in several key respects. Both theories agree that societal decision making occurs through elite interaction, not mass participation; that the key political actors are the leaders of large organizations and institutions, not individual citizens; and that public policy generally reflects the interests of large organizations and institutions, not majority preferences. Indeed, because of these similarities, some critics of pluralism assert that it is really a disguised form of elitism—that is, elitism hiding in democratic rhetoric.[13] Yet despite these recognized parallels with pluralist theory, elite theory offers a fundamentally different view of power and society.

First of all, elite theory asserts that the most important division in society is between elites and masses, between the few who govern and the many who do not. Elites in all organizations and institutions in society share a common experience—the exercise of power. Occupying positions of power provides elites with a common motive—the preservation of their organization and their position in it. Pluralism overlooks this central division of society into elites and masses and emphasizes the fragmentation of society and competition between leadership groups. Elitism emphasizes the importance to leaders of maintaining their positions of power, while pluralism emphasizes their devotion to their group interests.

Elite theory asserts that the mass membership of organizations, parties, interest groups, and institutions in society rarely exercises any direct control over the elite leadership. Group membership does *not* ensure effective individual participation in decision making. Rarely do corporations, unions, armies, churches, governmental bureaucracies, or professional associations have any internal democratic mechanisms. They are usually run by a small elite of officers and activists. Leaders of corporations, banks, labor unions, interest groups, television networks, churches, universities, think tanks, and civic associations remain in control year after year. Very few people attend meetings, vote in organizational elections, or make their influence felt within their organization. The pluralists offer no evidence that the giant organizations and institutions in American life really represent the views or interests of their individual members.

Elite theory suggests that accommodation and compromise among leadership groups is the prevailing style of decision making, not competition and conflict. Pluralism contends that competition among leadership groups protects the individual. But why should we assume that leadership groups compete with each other? More likely, each elite group allows other elite groups to govern in their own spheres of influence without interference. According to elite theory, accommodation rather than competition is the prevailing style of elite interaction: "You scratch my back and I'll scratch yours." Where interests occasionally overlap, elite differences are compromised in order to maintain stability. It is true that multiple, relatively autonomous elites exist in a democratic society; but this multiplicity does not guarantee competition or a balance among centers of power.

Elite theory takes account of *all* power holders in society, private as well as public. Pluralism focuses on governmental leaders and those who interact directly with them. Because governmental leaders are chosen in elections, pluralism asserts that leaders can be held accountable to the people. But even if governmental elites can be held accountable through elections, how can corporation executives, media elites, union leaders, and other persons in positions of private leadership be held accountable? Pluralism usually dodges this important question by focusing primary attention on *public*, government-elite decision making and largely ignoring *private*, nongovernment-elite decision making.

Elitism emphasizes the shared characteristics of leaders, not only their common interest in preserving the social system and their place in it, but also their many shared experiences, values, and goals. Pluralism emphasizes diversity among leaders—differences in backgrounds, ideologies, and viewpoints. Even when elitists show that a disproportionate share of America's leadership is composed of wealthy, educated, prestigiously employed, white, upper- and upper-middle-class males, pluralists respond by asserting that these background characteristics are poor predictors of the decision-making behavior of leaders. Instead, pluralists argue that leaders' decisions are a product of their role perceptions, institutional constraints, interest group pressures, public opinion, and so on. Elitism focuses on leadership consensus, asserting that elites differ more over the means than the ends of public policy. Pluralism focuses on elite conflict, asserting that elites differ on a wide variety of issues of vital importance to society.

Pluralism and elitism also differ over the nature and extent of mass influences over societal decision making. Elitism asserts that elites influence masses more than masses influence elites. Communication flows primarily downward from elites to masses. An enlightened elite may choose to consider the well-being of the masses in decision making, either out of ethical principles or a desire to avoid instability and revolution. But even when elites presume to act in the interests of the masses, the elites act on their *own* view of what is good for the masses, not what the masses decide for themselves. In contrast, pluralists, while acknowledging that elites rather than the masses make society's decisions, nonetheless assert that the masses influence policy through both their membership in organized interest groups and their participation in elections. Interest groups, parties, and elections, according to the pluralists, provide the means by which the masses can hold elites accountable for their decisions. But elite theory contends that the principal function of elections is not to provide policy mandates to elites, but rather to legitimize elite rule by providing symbolic reassurance that democratic elites govern on behalf of the masses.

In short, while elitism and pluralism share some common views on the preeminent role of elites in a democratic society, elitism differs from pluralism in several key respects, as summarized in Table 1-1.

ELITE AND MASS THREATS TO DEMOCRACY

It is the irony of democracy that the survival of democratic values—individual dignity, limited government, equality of opportunity, private property, freedom of speech and press, religious tolerance, and due process of law—depends on enlightened elites. The masses respond to the ideas and actions of elites. When elites abandon democratic principles or the masses lose confidence in elites, democracy is in peril.

Elite Distemper

Yet democratic elites do not always live up to their responsibilities to preserve the system and its values. Elite behavior is not always enlightened and farsighted, but is instead frequently shortsighted and narrowly self-serving. The relative autonomy of separate elites in a democracy—governmental, corporate, financial, media, legal, civic, and cultural—often encourages narrow visions of the common good and a willingness to sacrifice societal values for relative advantage.

Examples of narrowly self-serving elite behavior abound. Politicians resort to divisive, racial appeals or to class antagonisms—setting black against white or poor against rich—to win elections, even while knowing that these tactics undermine mass confidence in national leadership. Corporate officials sacrifice long-term economic growth for short-term, windfall, paper profits, knowing that the nation's competitive position in the world is

TABLE 1-1	How elitism and pluralism differ in their views of power and society

	ELITE THEORY	PLURALIST THEORY
Most Important Political Division(s) in Society	Elites who have power, and masses who do not.	Multiple competing groups (economic, racial, religious, ideological, etc.) that make demands upon government.
Structure of Power	Hierarchial, with power concentrated in a relatively small set of institutional leaders who make key social decisions.	Polyarchal, with power dispersed among multiple leadership groups who bargain and compromise over key societal decisions.
Interaction among Leaders	Consensus over values and goals for society, with disagreements largely limited to means of achieving common goals.	Conflict and competition over values and goals as well as means of achieving them.
Sources of Leadership	Common backgrounds and experiences in control of institutional resources; wealth, education, upper socio-economic status; slow continuous absorption of persons who accept prevailing values.	Diversity in backgrounds and experiences and activism in organizations; continuous formation of new groups and organizations; skills in organizational activity and gaining access to government.
Principal Institutions of Power	Corporations, banks, investment firms, media giants, foundations, "think tanks," and other private organizations, as well as government.	Interest groups, parties, and the legislative, executive, and judicial branches of government.
Principal Direction of Political Influence	Downward from elites to masses through mass media, education, civic, and cultural organizations.	Upward from masses to elites through interest groups, parties, elections, opinion polls, etc.
View of Public Policy	Public policy reflects elite preferences, as modified by both altruism and desire to preserve the political system from mass unrest; policy changes occur incrementally when elites redefine their own interests.	Public policy reflects balance of competing interest groups; policy changes occur when interest groups gain or lose influence, including mass support.
Principal Protection for Democratic Values	Elite commitments to individual liberty, free enterprise, and tolerance of diversity, and their desire to preserve the existing political system.	Competition among groups: countervailing centers of power each checking the ambitions of others.

undermined by shortsighted "bottom-line" policies. Elites move factories and jobs out of the United States in search of low-paid workers and higher profits. Global trade and unchecked immigration lower the real wages of American workers. Inequality in America increases, and elites and masses grow further apart. Members of Congress in pursuit of personal pay and perks as well as lifetime tenure cater to fat-cat political contributors and well-heeled interest groups. They devote more energy to running for office than to running the government. Bureaucrats, seeking to expand their powers and budgets, create a regulatory quagmire, disadvantaging the nation in global competition. Politicians and bureaucrats have burdened future generations with enormous debts. Interest group leaders pursue their quest for special privileges, treatments, and exemptions from law, at the expense of the public interest. Network television executives "hype" both news and entertainment shows with violence, scandal, sex, corruption, and scares of various sorts, knowing that these stories undermine mass confidence in the nation's institutions. Lawyers and judges pervert the judicial process for personal advantage, drowning the nation in a sea of litigation, clogging the courts and delaying justice, reinterpreting laws and the Constitution to suit their purposes, and undermining mass respect for the law.

In short, elites do not always act with unity and purpose. They all too frequently put narrow interests ahead of broader, shared values. These behaviors grow out of the relative autonomy of various elites in a democracy. They are encouraged by the absence of any external checks on the power of elites in their various domains. The only effective check on irresponsible elite behavior is their own realization that the system itself will become endangered if such behavior continues unrestrained. So periodically elites undertake reforms, mutually agreeing to curb the most flagrant abuses of the system. The stimulus to reform is the restoration of mass confidence in elite government, and ultimately the preservation of the elite system itself. But reforms often succeed only in creating new opportunities for abuse, changing the rules but failing to restrain self-interested elites.

Mass Unrest

But mass politics can also threaten democratic values. Despite a superficial commitment to the symbols of democracy, the masses have surprisingly weak commitments to the principles of individual liberty, toleration of diversity, and freedom of expression when required to apply these principles to despised or obnoxious groups or individuals. In contrast, elites, and the better-educated groups from which they are recruited, are generally more willing than the masses to apply democratic values to specific situations and to protect the freedoms of unpopular groups.

Masses are dangerously vulnerable to demagogic appeals to intolerance, racial hatred, anti-intellectualism, class antagonisms, anti-Semitism, and violence. Counterelites, or demagogues, are mass-oriented leaders who express hostility toward the established order and appeal to the mass sentiments. These counterelites, whether they are on the left or right, are extremist and intolerant, impatient with due process, contemptuous of individual rights, eager to impose their views by sweeping measures and often willing to use violence and intimidation to do so. Right-wing counterelites talk of "the will of the people," while left-wing radicals cry, "All power to the people." Both appeal to mass extremism: the notion that compromise and coalition-building, and working within the democratic system for change, is pointless or even immoral. Democratic politics is viewed with cynicism. Counterelites frequently resort to conspiracy theories to incite the masses. The left charges that the capitalist conspiracy exploits and oppresses the people for its own profit and amusement; the right charges that the nation is falling prey to an international conspiracy whose goal is to deprive the American people of their liberty and property. The historian Richard Hofstadter refers to this popularity of conspiracy theories as "the paranoid style of politics."[14]

FOCUS

The Unpolitics of College Students

For most college students, politics is *not* as interesting as football or basketball, or the sex lives of celebrities, or prime-time television sitcoms. When it comes to political issues, inattention, boredom, cynicism, and a sense of powerlessness are especially prevalent among college-age people today. The "baby boom" generation of students of the late 1960s and early 1970s were more active politically and more liberal in their views. This earlier generation of students confronted an unpopular war in Vietnam, the military draft, and the Watergate scandal and the forced resignation of a president.

This is the generation from which many current college instructors were recruited.

College students today are far less active politically than students a generation ago. Today's students are much more concerned with their financial futures and with raising a family than their predecessors. Students today are much less interested in "developing a meaningful philosophy of life." (See Table 1-2.)

It is not easy trying to develop an interest in politics on the campus today. Only 27 percent of students believe that "keeping up with political affairs" is important, and only 17 percent think that "influencing the political structure" is important. Only 14 percent even *discussed* politics in the last year! Why? One student replied: "I don't think our opinion matters in the grand scale of things," reflecting a widely shared feeling of powerlessness among young people.

			PERCENT WHO RESPONDED POSITIVELY	

QUESTIONS	1970	1998
Objectives considered important in life:		
Being very well off financially	41	75
Raising a family	65	73
Developing a meaningful philosophy of life	71	41
Keeping up with political affairs	49	27
Influencing the political structure	41	17
Political activities in past year:		
Discussed politics	30	14
Worked in a campaign	12	8
Political views, self-described:		
Far left	2	3
Liberal	33	22
Middle of the road	48	55
Conservative	16	19
Far right	1	2
Policy positions, agree that:		
Abortion should be legal	83	54
Death penalty should be abolished	33	24
Marijuana should be legalized	47	35
Affirmative action in college admissions should be abolished	NA	50

TABLE 1-2

Survey of college freshmen in 1970 and 1998

Source: Selected questions from the American Council on Education Annual Survey of College Freshmen, as reported in the *Chronicle of Higher Education,* January 16, 1998.

It is the irony of democracy that democratic values can survive only in the absence of mass political activism. Democratic values thrive best when the masses are absorbed in the problems of everyday life and involved in groups and activities that distract their attention from mass political movements. Political stability depends on mass involvement in work, family, neighborhood, trade union, hobby, church, group recreation, and other activities. When the masses become alienated from home, work, and community—when their ties to social organizations and institutions weaken—they become vulnerable to the appeals of demagogues, and democratic values are endangered.

Mass activism inspires elite repression. Mass political movements, when they gain momentum and give rise to hatred, generate fear and insecurity among elites. They respond by limiting freedom and strengthening security, banning demonstrations, investigating and harassing opposition, arresting activists, and curtailing speech, writing, and broadcasting—usually under the guise of preserving law and order. Universities, once heralded as society's bastions of free thought and expression, impose "speech codes," "sensitivity training," and other repressive measures on students and faculty, in the paradoxical pursuit of tolerance and "diversity." Ironically, elites resort to these repressive actions out of a genuine belief that they are necessary to preserve democratic values.

Elite theory, then, recognizes multiple threats to democracy: *elite misdeeds*—shortsighted and self-interested behavior that undermines popular support for the political system; *mass activism*—extremist and intolerant political movements, led by counterelites appealing to racial hatred, class antagonism, and personal fears; and *elite repression*—forced indoctrination in "political correctness"; limitations on dissent, speech, and assembly in the name of law and order; and the subversion of democratic values in a paradoxical effort to preserve the system.

AN ELITIST THEORY OF DEMOCRACY

All societies are governed by elites, even democratic societies. The elitist theory of democracy is not an attack upon democracy, but rather an aid in understanding the realities of democratic politics.

Elite theory is not an apology for elite rule; it is not defense of official misdeeds or repression. Rather, it is a realistic explanation of how democracy works, how democratic values are both preserved and threatened, how elites and masses interact, how public policy is actually determined, and whose interests generally prevail.

Critics of this elitist theory of democracy claim that it is "conservative," that it legitimizes elite rule, that it obstructs social progress of the masses. But elite theory neither endorses nor condemns elite governance, but rather seeks to expose and analyze the way in which elites function in a democracy.

Elite theory poses the central questions of American politics: Who governs the nation? How do people acquire power? How are economic and political power related? What interests shaped the U.S. Constitution? How have American elites changed over two centuries? How widely is power shared in the United States today? Are leaders in government, business, banking, the media, law, foundations, interest groups, and cultural affairs separate, distinct, and competitive—or are they concentrated, interlocked, and consensual? Do elites or masses give greater support to democratic values? Are elites becoming ever more isolated from masses? Are masses losing confidence in the nation's elite, and if so, what does this mean for democracy? Can democracy long survive when most people are distrustful of government and cynical toward politics?

Are masses generally informed, sensible, and considerate—or are they largely ill informed, apathetic, and intolerant? Does public opinion shape elite behavior—or do elites shape public opinion through the mass media? How successful are media elites in molding mass opinion and influencing public debate? Are American political parties "responsible" instruments of popular control of government—or are they weakened oligarchies, dominated by ideologically motivated activists? Do elections serve as policy mandates from the people—or are they primarily an exercise in citizenship, choosing personnel, not policy? Are political campaigns designed to inform voters and assess their policy preferences—or are they expensive, commercial adventures in image making? How politically active, informed, knowledgeable, and consistent in their views are the American people? Do organized interest groups fairly represent the views of their members—or do they reflect the views and interests of leaders who are largely out of touch with the members? Does competition among interest groups create a reasonable balance in public policy—or do the special interests dominate policy making at the expense of the mass public?

How much influence do masses have over the actions of presidents, Congress, and courts? What role does the president play in America's elite system? What effect does the president's behavior have on the way the masses view their government? Does presidential popularity with the masses affect the power of the president? Is power shifting from elected officials to "faceless bureaucrats"? What are the sources of bureaucratic power, and can bureaucracy be restrained? Whom do members of Congress really represent? Are members of Congress held accountable for their policy decisions by the voters back home—or are they free to pursue their personal interests in Washington, knowing that their constituents are generally unaware of their policy positions? Why are the nation's most important domestic policy questions usually decided by the most elitist branch of the government, the unelected, lifetime-tenured justices of the Supreme Court? Can political decentralization—decision making by subelites in states and communities—increase mass involvement in government? How do elites respond to mass protest movements? Do protest movements themselves become oligarchic over time and increasingly divorced from the views of the masses?

This text will address questions such as these from the perspective of *elite* theory. But it will also compare and evaluate the answers suggested by *pluralist* theory and *democratic* theory. The goal is a better understanding not only of American politics but also of elitism, pluralism, and democracy.

Notes

1. Harold Lasswell and Abraham Kaplan, *Power and Society* (New Haven, Conn.: Yale University Press, 1950), p. 219.

2. Gaetano Mosca, *The Ruling Class* (New York: McGraw-Hill, 1939), p. 50.

3. Roberto Michels, *Political Parties: A Sociological Study of the Oligarchical Tendencies of Modern Democracies* (1915; reprint, New York: Free Press, 1962), p. 70.

4. Harold Lasswell and Daniel Lerner, *The Comparative Study of Elites* (Stanford, Calif.: Stanford University Press, 1952), p. 7.

5. David Truman, "The American System in Crisis," *Political Science Quarterly* 74 (December 1959): 489.

6. Richard Hofstadter, *The American Political Tradition* (New York: Knopf, 1948), p. viii.

7. John Stuart Mill, *Representative Government* (New York: Dutton, Everyman's Library, 1962), p. 203.

8. For a discussion of John Locke and the political philosophy underlying democracy, see George Sabine, *A History of Political Theory* (New York: Holt, Rinehart & Winston, 1950), pp. 517–541.

9. James Madison, *The Federalist,* Number 10 (New York: Modern Library, 1937).

10. For a discussion of "Democracy in the States" and a list of states that allow initiative and referenda voting, see Thomas R. Dye, *Politics in States in Communities* (Upper Saddle River, N. J.: Prentice-Hall, 1997), Chapter 2.

11. E. E. Schattschneider, *Two Hundred Americans in Search of a Government* (New York: Holt, Rinehart & Winston, 1969), p. 63.

12. See Eva Etzioni-Halevy, *The Elite Connection* (Cambridge, Mass.: Polity Press, 1993).

13. Peter Bachrach, *The Theory of Democratic Elitism: A Critique* (Boston: Little, Brown, 1967), p. xi.

14. Richard Hofstadter, *The Paranoid Style of American Politics* (New York: Knopf, 1965).

Selected Readings

Dahl, Robert A. *Pluralist Democracy in the United States: Conflict and Consensus.* Chicago: Rand McNally, 1967. Most of Dahl's important theoretical work was at the community level. This book extended pluralism to the national level.

Etzioni-Halevy, Eva. *The Elite Connection.* Cambridge, Mass.: Polity Press, 1993. A scholarly description of "democratic elite theory," with comparisons to classical liberalism, traditional European elite theory, and modern American pluralism. It argues that although Western democracy is not "government by the people," it preserves democratic values through competition among separate and relatively autonomous elites both within and outside the state.

Etzioni-Halevy, Eva. (Ed.) *Classes and Elites in Democracy.* New York: Garland Press, 1997. Advanced students may wish to read key selections from the scholarly literature on classes, elites, and democracy. This well-edited volume contains thirty-eight brief selections from the works of such writers as Karl Marx, Roberto Michels, Gaetano Mosca,

Vilfredo Pareto, Joseph A. Schumpeter, C. Wright Mills, Robert A. Dahl, Samuel P. Huntington, and Seymour Martin Lipset.

Henry, William A., III. *In Defense of Elitism.* New York: Doubleday, 1994. A critical debunking of the myths that everyone is alike (or should be), that a just society will produce equal success for everyone, and that the common man is always right.

Michels, Roberto. *Political Parties: A Sociological Study of the Oligarchical Tendencies of Modern Democracies.* New York: Free Press, 1962. This classic book first appeared in 1911 in German. Michels was a disciple of Mosca. Like Mosca, he saw elitism as an outcome of social organization. Michels argued that the very fact of organization in society leads inevitably to an elite. His often-quoted thesis is, "Who says organization, says oligarchy." Political scientists have called this "the iron law of oligarchy."

Mosca, Gaetano. *The Ruling Class.* Edited by A. Livingston. New York: McGraw-Hill, 1939. This classic book was first published in 1896 in Italy. Mosca added to it in a 1923 edition that reflects the impact of World War I on his ideas. Along with the work of Vilfredo Pareto, Mosca's *Ruling Class* forms the basis of "classical elitism."

Pareto, Vilfredo. *The Mind and Society: Treatise of General Sociology.* New York: Harcourt, Brace & World, 1935 (originally published in 1915–1916 in four volumes). Pareto begins with a very broad definition of elite. He suggests that in any human activity, those who are the top practitioners are the elite in that activity. Thus he groups elites into two classes—the governing elite and the nongoverning elite—depending on whether the activity of which they are a top practitioner is important to government. Pareto also introduces psychological notions into his work. He speaks of "residues," which are human instincts, sentiments, or states of mind that remain constant over time and from state to state.

2

The Founding Fathers:
The Nation's First Elite

All communities divide themselves into the few and the many. The first are the rich and well-born, the other the masses of people.

—ALEXANDER HAMILTON

The Founding Fathers—those fifty-five men who wrote the Constitution of the United States and founded a new nation—were a truly exceptional elite, not only "rich and well-born" but also educated, talented, and resourceful. When Thomas Jefferson, then the nation's minister in Paris, first saw the list of delegates to the Constitutional Convention of 1787, he wrote to John Adams, the minister to London, "It is really an assembly of demigods."[1] The men at the Convention belonged to the nation's intellectual and economic elites; they were owners of landed estates, important merchants and importers, bankers and financiers, real estate and land speculators, and government bond owners. Jefferson and Adams were among the nation's very few notables who were not at the Constitutional Convention.

The Founding Fathers were not typical of the four million Americans in the new nation, most of whom were small farmers, tradespeople, frontier dwellers, servants, or slaves. However, to say that these men were not a representative sample of the American people, or that the Constitution was not a very democratic document, does not discredit the Founding Fathers or the Constitution. To the aristocratic society of eighteenth-century Europe, the Founding Fathers were dangerous revolutionaries who were establishing a government in which men with the talent of acquiring property could rise to political power even though not born into the nobility. And the Constitution has survived the test of time, providing the basic framework for an ever-changing society.

ELITES AND MASSES IN THE NEW NATION

Many visitors from the aristocratic countries of Europe noted the absence of an American nobility and commented on the spirit of equality that prevailed. Yet class lines existed in America. At the top of the social structure, a tiny elite dominated the social, cultural, economic, and political life of the new nation. The French chargé d'affaires reported in 1787 that America had "no nobles" but that certain "gentlemen" enjoyed "preeminence" because of "their wealth, their talents, their education, their families, or the offices they hold."[2] Some of these prominent gentlemen were Tories who fled America after the Revolution, but Charleston still had its Pinckneys and Rutledges; Boston its Adamses, Lowells, and Gerrys; New York its Schuylers, Clintons, and Jays; Philadelphia its Morrises, Mifflins, and Ingersolls; Maryland its Jenifers and Carrolls; and Virginia its Blairs and Randolphs.

Below this thin layer of educated and talented merchants, planters, lawyers, and bankers was a substantial body of successful farmers, shopkeepers, and independent artisans—of the "middling" sort, as they were known in revolutionary America. This early middle class was by no means a majority in the new nation; it stood considerably above the masses of debt-ridden farmers and frontier dwellers who made up most of the population. This small middle class had some political power, even at the time of the Constitutional Convention; it was entitled to vote, and its views were represented in governing circles, even if these views did not prevail at the Convention. The middle class was better represented in state legislatures and was championed by several men of prominence in the revolutionary period—Patrick Henry, Luther Martin, and Thomas Jefferson.

The great mass of white Americans in the revolutionary period were "freeholders," small farmers who worked their own land, scratching out a bare existence for themselves and their families. They had little interest in, or knowledge of, public affairs. Usually the small farmers who were not barred from voting by property-owning or tax-paying qualifications were too preoccupied with debt and subsistence, or too isolated in the wilderness, to vote anyway. Nearly eight out of ten Americans made a marginal living in the dirt; one in ten worked in fishing or lumbering; and one in ten worked in commerce in some way, whether as a dockhand, sailor, lawyer, or merchant.

At the bottom of the white social structure in the new republic were indentured servants and tenant farmers; this class, which was perhaps 20 percent of the population, exercised little, if any, political power. Finally, still
further below, were the black slaves. Although they made up almost another
20 percent of the population and were an important component of the
American economy, they were considered property, even in a country that
proclaimed the natural rights and equality of "all men."

ELITE PREFERENCES: INSPIRATION FOR A NEW CONSTITUTION

In July 1775, Benjamin Franklin proposed to the Continental Congress a
plan for a "perpetual union"; following the Declaration of Independence in
1776, the Congress appointed a committee to consider the Franklin proposal. The committee, headed by John Dickinson, made its report in the
form of the Articles of Confederation, which the Congress debated for more
than a year before finally adopting them on November 15, 1777. The Articles of Confederation were not to go into effect until every state approved;
Delaware withheld its consent until 1779, Maryland until 1781.

Government under the Articles of Confederation

The Articles of Confederation, effective from 1781 to 1789, established a
"firm league of friendship" among the states "for their common defense, the
security of their liberties, and their mutual and general welfare." The document reassured each state of "its sovereignty, freedom, and independence,
and every power, jurisdiction, and right, which is not by this confederation
expressly delegated to the United States, in Congress assembled." The Confederation's delegated powers included power to declare war, to send and
receive ambassadors, to make treaties, to fix standards of weights and measures, to regulate the value of coins, to manage Indian affairs, to establish
post offices, to borrow money, to build and equip an army and navy, and to
make requisitions (requests) to the several states for money and people.
However, certain key powers remained with the states, including two of
the most important ones of government: to regulate commerce and to
levy taxes.

Repayment of Loans Made to Congress

The inability of Congress to levy taxes under the Articles of Confederation
was a serious threat to those elites who had given financial backing to the

new nation during the Revolutionary War. The Continental Congress and the states had financed the war with money borrowed through the issuance of government bonds. Congress was unable to tax the people to pay off those debts, and the states became less and less inclined, as time passed, to meet their obligations to the central government. The states paid only one-tenth the sums requisitioned by the Congress under the Articles. During the last years of the Articles, the national government was unable even to pay interest on its debt. As a result, the bonds and notes of the national government lost most of their value, sometimes selling on the open market for only one-tenth their original value. Investors who had backed the American war effort were left with nearly worthless bonds.

Without the power to tax, and with the credit of the Confederation ruined, the prospects of the central government for future financial support—and survival—looked dim. Naturally the rich planters, merchants, and investors who owned government bonds had a direct financial interest in helping the national government acquire the power to tax and to pay off its debts.

Elimination of Barriers to Trade and Commerce

The inability of Congress under the Articles to regulate commerce among the states and with foreign nations, and the states' practice of laying tariffs on the goods of other states as well as on those of foreign nations, created havoc among commercial and shipping interests. "In every point of view," Madison wrote in 1785, "the trade of this country is in a deplorable condition."[3] The American Revolution had been fought, in part, to defend American commercial and business interests from oppressive regulation by the British government. Now the states themselves were interfering with the development of a national economy. Merchants and shippers with a view toward a national market and a high level of commerce were vitally concerned that the national government acquire the power to regulate interstate commerce and to prevent the states from imposing crippling tariffs and restrictions on interstate trade.

Protection of Bankers and Creditors from Cheap Money

State governments under the Articles posed a serious threat to investors and creditors through issuing cheap paper money and passing laws impairing contractual obligations. Paper money issued by the states permitted debtors to pay off their creditors with money worth less than the money originally loaned. Even the most successful farmers were usually heavily in debt, and many of them were gaining strength in state legislatures. They threatened to pass laws delaying the collection of debts and even abolishing the prevailing practice of imprisonment for unpaid debts. Obviously creditors had a direct financial interest in establishing a strong central government that could prevent the states from issuing public paper or otherwise interfering with debt collection.

Protection of Property against Radical Movements

A strong central government would help protect creditors against social upheavals by the large debtor class in America. In several states, debtors had already engaged in open rebellion against tax collectors and sheriffs attempting to repossess farms on behalf of creditors. The most serious rebellion broke out in the summer of 1786 in Massachusetts, when bands of insurgents—composed of farmers, artisans, and laborers—captured the courthouses in several western districts and briefly held the city of Springfield. Led by Daniel Shays, a veteran of Bunker Hill, the insurgent army posed a direct military threat to the governing elite of Massachusetts. Shays' Rebellion was put down by a smaller mercenary army, paid for by well-to-do citizens who feared a wholesale attack on property rights.

The states' growing radicalism intimidated the propertied classes, who began to advocate a strong central government to "insure domestic tranquility," guarantee "a republican form of government," and protect property "against domestic violence." The American Revolution had disturbed the masses' tradition of deferring to those in authority. Extremists like Thomas Paine, who reasoned that it was right and proper to revolt against England because of political tyranny, might also call for revolt against creditors because of economic tyranny. If debts owed to British merchants could be legislated out of existence, why not also the debts owed to American merchants? Acts of violence, boycotts, tea parties, and attacks on tax collectors frightened all propertied people in America.

Opening Western Land to Speculation

A strong central government with enough military power to oust the British from the Northwest and to protect western settlers against Indian attacks could open the way for the development of the American West. In addition, the protection and settlement of western land would cause land values to skyrocket and make land speculators rich.

Men of property in early America very actively speculated in western land. George Washington, Benjamin Franklin, Robert Morris, and even the popular hero Patrick Henry were involved in land speculation. During the Revolutionary War, the Congress had often paid the Continental soldiers with land certificates. After the war, most of the ex-soldiers sold the certificates to land speculators at very low prices. The Confederation's military weakness along its frontiers had kept the value of western lands low, for ravaging Indians discouraged immigration to the lands west of the Alleghenies, and the British threatened to cut off westward expansion by continuing to occupy (in defiance of the peace treaty) seven important fur-trading forts in the Northwest. The British forts were also becoming centers of anti-American influence among the Indians.

Protection of Shipping and Manufacturing

The development of a strong national navy was also important to American commercial interests, for the states seemed ineffective in preventing smuggling, and piracy was a very real danger and a vital concern of American shippers.

Manufacturing was still in its newborn stages during the revolutionary era in America, but farsighted investors were anxious to protect infant American industries against the import of British goods. Although all thirteen states erected tariff barriers against foreign goods, state tariffs could not provide the same protection for industry as a strong central government with a uniform tariff policy, because the state tariff system allowed low-tariff states to bring in foreign goods and circulate them throughout the country.

Ensuring the Return of Runaway Slaves

Southern planters and slaveholders also sought protection for their ownership of human "property." In 1787 slavery was lawful everywhere except Massachusetts. While many leaders in the South as well as the North recognized the moral paradox of asserting in the Declaration of Independence that "All men are created equal . . . ," yet at the same time owning slaves (as did the author of the Declaration, Thomas Jefferson), nonetheless the nation's Founders were fully prepared to protect "the peculiar institution" of slavery. (Interestingly, the Founders were too embarrassed to use the word "slave" in the new Constitution, preferring instead the euphemism "persons held to service or labor.") It was especially important to slave owners to guarantee the return of escaped slaves.

Exercising Power in World Affairs

Finally, a strong sense of nationalism appeared to motivate America's elites. While the masses focused on local affairs, the educated and cosmopolitan leaders in America were concerned about the weakness of America in the international community. Thirteen separate states failed to manifest a sense of national purpose and identity. The Confederation was held in contempt not only by Britain, as evidenced by the violations of the Treaty of Paris, but even by the lowly Barbary states. Hamilton expressed the indignation of America's leadership over its inability to swing weight in the world community:

> There is something . . . diminutive and contemptible in the prospect of a number of petty states, with the appearance only of union, jarring, jealous, and perverse, without any determined direction, fluctuating and unhappy at home, weak and insignificant by their dissentions in the eyes of other nations.[4]

In short, America's elite wanted to assume a respectable role in the international community and exercise power in world affairs.

FORMATION OF A NATIONAL ELITE

In the spring of 1785, delegates from Virginia and Maryland met at Alexandria, Virginia, to resolve certain difficulties that had arisen between the two states over the regulation of commerce and navigation on the Potomac River and Chesapeake Bay. It was fortunate for the new nation that the most prominent man in America, George Washington, took a personal interest in this meeting. As a rich planter and land speculator who owned more than 30,000 acres of western lands upstream on the Potomac, Washington was keenly aware of commercial problems under the Articles. He lent great prestige to the Alexandria meeting by inviting participants to his home at Mount Vernon. Out of this conference came the idea for a general economic conference for all the states. The Virginia legislature issued a call for such a convention to meet at Annapolis in September 1785.

Judged by its publicly announced purpose—securing interstate agreement on matters of commerce and navigation—the Annapolis Convention was a failure; only twelve delegates appeared, representing five commercial states: New York, New Jersey, Pennsylvania, Delaware, and Virginia. But these twelve men saw the opportunity to use the Annapolis meeting to achieve greater political successes. Alexander Hamilton, with masterful political foresight, persuaded the others in attendance to strike out for a full constitutional solution to America's ills. The Annapolis Convention adopted a report, written by Hamilton, that outlined the defects in the Articles of Confederation and called upon the states to send delegates to a new convention to suggest remedies for these defects. The new convention was to meet in May 1787 in Philadelphia. Rumors at the time suggested that Hamilton, with the behind-the-scenes support of James Madison in the Virginia legislature, had intended all along that the Annapolis Convention fail in its stated purposes and that it provide a stepping-stone to larger political objectives.

Shays' Rebellion was very timely for men like Hamilton and Madison, who sought to galvanize America's elite into action. Commencing in the fall of 1786, after the Annapolis call for a new convention, the rebellion convinced men of property in Congress and state legislatures that there was cause for alarm.

On February 21, 1787, Congress confirmed the call for a convention to meet in Philadelphia

> *for the sole and express purpose of revising the Articles of Confederation and reporting to Congress and the several legislatures such alterations and provisions therein as shall, when agreed to in Congress and confirmed by the states, render the federal Constitution adequate to the exigencies of government and the preservation of the union.*

Delegates to the Convention were appointed by the legislatures of every state except Rhode Island, the only state in which the debtor classes had wrested political control from the legislature.

The fifty-five men who met in the summer of 1787 to establish a new national government quickly chose George Washington, their most prestigious member—indeed the most prestigious man on the continent—to preside over the assembly. Just as quickly, the Convention decided to hold its sessions behind closed doors and to keep all proceedings a carefully guarded secret. Delegates adhered closely to this decision and informed neither close friends nor relatives of the nature of the discussions. Apparently the Founding Fathers were aware that elites are most effective in negotiation, compromise, and decision making when operating in secrecy.

The Convention was quick to discard its congressional mandate to "revise the Articles of Confederation"; without much hesitation, it proceeded to write an entirely new constitution. Only men confident of their powers and abilities, men of principle and property, could proceed in this bold fashion. Let us examine the characteristics of the nation's first elite more closely.

George Washington's Prestige

One cannot overestimate the prestige of George Washington at this time in his life. As the commander-in-chief of the successful revolutionary army and founder of the new nation, he had overwhelming charismatic appeal among both elites and masses. Preeminent not only as a soldier, statesman, and founder of the nation, he was also one of the richest men in America. Through all the years that he had spent in the revolutionary cause, he had refused any payment for his services. He often paid his soldiers from his own fortune. In addition to his large estate on the Potomac, he possessed many thousands of acres of undeveloped land in western Virginia, Maryland, Pennsylvania, Kentucky, and the Northwest Territory. He owned major shares in the Potomac Company, the James River Company, the Bank of Columbia, and the Bank of Alexandria. And he held large amounts in U.S. bonds and securities. Washington stood at the apex of America's elite structure.

Founders' Governing Experience

The Founding Fathers had extensive experience in governing. These same men had made all the key decisions in American history from the Stamp Act Congress to the Declaration of Independence to the Articles of Confederation. They controlled the Congress of the United States and had conducted the Revolutionary War. Eight delegates had signed the Declaration of Independence. Eleven delegates had served as officers in Washington's army. Forty-two of the fifty-five Founding Fathers had already served in the U.S. Congress. Even at the moment of the Convention, more than forty delegates held high offices in state governments; Franklin, Livingston, and Randolph were governors. The Founding Fathers were unsurpassed in political skill and experience.

Founders' Education

In an age when no more than a handful of men on the North American continent had gone to college, the Founding Fathers were conspicuous for their educational attainment. More than half the delegates had been educated at Harvard (founded in 1636), William and Mary (1693), Yale (1701), University of Pennsylvania (1740), Columbia College (1754), Princeton (1756), or in England. The tradition of legal training for political decision makers, which has continued in the United States to the present, was already evident. About a dozen delegates were still active lawyers in 1787, and about three dozen had had legal training.

Founders' Wealth

The fifty-five men at Philadelphia formed a major part of the nation's economic elite as well. The personal wealth represented at the meeting was enormous. It is difficult to determine accurately who were the richest men in America at that time because the finances of the period were chaotic and because wealth assumed a variety of forms—land, ships, credit, slaves, business inventories, bonds, and paper money of uncertain worth (even George Washington had difficulty at times converting his land wealth into cash). But at least forty of the fifty-five delegates were known to be holders of government bonds; fourteen were land speculators; twenty-four were moneylenders and investors; eleven were engaged in commerce or manufacturing; and fifteen owned large plantations.[5] (See Table 2-1.)

Robert Morris was perhaps the foremost business and financial leader in the nation in 1787. This Philadelphia merchant owned scores of ships that traded throughout the world; he engaged in iron manufacturing, speculated in land in all parts of the country, and controlled the Bank of North America in Philadelphia, probably the nation's largest financial institution at the time. He earned his title "the patriot financier" by underwriting a large share of the debts of the United States during and after the Revolutionary War. Later in his life, his financial empire collapsed, probably because of overspeculation, and he died in debt. But at the time of the Convention, he stood at the center of America's financial structure.

Founders' "Continental" View

Perhaps what most distinguished the men at Philadelphia from the masses was their cosmopolitanism. They approached political, economic, and

| TABLE 2-1 | Founding Fathers' known membership in elite groups |

HOLDERS OF PUBLIC SECURITY INTERESTS		REAL ESTATE AND LAND SPECULATORS	LENDERS AND INVESTORS	MERCHANTS, MANUFACTURERS, AND SHIPPERS	PLANTERS AND SLAVEHOLDERS
MAJOR	MINOR				
Baldwin	Bassett	Blount	Bassett	Broom	Butler
Blair	Blount	Dayton	Broom	Clymer	Davie
Clymer	Brearly	Few	Butler	Ellsworth	Jenifer
Dayton	Broom	Fitzsimons	Carroll	Fitzsimons	A. Martin
Ellsworth	Butler	Franklin	Clymer	Gerry	L. Martin
Fitzsimons	Carroll	Gerry	Davie	King	Mason
Gerry	Few	Gilman	Dickinson	Langdon	Mercer
Gilman	Hamilton	Gorham	Ellsworth	McHenry	C. C. Pinckney
Gorham	L. Martin	Hamilton	Few	Mifflin	C. Pinckney
Jenifer	Mason	Mason	Fitzsimons	G. Morris	Randolph
Johnson	Mercer	R. Morris	Franklin	R. Morris	Read
King	Mifflin	Washington	Gilman		Rutledge
Langdon	Read	Williamson	Ingersoll		Spaight
Lansing	Spaight	Wilson	Johnson		Washington
Livingston	Wilson		King		Wythe
McClurg	Wythe		Langdon		
R. Morris			Mason		
C. C. Pinckney			McHenry		
C. Pinckney			C. C. Pinckney		
Randolph			C. Pinckney		
Sherman			Randolph		
Strong			Read		
Washington			Washington		
Williamson			Williamson		

military issues from a "continental" point of view. Unlike the masses, members of the elite extended their loyalties beyond their states; they experienced the sentiment of nationalism half a century before it would begin to seep down to the masses.[6]

ELITE CONSENSUS IN 1787

By focusing on the debates *within* the Convention, many historical scholars have overemphasized the differences of opinion among the Founding Fathers. True, the Convention was the site of many conflicting views and innumerable compromises; yet the more striking fact is that the delegates were in almost complete accord on essential political questions.

Protecting Liberty and Property

They agreed that the fundamental end of government is the protection of liberty and property. They accepted without debate many of the precedents set by the English constitution and by the constitutions of the new states. Reflecting the advanced ideas of their times, the Founding Fathers were much less religious than most Americans today. Yet they believed in a law of nature with rules of abstract justice to which human laws should conform. They believed that this law of nature endowed each person with certain inalienable rights essential to a meaningful existence—the rights to life, liberty, and property—and that these rights should be recognized and protected by law. They believed that all people were equally entitled to respect of their natural rights regardless of their station in life. Most of the Founding Fathers were even aware that this belief ran contrary to the practice of slavery and were embarrassed by this inconsistency in American life.

But "equality" did *not* mean to the Founding Fathers that people were equal in wealth, intelligence, talent, or virtue. They accepted inequalities in wealth and property as a natural product of human diversity. They did not believe that government had a responsibility to reduce these inequalities; in fact, they saw "dangerous leveling" as a serious violation of the right to property and the right to use and dispose of the fruits of one's own industry.

Government as Contract

The Founding Fathers agreed that the origin of government is an implied contract among people. They believed that people pledge allegiance and obedience to government in return for protection of their persons and property. They felt that the ultimate legitimacy of government—sovereignty—rests with the people themselves and not with gods or kings and that the basis of government is the consent of the governed.

Republicanism

The Founding Fathers believed in republican government. They opposed hereditary monarchies, the prevailing form of government in the world at the time. Although they believed that people of principle and property should govern, they were opposed to an aristocracy or a governing nobility. To them, a "republican government" was a representative, responsible, and nonhereditary government. But they certainly did *not* mean mass democracy, with direct participation by the people in decision making. They expected the masses to consent to government by men of principle and property, out of recognition of their abilities, talents, education, and stake in the preservation of liberty and order. The Founding Fathers believed that the masses should have only a limited role in selecting government leaders. They bickered over how much direct participation is appropriate in selecting decision makers and they bickered over the qualifications necessary for public office, but they generally agreed that the masses should have only a limited, indirect role in selecting decision makers and that decision makers themselves should be men of wealth, education, and proven leadership ability.

Limited Government

The Founding Fathers believed in limited government that could not threaten liberty or property. Since the Founding Fathers believed that power is a corrupting influence and that the concentration of power is dangerous, they believed in dividing government power into separate bodies capable of checking, or thwarting, one another should any one branch pose a threat to liberty or property. Differences of opinion among honest people, particularly differences among elites in separate states, could best be resolved by balancing representation of these several elites in the national government and by creating a decentralized system that permits local elites to govern their states as they see fit, with limited interference from the national government.

_____

Nationalism

Finally, and perhaps most important, the Founding Fathers believed that only a strong national government, with power to exercise its will directly on the people, could "establish justice, insure domestic tranquility, provide for the common defense, promote the general welfare, and secure the blessings of liberty."

This consensus on fundamentals dwarfed the differences requiring compromise in the Convention. It was the existence of a national elite and its agreement on the fundamentals of politics that made possible the formation of the U.S. government. If the elites had faced substantial divisiveness in 1787, any substantial competition or conflict, or any divergent centers of influence, a new government would never have emerged from the Philadelphia Convention. Elite consensus in 1787 was profoundly conservative; the elites wished to preserve the status quo in the distribution of power and property in the United States. Yet at the same time, this elite consensus was radical compared with the beliefs of their elite contemporaries elsewhere in the world. Nearly every other government adhered to the principles of hereditary monarchy and privileged nobility, whereas American elites were committed to republicanism. Other elites asserted the divine rights of kings, but American elites talked about government by the consent of the governed. While the elites in Europe rationalized and defended a rigid class system, American elites believed in equality and inalienable human rights.

AN ELITE IN OPERATION: CONCILIATION AND COMPROMISE

On May 25, 1787, sessions of the Constitutional Convention opened in Independence Hall, Philadelphia. After the delegates had selected Washington as president of the Convention and decided to keep the proceedings of the Convention secret, Governor Edmund Randolph, speaking for the Virginia delegation, presented a draft of a new constitution.*

_____

*James Madison kept secret notes on the Convention, which he published many years later. Most of our knowledge about the Convention comes from Madison's notes. See Max Ferrand, ed., *The Records of the Federal Convention of 1787* (New Haven, Conn.: Yale University Press, 1911).

Representation Compromise

The Virginia plan gave little recognition to the states in its proposed composition of the national government. The plan suggested a two-house legislature, the lower house to be chosen by the people of the states, with representation according to the population. The upper house was to be chosen by the first house. This Congress would have power to "legislate in all cases in which the separate states are incompetent, or in which the harmony of the United States may be interrupted by the exercise of individual legislation." Moreover, Congress would have the authority to nullify state laws that it felt violated the Constitution, thus ensuring national supremacy. The Virginia plan also proposed a parliamentary form of government, with Congress choosing members of the executive and judiciary branches.

The most important line of cleavage at the Convention was between elites of large states and elites of small states over the representation scheme in the Virginia plan. This question was not one of economic interest or ideology, since delegates from large and small states did not divide along economic or ideological lines. After several weeks of debate over the Virginia plan, delegates from the small states presented a counterproposal in a report by William Paterson of New Jersey. The New Jersey plan may have been merely a tactic by the small-state elites to force the Convention to compromise on representation, for the plan was set aside after only a week of debate with little negative reaction. The New Jersey plan proposed to retain the representation scheme outlined in the Articles of Confederation, which granted each state a single vote. But the plan went further, proposing separate executive and judiciary branches and expansion of the powers of Congress to include the right to levy taxes and regulate commerce.

The New Jersey plan was not an attempt to retain the Confederation. Indeed, the plan included words that later appeared in the Constitution as the famous national supremacy clause that provides that the U.S. Constitution and federal laws supersede each state's constitution and laws. Thus even the small states did not envision a confederation. Both the Virginia and New Jersey plans were designed to strengthen the national government; they differed only on how much to strengthen it and on its system of representation.

On June 29, William Samuel Johnson of Connecticut proposed the obvious compromise: that representation in the lower house of Congress be based upon population, whereas representation in the upper house would be equal—two senators from each state. The Connecticut compromise also provided that equal representation of states in the Senate could not be abridged, even by constitutional amendment.

Slavery Compromises

The next question requiring compromise was that of slavery and the role of slaves in the system of representation, an issue closely related to economic differences among America's elite. It was essentially the same question that seventy-four years later divided that elite and provoked the nation's bloodiest war. Planters and slaveholders generally believed that wealth, particularly wealth in slaves, should count in apportioning representation. Nonslaveholders felt that "the people" should include only free inhabitants. The decision to apportion direct taxes among the states in proportion to population opened the way to compromise, since the attitudes of slaveholders and nonslaveholders reversed when counting people in order to apportion taxes. The result was the famous three-fifths compromise: three-fifths of the slaves of each state would be counted for the purpose of both representation and apportioning direct taxes.

A compromise was also necessary on the question of trading in slaves. On this issue, the men of Maryland and Virginia, states already well supplied with slaves, were able to indulge in the luxury of conscience and support proposals for banning the further import of slaves. But the less-developed southern states, particularly South Carolina and Georgia, could not afford this posture since they still wanted additional slave labor. Inasmuch as the southern planters were themselves divided, the ultimate compromise permitted Congress to prohibit slave trade—but not before the year 1808. The twenty-year delay would allow the undeveloped southern states to acquire all the slaves they needed before the slave trade ended.

Export Tax Compromise

Agreement between southern planters and northern merchants was still relatively easy to achieve at this early date in American history. But latent conflict was evident on issues other than slavery. Although all elite groups agreed that the national government should regulate interstate and foreign commerce, southern planters feared that the unrestricted power of Congress over commerce might lead to the imposition of export taxes. Export taxes would bear most heavily on the southern states, which depended on foreign markets in order to sell the indigo, rice, tobacco, and cotton the southern states produced. However, planters and merchants were able to compromise again in resolving this issue: articles exported from any state should bear no tax or duty. Only imports could be taxed by the national government.

Voter Qualification Compromise

Another important compromise, one that occupied much of the Convention's time (though it has received little recognition from later writers), concerned qualifications for voting and holding office in the new government. Although no property qualifications for voters or officeholders appear in the text of the Constitution, the debates revealed that members of the Convention generally favored property qualifications for officeholding. The delegates showed little enthusiasm for mass participation in democracy. Elbridge Gerry of Massachusetts declared that "the evils we experience flow from the excess of democracy." Roger Sherman protested that "the people immediately should have as little to do as may be about the government." Edmund Randolph continually deplored the turbulence and follies of democracy, and George Clymer's notion of republican government was that "a representative of the people is appointed to think for and not with his constituents." John Dickinson considered property qualifications a "necessary defense against the dangerous influence of those multitudes without property and without principle, with which our country like all others, will in time abound." Charles Pinckney later wrote to Madison, "Are you not . . . abundantly depressed at the theoretical nonsense of an election of Congress by the people; in the first instance, it's clearly and practically wrong, and it will in the end be the means of bringing our councils into contempt." Many more such elitist statements appear in the records of the Convention.[7]

Given these views, how do we explain the absence of property qualifications in the Constitution? Actually a motion was carried in the Convention instructing a committee to fix property qualifications for officeholding, but the committee could not agree upon what qualifications to impose. Various propositions to establish property qualifications met defeat on the floor, not because delegates believed they were inherently wrong but, interestingly enough, because the elites at the Convention represented different kinds of property holdings. Madison pointed out that fact in the July debate, noting that a land ownership requirement would exclude from Congress the mercantile and manufacturing classes, who would hardly be willing to turn their money into landed property just to become eligible for a seat in Congress. Madison rightly observed that "landed possessions were no certain evidence of real wealth. Many enjoyed them to a great extent who were more in debt than they were worth." The objections by merchants and investors defeated the "landed" qualifications for congressional representatives.

Thus the Convention approved the Constitution without property qualifications on officeholders or voters, except those that the states themselves might see fit to impose. Failing to come to a decision on this issue of suffrage, the delegates merely returned the question to state legislatures by providing that "the electors in each state should have the qualifications requisite for electors of the most numerous branch of the state legislatures." At the time, this expedient course of action did not seem likely to produce mass democracy. Only one branch of the new government, the House of Representatives, was to be elected by popular vote. The other three controlling bodies—the president, the Senate, and the Supreme Court—were removed from direct voter participation. The delegates were reassured that nearly all the state constitutions then in force included property qualifications for voters.

Finally, the Constitution did not recognize women as legitimate participants in government. For nearly one hundred years, no state accorded women the right to vote. (The newly formed Wyoming Territory first gave women the right to vote and hold public office in 1869.) Not until 1920 was the U.S. Constitution amended to guarantee women the right to vote.

THE CONSTITUTION AS ELITIST DOCUMENT

The text of the Constitution, together with interpretive materials in *The Federalist* papers written by Hamilton, Madison, and Jay, provides ample evidence that elites in America benefited both politically and economically from the adoption of the Constitution.* Although both elites and nonelites—indeed all Americans—may have benefited from the Constitution, *elites benefited more directly and immediately than did nonelites.* And we can infer that the elites would not have developed and supported the Constitution if they had not stood to gain substantially from it.

Let us examine the text of the Constitution itself and its impact on American elites. Article I, Section 8, grants seventeen types of power to Congress, followed by a general grant of power to make "all laws which shall be necessary and proper for carrying into execution the foregoing powers."

Levying Taxes

The first and perhaps most important power is the "power to lay and collect taxes, duties, imposts, and excises." The taxing power is the basis of all

*See the Appendix for a complete document of the Constitution of the United States of America.

"You know, the idea of taxation <u>with</u> representation doesn't appeal to me very much, either."

other powers, and it enabled the national government to end its dependence upon states. This power was essential to the holders of public securities, particularly when combined with the provision in Article VI, "All debts contracted and engagements entered into, before the adoption of this Constitution, shall be as valid against the United States under this Constitution, as under the Confederation." Thus the national government was committed to paying off all those investors who held bonds of the United States, and the taxing power guaranteed that commitment would be fulfilled.

The text of the Constitution suggests that the Founding Fathers intended Congress to place most of the tax burden on consumers in the form of custom duties and excise taxes rather than direct taxes on individual income or property. Article I, Section 2, states that government can levy direct taxes only on the basis of population; it follows that it could not levy such taxes in proportion to wealth. This provision prevented the national government from levying progressive income taxes; not until the Sixteenth Amendment in 1913 did this protection for wealth disappear from the Constitution.

Southern planters, whose livelihoods depended on the export of indigo, rice, tobacco, and cotton, strenuously opposed giving the national government the power to tax exports. Article I, Section 9, offered protection for their interests: "No tax or duty shall be laid on articles exported from any State." However, Congress was given the power to tax imports so that northern manufacturers could erect a tariff wall to protect American industries against foreign goods.

Regulating Commerce

Congress also had the power to "regulate commerce with foreign nations, and among the several States." The interstate commerce clause, together with the provision in Article I, Section 9, prohibiting the states from taxing either imports or exports, created a free trade area over the thirteen states. This arrangement was very beneficial for American merchants.

Protecting Money and Property

Following the Article I, Section 8, powers to tax and spend, to borrow money, and to regulate commerce is a series of specific powers designed to enable Congress to protect money and property. Congress is given the power to make bankruptcy laws, to coin money and regulate its value, to fix standards of weights and measures, to punish counterfeiting, to establish post offices and post roads, to pass copyright and patent laws to protect authors and inventors, and to punish piracies and felonies committed on the high seas. Each of these powers is a specific asset to bankers, investors, and shippers, respectively. Obviously the Founding Fathers felt that giving Congress control over currency and credit in the United States would result in better protection for financial interests than would leaving the essential responsibility to the states. Similarly, they believed that control over communication and transportation (by establishing post offices and post roads) was too essential to trade and commerce to be left to the states.

Creating the Military

The remaining powers in Article I, Section 8, deal with military affairs: raising and supporting armies; organizing, training, and calling up the state militia; declaring war; suppressing insurrections; and repelling invasions. These powers—together with the provisions in Article II making the president the commander-in-chief of the army and navy and of the state militia when called into the federal service, and giving the president power to make treaties with the advice and consent of the Senate, and to send and receive ambassadors—centralized diplomatic and military affairs at the national level. Article I, Section 10, confirms this centralization of diplomatic and military powers by prohibiting the states from entering into treaties with foreign nations, maintaining ships of war, or engaging in war unless actually invaded.

Clearly the Founding Fathers had little confidence in the state militias, particularly when they were under state control; General Washington's painful experiences with state militias during the Revolutionary War were still fresh in his memory. The militias had proved adequate when defending their own states against invasion, but when employed outside their own states, the militias were often a disaster. Moreover, if western settlers were to be protected from the Indians and if the British were to be persuaded to give up their forts in Ohio and open the way to westward expansion, the national government could not rely upon state militias but must have an army of its own. Similarly, a strong navy was essential to the protection of U.S. commerce on the seas (the first significant naval action under the new government was against the piracy of the Barbary states). Thus a national army and navy were not so much protection against invasion (for many years the national government continued to rely primarily upon state militias for this purpose) as they were protection and promotion of the government's commercial and territorial ambitions.

Protecting against Revolution

A national army and navy, as well as an organized and trained militia that could be called into national service, also provided protection against class wars and debtor rebellions. In an obvious reference to Shays' Rebellion, Hamilton warned in *The Federalist*, Number 21:

> *The tempestuous situation from which Massachusetts has scarcely emerged evinces that dangers of this kind are not merely speculative. Who could determine what might have been the issue of her late convulsions if the malcontents had been headed by a Caesar or a Cromwell? A strong military force in the hands of the national government is a protection against revolutionary action.*[8]

Further evidence of the Founding Fathers' intention to protect the government classes from revolution is found in Article IV, Section 4, where the national government guarantees to every state "a republican form of government" as well as protection against "domestic violence." Thus in addition to protecting western land and commerce on the seas, a strong army and navy would enable the national government to back up its pledge to protect governing elites in the states from violence and revolution.

Protection against domestic insurrection also appealed to the southern slaveholders' deep-seated fear of a slave revolt. Madison drove this point home in *The Federalist*, Number 23:

> *I take no little notice of an unhappy species of population abounding in some of the states who, during the calm of regular government were sunk below the level of men; but who, in the tempestuous seeds of civil violence, may emerge into human character and give a superiority of strength to any party with which they may associate themselves.*[9]

Protecting Slavery

The Constitution permitted Congress to outlaw the import of slaves after 1808. But most southern planters were more interested in protecting their existing property and slaves than they were in extending the slave trade, and the Constitution provided an explicit advantage to slaveholders in Article IV, Section 2:

> *No person held to service or labor in one State, under the laws thereof, escaping into another, shall in consequence of any law or regulation therein, be discharged from such service or labor, but shall be delivered up on claim of the party to whom such service or labor may be due.*

This provision was an extremely valuable protection for one of the most important forms of property in the United States at the time. Although the U.S. slave trade lapsed after twenty years, slavery itself, as a domestic institution, was better safeguarded under the new Constitution than under the Articles.

Limiting States in Monetary Affairs

The restrictions placed upon state legislatures by the Constitution also provided protection to economic elites in the new nation. States could not coin money, issue paper money, or pass legal-tender laws that would make any money other than gold or silver coin tender in the payment of debts. This restriction would prevent the states from issuing cheap paper money, which debtors could use to pay off creditors with less valuable currency. Moreover, the states were prohibited from passing legal-tender laws obliging creditors to accept paper money in payment of debts.

Limiting States in Business Affairs

The Constitution also prevents states from passing any law "impairing the obligation of contracts." The structure of business relations in a free-enterprise economy depends on governmental enforcement of private contracts, and economic elites seek to prevent government from relieving people of their contractual obligations. If state legislatures could relieve debtors of their contractual obligations, relieve indentured servants of their obligations to their masters, prevent creditors from foreclosing on mortgages, declare moratoriums on debt, or otherwise interfere with business obligations, then the interests of investors, merchants, and creditors would be seriously damaged.

ELITISM AND THE STRUCTURE OF THE NATIONAL GOVERNMENT

The structure of the national government clearly reflects the desire of the Founders to protect liberty and property, especially from mass *majorities*.

Those who criticize the U.S. government for its slow, unwieldy processes should realize that the government's founders deliberately built in this characteristic. These cumbersome arrangements—the checks and balances and the fragmentation of authority that make it difficult for government to realize its potential power over private interests—aim to protect private interests from governmental interference and to shield the government from an unjust and self-seeking majority. If the system handcuffs government and makes it easy for established groups to oppose change, then the system is working as intended.

This system of intermingled powers and conflicting loyalties is still alive today. Of course, some aspects have changed; for example, voters now elect senators directly, and the president is more directly responsible to the voters than was originally envisioned. But the basic arrangement of checks and balances endures. Presidents, senators, representatives, and judges are chosen by different constituencies; their terms of office vary, and their responsibilities and loyalties differ. This system makes majority rule virtually impossible.

National Supremacy

The heart of the Constitution is the supremacy clause of Article VI:

> *This Constitution, and the laws of the United States which shall be made in pursuance thereof; and all treaties made, or which shall be made, under the authority of the United States, shall be the supreme law of the land; and the judges in every State shall be bound thereby, any thing in the Constitution or laws of any State to the contrary notwithstanding.*

This sentence made it abundantly clear that laws of Congress would supersede laws of the states, and it made certain that Congress would control interstate commerce, bankruptcy, monetary affairs, weights and measures, currency and credit, communication, transportation, and foreign and military affairs. Thus the supremacy clause ensures that the decisions of the national elite will prevail over those of the local elites in all vital areas allocated to the national government.

Republicanism

The structure of the national government—its republicanism and its system of separated powers and checks and balances—was also designed to protect liberty and property. To the Founding Fathers, a republican government meant the delegation of powers by the people to a small number of citizens "whose wisdom may best discern the true interest of their country, and whose patriotism and love of justice will be least likely to sacrifice it to temporary or partial consideration."[10] Madison explained, in classic elite fashion, "that the public voice, pronounced by representatives of the people, will be more consonant to the public good than if pronounced by the people themselves." The Founding Fathers clearly believed that representatives of the people were more likely to be enlightened persons of principle and property than the voters who chose them and would thus be more trustworthy and dependable.

Voters also had a very limited voice in the selection of decision makers. Of the four major decision-making entities established in the Constitution—the House of Representatives, the Senate, the presidency, and the Supreme Court—the people were to elect only one. The others were to be at least twice removed from popular control. In the constitution of 1787, the people elected only House members, and for short terms of only two years. In contrast, state legislatures were to elect U.S. senators for six-year terms. Electors, selected as state legislatures saw fit, selected the president. The states could hold elections for presidential electors, or the state legislatures could appoint them. The Founding Fathers hoped that presidential electors would be prominent men of wealth and reputation in their respective states. Finally, federal judges were to be appointed by the president for life, thus removing those decision makers as far as possible from popular control.

Separation of Powers and Checks and Balances

The Founding Fathers also intended the system of separated powers in the national government—separate legislative, executive, and judicial branches—as a bulwark against majoritarianism (government by popular majorities) and an additional safeguard for elite liberty and property. The doctrine derives from the French writer Montesquieu, whose *Spirit of Laws* was a political textbook for these eighteenth-century statesmen. *The Federalist,* Number 51, expressed the logic of the system of checks and balances:

> *Ambition must be made to counteract ambition. . . . It may be a reflection on human nature, that such devices should be necessary to control the abuses of government. But what is government itself, but the greatest of all reflections on human nature? If men were*

> *angels, no government would be necessary. If angels were to govern men, neither external or internal controls on government would be necessary. In framing a government which is to be administered by men over men, the greatest difficulty lies in this: you must first enable the government to control the governed; and in the next place oblige it to control itself.*[11]

The Constitution states the separation-of-powers concept in the opening sentences of the first three articles:

> *[Article I:] All legislative powers herein granted shall be vested in a Congress of the United States, which shall consist of a Senate and House of Representatives. [Article II:] The executive power shall be vested in a President of the United States. . . . [Article III:] The*

FOCUS

James Madison, Suppressing Majority "Factions"

Perhaps the most important contributor to the Constitution was James Madison (1751–1836). Not only did he place a key role in writing the Constitution but his insightful and scholarly defense of it also helped immeasurably in securing its ratification. Indeed, Madison is more highly regarded by political scientists and historians as a *political theorist* than as the fourth president of the United States.

Madison's family owned a large plantation, Montpelier, near present-day Orange, Virginia. Private tutors and prep schools provided him with a thorough background in history, science, philosophy, and law. He graduated from the College of New Jersey (now Princeton University) at eighteen and assumed a number of elected and appointed posi-

tions in Virginia's colonial government. In 1776, Madison drafted a new Virginia Constitution. While serving in Virginia's Revolutionary assembly, he met Thomas Jefferson; the two became lifetime political allies and friends. In 1787, Madison represented Virginia at the Constitutional Convention and took a leading role in its debates over the form of a new federal government. Madison's *Notes on the Constitutional Convention of 1787,* published twenty years after the event, is the only recount of the secret meeting.

Madison's political philosophy is revealed in *The Federalist Papers,* a series of eighty-five essays published in major newspapers in 1787–88, all signed simply "Publius." Alexander Hamilton and John Jay contributed some of them, but Madison wrote the two most important essays: Number 10, which explains the nature of political conflict (faction) and how it can be "controlled"; and Number 51, which explains the system of separation of powers and checks and balances.

According to Madison, "controlling faction" was the principal task of government. What creates factions? According to Madison, conflict is part of human nature. In all societies, we find "a zeal for different opinions concerning religion, concerning government, and many other points," as well as "an

> *judicial power of the United States shall be vested in one Supreme Court, and in such inferior courts as the Congress may from time to time ordain and establish.*

Insofar as this system divides responsibility and makes it difficult for the masses to hold government accountable for public policy, it achieves one of the purposes intended by the Founding Fathers. Each of the four major decision-making bodies of the national government—House, Senate, President, and Supreme Court—is chosen by different constituencies. Because the terms of these decision-making bodies are of varying length, a complete renewal of government at one stroke is impossible. Thus the people cannot wreak havoc quickly through direct elections. To make their will felt in all

---

attachment to different leaders ambitiously contending for preeminence and power." Even when there are no serious differences among people, these "frivolous and fanciful distinctions" will inspire "unfriendly passions" and "violent conflicts."

However, according to Madison,

> "the most common and durable source of factions has been the various and unequal distribution of property. Those who hold and those who are without property have ever formed distinct interests in society. Those who are creditors and those who are debtors fall under like discrimination. A landed interest, a manufacturing interest, a mercantile interest, a monied interest, with many lesser interests, grow up of necessity in civilized nations, and divide them into different classes, actuated by different sentiments and views [The Federalist, *Number 10*].

In Madison's view, a national government is the most important protection against mass movements that might threaten property. By creating such a government, encompassing a large number of citizens and a great expanse of territory,

> *you take in a greater variety of parties and interests; you make it less probable that a majority of the whole will have a common motive to invade the rights of other citizens; or if such a common motive exists it will be more difficult for all who feel it to discover their own strength, and to act in unison with each other.*

The structure of the new national government should ensure suppression of "factious" issues (those that would generate factions). And Madison did not hedge in naming these factious issues: "A rage for paper money, for an abolition of debts, for an equal division of property, of any other improper or wicked project." Note that Madison's factious issues are all challenges to the dominant economic elites. His defense of the new Constitution was that its republican and federal features would help keep certain threats to property from ever becoming public issues. In short, the Founding Fathers deliberately designed the new U.S. government to make it difficult for any mass political movement to challenge property rights.

the decision-making bodies of the national government, they must wait years.

Moreover, each of these decision-making bodies has an important check on the decisions of the others. No bill can become law without the approval of both the House and the Senate. The president shares in the legislative power through the veto and the responsibility to "give to the Congress information of the state of the Union, and recommend to their consideration such measures as he shall judge necessary and expedient. . . . "The president can also convene sessions of Congress. But the appointing power of the president is shared by the Senate; so is the power to make treaties. Also Congress can override executive vetoes. The president must execute the laws but cannot do so without relying on executive departments, which Congress must create. The executive branch can spend only money appropriated by Congress. Indeed, "separation of powers" is a misnomer, for we are really talking about sharing, not separating, power; each branch participates in the activities of every other branch.

Even the Supreme Court, which was created by the Constitution, must be appointed by the president with the consent of the Senate, and Congress may prescribe the number of justices. Congress must create lower and intermediate courts, establish the number of judges, and fix the jurisdiction of lower federal courts.

Judicial Review

Perhaps the keystone of the system of checks and balances is the idea of judicial review, an original contribution by the Founding Fathers to the science of government. In *Marbury* v. *Madison* in 1803, Chief Justice John Marshall argued convincingly that the Founding Fathers intended the Supreme Court to have the power to invalidate not only state laws and constitutions but also any laws of Congress that came into conflict with the Constitution. The text of the Constitution nowhere specifically authorizes federal judges to invalidate acts of Congress; at most, the Constitution implies this power. (But Hamilton apparently thought that the Constitution contained this power, since he was careful to explain it in *The Federalist*, Number 78, before the ratification of the Constitution.) Thus, the Supreme Court stands as the final defender of the fundamental principles agreed upon by the Founding Fathers against the encroachments of popularly elected legislatures.

RATIFICATION: AN EXERCISE IN ELITE POLITICAL SKILLS

When its work ended on September 17, 1787, the Constitutional Convention sent the Constitution to New York City, where Congress was then in session. The Convention suggested that the Constitution "should afterwards be submitted to a convention of delegates chosen in each state by the people thereof, under the recommendation of its legislature for their assent and ratification." Convention delegates further proposed that ratification by nine states be sufficient to put the new constitution into effect. On September 28, Congress sent the Constitution to the states without further recommendations.

Extraordinary Ratification Procedure

The ratification procedure suggested by the Founding Fathers was a skillful political maneuver. Since Convention proceedings had been secret, few people knew that the delegates had gone beyond their instructions to amend the Articles of Confederation and had created a whole new scheme of government. Their ratification procedure was a complete departure from what was then the law of the land, the Articles of Confederation. The Articles provided that Congress make amendments only with the approval of *all* states. But since Rhode Island was firmly in the hands of small farmers, the unanimity required by the Articles was obviously out of the question. The Founding Fathers felt obligated to act outside the existing law.

The Founding Fathers also called for special ratifying conventions in the states rather than risk submitting the Constitution to the state legislatures. This extraordinary procedure gave clear advantage to supporters of the Constitution, since submitting the plan to the state legislatures would weaken its chances for success. Thus the struggle for ratification began under ground rules designed by the national elite to give them the advantage over any potential opponents.

Limited Participation in Ratification

In the most important and controversial study of the Constitution to date, Charles A. Beard compiled a great deal of evidence supporting the hypothesis "that substantially all of the merchants, moneylenders, security holders, manufacturers, shippers, capitalists and financiers, and their professional associates are to be found on one side in support of the Constitution, and that substantially all of the major portion of the opposition came from the non-slaveholding farmers and debtors."[12] While historians disagree over the solidarity of class divisions in the struggle for ratification, most concede that only about 160,000 people voted in elections for delegates to state ratifying conventions and that not more than 100,000 of these voters favored the adoption of the Constitution. This figure represents about one in six of the adult males in the country, and no more than 5 percent of the general population. Thus, whether or not Beard is correct about class divisions in the struggle for ratification, it is clear that the number of people who participated in any fashion in ratifying the Constitution was an extremely small minority in the population.*

Emergence of Anti-Federalist Opposition

Some men of property and education did oppose the new Constitution. These were men who had greater confidence in their ability to control state governments than to control the new federal government. They called themselves "Anti-Federalists," and they vigorously attacked the Constitution as a counterrevolutionary document that could undo much of the progress made since 1776 toward freedom, liberty, and equality. According to the opponents of the Constitution, the new government would be "aristocratic," all powerful, and a threat to the "spirit of republicanism" and the "genius of democracy." They charged that the new Constitution created an aristocratic upper house and an almost monarchical presidency. The powers of the national government could trample the states and deny the people of the states the opportunity to handle their own political and economic affairs. The Anti-Federalists repeatedly asserted that the Constitution removed powers from the people and concentrated them in the hands of a few national officials who were largely immune to popular control; moreover, they attacked the undemocratic features of the Constitution and argued that state govern-

*Beard's economic interpretation differs from an elitist interpretation in that Beard believes that the economic elites supported the Constitution and the masses opposed it. Our elitist interpretation asserts only that the masses did not participate in writing or adopting the Constitution and that elites benefited directly from its provisions. Our interpretation does not depend upon showing that the masses opposed the Constitution but merely that they did not participate in its establishment. Attacks on Beard appear in Forrest McDonald, *We the People: The Economic Origins of the Constitution* (Chicago: University of Chicago Press, 1958) and Robert E. Brown, *Charles Beard and the Constitution* (Princeton, N.J.: Princeton University Press, 1956). Lee Benson provides a balanced view in *Turner and Beard: American Historical Writing Reconsidered* (New York: Free Press, 1960).

ments were much more representative of the people. Also under attack were the secrecy of the Constitutional Convention and the actions of the Founding Fathers, both contrary to the law and the spirit of the Articles of Confederation.

The Bill of Rights as an Afterthought

While the Anti-Federalists deplored the undemocratic features of the new Constitution, their most effective criticism centered on the absence of any bill of rights. The omission of a bill of rights was particularly glaring since the idea was very popular at the time, and most new state constitutions contained one. It is an interesting comment on the psychology of the Founding Fathers that the idea of a bill of rights did not come up in the Convention until the final week of deliberations; even then it received little consideration. The Founding Fathers certainly believed in limited government, and they did write a few liberties into the body of the Constitution, such as protection against bills of attainder and *ex post facto* laws, a guarantee of the writ of *habeas corpus,* a limited definition of treason, and a guarantee of jury trial. However, they did not include a bill of rights in the Constitution.

When criticism about the absence of a bill of rights began to mount, supporters of the Constitution presented an interesting argument to explain the deficiency: (1) the national government was one of enumerated powers and could not exercise any powers not expressly delegated to it in the Constitution; (2) the power to interfere with free speech or press or otherwise to restrain liberty was not among the enumerated powers in the Constitution; (3) it was therefore unnecessary to deny the new government that power specifically. But this logic was unconvincing; the absence of a bill of rights seemed to confirm the suspicion that the Founding Fathers were more concerned with protecting property than with protecting the personal liberties of the people. Many members of the elite and nonelite alike were uncomfortable with the thought that personal liberty depended on a thin thread of inference from enumerated powers. Supporters of the Constitution thus had to retreat from their demand for unconditional ratification; the New York, Massachusetts, and Virginia conventions agreed to the new Constitution only after receiving the Federalists' solemn promise to add a bill of rights as amendments. Thus the fundamental guarantees of liberty in the Bill of Rights were political concessions by the nation's elite. Whereas the Founding Fathers deserved great credit for the document that they produced at

Philadelphia, the first Congress to meet under that Constitution was nonetheless obliged to submit twelve amendments to the states, ten of which were ratified by 1791.

Summary

Elite theory provides us with an interpretation of the U.S. Constitution and the basic structure of U.S. government. Our analysis of constitutional policies centers on the following propositions:

1. The Constitution of the United States was not "ordained and established" by "the people." Instead it was written by a small, educated, talented, wealthy elite in America, representative of powerful economic interests: bondholders, investors, merchants, real estate owners, and planters.

2. The Constitution and the national government that it established had its origins in elite dissatisfaction with the inability of the central government to pay off its bondholders, the interference of state governments with the development of a national economy, the threat to investors and creditors posed by state issuance of cheap paper money and laws relieving debtors of contractual obligations, the threat to propertied classes arising from post–Revolutionary War radicalism, the inability of the central government to provide an army capable of protecting western development or a navy capable of protecting American commercial interests on the high seas, and the inability of America's elite to exercise power in world affairs.

3. The elite achieved ratification of the Constitution through its astute political skills. The masses of people in the United States did not participate in the writing of the Constitution or in its adoption by the states, and they probably would have opposed the Constitution had they had the information and resources to do so.

4. The Founding Fathers shared a consensus that the fundamental role of government is the protection of liberty and property. They believed in a republican form of government by men of principle and property. They opposed an aristocracy or a governing nobility, but they also opposed mass democracy with direct participation by the people in decision making. They feared mass movements seeking to reduce inequalities of wealth, intelligence, talent, or virtue. "Dangerous leveling" was a serious violation of men's rights to property.

5. The structure of American government was designed to suppress "factious" issues—threats to dominant economic elites. Republicanism, the division of power between state and national governments, and the complex system of checks and balances and divided power were all designed as protections against mass movements that might threaten liberty and property.

6. The text of the Constitution contains many direct and immediate benefits to America's governing elite. Although all Americans, both elite and mass, may have benefited by the adoption of the Constitution, the advantages and benefits for U.S. elites were their compelling motives for supporting the new Constitution.

Notes

1. Lester Cappon, ed., *The Adams-Jefferson Letters* (Chapel Hill: University of North Carolina Press, 1959), vol. I, p. 106.

2. Max Ferrand, ed., *The Records of the Federal Convention of 1787* (New Haven, Conn.: Yale University Press, 1937), vol. III, p. 15.

3. Ibid., p. 32.

4. See Clinton Rossiter, *1787, The Grand Convention* (New York: Macmillan, 1966), p. 45.

5. Charles A. Beard, *An Economic Interpretation of the Constitution of the United States* (New York: Macmillan, 1913), pp. 73–151.

6. John P. Roche, "The Founding Fathers: A Reform Caucus in Action," *American Political Science Review* 55 (December 1961): 799.

7. See especially Beard, *Economic Interpretation.*

8. James Madison, Alexander Hamilton, and John Jay, *The Federalist* (New York: Modern Library, 1937).

9. Ibid.

10. Ibid.

11. Ibid.

12. Beard, *Economic Interpretation,* pp. 16–17.

Selected Readings

Beard, Charles A. *An Economic Interpretation of the Constitution of the United States.* New York: Macmillan, 1913. The Free Press issued a paperback edition in 1965. Much of this chapter reflects data presented by Beard in this classic work. Beard traces the events leading up to the writing of the Constitution and the events surrounding ratification from an economic point of view. He discovers that economic considerations played a major, if not central, role in the shaping of the Constitution.
For several critiques of Beard, see:

1. Beale, Howard K., ed. *Charles A. Beard: An Appraisal.* Lexington: University of Kentucky Press, 1954.

2. Benson, Lee. *Turner and Beard: American Historical Writing Reconsidered.* New York: Free Press, 1960.

3. McDonald, Forrest. *We the People: The Economic Origins of the Constitution.* Chicago: University of Chicago Press, 1958.

Madison, James, Alexander Hamilton, and John Jay. *The Federalist.* New York: Modern Library, 1937. This collection of the articles published in support of the Constitution offers perhaps the most important contemporary comments available on the Constitution.

Peltason, J. W. *Understanding the Constitution,* 13th ed. New York: Harcourt Brace, 1994. Of the many books that explain parts of the Constitution, this is one of the best. It contains explanations of the Declaration of Independence, the Articles of Confederation, and the Constitution. The book is written clearly and is well suited for undergraduate as well as graduate and faculty use.

Rossiter, Clinton L. *1787, The Grand Convention.* New York: Macmillan, 1966. This readable and entertaining account of the men and events of 1787 contains many insights into the difficulties the Founding Fathers had writing the Constitution.

Wood, Gordon S. *The Creation of the American Republic 1776–1787.* New York: Norton, 1993. A study of the political conflicts in the new nation that led to the Constitutional Convention.

3

The Evolution of American Elites

The fierceness of political struggles has often been misleading; for the range of vision embodied by the primary contestants in the major parties has always been bounded by the horizons of property and enterprise.

—RICHARD HOFSTADTER

A stable elite system depends on the "circulation of elites"—the movement of talented and ambitious individuals from the lower strata into the elite. An open elite system providing for "a slow and continuous modification of the ruling classes" is essential for continuing the system and avoiding revolution. *Popular elections, party competition, and other democratic institutions in the United States have not enabled the masses to govern, but these institutions have helped keep the elite system an open one.* They have assisted in the circulation of elites, even if they have never been a means of challenging the dominant elite consensus.

In this chapter, a historical analysis of the evolution of American elites, we show that American elite membership has evolved slowly, without any serious break in the ideas or values underlying the U.S. political and economic system. The United States has never experienced a true revolution that forcibly replaced governing elites with nonelites. Instead American elite membership has been open to those who acquire wealth and property and who accept the national consensus about private enterprise, limited government, and individualism. Industrialization, technological change, and new sources of wealth in the expanding economy have produced new elite members, and the U.S. elite system has permitted the absorption of the new elites without upsetting the system itself.

Policy changes and innovations in the structure of American government over the decades have been *incremental* (step-by-step) rather than revolutionary. Elites have modified public policies but seldom replaced them. They have made structural adaptations in the constitutional system designed by the Founding Fathers but have kept intact the original framework of U.S. constitutionalism.

Political conflict in the United States has centered on a very narrow range of issues. Only once, in the Civil War, have elites been deeply divided over the nature of American society. The Civil War reflected a deep cleavage between southern elites—dependent upon a plantation economy, slave labor, and free trade—and northern industrial and commercial elites, who prospered under free labor and protective tariffs.

HAMILTON AND THE NATION'S FIRST PUBLIC POLICIES

The most influential figure in George Washington's administration was Alexander Hamilton, secretary of the treasury. More than anyone else, Hamilton was aware that the new nation had to win the lasting confidence of business and financial elites in order to survive and prosper. Only if the United States were established on a sound financial basis could it attract investors at home and abroad and expand its industry and commerce. Great Britain remained the largest source of investment capital for the new nation, and Hamilton was decidedly pro-British. He also favored a strong central government as a means of protecting property and stimulating the growth of commerce and industry.

Paying the National Debt

Hamilton's first move was to refund the national debt at face value. Most of the original bonds were no longer in the hands of the original owners but had fallen to speculators who had purchased them for only a fraction of their face value. Since these securities were worth only about twenty-five cents on the dollar, the Hamilton refund program meant a 300 percent profit for the speculators. Hamilton's program went beyond refunding the debts owed by the United States; he also undertook to pay the debts incurred by the states themselves during the Revolutionary War. His object was to place the creditor class under a deep obligation to the central government.

Establishing a National Bank

Hamilton also acted to establish a Bank of the United States, which would receive government funds, issue a national currency, facilitate the sale of national bonds, and tie the national government even more closely to the banking community. The Constitution did not specifically grant Congress the power to create a national bank, but Hamilton was willing to interpret the "necessary and proper" clause broadly enough to include the creation of a bank to help carry out the taxing, borrowing, and currency powers enumerated in the Constitution. Hamilton's broad construction of the "necessary and proper" clause looked in the direction of a central government that would exercise powers not specifically enumerated in the Constitution. Thomas Jefferson, who was secretary of state in the same cabinet with Hamilton, expressed growing concern over Hamilton's tendency toward national centralization. Jefferson argued that Congress could not establish the bank because the bank was not strictly "necessary" to carry out delegated functions. But Hamilton won out, with the support of President Washington; in 1791 Congress voted to charter the Bank of the United States. For twenty years the bank was very successful, especially in stabilizing the currency of the new nation.

Expanding the "Necessary and Proper" Clause

Not until 1819 did the Supreme Court decide the constitutionality of the Bank of the United States. In the famous case of *McCulloch* v. *Maryland,* the Supreme Court upheld the broad definition of national power suggested by Hamilton under the "necessary and proper" clause. At the same time, the Court established the principle that a state law that interferes with a national activity is unconstitutional.[1] "Let the end be legitimate," Chief Justice John Marshall wrote, "let it be within the scope of the Constitution, and all means which are appropriate, which are plainly adopted to that end, which are not prohibited, but consistent with the letter and spirit of the Constitution, are constitutional." The *McCulloch* case firmly established the principle that Congress has the right to choose any appropriate means for carrying out the delegated powers of the national government. The "necessary and proper" clause is now sometimes called the "implied powers" clause or the "elastic" clause because it gives to Congress many powers that the Constitution does not explicitly grant. Congress still traces all its activities to some formal grant of power, but this task is usually not difficult.

RISE OF THE JEFFERSONIANS

The centralizing effect of Hamilton's programs and their favoring of merchants, manufacturers, and shipbuilders aroused some opposition in elite circles. Southern planters and large landowners benefited very little from Hamilton's policies, and they were joined in their opposition by local and state elites who feared that a strong central government threatened their own powers. These agrarian groups were first called "Anti-Federalists," and later "Republicans" and "Democratic Republicans" when those terms became popular after the French Revolution. When Thomas Jefferson resigned from Washington's cabinet in protest of Hamilton's program, Anti-Federalists began to gather around Jefferson.

Jefferson as a Wealthy Plantation Owner

Historians portray Jefferson as a great democrat and champion of the "common man." And in writing the Declaration of Independence, the Virginia Statute for Religious Freedom, and the famous *Notes on Virginia,* Jefferson indeed expressed concern for the rights of all "the people" and a willingness to trust in their wisdom. But when Jefferson spoke warmly of the merits of "the people," he meant those who owned and managed their own farms and estates. He firmly believed that only those who owned their own land could make good citizens. Jefferson disliked aristocracy, but he also held the urban masses in contempt. He wanted to see the United States become a nation of free, educated, landowning farmers. Democracy, he believed, could be founded only on a propertied class in a propertied nation. His belief that land ownership is essential to virtuous government explains in part his Louisiana Purchase, which he hoped would provide the American people with land "to the hundredth and thousandth generation."[2]

The dispute between Federalists and Anti-Federalists in the early United States was not between elites and masses. It was a dispute within elite circles between two propertied classes: merchants and bankers on one side, and plantation owners and slaveholders on the other.[3]

Rise of Political Parties

The Anti-Federalists, or Republicans, did not elect their first president, Thomas Jefferson, until 1800. John Adams, a Federalist, succeeded Washington in the election of 1796. Yet the election of 1796 was an important milestone in the development of the American political system. For the first time, two candidates, Adams and Jefferson, campaigned not as individuals but as members of political parties. For the first time, the candidates for the electoral college announced themselves before the election as either "Adams's men" or "Jefferson's men." Most important, for the first time, American political leaders realized the importance of molding mass opinion and organizing the masses for political action. The Republican party first saw the importance of working among the masses to rally popular support. The Federalist leaders made the mistake of assuming that they could maintain the unquestioning support of the less educated and less wealthy without bothering to mold their opinions.

Early Attempts at Elite Repression

Rather than trying, as the Republicans did, to manipulate public opinion, the Federalists tried to outlaw public criticism of the government by means of the Alien and Sedition Acts of 1798. Among other things, these acts made it a crime to publish any false or malicious writing directed against the president or Congress, or to "stir up hatred" against them. The acts directly challenged the newly adopted First Amendment guarantee of freedom of speech and press.

In response to the Alien and Sedition Acts, Jefferson and Madison put forward their famous Kentucky and Virginia resolutions. These measures proposed that the states assume the right to decide whether Congress has acted unconstitutionally and, furthermore, that the states properly "interpose" their authority against "palpable and alarming infractions of the Constitution." The Virginia and Kentucky legislatures passed these resolutions and declared the Alien and Sedition Acts "void and of no force" in these states.

REPUBLICANS IN POWER: THE STABILITY OF PUBLIC POLICY

In the election of 1800, the Federalists went down to defeat; Thomas Jefferson and Aaron Burr were elected over John Adams and C. C. Pinckney. Only the New England states, New Jersey, and Delaware, where commercial and manufacturing interests were strongest, voted Federalist. Because the vast majority of American people won their living from the soil, the landed elites were able to mobilize those masses behind their bid for control of the government. The Federalists failed to recognize the importance of agrarianism in the nation's economic and political life. Another half-century would pass and America's Industrial Revolution would be in full swing before manufacturing and commercial elites would reestablish their dominance.

The election of 1800 enabled landed interests to gain power in relation to commercial and industrial interests. Yet the fact that an "out" party peacefully replaced an "in" party is testimony to the strength of the consensus among the new nation's elite.* The "Virginia dynasty"—Thomas Jefferson, James Madison, and finally James Monroe—governed the country for six presidential terms, nearly a quarter of a century. Interestingly, once in office, the Republicans made few changes in Federalist and Hamiltonian policy. (The only major pieces of legislation repealed by the Republicans were the Alien and Sedition Acts. And it seems clear that in passing these acts the Federalists had violated elite consensus.) The Republicans did not attack commercial or industrial enterprise; in fact commerce and industry prospered under Republican rule as never before. They did not attempt to recover money paid out by Hamilton in refunding national or state debts. They allowed public land speculation to continue. Instead of crushing the banks, Republicans soon supported the financial interests they had sworn to oppose.

Jefferson was an ardent expansionist; to add to America's wealth in land, he purchased the vast Louisiana Territory. Later a stronger army and a system of internal roads were necessary to help develop western land. Jefferson's successor, James Madison, built a strong navy and engaged in another war with England, the War of 1812, to protect U.S. commerce on the high seas. The Napoleonic wars and the War of 1812 stimulated American manufacturing by depressing trade with Britain. In 1816 Republicans passed a

*The original text of the Constitution did not envision an opposing faction. Presidential electors could cast two votes for president, with the understanding that the candidate with the second highest vote total would be vice-president. Seventy-three Republican electors pledged to Jefferson and sixty-five Federalists pledged to Adams went to the electoral college. Somewhat thoughtlessly, all the Republicans cast one vote for Jefferson and one vote for Aaron Burr, his running mate, with the result that each man received the same number of votes for the presidency. Because of the tie vote, the decision went to the Federalist-controlled House of Representatives, where a movement was begun to elect Burr, rather than Jefferson, in order to embarrass the Republicans. But Alexander Hamilton used his influence in Congress to swing the election to his old political foe Jefferson, suggesting again that their differences were not so deep that either would deliberately undermine the presidency to strike at the other. Once in power, the Republicans passed the Twelfth Amendment to the Constitution, providing that each presidential elector should thereafter vote separately for president and vice president. Both Federalists and Republicans in the states promptly agreed with this reform and ratification was completed by the election of 1804.

high tariff in order to protect domestic industry and manufacturing from foreign goods. As for Republican tax policies, Jefferson wrote in 1816:

> To take from one, because it is thought his own industry and that of his fathers has acquired too much, in order to spare to others, who, or whose fathers, have not exercised equal industry and skill, is to violate arbitrarily the first principle of association, "the guarantee to everyone the free exercise of his industry and the fruits acquired by it."[4]

In short, the Republicans had no intention of redistributing wealth in the United States. Indeed, before the end of Madison's second term in 1817, the Republicans had taken over the whole complex of Hamiltonian policies: a national bank, high tariffs, protection for manufacturers, internal improvements, western land development, a strong army and navy, and a broad interpretation of national power. So complete was the elite consensus that by 1820 the Republicans had completely driven the Federalist party out of existence, largely by taking over its programs.

RISE OF THE WESTERN ELITES

According to Frederick Jackson Turner, "The rise of the New West was the most significant fact in American history."[5] Certainly the American West had a profound impact on the political system of the new nation. People went west because of the vast wealth of fertile lands that awaited them there; nowhere else in the world could one acquire wealth so quickly as in the new American West. Because aristocratic families of the eastern seaboard seldom had reason to migrate westward, the western settlers were mainly middle- and lower-class immigrants. With hard work and good fortune, penniless migrants could become wealthy plantation owners or cattle ranchers in a single generation. Thus the West offered rapid upward social mobility.

New elites arose in the West and had to be assimilated onto America's governing circles. No one exemplifies the new entrants into the U.S. elite better than Andrew Jackson. Jackson's victory in the presidential election of 1828 was not a victory of the common people against the propertied classes but rather one of the new western elites against established Republican leadership in the East. Jackson's victory forced established U.S. elites to recognize the growing importance of the West and to open their ranks to the new rich west of the Alleghenies.

The "Natural Aristocracy"

Since Jackson was a favorite of the people, it was easy for him to believe in the wisdom of the common people. But Jacksonian democracy was by no means a philosophy of leveling egalitarianism. The ideal of the frontier society was the self-made man, and people admired wealth and power won by competitive skill. Wealth and power obtained only through special privilege offended the frontiersmen, however. They believed in a *natural aristocracy* rather than an aristocracy by birth, education, or special privilege. Jacksonians demanded not absolute equality but a more open elite system—a greater opportunity for the rising middle class to acquire wealth and influence through competition.

Expansion of the Electorate

In their struggle to open America's elite system, the Jacksonians appealed to mass sentiment. Jackson's humble beginnings, his image as a self-made man, his military adventures, his frontier experience, and his rough, brawling style endeared him to the masses. As beneficiaries of popular support, the new elites of the West developed a strong faith in the wisdom and justice of popular decisions. The new western states that entered the Union granted universal white male suffrage, and gradually the older states fell into step. Rising elites, themselves often less than a generation away from the masses, saw in a widened electorate a chance for personal advancement that they could never have achieved under the old regime. Therefore, the Jacksonians became noisy and effective advocates of the principle that all men should have the right to vote and to hold public office. They also successfully attacked the congressional caucus system of nominating presidential candidates. After his defeat in Congress in 1824, Jackson wished to sever Congress from the presidential nominating process. In 1832, when the Democrats held their first national convention, they renominated Andrew Jackson by acclamation. The tradition of nominating presidential candidates by national party convention was viewed as a democratizing reform. But it really originated out of Jackson's frustration at not being nominated by the Democratic party's congressional caucus in 1824.

ELITE CLEAVAGE: THE CIVIL WAR

During the nation's first sixty years, American elites substantially agreed about the character and direction of the new nation. Conflicts over the national bank, the tariff, internal improvement (such as roads and harbors), and even the controversial war with Mexico in 1846 did not threaten the basic underlying consensus. In the 1850s, however, the status of blacks in American society—the most divisive issue in the history of American politics—drove a wedge into the elites and ultimately led to the nation's bloodiest war. The national political system was unequal to the task of negotiating a peaceful settlement to the slavery problem because America's elites divided deeply over the question.

Southern Elites

In 1787 the southern elites—cotton planters, landowners, exporters, and slave traders—foresaw an end to slavery, but after 1820 the demand for cotton became insatiable, and southern planters could not profitably produce cotton without slave labor. Cotton accounted for more than half the value of all U.S. goods shipped abroad before the Civil War. Although Virginia did not depend on cotton, it sold great numbers of slaves to the cotton states, and "slave raising" itself became immensely profitable.

It was the white *elites* and not the white *masses* of the South who had an interest in the slave and cotton culture. On the eve of the Civil War, probably no more than 400,000 southern families—approximately one in four—held slaves, and many of those families held only one or two slaves each. The number of great planters—men who owned fifty or more slaves and large holdings of land—was probably not more than 7,000, yet their views dominated southern politics.

Northern Elites

The northern elites were merchants and manufacturers who depended on free labor, yet they had no direct interest in abolishing slavery in the South. But both northern and southern elites realized that control of the West was the key to future dominance of the nation. Northern elites wanted a West composed of small farmers who produced food and raw materials for the industrial and commercial East and provided a market for eastern goods. Southern planters feared the voting power of a West composed of small farmers and wanted western lands for expansion of the cotton and slave culture. Cotton ate up the land and, because it required continuous cultivation and monotonous rounds of simple tasks, was suited to slave labor. Thus to protect the cotton economy, it was essential to protect slavery in western lands. This conflict over western land eventually precipitated the Civil War.

Attempts at Compromise

Despite these differences, the underlying consensus of American elites was so great that they devised compromise after compromise to maintain unity. The Missouri Compromise of 1820 divided the land in the Louisiana Purchase exclusive of Missouri between free territory and slave territory at 36° 30' and admitted Maine and Missouri as free and slave states, respectively. After the war with Mexico, the elaborate Compromise of 1850 caused one of the greatest debates in American legislative history, with Senators Henry Clay, Daniel Webster, John C. Calhoun, Salmon P. Chase, Stephen A. Douglas, Jefferson Davis, Alexander H. Stevens, Robert Tombs, William H. Seward, and Thaddeus Stevens all participating. Elite divisiveness was apparent, but it was not yet so destructive as to split the nation. Congress achieved a compromise by admitting California as a free state; creating two new territories, New Mexico and Utah, out of the Mexican cession; enacting a drastic fugitive slave law to satisfy southern planters; and prohibiting slave trade in the District of Columbia. Even the Kansas-Nebraska Act of 1854 was to be a compromise; each new territory would decide for itself whether to be slave or free, with the expectation that Nebraska would vote free and Kansas slave. But gradually the spirit of compromise gave way to cleavage and conflict.

Cleavage, Violence, and Secession

Beginning in 1856, proslavery and antislavery forces fought it out in "bleeding Kansas." Intemperate language in the Senate became commonplace, with frequent threats of secession, violence, and civil war.

In 1857 the Supreme Court decided, in *Dred Scott* v. *Sandford,* that the Missouri Compromise was unconstitutional because Congress had no authority to forbid slavery in any territory.[6] The Constitution protected slave property, said Chief Justice Roger B. Taney, as much as any other kind of property.

In 1859 John Brown and his followers raided the U.S. arsenal at Harpers Ferry as a first step to freeing the slaves of Virginia by force. Brown was captured by Virginia militia under the command of Colonel Robert E. Lee, tried for treason, found guilty, and executed. Southerners believed that northerners had tried to incite the horror of a slave insurrection, while northerners believed that Brown had died a martyr.

The conflict between North and South led to the complete collapse of the Whig party and the emergence of a new Republican party composed exclusively of northerners and westerners. For the first time in the history of American parties, one of the two major parties did not spread across both sides of the Mason-Dixon line; 1860 was the only year in American history that four major parties sought the presidency. The nation was so divided that no party came close to winning the majority of popular votes. Lincoln, the Republican candidate, and Douglas, the Democratic candidate, won most of their votes from the North and West, while John C. Breckinridge (Kentucky), the Southern Democratic candidate, and John Bell (Tennessee), the Constitutional Union candidate, received most of their votes from the South.

More important, the cleavage had become so deep that many prominent southern leaders announced that they would not accept the outcome of the presidential election if Lincoln won. Threats of secession were not new, but this time it was no bluff. For the first and only time in American history, prominent elite members were willing to destroy the American political system rather than compromise their interests and principles. Shortly after the election, on December 20, 1860, the state of South Carolina seceded from the Union. Within six months, ten other southern states followed.

Lincoln and Slavery

Abraham Lincoln never attacked slavery in the South; his exclusive concern was to halt the spread of slavery in the western territories. He wrote in 1845, "I hold it a paramount duty of us in the free states, due to the union of the states, and perhaps to liberty itself (paradox though it may seem), to let the slavery of the other states alone."[7] Throughout his political career, he consistently held this position. On the other hand, with regard to the western territories he said, "The whole nation is interested that the best use shall be made of these territories. We want them for homes and free white people. This they cannot be, to any considerable extent, if slavery shall be planted within them."[8] In short, Lincoln wanted to tie the western territories economically and culturally to the northern system. As for Lincoln's racial views, as late as 1858 he said:

> *I will say, then, that I am not, nor ever have been, in favor of bringing about in any way the social and political equality of the white and black races; that I am not, nor ever have been, in favor of making voters or jurors of Negroes, nor qualifying them to hold office, nor to intermarry with white people . . . and in as much as*

> *they cannot so live while they do remain together, there must be a*
> *position of superior and inferior; and I as much as any other man*
> *am in favor of having the superior position assigned to the white*
> *race.*[9]

Lincoln's political posture was essentially conservative. He wished to preserve the long-established order and consensus that had protected American principles and property rights so successfully in the past. He was not an abolitionist, and he did not want to destroy the southern elites or to alter the southern social fabric. His goal was to bring the South back into the Union, to restore orderly government, and to establish the principle that the states cannot resist national authority with force.

Emancipation as Political Opportunism

As the war continued and casualties mounted, northern opinion toward southern slaveowners became increasingly bitter. Many Republicans joined the abolitionists in calling for emancipation of the slaves simply to punish the "rebels." They knew that the South's power depended on slave labor. Lincoln also knew that if he proclaimed that the war was being fought to free the slaves, foreign intervention was less likely. Yet even in late summer of 1862, Lincoln wrote:

> *My paramount object in this struggle is to save the Union. If I could*
> *save the Union without freeing any slaves, I would do it; if I could*
> *save it by freeing some and leaving others alone, I would also do*
> *that. I shall do less whenever I shall believe what I am doing hurts*
> *the cause, and I shall do more whenever I believe doing more will*
> *help the cause. I shall adopt new views as fast as they shall appear*
> *to be true views.*[10]

Finally, on September 22, 1862, Lincoln issued his preliminary Emancipation Proclamation. Claiming his right as commander-in-chief of the army and navy, he promised that "on the first day of January 1863, all persons held as slaves within any state or designated part of a state, the people whereof shall then be in rebellion against the United States shall be then, thence forward, and forever free." Thus one of the great steps forward in human freedom in this nation, the Emancipation Proclamation, did not come about as a result of demands by the people, and certainly not as a result of demands by the slaves themselves. It was a political and military action by the president for the sake of helping to preserve the Union. It was not a revolutionary action but a conservative one.

RISE OF THE NEW INDUSTRIAL ELITE

The Civil War's importance to U.S. elite structure lies in the commanding position that the new industrial capitalists won in the course of struggle. Even before 1860, northern industry had been altering the course of American life; the economic transformation of the United States from an agricultural to an industrial nation reached the crescendo of a revolution in the second half of the nineteenth century. Canals and steam railroads had been opening new markets for the growing industrial cities of the East. The rise of corporations and of stock markets for the accumulation of capital upset old-fashioned ideas of property. The introduction of machinery in factories revolutionized the conditions of American labor and made the masses dependent on industrial capitalists for their livelihood. Civil War profits compounded the capital of the industrialists and placed them in a position to dominate the economic life of the nation. Moreover, when the southern planters were removed from the national scene, the government in Washington became the exclusive domain of the new industrial leaders.

Political Plunder

The protective tariff, long opposed by the southern planters, became the cornerstone of the new business structure of the United States. The industrial capitalists realized that the Northwest Territory was the natural market for their manufactured goods, and the protective tariff restricted the vast and growing American market to American industry alone. The passage of the Homestead Act in 1862 threw the national domain wide open to settlers, and the Transcontinental Railroad Act of 1862 gave the railroads plentiful incentives to link expanding western markets to eastern industry. The northeastern United States was rich in the natural resources of coal, iron, and water power; and the large immigrant population streaming in from Europe furnished a dependable source of cheap labor. The Northeast also had superior means of transportation—both water and rail—to facilitate the assembling of raw materials and the marketing of finished products. With the rise of the new industrial capitalism, power in the United States flowed from the South and West to the Northeast, and Jefferson's dream of a nation of small free farmers faded.

Social Darwinism

The new industrial elite found a new philosophy to justify its political and economic dominance. Drawing an analogy from the new Darwinian biology, Herbert Spencer undertook to demonstrate that just as an elite was selected in nature through evolution, so also society would near perfection as it allowed natural social elites to be selected by free competition. In defense of the new capitalists, Herbert Spencer argued: "There cannot be more good done than that of letting social progress go on unhindered; an immensity of mischief may be done in . . . the artificial preservation of those least able to care for themselves."[11] Spencer hailed the accumulation of new industrial wealth as a sign of "the survival of the fittest." The "social Darwinists" found in the law of survival of the fittest an admirable defense for the emergence of a ruthless ruling elite, an elite that defined its own self-interest more narrowly, perhaps, than any other in American history.

Industrial Capitalism

As business became increasingly national in scope, only the strongest or most unscrupulous of the competitors survived. Great producers tended to become the cheapest ones, and little companies tended to disappear. Industrial production rose rapidly, while the number of industrial concerns steadily diminished. Total capital investment and total output of industry vastly increased, while ownership became concentrated. One result was the emergence of monopolies and near monopolies in the major industries of the United States. Another result was the accumulation of great family fortunes.[12] (See Table 3-1, compiled from 1924 tax returns. Admittedly it fails to record other great personal fortunes, such as Armour and Swift in meat packing, Candler in Coca-Cola, Cannon in textiles, Fleischmann in yeast, Pulitzer in publishing, Golet in real estate, Harriman in railroads, Heinz in foods, Manville in asbestos, Cudahy in food processing, Dorrance in Campbell's Soup, Hartford in A&P, Eastman in film, Firestone in rubber, Sinclair in oil, Chrysler in automobiles, Pabst in beer, and others.)

Elite Political Dominance

The only serious challenge to the political dominance of eastern capital came over the issue of "free silver." Leadership of the "free silver" movement came from mine owners in the silver states of the Far West. Their campaigns

| TABLE 3-1 | The great industrial fortunes, 1924 |

RANKING BY 1924 INCOME TAX	FAMILY	PRIMARY SOURCE OF WEALTH
1	Rockefeller	Standard Oil Co.
2	Morgan Inner Group (including Morgan partners and families and eight leading Morgan corporation executives)	J. P. Morgan & Co., Inc.
3	Ford	Ford Motor Co.
4	Harkness	Standard Oil Co.
5	Mellon	Aluminum Company
6	Vanderbilt	New York Central Railroad
7	Whitney	Standard Oil Co.
8	Standard Oil Group (including Archbold, Bedford, Cutler, Flagler, Pratt, Rogers, and Benjamin, but excepting others)	Standard Oil Co.
9	Du Pont	E. I. Du Pont de Nemours
10	McCormick	International Harvester Co. and Chicago Tribune, Inc.
11	Baker	First National Bank
12	Fisher	General Motors
13	Guggenheim	American Smelting and Refrigerating Co.
14	Field	Marshall Field & Co.
15	Curtis-Bok	The Curtis Publishing Company
16	Duke	American Tobacco Co.
17	Berwind	Berwind-White Coal Co.
18	Lehman	Lehman Brothers
19	Widener	American Tobacco and Public Utilities
20	Reynolds	R. J. Reynolds Tobacco Company
21	Astor	Real estate
22	Winthrop	Miscellaneous
23	Stillman	National City Bank
24	Timken	Timken Roller Bearing Company
25	Pitcairn	Pittsburgh Plate Glass Company
26	Warburg	Kuhn, Loeb & Company
27	Metcalf	Rhode Island textile mills
28	Clark	Singer Sewing Machine Company
29	Phipps	Carnegie Steel Company

| TABLE 3-1 | The great industrial fortunes, 1924 *(continued)* |

RANKING BY 1924 INCOME TAX	FAMILY	PRIMARY SOURCE OF WEALTH
30	Kuhn	Kuhn, Loeb & Company
31	Green	Stocks and real estate
32	Patterson	Chicago Tribune, Inc.
33	Taft	Real estate
34	Deering	International Harvester Co.
35	De Forest	Corporate law practice
36	Gould	Railroads
37	Hill	Railroads
38	Drexel	J. P. Morgan & Company
39	Thomas Fortune Ryan	Stock market
40	H. Foster (Cleveland)	Auto parts
41	Eldridge Johnson	Victor Phonograph
42	Arthur Curtiss James	Copper and railroads
43	C. W. Nash	Automobiles
44	Mortimer Schiff	Kuhn, Loeb & Company
45	James A. Patten	Wheat market
46	Charles Hayden	Stock market
47	Orlando F. Weber	Allied Chemical & Dye Corp.
48	George Blumenthal	Lazard Freres & Co.
49	Ogden L. Mills	Mining
50	Michael Friedsam	Merchandising
51	Edward B. McLean	Mining
52	Eugene Higgins	New York real estate
53	Alexander S. Cochran	Textiles
54	Mrs. L. N. Kirkwood	
55	Helen Tyson	
56	Archer D. Huntington	Railroads
57	James J. Storrow	Lee Higgins & Co.
58	Julius Rosenwald	Sears, Roebuck and Co.
59	Bernard M. Baruch	Stock market
60	S. S. Kresge	Merchandising

Source: Ferdinand Lundberg, *America's Sixty Families* (Secaucus, N.J.: Citadel Press, 1937). Reprinted by permission.

convinced thousands of western farmers that the unrestricted coinage of silver was the answer to their economic distress. The western mine owners did not care about the welfare of small farmers, but the prospect of inflation, debt relief, and expansion of the supply of money and purchasing power won increasing support among the masses in the West and South.

When William Jennings Bryan delivered his famous Cross of Gold speech at the Democratic convention in 1896, he undid the Cleveland "Gold Democrat" control of the Democratic party. Bryan was a westerner, a talented orator, an anti-intellectual, and a deeply religious man; he was antagonistic to the eastern industrial interests and totally committed to the cause of free silver. Bryan tried to rally the nation's have-nots to his banner; he tried to convince them that Wall Street was exploiting them. Yet he did not severely criticize the capitalist system, nor did he call for increased federal regulatory powers. In his acceptance speech he declared, "Our campaign has not for its object the reconstruction of society. . . . Property is and will remain the stimulus to endeavor and the compensation for toil."[13]

The Republican campaign, directed by Marcus Alonzo Hanna of Standard Oil, aimed to persuade the voters that what was good for business was good for the country. Hanna raised an unprecedented $16 million campaign fund from his wealthy fellow industrialists (an amount unmatched in presidential campaigns until the 1960s) and advertised his candidate, William McKinley, as the man who would bring a "full dinner pail" to all.

Bryan's attempt to rally the masses was a dismal failure; McKinley won by a landslide. Bryan ran twice again under the Democratic banner, in 1900 and 1908, but he lost by even greater margins. Although Bryan carried the South and some western states, he failed to rally the masses of the populous eastern states or of the growing cities. Republicans carried working-class, middle-class, and upper-class neighborhoods in the urban industrial states.

LIBERAL ESTABLISHMENT: REFORM AS ELITE SELF-INTEREST

In 1882 William H. Vanderbilt of the New York Central Railroad expressed the ethos of the industrial elite: "The public be damned." This first generation of great American capitalists had little sense of public responsibility. They had built their empires in the competitive pursuit of profit. They believed that their success arose from the immutable laws of natural selection, the survival of the fittest; they believed that society was best served by allowing those laws to operate freely.

"My strength is as the strength of ten, because I'm rich."

Wilson's Early Warning

In 1912 Woodrow Wilson, forerunner of a new elite ethos, criticized America's elite for its lack of public responsibility. Wilson urged America's elite to value the welfare of the masses as an aspect of its own long-run welfare. Wilson did not wish to upset the established order; he merely wished to develop a sense of public responsibility within the establishment. He believed that the national government should see that industrial elites operate in the public interest, and his New Freedom program reflected his high-minded aspirations. The Federal Reserve Act (1914) placed the nation's banking and credit system under public control. The Clayton Antitrust Act (1914) attempted to define specific business abuses, such as charging different prices to different buyers, granting rebates, and making false statements about competitors. Wilson's administration also established the Federal Trade Commission (1914) and authorized it to function in the "public interest" to prevent "unfair methods of competition and unfair and deceptive acts in commerce." Congress established an eight-hour day for railroad workers in

FOCUS

Elites in American History

What has been the relationship between economic elites and governmental leadership in American history? Political scientist Phillip H. Burch has explored this central question in a three-volume study evaluating the social and economic backgrounds of top cabinet-level and diplomatic appointments from the administration of President George Washington to that of President Jimmy Carter.[a] Burch defines one of the "economic elite" as a person who has held an important post (executive or director) in a major business enterprise or corporate law firm and/or whose family owned great wealth or occupied an important corporate position. Collectively, the economic elite never constituted more than 1 percent of the U.S. population. Yet, according to Burch, over the years since 1789 they constituted 78.7 percent of top governmental leaders.

According to Burch, the accompanying table shows that "the United States has certainly not been a land of equality of political opportunity. Rather, it has been an elitist-dominated nation." Nonetheless, economic elites occupied fewer top governmental posts in some periods than in others. During the New Deal years and World War II, President Roosevelt brought many noneconomic elites into top government posts, although Roosevelt himself possessed the very highest elite credentials. In earlier periods of American political history, government was almost exclusively directed by economic elites (95.8 percent elite-dominated in the pre–Civil War period, compared with 74.4 percent in more recent years).

Overall, nearly 80 percent of the nation's top appointed leaders have been elite figures, a considerably higher percentage than the proportion of presidents with elite backgrounds (only 58 percent by Burch's estimate). Burch concludes: "Regardless of its changing form, America has almost always been dominated by some form of wealth"[b]

[b]Ibid., vol. III, p. 388.

Elites in government, 1789–1980

	ELITE CABINET AND DIPLOMATIC APPOINTEES
Federalist period (1789–1801)	100.0%
Jeffersonian Republican years (1801–1829)	95.7
Jackson era (1829–1841)	93.8
Pre–Civil War decades (1841–1861)	95.2
Pre–Civil War period (1789–1861)	**95.8**
Civil War and Reconstruction (1861–1877)	81.1
Late nineteenth-century period (1877–1897)	86.8
McKinley–Taft years (1897–1913)	91.7
Wilson regime (1913–1921)	57.1
Harding–Hoover years (1921–1933)	80.9
Post–Civil War to New Deal period (1861–1933)	**83.5**
New Deal years (1933–1940)	47.4
World War II years (1940–1945)	57.9
Truman years (1945–1953)	55.6
Eisenhower years (1953–1961)	81.1
Kennedy–Johnson years (1961–1969)	62.7
Nixon–Ford years (1969–1977)	68.6
Carter years (1977–1980)	65.4
New Deal to Carter period (1933–1980)	**64.4**
Overall (1789–1980)	**78.7**

Note: An elite appointee is a person who has held a prior important position (executive or director) in a major business enterprise or corporate law firm and/or whose family has considerable wealth or an important corporate link.

Source: Phillip H. Burch, Jr., *Elites in American History,* vol. III (New York: Holmes and Meier, 1980), p. 383. Reprinted by permission.

[a]Phillip H. Burch, Jr., *Elites in American History*, 3 vols. (New York: Holmes and Meier, 1980).

interstate commerce (1914) and passed the Child Labor Act (1914) in an attempt to eliminate the worst abuses of children in industry (the Supreme Court, much less "public-regarding," declared this act unconstitutional). Wilson's program aimed to preserve competition, individualism, enterprise, opportunity—all considered vital in the American heritage. But he also believed fervently that elites must function in the public interest and that some government regulation might be required to see that they do so.

The Great Depression

Herbert Hoover was the last great advocate of the rugged individualism of the old order. The economic collapse of the Great Depression undermined the faith of both elites and nonelites in the ideals of the old order. Following the stock market crash of October 1929, and despite elite assurances that prosperity lay "just around the corner," the American economy virtually stopped. Prices dropped sharply, factories closed, real estate values declined, new construction practically ceased, banks went under, wages dropped drastically, and unemployment figures mounted. By 1932 one out of every four persons in the United States was unemployed, and one out of every five persons was on welfare.

Elite Reform

The election of Franklin Delano Roosevelt to the presidency in 1932 ushered in a new era in American elite philosophy. The Great Depression did not bring about a revolution or the emergence of new elites, but it did have an important impact on the thinking of America's governing elites. The victories of fascism in Germany and communism in the Soviet Union and the growing restlessness of the masses in America combined to convince America's elite that reform and regard for the public welfare were essential to the continued maintenance of the American political system and their dominant place in it.

Roosevelt sought a New Deal philosophy that would permit government to devote much more attention to the public welfare than did the philosophy of Hoover's somewhat discredited "rugged individualism." The New Deal was not new or revolutionary but rather a necessary reform of the existing capitalist system. It had no consistent unifying plan; it was a series of improvisations, many of them adopted very suddenly and some of them even contradictory. Roosevelt believed that government needed to undertake more careful economic planning to adapt "existing economic organizations to the service of the people." And he believed that the government must act humanely and compassionately toward those who were suffering hardship. Relief, recovery, and reform—not revolution—were the objectives of the New Deal.

Noblesse Oblige

For anyone of Roosevelt's background, it would have been surprising indeed to try to do anything other than preserve the existing social and economic order. Roosevelt was a descendant of two of America's oldest elite families, the Roosevelts and the Delanos, patrician families whose wealth predated the Civil War and the Industrial Revolution. The Roosevelts were not schooled in the scrambling competition of the new industrialists. From the beginning Roosevelt expressed a more public-regarding philosophy. Soon his personal philosophy of noblesse oblige—elite responsibility for the welfare of the masses—became the prevailing ethos of the new liberal establishment. (See the section, "The Liberal Establishment," in Chapter 4.)

VIETNAM: ELITE FAILURE TO LEAD

America's failure in Vietnam—the nation's longest war and only decisive loss—was not the result of military defeat. Rather, it resulted from the failure of the nation's political leadership to set forth clear objectives in Vietnam, to develop a strategy to achieve those objectives, and to rally mass support behind the effort.

A national elite that seeks to lead a society into war must clearly set forth the objectives of the war and convince itself and the mass of citizens that the objectives are worth the costs. But the objectives of the United States in Vietnam were vague and continually shifting. U.S. involvement was initiated by an intelligent and well-meaning liberal elite convinced of its wisdom and idealism and confident that government power, including military force, could be used to do good in the world.

Incremental Involvement

Initially the United States sought to resist communist aggression from North Vietnam and ensure a strong and independent democratic South Vietnamese government. President John F. Kennedy sent a large force of military advisors and counterinsurgency forces to assist in every aspect of training and support for the Army of the Republic of Vietnam (ARVN). President Kennedy personally inspired the development and deployment of U.S. counterinsurgency Special Forces ("Green Berets") to deal directly with a guerrilla enemy and help "win the hearts and minds" of the Vietnamese people.

President Kennedy's actions were consistent with long-standing U.S. policy of containing the spread of communism and assisting free people in resisting internal subversion and external aggression. The "best and the brightest" of the nation's liberal leadership in the early 1960s were convinced of the wisdom of using American power in Southeast Asia; these key decision makers included Secretary of State and former Rockefeller Foundation President Dean Rusk, Secretary of Defense and former Ford Motor Company President Robert McNamara, and National Security Advisor and former Harvard University Dean McGeorge Bundy.[14]

By 1964 units of the North Vietnamese Army (NVA) had begun to supplement the communist guerrilla forces (Vietcong) in the south. Unconfirmed reports of an attack on U.S. Navy vessels by North Vietnamese torpedo boats led to the "Gulf of Tonkin" resolution by the Congress, authorizing the president to take "all necessary measures" to "repel any armed attack" against any U.S. forces in Southeast Asia. In February 1965 President Lyndon B. Johnson ordered U.S. combat troops into South Vietnam and authorized a gradual increase in air strikes against North Vietnam.

Political Limits

The fateful decision to commit U.S. ground combat forces to Vietnam was made without any significant effort to mobilize American public opinion, the government, or the economy for war. On the contrary, the president minimized the U.S. military effort, placed numerical limits on U.S. troop strength in Vietnam, limited bombing targets, and underestimated North Vietnam's military capabilities as well as expected U.S. casualties. No U.S. ground troops were permitted to cross into North Vietnam, and only once (in Cambodia in 1970) were they permitted to attack NVA forces elsewhere in Indochina. President Johnson's gradualist approach (operation "Rolling Thunder" called for U.S. air strikes to move northward from the South Vietnamese border toward Hanoi at a slow and steady pace) gave the enemy precious time to construct a heavy air defense system, organize civilian repair brigades, disperse its military depots, and develop alternative transportation routes to the south. But more important, the U.S. leadership provided no clear-cut military objectives.

Military Victory, Political Defeat

The failure of the nation's leadership to set forth a clear military objective in Vietnam made "victory" impossible. *The Pentagon Papers*,[15] composed of official memos and documents of the war, reveal increasing disenchantment with military results throughout 1967 by Secretary of Defense Robert McNamara and others who had originally initiated U.S. military actions. But President Johnson sought to rally support for the war by claiming that the United States was "winning." General Westmoreland was brought home to tell Congress that there was a light at the end of the tunnel. "We have reached an important point where the end begins to come into view."[16] But these pronouncements only helped set the stage for the enemy's great political victory—the Tet offensive.

On January 30, 1968, Vietcong forces blasted their way into the U.S. embassy compound in Saigon and held the courtyard for six hours. The attack was part of a massive, coordinated Tet offensive against all major cities of South Vietnam. The offensive caught the United States and ARVN forces off guard. The ancient city of Hue was captured and held by Vietcong for nearly three weeks. But U.S. forces responded and inflicted very heavy casualties on the Vietcong. The Vietcong failed to hold any of the positions they captured; the people did not rise up to welcome them as "liberators," and their losses were high. Indeed, after Tet the Vietcong were no longer an effective fighting force; almost all fighting would be conducted thereafter by regular NVA troops. (Hanoi may have planned the elimination of Vietcong forces this way in order to ensure its eventual domination of the South.) By any *military* measure, the Tet offensive was a "defeat" for the enemy and a "victory" for U.S. forces.

Yet the Tet offensive was Hanoi's greatest political victory. "What the hell is going on?" asked a shocked television anchorman, Walter Cronkite. "I thought we were winning the war."[17] Television pictures of bloody fighting in Saigon and Hue seemed to mock the administration's reports of an early end to the war. The media, believing they had been duped by Johnson and Westmoreland, launched a long and bitter campaign against the war effort. Elite support for the war plummeted.

Elite Opinion Shifts

Elite opinion in the United States shaped the course of the Vietnam War, not mass opinion. Evidence for this thesis is provided by John F. Mueller, who

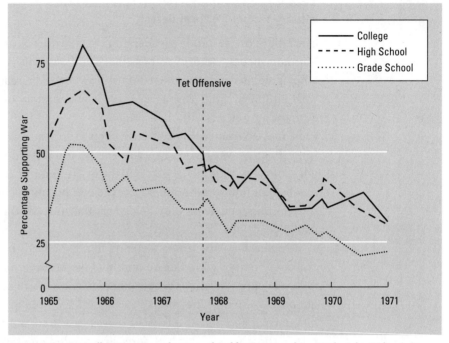

FIGURE 3-1

Trends in support of the Vietnam War, by education

Source: John F. Mueller, *War, Presidents, and Public Opinion* (New York: John Wiley & Sons, Inc., 1973), p. 125. Used with permission of the author.

traced support for the war over time among various segments of the nation's population.[18] In the early stages of the war, there was great public support for the fighting, especially among college-educated groups (see Figure 3-1), from which elites are drawn. The masses supported the war at the outset, but not as strongly as did the better-informed and better-educated groups. But after the Tet offensive in 1968, support of the Vietnam War by college-educated Americans declined. When elites supported the war in its early stages, the United States escalated its participation, despite less-than-enthusiastic support by less-educated groups. The United States withdrew from the war and sought a negotiated settlement after elites, not masses, made a dramatic shift in opinion. Elites agreed on escalation in the early phases of the Vietnam War, and they agreed on withdrawal in its later phases. Their only disagreements among themselves occurred over the speed of withdrawal.

The antiwar protesters had no significant effect on the course of the war. Mueller concludes, "The protest against the war in Vietnam may have been counterproductive in its impact on public opinion: that is, the war might have been somewhat more unpopular if protest had not existed."[19]

Most Americans disapproved of Jane Fonda's broadcasting enemy propaganda from Hanoi while U.S. prisoners were being tortured in prisons a few blocks away.

Deserted by the very elites who had initiated American involvement in the war, hounded by hostile media, and confronting a bitter and divisive presidential election, Lyndon Johnson made a dramatic announcement on national television on March 31, 1968: he halted the bombing of North Vietnam and asked Hanoi for peace talks, and concluded: "I shall not seek, and I will not accept, the nomination of my party for another term as your president." Formal peace talks opened in Paris on May 13.

Shifting Political Objectives

U.S. objectives in Vietnam shifted again with the arrival in Washington of the new president, Richard M. Nixon, and his national security advisor, Henry A. Kissinger. In the presidential election campaign of 1968, both candidates—Democratic Vice President Hubert H. Humphrey and Republican Richard Nixon—presented nearly identical positions supporting U.S. military efforts and endorsing a negotiated peace. But when the Nixon administration took office, it immediately began a gradual withdrawal of U.S. forces from Vietnam.

Nixon and Kissinger knew the war must be ended. But they sought to end it "honorably." The South Vietnamese could not be abruptly abandoned without threatening the credibility of U.S. commitments everywhere in the world. They sought a peace settlement that would give South Vietnam a reasonable chance to survive. They hoped that "detente" with the Soviet Union, and a new relationship with the People's Republic of China, might help to bring about "peace with honor" in Vietnam. But even in the absence of a settlement, they began the withdrawal of U.S. troops under the guise of "Vietnamization" of the war effort. ARVN forces were required to take up the burden of fighting as U.S. forces withdrew.

The End Game

Meanwhile, National Security Advisor Henry Kissinger and Hanoi's Le Duc Tho had begun meeting secretly in Paris, away from the formal negotiations, to work out "the shape of a deal." U.S. prisoners of war were a major bargaining chip for Hanoi. In the presidential election of 1972, the war became a partisan issue. Democratic candidate George McGovern had earlier stated that he would "crawl on his hands and knees to Hanoi" for peace, while Nixon continued his "peace with honor" theme. Nixon's landslide reelection strengthened his position in negotiations. In October Kissinger believed he had worked out a peace agreement, and he announced prematurely that "peace is at hand." But the agreement collapsed, in part because of the reluctance of the South Vietnamese to go along with the provisions worked out between Hanoi and Washington and in part because of last-minute new demands by Hanoi.[20]

The United States unleashed a devastating air attack directly on Hanoi for the first time in December 1972. U.S. B-52s from Guam joined with bombers based in Thailand to destroy factories, power plants, and transportation facilities in Hanoi itself. Critics at home labeled Nixon's action "the Christmas bombing," and congressional doves again planned to force an end to the war by law. But when negotiations resumed in Paris in January, the North Vietnamese quickly agreed to peace on the terms that Kissinger and Le Duc Tho had worked out earlier. Both Nixon and Kissinger contend that the Christmas bombing secured the final peace.[21]

The Paris Peace Agreement of 1973 called for a cease-fire in place, with NVA troops remaining in its areas of control in the south. The South Vietnamese government and the ARVN also remained in place. All U.S. forces were withdrawn from South Vietnam and U.S. prisoners returned. But the major question of the war—the political status of South Vietnam—was unresolved. The United States promised "full economic and military aid" to the South Vietnamese government and promised to "respond with full force" should North Vietnam violate the cease-fire. The United States also agreed to provide Hanoi with billions of dollars in aid for reconstruction.

Abandoning Commitments

The South Vietnamese government lasted two years after the Paris Peace Agreement. The United States fulfilled none of its pledges, either to South or North Vietnam. Congress refused to provide significant military aid to the South Vietnamese. Congress passed the War Powers Act in 1973 over Nixon's veto, obligating the president to withdraw U.S. troops from combat within sixty days in the absence of an explicit congressional endorsement. The Watergate affair forced Nixon's resignation in August 1974. In early 1975 Hanoi decided that the United States would not "jump back in," and therefore "the opportune moment" was at hand. The NVA attacked first in the central highlands, and South Vietnamese President Nguyen Van Thieu unwisely ordered a withdrawal to the coast. The retreat quickly became a rout. When NVA forces attacked Hue and Da Nang, the ARVN and thousands of civilians fled southward toward Saigon.

President Gerald Ford never gave serious consideration to the use of U.S. military forces to repel the new invasion, and his requests to Congress for emergency military aid to the South Vietnamese fell on deaf ears. U.S. Ambassador Graham Martin, embarrassed by his government's abandonment of Vietnam, delayed implementation of escape plans until the last moment. The United States abandoned hundreds of thousands of loyal Vietnamese who had fought alongside the Americans for years.[22] The spectacle of U.S. Marines using rifle butts to keep desperate Vietnamese from boarding helicopters on the roof of the U.S. embassy "provided a tragic epitaph for twenty-five years of American involvement in Vietnam."[23] Unlike past wars, there were no victory parades, and no one could answer the question of the mother whose son was killed in Vietnam: "What did he die for?"

THE GULF WAR: ELITE LEADERSHIP RESTORED

America's leadership performed markedly better in the Gulf War. Clear strategic objectives were established by President George Bush: to force the immediate and unconditional withdrawal of Iraqi troops from Kuwait; to destroy Saddam Hussein's nuclear, chemical, and biological weapons facilities; and to ensure that Iraqi military forces would no longer be capable of posing a threat to the region. The president relied upon his military commanders to devise a plan to achieve these objectives, to assemble the necessary forces to carry out the plan without artificial ceilings or limitations, and to execute the plan effectively and with minimum casualties. The president relied on a single direct chain of military command, from Secretary of Defense Richard Cheney, to the Chairman of the Joint Chiefs of Staff, General Colin Powell, to a single battlefield commander, General Norman Schwarzkopf, who controlled all Army, Navy, Air Force, and Marine units in the operation, as well as all allied forces.

The U.S. military leadership had learned its lessons from Vietnam: define clear military objectives, use overwhelming and decisive military force, move swiftly and avoid protracted stalemate, minimize casualties, and be sensitive to the image of the war projected back home. The president concentrated his attention on winning political support for the war in world capitals, at the United Nations, and, most important, at home.

Operation Desert Shield

Saddam Hussein's miscalculations contributed heavily to the U.S. political and military victory. His invasion of Kuwait on August 2, 1990, was apparently designed to restore his military prestige following eight years of indecisive war against Iran, to secure additional oil revenues to finance the continued buildup of Iraqi military power, and to intimidate and perhaps to invade Saudi Arabia and the Gulf states and thereby secure control over a major share of the world's oil reserves. The Iraqi invasion met with surprisingly swift response from the United Nations in Security Council Resolution 660, condemning the invasion and demanding an immediate withdrawal, and Resolution 661, imposing a trade embargo and economic sanctions. A summit meeting of Arab states reinforced the condemnation and sanctions, with only Libya, Yemen, and the Palestine Liberation Organization (PLO) supporting Iraq. And President Bush immediately sent Secretary of Defense Cheney to Saudi Arabia to arrange for U.S. deployment of force to resist an Iraqi attack. The Saudi king was initially skeptical of U.S. resolve; the United States had deserted its friends too often in the past when the fighting got tough and public opinion shifted. But on August 7, the first U.S. forces were sent to Saudi Arabia in Operation Desert Shield to assist in the defense of the kingdom.

President Bush immediately set to work to stitch together a coalition military force that would eventually include thirty nations. While the military contributions made by many coalition nations were very modest (for example, Poland sent a hospital ship), the political symbolism was important: it was not Saddam Hussein against the United States, but Saddam Hussein against the world.

Massive Military Buildup

Early on, the president described the U.S. military deployment as "defensive," but he soon became convinced that neither diplomacy nor an economic blockade would dislodge Saddam from Kuwait. The president ordered the military to prepare an "offensive" option. The top U.S. military commanders, including Generals Powell and Schwarzkopf, had been field officers in Vietnam, and they were resolved not to repeat the mistakes of that war. They were reluctant to go into battle without the full support of the American people. If ordered to fight, they wanted to employ overwhelming and decisive military force; they wanted to avoid gradual escalation, protracted conflict, target limitations, and political interference in the conduct of the war. They presented the president with an "offensive" plan that called for a very large military buildup: elements of six Army divisions and two Marine divisions; more than a thousand combat aircraft, plus hundreds of tanker and transport aircraft; and six Navy carrier battle groups with nearly 500 combat aircraft. Coalition forces included British and French heavy armored units and Egyptian, Syrian, Saudi, and other Arab units.

The president announced this massive buildup of forces on November 8, but immediately faced a barrage of criticism at home for abandoning his earlier defensive posture. U.S. Senator Sam Nunn, respected chairman of the Senate Armed Forces Committee, opened hearings that urged the president to continue economic sanctions and avoid the heavy casualties that a land war was expected to produce. But the president was convinced that sanctions would not work, that Saddam would hold out for years, that eventually the political coalition backing the embargo would break up, and that Saddam would become increasingly powerful on the world stage. He argued that Saddam would soon acquire nuclear weapons, that if unchecked he could soon dominate the Arab world and Mideast oil reserves, and that aggression must not be allowed to succeed. Secretary of State James Baker convinced the UN Security Council members, including the Soviet Union (with China abstaining), to support Resolution 678 authorizing states to "use all necessary means" against Iraq unless it withdrew from Kuwait by January 15. Bush had won the support of the world body for offensive action, but the Democratic-controlled Congress balked. The president believed he had constitutional authority as commander-in-chief to attack Baghdad, whether or not Congress approved. The Democratic leadership thought otherwise, but after long debate in the Senate, enough Democrats deserted their party to give the president a close 52–47 vote in favor of the use of force.

Operation Desert Storm

From Baghdad, CNN reporters Bernard Shaw and Peter Arnett were startled the early morning of January 17 when Operation Desert Storm began with an air attack on key installations in the city. Iraqi forces were also surprised, despite the prompt timing of the attack; Saddam had assured them that the United States lacked the resolve to fight, and that even if war broke out, U.S. public opinion would force a settlement as casualties rose. Air forces quickly won air supremacy and then went on to attack strategic targets, including nuclear facilities, chemical warfare plants, command centers, and military communications; and later to degrade Iraqi military forces by cutting off supplies, destroying tanks and artillery, and demoralizing troops with round-the-clock bombardment. U.S. television audiences were treated to videotapes of laser-guided smart bombs entering the doors and air shafts of enemy bunkers. Collateral civilian damage was lower than in any previous air war. After five weeks of air war, intelligence estimated that nearly half the Iraqi tanks and artillery in the field had been destroyed, demoralized troops were hiding in deep shelters, and the battlefield had been isolated and "prepared" for ground operations.

General Schwarzkopf's plan for the ground war emphasized deception and maneuver. While Iraqi forces prepared for attacks from the south and the east coast, Schwarzkopf sent heavy armed columns in a "Hail Mary" play—a wide sweep to the west, outflanking and cutting off Iraqi forces in the battle area. On the night of February 24, the ground attack began with Marines easily breaching berms, ditches, and mine fields and racing directly to the Kuwait city airport; helicopter air assaults lunged deep into Iraq; armored columns raced northward across the desert to outflank Iraqi forces and then attack them from the west; and a surge in air attacks kept Iraqi forces holed up in their bunkers. Iraqi troops surrendered in droves; highways from Kuwait city were turned into massive junkyards of Iraqi vehicles; Iraqi forces that tried to fight were quickly destroyed. After one hundred hours of ground fighting, President George Bush declared a cease-fire.

Triumph without Victory?

In retrospect, the president's decision to end the war after only one hundred hours of ground operations appears to have been premature. Not all of the president's original objectives were fully accomplished. Units of Saddam's elite Republican Guard, which would have been surrounded and destroyed with another day's fighting, escaped back to Baghdad. With these surviving forces, Saddam maintained his cruel grip on the country and proceeded to attack his regime's opponents brutally, especially the Kurdish minority in northern Iraq. Later investigations revealed that his nuclear weapons facilities had not been completely destroyed. And finally, Saddam's continuation in power appeared to mock the sacrifices in lives exacted by the war.

Nonetheless, America's elite learned important political lessons from the Gulf War:

★ Decisive military victory inspires confidence in a nation's elite. It inspires patriotism, national unity, and support for the nation's values and institutions. George Bush achieved an all-time high in presidential approval ratings in the polls immediately following the Gulf War victory. The military rose to the top of the list of "trusted" institutions in American society.

★ A rapid conclusion of hostilities ensures that public support will not erode over time and that protracted combat and a steady stream of casualties will not fuel antiwar sentiments.

★ The rapid employment of overwhelming forces is both politically and militarily superior to gradual escalation and the employment of minimum force. The use of overwhelming force reduces total casualties and achieves an earlier and more decisive victory. Such force reduces the opportunity for diplomatic interventions that may produce compromised, indecisive resolutions.

★ The nation's political leadership is vastly more effective when it concentrates on developing and maintaining foreign and domestic political support for the war, while leaving the planning and execution of military operations to the military leadership.

Summary

According to elite theory, the movement of nonelites into elite positions must be slow and continuous in order to maintain stability and avoid revolution. Furthermore, potential elite members must demonstrate their commitment to the basic elite consensus before being admitted to elite positions. Elite theory recognizes competition among elites but contends that elites share a broad consensus about preserving the system essentially as it is. It views public-policy changes as a response to elites' redefinition of their own self-interest rather than as a product of direct mass influence. Finally, elite theory views changes in public policy as incremental rather than revolutionary. American political history supports these propositions:

1. America's elite membership evolved slowly, with no serious break in the ideas or values of the American political and economic system. When the leadership of Hamilton and Adams (Federalists) shifted to that of Jefferson, Monroe, and Madison (Republicans), government policies changed very little because of the fundamental consensus among elite members.

2. As new sources of wealth opened in an expanding economy, America's elite membership opened to new groups and individuals who had acquired wealth and property and who accepted the national consensus about private

enterprise, limited government, and individualism. The West produced new elites, who were assimilated into the governing circle. Public policies changed but were not replaced. The Jacksonians wanted a more open elite system in which the newly wealthy could acquire influence, but they were no more in favor of "dangerous leveling" than were the Founding Fathers.

3. The Civil War reduced southern planters' influence in America's elite structure and paved the way for the rise of the new industrial capitalists. The Industrial Revolution produced a narrowly self-interested elite of industrial capitalists. Mass movements resulted—chiefly one for free silver—but they met with failure.

4. America's elites have divided deeply on the nature of American society only once. This division produced the Civil War, the nation's bloodiest conflict. The Civil War was a conflict between southern elites, dependent on a plantation economy, slave labor, and free trade, and northern industrial commercial elites, who prospered under free labor and protective tariffs. But before, during, and after the Civil War, northern and southern elites continued to strive for compromise in recognition of shared consensus on behalf of liberty and property.

5. The new liberal establishment sought to preserve the existing social and economic order, not to overthrow it. The Great Depression, the victories of fascism in Germany and communism in the Soviet Union, and growing restlessness of the American masses combined to convince America's elites that a more public-regarding philosophy was essential to preserving the American political system and their prominent place in it. Eventually Franklin D. Roosevelt's philosophy of noblesse oblige—elite responsibility for the welfare of the masses—won widespread acceptance among established American leadership.

6. Policy changes have been incremental. Policy changes, including those launched by the New Deal, occurred when events threatened the system; governing elites—acting on the basis of enlightened self-interest—instituted reforms to preserve the system. Even the reforms and welfare policies of the New Deal were designed to strengthen the existing social and economic fabric of society while minimally dislocating elites.

7. America's defeat and humiliation in Vietnam was a result of the failure of the nation's elite to set forth clear policy objectives, develop a strategy to achieve those objectives, and rally mass support behind the war. Elites, not masses, initially favored the war; and the United States began its withdrawal when elite, not mass, opinion shifted against the war.

8. America's political and military leadership performed much better in the Gulf War. The decisive use of overwhelming military force to achieve quick victory with minimum U.S. casualties propelled President Bush to all-time highs in approval ratings and established the military as the most trusted institution in American society.

Notes

1. *McCulloch* v. *Maryland,* 4 Wheaton 316 (1819).

2. See Richard Hofstadter, *The American Political Tradition* (New York: Knopf, 1948), pp. 18–44.

3. Ibid., pp. 32–33.

4. Ibid., p. 38.

5. Frederick Jackson Turner, "The West and American Ideals," in *The Frontier in American History* (New York: Holt, Rinehart & Winston, 1921).

6. *Dred Scott* v. *Sandford,* 19 Howard 393 (1857).

7. Hofstadter, op. cit., p. 109.

8. Ibid., p. 113.

9. Ibid., p. 116.

10. Ibid., p. 119.

11. Herbert Spencer, *Social Statics* (1851).

12. See Gustavus Myers, *A History of the Great American Fortunes,* 3 vols. (Chicago: Kerr, 1910).

13. V. O. Key, Jr., *Politics, Parties, and Pressure Groups* (New York: T. Y. Crowell, 1942), pp. 189–191.

14. See David Halberstam, *The Best and the Brightest* (New York: Random House, 1973).

15. New York Times, *The Pentagon Papers* (New York: Bantam Books, 1971).

16. George C. Herring, *America's Longest War* (New York: Random House, 1979), p. 182.

17. Ibid., p. 188.

18. John F. Mueller, *War, Presidents, and Public Opinion* (New York: Wiley, 1973).

19. Ibid., p. 164.

20. See Henry Kissinger, *The White House Years* (Boston: Little, Brown, 1979), pp. 1301–1446.

21. Ibid., p. 1461; see *RN: The Memoirs of Richard Nixon,* vol. 2 (New York: Warner Books, 1978), p. 251.

22. See Frank Snepp, *Decent Interval* (New York: Random House, 1977).

23. Herring, op. cit., p. 262.

Selected Readings

Burch, Phillip H., Jr. *Elites in American History.* Vol. I: *The Federalist Years to the Civil War.* Vol. II: *The Civil War to the New Deal.* Vol. III: *The New Deal to the Carter Administration.* New York: Holmes and Meier, 1980. The most thorough study available of the class backgrounds of American leaders throughout history. Burch describes the socioeconomic status and financial interests of top government officials from the Washington to the Carter administrations. He links the elite status of these decision makers to their public actions and policy positions.

Elkins, Stanley, and Eric McKitrick. *The Age of Federalism.* New York: Oxford University Press, 1993. An examination of politics in America at the close of the eighteenth century, leading up to the election of 1800.

Hartz, Louis. *The Liberal Tradition in America*. New York: Harcourt, Brace, & World, 1955. The absence of a feudal aristocracy in the United States obstructed the development of social class consciousness, which in turn prevented the emergence of socialism in this country. The United States as a nation was "born free," and most Americans consider themselves middle class.

Hofstadter, Richard. *The American Political Tradition*. New York: Knopf, Vintage Books, 1948. This book is an important political history from an elite perspective. Hofstadter traces the development of American political elites and their philosophies from Jefferson and the Founding Fathers through Jackson, Bryan, Wilson, and Franklin Roosevelt. He emphasizes that at every stage of U.S. history, elites have been in considerable agreement over major issues (with the possible exception of the Civil War). Finally Hofstadter discusses the elite practice of incrementalism: that elite leaders have always moved to preserve the established order with as little change in the system as possible.

4

Elites in America

There has always been a privileged class, even in America, but it has never been so dangerously isolated from its surroundings.

—CHRISTOPHER LASCH

Power in the United States is organized into large institutions. Positions at the top of the major institutions in American society are sources of great power. Sociologist C. Wright Mills described the relationship between institutional authority and power in this way:

> *If we took the one hundred most powerful men in America, the one hundred wealthiest, and the one hundred most celebrated away from the institutional positions they now occupy, away from their resources of men and women and money, away from the media of mass communication that are now focused upon them—then they should be powerless and poor and uncelebrated. For power is not of a man. Wealth does not center in the person of the wealthy. Celebrity is not inherent in any personality. To be celebrated, to be wealthy, to have power, requires access to major institutions, for the institutional positions men occupy determine in large part their chances to have and to hold these values experiences.*[1]

In this chapter we describe the people who occupy high positions in the major private and governmental institutions of American society. We include the major *private* institutions—in industry, finance, media, law, and other "nongovernmental institutions"—because we believe that they allocate values for our society and shape the lives of all

Americans. Remember, we defined an elite member as anyone who participates in decisions that allocate values for society, not just those who participate in decision making as part of the government. The decisions of automobile companies to raise prices, of banks to raise or lower interest rates, of computer companies to market new products, of the mass media to determine what is "news," and of schools and colleges to decide what shall be taught—all affect the lives of Americans as much as do government decisions.

We will argue that the globalization of corporate power is moving economic elites in America even further away from the people. International elites in industry, banking, finance, and the media are increasingly removed from the values, beliefs, and concerns of the masses of people in their countries. Indeed, global elites are becoming increasingly free from the restraints of national governments. America's global elite is becoming ever more isolated from the masses. Social historian Christopher Lasch observes:

> *It is a question whether they think of themselves as Americans at all. Patriotism, certainly, does not rank very high in their hierarchy of virtues. "Multiculturalism," on the other hand, suits them to perfection, conjuring up the agreeable images of a global bazaar. . . . The new elites are at home only in transit, en route to a high-level conference, to the grand opening of a new franchise, to an international film festival, or to an undiscovered resort. Theirs is essentially a tourist's view of the world—not a perspective likely to encourage a passionate devotion to democracy.[2]*

THE CONCENTRATION OF CORPORATE POWER

Economic power in the United States is concentrated in a small number of large corporations and banks. Traditionally, pluralism portrays business as just another interest group, competing with all other interest groups to influence public policy. Corporate power, according to the pluralists, depends on the political skills and resources of particular individuals, groups, and industries within the corporate world, on the performance of the economy, on the climate of public opinion, and on the relative strength of competing groups. In contrast, elitism views economic elites as distinctly powerful, not only in shaping government policy, but, more important, in making decisions that directly influence all our lives.

Economic elites decide what will be produced, how it will be produced, how much it will cost, how many people will be employed, who will be employed, and what their wages will be. They decide how goods and services will be distributed, how much money will be available for loans, what interest rates will be charged, and what new technologies will be developed. Of course, these decisions are influenced by governmental regulations, consumer demand, international competition, federal fiscal and monetary policy, and other public and private market forces. But in a free-market economy, corporate elites, not government officials, make most of the key economic decisions.[3]

Industrial Concentration

Formal control of the nation's economic life rests in the hands of a relatively small number of senior officers and directors of the nation's largest corporate institutions. This concentration has occurred chiefly because economic enterprise has increasingly consolidated into a small number of giant corporations. The following statistics only suggest the scale and concentration of modern U.S. corporate enterprise.

There are over 200,000 industrial corporations in the United States, but the 50 corporations listed in Table 4-1 control nearly 60 percent of all industrial assets in the nation. The 5 largest industrial corporations (General Motors, Ford Motor Co., Exxon, General Electric, IBM) control 15 percent of the nation's industrial assets. Concentration in other sectors of the American economy (commercial banking, insurance, retail stores, investment firms, etc.) is even greater.

Financial Concentration

The financial elite of America is even more concentrated than the industrial elite and becoming ever more so each year. Table 4-2 lists the 25 largest commercial banks in the nation; together they control over 50 percent of all banking assets. Yet banking "megamergers" continue to increase financial concentration in America. Citicorp merged with the Travelers Group, the nation's largest diversified financial investment corporation, in 1998. Likewise, BankAmerica and NationsBank merged, as did Banc One and First Chicago. These banks, together with just three giant Wall Street securities

TABLE 4-1	RANK	CORPORATION	RANK	CORPORATION
	1	General Motors	26	Compaq Computer
America's fifty	2	Ford Motor Co.	27	Conagra
largest industrial	3	Exxon	28	Merck
corporations	4	General Electric	29	GTE
	5	Intl. Business Machines	30	Johnson & Johnson
	6	Chrysler	31	Walt Disney
	7	Mobil	32	United Parcel Service
	8	Philip Morris	33	USX
	9	AT&T	34	BellSouth
	10	Boeing	35	Enron
	11	Texaco	36	International Paper
	12	Hewlett-Packard	37	Dow Chemical
	13	E. I. Du Pont de Nemours	38	Sara Lee
	14	Chevron	39	MCI Communications
	15	Procter & Gamble	40	Loews
	16	Amoco	41	Atlantic Richfield
	17	Bell Atlantic	42	Caterpillar
	18	Motorola	43	Coca-Cola
	19	PepsiCo	44	Xerox
	20	Lockheed Martin	45	UAL
	21	Dayton Hudson	46	RJR Nabisco Holdings
	22	Lucent Technologies	47	Bristol-Myers Squibb
	23	Intel	48	Ingram Micro
	24	SBC Communications	49	Duke Energy
	25	United Technologies	50	Ameritech

Note: Ranked by annual revenue. Banking, retail, and investment firms separately ranked.
Source: Derived from data provided in *Fortune,* April 20, 1998.

TABLE 4-2	RANK	COMMERCIAL BANK	RANK	COMMERCIAL BANK
	1	Citicorp	14	PNC Bank
America's largest	2	Chase Manhattan Corp.	15	BankBoston Corp.
commercial banks	3	BankAmerica Corp.*	16	Keycorp
	4	NationsBank Corp.*	17	Bank of New York Co.
	5	J. P. Morgan & Co.	18	Wachovia Corp.
	6	First Union Corp.	19	National City Corp.
	7	Banc One Corp.*	20	Mellon Bank Corp.
	8	Bankers Trust N.Y. Corp.	21	Suntrust Banks
	9	First Chicago NBD Corp.*	22	MBNA
	10	Norwest Corp.	23	Corestates Finan. Corp
	11	Wells Fargo & Co.	24	Barnett Banks
	12	Fleet Financial Group	25	Republic New York Corp.
	13	U.S. Bancorp		

*megamerged 1998
Note: Ranked by revenues in 1997. Megamergers in 1998 shown but not ranked.

Source: Data from *Fortune,* April 20, 1998.

firms—Merrill Lynch, Morgan Stanley Dean Witter, and Lehman Brothers—largely decide how America will invest in its future. They decide whether, when, and under what terms American corporations can borrow money and sell stocks and bonds. That is to say, they decide upon the allocation of capital in our capitalist system.

FOCUS

Corporate Merger Mania

America's corporate elite is becoming ever more concentrated. Indeed, "merger mania" has largely swept away community banks, smaller stock brokerage firms, and independent newspapers, publishers, and media companies. All but a very few successful independent business entrepreneurs—those who create most of America's new products and services—eventually sell out to the corporate conglomerates.

The U.S. government has relaxed enforcement of its antitrust laws, laws that date back to the Sherman Antitrust Act of 1890. In a mega-merger labeled "Rockefeller's Revenge," Exxon, the nation's third largest industrial corporation, and Mobil, the nation's seventh largest, agreed to combine their power in 1998. Actually, their merger is a *recombination* of giant oil companies once owned by John D. Rockefeller's Standard Oil Company monopoly. The U.S. Supreme Court approved President Theodore Roosevelt's trust-busting breakup of Standard Oil in 1911. But today it is argued that global competition in the oil industry requires a reconcentration of economic power in U.S. corporations. The new Exxon-Mobil giant claims that it must compete with global oil conglomerates such as Royal Dutch Shell (Netherlands) and British Petroleum (which itself recently bought up Amoco).

In 1998 Citicorp (banking) and Travelers Group (insurance) merged their assets to be the *world's* largest financial institution with nearly one trillion dollars in assets. The new Citigroup boasts of over one hundred million customers in more than one hundred countries.

Defenders of corporate and financial mega-mergers argue that these deals are needed to make American firms large enough to compete successfully against giant conglomerates in Japan and Europe. (Before its merger with Travelers, Citicorp, America's largest commercial bank, was *not* ranked among the top twenty global financial institutions.) And they argue that in any business—manufacturing, retail sales, or service—larger size grants easier access to capital and supplies and therefore allows the giants to keep prices down. Few locally owned retail stores, for example, can compete in prices with K-Mart or J. C. Penney, let alone the nation's largest retailer, Wal-Mart.

Each year the nation posts a new record number of mergers and acquisitions (see Figure 4-1). Merger mania helps drive a soaring stock market. Costs and prices are kept low and profits driven up. Perhaps more importantly, elites further concentrate their power and resources.

But masses face continuing disruption in their lives. Employees face job losses, dislocations, and "downsizing" of their positions and salaries. Even in a strong economy workers must be prepared constantly to move on to new jobs. It is not only factory workers who are regularly displaced, but also bank tellers, retail sales persons, stockbrokers, and many other middle-class "white-collar" employees.

"Do you, Scofield Industries, take Amalgamated Pipe?"

CORPORATE ELITES

Following the Industrial Revolution in America in the late nineteenth century and well into the twentieth century, the nation's largest corporations were controlled by the tycoons who created them—Andrew Carnegie (Carnegie Steel, later United States Steel, and today USX); Andrew Mellon (Alcoa and Mellon banks); Henry Ford (Ford Motor Co.); J. P. Morgan (J. P. Morgan); and, of course, John D. Rockefeller (Standard Oil Company, later broken into Exxon, Mobil, Chevron, Atlantic Richfield, and other large oil companies). But by the 1930s control of most large corporations had passed to professional managers. As early as 1932, Adolf Berle and Gardiner Means, in their classic book, *The Modern Corporation and Private Property,* described the separation of ownership from control. The theory of "managerialism" became the conventional wisdom about corporate governance. Liberal economist John Kenneth Galbraith summarized the triumph of managerialism:

| FIGURE 4-1 | Big deals: Estimated value of corporate mergers each year

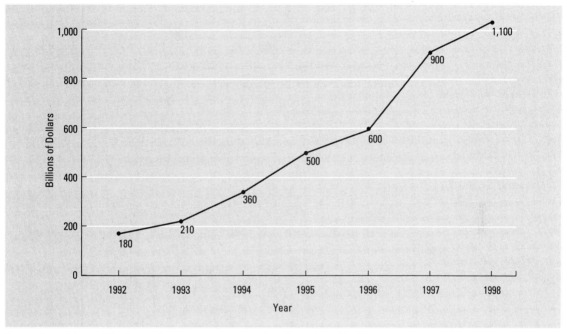

Source: Securities and Exchange Commission as reported in *Time,* April 20, 1998.

Seventy years ago the corporation was the instrument of its owners and a projection of their personalities. The names of these principals—Carnegie, Rockefeller, Harriman, Mellon, Guggenheim, Ford—were well known across the land. They are still known, but for the art galleries and philanthropic foundations they established and their descendants who are in politics. The men who now head the great corporations are unknown. . . . The men who now run the large corporations own no appreciable share of the enterprise. They are selected not by the stockholders but, in the common case, by a board of directors which narcissistically they selected themselves.[4]

Corporate power thus does not rest in the hands of the masses of corporate employees or even in the hands of the millions of middle- and upper-class Americans who own corporate stock.

Management Power

Corporate power is generally wielded by the top managers of the nation's large industrial corporations and financial institutions. Theoretically, stockholders have ultimate power over management, but in fact individual stockholders seldom have any control over the activities of the corporations they own. When confronted with mismanagement, individual stockholders simply sell their stock, rather than try to challenge the powers of the managers. Indeed, most stockholders sign over "proxies" to top management so that top management may cast these proxy votes at the annual meetings of stockholders. Management itself usually selects its own slate for the board of directors and easily elects them with the help of proxies.

Large control blocks of stock in corporations are usually held by banks and financial institutions or pension trusts or mutual funds. Occasionally, the managers of these institutions will demand the replacement of corporate managers who have performed poorly. But more often than not, banks and trust funds vote their stock for the management slate. Institutional investors usually allow the management of corporations essentially to appoint themselves and their friends to the board of directors and thus to become increasingly unchallengeable.

Board membership in major U.S. banks and corporations averages between twelve and fifteen. Board members are divided among "inside" directors (top executive officers of the corporation itself), "outside" directors (usually top executive officers of other banks or corporations), and "public interest" directors (persons selected to give symbolic representation to consumers, or minorities, or civic groups). (See Table 4-3.)

Interlocking Directorates

Corporate power is further concentrated by a system of interlocking directorates. Interlocking directorates, in which a director of one corporation also sits on the boards of other corporations, enable key corporate elites to wield influence over a large number of corporations. It is not uncommon for top members of the corporate elite to hold four, five, or six directorships.

The Legal Elite

Sociologist C. Wright Mills asserted that lawyers are a key segment of the nation's aristocracy of power:

> *The inner core of the power elite also includes men of the higher legal and financial type from the great law factories and investment firms who are professional go-betweens of economic, political, and military affairs, and who thus act to unify the power elite.*[5]

TABLE 4-3	INSIDE	OUTSIDE (CORPORATE)

Directors of Chase Manhattan Bank	Thomas G. Labrecque
	  Chairman and chief executive officer
	Arthur F. Ryan
	  President and chief operating officer
	Richard J. Boyle
	  Vice chairman
	Robert R. Douglass
	  Vice chairman
		M. Anthony Burns
		  Chairman and CEO, Ryder System
		James L. Ferguson
		  Chairman and CEO, General Foods
		Edward S. Finkelstein
		  Chairman and CEO, R. H. Macy
		Robert E. Floweree
		  Retired chairman, Georgia Pacific
		H. Lawrence Fuller
		  Chairman and CEO, Amoco Oil
		Howard C. Kauffmann
		  Retired president, Exxon
		Edmund T. Pratt, Jr.
		  Chairman, Pfizer
		Henry B. Schacht
		  Chairman and CEO, Cummins Engine
		A. Alfred Taubman
		  President, Taubman, Inc.
		Donald H. Trautlein
		  Retired chairman, Bethlehem Steel
		Kay R. Whitmore
		  Chairman and CEO, Eastman Kodak

	OUTSIDE (PUBLIC INTEREST)	

	Joan Ganz Cooney
	  Chairman, Children's Television Workshop
	Richard W. Lyman
	  Former president, Stanford University
	A. John H. McArthur
	  Dean, Harvard School of Business
	David T. McLaughlin
	  President, Aspen Institute	

Source: Based on data from *Moody's Banking Manual,* 1992.

The prevalence of lawyers in *politics* is an American tradition. Among the fifty-five delegates to the Constitutional Convention in 1787, some twenty-five were lawyers. The political dominance of lawyers is even greater today, with lawyers filling more than half of U.S. Senate seats and nearly half of the seats in the U.S. House of Representatives.

Within the *corporate* elite—presidents and directors of the nation's largest industries, banks, utilities, and insurance companies—over 15 percent are lawyers. But neither the politician-lawyer nor the businessperson-lawyer really stands at the top of the legal profession. The "superlawyers" are the senior partners of the nation's most highly esteemed New York and Washington law firms. These are the firms that represent clients such as General Motors, AT&T, Du Pont, CBS, and American Airlines,[6] not only in the courts but, perhaps more importantly, before Congress and the federal regulatory agencies. Of course, the nation's largest corporate and financial institutions have their own legal departments; but attorneys in these departments, known as "house counsels," usually handle routine matters. When the stakes are high, the great corporations turn to the superlawyers. (See Table 4-4.)

TABLE 4-4	WALL STREET	WASHINGTON
The top law firms	Shearman & Sterling Cravath, Swaine, & Moore White & Case Dewey, Ballantine, Bushby, Palmer & Wood Simpson, Thacher & Bartlett Davis, Polk & Wardwell Milbank, Tweed, Hadley & McCloy Cahill, Gordon & Reindel Sullivan & Cromwell Chadbourne, Parke, Whiteside & Wolff Breed, Abbott & Morgan Winthrop, Simpson, Putnam & Roberts Cadwalader, Wickersham & Taft Wilkie, Farr & Gallagher Donovan, Leisure, Newton & Irvine Lord, Day & Lord Dwight, Royall, Harris, Koegel & Caskey Mudge, Rose, Guthrie & Alexander Kelley, Drye & Warren Cleary, Gottlieb, Steen & Hamilton	Arnold & Porter Covington & Burling Arrent, Fox, Kintner, Plotkin & Kahn Wilmer, Cutler & Pickering Clifford, Warnke, Glass, McIlwain & Finney Fried, Frank, Harris, Shriver & Kampelman Rodgers & Wells

These firms were selected on the basis of reputed power and prestige. If gross revenues were considered, the following firms would be at the top of the list: Skadden, Arps, Slate, Meagler & Flom (New York); Finley, Kumble, Wagner, Heine, Underberg, Manley, Myerson & Casey (New York); Baker and McKenzie (Chicago); Gibson, Dunn & Crutcher (Los Angeles); O'Melveny & Myers (Los Angeles).

THE GLOBAL ELITES

International trade—the buying and selling of goods and services between individuals and firms located in different countries—has expanded very rapidly in recent decades. Today, almost one-quarter of the *world's* total output is sold in a country other than the one in which it was produced. Today the United States exports about 11 percent of the value of its gross domestic product (GDP) and imports about 12 percent. Exports and imports were only about 3 percent of GDP in 1970 (see Figure 4-2). Global competition heavily impacts the American economy.

Changing Elite Preferences for World Trade

Historically, American business supported high tariffs, but as the U.S. economy matured and the costs of global transportation and communication declined, America's largest corporations began to look beyond the nation's borders.

FIGURE 4-2 | U. S. world trade

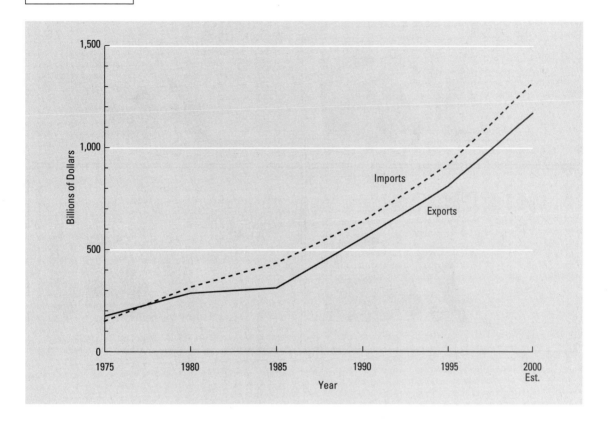

Prior to World War II, U.S. tariffs on all imported goods averaged 30 to 50 percent in various decades. This suited U.S. manufacturers very well, eliminating most foreign competition from the U.S. market. U.S. firms enjoyed sheltered markets; they could raise prices to levels just below the price of imported goods with their high tariffs attached. American consumers, of course, paid higher prices than they otherwise would if foreign goods could enter the country without tariffs. But the U.S. steel, automobile, and electrical appliance industries grew powerful economically and politically.

After World War II, the American economy was the most powerful in the world. American manufacturing corporations had few international competitors in most industries. Given their dominant position in world trade, American corporations sought to lower trade barriers around the world. The Council on Foreign Relations and the global-membership Trilateral Commission (see "The Elite Think Tanks" in Chapter 14) and America's largest

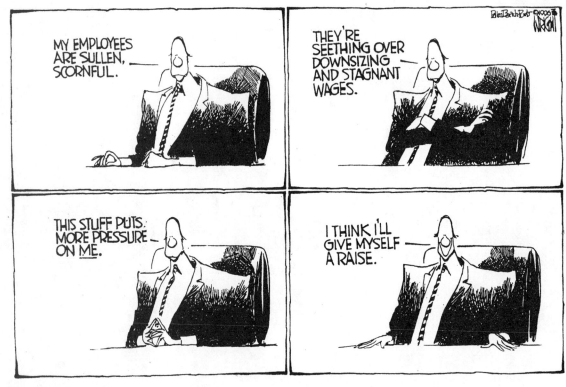

Palm Beach Post © 1996 Wright.

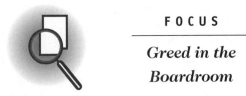

FOCUS

Greed in the Boardroom

There is abundant evidence that the corporate managers put *personal motives*—especially their own pay, benefits, and perquisites—above the interests of the corporation and its stockholders. The pay of chief executive officers (CEOs) of the largest corporations has mushroomed in recent years, as has the pay of corporate directors. The average CEO in the 365 largest corporations in 1996 took home nearly $2.3 million in pay and benefits.[a] According to business professor Edward E. Lawler, "It just seems to get more absurd each year. What is outrageous one year becomes a standard for the next. And no one is in a position to say no."[b] Boards of directors are supposed to oversee top executive pay and protect stockholders. But CEOs generally win approval for their own salaries from compliant directors.

The pay gap in the United States between corporate chieftains and average factory workers has increased dramatically over the last few decades (see the figure). In the early 1980s the median pay package (pay, benefits, and perquisites) of a corporate CEO was approximately fifty times greater than the pay of the average factory worker. By 1996 that gap had quadrupled, with the median CEO

FIGURE 4-2   Declines in U.S. tariffs over time

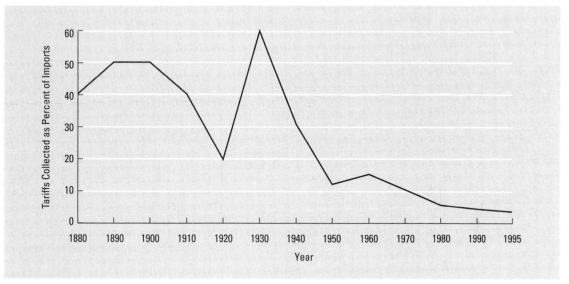

Source: Data from *Statistical Abstract of the United States,* 1997 pp. 333, 861.

corporations lobbied Congress for reductions in U.S. tariffs in order to encourage other nations to reduce their own tariffs. The result was a rapid decline in average U.S. tariff rates (see Figure 4-2). In effect, the United States

earning 209 times the pay of the average factory worker. (In Japan, by contrast, the average CEO receives only seventeen times the pay of an ordinary worker.) It is difficult to explain to workers, whose average real hourly earnings have *declined* steadily since 1970,[c] why the pay packages of top corporate (and governmental) leaders have skyrocketed. Comparable data on Japanese and German top executives are plagued by measurement problems, but it is estimated that American CEOs are paid three to four times more than their foreign counterparts.[d]

In 1992 the U.S. Securities and Exchange Commission tightened its reporting requirements so that public corporations must now provide more information about executive pay packages. In 1993 Congress increased corporate taxes on corporations that pay their executives more than $1 million a year. But these regulations have been totally ineffective in slowing the growth of CEO compensation.

If factory workers had received pay raises comparable to those given their bosses between 1980 and 1995, they would now be paid an average of $90,000 a year.

[a]*Business Week* (April 21, 1997).

[b]See Thomas A. Stewart, "The King Is Dead," *Fortune* (January 11, 1993): 34–40.

[c]*Statistical Abstract of the United States, 1997* (Washington, D.C.: U.S. Government Printing Office, 1997).

[d]Margaret M. Blair, "CEO Pay," *Brookings Review* (Winter 1994): 23–27.

became an open market. Inasmuch as U.S. firms largely dominated their domestic markets in the 1950s and 1960s (steel, automobiles, aircraft, computers, drugs, electronics, appliances, agriculture, and so forth), they had little fear of foreign competition. On the contrary, they expanded their own international sales, becoming multinational corporations.

The Rise of the Multinationals

America's top exporting corporations (see Table 4-5) have largely dictated U.S. trade policy. In 1947 GATT (General Agreement on Tariffs and Trade) was created to advance international trade. The World Bank and International Monetary Fund (IMF) were initially formed to assist in the post–World War II recovery of European economies; today their mission has shifted to assisting developing nations in becoming world trading partners.

Prior to 1980 the United States regularly incurred a *positive* annual trade balance, that is, exporting more goods and services than it imported. But since 1980 the United States has incurred balance of trade *deficits* every year. However, today U.S. multinational corporations receive substantial revenues from their exports. Moreover, most have manufacturing facilities as well as sales and distribution staffs worldwide. They stand to gain much more from the globalization of trade than they might lose from domestic competition from foreign firms.

In 1993 the United States, Canada, and Mexico signed the North American Free Trade Agreement (NAFTA). Objections by labor unions in the United States (and independent presidential candidate Ross Perot) were drowned out in a torrent of support by the American corporate community, Democrats and Republicans in Congress, President Bill Clinton and former President George Bush. NAFTA envisions the removal of tariffs on virtually all products by all three nations over a period of ten to fifteen years. It also allows banking, insurance, and other financial services to cross these borders.

While the U.S. economy has performed very well in recent years, the benefits from that performance have been very unevenly distributed. The global economy has produced growth and profit for America's largest corporations and amply rewarded the nation's highest skilled workers. Indeed, global trade has *raised aggregate income* for the nation. But at the same time, it has contributed to a *decline in average earnings* of American

TABLE 4-5	RANK	COMPANY	FOREIGN REVENUE ($ BILLIONS)
U.S. top exporting corporations	1	Exxon	89.6
	2	General Motors	51.0
	3	Mobil	48.5
	4	Ford Motor	48.1
	5	IBM	46.6
	6	Texaco	31.4
	7	General Electric	23.4
	8	Chevron	22.2
	9	Hewlett-Packard	21.4
	10	Citicorp	19.8
	11	Philip Morris Cos.	19.6
	12	Procter & Gamble	17.6
	13	E.I. Du Pont de Nemours	16.6
	14	American International Group	15.0
	15	Motorola	12.6
	16	Coca-Cola	12.5
	17	Intel	12.2
	18	Xerox	12.0
	19	Dow Chemical	11.3
	20	Johnson & Johnson	10.7
	21	United Technologies	10.1
	22	Digital Equipment	9.4
	23	PepsiCo	9.2
	24	Eastman Kodak	8.6
	25	Compaq Computer	8.4
	26	Chrysler	8.2
	27	Amoco	8.0
	28	Chase Manhattan	7.9
	29	Minnesota Mining & Manufacturing	7.6
	30	Sara Lee	

Source: Data derived from *Forbes* Magazine, April 20, 1998.

workers and *worsened inequality* in America. Elite gains have been accompanied by mass losses (see Chapter 5).

GOVERNING ELITES

Politicians specialize in office seeking. They know how to run for office, but they may not know how to run the government. After victory at the polls, wise politicians turn to experienced executive elites to run the government. Both Democratic and Republican presidents select essentially the same type of executive elite to staff the key positions in their administrations. Frequently, these top government executives—cabinet members, presidential advisors, special ambassadors—have occupied key posts in private industry, finance, or law or influential positions in education, the arts and sciences, or social, civic, and charitable associations. The executive elites move easily in and out of government posts from their positions in the corporate, financial, legal, and educational world. They often assume government jobs at a financial sacrifice, and many do so out of a sense of public service.

Revolving Doors

The elitist model of power envisions a single group of people exercising power in many sectors of American life. Elitists do not necessarily expect to see individuals simultaneously occupying high positions in both business and government, but they do expect to see a "revolving door" by which elites move from power positions in banking, industry, the media, law, the foundations, and education to power positions in government, then frequently returning to prestigious private posts after a term of "public service." This revolving door pattern contrasts with the pluralist model of power (described in Chapter 1), which suggests very little overlapping among centers of power. Pluralists envision *different* groups of people exercising power in the various sectors of American life.

Consider the career backgrounds of former occupants of the three key cabinet posts of U.S. government—secretaries of state, defense, and the treasury—over the past four decades. (See Table 4-6.) We believe these biographies clearly illustrate the elitist notion of a "revolving door" of power. It is true that less important cabinet and executive staff positions sometimes have been filled with career government bureaucrats or people with few elite credentials. But historically presidents have almost always turned to the "heavyweights" to staff the key posts in the federal government.

ELITE RECRUITMENT: GETTING TO THE TOP

How do people at the top get there? Certainly we cannot provide a complete picture of the recruitment process in all sectors of society, but we can learn whether the top leadership in government comes from the corporate world or whether these two worlds depend on separate and distinct channels of recruitment.

| TABLE 4-6 | | Governing elites: Eisenhower through Bush |

POSITION	NAME	DATES SERVED	BACKGROUND
Secretaries of State	John Foster Dulles	1953–1960	Partner of Sullivan and Cromwell (one of the twenty largest law firms on Wall Street); member of the board of directors of the Bank of New York, the Fifth Avenue Bank, the American Bank Note Company, and numerous industrial corporations; a trustee of the New York Public Library, the Union Theological Seminary, the Rockefeller Foundation, and the Carnegie Endowment for International Peace.
	Dean Rusk	1961–1968	Former president of the Rockefeller Foundation.
	William P. Rogers	1969–1973	U.S. attorney general during Eisenhower Administration; senior partner in Royall, Koegal, Rogers, and Wells (one of the twenty largest Wall Street law firms).
	Henry Kissinger	1973–1977	Former special assistant to the president for national security affairs; former Harvard professor of international affairs and project director for Rockefeller Brothers Fund and for the Council on Foreign Relations.
	Cyrus Vance	1977–1980	Senior partner in New York law firm of Simpson, Thatcher, and Bartlett; a director of IBM and Pan American World Airways; a trustee of Yale University, chairman of the board of trustees of the Rockefeller Foundation, and member of the Council on Foreign Relations; former secretary of the army and undersecretary of defense; U.S. negotiator in the Paris Peace Conference on Vietnam.
	Edmund S. Muskie	1980–1981	The only "political" figure to serve in this office in recent times; U.S. senator (D-Maine), 1959–1980, and chairman of the Senate Budget Committee; governor of Maine, 1955–1959; member of Maine House of Representatives, 1946–1951; small-town attorney.
	Alexander Haig, Jr.	1981–1982	President of United Technologies and former four-star general, U.S. Army; former supreme allied commander, NATO; former White House chief of staff under President Richard Nixon; former deputy assistant for national security affairs under Henry Kissinger.
	George P. Shultz	1982–1988	President of Bechtel Corporation, the world's largest construction company; former secretary of the treasury and secretary of labor; former dean of the Graduate School of Business of the University of Chicago; a director of J. P. Morgan & Company, Morgan Guaranty Trust Co., Sears, Roebuck and Co., and the Alfred P. Sloan Foundation.
	James A. Baker	1989–1993	Former secretary of the treasury; former White House chief of staff; Bush campaign manager; wealthy Houston attorney and oilman.
Secretaries of Defense	Charles E. Wilson	1953–1957	President and member of the board of directors of General Motors Corporation.

(continued)

TABLE 4-6		Governing elites: Eisenhower through Bush (continued)	

POSITION	NAME	DATES SERVED	BACKGROUND
Secretaries of Defense (continued)	Neil H. McElroy	1957–1959	Former president and member of the board of directors of Procter & Gamble Co.; member of the board of directors of General Electric Co., Chrysler Corporation, and Equitable Life Insurance Company; member of the board of trustees of Harvard University.
	Thomas A. Gates	1959–1960	Secretary of the navy, 1957–1959; chairman of the board and chief executive officer, Morgan Guaranty Trust Co. (J. P. Morgan, New York); member of the board of directors of General Electric Co., Bethlehem Steel Corp., Scott Paper Co., Campbell Soup Co., and so on.
	Robert S. McNamara	1961–1967	President and member of the board of directors of the Ford Motor Co.; member of the board of directors of Scott Paper Co.; president of the World Bank, 1967–1982.
	Clark Clifford	1967–1969	Senior partner of Clifford and Miller (Washington law firm); member of the board of directors of the National Bank of Washington and the Sheraton Hotel Corporation; special counsel to the president, 1949–1950; member of the board of trustees of Washington University in St. Louis.
	Melvin Laird	1969–1973	Former Republican congressman from Wisconsin.
	James R. Schlesinger	1973–1977	Former director, Central Intelligence Agency; former chairman, Atomic Energy Commission; former economics professor and research associate, Rand Corporation.
	Harold Brown	1977–1981	Former president, California Institute of Technology; member of the board of directors of IBM and the Times-Mirror Corporation; secretary of the air force under President Lyndon Johnson; U.S. representative to the Strategic Arms Limitation Treaty talks under President Richard Nixon.
	Caspar W. Weinberger	1981–1988	Former vice president of Bechtel Corporation; former secretary of health, education, and welfare; former director of Office of Management and Budget; former chairman of Federal Trade Commission; a director of PepsiCo. and Quaker Oats Co.; former San Francisco attorney and California state legislator.
	Richard B. Cheney	1989–1993	Former Wyoming congressman and Republican whip in the House of Representatives; assistant to the president under Gerald Ford; White House chief of staff under Richard Nixon; former Washington attorney and congressional staffer.
Secretaries of the Treasury	George M. Humphrey	1953–1957	Former chairman of the board of directors of M. A. Hanna Company; member of the board of directors of National Steel Corp., Consolidated Coal Company, Canada, and Dominion Sugar Company; a trustee of the Massachusetts Institute of Technology.
	Robert B. Anderson	1957–1961	Secretary of the navy, 1953–1954; deputy secretary of defense, 1954–1955; member of the board of directors of the Goodyear Tire & Rubber Company; member of the executive board of the Boy Scouts of America.

TABLE 4-6			Governing elites: Eisenhower through Bush (continued)

POSITION	NAME	DATES SERVED	BACKGROUND
Secretaries of the Treasury (continued)	C. Douglas Dillon	1961–1965	Chairman of the board of Dillon, Reed and Company (Wall Street investment firm); member of the New York Stock Exchange; director of U.S. and Foreign Securities Corporation and of International Securities Corporation; member of the board of governors of the New York Hospital and of the Metropolitan Museum.
	Henry H. Fowler	1965–1969	Senior partner, Washington law firm of Fowler, Leva, Hawes and Symington; undersecretary of the treasury, 1961–1964.
	David Kennedy	1969–1971	President and chairman of the board of Continental Illinois Bank and Trust Company; a director of International Harvester Company, Commonwealth Edison, Pullman Company, Abbot Laboratories, Swift and Company, U.S. Gypsum, and Communications Satellite Corporation; trustee of the University of Chicago, the Brookings Institution, the Committee for Economic Development, and George Washington University.
	John B. Connally	1971–1972	Former secretary of the navy, governor of Texas, administrative assistant to Lyndon B. Johnson; attorney for Murcheson Brothers Investment (Dallas); former director of New York Central Railroad.
	George P. Shultz	1972–1974	Former secretary of labor and director of the Office of Management and Budget; former dean of the University of Chicago Graduate School of Business; former senior partner of Salomon Brothers (one of Wall Street's largest investment firms) and Stein, Roe and Farnham (investments).
	William E. Simon	1974–1977	Former director, Federal Energy Office, and former deputy secretary of the treasury; former senior partner of Salomon Brothers.
	Werner Michael Blumenthal	1977–1979	Former president of the Bendix Corporation; a trustee of Princeton University and member of the Council on Foreign Relations.
	G. William Miller	1979–1981	Chairman and chief executive officer of the Textron Corporation; formerly a partner in the New York law firm of Cravath, Swaine, and Moore; a director of Allied Chemical and Federated Department Stores; former chairman of the Council of Economic Advisors.
	Donald T. Regan	1981–1985	Former chairman of Merrill Lynch & Co., the nation's largest investment firm; former vice chairman of the New York Stock Exchange; a trustee of the University of Pennsylvania, Committee for Economic Development, and the Business Roundtable.
	James A. Baker	1985–1988	Wealthy Houston attorney and White House chief of staff in Reagan's first term.
	Nicholas Brady	1988–1993	Former chairman of the Wall Street firm of Dillon, Read and Company; a director of Purolator, Bessermer Securities, Doubleday & Co., George International, ASA Ltd., Media General Inc., and NCR Corp.

FOCUS

The Friends of Bill and Hillary

If the Clinton administration "looks like America," then we have become a nation of lawyers and lobbyists.

Perhaps it should come as no surprise that almost all of the top jobs in the Clinton administration are filled by lawyers, lobbyists, politicians, and bureaucrats. Unlike his predecessors in the White House, Bill Clinton never had any experience outside of politics and government. Among Clinton's top advisors, very few were recruited from the business world. Nor is there any significant military experience represented on Clinton's top team, although several members are veterans.

Clinton's pledge to bring to Washington an administration that "looks like America" presumably meant more minorities and women appointed to cabinet-level positions. Clinton's initial cabinet team included three women—Attorney General Janet Reno, Health and Human Services Secretary Donna Shalala, and Energy Secretary Hazel O'Leary. Three African Americans served in the Clinton cabinet—Commerce Secretary Ron Brown, Agricultural Secretary Mike Espy, and Veterans Affairs Secretary Jesse Brown; and two Hispanics headed departments—Housing and Urban Development Secretary Henry Cisneros and Transportation Secretary Federico Peña. It appears that the Clinton administration is slightly more "diverse" than that of his immediate predecessor.

But like all previous administrations, the friends of Bill and Hillary are drawn overwhelmingly from among the most-privileged, best-educated, well-connected, upper- and upper-middle-class segments of America. There is very little "diversity" in the educational and social backgrounds of top Clinton advisors. Nearly half received their educations, either graduate or undergraduate, at just three of the nation's most prestigious private universities—Harvard, Yale, and Stanford. Nearly 90 percent hold *advanced* degrees. Law degrees predominate.

The profusion of lawyers on the Clinton team exceeds any previous presidential administration. However, even though two-thirds of Clinton's top appointees are educated in law, few of these people actually practiced law for any extended period of their careers. Only Attorney General Janet Reno can really be said to have devoted her career to law. All of the other lawyers devoted their careers principally to elected and appointed governmental office.

While experience in the private sector is limited, Clinton's team can boast a wealth of experience in government—in both elected offices and bureaucratic posts.

Overall, the Clinton administration is clearly distinguishable from the previous administration in its heavy reliance on politicians and bureaucrats, its oversupply of lawyers, and its absence of experience in business and the military.

By custom, cabinet officials who served during a president's first term offer their resignations at the beginning of a second term. This allows the president to reshape his administration and allow cabinet members to exit more or less gracefully. Following his reelection, Clinton was given the opportunity to retain some of his top officials (for example, Treasury Secretary Robert Rubin, HHS Secretary Donna Shalala, Interior Secretary Bruce Babbitt, Education Secretary Richard Riley, Attorney General Janet Reno, and Veterans Affairs Secretary Jesse Brown), while replacing others (for example, former Secretary of State Warren Christopher, former HUD Secretary Henry Cisneros, former Labor Secretary Robert Reich, former Agriculture Secretary Mike Espy, and former Energy Secretary Hazel O'Leary). (See Table 4-7.)

Source: Adapted from Thomas R. Dye, "The Friends of Bill and Hillary," *PS Political Science and Politics,* Vol. 26 (December 1993): 693–695. For additional information on leadership in the Clinton administration, see Thomas R. Dye, *Who's Running America? The Clinton Years* (Englewood Cliffs, NJ: Prentice-Hall, 1994).

TABLE 4-7 Clinton's cabinets

POSITION	FIRST TERM			SECOND TERM		
	NAME	EDUCATION	EXPERIENCE	NAME	EDUCATION	EXPERIENCE
Vice President	Albert Gore, Jr.	Harvard U., B.A.; Vanderbilt U., L.L.B.	Newspaper reporter, real estate developer, lawyer	*continued in office*		
Secretary of State	Warren M. Christopher	U. of Southern Calif., B.S.; Stanford U., L.L.B.	Lawyer, government official	Madeleine K. Albright	Columbia University, Ph.D.	Professor at Georgetown University; National Security Council staff; U.S. Ambassador to United Nations
Secretary of Treasury	Lloyd Bentsen	U. of Texas, L.L.B.	Lawyer, financial executive	Robert E. Rubin	Harvard U., B.A.; Yale Law School, J.D.	Multi-millionaire investor chair of investment firm of Goldman, Sacks & Co.
Secretary of Defense	Les Aspin*	Yale U., B.A.; Oxford U., M.A.; Massachusetts Institute of Technology, Ph.D.	Economics professor	William S. Cohen	Bowdoin College, B.A.; Boston U. Law School, J.D.	U.S. Senator from Maine; Senate Armed Forces and Intelligence committees; never served in military
Attorney General	Janet Reno	Cornell, B.A.; Harvard, L.L.B.	Lawyer, state attorney	*continued in office*		
Secretary of Commerce	Ronald H. Brown	Middlebury College, B.A.; U. of St. John's, J.D.	Lawyer, party chair, lobbyist	William Daley	Loyola U., B.A.; John Marshall Law School, J.D.	Banker, major Democratic party fundraiser
Secretary of Housing and Urban Development	Henry G. Cisneros	Texas A&M U., M.A.; John F. Kennedy School of Govt., M.A.; George Washington U., doctor of public administration.	Public official	Andrew M. Cuomo	Fordham U., B.A.; Albany Law School, J.D.	Campaign manager for his father (former NY Governor Mario Cuomo); assistant HUD secretary
Secretary of Labor	Robert B. Reich	Dartmouth College; Yale Law School, J.D.; and Oxford U.	Lawyer, lecturer, author	Alexis M. Herman	Xavier U., B.A.	Director of Women's Bureau in Dept. of Labor; Consultant to businesses and government on employment of minorities, and women

Clinton's cabinets (continued)

	FIRST TERM			SECOND TERM		
POSITION	NAME	EDUCATION	EXPERIENCE	NAME	EDUCATION	EXPERIENCE
Secretary of Transportation	Federico F. Peña	U. of Texas-Austin, B.A., J.D.;	Lawyer, public official	Rodney E. Slater	Eastern Michigan University, B.A.; University of Arkansas, J.D.	Head of Federal Highway Administration; Arkansas State Highway Commission and special assistant for minority affairs under Gov. Clinton
Secretary of Interior	Bruce Babbitt	U. of Notre Dame, B.S.; U. of Newcastle, England, M.A.; Harvard Law School, L.L.B.	Lawyer, public official, lobbyist	continued in office		
Secretary of Health and Human Services	Donna E. Shalala	Western College, A.B.; Syracuse U., Ph.D.	University administrator, professor	continued in office		
Secretary of Education	Richard W. Riley	Furman U., B.A.; U. of South Carolina Law School, L.L.D.	Lawyer, public official	continued in office		
Secretary of Agriculture	Mike Espy	Howard U., B.A.; Santa Clara U., J.D.	Lawyer, businessman, public official	Dan Glickman	University of Michigan, B.A.; George Washington University Law School, J.D.	U.S. Congressman from Kansas; House Agriculture Committee
Secretary of Energy	Hazel R. O'Leary	Fisk College, B.A.; Rutgers Univ. School of Law, J.D.	Lawyer, energy company executive, lobbyist	Federico F. Peña	University of Texas-Austin, B.A., J.D.	Mayor of Denver; Secretary of Transportation
Secretary of Veterans Affairs	Jesse Brown	Chicago City College	Veterans advocate, lobbyist	continued in office		

*Data covers *initial* Clinton appointments in 1993. Early replacements include Secretary of Defense William William Perry (defense industry executive, Stanford Ph.D. in mathematics, and developer of the "Stealth" technology) for Les Aspin.

FIGURE 4-3

Recruitment to
top institutional
positions

*Presidents and
directors of the largest
corporations in
industry,
communication,
transportation,
utilities, banking, and
insurance. N = 3,572.

†Trustees of prestigious
private colleges and
universities; directors
of the twelve largest
private foundations;
senior partners of top
law firms; directors or
trustees of twelve
prestigious civic and
cultural organizations.
N = 1,345.

‡President and vice
president; secretaries,
undersecretaries, and
assistant secretaries of
all executive
departments; White
House presidential
advisors; congressional
leaders, committee
chairpersons, and
ranking minority-party
members; Supreme
Court justices; Federal
Reserve Board; Council
of Economic Advisors;
all four-star generals
and admirals. N = 286.

§Labor, press, religion,
and so forth.

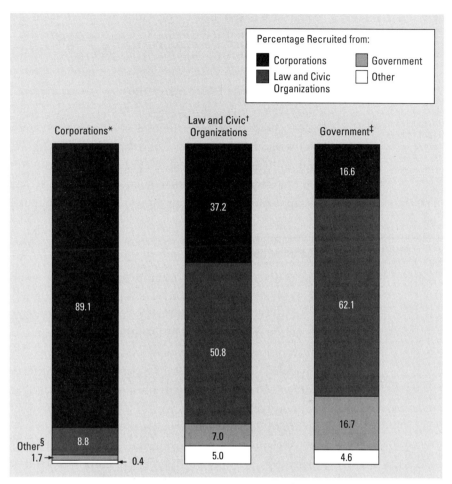

Source: Thomas R. Dye, *Who's Running America? The Clinton Years* (Englewood Cliffs, N.J.: Prentice-Hall, 1994).

Biographical information on individuals in positions of authority in society's top institutions reveals separate paths to authority. Figure 4-3 shows the principal lifetime occupational activity of individuals at the top of separate sectors of the elite. (This categorization depends largely on the way they identified their principal occupation in *Who's Who*.)

It turns out that the corporate sector supplies a majority of the occupants of top positions only in the corporate sector (89.1 percent). The corporate sector supplies just 37.2 percent of the top elites in law and civic organizations and only 16.6 percent of government elites. Top leaders in government are recruited primarily from the legal profession (62.1 percent);

some have based their careers in government itself (16.6 percent). This finding is important. *Government and law apparently provide independent channels of recruitment for high public office.* High position in the corporate world is *not* a prerequisite to high public office.

What do we know about those who occupy authoritative positions in American society? A number of excellent social-background studies of political decision makers,[7] federal government executives,[8] military officers,[9] and corporate executives[10] consistently show that top business executives and political decision makers are *atypical* of the American public.[11] They are recruited from the well-educated, prestigiously employed, older, affluent, urban, white, Anglo-Saxon, upper- and upper-middle-class male population.

Age and Education

The average age of the corporate leaders (directors and chief executive officers) identified in one study was sixty-one. Leaders in foundations, law, education, and civic and cultural organizations are slightly older. Top positions in government are filled by slightly younger people.

Nearly all top U.S. leaders are college educated, and more than half hold advanced degrees. About 25.8 percent hold law degrees, and 31.1 percent hold advanced academic or professional degrees (earned degrees only, not honorary degrees). Government leaders are somewhat more likely than corporate leaders to hold advanced degrees.

A glance at the precollegiate education of our top elites reveals that many are "preppies": 11 percent of corporate leaders and 6 percent of government leaders attended one of the thirty prestigious preparatory schools in America—Groton, Hotchkiss, Exeter, Loomis, Choate, and so on. Needless to say, only an infinitesimal proportion of the population receives an education at a prestigious preparatory school. Even more impressive, 55 percent of corporate leaders and 44 percent of government leaders are alumni of twelve prestigious, heavily endowed private universities: Harvard, Yale, Chicago, Stanford, Columbia, MIT, Cornell, Northwestern, Princeton, Johns Hopkins, University of Pennsylvania, and Dartmouth. *Elites in America are notably "Ivy League,"* as Table 4-8 shows.

Women and Minorities at the Top

Women and minorities have made significant inroads into America's power elite over the last three decades.[12] Among the directors of the nation's

TABLE 4-8		CORPORATE	LAW AND CIVIC ORGANIZATIONS	GOVERNMENT
AVERAGE AGE		61 YEARS	64 YEARS	58 YEARS
Schools				
	Public	81.8	73.2	90.9
	Private	7.0	8.8	3.0
	Prestigious*	11.2	18.0	6.1
Colleges				
	Public	25.3	8.4	37.9
	Private	18.2	8.4	17.2
	Prestigious†	54.9	83.2	41.9
Education				
	College educated	97.0	100.0	100.0
	Advanced degree	52.4	98.5	77.4

Social characteristics of corporate, public-interest, and government elites

*Andover, Buckley, Cate, Catlin, Choate, Cranbrook, Country Day, Deerfield, Exeter, Episcopal, Gilman, Groton, Hill, Hotchkiss, Kent, Kingswood, Lakeside, Lawrenceville, Lincoln, Loomis, Middlesex, Milton, St. Andrew's, St. Christopher's, St. George's, St. Mark's, St. Paul's, Shatluck, Taft, Thatcher, Webb, Westminster, Woodbary Forest.

†Harvard, Yale, Chicago, Stanford, Columbia, MIT, Cornell, Northwestern, Princeton, Johns Hopkins, University of Pennsylvania, and Dartmouth.

Source: Thomas R. Dye, *Who's Running America? The Clinton Years* (Englewood Cliffs, N.J.: Prentice-Hall, 1994).

largest corporations, for example, women have increased their representation from less than one percent in 1970 to nearly nine percent in 1995. There are few large corporations that do not have at least one woman on their governing boards; most have two. (The average corporate board has about twelve members.)

Women are better represented in government than in the boardroom. Recent presidents have been careful to appoint two or more women to the fourteen-member cabinet. President Clinton has appointed more female cabinet members than any previous president. His appointees include top cabinet positions—Madeleine Albright as secretary of state and Janet Reno as attorney general (see Focus: "The Friends of Bill and Hillary"). President Reagan appointed the first woman to the Supreme Court, Sandra Day O'Connor, in 1981, and President Clinton added Ruth Bader Ginsberg in 1993 (see Chapter 13). And in the 1990s women's representation in the House and Senate rose markedly (see Chapter 12). Nevertheless, the nation's elite remains overwhelmingly male.

TABLE 4-9	CORPORATE ELITES*	GOVERNMENTAL ELITES†		
Women and minorities at the top		SENATE	HOUSE	CABINET	SUPREME COURT
	N = 11,800	N = 100	N = 435	N = 14	N =9
Women	8.6%	9.0%	11.7%	28.6%	22.2%
African-Americans	3.6	1.0	8.5	14.3	11.1
Hispanics	0.7	0	4.1	7.1	0
Asians	0.4	2.0	0.7	0	0
Native Americans	0	1.0	0	0	0

*Directors of *Fortune* 1000 companies, 1995.

†House and Senate of the 105th Congress; cabinet as of Clinton's second term.

African-Americans have also gained representation among the nation's elite in recent years. Yet with roughly 12.8 percent of the total population, African-Americans remain seriously underrepresented at the top of the corporate world (see Table 4-9). In contrast, African-American representation among governmental elites is approaching parity. Congressional reapportionment after 1990, under the close supervision of the Justice Department and the federal courts, significantly increased the number of African-Americans in the House of Representatives.

Although Hispanics now account for about 10 percent of the U.S. population (and may soon become the nation's largest minority), they are virtually absent from top corporate positions, and their representation in government is well below their proportion of the population.

Upward Mobility

The United States describes itself as the land of opportunity. An important political question may be how much real opportunity exists for individual Americans to move from masses to elites. Are top institutional positions largely limited to the sons and daughters of upper-class families? Our own estimate is that approximately *30 percent* of our total institutional elite are upper class in social origin.

Certainly individuals with upper-class family origins are disproportionately represented in institutional leadership positions. (Far less than 1 percent of the general population would meet our definition of upper-class origin). But we cannot conclude that the upper class "dominates" on the basis of our estimate of 30 percent upper-class origins. On the contrary, 70 percent of our institutional elite appeared to be middle class in family origin; their parents were able to send them to college, but there is no indication that their parents themselves ever achieved high institutional position.

This estimate derives from a sample of our elite for whom we endeavored to learn their parents' class circumstances. We attributed *upper-class social origin* on the basis of the following: (1) attendance at a private prestigious preparatory school; (2) parent is an officer or a director of a major corporation, bank, insurance company, or utility; (3) parent is a high government official or general in the military; (4) parent is an attorney in a top law firm, a newspaper owner or director, or a university president or trustee of a university, foundation, or major civic or cultural association.[13]

THE LIBERAL ESTABLISHMENT

Elites in the United States share a consensus about the fundamental values of private property, limited government, individual liberty, and due process of law. Moreover, since the Roosevelt era, American elites have generally supported liberal, public-regarding social-welfare programs, including social security, fair labor standards, unemployment compensation, a progressive income tax, a federally aided welfare system, governmental regulation of public utilities, and countercyclical fiscal and monetary policies. Today elite consensus also includes a commitment to equality of opportunity for black Americans and desire to remove direct discrimination from the law.

The prevailing philosophy of the American elite is liberal and public-regarding, with a willingness to take the welfare of others into account as part of one's own well-being and a willingness to use governmental power to correct perceived wrongs done to others. It is a philosophy of noblesse oblige—elite responsibility for the welfare of the poor and downtrodden, particularly blacks. Traditionally the liberal elite has believed that it could change people's lives—end discrimination, abolish poverty, eliminate slums, ensure employment, uplift the poor, eliminate sickness, educate the masses, and instill dominant cultural values in everyone. America's masses do not widely share this philosophy.

Leadership for liberal reform has always come from the upper social classes—usually from established old family segments of the elite, rather than the newly rich, self-made segments. Before the Civil War, abolitionist leaders were "descended from old and socially dominant Northeastern families" and were clearly distinguished from the new industrial leaders of that era. Later, when the children and grandchildren of the rugged individualists of the Industrial Revolution inherited positions of power, they turned away from the social-Darwinist philosophy of their parents and moved toward the more public-regarding ideas of the New Deal. Liberalism was championed not by the working class but by men like Franklin D. Roosevelt (Groton and Harvard), Adlai Stevenson (Choate School and Princeton), Averell Harriman (Groton and Yale), and John F. Kennedy (Choate School and Harvard).

The liberal, public-regarding character of the U.S. elite defies simplistic Marxian interpretations of American politics; wealth, education, sophistication, and upper-class cultural values foster attitudes of public service and do-goodism. Liberal elites are frequently paternalistic toward segments of the masses they define as "underprivileged," "culturally deprived," and "disadvantaged," but they are seldom hostile toward them. Indeed, hostility toward blacks is more characteristic of white masses than of white elites.

The liberal philosophy of noblesse oblige leads inevitably to a sense of national responsibility for the welfare of the world. The missionary spirit of liberalism strives to bring freedom—self-determination, civil liberty, limited government, and private enterprise—to all the peoples of the world. America's major wars of the twentieth century occurred during the administrations of liberal Democratic presidents: Wilson (World War I), Roosevelt (World War II), Truman (Korea), and Kennedy and Johnson (Vietnam). The United States fought both world wars to "make the world safe for democracy." Following World War II, the nation embarked upon a policy of worldwide involvement in the internal and external affairs of nations in an effort to halt the expansion of communism. The "good" that liberal U.S. leadership seeks to do throughout the world is neither appreciated nor understood by the elites and masses of many nations. The result has been a great deal of bloodshed and violence committed by well-meaning liberal administrations for the finest of motives.

But the public regardingness of America's liberal elite is not confidence in the wisdom or judgment of the people. On the contrary, despite popular Democratic rhetoric about the "common sense" of the American people, few elites have much confidence in the ability of the masses to know what is good for them (see Focus: "Elite Attitudes toward Mass Governance").

Congress members, perhaps because they are elected by the people, appears to have somewhat more confidence in mass judgment than other elites in Washington. (At least, Congress members believe the people made the right choice on election day.) Yet fewer than one-third of Congress members believe the American people know enough to form wise opinions on public issues. Nonelected elites have far less confidence in the wisdom of the people (or they are more honest in their responses because they are not subject to popular election). Over three-quarters of top executive and bureaucratic elites in Washington do not believe that the American public can form wise opinions on public issues.

FOCUS

Elite Attitudes toward Mass Governance

Since the early days of the Republic, American elites have adopted a democratic rhetoric that obscures their disdain for the masses. Alexander Hamilton may have been the last national leader to publicly acknowledge elitist views:

> *All societies divide themselves into the few and the many. The first are the rich and the well-born; the other the masses of people. And however often it is said that the voice of the people is the voice of God, it is not true in fact. The people are forever turbulent and changing; they seldom judge right.*

Today, as well as 200 years ago, elites have very little confidence in the judgment of the masses.

It is difficult to query elites about their true opinion of the masses. Elites are difficult to survey by standard polling methods, and even when questioned they know enough to give socially acceptable responses. The rhetoric of democracy is so ingrained that elites instinctively recite democratic phrases. But consider the following responses obtained in a special survey of congressional, executive, and bureaucratic elites in Washington conducted by the Princeton Survey Research Associates:

	CONGRESS MEMBERS	PRESIDENTIAL STAFF	SENIOR BUREAUCRATS

QUESTION: *"How much trust and confidence do you have in the wisdom of the American people when it comes to making choices on election day: a great deal, a fair amount, not very much, or none at all?"*

	CONGRESS MEMBERS	PRESIDENTIAL STAFF	SENIOR BUREAUCRATS
Great deal	64	34	34
Fair amount	31	51	44
Not very much	1	12	20
None at all	0	1	1
Don't know/ No answer	4	2	1

QUESTION: *"Do you think the American public knows enough about the issues you face to form wise opinions about what should be done about these issues, or not?"*

	CONGRESS MEMBERS	PRESIDENTIAL STAFF	SENIOR BUREAUCRATS
Yes	31	13	14
No	47	77	81
Maybe/ Depends (vol.)	17	7	3
Don't know/ No answer	5	3	2

Source: Pew Research Center/*National Journal* survey conducted under the direction of Princeton Survey Research Associates. October 1997–February 1998. N = 81 members of Congress, 98 presidential appointees, and 151 members of the Senior Executive Service of the federal government. As reported in *The Polling Report,* May 4, 1998.

THE CONSERVATIVE MOOD

A mood of disillusionment penetrated elite circles in the 1980s and dampened enthusiasm for government intervention in society. The war in Vietnam, President Lyndon Johnson's Great Society, urban rioting, campus unrest, Watergate, and inflation all had raised doubts about the size and scope of government power. Elite interest in liberal reforms was tempered by the failures and costs of well-meaning yet ineffective (and sometimes harmful) public programs. Elites learned that government cannot solve society's problems simply by passing a law, creating a new bureaucracy, and spending a few billion dollars. War, poverty, ill health, discrimination, joblessness, inflation, crime, ignorance, pollution, and unhappiness have afflicted society for a long time. Elites no longer assume that these problems can be erased from society by finding and implementing the "right" public policies.

The Neoconservatives

The "neoconservatives" among America's elite continue to be liberal, reformist, and public-regarding, but they oppose the paternalistic state.

FOCUS

Where to Find the Establishment

The American establishment—with its old school ties, inherited wealth, upper-class lifestyle, position, and privilege—flourishes even in a democratic society. Not only is the establishment found in the higher echelons of business and government but, more important, it is said to "inhabit" the nation's most influential universities, foundations, and think tanks. Its unifying mission is to advance a public ethos—a civic morality emphasizing tolerance, individual liberty, reform, and do-goodism. Members of the establishment are generally from the upper social class in origin and have benefited from educations at prestigious private preparatory schools and Ivy League universities.

The establishment is not an institution itself but rather a "collective entity" or "third force" (the other two being business and government) that links all the institutions of American society together to pursue liberal values and goals. The establishment seeks to protect the United States from vulgar mass impulses—religious fundamentalism, racism, narrow patriotism, and selfish, short-sighted competition. *New York Times* columnist Leonard Silk and his son Harvard historian Mark Silk write:

> *Although the origins of the Establishment are ecclesiastical and aristocratic, in America it is firmly joined to both democratic and capitalist institutions. But its ambitions go beyond: it seeks to protect and advance social, moral, and aesthetic values that transcend the interest of any single person, economic group, or political organization; it affects to be a harmonizer,*

They are not as confident or ambitious (bordering on arrogant) as the liberals of the 1960s were. The neoconservatives have more faith in the free-market system and less confidence that governmental regulations will be effective. They have more respect for the traditional values and institutions, including religion, family, and the community. They believe in equal opportunity for everyone, but they do not believe in absolute equality, whereby the government ensures that everyone gets equal shares of everything. Neoconservatives, like all other liberals, disapprove of unequal treatment of racial minorities, but they generally oppose affirmative action that involves racial quotas. Finally, neoconservatives believe that the United States must maintain a strong national defense and that American democracy cannot survive for long in a world that is hostile to American values.[14]

The conservative mood does not alter the underlying commitment to liberal, reformist values. But it represents a more realistic view of what government can achieve and a more traditional view of the importance of personal initiative, enterprise, work, and family. This view did not reside solely in the Reagan and Bush administrations; it enjoys wide acceptance among the nation's top leaders in every sector of society.

---

an arbiter, a wise instructor of the nation—and particularly of its political and business leaders.[a]

The "familiar Establishment type" is "one of those Ivy League lawyer-doers able to move lightly among the worlds of business, government, and good works." The politics of the establishment run from "the reasonable right to the responsible left." The establishment is influential whether a Republican or Democratic administration is in Washington. "A change in the guard in Washington pulls to the new President those prominent establishmentarians most friendly to his aims, while pushing their counterparts from the previous administration back to the staffs and boards of the Establishment's private institutions."

The institutions that the establishment "inhabits" are said to be Harvard University, the *New York Times,* the Ford Foundation, the Brookings Institution, the Council on Foreign Relations, and the Committee for Economic Development. Not every person associated with these institutions is a member of the establishment. And there are other institutions that also possess establishment connections: Yale University, Princeton University, Columbia University, the University of Chicago, Stanford University, the Carnegie Endowment, the RAND Corporation, Twentieth Century, the Russell Sage Foundation, the Century Club, the Metropolitan Museum of Art, the Museum of Modern Art, and the Metropolitan Opera. But the establishment is not defined by these instruments. Instead the establishment is defined as "a national force, outside of government, dedicated to truth, liberty, and, however defined, the broad public interest."[b]

[a]Leonard Silk and Mark Silk, *The American Establishment* (New York: Basic Books, 1980), p. 325.

[b]Ibid., p. 20.

The Neoliberals

Today many liberals retain their faith in the power of government to "do good" and to solve society's problems, yet they reject many traditional liberal programs as unworkable. Neoliberalism "is an attempt to combine the traditional Democratic compassion for the downtrodden and outcast elements of society with different vehicles than the categorical aid programs or quota systems or new federal bureaucracies."[15] More than anything else, neoliberalism is a search for *new ideas* for government programs to restore the nation's economic health, uplift the poor, end discrimination, distribute income more equally, and provide education and medical care to all.

Chief among the neoliberal concerns is the nation's economy. Unlike old liberals, who placed social issues first on their agenda, the neoliberals are aware that little progress on social problems can be expected unless the economy is healthy. Instead of the antibusiness attitudes of liberals in the 1970s with their hostility toward industry, science, and technology, the neoliberals argue that government must take an active role in promoting and directing the nation's industrial growth.

Neoliberals are generally critical of the traditional "interest group" liberals who would sacrifice America's growth, productivity, and competitive edge in world markets in order to satisfy the demands of union leaders, protectionist-seeking industries, and other special interests. The struggle between the neoliberals and traditional liberals is being fought mainly *within* the Democratic party.

Prior to his presidential candidacy, Bill Clinton generally aligned himself with the neoliberal agenda. As chairman of the Democratic Leadership Caucus, he joined in efforts to move the Democratic party away from traditional interest group liberalism and toward more moderate, centrist policy positions. Much of Clinton's campaign rhetoric incorporated neoliberal ideas: ending "welfare as we know it" by requiring welfare recipients to work; guaranteeing health insurance to all Americans through "managed competition"; and calling for government "investment" (not "spending") in education and training for workers, infrastructure such as communications and transportation, and advanced technology.[16] At the beginning of his second term he announced that "The era of big government is over."

Summary

Elite theory does not limit its definition of elites to those who participate in *government* decision making. Anyone who participates in decisions that allocate values for society is an elite. Power in the United States is organized into large institutions, private as well as public: corporations, banks and financial institutions, universities, law firms, churches, professional associations, and military and government bureaucracies. This chapter develops several propositions in analyzing power and the institutional structure of the United States:

1. The giant institutions and bureaucracies of American society carry great potential for power.

2. The institutional structure of American society concentrates great authority in a relatively small number of positions. Fifty of the largest industrial corporations control nearly 60 percent of the nation's industrial assets, and fifty large banks control over two-thirds of the nation's banking assets.

3. In the early twentieth century, managerial elites largely replaced the great entrepreneurial elites of the Industrial Revolution. Top corporate management continues to wield corporate power, rather than the mass of employees or individual stockholders. However, in recent years large institutional investors such as pension funds, investment firms, banks, and insurance companies have increasingly challenged top management.

4. There is ample evidence of excessive greed in corporate boardrooms, especially in the pay, benefits, and perquisites of top managers. The average CEO of a large corporation earns 209 times the pay of an average factory worker.

5. American elites disproportionately represent the well-educated, prestigiously employed, older, affluent, urban, white, Anglo-Saxon, upper- and upper-middle-class male population.

6. Elites in the United States share a consensus about the fundamental values of private enterprise, due process of law, liberal and public-regarding social-welfare programs, equality of opportunity, and opposition to the spread of communism. The prevailing impulse of the "liberal establishment" is to do good, to perform public services, and to use governmental power to change lives. In world affairs, this missionary spirit has involved the United States in a great deal of bloodshed and violence, presumably in pursuit of high motives: the self-determination of free peoples resisting aggression and suppression.

7. Despite democratic rhetoric, American elites doubt that the masses of people have the knowledge or judgment to make wise decisions about public affairs.

8. In recent years American elites have reflected a more conservative mood, derived from their disappointments with government—Vietnam, Watergate, and the failures of many Great Society programs. This "neoconservatism" is skeptical of large-scale governmental interventions to achieve social good and more respectful of free markets, traditional values, and private institutions.

9. Neoliberals retain their faith in the power of government to "do good" but reject many of the traditional bureaucratic solutions of the New Deal of the 1930s and Great Society of the 1960s. Neoliberals believe that little progress can be made on social issues unless the economy remains strong.

10. The term *establishment* has been employed to describe an upper-class, educated "third force" in American society, separate from business and government yet frequently moving between those sectors of society. The establishment is concerned primarily with advancing a broad civic ethos— good government, tolerance, reformism, and internationalism. The establishment is said to "inhabit" the nation's most prestigious private universities, foundations, and think tanks.

Notes

1. C. Wright Mills, *The Power Elite* (New York: Oxford University Press, 1956), pp. 10–11.

2. Christopher Lasch, *The Revolt of the Elites* (New York: W. W. Norton, 1995), p. 6.

3. Even the leading pluralist scholars have revised their views about corporate power in the United States. For many years pluralist political scientists, notably Yale University's Robert A. Dahl and Charles E. Lindblom, argued that no single interest group, including "business," dominated American politics. But later Dahl and Lindblom publicly confessed their "error":

   > In our discussion of pluralism we made another error—and it is a continuing error in social science—in regarding business and business groups as playing the same interest group role as the other groups in polyarchal systems, though more powerful. Businessmen play a distinctive role in polyarchal politics that is qualitatively different from that of any interest group. It is also much more powerful than an interest group role.

   Robert A. Dahl and Charles E. Lindblom, *Politics and Economic Welfare,* 2nd ed. (Chicago: University of Chicago Press, 1976). See preface.

4. John Kenneth Galbraith, *The New Industrial State* (Boston: Houghton Mifflin, 1967), p. 323.

5. C. Wright Mills, *The Power Elite* (New York: Oxford, 1956), p. 289.

6. Quoted as clients of Covington & Burling by Joseph C. Goulden, *The Superlawyers* (New York: Dell, 1971), p. 27.

7. Donald R. Matthews, *The Social Background of Political Decision-Makers* (New York: Doubleday, 1954).

8. David T. Stanley, Dean E. Mann, and Jameson W. Doig, *Men Who Govern* (Washington, D.C.: Brookings, 1967).

9. Morris Janowitz, *The Professional Soldier: A Social and Political Portrait* (New York: Free Press, 1960).

10. Lloyd Warner and James C. Abegglen, *Big Business Leaders in America* (New York: Harper & Brothers, 1955).

11. Thomas R. Dye, *Who's Running America? The Clinton Years* (Englewood Cliffs, N.J.: Prentice-Hall, 1994), p. 172.

12. Ibid.

13. See Thomas R. Dye, *Who's Running America? The Clinton Years.* (Englewood Cliffs, N.J.: Prentice-Hall, 1994.)

14. Irving Kristol, "What Is a Neoconservative?" *Newsweek* (January 19, 1976): 87.

15. Randall Rothenberg, *The Neoliberals* (New York: Simon & Schuster, 1984).

16. Bill Clinton and Al Gore, *Putting People First* (New York: New York Times Books, 1992).

Selected Readings

Dionne, E. J., Jr. *Why Americans Hate Politics.* New York: Simon & Schuster, 1991. A review of recent political history intended to show why Americans are increasingly distrustful of government and cynical toward politics.

Domhoff, G. William. *Who Rules America?* Englewood Cliffs, N.J.: Prentice-Hall, Spectrum Books, 1967. *The Higher Circles.* New York: Random House, Vintage Books edition, 1970. *Who Rules America Now?* Englewood Cliffs, N.J.: Prentice-Hall, 1983. In these books, Domhoff argues that there is a governing class in the United States. By the term *governing class,* he means the part of the national upper class that holds positions of power in the federal government and industry and their upper-middle-class hired executives. He spends a great deal of time in these books developing the notion of class indicators. In *Who Rules America?* he examines elite control of the federal government; in *The Higher Circles* he develops in detail the role of private planning organizations in the formation of foreign and domestic policy; and in *Who Rules America Now?* he revises and updates his theory of upper-class dominance of American life.

Dye, Thomas R. *Who's Running America? The Clinton Years.* Englewood Cliffs, N.J.: Prentice-Hall, 1994. This book studies 5,000 top institutional leaders in industry, banking, utilities, government, the media, foundations, universities, and civic and cultural organizations. The book names names, studies concentration of power and interlocking at the top, examines recruitment and social backgrounds, discusses elite values, examines cohesion and competition among leaders, and outlines the policy-making process.

Halberstam, David. *The Best and the Brightest.* New York: Random House, 1973. This book assesses the men who advised presidents Kennedy and Johnson on conduct of the war in Vietnam. Based on interviews conducted by the author, a former *New York Times* Vietnam correspondent, the book reveals an excellent view of the men and processes responsible for decision making at the highest levels of the federal executive branch.

Lasch, Christopher. *The Revolt of the Elites.* New York: W. W. Norton, 1998. Lasch believes that the decline of public-regarding elites is a greater threat to democracy than a mass revolt led by demagogues (counterelites; see Chapter 5). He is, therefore, in accord with our premise that elites have squandered their positions of trust.

Mills, C. Wright. *The Power Elite.* New York: Oxford University Press, 1956. This book is a classic of elite literature. Mills takes an institutional approach to roles within an "institutional landscape." Three institutions—the big corporations, the political executive, and the military—are of great importance. The individuals who fill the positions within these institutions form a power elite. These higher circles share social attributes (such as similar lifestyles, preparatory schools, and clubs) as well as positions of power. Thus Mills's power elite is relatively unified. It is also practically free from mass accountability, which leads Mills to complain of the "higher immorality" of the power elite.

Silk, Leonard, and Mark Silk. *The American Establishment.* New York: Basic Books, 1980. A lively description of the establishment and the institutions it "inhabits," including Harvard University, the *New York Times,* the Ford Foundation, the Brookings Institution, the Council on Foreign Relations, and the Committee for Economic Development. The Silks portray the establishment as a largely upper-class "third force" linking the leadership of the corporate and government sectors of American society.

5

Masses in America

Let us transport ourselves into a hypothetical country that, in a democratic way, practices the persecution of Christians, the burning of witches, and the slaughtering of Jews. We should certainly not approve of these practices on the ground that they have been decided on according to the rules of democratic procedure.

—JOSEPH SCHUMPETER

Democratic government envisions an active, informed, participating citizenry. It also envisions a citizenry committed to democratic values—liberty and equality, freedom of speech and press, tolerance of diversity, and due process of law. And perhaps most importantly, democracy envisions a people who believe in equality of opportunity—that is, people who believe that they or their children have a reasonable opportunity to improve their lives, if they study and work hard, save and invest wisely, and display initiative and enterprise. The United States describes itself as the "land of opportunity." The promise of upward mobility, and the absence of extreme difference between rich and poor, diminishes class consciousness, that is, an awareness of one's class position and a motive for class conflict.

But in this chapter we shall argue that despite a robust economy, the masses in America—especially unskilled and semiskilled workers—have seen their average wages *decline* over time. The nation's labor force has been *de*unionized. Despite mass opposition, immigration, both legal and illegal, has skyrocketed. More importantly, *inequality* in America is increasing. Differences between rich and poor in both income and wealth are growing. These disturbing trends are largely a product elite support for the globalization of trade. Elites in America benefit directly from the expansion of international trade, the globalization of capital markets, and worldwide competition among workers for jobs.

Finally, we shall argue that most Americans are ignorant of public affairs and apathetic about politics. While they may voice superficial agreement with abstract statements of democratic values, they do not translate these values into specific attitudes or behaviors, especially toward people and ideas that they despise. We believe the real question is how democracy and individual freedom can survive in a society where the masses give only limited support to these values.

ELITE GAINS, MASS LOSSES

While the U.S. economy has performed very well in recent years, the benefits from that performance have been very unevenly distributed. The global economy has produced growth and profit for America's largest corporations and amply rewarded the nation's highest skilled workers. Indeed, global trade has *raised aggregate income* for the nation. But at the same time, it has contributed to a *decline in average earnings* of American workers and *worsened inequality* in America. Elite gains have been accompanied by mass losses.

Declining Worker Earnings

Average hourly and weekly earnings of American workers have declined significantly over the past two decades (see Figure 5-1). In real dollars (controlling for the effects of inflation), average hourly earnings declined from $8.10 in 1970 to $7.40 in 1995. The earnings of unskilled and semiskilled workers have fallen even more dramatically, by 25 to 33 percent since 1980.

This decline in the earnings of American workers, especially the less skilled, has occurred simultaneously with the growth of international trade. While this coincidence does not prove that trade is causing earnings to decline, it raises a question: whether in a global economy the huge supply of unskilled labor is pushing down the wages of American workers. Increased trade, especially with less developed economies such as Mexico, China, and India, with their huge numbers of low-wage workers, creates competition for American workers. It is difficult to maintain the wage levels of American jobs, especially in labor intensive industries, in the face of such competition. Moreover, it is not uncommon for U.S. corporations to move their manufac-

| FIGURE 5-1 | Declining earnings for American workers |

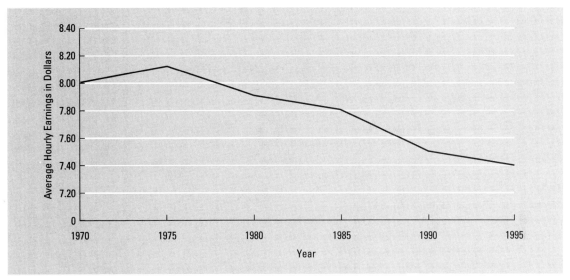

Source: Bureau of Labor Statistics, as reported in Council of Economic Advisers, *Economic Report of the President 1995*, Washington, D.C.: Government Printing Office, 1995.

turing plants to low-wage countries, especially to northern Mexico, where the transportation costs of moving finished products back to the U.S. market are minimal.

Capital Mobility

The global economy encourages the unrestricted movement of investment capital across borders. Large investors—banks, investment firms, corporations, mutual funds—regularly transfer assets from New York to London to Tokyo to Hong Kong to Singapore and to other financial centers around the world. Communications technology has greatly accelerated multinational capital flows in recent years. This allows companies to buy products and build factories where they can take advantage of cheaper unskilled and semiskilled labor.

Deunionization

Fifty years ago American unions were a significant force in determining workers' wages, especially in manufacturing. Industrial unions, such as

"Human Resources."

the United Steel Workers, United Automobile Workers, and United Mine Workers, set wage rates that influenced the entire national wage structure. Nearly forty percent of the nation's labor force was unionized.

Today fewer than 15 percent of the nation's labor force is unionized (see Figure 5-2). The major industrial unions have shrunk in membership; only unions of government employees (American Federation of State, County and Municipal employees), teachers (National Education Association), and some transportation and service workers (International Brotherhood of Teamsters) have gained members in recent years.

The AFL-CIO (American Federation of Labor–Congress of Industrial Organizations) is a federation of national unions. Today the AFL-CIO and its members appear to devote more attention to Washington lobbying than to negotiating wage contracts with employers. Indeed, union wage demands have been modest in recent years and nationwide strikes rare.

Deunionization is largely a product of the globalization of the economy. Employers can move, or threaten to move, their factories outside the

| FIGURE 5-2 | Deunionization |

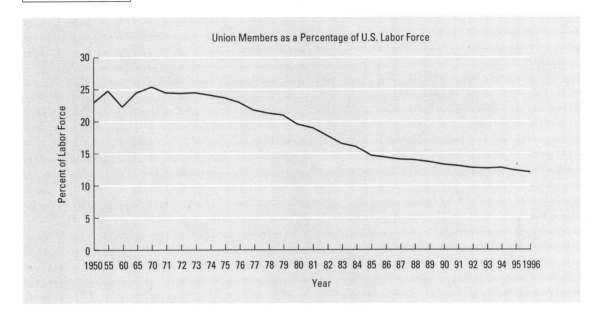

Union Members as a Percentage of U.S. Labor Force

country in response to union demands. Or they can replace striking union members with nonunion workers. Heavy immigration into the United States maintains a large pool of available low-wage workers.

Elite-Mass Differences Over Immigration

The United States accepts more immigrants than all other nations of the world combined. (See Figure 5-3.) The vast majority of immigrants in recent years come from the less-developed nations of Asia (43 percent) and Latin America (47 percent). Most immigrants come to the United States for economic opportunity. Most personify the traits we typically think of as American: opportunism, ambition, perseverance, initiative, and a willingness to work hard. As immigrants have always done, they frequently take dirty, low-paying, thankless jobs that other Americans shun.

Elites, notably the nation's business and corporate leaders, tend to support immigration, in principle, as an increase in the supply of low-wage workers in the United States. But mass support for *legal* immigration has declined over the years.

FIGURE 5-3	Immigration to the United States

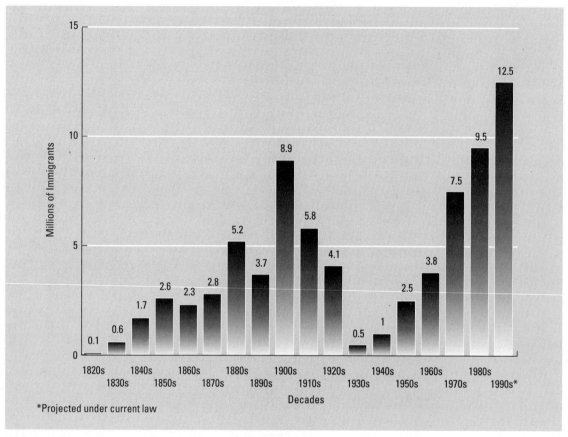

*Projected under current law

Source: *Manhattan Abstract of the United States, 1995,* p. 10.

QUESTION: *In your view should immigration be kept at its present level, increased, or decreased?*[1]

	1965	1977	1994	1995
Decreased	33%	42%	63%	62%
Kept at present level	39%	37%	27%	27%
Increased	8%	7%	6%	7%

Most Americans agree that immigrants make valuable contributions—that they "are productive citizens once they get their feet on the ground" (63 percent), "are hard-working" (58 percent), "are basically good honest people" (55 percent). However, majorities also believe that immigrants "are a burden on taxpayers" (66 percent). "take jobs from Americans" (58 percent), and "add to the crime problem" (56 percent).

Illegal Immigration

Estimates of illegal immigration vary wildly, from the official U.S. Immigration and Naturalization Service (INS) estimate of 400,000 per year (about 40 percent of the legal immigration), to unofficial estimates ranging up to three million per year. The INS estimates that about four million illegal immigrants currently reside in the United States; unofficial estimates range up to ten million or more. Many illegal immigrants slip across U.S. borders, or enter ports with false documentation, while many more overstay tourist or student visas (and are not counted by the INS as illegal immigrants).

As a free society, the United States is not prepared to undertake massive roundups and summary deportations of millions of illegal residents. The Fifth and Fourteenth Amendments to the U.S. Constitution require that every *person* (not just *citizen*) be afforded "due process of law." The INS may turn back persons at the border or even hold them in detention camps. The Coast Guard may intercept boats at sea and return persons to their country of origin.[2] Aliens have no constitutional right to come to the United States. However, *once in the United States, whether legally or illegally, every person is entitled to due process of law and equal protection of the laws.* People are entitled to a fair hearing prior to any government attempt to deport them. Aliens are entitled to apply for asylum and present evidence at a hearing of their "well-founded fear of prosecution" if returned to their country.

A national bipartisan commission on immigration reform, chaired by the late Texas Democratic Congresswoman Barbara Jordan, recommended the enforcement of existing federal laws barring the hiring of illegal aliens by establishing a national computerized verification system that employers could easily access when considering job applicants. But industry groups managed to bury the recommendation in Congress.

Elite Support for Immigration

Powerful industry groups that benefit from the availability of legal and illegal immigrants have led the fight in Washington to keep America's doors open. They have fought not only to expand legal immigration but also to weaken enforcement of laws against illegal immigration.

Current U.S. immigration policy—the admission of more than one million *legal* immigrants per year and weak enforcement of laws against *illegal* immigration—is largely driven by industry groups seeking to lower their labor costs. Agriculture, restaurants, clothing, manufacturers, and hospitals, for example, all lobby heavily in Washington to weaken immigration laws and their enforcement. Large agribusinesses benefit from a heavy flow of unskilled immigrants who harvest their crops at very low wages. Clothing, textile, and shoe companies that have not already moved their manufacturing overseas are eager to hire low-paid immigrants for their assembly lines. Even high-tech companies have found that they can recruit skilled computer analysts and data processors from English-speaking developing nations (India, for example) for wages well below those paid to American citizens with similar skills. These business interests frequently operate behind the scenes in Washington, allowing pro-immigration ethnic and religious groups to capture media attention. And indeed, large numbers of Americans identify with the aspirations of people striving to come to the United States, whether legally or illegally. Many Americans still have family and relatives living abroad who may wish to immigrate. Hispanic groups have been especially concerned about immigration enforcement efforts that may lead to discrimination against all Hispanic Americans. Foreign governments, especially Mexico, have also protested U.S. enforcement policies.

INEQUALITY IN AMERICA

Income inequality is and has always been a significant component of the American social structure. The top fifth (20 percent) of income recipients in the United States receives more than 45 percent of all income in the nation, while the bottom fifth receives less than 5 percent (see Table 5-1). The income share of the top fifth has declined since the pre-World War II years. And the income share of the top 5 percent of families has declined from 30.0 to 17.6 percent. But the bottom fifth of the population still receives a very small share of the national income—4.4 percent. In 1996 the bottom fifth was composed of families receiving less than $19,000 per year; the top 5 percent were those families receiving more than $127,000.

Inequality has worsened in the United States in recent decades. Various theories have been put forward to explain this trend: the decline of the manufacturing sector of the economy with its relatively high-paying blue-collar jobs; a rise in the number of two-wage families, making

TABLE 5-1	Distribution of family income in the United States

PERCENTAGE OF TOTAL INCOME RECEIVED

QUINTILES*	1929	1936	1950	1962	1972	1980	1990	1996
Lowest	3.5	4.1	4.8	4.6	5.5	5.2	4.6	4.4
Second	9.0	9.2	10.9	10.9	12.0	11.6	10.8	10.1
Third	13.8	14.1	16.1	16.3	17.4	17.5	16.6	15.8
Fourth	19.3	20.9	22.1	22.7	23.5	24.2	23.8	23.2
Highest	54.4	51.7	46.1	45.5	41.6	41.5	44.3	45.8
Total	100.0	100.0	100.0	100.0	100.0	100.0	100.1	100.3
Top 5 percent	30.0	24.0	21.4	19.6	14.4	15.7	17.4	20.0

*Each quintile is 20 percent of the population.

Source: U.S. Bureau of the Census, *Current Population Reports.*

single-wage households relatively less affluent; and demographic trends, which include larger proportions of aged as well as larger proportions of female heads of households.

But the globalization of trade is emerging as the principal cause of increasing inequality in America. Americans are now competing economically with peoples around the world. Our unskilled and semiskilled workers are obliged to compete with very low-wage workers in developing nations, from China, Taiwan, and South Korea, Mexico, and the Caribbean. In contrast, our highly skilled workers, entrepreneurs, executives, and investors, are well-positioned to gain from trade. The result is that inequality worsens even though the aggregate income of the nation rises.

Figure 5-4 shows the percentage of losses and gains since 1979 of families in each income class. Lowest income families have lost nearly 15 percent of their real income over these years, while the highest income families have gained nearly 30 percent in real income.

Inequality of Wealth

Wealth is even more unequally distributed than income. (Wealth is the total value of a person's assets—bank accounts, stocks, bonds, mutual funds,

FIGURE 5-4 | Worsening inequality

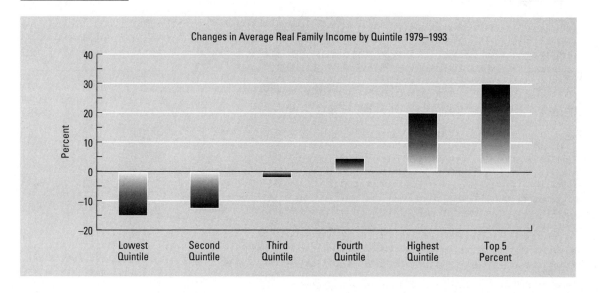

Changes in Average Real Family Income by Quintile 1979–1993

business equity, houses, properties, etc.—minus debts, mortgages, and un-paid bills.) Millionaires in America are no longer considered rich. More than two million people have a net worth exceeding $1 million. To be truly rich today, one must be worth more than $300 million. Most of the nation's wealthy are reluctant to reveal their net worth; thus any listing is only an es-timate. There may be 200 individuals and families in the world worth more than $1 *billion.* The richest person in the world is the Sultan of Brunei, who is worth around $25 *billion. Forbes* magazine lists over 70 *billionaires* in the United States.[3]

The top 1 percent of families in the United States currently owns about 40 percent of all family wealth.[4] Moreover, inequality of wealth has worsened in recent years; between 1950 and 1980 this figure fluctuated between 25 and 30 percent.

Harvard economist Richard B. Freeman summarizes these distress-ing views:

> *An economic disaster has befallen low-skilled Americans,*
> *especially young men, Researchers using several data sources—*
> *including household survey data from the Current Population*
> *Survey, other household surveys, and establishment surveys—have*
> *documented that wage inequality and skill differentials in earnings*

> *and employment increased sharply in the United States from the mid-1970s through the 1980s and into the 1990s. The drop in the relative position of the less skilled shows up in a number of ways: greater earnings differentials between those with more and less education; greater earnings differentials between older and younger workers; greater differentials between high-skilled and low-skilled occupations; in a wider earnings distribution overall and within demographic and skill groups; and in less time worked by low-skill and low-paid workers.*[5]

MASS DISAFFECTION FROM POLITICS

Distrust and cynicism characterize mass attitudes toward government and politics. Surveys of American public opinion since the 1960s have shown dramatic increases in public disdain of politics and politicians—"Public officials don't care what people like me think!"; "Government is run by a few big interests looking out for themselves!"; "Quite a few government officials are crooked!" (See Figure 5-5.)

The rise in a mass cynicism together with the decline in mass trust of government (see Focus: "Mass Distrust of America's Elite" in Chapter 1), deeply concerns American elites. Their concerns are that if the masses' trust in government is weakened, "citizens may become less likely to comply with the laws, to support government programs through taxes, and to enter government service. Without those critical resources, government will be unable to perform well, and people will become even more disaffected—a dangerous downward spiral that can weaken democratic institutions."[6]

Studies by elite institutions frequently conclude that "the underlying causes of declining confidence in government are complex." While acknowledging that elite actions themselves—notably the Vietnam War and the Watergate scandal—were influential in causing mass disaffection, these studies also point to several other underlying factors. First, they bemoan a long-term trend toward disrespect of authority (as elites throughout the ages have done). Second, they acknowledge that globalization of the economy involves some "creative destruction"—disruption of the lives of many people and a resulting insecurity that is blamed on government. Thirdly, they contend that changes in the political process—the decline in allegiance to political parties, the increased role of television in political campaigns, the professionalization of politics—"have increased the distance between

| FIGURE 5-5 | Mass disaffection from politics |

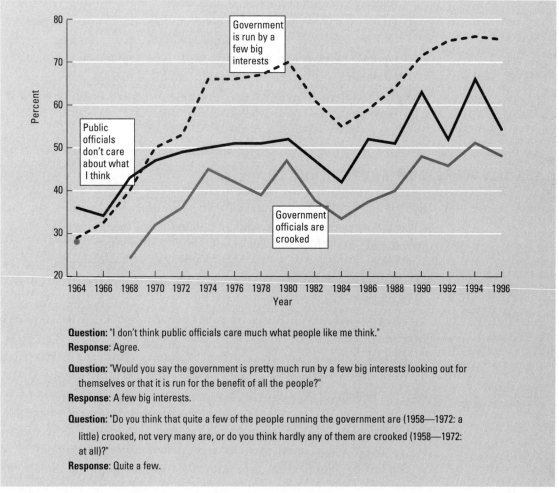

Question: "I don't think public officials care much what people like me think."
Response: Agree.

Question: "Would you say the government is pretty much run by a few big interests looking out for themselves or that it is run for the benefit of all the people?"
Response: A few big interests.

Question: "Do you think that quite a few of the people running the government are (1958—1972: a little) crooked, not very many are, or do you think hardly any of them are crooked (1958—1972: at all)?"
Response: Quite a few.

Source: National Election Studies.

political activists and the public at large, making average citizens feel that they have less control over their elected representatives." Finally, some elite studies have also acknowledged the effect of negative reporting on popular attitudes toward government and politics.

But solutions to the perceived problem of mass disaffection are elusive. Elites generally recognize that *a strong economy is the best defense against the masses acting on their discontents.* Indeed, the strong economy of recent years already appears to have reduced mass distrust and cynicism by a small yet significant degree. Elites regularly recommend that "politicians stop campaigning against government and start stressing the crucial roles that it plays." Elites correctly observe that masses continue to want government to play a significant role in many different areas of life.

QUESTION: *"It should be the responsibility of the federal government to . . .*

Guarantee national security	91%
Ensure health standards	70%
Ensure fair treatment of women and minorities	67%
Protect the natural environment	65%
Finance health care	63%
Ensure that the poorest Americans have enough to eat	58%

Finally, elites are encouraged that mass opinion remains very positive toward the constitutional framework of American government, even while it is critical of the people who run it.

ANTIDEMOCRATIC ATTITUDES AMONG THE MASSES

The masses give only superficial support to fundamental democratic values—freedom of speech and press and due process of law. People *say* they believe in those values when they are expressed as abstract principles; for example, they answer yes to the question "Do you believe in freedom of speech for everyone?" However, the public is unable or unwilling to apply the principles to specific situations, especially situations involving despised or obnoxious groups or individuals. In contrast, elites and the well-educated groups from which they are recruited are much more willing than the masses to apply democratic values in specific situations and to protect the freedoms of unpopular groups.

After years of studying the differences between elites and masses in their attitudes toward freedom, political scientists Herbert McClosky and Alida Brill reached the following conclusions regarding the masses in the United States:

> *If one judges by the responses of the mass public to survey questions, one has little reason to expect that the population as a whole will display a sensitive understanding of the constitutional norms that govern the free exercise of speech and publication. Only a minority of the mass public fully appreciate why freedom of speech and press should be granted to dissenters and to others who challenge conventional opinion.*[8]

In contrast, these scholars are much more optimistic regarding freedom and tolerance among elites:

> *Insofar as these matters are better understood and more firmly believed by those who, in one role or another, help to govern the society, one is tempted to conclude that, owing to the vagaries of the social process, the protection of First Amendment rights rests principally upon the very groups the Amendment was mainly designed to control—the courts, the legislature, political leaders, and the opinion elites of the society.*[9]

Differences between elites and masses in support of democratic values are illustrated in Table 5-2. These questions were asked of a national sample of community leaders (the press, clergy, teachers, men and women in business, lawyers and judges, union officials, and leaders of voluntary organizations), as well as a national sample of the public.

Social Class and Democratic Attitudes

Clearly the masses do not fully understand or support the ideas and principles on which the U.S. political system rests. We are left asking how the system survives.

The distribution of antidemocratic attitudes among various social classes may provide part of an answer. Upper social classes (from which members of elites are largely recruited) give greater, more consistent support to democratic values than do lower social classes. Political sociologist Seymour Martin Lipset has observed that "extremist and intolerant movements in modern society are more likely to be based on the lower classes than on the middle and upper classes."[10] Analyzing the ideologies of the lower class, Lipset notes:

> *The poorer strata everywhere are more liberal or leftist on economic issues; they favor more welfare state measures, higher wages, graduated income taxes, support of trade unions, and so*

TABLE 5-2	Elite versus mass support of democratic values	% MASS PUBLIC	% COMMUNITY LEADERS

ACADEMIC FREEDOM
When inviting guest speakers to a college campus:

	% MASS PUBLIC	% COMMUNITY LEADERS
____ students should be free to invite the ones they want to hear.	41	60
____ speakers should be screened beforehand to be sure they don't advocate dangerous or extreme ideas.	45	26

FREEDOM OF SPEECH
Should foreigners who dislike our government or criticize it be allowed to visit or stay here?

____ yes	41	69
____ no	47	24

If a group asks to use a public building to hold a meeting denouncing the government, their request should be:

____ granted	23	51
____ denied	57	26

RELIGIOUS FREEDOM
The freedom of atheists to make fun of God and religion:

____ should be legally protected no matter who might be offended.	26	53
____ should not be allowed in a public place where religious groups gather.	53	30

DUE PROCESS OF LAW
A person suspected of serious crimes:

____ should have the right to be let out on bail.	16	31
____ should be kept safely in prison until the trial.	68	36

HOMOSEXUALITY
Should a community allow its auditorium to be used by gay liberation movements to organize for homosexual rights?

____ yes	26	46
____ no	58	40

Complete equality for homosexuals in teaching and other public service jobs:

____ should be protected by law.	29	49
____ may sound fair but is not really a good idea.	51	33

Note: Percentages exclude "neither," "undecided," and no response.

Source: Herbert McClosky and Alida Brill, *Dimensions of Tolerance: What Americans Believe About Civil Liberties,* Russell Sage Foundation, 1983. Reprinted by permission.

> forth. But when liberalism is defined in noneconomic terms—as support of civil liberties, internationalism, and so forth—the correlation is reversed. The more well-to-do are more liberal; the poorer are more intolerant.[11]

| FIGURE 5-6 | Educational levels and tolerance |

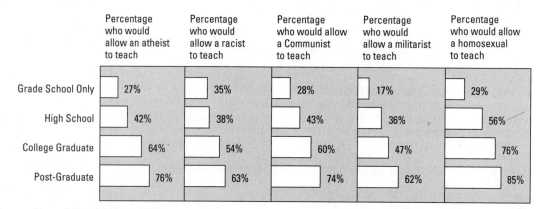

	Percentage who would allow an atheist to teach	Percentage who would allow a racist to teach	Percentage who would allow a Communist to teach	Percentage who would allow a militarist to teach	Percentage who would allow a homosexual to teach
Grade School Only	27%	35%	28%	17%	29%
High School	42%	38%	43%	36%	56%
College Graduate	64%	54%	60%	47%	76%
Post-Graduate	76%	63%	74%	62%	85%

Source: General Social Survey, 1996.

Education and Democratic Attitudes

Education is a very important factor in developing tolerance and respect for civil liberty. Clearly, Americans' level of education is related to their degree of tolerance, as is illustrated by Figure 5-6. Each increment of education adds to the respondents' willingness to allow racists, Communists, or homosexuals to teach. In two of three examples, only those groups educated above the high school level contain tolerant majorities.

Indeed, a lack of education may be more important than any other characteristic in shaping antidemocratic attitudes. Within occupational levels, higher educational status makes for greater tolerance. Increases in tolerance associated with educational level are greater than those related to occupation. No matter what the occupation, tolerance and education are strongly related.

Education also affects tolerance by influencing an individual's ability to apply an abstract principle to a concrete situation. It is one thing to agree that peaceful demonstrations are legitimate; it is quite another to allow an *unpopular* demonstration. For example, even when less-educated people agree with the general statement "People should be allowed to hold a protest demonstration to ask the government to act on some issue," only about one-third of them would allow a demonstration in favor of legalizing marijuana. But well-educated people are able to apply their abstract principles to specific situations: among the well-educated who agree with this general statement, more than 80 percent would allow a pro-marijuana demonstration.[12]

Elite Experience and Democratic Attitudes

Finally, leadership experience itself may also contribute to tolerance. While education is the most influential factor in promoting tolerance, leadership and activity in public affairs also develops tolerance. Political scientists Herbert McClosky and Alida Brill compared mass attitudes with those of community leaders—local government officials, judges and lawyers, journalists, clergy, school administrators, and leaders of unions and civic organizations. McClosky and Brill asked a variety of questions designed to ascertain support for civil liberty. For example, they asked, "Should demonstrators be allowed to hold a mass protest march for some unpopular cause?" with possible answers being "Yes, even if most people in the community do not want it" and "No, not if the majority is against it." (Among community leaders, 71 percent said yes, but among the mass public only 41 percent would allow a mass demonstration protest for an unpopular cause.)[13]

Perhaps leadership activity socializes people to democratic norms; they may become more familiar with democratic values because they are active in the democratic process. Or perhaps their public activity exposes them to a wider variety of attitudes, opinions, and lifestyles, broadens their perspective, and generates empathy for people different from themselves.

ARE THE MASSES BECOMING MORE DEMOCRATIC?

There is some evidence suggesting that over time Americans are becoming more tolerant of different social groups. This is particularly true of groups that elites themselves have come to accept and have undertaken to instruct the masses on what should be their proper attitudes.

Consider, for example, the historic change in white mass attitudes toward school integration that occurred in the years following the historic Supreme Court decision of *Brown v. Board of Education of Topeka, Kansas,* holding that racial segregation violated the equal protection clause of the U.S. Constitution.

From 1942 to 1982, a national sample of white Americans was asked the question "Do you think white and black students should go to the same

| TABLE 5-3 | White attitudes toward school integration following *Brown* v. *Board of Education* |

QUESTION: *Do you think white students and Negro students should go to the same schools or to separate schools?*

PERCENTAGE ANSWERING "SAME SCHOOLS"

	1942	1956	1963	1966	1973	1980	1982
Total whites	30%	49%	62%	67%	82%	88%	91%

QUESTION: *Would you send your child to a school where more than half the children are black?*

PERCENTAGE ANSWERING "YES"

	1942	1956	1963	1966	1973	1980	1982
Total whites	*	*	25%	33%	45%	36%	46%

*Question not asked in these years.

Sources: Paul B. Sheatsley, "White Attitudes Toward the Negro," *Daedalus* 95, no. 1 (Winter 1966). Reprinted by permission of *Daedalus, Journal of American Academy of Arts and Sciences,* Boston, Mass., Winter 1966, *The Negro American*-2. Updating from *Gallup Opinion Index* (October 1973) and *Public Opinion* (April/May 1981 and October/November 1982). Prior to 1973 the term *Negro* was used in the question instead of *black.*

schools or separate schools?" In 1942, not one white American in three approved of integrated schools (see Table 5-3). In 1956, two years after the historic *Brown* v. *Board of Education* court decision, white attitudes had shifted markedly. Nationwide support for integration characterized about half of the white population. By 1963, two out of every three whites supported integrated schools, and there was a continuation of the upward trend until over 90 percent of white Americans favored school integration by the 1980s. (Note, however, that despite increasing tolerance of integration *in principle,* white parents do not want their children to become a minority in their schools.) Additional survey information suggests that whites are becoming increasingly accommodating toward equal rights for blacks over time in other areas as well. But it should be noted that white opinion generally *follows* public policy, rather than leading it.

Over time Americans also appear to have become more tolerant of certain out-groups. Specifically Americans have become more willing to allow "communists" "atheists," and others to hold meetings, make speeches, and place their books in public libraries (see Table 5-4). One explanation of this

TABLE 5-4	PERCENT AGREE			
	1954	1972	1980	1994
An admitted communist should be allowed to make a speech.	28	52	59	70
An admitted communist's book should be allowed in the library.	29	53	60	69
Someone who is against church and religion should be allowed to make a speech.	38	65	62	72
Someone who is against church and religion's book should be allowed in the library.	29	53	64	70

Increased tolerance toward "communists" and "atheists"

Source: General Social Survey.

trend is the increased exposure of the masses to media messages of tolerance (see Chapter 6).

A more cynical interpretation is that there has been little change in "real" tolerance for unpopular groups but rather a change in *which* groups are considered particularly obnoxious. Over time, communists and atheists have become less threatening. But people are still willing to restrict the liberties of those they dislike; for example, racists, pro-abortion or anti-abortion groups, homosexuals, and neo-Nazis. In other words, some people who would defend the liberties of communists and atheists may be willing to deny the same liberties to racists or Nazis. "Liberty" may depend on who says what.

Indeed, "content-controlled" questions in which respondents were first given a list of groups and asked which they liked least, and then asked whether they would restrict the liberties of their "least-liked" group, revealed surprising levels of intolerance. (See Table 5-5.)

Putting Civil Rights to Popular Vote

In states with the initiative and referendum, civil rights issues often come up for popular vote. And when they do, *the restrictive, anti-civil-rights side regularly wins!* Indeed, one study of seventy-four referenda votes in the states on civil rights issues—housing and public accommodation laws protecting minorities, school desegregation, protection for homosexuals, English-only laws, and protection for AIDS victims—reports anti-minority victories on over three-quarters of the votes.[14] James Madison's concerns

TABLE 5-5	PERCENT AGREE
Continuing intolerance toward despised groups	*Members of the [least-liked group] should be allowed to teach in public schools.* 19
	The [least-liked group] should be outlawed. 29
	Members of the [least-liked group] should be allowed to make a speech in this city. 50
	The [least-liked group] should have their phones tapped by our government. 59
	The [least-liked group] should be allowed to hold public rallies in our city. 34

Source: Data from John L. Sullivan, James Pierson, and George Marcus, *Political Tolerance and American Democracy* (Chicago: University of Chicago Press, 1982), p. 67.

about "the tyranny of the majority" appear to be as well founded today as they were two hundred years ago.

Changing Targets of Intolerance

The targets of intolerance change over time, and attacks on freedom come from both liberals and conservatives. Radical right groups strive to control instruction and reading material in public schools by removing literature that they consider offensive. For decades, such groups have sought to eliminate science books with an evolutionary bias, sex education materials judged to be threatening to the institution of marriage, political literature judged to be anti-American, and economic material assessed as hostile to capitalism. Now, however, liberal groups are becoming equally vocal on behalf of censorship. These groups seek to remove literature they consider sexist and racist from schools and libraries, to ban pornography, and to reduce the display of violence on television. Television networks and public schools both report increased activity by liberal groups seeking to impose their values.

In short, the targets of discrimination are changeable; they vary with the times. In the 1950S when the Cold War was at its zenith, the masses' fear of communist activity led them to reject the legitimacy of Communists speaking, writing, or seeking public office. But by the 1960s many people saw internal social protest as the greatest threat. The percentage of people who believed that members of the Communist party were harmful decreased, while the percentage believing student demonstrators were harmful increased. Later, increased fear of crime led to growing mass willingness to curtail the rights of accused criminals.

TABLE 5-6	Personal ideology and least-liked group		
"SHOULD BE OUTLAWED"	PERCENTAGE OF LIBERALS SAYING	PERCENTAGE OF MODERATES SAYING	PERCENTAGE OF CONSERVATIVES SAYING
Communists/Socialists	21	32	44
New Left	7	15	21
Radical Right	59	34	17
Others	8	11	7

Source: Data from John L. Sullivan, James Pierson, and Gregory E. Marcus, *Political Tolerance and American Democracy* (Chicago: University of Chicago Press, 1982), p. 276.

Hatred tends to vary with individual ideology. As we can see in Table 5-6, self-identified liberals hate the radical right, and self-identified conservatives hate Communists and Socialists. Overall, two-thirds of the sample wanted to *outlaw* the group named as least liked! These polls contradict the notion that the masses in America are becoming more tolerant over time.

MASS POLITICAL IGNORANCE

If elections are to be a means of popular control over public policy, voters must be reasonably well informed about policy issues and must hold opinions about them. Yet large numbers of the electorate are politically uninformed, have no real opinions on policy issues, and therefore respond inconsistently to policy questions.

Ignorance

Public opinion surveys regularly report what is now the typical finding of a low level of political information among adult Americans (see Figure 5-7). Only about half the public knows the elementary fact that each state has two U.S. senators; fewer still know the terms of members of Congress or the number of Supreme Court justices. While most Americans can name the president, less than half can name their congressional representative, and fewer still can name both of their U.S. senators. Knowledge of state and local officeholders is even worse. Elites view such political ignorance as irrational. For active and influential elites, the stakes of competition in politics are high, and the cost of information is cheap; their careers, self-esteem, and

| FIGURE 5-7 | Mass political ignorance |

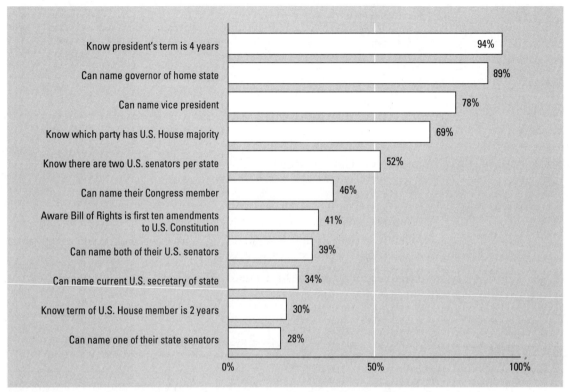

Source: Data from Robert S. Erikson, Norman R. Luttbeg, and Kent L. Tedin, *American Public Opinion,* 3rd ed. (New York: Macmillan, 1988), p. 42; citing various polls by Gallup, Harris, National Opinion Research Center (NORC), and CBS/*New York Times.* Similar "shocking" results are regularly reported in national polls; see, for example, Richard Morin, "Who's in Control? Many Don't Know or Care," *Washington Post,* January 29, 1996.

prestige are directly and often daily affected by political decisions. For such elites, ignorance would be irrational.

Ignorance diminishes with education, of course. Yet over time Americans are becoming more ignorant of government and politics than previous generations (see Table 5-7). This leads to an apparent paradox: Americans are becoming more educated in terms of years of schooling completed, yet less knowledgeable about public affairs.

Among the masses, however, political ignorance may be a rational stance—that is, the cost of informing oneself about politics may outweigh the benefits. Most people do not have friends in public office and do not benefit directly from the victory of one candidate or another. Moreover, because

TABLE 5-7	AMERICANS WHO KNEW THE NAME OF THE U.S. VICE PRESIDENT		
Political ignorance and education over time		1995	1952
	School dropout	33%	57%
	High school graduate	56	80
	Some college	69	80
	College graduate	82	94

	AMERICANS WHO KNEW WHICH PARTY CONTROLLED THE HOUSE OF REPRESENTATIVES		
		1995	1947
	School dropout	40%	59%
	High school graduate	54	77
	Some college	63	87
	College graduate	80	90

Source: Data from *The American Enterprise,* "Ill-Educated Americans," March/April 1997, p. 19.

one vote among millions is only infinitesimally influential, to most people it must seem quite reasonable to remain ignorant about politics. Thus the average voter generally tunes out political information.

Phantom Opinions

Contradictions in mass opinion are frequently revealed in public opinion polls. Because opinion polls ask questions that are meaningless to many people, the answers are often meaningless as well. Many people have never thought about the question before it is asked and will never think about it again. Their spontaneous responses do not reflect preexisting opinion. Many respondents do not wish to appear uninformed, and therefore they offer an "opinion" even though they had never thought about the issue prior to the interview. Few people acknowledge they have no opinion, even when that option is provided on a survey question. Many respondents simply react to question wording, responding positively to positive phrases ("helping poor people," "improving education," "cleaning up the environment," and the like) and negatively to negative phrases (such as "raising taxes," "expanding governmental power," "restricting choice"). Many respondents succumb to a "halo effect"—giving socially approved responses to questions, regardless of their true feelings.

Inconsistent Opinions

Since so many people hold no real opinion on political issues, question wording frequently produces inconsistent responses. For example, when

FOCUS

What If the People Voted on National Issues

What would happen if we allowed the American people to vote on nationwide referenda voting on key public issues? Perhaps Congress should be authorized to place particularly controversial issues on a national ballot. Perhaps a petition signed by one million voters should also result in a question being placed on a national ballot.

Democratic *proponents* of direct voting on national issues argue that national referenda would:

★ Enhance government responsiveness and accountability to the people.

★ Stimulate national debate over policy questions.

★ Increase voter interest and turnout on election day.

★ Increase trust in government and diminish feelings of alienation from Washington.

★ Give voters a direct role in policy making.

Elitist *opponents* of direct democracy, from our nation's Founders to the present, argue that national referenda voting would:

★ Encourage majorities to sacrifice the rights of individuals and minorities.

★ Lead to the adoption of unwise and unsound policies, because voters are not sufficiently informed to cast intelligent ballots on many issues.

★ Does not allow consideration of alternative policies or modifications or amendments to the proposition set forth on the ballot. (In contrast, legislators devote a great deal of attention to writing, rewriting, and amending bills, and seeking out compromises among interests.)

★ Enable special interests to mount expensive referendum campaigns; the outcomes of referenda would be heavily influenced by paid television advertising.

How would voters' decisions in national referenda differ from current government policies? A national poll on twenty-seven key policy issues produced the results shown on the next page. We have placed an asterisk in front of each issue in which *current public policy differs from popular preference*—almost half of the issue polled.

asked whether they agreed or disagreed with the statement "Professors in state-supported institutions should have freedom to speak and teach the truth as they see it," Californians appeared to support academic freedom by a ratio of 52 to 39. But when opinions were sought on the statement "Professors who advocate controversial ideas or speak out against official policy have no place in a state-supported college or university," the same ratio of 52 to 39 was found, but this time the majority was on the side favoring restrictions on academic freedom.[15] A study of attitudes toward pornography

"SUPPOSE THAT ON ELECTION DAY THIS YEAR YOU COULD VOTE ON KEY ISSUES AS WELL AS CANDIDATES. PLEASE TELL ME WHETHER YOU WOULD VOTE FOR OR AGAINST EACH ONE OF THE FOLLOWING PROPOSITIONS." (27 ITEMS READ IN RANDOM ORDER)

		% FOR	% AGAINST	% NO OPINION
1.	* Balanced budget amendment	83	14	3
2.	Raising the minimum wage	83	15	2
3.	* English as the official language	82	16	2
4.	Life sentences for drug dealers	80	17	3
5.	Death penalty for murder	79	18	3
6.	* Congressional term limits amendment	74	23	3
7.	* Prayer in public schools amendment	73	25	2
8.	* Reducing all government agencies	71	23	6
9.	2-year cutoff for welfare without work	71	24	5
10.	Mandatory job retraining	69	25	6
11.	* Doctor-assisted suicide	68	29	3
12.	* School choice	59	37	4
13.	* Teaching creationism in public schools	58	36	6
14.	* Ban on partial-birth abortions	57	39	4
15.	Ban on assault rifles	57	42	1
16.	* 5-year freeze on legal immigration	50	46	4
17.	* Federal flat tax system	49	39	12
18.	Reducing social spending	44	53	3
19.	Reducing defense spending	42	54	4
20.	Abortion ban except to save mother's life	42	56	2
21.	Reestablishing relations with Cuba	40	49	11
22.	* School busing for racial balance	34	62	4
23.	Legalization of gay marriages	28	67	5
24.	Selling off public lands	24	70	6
25.	Legalization of marijuana	24	73	3
26.	Withdrawal of U.S. from United Nations	17	77	6
27.	* Racial preferences in jobs and school	14	83	3

Source: *The Gallup Poll Monthly,* May 1996.

provides an even clearer example of inconsistent response. When respondents were asked whether they agreed that "people should have the right to purchase a sexually explicit book, magazine, or movie, if that's what they want to do," an overwhelming 80 percent endorsed the statement. However, when the same respondents were also asked whether they agreed with the opposite statement that "community authorities should be able to prohibit the selling of magazines or movies they consider to be pornographic," 65 percent approved of this view as well.[16]

MASS POLITICAL APATHY

Political apathy also characterizes mass politics (see Figure 5-8). Nearly half of eligible voters in the United States stay away from the polls, even in presidential elections. Voter turnout is lower yet in off-year congressional elections, when it falls to 35 percent of the voting-age population. City or county elections, when they are held separately from state or national elections, usually produce turnouts of 20 to 35 percent of eligible voters. Less than 1 percent of the American adult population ever run for public office. Only about 5 percent ever actively participate in parties and campaigns, and about 10 percent ever make financial contributions. About 15 percent wear political buttons or display bumper stickers. Less than 20 percent ever write their congressman or contact any other public official. About one-third of the population belongs to organizations that could be classified as interest groups, and only a few more ever try to convince their friends to vote for a certain candidate.

Sustained political participation—voting consistently in election after election for state and local offices as well as Congress and the president—is very rare. One study of voter participation over ten elections (including presidential, congressional, gubernatorial, and state and local legislative elections) showed that only 4 percent of the voting-age population voted in nine or all ten of the elections; only 26 percent voted in half of the ten elections, and 38 percent did not vote in any election.[17] Age is the best predictor of sustained political activity; older citizens are more likely than young people to be regular voters.

HOW DOES DEMOCRACY SURVIVE?

It is the irony of democracy that democratic ideals survive because the masses are generally apathetic and inactive. Thus the capacity of the

FIGURE 5-8   Mass political apathy

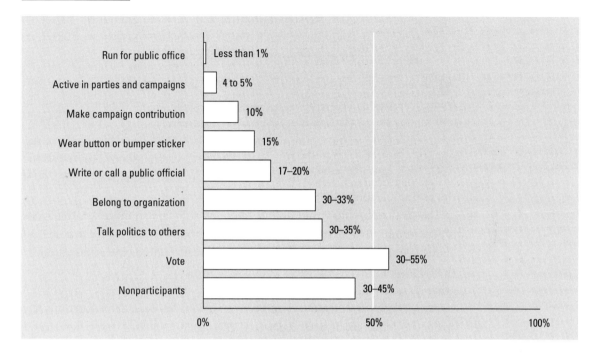

Run for public office	Less than 1%
Active in parties and campaigns	4 to 5%
Make campaign contribution	10%
Wear button or bumper sticker	15%
Write or call a public official	17–20%
Belong to organization	30–33%
Talk politics to others	30–35%
Vote	30–55%
Nonparticipants	30–45%

American masses for intolerance, authoritarianism, scapegoating, racism, and violence seldom translates into organized, sustained political movements.

The survival of democracy does *not* depend on mass support for democratic ideals. It is apparently not necessary that most people commit themselves to a democracy; all that is necessary is that they fail to commit themselves actively to antidemocratic movements. The masses' tendency to avoid political activity makes their antidemocratic attitudes less destructive. Those with the attitudes most dangerous for democracy are the least involved in politics.

Occasionally, however, mass apathy gives way to mass activism. Reflecting the masses' antidemocratic, extremist, hateful, and violence-prone sentiments, this activism occasionally threatens democratic values.

Mass activism tends to occur in crises—defeat or humiliation in war, economic depression and unemployment, or threats to public safety. Political sociologist William Kornhauser correctly observes:

> *There appears to be a close relation between the severity of crises and the extent of mass movements in Western societies. The more severe the depression in industrial societies, the greater the social*

> *atomization, and the more widespread are mass movements. . . .*
> *The stronger a country's sense of national humiliation and defeat in*
> *war, the greater the social atomization, and the greater the mass*
> *action (for example, there is a close association between military*
> *defeat and the rise of strong mass movements.*[18]

Defeat in war, or even failure to achieve any notable victories in a protracted military effort, reduces mass confidence in established leadership and makes the masses vulnerable to the appeals of counterelites. Both fascism in Germany and communism in Russia followed on the heels of national humiliation and defeat in war. The antiestablishment culture of the late 1960s and early 1970s owed a great deal to the mistakes and failures of the nation's leadership in Vietnam.

Mass anxiety and vulnerability to counterelites also increase in periods of economic dislocation—depression, unemployment, or technological change—that threaten financial security. Poverty alone causes less anxiety than does change or the threat of change in people's level of affluence. Another source of anxiety among the masses is their perceived level of personal safety. Crime, street violence, and terrorism can produce disproportionately strong anxieties about personal safety. Historically, masses that believe their personal safety is threatened have turned to vigilantes, the Ku Klux Klan, and "law and order" movements.

The masses are most vulnerable to extremism when they are alienated from group and community life and when they feel their own lives are without direction or purpose. Mass participation in the established organizations of the community—church groups, PTAs, Little League, fraternal orders—provides a sense of participation, involvement, and self-esteem. Involvement shields the masses from the despairing appeals of demagogues who play on latent mass fears and hatreds. People who are socially isolated are most likely to become mobilized by totalitarian movements. Thus a thriving group and community life very much serves the interest of elites; it helps protect them from the threat of demagogues who wish to challenge the established system of values.

THE DANGERS OF MASS ACTIVISM

Mass activism presents serious threats to Democratic values. Demagogues (or counterelites) seek to exploit in the worst attributes of mass politics—intolerance, racial hatred, class antagonism, anti-Semitism, impatience with democratic processes and the tendency to resort to violence to achieve "the will of the people."

Counterelites have arisen in American politics from both the extreme left and the extreme right. But all appeal to similar mass sentiments.

Although left counterelites in the United States are just as antidemocratic, extremist, and intolerant as are right counterelites, their appeal is not as broadly based as is the appeal to the right. Left counterelites have no mass following among workers, farmers, or middle-class Americans. In contrast, right counterelites in the United States historically have been more successful in appealing to broad mass followings.

Right-wing Extremism

Many changes in American society over the years have contributed to the popular appeal of right counterelites: shifts in power and prestige from the farms to the cities, from agriculture to industry, from the North to the West; shifts away from racial segregation toward special emphasis on opportunities for blacks; shifts from religion to secularism; shifts in scale from small to large, from personal to impersonal, from individual to bureaucratic; increases in crime, racial disorder, and threats to personal safety. Any genuine "people's" revolution in the United States would undoubtedly take the form of a right-wing, nationalist, patriotic, religious-fundamentalist racist, anti-intellectual, "law and order" movement.[19]

The Wallace Movement

Right-wing extremism is nothing new in American history. The early career of George C. Wallace was typical of many counterelites in its populism, extremism, antielitism, and egalitarianism. (As an independent candidate, Wallace won 14 percent of the popular vote in the 1968 presidential election.) In both North and South, Wallace appealed to *racial sentiments*—a mass characteristic of whites that he exploited. But it is a mistake to dismiss Wallace as merely a racist. He appealed to "little people" throughout the nation by expressing a wide variety of mass sentiments. He attacked the "Eastern money interests" and the "over-educated ivory tower folks with pointed heads looking down their nose at us." Republicans were attacked as "bankers and big money people" who exploit "us ordinary folks." Wallace's welfare and public-works programs, when he was governor of Alabama, were the most liberal in the state's history, and he was regarded as a threat to conservative business interests in that state. Wallace also exploited *fears about personal safety*. Wallace frequently referred to demonstrators as "the scum of the earth"; he pledged that if a demonstrator ever tried to lie down in front of a Wallace motorcade "it would be the last car he ever lies down in front of." Wallace's simplistic solution to rioting was "to let the police run this country for a year or two and there wouldn't be any riots." Wallace correctly judged that this mass audience would welcome a police state in order to ensure their personal safety.

Citizen Militias

In recent years self-styled citizen "militias" have cropped up across the nation—armed groups that more or less regularly get together dressed in camouflage to engage in military tactics and training. Their politics are generally superpatriotic, occasionally racist, and often conspiracy-minded. They frequently view federal government agencies as the enemy and the United Nations as a threat to American independence. They view themselves as modern-day descendants of the American patriot militias who fought the Revolutionary War. They believe the Constitution's Second Amendment "right to bear arms" guarantees individual Americans the right to arm themselves against tyrannical government. This often places them in conflict with regulatory efforts of the Bureau of Alcohol, Tobacco, and Firearms (ATF). It was the ATF's violent efforts to enforce federal gun-control laws that led to the deaths of more than seventy people near Waco, Texas, in 1993; this incident reportedly inspired the bombing of the Oklahoma City federal building and the deaths of 168 people there in 1995.

Elite Repression in Response to Mass Activism

Elites are more committed to democratic values than the masses, but they frequently abandon those values in periods of crisis and become repressive. Antidemocratic mass activism has its counterpart in elite repression. Both endanger democratic values.

Mass activism and elite repression frequently interact to create twin threats to democracy. Mass activism—riots, demonstrations, extremism, violence—generates fear and insecurity among elites, who respond by curtailing freedom and strengthening security. Convincing themselves that they are preserving liberal democratic values, elites may cease tolerating dissent, curtail free speech, jail potential counterelites, and strengthen police and security forces in the name of "national security" or "law and order." Ironically, these steps make society less democratic rather than more so.

Repressive behavior is typical of elites who feel threatened in crises, as some notable events in American history show. The Alien and Sedition Acts (1798), passed in the administration of John Adams, closed down Jeffersonian newspapers and jailed their editors. Abraham Lincoln suspended due process rights and imposed military law in many areas, both North and South, where citizens opposed his efforts to preserve the Union. The "Red Scare" of 1919–1920 resulted in the roundup of suspected Bolsheviks in the administration of Woodrow Wilson, even after the end of World War I. During World War II the Roosevelt administration imprisoned thousands of Japanese-American families in West Coast detention camps. And during the Truman and Eisenhower administrations, suspected Communists and "fellow travelers" were persecuted by dismissal from their jobs, blacklisting, and, occasionally, imprisonment. During the Cold War federal security agencies used such means as wiretapping, monitoring mail, paid informants, surveillance, infiltration, and "surreptitious entry" (burglary). These practices began with the Roosevelt administration and continued through the Truman, Eisenhower, Kennedy, Johnson, and Nixon years. The Watergate affair (the break-in at Democratic party headquarters in the Watergate apartments, Washington, D.C., in June 1972, and subsequent White House attempts at a coverup of those involved) grew out of a more general atmosphere of fear and repression that surrounded the White House in the early 1970s. No evidence suggests that the major figures participated in Watergate for personal financial gain. Rather, they appeared genuinely to believe that the political system was in jeopardy and that only extraordinary measures could preserve it (see the section "Watergate and the Limits of Presidential Power" in Chapter 10).

Elite theory inspires a reluctance to rely upon majority sentiments for the protection of individual liberty. Elitists do not trust the masses to protect "the weaker party or the obnoxious individual." They share with the Founders the fear that government by majority is incompatible with "personal security or the rights of property," the fear that the masses are fatally vulnerable to the appeals of intolerance, racism, authoritarianism, and even occasional violence. This aspect of elite theory—distrust of the masses—runs contrary to what Americans have been taught throughout their lives. It directly challenges the vision of "the people" as wise, honorable, and compassionate. It is, perhaps, the most controversial tenet of elitism.

Summary

Democratic theory envisions an active, informed citizenry who believe in equality of opportunity. Democracy is said to thrive in the absence of extreme differences between rich and poor, in the promise of upward social mobility. Democracy is said to depend upon popular support for individual liberty, freedom of expression, and due process of law. But our analysis of mass conditions and attitudes in America today suggests the following propositions:

1. The earnings of American workers have declined significantly over the past three decades. This decline, especially among unskilled and semiskilled workers, has occurred simultaneously with the growth of international trade.

2. Inequality in America has worsened since 1970. The gap between rich and poor has widened as elites have moved investment capital across national borders, lowered tariffs for foreign goods coming to America, and encouraged legal and illegal immigration.

3. Distrust and cynicism characterized mass attitudes toward government and politics. However, elites have benefited politically, from a strong economy that has dampened mass enthusiasm for political activism.

4. Despite mass disaffection from government and politics, the masses expect their government to provide for their economic security.

5. Mass support for democratic values is at best superficial. Elites are more consistent than masses in applying general principles of democracy to specific individuals and groups.

6. While the targets of mass hatred and intolerance change over time, giving the appearance of increasing respect for democratic values, in fact the willingness of the masses to deny fundamental liberties to despised groups remains unchanged.

7. The survival of democracy depends on elite rather than mass commitment to democratic ideals. Political apathy and nonparticipation among the masses contribute to the survival of democracy. Fortunately for democracy, the antidemocratic masses are generally more apathetic than elites are. Only an unusual demagogue or counterelite can arouse the masses from their apathy and create a threat to the elite consensus.

8. Occasionally mass apathy turns into mass activism, which is generally extremist, intolerant, antidemocratic, and violence-prone. Conditions that encourage mass activism include defeat or humiliation in war, economic dislocation, and perceived threats to personal safety.

9. Although left counterelites are as antidemocratic as right counterelites, their appeal is not as broadly based as the appeal of the right. Right counterelites have mobilized mass support among large numbers of farmers, workers, and middle-class Americans.

10. Although more committed to democratic values than the masses are, elites may abandon these values in crises. When war or revolution threatens the existing order, elites may deviate from democratic values to maintain the system. They may then cease tolerating the dissent, censor mass media, curtail free speech, jail counterelites, and strengthen police and security forces.

Notes

1. National polls reported in *The American Enterprise* March/April 1995, p. 105; and *USA Today,* July 10, 1995.

2. *Sale v. Haitian Centers Council,* 125 L. ed. 2d 128 (1993).

3. *Forbes,* "The *Forbes* Four Hundred," published annually in the October issue.

4. Edward N. Wolff, *Top Heavy* (New York: Twentieth Century Fund, 1995), p. 104.

5. Richard B. Freeman, "Are Your Wages Set in Beijing?" *Journal of Economic Perspectives* vol. 9 (Summer 1995): 15.

6. Quotations attributed to elites are taken from Harvard professor Joseph S. Nye, Jr., "Finding Ways to Improve the Public's Trust in Government," *Chronicle of Higher Education* (January 16, 1998), pp. B6–7. See also Joseph S. Nye, Jr., *Why People Don't Trust Government* (Cambridge, Mass.): Harvard University Press, 1997).

7. National poll reported in *American Enterprise,* (November/December 1997): 91.

8. Herbert McClosky and Alida Brill, *Dimensions of Tolerance* (New York: Russell Sage Foundation, 1983), p. 249.

9. Ibid.

10. Seymour Martin Lipset, *Political Man* (Garden City, N.Y.: Doubleday, 1963), p. 87.

11. Ibid., p. 92.

12. William Kornhauser, *The Politics of Mass Society* (Glencoe, Ill.: Free Press, 1959), p. 174.

13. McClosky and Brill, op. cit., p. 249.

14. See Barbara S. Gamble, "Putting Civil Rights to a Popular Vote," *American Journal of Political Science,* vol. 41 (January 1997), 245–269.

15. *Gallup Opinion Index* (March 1968): 11; cited in Robert S. Erikson, Norman R. Luttbeg, and Kent L. Tedin, *American Public Opinion,* 3rd ed. (New York: Macmillan, 1988), p. 55.

16. *Public Opinion* (September/October 1986): 32; also cited by Erikson et al., op. cit., p. 55.

17. Lee Sigelman et al., "Voting and Nonvoting: A Multi-Election Perspective," *American Journal of Political Science* 29 (November 1985): 749–765.

18. Kornhauser, op. cit., p. 174.

19. Seymour Martin Lipset and Earl Raab, *The Politics of Unreason* (New York: Harper & Row, 1970), p. 348.

Selected Readings

Kornhauser, William. *The Politics of Mass Society.* Glencoe, Ill.: Free Press, 1959. A classic work in political sociology arguing that "atomization" of individuals in the masses makes them vulnerable to the appeals of demagogues and leads to mass movements of intolerance, hatred, and violence. The survival of democracy, Kornhauser argues, depends on "insulating" elites from mass movements by involving the masses in community, family, church, and recreational activities.

Lipset, Seymour Martin, and Earl Raab. *The Politics of Unreason.* New York: Harper & Row, 1970. A historical recounting of right-wing extremism in America from colonial times through the 1960s.

McClosky, Herbert, and Alida Brill. *Dimensions of Tolerance.* New York: Russell Sage Foundation, 1983. A report of survey results of support for civil liberties among the mass public and a selected sample of civic leaders. The results reveal consistent differences in levels of tolerance between the mass public and elites in speech and press, due process, fair trial, equal opportunity, privacy, and women's and homosexuals' rights.

McClosky, Herbert, and John Zaller. *The American Ethos.* Cambridge: Harvard University Press, 1984. A report of public attitudes toward capitalism and democracy showing that "influentials" (in other words, elites) both understand and support these components of the American ethos more than the general public.

Stouffer, Samuel A. *Communism, Conformity, and Civil Liberties.* New York: Wiley, 1955. The earliest study, now a classic, of intolerance and authoritarianism among the American people. Based on surveys during the McCarthy period, Stouffer shows that the willingness to curtail the liberties of atheists, Socialists, and Communists is greatest among the least educated segments of the population.

Sullivan, John L., James Pierson, and Gregory Marcus. *Political Tolerance and American Democracy.* Chicago: University of Chicago Press, 1982. The authors demonstrate that tolerance has *not* increased over time but rather that the objects of intolerance change. Americans, both liberal and conservative, are willing to curtail the freedoms of groups that they most despise.

Wolff, Edward N. *Top Heavy.* New York: Twentieth Century Fund, 1995. A fact-filled report on the increasing inequality of wealth in America, together with a proposal to tax wealth as well as income.

6

Elite–Mass Communication

For most people most of the time politics is a series of pictures in the mind, placed there by television news, newspapers, magazines, and discussions. . . . Politics for most of us is a passing parade of symbols.

—MURRAY EDELMAN

Communication in the American political system flows downward from elites to masses. Television and the press are the means by which elites communicate to the masses not only information but also values, attitudes, and emotions. Professional pollsters in turn try to measure mass response to these elite communications. But elite-mass communication often fails. Masses frequently misinterpret elite messages to them, and elites cannot always shape mass opinion as they intend.

THE NEWSMAKERS

Elites instruct masses about politics and social values chiefly through television, the major source of information for the vast majority of Americans. Those who control this flow of information are among the most powerful people in the nation.

Television is the first true *mass* communication form. Nearly everyone, including children, watches the evening news. Over two-thirds of the public testifies that television provides "most of my views about what is going on in the world." And most Americans say that television is their "most believable" news source. (See Figure 6-1.)

Television has great impact because it is visual: it can convey emotions as well as information. Police dogs attacking blacks, people loading sacks of

FIGURE 6-1

Where the masses get their news and which source they believe

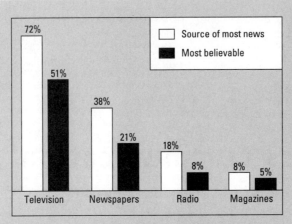

Questions: First, I'd like to ask you where you usually get most of your news about what's going on in the world today—from the newspapers or radio or television or magazines or talking to people or where?

If you got conflicting or different reports of the same news story from radio, television, the magazines, and the newspapers, which of the four versions would you be most inclined to believe—the one on radio or television or magazines or newspapers?

Note: Percentages (for sources of news) add up to 125 percent due to multiple responses. For trend line on these questions, see Harold W. Stanley and Richard G. Niemi, *Vital Statistics on American Politics, 1997–1998* (Washington: Congressional Quarterly Press, 1998). Between 1962 and 1964, television passed newspapers as a source of most news. Between 1958 and 1960, television passed newspapers as the most believable medium.

dead American soldiers onto helicopters, angry crowds burning and looting in cities—all convey emotions as well as information.

The power to determine what most Americans will see and hear about the world rests largely with a few private corporations: Capital Cities–ABC Inc. (ABC); CBS Inc. (CBS); and the National Broadcasting Corporation (NBC), a division of General Electric Corporation; Fox Broadcasting (Fox Network); and Turner Communications (CNN). Local television stations are privately owned and licensed to use broadcast channels by a government regulatory agency, the Federal Communications Commission (FCC). But because of the high cost of producing news and entertainment at the station level, virtually all stations must use news and programming from the major networks.

The top network executives—presidents, vice presidents, and producers—determine the news and entertainment Americans see. These executives are indeed "a tiny, enclosed fraternity of privileged men."* Top news anchors like Dan Rather, Peter Jennings, and Tom Brokaw assist in putting together the evening news show, but decisions about stories are made by the producers under supervision of the network executives. The leading

---

*So called by former Vice President Spiro T. Agnew, who also described them more colorfully as "super-sensitive, self-anointed, supercilious electronic barons of opinion." See *Newsweek* (November 9, 1970): 22.

television reporters—Sam Donaldson, Ed Bradley, Mike Wallace, Cokie Roberts, and others—occasionally pursue their own story ideas, but the decision to put their stories on the air rests with the news executives. Moreover, network executives exchange views with the editors of the *New York Times,* the *Washington Post, Newsweek, Time,* and a few of the largest newspaper chains. The television executives and producers and print editors and publishers collectively are the "newsmakers."

The newsmakers frequently make contradictory remarks about their own power. They sometimes claim that they do no more than "mirror" reality. The "mirror" myth is nonsense. A mirror makes no choices about what images it reflects, but television executives have the power to create some national issues and ignore others; to elevate obscure people to national prominence; to reward politicians they favor and punish those they disfavor. Indeed, at times the newsmakers proudly credit themselves with the success of the civil rights movement, ending the Vietnam War, and forcing two presidents—Johnson and Nixon—out of office. These claims contradict the mirror image theory, but they more accurately reflect the power of the mass media.

THE MEDIA'S POLITICAL FUNCTIONS

The political power of the mass media arises from several of its vital functions: newsmaking, interpretation, socialization, persuasion, and agenda setting.

Newsmaking

Newsmaking is deciding what and who are "newsworthy" and allocating precious television time and newspaper space accordingly. Television producers and newspaper and magazine editors focus attention on certain people, issues, and events, and that attention in turn generates public concern and political action. Without media coverage, the mass public would not know about these personalities, issues, or events. And without public interest, government officials would not consider the topics important.

The media must select from a tremendous oversupply of information and decide what is "news," and the selection process is the root of their power. Television cannot be "a picture of the world" (as some television executives pretend) because the whole world cannot squeeze into the picture (or into the twenty-four noncommercial minutes of the network evening news). Media attention creates events, issues, and personalities; media inattention means obscurity, even nonexistence. Of course, politicians, public relations people, interest group leaders, and aspiring "celebrities" know that the decisions of news executives are vital to their success and even to their existence. So they try, sometimes desperately, to attract the media's attention—to get just fifteen seconds on the network news. The result is the "media event"—an activity arranged primarily to stimulate media coverage and attract public attention to an issue or personality. The more bizarre, dramatic, and sensational the event, the more likely it is to attract media attention. It may be a march or demonstration, a dramatic confrontation, an illustration of injustice, a press conference, a visit to a home for the elderly, or a walk down a ghetto street. A media event for television must provide opportunities for interesting or dramatic pictures; television networks are likely to ignore topics or issues without such "good visuals."

Interpretation

Interpretation of events, issues, and personalities begins when newsmakers search for an "angle" on the story—a way to put it into context and speculate about its meaning and consequences. Through interpretation, newsmakers provide the masses with explanations and meanings for events and personalities.

Most network news broadcasts now include a "special segment" or "news special"—two or three minutes of "in-depth" coverage of a particular topic, such as gun control, nuclear plant safety, or international terrorism. News staffs prepare the specials well in advance of their showing and use film or videotape and a script with a "lead-in," "voice-over," and "recapitulation." The interpretive function is clearest in these stories, but interpretation takes place in every news story.

Socialization

The media's socialization function is to teach mass audiences the elite's preferred political norms and values. Both news and entertainment programming contribute to socialization. Election night coverage shows "how democracy works" and reinforces the values of political participation. Advertising shows Americans how they should live—it illustrates desirable lifestyles and encourages viewers to buy such products as automobiles, beer, soap, and perfume.

Entertainment programs also socialize the mass public by introducing social themes and ways of life—for example, racial tolerance (racially mixed neighborhoods as settings, situation comedies with cute black children), new sexual mores (sex outside marriage, unmarried couples living together), divorce and feminism (divorced mothers raising children and living happily outside marriage; successful, happy, and single professional women), and even homosexuality (well-adjusted, likable, sensitive, humorous homosexuals). Television executives and producers frequently congratulate themselves on such socially progressive themes.

Persuasion

Persuasion occurs when governments, corporations, unions, political parties, and candidates make deliberate attempts, usually but not always through paid advertising, to affect people's beliefs, attitudes, or behavior. The Department of Defense has become a major advertiser in its efforts to recruit for all-volunteer forces—"Be all that you can be!" Corporate advertisers ask Americans not only to buy products but also to believe that the corporations are concerned with the environment or with health or with the economic welfare of the nation. Unions ask television viewers to "Look for the union label."

The most obvious efforts at political persuasion take place during political campaigns. Candidates no longer rely on Democratic and Republican party organizations to run their campaigns but instead seek out advertising and public relations specialists to direct sophisticated media campaigns. Candidates can use television to bypass party organizations and go directly to the people. As the image makers have taken over political campaigns, the importance of political parties has declined. When voters can see and hear candidates in their own living rooms, they need not rely so heavily on party leaders to provide them with information and advice. Television has made candidate *image* a major factor in voters' choices.

Agenda Setting

The *real power of the mass media lies in deciding what will be decided.* Defining the issues, identifying alternative policies, focusing on political, economic, or social "crises"—these are critical aspects of national policy making. We can refer to these activities as *agenda setting.* Conditions in society that are *not* defined as "crises," or even as "problems," by the mass media never become policy issues. Such conditions do not get on political leaders' agendas. Political leaders, eager to get coverage on the evening news programs, speak out on the issues the mass media have defined as important. These issues are placed on the agenda of decision makers. Governments must then decide what to do about them.

Clearly, then, the power to decide what will be a "crisis" or "problem" or "issue" is critical to the policy-making process. Deciding what the problems are is even more important than deciding what the solutions will be.

Pluralist textbooks imply that issues or problems or crises just happen. Pluralists argue that in a free, competitive society such as ours, channels of access and communication to government are open to everyone, so any problem can be discussed and placed on the agenda of decision makers.

But in reality, policy issues do not just happen. Creating an issue, dramatizing it, calling attention to it, turning it into a "crisis," and pressuring government to do something about it are important political tactics. Influential individuals, organized interest groups, political candidates and officeholders, and, perhaps most important, the mass media all employ these tactics.

The power of television is not in persuading viewers to take one side of an issue or another or to vote for one candidate or another. Instead, the power of television is in setting the agenda for decision making: deciding which issues and candidates will be given attention and which will be ignored. Systematic research has shown that issues that receive the greatest attention in the mass media are most likely to be viewed by voters as "important."

BASHING AMERICA FOR FUN AND PROFIT

American television and the news media in general have a bad-news bias. They cover bad news very well. They do not cover good news very well or very often. Bad news is big news: it is dramatic and sensational. Scandals, rip-offs, violent crimes, threatening budget cuts, sexual deviance, environmental scares, and similar fascinations all capture audience attention. But the goods news—improved health statistics, longer life spans, better safety records, higher educational levels, and so on—does not stir audience interest so easily. The result is an overwhelming bias toward negative news stories in the media, especially on television. Bad news stories outnumber good news stories ten to one.

The networks select news for its emotional impact. Stories that inspire mass fears (bombing and terrorism, mass killings, nuclear power plant accidents, AIDS, global warming, and so on) are especially favored. Violence, sex, and government corruption are favorite topics because they attract popular interest. When faced with more complex problems—inflation, government deficits, foreign policy—the newsmakers feel they must simplify, dramatize, or else altogether ignore them.

Entertainment programs reinforce the negative picture of American life. Consider the popularity of crime programs. In the real world, about three out of a hundred Americans will be victims of a crime *in a year.* In prime-time television entertainment, approximately ten crimes are committed *each night.* Murder is the least common crime in the real world, but it is by far the most common crime on television, which averages one killing every two and a half programs! It is little wonder that Americans who watch a great deal of television tend to overestimate the real amount of crime in society greatly.

Crime is the leading topic of television network news.[1] Crime stories are twice as frequent as the next leading topic—health scares of various sorts. Sex scandals are the fastest growing category of news story.

Sex Sells

Historically, reputable newspapers and magazines declined to carry stories about the sex lives of political figures. This unwritten ethic of journalism protected Presidents Franklin D. Roosevelt, Dwight D. Eisenhower, and especially John F. Kennedy during their political careers. But today, journalistic ethics (if there are any at all) do not limit reporting of sexual charges, rumors, or innuendoes or public questioning of candidates and appointees about whether they ever "cheated on their spouse," "smoked marijuana," or "watched pornographic movies."

The media's rationale is that these stories reflect on the *character* of a candidate and hence deserve reporting to the general public as information relevant to their choice for national leadership. Yet it seems clear that scandalous stories are pursued by the media primarily for their commercial value. Sex sells; it attracts viewers and readers. But the media's focus on sexual scandal and other misconduct obscures other issues. Politicians defending themselves from personal attack cannot get their political themes and messages across to voters. Moreover, otherwise qualified people may stay out of politics to avoid the embarrassment to themselves and their families that results from invasion of personal privacy.

America's entertainment industry—its movie studios, TV show producers, and record companies—deluge America with graphic violence, endless profanity, and irresponsible sex. That is the view of an increasing number of serious critics, not just religious "fanatics." National surveys regularly report that the vast majority of Americans believe that today's movies contain "too much violence" (82 percent), "too much profanity" (80 percent), and "too much sex" (72 percent). Most TV viewers believe that television shows "ridicule and make fun of religion" (72 percent) as well as "ridicule and make fun of traditional values such as marriage and motherhood" (64 percent).[2]

Television shows have become increasingly sex obsessed and profanity-ridden; they glamorize unmarried motherhood and celebrate homosexual lifestyles. Recordings are released with lyrics that glamorize cop-killing, rape, and suicide. Critic Michael Medved writes:

> *Our fellow citizens cherish the institution of marriage and consider religion an important priority in life; but the entertainment industry promotes every form of sexual adventurism and regularly ridicules religious believers as crooks or crazies. . . .*[3]

Hollywood claims its movies simply reflect the sex, vulgarity, and violence already present in our culture, that restraints on movie makers would inhibit "creative oratory," and that censorship would violate "freedom of expression." They argue that politicians from Dan Quayle (who attacked *Murphy Brown* for glamorizing unmarried motherhood) to Bob Dole (who attacked Time-Warner for promoting "gangsta rap"), are merely pandering for the votes of religious conservatives. And they contend that the popularity of their movies, television shows, and records (judged in terms of money received from millions of movie-goers, viewers, and listeners) prove that Americans are entertained by the current Hollywood output, regardless of what socially approved responses they give to pollsters. "Movies drenched in gore, gangster rap, even outright pornography are not some sort of alien interstellar dust malevolently drifting down to us, but products actively sought out and beloved by millions."[4]

Explaining the Bad-News Bias

Why are the media so negative? One explanation is the commercial value of exciting and sensational news. It attracts viewers and increases television ratings. Higher ratings mean more advertisers and more profit for the networks. The business of the media is to attract viewers and readers and then sell them to advertisers. Indeed, advertising rates, and hence media corporate revenues, are largely determined by "ratings"—estimates made by independent companies, notably A. C. Nielsen, of the number of viewers watching a particular program. Advertising prices can run from $200,000 for a single thirty-second time spot during prime-time evening broadcasting on a major network, to as much as $2 million for thirty seconds on the Super Bowl with its estimated 60 million to 70 million viewers.

Another contributing explanation is the liberal ideology of the newsgathering establishments. The most influential journalists at the television networks and influential newspapers are political liberals. They believe that spotlighting negative aspects of American life will lead to social reforms. Their focus on the problems of American society leaves little time or space for good news. Still another explanation derives from the professional norms of journalism today. Many journalists believe that the media should be adversarial—that is, the media should act as critics of society. Investigative journalism is popular among young journalists; they believe that a vigilant, investigative press must aggressively seek to expose corruption and scandal in high places.

Mass Reaction

But fun and profit for the media come with high costs for American society. People heavily exposed to political scandal and corruption by the media lose trust and confidence in government and its institutions. Increased mass cynicism and declining voter participation can be attributed to "television malaise"—feelings of distrust, powerlessness, and disaffection from government stemming from television's emphasis on the negative in politics.[5] Taxpayers who believe that—despite billions of dollars of government spending—poverty is always getting worse, education and housing are declining, crime is worsening, and the environment is deteriorating, are likely to revolt. Why would anyone want to pay taxes if the prevailing image of government is one of scandals, waste, and rip-offs?

Most Americans object to government censorship. Rather, they believe that the entertainment industry itself should exercise self-restraint.

QUESTION: *Do you favor or oppose each of the following as a way to reduce the amount of sex and violence in popular entertainment?*

	FAVOR	OPPOSE
Tighten parental supervision	93%	6%
Warning labels on records	83%	15%
Voluntary self-restraint by entertainment companies	81%	15%
Government censorship	27%	69%

Thus, a free society must rely on the virtue and social responsibility of the entertainment industry directors, as well as public pressure for moral sensitivity. Or as former U.S. Senator Bill Bradley put it: "The answer has got to be more citizenship in the boardroom, not censorship. The public has got to hold boards of directors, executives, and corporations accountable for making money out of trash."[6]

LIBERAL BIAS IN TELEVISION NEWS

Network television—through entertainment, newscasts, and news specials—communicates established liberal elite values to the masses. These are the values of the media elite: liberal reform and social welfare, a concern for the problems of minorities and the poor, skepticism toward organized religion and the "traditional" family, suspicion of business, hostility toward the military, and an urge to use government power to "do good." (See the Focus: "The Hollywood Liberals.")

There is far less diversity of views on television than in the press. Individual newspapers and magazines present conventionally "liberal" or "conservative" views—for example, the *New York Times* versus the *Wall Street Journal, Newsweek* versus *U.S. News & World Report,* or *Harper's* versus the *National Review*—and thus balance one another to some degree. But the major television networks present a conventional liberal point of view. (William F. Buckley's *Firing Line,* representing a "conservative" viewpoint, is carried only by public television stations; CNN's program *Crossfire* presents a liberal and a conservative commentator, often Pat Buchanan, together; and ABC allows George Will to sit in on its Sunday talk shows.) Talk *radio* is the one medium where conservatism prevails, both among mass callers and the hosts, for example, Rush Limbaugh, Gordon Liddy.

The liberal bias of the news originates in the values of the newsmakers. The owners (stockholders) of the major corporations that own the television networks, magazines, and newspaper chains usually share the moderate conservatism and Republicanism of the business community, but the producers, directors, and reporters are clearly left-leaning and Democratic in their political views. One study of news executives reported that 63 percent described themselves as "left-leaning," only 27 percent as "middle-of-the-road," and 10 percent as "right leaning."[7] Newsmakers describe themselves as either "independent" (45 percent) or Democratic (44 percent); very few (9 percent) admit to being Republican. And most are male and upper middle class in origin. Another study asked members of the Washington press corps to describe their own politics: 42 percent of the press corps called themselves "liberal," 39 percent "middle-of-the-road," and 19 percent "conservative."[8]

In summarizing the social and political bias of the mass media in America, political scientist Doris A. Graber wrote, "Economic and social liberalism prevails, as does a preference for an internationalist foreign policy, caution about military intervention, and some suspicion about the ethics of established large institutions, particularly government."[9]

FOCUS

The Hollywood Liberals

The motion picture and television industry centered in Hollywood has a profound effect on the nation's political culture. Much of the commercial product of Hollywood—both television entertainment programming and motion pictures—is directed toward young people. They are the heaviest watchers of television and the largest buyers of movie tickets. Thus Hollywood plays an important role in socializing young Americans to their political world.

With a few exceptions, Hollywood producers, directors, writers, studio executives, and actors are decidedly liberal in their political views, especially when compared with the general public. Of the Hollywood elite, over 60 percent describe themselves as liberal and only 14 percent as conservative, whereas in the general public, self-described conservatives outnumber liberals by a significant margin. Hollywood leaders are five times more likely to be Democrats than Republicans, although many claim to be independents. And on both economic and social issues, the Hollywood elite is significantly more liberal than the nation's general public or college-educated public.

	HOLLYWOOD LEADERS	AMERICAN PUBLIC
★ When it comes to politics do you usually think of yourself as:		
Liberal	60%	30%
Conservative	14	43
Other	23	3
Neither/Don't Know	3	24
★ In politics of today, do you consider yourself:		
Republican	9	28
Democrat	49	33
Independent	40	28
Other/ None /Don't Know	2	11
★ Favor a constitutional amendment to permit prayer in public schools		
Favor	16	74
★ Describe themselves as		
A religious person	24	62
An anticommunist	37	69
Support gay rights	68	12
Support women's movement (men only)	75	46

Source: David. Prindle, "Hollywood Liberalism," *Social Science Quarterly* 74 (March 1993): 121.

BIAS AND SLANDER: FREEDOMS OF THE PRESS

Media elites claim that the First Amendment's guarantee of freedom of the press gives them a constitutional right to be biased. Certainly the drafters of the Bill of Rights agreed with Thomas Jefferson that a free and critical press was essential to the proper functioning of democracy. The media argue that they must be free to say and print whatever they wish, whether or not it is biased, unfair, negative, sensational, unfounded, dangerous, or offensive. Generally, the U.S. Supreme Court has agreed.

No Prior Restraint

The Court has interpreted freedom of the press to mean that government may place "no prior restraint" on speech or publication (that is, *before* it is said or published). Originally this doctrine was designed to prevent the government from closing down or seizing newspapers. Today the doctrine prevents the government from censoring any news items. For example, the Supreme Court ruled against the federal government and in favor of the *New York Times* in the famous case of the Pentagon Papers. The *New York Times* and the *Washington Post* undertook to publish secret information stolen from the files of the State Department and Defense Department regarding U.S. policy in Vietnam while the war was still in progress. No one disputed the fact that stealing the secret material was illegal. What was at issue was the ability of the government to prevent publication of the stolen materials in order to protect national security. But the Supreme Court rejected the national security argument and reaffirmed that the government may place no prior restraint on publication. If the government wishes to keep military secrets, it must not let them fall into the hands of the U.S. press.

Absence of "Fairness"

In the early days of radio, broadcast channels were limited and anyone with a radio could broadcast on any frequency. Interference was a common frustration of early broadcasters. The industry petitioned the federal government to regulate and license the assignment and use of broadcast frequencies.

The Federal Communications Commission (FCC) was established in 1934 to allocate broadcast frequencies and license stations for the "public interest, convenience, and necessity." The enabling act clearly instructed the FCC: "Nothing in this Act shall be understood or construed to give the Commission the power of censorship." For many years a "fairness doctrine" required radio and television stations that provided air time to a political candidate to offer competing candidates the same amount of air time at the same price. In addition, stations that broadcast editorials had to provide an opportunity for responsible individuals to present conflicting views. But there was always a huge hole in the fairness doctrine: news programs were exempt. Newscasts, news specials, even long documentaries were all exempt from the fairness doctrine. A biased news presentation did *not* require the network or station to grant equal time to opponents of its views. Moreover, the FCC did little to enforce the fairness doctrine. No station ever lost its license because of the doctrine.

But this modest check on media bias was eliminated by the FCC itself in 1987. As part of an effort to deregulate the broadcasting industry, the FCC scrapped the fairness doctrine despite strong opposition from Congress and watchdog groups. (The decision did not affect the equal-time provision for political candidates.) The FCC defended its decision by arguing that (1) the doctrine chilled debate by leading broadcasters to avoid controversy, and (2) the rapid rise in the number of broadcast outlets (for example, through cable television) showed that market competition rather than government regulation best served the public interest in receiving a variety of perspectives on public affairs. Congress tried to overrule the FCC by passing legislation designed to make the fairness doctrine legally binding, but President Reagan successfully vetoed it. Thus, broadcasters have no legal obligation to be "fair" in their presentation of public issues.

"Absence of Malice"

Communications that wrongly damage an individual are known in law as libel (written) and slander (spoken). The injured party must prove in court that the communication caused actual damage and that it was either false or defamatory. A damaging falsehood, or words or phrases that are inherently defamatory ("Joe Jones is a rotten son of a bitch"), are libelous and not protected by the First Amendment from lawsuits seeking compensation.

But media elites have successfully sought over the years to narrow the individual's protection against libel and slander. They were successful in *New York Times* v. *Sullivan* (1964) in depriving *public officials* of the right to recover damages for false statements unless they are made with "malicious intent." The "Sullivan rule" requires public officials not only to show that the media published or broadcast false and damaging statements but also to prove that they did so *knowing at the time* that their statements were false and damaging, or that they did so with "reckless disregard" for the truth or falsehood of their statements. The effect of the Sullivan rule is to free the media to say virtually anything about public officials. Indeed, the media have even sought to expand the definition of "public officials" to "public figures"— that is, virtually anyone the media choose as the subject of a story.

Media Power

In summary, no effective governmental checks on media power really exist. The constitutional guarantee of freedom of the press is more broadly interpreted in the United States than in any other democracy. The First Amendment guarantees a powerful, independent, and critical media elite.

MEDIA CAMPAIGNS

Television has contributed to the decline of political parties; it has replaced party leaders as "kingmakers"; it has encouraged voting on the basis of candidate image; it has fostered the development of media campaigns with professional advertising techniques; and it has significantly increased the costs of running for public office. All these changes reduce the influence of masses in politics and contribute to the power of elites.

The Decline of Parties

The media have replaced the party organizations as the principal link between the candidates and the voters. Candidates can take their campaigns directly to the voters. They can capture party nominations in primary elections dominated by television advertising. Party organizations have little to say about who wins the party's nomination and next to nothing to say about who wins in the general election. Aspiring candidates no longer begin their quest for public office by calling on party leaders but start instead by hiring professional media advertising firms. Both primary and general elections are now fought largely in the media.

Media as Kingmakers

Heavy media coverage creates candidates (see the Focus: "Media Coverage of Presidential Elections"). The media provide name recognition, the first requirement for a successful candidate. Indeed, heavy media attention can transform unknown figures into instant candidates; candidates no longer need to spend years in political apprenticeship in minor offices to run for Congress or a governorship. The media can also condemn an aspiring candidate to obscurity and defeat simply by failing to report his or her activities. Newsmakers select the "serious" candidates for coverage at the beginning of a race. In primary elections, the media even select "the real winner": if the favorite does not win by as large a margin as the media predicted, the media may declare the runner-up "the real winner" even when his or her vote total is less than that of the favorite. People who cannot perform well in front of a camera are no longer feasible candidates for major public office.

FOCUS

Media Coverage of Presidential Elections

How well does television cover presidential elections? The media treat election campaigns as horse races—reporting on who is ahead or behind, what the candidates' strategies are, how much money they are spending, and, above all, what their current standing in the polls is. Such stories account for about half of all television news coverage of an election. Additional stories are centered on campaign issues—controversies that arise on the campaign trail itself, including verbal blunders by the candidates—and character issues, such as the sex life of the candidate. In contrast, policy issues typically account for about one-third of the television news stories on a presidential election campaign. (See Table 6-1.)

When there is no real horse race to report—that is, when one candidate (Bill Clinton) leads his opponent (Bob Dole) by 10 to 20 percentage points throughout the campaign as in 1996, the media simply turn their attention away from the campaign. Indeed, from Labor Day to Election Day 1996, nine weeks of presidential election coverage,

the major television networks (ABC, CBS, and NBC) devoted only 483 stories to the lackluster Clinton-Dole campaign. That race was never close, so the media reduced their coverage dramatically—well below the nearly 800 stories over the same time period that had been given to the volatile three-way campaign (Bush, Clinton, and Perot) in 1992. Perhaps that is one reason why voter turnout in 1996 dropped to an all-time low (see Chapter 7).

Typically news stories about presidential candidates are *negative*. This usually applies to both Republican and Democratic candidates, although Republicans regularly suffer more negative coverage than Democrats. Clinton fared better on television than any recent presidential candidate, receiving 50 percent positive coverage in 1996.

Perhaps most distorting of all television news practices is the reluctance of anchors and reporters to allow the candidates to speak for themselves during the campaign. Instead, about three-fourths of campaign news airtime is used by anchors and reporters discussing the campaigns. *Only 13 percent* of television news story time features comments by the candidates themselves. In other words, viewers hear almost six times more campaign talk from journalists than from candidates! And the average sound bite for a presidential candidate—words actually spoken by these candidate—has shrunk to eight seconds.[a]

[a]Thomas Patterson, *Out of Order* (New York: Random House, 1993).

TABLE 6-1	COVERAGE	1996 CLINTON—DOLE	1992 CLINTON—BUSH
TV news coverage of the presidential campaign	Total stories	483	774
	Horse race stories	48%	57%
	Policy issues	37%	32%
	Other (voter interest, candidate background and record, fund-raising, etc.)		

TONE	NEGATIVE COMMENTS 1996	
	CLINTON	DOLE
Overall	50%	67%
Issues/record	53%	66%
Campaign performance	51%	84%
Economic policy	43%	69%
Social policy	49%	71%

Source: Derived from figures provided in *Media Monitor,* December 1996.

Image Elections

In covering elections, television largely ignores policy questions and focuses on candidate image—the personal traits of the candidates. Candidates are presented on television not in terms of their voting records or policy positions but instead on their ability to project a personal image of charm, warmth, "compassion," youth and vigor, honesty and integrity, and so forth. Elections are presented on television as struggles between competing personalities.

The media cover elections as a political game, consisting of speeches, rallies, press conferences, travels, and perhaps debates. The media report on who is winning or losing, what their strategies are, how much money they are spending, how they look in their public appearances, the response of their audiences, and so on. It is not surprising that policy issues do not play a very large role in voters' decisions, because the media do not pay much attention to policy issues.

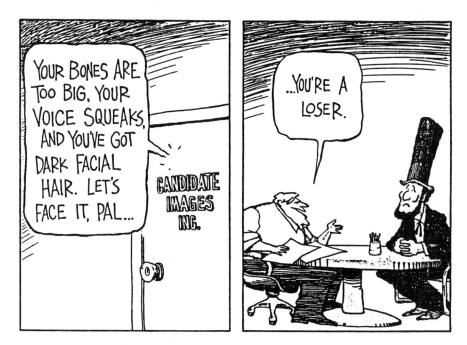

The Media Campaign

Professional media campaigns, usually directed by commercial advertising firms, have replaced traditional party-organized or amateur grass-roots campaigns. Today, professional media people may plan an entire campaign; develop computerized mailing lists for fund-raising; select a (simple) campaign theme and desirable candidate image; monitor the progress of the campaign with continuous voter polls; produce television tapes for commercials, as well as signs, bumper stickers, and radio spots; select the candidate's clothing and hairstyle; write speeches, schedule appearances that will attract new coverage; and even plan the victory party.

Professional campaign management begins with assessing the candidate's public strengths and weaknesses, evaluating those of the opponent, and determining the concerns uppermost in voters' minds. Early polls can test for name recognition, favorable or unfavorable images, and voter concerns; these polls then feed into the campaign strategy. Polls during the campaign chart the candidate's progress, assess the theme's effectiveness, and even identify undecided groups as targets for last-minute campaign efforts.

"Negative" campaigns can stress the opponent's weaknesses. Most professional campaigning takes the form of paid television commercials, produced by experienced advertising agencies and shown in specific voter "markets." But a good media campaign manager also knows how to get the candidate "free" time on the evening news. Candidates must attract the media and convey a favorable image: they may visit an old people's home, a coal mine, a ghetto, or a pig farm to appeal to specific groups of voters. A candidate may work a day digging ditches (particularly if perceived as a playboy millionaire), or walk from city to city (particularly if the opponent flies in a chartered airplane), or participate in a hog-calling contest (particularly if viewed as too intellectual). Such activities are more likely to win a spot on the evening news than is a thoughtful speech on nuclear disarmament.

Elitist Effects of the Media

All these media effects on elections contribute to the relative power of elites. Local party organizations have been replaced by national media campaigns. Policy questions are largely ignored in elections, in favor of easily manipulated candidate images. (More about campaigning and voter choice appears in Chapter 8.) Grass-roots campaigning has been displaced by expensive, professional media campaigns, usually directed by commercial advertising agencies. The costs of campaigning have risen dramatically because of the high cost of television advertising. The first question any aspiring candidate faces today—from city hall to county courthouse to state capital to Washington—is how much money can be raised for the campaign. The high costs of a media campaign require that (1) the candidate be personally wealthy or have wealthy friends or (2) the candidate receive financial support from organized interests, usually the political action committees (or PACs) established by corporations, banks, professional associations, industry groups, unions, and other special interests. (The power of interest groups is discussed in Chapter 9.)

ASSESSING MEDIA IMPACT

What impact do media elites have on mass opinion and behavior? For many years political scientists advanced the curious notion that the mass media had only "minimal effects" on political behavior. Of course, wiser business elites never believed the minimal-effects theory, as the growth of the multibillion-dollar advertising industry attests. Nor did the politicians believe it, as they turned increasingly to expensive television advertising. Presumably political scientists were basing their theory on the fact that newspaper editorial endorsements seldom changed people's votes. Systematic research on the political effects of the mass media, particularly television, is fairly recent. This research tells a far different story.

It is not easy to sort out the effects of media communications from the effects of many other social, cultural, political, economic, and psychological influences on mass attitudes and behavior. Even when we find strong correlations between the opinions expressed in the mass media and the opinions expressed by the general public, it is difficult to determine systematically whether the media shaped public opinion, public opinion shaped media broadcasts, or both were shaped simultaneously by political events. In other words, it is difficult to prove that the media *cause* changes in opinions or behavior. Nonetheless, systematic research on media effects has progressed to the point where some generalizations are possible.

Media effects can be categorized as influencing (1) cognition and comprehension, (2) attitudes and values, and (3) behavior. These categories of effects are ranked by the degree of influence the media are likely to have over us. That is to say, the strongest effects of the media are in cognition and comprehension—in generating awareness and increasing information levels. The media also influence attitudes and values, but the strength of media effects is diluted by many other sources of attitudes and values. Finally, it is most difficult to establish the independent effect of the media on behavior.

Cognition and Comprehension

Media elites strongly influence what we know about our world and how we think and talk about it. Years ago foreign policy expert Bernard Cohen, in the first book to assess the effects of media on foreign policy, put it this way: "The mass media may not be successful in telling people what to think, but the media are stunningly successful in telling their audience what to think about."[10]

However, the masses generally suffer from *information overload;* so many communications are directed at them that they cannot possibly process them all in their minds. A person's ability to recall a media report is dependent upon repeated exposure to it and reinforcement through personal experience. For example, an individual who has a brother in a trouble spot in the Middle East is more likely to be aware of reports from that area of the world. But most viewers become narcotized by information overload; too many voices with too many messages cause them to block out nearly all information. Information overload may be especially heavy in political news.

Television tells most viewers more about politics than they really want to know. Political scientist Austin Ranney writes: "The fact is that for most Americans politics is still far from being the most interesting and important thing in life. To them, politics is usually confusing, boring, repetitious, and above all irrelevant to the things that really matter in their lives."[11]

Attitudes and Values

Media elites can create new opinions more easily than they can change existing ones. The media often tell the masses how they should feel about news events or issues—those about which the masses have no prior feelings or experiences. And the media can reinforce values and attitudes that the masses already hold. But there is very little evidence that the media can change existing mass values.

The masses defend against bias in news and entertainment programming by *selective perception*—mentally screening out information or images with which one disagrees. Selective perception causes people to tend to see and hear only what they want to see and hear. Selective perception reduces the impact of media elites on mass attitudes and behavior.

The networks' concentration on scandal, abuse, and corruption in government, for example, has not always produced the desired liberal, reformist notions in the minds of the masses of viewers. Contrary to the expectations of network executives, their focus on governmental scandals—Watergate, illicit activities by the Central Intelligence Agency, abuses by the Federal Bureau of Investigation, congressional sex scandals, and power struggles between Congress and the executive branch—has produced feelings of general political distrust and cynicism toward government and the political system.

Public Opinion

Can media elites change public opinion? This question was directly confronted by political scientists Benjamin I. Page, Robert Y. Shapiro, and Glenn R. Dempsey in an extensive study of eighty policy issues over fifteen years. They examined public opinion polls on various policy issues at a first point in time, then media content over a following interval of time, and finally public opinion on these same issues at the end of the interval. The purpose was to learn whether media content—messages scored by their relevance to the issue, their salience in the broadcast, their pro or con direction, the credibility of the news source, and quality of the reporting—changed public opinion. Although most people's opinions remained constant over time (opinion at the first time period is the best predictor of opinion at the second time period), opinion changes were heavily influenced by media messages. Page, Shapiro, and Dempsey concluded that "news variables alone account for nearly half the variance in opinion change."

They also learned that:

★ *Anchors, reporters, and commentators* had the greatest impact on opinion change. Television newscasters have high credibility and trust with the general public. Their opinions are crucial in shaping mass opinion.

★ *Independent experts* interviewed by the media have a substantial impact on opinion but not as great as newscasters themselves.

★ *A popular president* can also shift public opinion somewhat. On the other hand, unpopular presidents do not have much success as opinion movers.

★ *Interest groups* on the whole have a slightly negative effect on public opinion. "In many instances they seem to actually have antagonized the public and created a genuine adverse effect"; such cases include Vietnam War protesters, nuclear freeze advocates, and other demonstrators and protesters, even peaceful ones.[12]

Behavior

Media elites have a difficult task in *changing* behavior. But television can motivate people who are already predisposed to act in a certain way.

Many studies have been conducted concerning the effect of the media on behavior—the effect of TV violence, the effect of television on children, and the effects of obscenity and pornography. It is difficult to generalize from these studies. However, it appears that television is more likely to reinforce behavioral tendencies than to change them. For example, televised violence may trigger violent behavior in children who are already predisposed to such behavior, but televised violence has little behavioral effect on the average child. Likewise, there is little evidence that pornography itself causes rape or other deviant sexual behavior among viewers.

Nonetheless, we know that television advertising sells products. And we know that political candidates spend millions to persuade audiences to go out and vote for them on election day. Both manufacturers and politicians create name recognition, employ product differentiation, try to associate with audiences, and use repetition to communicate their messages. These tactics are designed to affect our behavior both in the marketplace and in the election booth.

Political ads are more successful in motivating a candidate's supporters to go to the polls than they are in changing opponents into supporters. It is unlikely that a voter who dislikes a candidate or is committed to a candidate, and who has a lot of information about both candidates, will be persuaded by political advertising to change his or her vote. But many potential voters are undecided, and the support of many others is "soft." Going to the polls on election day requires effort—people have errands to do, it may be raining, they may be tired. Television advertising is more effective with the marginal voters.

Summary

Communications in the American political system flow downward from elites to masses. Elites influence mass opinion more than masses influence elite opinion.

1. Television is the principal means by which elites communicate to masses. Control of the flow of information to the masses is highly concentrated. A handful of prestigious news organizations decides what will be the "news."

2. The political functions of the mass media include newsmaking (deciding what to report), interpretation (providing the masses with explanations of events), socialization (teaching about preferred norms, values, and lifestyles), persuasion (making direct efforts to affect behavior), and agenda setting.

3. The most important power of the mass media is agenda setting—deciding what will be decided. The media decide what conditions in society to label "crises" or "problems" or "issues" and thereby place these topics on the agenda of national decision makers.

4. Bias in the news arises from the newsmakers' own liberal-establishment views, plus the need to dramatize and sensationalize the news. However, the newsmakers' concentration on scandal and corruption in government often produces "television malaise"—social distrust, political cynicism, and feelings of powerlessness—instead of reform.

5. The First Amendment's guarantee of freedom of the press has been expanded by the Supreme Court to remove virtually all checks on media power. The Sullivan rule renders public officials especially vulnerable to media attacks.

6. The talk-show culture contributes to sleazy, conspiracy-oriented, scandal-ridden views of politics among the masses. It creates a favorable environment for independent anti-Washington candidates such as Ross Perot.

7. The media have largely replaced political parties as the principal link between the candidates and the voters. The media focus on the personal image of candidates rather than issues. The high cost of media campaigning adds to the influence of wealthy contributors.

8. The media are most effective at influencing mass cognition and comprehension—what people know, think, and talk about. The media are somewhat less effective in shaping attitudes and values; "selective perception" enables the masses to screen out media messages with which they disagree. The media are least effective at directly influencing behavior; for example, political ads are more successful in motivating a candidate's supporters to go to the polls than they are in changing opponents into supporters.

Notes

1. *Media Monitor,* January 1998.

2. *Time*/CNN national poll reported in *Time,* June 12, 1995.

3. Michael Medved, *Hollywood vs. America* (New York: Harper, 1992), p. 70.

4. Quoting Katha Pollit, *Time,* June 12, 1995, p. 33–36.

5. See Michael J. Robinson, "Public Affairs Television and the Growth of Political Malaise," *American Political Science Review* 70 (June 1976): 409–432.

6. *Time,* June 12, 1995, p. 34.

7. John Johnstone, Edward Slawski, and William Bowman, *The Newspeople* (Urbana: University of Illinois Press, 1976), pp. 225–226.

8. Stephen Hess, *The Washington Reporters* (Washington, D.C.: Brookings Institution, 1981).

9. Doris A. Graber, *Mass Media and American Politics* (Washington, D.C.: Congressional Quarterly, 1980), p. 41.

10. Bernard Cohen, *The Press and Foreign Policy* (Princeton: Princeton University Press, 1963), p. 10.

11. Austin Ranney, *Channels of Power* (New York: Basic Books, 1983), p. 11.

12. Benjamin I. Page, Robert Y. Shapiro, and Glenn R. Dempsey, "What Moves Public Opinion," *American Political Science Review* 81 (March 1987): 23–24, 37.

Selected Readings

Ansolabehere, Stephen, Roy Behr, and Shanto Iyengar. *The Media Game.* New York: Macmillan, 1993. A comprehensive text assessing the changes in the political system brought about by television since the 1950s.

Dye, Thomas R., Harmon Zeigler, and S. Robert Lichter. *American Politics in the Media Age,* 4th ed. Pacific Grove, Calif.: Brooks/Cole, 1992. A comprehensive examination of the influence of the mass media in all aspects of American politics.

Fallows, James. *Breaking the News: How the Media Undermine American Democracy.* New York: Pantheon Books, 1996. A well-known reporter describes how the media distort democracy and lose the trust of the American people.

Graber, Doris A. *Mass Media and American Politics,* 4th ed. Washington, D.C.: Congressional Quarterly Press, 1992. A wide-ranging description of media effects on campaigns and elections, as well as on social values and public policy.

Lichter, S. Robert, Stanley Rothman, and Linda S. Lichter, *The Media Elite.* Bethesda, Md.: Adler & Adler, 1986. A comprehensive study of the social, psychological, and political orientations of the leadership of the mass media, based on extensive interviews in the most influential media outlets.

Medved, Michael. *Hollywood vs. America.* New York: HarperCollins, 1992. An informative and amusing description of the ongoing cultural war between Hollywood and its audiences.

Patterson, Thomas E. *Out of Order.* New York: Random House, 1993. A devastating attack on television news coverage of political campaigns, its negativism, and the resulting cynicism it inspires among citizens.

Prindle, David F. *Risky Business: The Political Economy of Hollywood.* Boulder, Colo.: Western Press, 1993. The politics and economics that drives Hollywood's political liberalism and activism.

Ranney, Austin. *Channels of Power.* New York: Basic Books, 1983. A general assessment of how television has changed American politics, especially how television has weakened political parties, undermined the credibility of political leaders, and reduced the time available to elected officials to put their programs into effect.

Sabato, Larry. *Feeding Frenzy.* New York: Free Press, 1992. An assessment of "how attack journalism has transformed American politics," produced "titillation rather than scrutiny," and resulted in "trivialization rather than enlightenment."

7

American Political Parties: A System in Decay

Organization implies the tendency to oligarchy. Every party ... becomes divided into a minority of directors and a majority of directed.

—ROBERTO MICHELS

Traditional political science asserted that parties were necessary instruments of popular control of government. But we will show, in this chapter, that the two major political parties in the United States have little incentive to offer clear policy alternatives; that Democratic and Republican voters do not divide clearly along liberal and conservative lines; that party organizations are oligarchic and dominated by activists who are largely out of touch with the voters; that candidates are selected in primary elections in which personal organization and financial assets, not party organizational support, are crucial to victory; that party voting in general elections is declining over time; and that television has replaced party organizations as a means of linking candidates to voters. In short, the American party system fails to provide the masses with an effective means to direct public policy.

THE RESPONSIBLE PARTY MODEL IN DISARRAY

Pluralist political theory developed a "responsible party" model of the American system that viewed the parties as principal instruments of popular control of government. "Responsible parties" were supposed to:

★ Develop and clarify alternative policy positions for the voters;

★ Educate the people about the issues and simplify choices for them;

★　Recruit candidates for public office who agreed with party policy positions;

★　Organize and direct their candidates' campaigns to win office;

★　Hold their elected officials responsible for enacting party policy positions after they were elected; and

★　Organize legislatures to ensure party control of policy making.

In carrying out these functions, responsible parties were supposed to modify the demands of special interests, build a consensus that could win majority support, and provide simple and identifiable, yet meaningful, choices for the voters on election day. In this way, disciplined, issue-oriented, competitive parties would be the principal means by which the people would direct public policy.

But this responsible party model fell into disarray over the years, if indeed it ever accurately described the American political system. There are some fundamental problems with this pluralist model of the parties:

1. *The parties do not offer the voters clear policy alternatives.* Instead, each tries to capture the broad center of most policy dimensions, where it believes most Americans can be found. There is no incentive for parties to stand on the far right or far left when most Americans are found in the center. So the parties echo each other, and critics refer to them as "Tweedledee and Tweedledum." Indeed, *voter decisions are seldom based on the policy stands of candidates or parties.*

2. *The parties themselves are oligarchies, dominated by active, ideologically motivated elites.* The active party elites, for example, delegates to the national conventions, hold policy views that do not reflect the opinions of the rank and file. Democratic party activists are far more liberal than Democratic voters, and Republican party activists are more conservative than Republican voters.

3. *Primary elections determine nominees, not party organizations.* The progressive reformers who introduced primary elections at the beginning of the twentieth century wanted to undercut the power of party machines in determining who runs for office, and the reformers succeeded in doing so. Nominees now establish personal organizations in primary elections; they do not have to negotiate with party leaders.

4. *Party loyalties have been declining over the years.* Most people remain registered as Democrats or Republicans in order to vote in party

primary elections, but increasing numbers of people identify themselves as Independent and cast their vote in general elections without reference to party. Split-ticket voting (where a single voter casts his or her vote for a Democrat in one race and a Republican in another) is also increasing.

5. *The mass media, particularly television, have replaced the party as a means of political communication.* Candidates can come directly into the voter's living room via television. Campaigning is now largely a media activity. Candidates no longer need party workers to carry their message from block to block.

Despite these problems, the American political parties survive. They are important in the selection of *personnel* for public office, if not for the selection of public policy. Very few Independents are ever elected to high political office. Serious candidates for the presidency, the U.S. Senate, the House of Representatives, state governorships, and state legislatures (in every state except nonpartisan Nebraska) must first win Democratic or Republican party nomination.

DEMOCRATIC AND REPUBLICAN PARTIES: CONSENSUS OR COMPETITION?

The "Tweedledee and Tweedledum" image of American political parties contains a great deal of truth. Both parties reflect prevailing elite consensus on basic democratic values: the sanctity of private property, a free-enterprise economy, individual liberty, limited government, majority rule, and due process of law. Moreover, since the 1930s both parties have supported the public-oriented, mass-welfare domestic programs of the "liberal establishment": social security, fair labor standards, unemployment compensation, a national highway program, a federally aided welfare system, countercyclical fiscal and monetary policies, and government regulation of banking, transportation, food and drugs, labor relations, and the environment. Finally, both parties have supported the basic outlines of U.S. foreign and military policy since World War II: international involvement, containing Soviet expansion, European recovery, the North Atlantic Treaty Organization, military preparedness, and the Korean, Vietnam, and Persian Gulf wars. Rather than promoting competition over national goals, the parties reinforce social consensus and limit the area of legitimate political conflict.

*"Listen, pal! I didn't spend seven million bucks to
get here so I could yield the floor to you."*

The major parties are not, of course, identical. While both parties draw
their support from all social groups in the United States, the social bases of
the parties are somewhat different. Democratic voters are drawn disproportionately from labor, union members and their families, big-city dwellers,
Jews, Catholics, and blacks. The core activists in the Democratic party
are often drawn from labor and teachers' unions, government employees,
and feminist, civil rights, and environmental organizations. Republican
voters are drawn disproportionately from rural, small-town, and suburban

FIGURE 7-1   Comparison of party officials to public in political ideology (self-described)

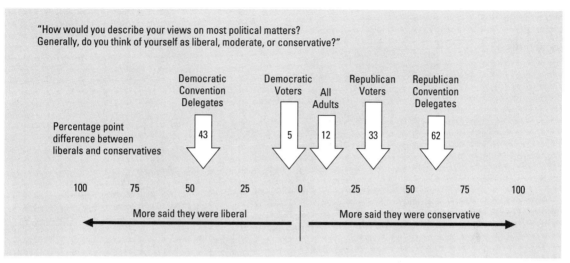

"How would you describe your views on most political matters?
Generally, do you think of yourself as liberal, moderate, or conservative?"

Source: *New York Times* (August 21, 1992): A-12. Copyright © 1992 by The New York Times Company. Reprinted by permission.

Protestants, and business and professional people. The core Republican activists are often drawn from small businesses and business organizations, religious and church groups, and civic and service organizations. To the extent that the aspirations of these groups differ, the thrust of party ideology also differs. The difference, however, is not very great. Democratic identifiers—those who identify themselves as Democrats—are only slightly more liberal than Republicans are. The more active partisans, however, are more ideologically distinct. Republican and Democratic activists are more conservative and more liberal, respectively, than less active supporters of the parties are (see Figure 7-1).

However, both parties' nominees, if they are to succeed, must appeal to the center. With only two parties and an overwhelmingly nonideological electorate, "consumer demand" requires that party ideologies be ambiguous and moderate. Therefore we cannot expect the parties, which seek to attract the maximum number of voters, to take up liberal and conservative positions supported by only minorities in the population.

Why can't we have a strongly principled party system, with a liberal party and a conservative party, each offering the voters a clear ideological

FIGURE 7-2

Why the parties
strive for
moderation

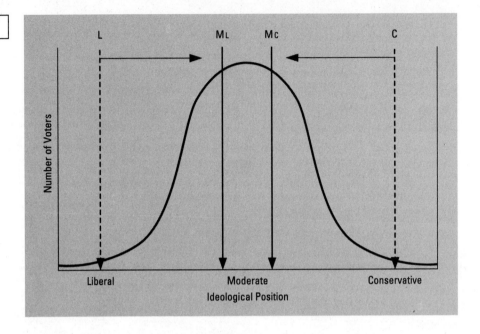

choice? We can diagram the centrist tendencies of the American party system as in Figure 7-2. Let us assume that the parties seek to win public office by appealing to a majority of voters, and let us assume that voters choose the party that is *closest* to their own ideological position. If the voters distribute themselves along a normal curve on these liberal–conservative dimensions, with most voters occupying the moderate center and only small numbers of voters occupying the far left and far right positions, then both parties would have a strong incentive to move to the center. If the liberal party (L) took a strong ideological position to the left of most voters, the conservative party (C) would move toward the center, winning more moderate votes, even while retaining its conservative supporters, who would still prefer it to the more liberal opposition party. Likewise, if the conservative party took a strong ideological position to the right of most voters, the liberal party would move to the center and win. Thus both parties must abandon strong ideological positions and move to the center, becoming moderate in the fight for support of the majority of voters—the moderates.

Republican conservative Barry Goldwater in 1964 and Democratic liberal George McGovern in 1972 demonstrated that strong ideological stances will *not* win presidential elections in the United States. In 1964 the Republicans offered a clear ideological alternative to the majority party that is notable in recent American political history. Goldwater, the Republican presidential candidate challenging Democrat Lyndon Johnson, specifically rejected moderation ("Moderation in defense of liberty is no virtue") and defended extremism ("Extremism in defense of liberty is no vice"). His overwhelming defeat counters the argument that the masses want a party that offers a clear ideological choice. A party with a pure liberal position will suffer disastrous defeat as well. In 1972 Democrat McGovern seriously overestimated the liberalism of the electorate in his race against Republican Richard Nixon. Like Goldwater, McGovern lost in a landslide. It is true that Ronald Reagan won two presidential elections with conservative rhetoric. But Reagan's conservatism was closer to mainstream opinion than Goldwater's. More important, Reagan's personal charm, relaxed manner, and reassuring words convinced voters that he was no extremist. In the 1988 presidential election, George Bush sought to avoid a conservative label, calling for a "kinder, gentler America" and successfully labeling his opponent Michael Dukakis an extreme liberal "out there, out of the mainstream." In 1992 Bill Clinton offered himself to the voters as a "new" Democrat, prepared to move beyond the old liberal solutions to appeal to the broad "middle class." Again in 1996 Clinton avoided public association with his liberal supporters; adopted conservative rhetoric, "The end of big government is over!"; and sailed to victory on the tide of economic prosperity.

In short, since the first goal of a party is to win elections, strong ideology and policy innovation are counterproductive. Firmer, more precise statements of ideology by the political parties would probably create new lines of cleavage and eventually fragment the parties. The development of a clear liberal or conservative ideology by either party would only cost it votes.

DECLINING MASS ATTACHMENTS TO PARTIES

For many years party identification among voters remained remarkably stable. (Party identification is determined by survey responses to the question, "Generally speaking, do you usually think of yourself as a Republican, a Democrat, an Independent, or what?") However, indications of a weakening of the American party system are found in the steady rise of self-described "Independents" over the years and the relatively few voters who describe themselves as "strong" Democrats and Republicans (see Figure 7-3).

| FIGURE 7-3 | Party identification, 1952–2000

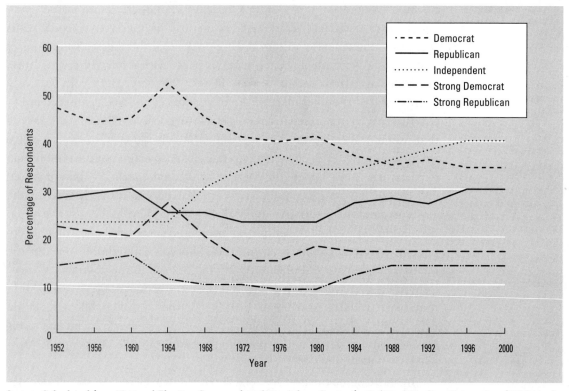

Source: Calculated from National Election Surveys data (Ann Arbor: Center for Political Studies, University of Michigan).

The Democratic party has long held a decided edge among American voters in both registration and self-identification. Nationwide Democratic registration exceeds Republican registration by almost two to one. But this Democratic party loyalty has been gradually eroded by popular Republican presidents.

Party identification is very closely associated with voter choice at the polls. Most voters cast their ballots for the candidates of their party. This is true in presidential elections (see Table 7-1) and even more true in congressional and state elections. Democratic party identifiers are somewhat more likely to vote for a Republican presidential candidate than Republican party identifiers are likely to vote for a Democrat. Prior to 1992 Independents tended to vote Republican in presidential elections. Indeed, the key to success for Republican presidential candidates is to win the votes of Independents and Democrats.

TABLE 7-1		PERCENTAGE OF REPUBLICANS	PERCENTAGE OF DEMOCRATS	PERCENTAGE OF INDEPENDENTS
Party and voter choice in presidential elections				
	1996			
	Republican: Dole	80	10	35
	Democrat: Clinton	13	84	43
	Independent: Perot	6	6	17
	1992			
	Republican: Bush	73	10	32
	Democrat: Clinton	10	77	38
	Independent: Perot	17	13	30
	1988			
	Republican: Bush	92	17	55
	Democrat: Dukakis	8	82	43
	1984			
	Republican: Reagan	92	26	63
	Democrat: Mondale	7	73	35
	1980			
	Republican: Reagan	86	26	55
	Democratic: Carter	8	69	29
	Independent: Anderson	5	4	14
	1976			
	Republican: Ford	91	18	57
	Democrat: Carter	9	82	38
	1972			
	Republican: Nixon	95	33	69
	Democrat: McGovern	5	67	31

ARE DEMOCRATS LIBERAL AND REPUBLICANS CONSERVATIVE?

Democratic and Republican voters cannot be clearly differentiated along liberal and conservative lines. If they could be—if the Republican party attracted all conservatives and the Democratic party all liberals—the Democratic party would no longer be the majority party, because more voters describe themselves as conservative than liberal.

The terms *liberal* and *conservative* have been used with different meanings over the years, so it is difficult to know whether Americans are really liberal or conservative. We can ask them questions like "How would you describe your own political philosophy—conservative, moderate, or liberal?" The results of surveys over recent years are shown in Figures 7-4a and 7-4b. Self-described conservatives outnumber liberals.

What do Americans mean when they label themselves as liberal, moderate, or conservative? This question has no clear answer. People who label themselves conservative do not consistently oppose social-welfare programs or government regulation of the economy. People who label themselves liberals do not consistently support social-welfare programs or government regulation of the economy. Nonetheless, more people prefer to label themselves conservative than liberal.

FOCUS

Mass Perceptions of the Parties

Over the years the Democratic party has usually managed to maintain an image among the masses of being "the party of the common people." The Republican party (also called the Grand Old Party, or GOP) has been saddled with an image of being "the party of the rich." And the Democratic party is seen as the party "more concerned with people like yourself." (See the figure below.)

When asked about each party's ability to handle various problems confronting the nation, however, the respondents rated the two parties about the same. The Republican party is trusted to do a better job in handling foreign affairs and maintaining a strong national defense. It is also seen as better at fighting crime and illegal drugs, and holding down taxes.

In contrast, the Democratic party is perceived to hold an advantage in many key domestic concerns of Americans. The Democrats are seen as better in protecting the environment and helping the middle class. The strongest Democratic advantage appears in protecting social security, and helping the poor and elderly (see the figure "The Parties' Images").

Party more concerned with people like me

Note: Chart excludes "favors the middle class" and unknown.

Source: Drawn from CBS/*New York Times* poll data reported in *The American Enterprise* (May/June 1991): 90.

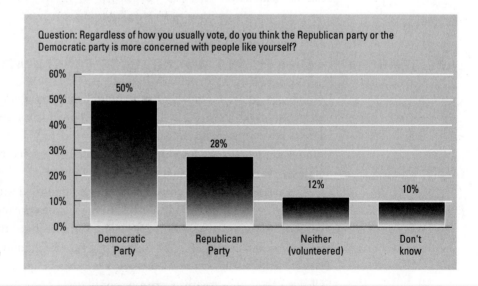

Question: Regardless of how you usually vote, do you think the Republican party or the Democratic party is more concerned with people like yourself?

Recall, however (Figure 7-1) that Democratic and Republican elites are ideologically separated from their voters. While exact percentages and specific questions vary from one election to the next, the general pattern is clear: Democratic party activists are far more liberal than Democratic party voters or the general electorate. Republican leaders are more conservative than either Republican voters or the general electorate.

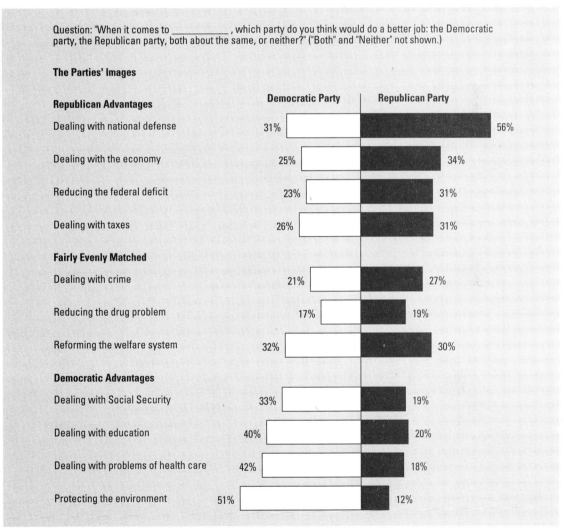

Question: "When it comes to _____ , which party do you think would do a better job: the Democratic party, the Republican party, both about the same, or neither?" ("Both" and "Neither" not shown.)

The Parties' Images

	Democratic Party	Republican Party
Republican Advantages		
Dealing with national defense	31%	56%
Dealing with the economy	25%	34%
Reducing the federal deficit	23%	31%
Dealing with taxes	26%	31%
Fairly Evenly Matched		
Dealing with crime	21%	27%
Reducing the drug problem	17%	19%
Reforming the welfare system	32%	30%
Democratic Advantages		
Dealing with Social Security	33%	19%
Dealing with education	40%	20%
Dealing with problems of health care	42%	18%
Protecting the environment	51%	12%

Source: Drawn from NBC/*Wall Street Journal* poll reported in *The Polling Report*, September 29, 1997.

FIGURE 7-4a   Liberals, moderates, and conservatives in the electorate

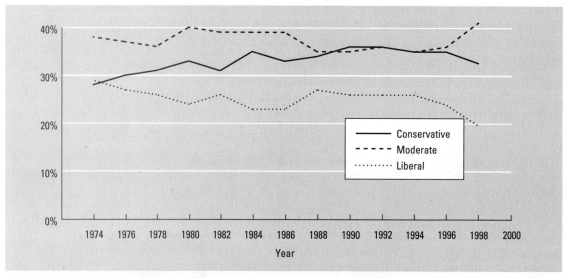

Source: Data from National Election Surveys, University of Michigan, and *New York Times,* June 9, 1997.

FIGURE 7-4b   All years combined, 1972–1996.

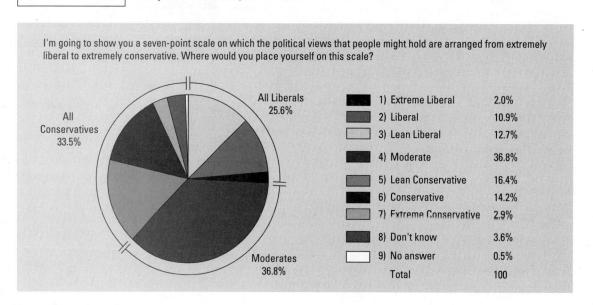

Source: General Social Survey, 1996.

POLITICAL PARTIES AS OLIGARCHIES

It is something of an irony that the parties, as the agents of democratic decision making, are not themselves democratic in their structures. American political parties are skeletal organizations, "manned generally by small numbers of activists and involving the great masses of their supporters scarcely at all."[1] In essence, power in the parties rests in the hands of those who have the time and the money to make it a full-time, or nearly full-time, occupation. Party activists—people who occupy party offices and committee posts, who attend local, county, state, or national party meetings and conventions, and people who regularly solicit and/or contribute campaign funds to their party and its candidates—are no more than 3 or 4 percent of the adult population.

Who are the party activists? We know, from research cited earlier, that the activists are strongly ideological. And it is not surprising that party activists are of relatively high socioeconomic status and come from families with a history of party activity. The highest socioeconomic levels are found in the highest echelons of the party organization. More than 70 percent of delegates to the Democratic and Republican national conventions are college graduates and almost half have graduate degrees. All but a handful are professionals or managers, and most enjoy incomes well above that of the average American. As political scientist Frank Sorauf notes, "The parties . . . attract men and women with the time and financial resources to be able to afford politics, with the information and knowledge to understand it, and with the skills to be useful in it."[2]

Most Republican and Democratic primary voters pay little or no attention to candidates for *party* offices. Indeed, there is seldom much competition for these offices at the local level, with only a single name appearing on the ballot for each party post.

Voters in party primary elections decide who will be their party's nominee for public office. Party primary elections decide state legislative candidates (in every state except nonpartisan Nebraska), gubernatorial candidates, congressional candidates, and in presidential party primaries, delegates pledged to support one or another of the candidates for the party's presidential nomination.

Mass participation in party affairs resembles a pyramid, with *all eligible voters* in the United States (about 200 million) at the bottom. (See Figure 7-5.) About half of all eligible voters go to the polls in a November general

FIGURE 7-5   Parties as oligarchies

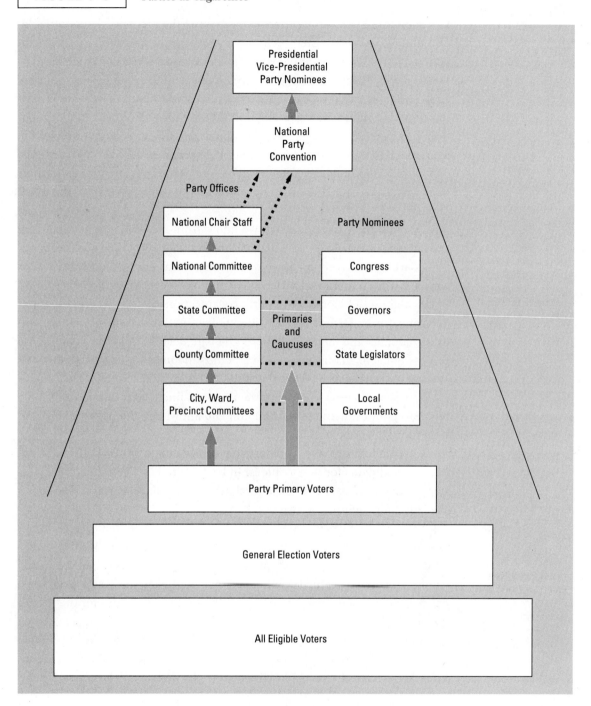

presidential election (90 million to 100 million). Between 30 and 40 percent of eligible voters cast ballots in off-year congressional elections. But *party primary elections,* even in presidential years, draw only about 25 percent of eligible voters. Yet these elections in effect choose the Democratic and Republican presidential candidates. Finally, as mentioned earlier, party activists are no more than 3 or 4 percent of the electorate.

The Democratic and Republican party organizations formally resemble the American federal system, with national committees, officers and staffs, and national conventions, 50 state committees, and more than 3,000 county committees with city, ward, and precinct levels under their supervision. Members of local and county party committees are usually elected in their party's primary election, although many of these posts across the country are vacant and/or filled with appointees. Both the Democratic and Republican parties have national committees with full-time staffs, and both parties have various policy commissions and caucuses that attract the attention of the energetic few.

PRESIDENTIAL PRIMARIES AND THE DETERIORATION OF PARTIES

The growth of presidential primaries has contributed a great deal to the decline in importance of party organizations. In their efforts to make the parties' presidential nominations more "democratic," reformers forced more and more states over the years to use primary elections for selecting delegates to their national nominating conventions. (See Table 7-2.) It was not until 1972 that a majority of party convention delegates were selected in presidential primary elections. The increased use of primaries has been written into state laws and now generally applies to both parties.

Given the expanded role of primaries, do "the voters" now select the presidential nominees? Actual participation in presidential primaries is far less than in general elections. Whereas voting for president in *general* elections hovers around 50 percent, participation in presidential *primaries* usually does not exceed 20 to 30 percent of eligible voters. Clearly, with an average turnout of this size, primaries do not represent the voice of "the people."

In low-turnout elections, the higher social classes are the principal participants. Such is the case in primary elections. Participants come disproportionately from the college-educated, professionally employed,

| TABLE 7-2 | Influence of presidential primaries in convention votes, 1968–1992 |

	DEMOCRATS		REPUBLICANS	
YEAR	NO. OF PRIMARIES	PERCENTAGE OF DELEGATES ELECTED IN PRIMARIES	NO. OF PRIMARIES	PERCENTAGE OF DELEGATES ELECTED IN PRIMARIES
1960	16	38.4	15	38.6
1964	16	41.4	17	45.6
1968	17	48.7	16	47.0
1972	23	66.5	22	58.2
1976	30	76.1	29	70.4
1980	35	81.1	36	78.0
1984	25	67.1	30	66.6
1988	35	88.4	36	80.7
1992	37	88.7	38	85.4
1996	35	70.9	43	85.9

upper-middle classes. Conspicuously underrepresented in the primary electorate are working-class voters and ethnic minorities.

Primary elections strengthen the influence of the ideological activists in each party. Liberals are overrepresented among Democratic primary voters and conservatives are overrepresented among Republican primary voters (see Table 7-3). But as the national electorate has been somewhat more conservative in its self-identification over the last decade, the Republican party has not suffered as much from the primary system as the Democratic party.

The nomination process begins with the Iowa caucuses in February, followed by the first primary election: New Hampshire, a tiny state that jealously guards its position as the first state to hold a primary in every presidential year. The tradition certainly has nothing to do with the strategic importance of New Hampshire in terms of delegate strength. New Hampshire's voters account for less than 1 percent of all votes cast in Democratic primaries, and they choose less than 1 percent of the delegates to the Democratic convention. Were it not for the fact that New Hampshire kicks off the season, its primary election would be ignored. However, the extensive

TABLE 7-3	Primary and general election voters' ideology			
	FLORIDA	ILLINOIS	TENNESSEE	TEXAS
Percentage of Democratic primary voters who call themselves liberals	30	38	30	34
Percentage of general election voters who call themselves liberals	21	25	18	21
Percentage of Republican primary voters who call themselves conservatives	60	55	59	65
Percentage of general election voters who call themselves conservatives	49	42	46	49

Source: Derived with permission from Elaine Ciyulla Kamark, "Structure as Strategy: Presidential Nominating Politics in the Post-Reform Era," in L. Sandy Maisel, ed., *The Parties Respond* (Boulder, Colo.: Westview Press, 1990), p. 174.

media coverage in the state might lead one to conclude that New Hampshire is a crucial state in the general election. New Hampshire *is* crucial—but as a media event.

Primaries provide an ideal opportunity for the media to separate the serious candidates from the aspirants (see Chapter 6). Although the primary electorate is more ideological than the electorate in general elections, the candidates rarely develop the issues well. Not only are early primaries frequently crowded with candidates, but the fact that the candidates are from the same party reduces the opportunity for exploring issues.

Thus, a candidate's media image becomes crucial. Before the primary season, candidates seek to establish credibility as serious contenders of presidential caliber. They attempt to generate name familiarity (as revealed in public opinion surveys) and thus recognition first as serious candidates, not necessarily as front-runners. The proliferation of primaries and attendant media attention makes it possible for a candidate to become well known quickly. A reputation can be created by "a strong organization, plenty of funds, shrewd advisors, an appealing campaign style, and a good image on television, even if his position on issues is not well known and is likely to antagonize many voters once they have become familiar with it."[3]

The consequence of the primary system is that political party leaders— governors, senators, representatives, mayors, the heads of state party organizations, and the like—cannot control the selection of presidential candidates. Without the anchor of party identification, public opinion becomes more volatile, more susceptible to media manipulation. Politics without parties becomes even more issueless than it was in the past. The primary system has been a major factor in the demise of parties and the creation of the new media elite: "Because the competing candidates often share most ideological orientations, personal attributes such as appearance, style, and wit attain new importance (presidents today must be fit and not fat, amusing not dull, with cool not hot personalities)."[4]

REALIGNMENT OR DEALIGNMENT?

In recent decades two clear trends have appeared in party identification among the public. First, the percentage of voters preferring *neither* party has increased substantially, and, second, the Democratic party has lost adherents. (See Figure 7-3.) The rise of Independents and the decline of Democratic partisans are two major developments that tend to complement one another.

Dealignment

Dealignment refers to the decline in the attractiveness of both parties. Dealignment is suggested by the growing number of people who have negative or neutral images of the parties and the growth in the belief that neither party can provide solutions for important problems.

There are several other indicators of party dealignment. Almost two-thirds of Americans say they split their votes between Democratic and Republican candidates for separate offices on election day. A majority say that they have voted for different parties in past presidential elections, and over one-third say they have voted for an independent or a third-party candidate. However, relatively few voters register as Independents. (See Table 7-4.) This is because many states (twenty-seven) have "closed" primaries which allow only registered Democratic and Republican party members to vote in their party's primary elections.[5] In these states voters *must* register as either Republicans or Democrats in order to vote in a primary election.

Realignment

Realignment is a more long-term change. Scholars are not in agreement as to whether a single election can be said to realign party identification, or

TABLE 7-4	VOTERS WHO:	
Indicators of party dealignment	Typically split their ticket	65%
	Have voted for different parties in past presidential elections	58%
	Have voted for independent/third-party candidates	37%
	Are currently registered as Independent	19%

Source: Data reported in *The Public Perceptive,* October/November 1996, p. 51.

whether it takes several elections. But scholars do share a basic under-standing of what realignment looks like; it occurs when

> *social groups change their party alignment; the party system realigns when the partisan bias of groups changes in ways that alter the social group profile of the parties. The changes may result from a previously Democratic group becoming Republican, [they] may reflect the development of a partisan cleavage among a group of voters who had not displayed any distinctive partisan bias, [and they] might also come about as a highly aligned group begins to lose its partisan distinctiveness.*[6]

The major party realignment in recent decades has been the erosion of the Democratic party loyalty of white southern voters. White southerners, conservatives in disposition, have been drifting away from their traditional Democratic ties. Republican candidates swept the southern states in four presidential elections (Nixon in 1972, Reagan in 1980 and 1984, and Bush in 1988). In 1992 and 1996 Arkansan Bill Clinton and Tennessean Al Gore moved several southern states back into the Democratic column. (See Figure 7-6.)

Yet many of the characteristics of great historical party realignments (such as the creation of the New Deal coalition that elected Franklin Roosevelt in the 1930s) are absent. Realignments in the past resulted in increased turnout, because massive shifts in preference generally were accompanied by increased interest in politics. But this effect has been notably absent in recent elections. Turnout has declined, not risen (see Figure 8-3 in Chapter 8.)

| FIGURE 7-6 | Democratic loss of southern and Protestant voters |

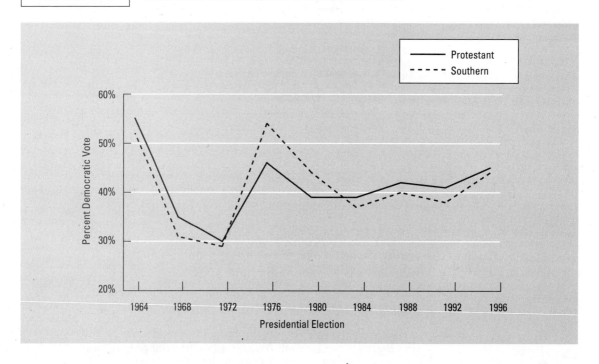

INDEPENDENT AND THIRD-PARTY POLITICS

Dealignment from the parties would seem to create a favorable environment for Independent candidates and third parties. The American tradition of the two-party system, however, combined with winner-take-all elections by district (for the House) and state (for the Senate), work against the development of third parties. In addition, the laws of the fifty states governing access to the November *general election* ballot erect high barriers to Independent candidates who would challenge the Democratic and Republican nominees. The major parties' candidates are automatically included on general election ballots, but Independents and third parties must meet varied requirements in the fifty states to get their names printed on the ballot. These requirements often include filing petitions signed by 5 or 10 percent of the registered voters; this means securing tens of thousands of signatures in smaller states, and hundreds of thousands in larger states.

At the presidential level, an Independent candidate must expend considerable financial and human resources just to get on the ballot in fifty states. In 1980, independent John Anderson was able to do so, and in 1992 Texas billionaire Ross Perot spent a small fortune organizing successful petition drives in all fifty states, and his Reform Party remained on the ballot in 1996.

The Perot Factor, 1992, 1996

While no Independent candidate has ever made it to the White House, Independent presidential candidates have affected the outcome of the race between the major party candidates. For example, Teddy Roosevelt's 1912 "Bull Moose" effort split off enough votes from Republican William Howard Taft to allow Democrat Woodrow Wilson to win. But historically the American two-party system has discounted Independent candidates.

In 1992 Ross Perot initially defied the conventional wisdom about Independent candidates. He motivated tens of thousands of supporters in a grassroots effort, "United We Stand, America," that succeeded in placing his name on the ballot in all fifty states. Perot promised to resolve the financial obstacle by spending "whatever it takes" from his own huge fortune to mount a "world-class campaign." (He ended up spending about $70 million.)

Perot's popular support (35 percent in the polls) quickly rose higher than any Independent candidate's in the history of modern polling. His twangy Texas quotes on *Larry King Live* captivated audiences, yet he carefully avoided taking clear policy positions. "Perot mania" began to fade, however, once the media started tearing down the candidate they had helped to create. By midsummer, Perot's media image had taken a beating and he was below 25 percent in the polls and mired in third place. Perot announced his exit from the race on July 16, at the start of the Democratic convention, although he never withdrew his name from the ballot in any state and actually continued to fund his petition drives. In September, he staged a "poll" of his "volunteers" and cited the results as a call to reenter the campaign.

With his own personal fortune, Perot launched the first real electronic campaign—shunning the traditional cross-country airport speeches, rallies, photo ops, and press conferences in favor of TV talk-show appearances, spot commercials, and paid half-hour "infomercials." In all three televised presidential debates, Clinton and Bush treated Perot with kid gloves, not wanting to alienate his middle-class supporters.

In the past, support for Independent candidates had vanished in the voting booth when voters decided not to "waste" their votes on a long shot. But Perot commercials during the last days of the campaign claimed that the real "wasted vote" would be a vote for "politics as usual." Five half-hour infomercials touted his character as husband, father, businessman, benefactor, and man of action. In the end, Perot garnered 19 percent of the popular vote, the highest percentage won by a third candidate since Teddy Roosevelt in 1912. Moreover, the Perot campaign played a major part in increasing overall voter turnout for the first time in over thirty years. Perot's candidacy prevented Bill Clinton from claiming majority support, holding the winner to 43 percent of the total votes cast. But Perot's voters were spread across the nation. He failed to win in a single state, and thus came up with *no* electoral votes.

In his second national campaign Perot was no longer a media novelty. Indeed, in many TV appearances he often appeared brusque, prickly, irritating, and autocratic. His key issues—deficit reduction and opposition to international trade agreements—seemed less compelling to voters in a thriving economy. With only 5 to 6 percent support in the early polls and no real chance of winning any electoral votes, Perot was excluded from the presidential debates. Rather than spend his own money this time, he accepted taxpayer-funded presidential campaign money. On election day he won fewer than half of the votes he had garnered four years earlier, and again failed to win any state's electoral votes.

A Third Party for America?

Yet Perot's candidacies raised a variety of questions for the future of American politics. Has dealignment proceeded to the point where the nation is ripe for a new third party? Can Perot voters be reintegrated into the Democratic or Republican parties? Can a new Independent challenger emerge in future presidential elections with enough financial and human resources to fully mobilize the disaffected and win electoral as well as popular votes? Would a constitutional crisis develop if three candidates divided the electoral vote and the House of Representatives chose as president a candidate who did *not* win the popular vote? How would an Independent president deal with a Congress still organized along party lines?

Political scientist Theodore J. Lowi argues that a strong third-party movement in America would reinvigorate politics and inspire national leaders to confront real policy issues:

> *With three parties, no party needs to seek a majority or pretend that it is a majority. What a liberating effect this would have on party leaders and candidates to go after constituencies composed of 35 percent rather than 51 percent of the voters. A three-party system would be driven more by issues, precisely because parties fighting for pluralities can be clearer in their positions.*[7]

Not only would a new third party be a source of new ideas, but also the Democratic and Republican parties would have stronger incentives to be more policy-oriented because they would no longer seek to win over a majority of voters. With real issues at stake in a three-party election, voter turnout would increase, as would all forms of political participation. Finally, a three-party system in Congress would allow that body to function more like a parliamentary system. (If three parties caused the president to be chosen by the House of Representatives, so much the better, says Lowi.)

However, it is also possible that a strong third party would further divide the American people, further complicate the problem of finding consensus, and lead to even more party squabbling and bickering in Congress.

Summary

Elitism asserts that elites share a consensus about the fundamental values of the political system. The elite consensus does not mean that elite members never disagree or never compete with one another for preeminence. But elitism implies that competition centers on a narrow range of issues and that elites agree on more matters than they disagree on. Our elite model suggests that parties agree about the general direction of public policy and limit their disagreement to relatively minor matters. Our analysis of the party system in the United States suggests the following propositions:

1. The parties share a consensus both on basic democratic values and on major directions of U.S. policy. They believe in the sanctity of private property, the free enterprise economy, and individual liberty. Moreover, both parties have supported the same general domestic and foreign policies—including social security, a graduated income tax, countercyclical fiscal and monetary policies, the Cold War, the Korean and Vietnam wars, and the Persian Gulf War.

2. The parties do not present clear ideological alternatives to the American voter. Both major parties are overwhelmingly middle class in organization, values, and goals. Deviation from the shared consensus by either party is more likely to lose than attract voters.

3. Both parties draw support from all social groups in the United States, but the Democrats draw disproportionately from labor, union members and their families, big-city dwellers, Jews, Catholics, and blacks, and the Republicans draw disproportionate support from rural, small-town, and suburban Protestants, and business and professional people.

4. Democratic and Republican party leaders differ over public policy more than Democratic and Republican mass followers do. However, all observed party differences fall well within the range of elite consensus on the values of individualism and capitalism.

5. The parties are dominated by small groups of activists who formulate party objectives and select candidates for public office. The masses play a passive

role in party affairs. They are not really members of the party; they are more like consumers. Party activists differ from the masses because they have the time and financial resources to be able to "afford" politics, the information and knowledge to understand it, and the organization and public relations skills to be successful in it.

6. Individual political party identification is reasonably stable. However, recent years have seen dealignment from both parties—a growth of Independent voters, a decline in "strong" party identifiers, and more split-ticket voting.

7. Despite mass disenchantment with the Democratic and Republican parties, Independent third party candidates face formidable barriers in the American electoral system, including winner-take-all district and state elections and state laws limiting access to the ballot.

Notes

1. Frank J. Sorauf, *Party Politics in America* (Boston: Little, Brown, 1968), pp. 79–80.

2. Ibid., p. 94.

3. Malcom E. Jewell, "A Caveat on the Expanding Use of Presidential Primaries," *Policy Studies Journal* (Summer 1974): 282.

4. Jeane Kirkpatrick, *Dismantling the Parties* (Washington, D.C.: American Enterprise Institute, 1978), p. 7.

5. Thomas R. Dye, *Politics in States and Communities,* 9th ed. (Upper Saddle River, N.J.: Prentice-Hall, 1998), p. 135.

6. John Petrocik, "The Post New Deal Party Coalitions and the Election of 1984," paper presented at the meeting of the American Political Science Association, New Orleans, 1985, p. 7.

7. Theodore J. Lowi, "The Party Crasher," *New York Times Magazine* (August 30, 1992).

Selected Readings

Beck, Paul Allen. *Party Politics in America.* 8th ed. New York: Longman, 1997. An authoritative text on the American party system—party organizations, the parties-in-government, and the parties-in-the-electorate.

Downs, Anthony. *An Economic Theory of Democracy.* New York: Harper & Row, 1959. Downs develops his now classic abstract model of party politics based on rational theory. He discusses the relationships among voters, parties, and governmental policy according to this theory and deduces empirical propositions.

Lowi, Theodore E., and Joseph Romange. *Debating the Two-Party System.* Boulder, Colo.: Rowman & Littlefield, 1997. Lowi argues that the two-party system is no longer adequate to represent the people of a diverse nation; Romange counters that two parties help unify the country and instruct Americans about the value of compromise.

Miller, Warren E. *Without Consent.* Lexington: University of Kentucky Press, 1988. Miller provides an analysis of the attitudes of party activists—delegates to the Democratic and Republican national conventions.

Shafer, Byron E. *Bifurcated Politics.* Cambridge: Harvard University Press, 1988. Shafer examines how the primary system has undermined the parties and reduced accountability.

Wattenberg, Martin P. *The Decline of American Political Parties.* Cambridge: Harvard University Press, 1990. An illuminating discussion of growing negative views of the parties and the increasing dealignment of the electorate from the party system.

8

Elections, Money, and the Myths of Democracy

As long as people are people, democracy, in the full sense of the word, will always be no more than an ideal. One may approach it as one would the horizon in ways that may be better or worse, but it can never be fully attained. In this sense, you, too, are merely approaching democracy.

—VACLAV HAVEL

Traditional democratic and "pluralist" textbooks in American government tell us that elections are a means by which masses can hold elites responsible for their policy decisions, that elections enable masses to direct public policy by voting for one candidate or party or another on election day.

But we argue that elections *do not* serve as policy mandates; instead, they function as symbolic reassurance to the masses. By allowing the masses to participate in a political activity, elections contribute to the legitimacy of government. Elected officeholders can claim that their selection by the voters legitimizes what they do in office; that the voters' collective decision to install them in office morally binds citizens to obey the laws; that the masses' only recourse to unjust laws is to wait until the next election to "throw the bums out." Yet even if the "bums" could be thrown out of office (and we will show that over 90 percent of them are regularly reelected), there is no guarantee that public policy would change.

Finally, we will argue that money drives political campaigns in America, not policy positions, nor voting records, nor even party or ideology. The influence of money in elections, and the influence of those who make campaign contributions, has grown dramatically in recent decades.

THE MYTH OF THE POLICY MANDATE

For elections to serve as policy mandates—that is, for voters to exercise influence over public policy through elections—four conditions would be necessary: (1) competing parties and candidates would offer clear policy alternatives, (2) voters would be concerned with policy questions, (3) election results would clarify majority preferences on these questions, and (4) elected officials would be bound by their campaign positions.

However, politics in the United States fulfills none of these conditions. Voters consequently cannot directly control public policy, for several reasons:

★ The *parties do not offer clear policy alternatives.* Because both parties agree on the major direction of public policy (see Chapter 7), the voters cannot influence it by choosing between the parties. Indeed, inasmuch as more voters describe themselves as "moderate" or "middle-of-the-road" than "liberal" or "conservative," it would be irrational for the Democratic or Republican parties to clearly differentiate their policy positions.

★ *Policy considerations are not the primary motivators of voter decisions.* For a mandate to be valid, the electorate must make informed, policy-oriented choices. But most voters are poorly informed on policy questions and have no strong, consistent policy positions. Traditional party ties and candidate personalities influence voters more than policy questions do. These factors dilute the voters' influence over policy.

★ *Majority preferences on policy questions cannot be determined from election results.* Victory for a candidate's party need not mean that the voters support all of its programs. Among the voters for a candidate are opponents as well as advocates of the candidate's position on a given issue. A popular majority may be composed of many policy minorities. How is a candidate to know which (if any) of his or her policy positions brought electoral victory?

★ Finally, for voters to exercise control over public officials, elected officials would have to be bound by their campaign pledges. However, *elected officials frequently ignore their campaign pledges.*

THE MYTH OF THE POLICY-ORIENTED VOTER

For the masses to influence policy through elections, not only would the parties have to offer clear and divergent policy alternatives to the voters, but also the voters would have to make their electoral choices on the basis of their policy preferences. But as we have already noted (see Chapter 5), most voters have no information or opinion about many specific policy issues and therefore cannot be expected to base their electoral choices on these issues. However, it is sometimes argued that, in lieu of specific policy stances, voters have broad liberal or conservative policy dispositions they use as a basis for voting. The pluralist "responsible party" model would be strengthened if it could be shown that voters think of themselves ideologically as liberals or conservatives and select candidates to match their own ideological position. In contrast, if voters largely overlook ideology as well as specific policy positions in their electoral decisions, then the argument of elite theory that elections fail to give the masses control over policy is strengthened.[1]

Determinants of Voter Choice

To assess the determinants of voters' choice, the University of Michigan Survey Research Center (SRC) regularly examines the responses of samples of voters in presidential and congressional elections. Researchers have derived the following categories as a result. *Ideologues* are respondents who are either "liberal" or "conservative" and are likely to rely on these principles in evaluating candidates and issues. *Near ideologues* are those who mentioned liberalism or conservatism, but did not rely on these dimensions as much as the ideologues did and may not have clearly understood the meaning of these political terms. At the next level, the *group benefits* class contained those who did not exhibit any ideological thinking but were able to evaluate parties and candidates by expected favorable or unfavorable treatment for social groups. Subjects favored candidates they considered sympathetic to a group with which they identified. A fourth group is respondents who base their judgment on their perception of the "goodness" or "badness" of the times. They blame or praise parties and candidates because of their association with conditions of war or peace, prosperity or depression. The last level includes respondents whose evaluations of the political scene hold *no relationship whatever to policy,* even in the broadest and most symbolic sense. Some of these profess loyalty to one of the two parties but have no understanding of the party's positions.

TABLE 8-1	Issues/ideology	19.4%
	Group benefits	30.0
Determinants of voter choice	Nature of the times (economy)	28.1
	Candidate image/other	21.5

Source: Calculated by the authors as averages over elections from 1986 through 1996 from data supplied by the University of Michigan Survey Research Center.

When social scientists first examined the entire electorate, they found that ideological commitments were significant for only a very small fraction of people. Of the total electorate, 3 percent were ideologues, 10 percent were near ideologues, and the remainder displayed no ideological content in their evaluations. Since these initial investigations, the proportion of the electorate that casts a vote based on ideology has stabilized at around 20 percent (see Table 8-1). Moreover, this ideological voting is most likely to occur among college-educated voters. There is no evidence that ideological voting is increasing over time.

Clearly, then, the majority of voters do *not* base their decision on the same factors as the minority of ideologically oriented voters. The ideological debate between liberals and conservatives has very little meaning for the masses of Americans.

The Ideology-Policy Linkage

It *is* true that self-identified "liberals" tend to vote Democratic and self-identified "conservatives" tend to vote Republican. This relationship appears to strengthen the pluralist argument that the party system reflects voters' policy preferences.

However, voters who label themselves "liberals" do not always take liberal positions on policy issues, nor do voters who label themselves "conservative" take conservative positions. *Elites* link attitudes toward various policies with an overreaching liberal or conservative ideology. For elites, ideology is a summary of various specific policy attitudes. But *masses* do not link their policy positions with their "liberalism" or "conservatism."

For example, the proper role of the federal government in guaranteeing jobs and a good standard of living has been the source of enduring partisan debate between liberal and conservative party activists and officeholders. Liberal elites, especially liberal Democratic elites, believe that the federal government should take an active role in the economy. Thus a self-described

TABLE 8-2	POLITICAL STANCE OF RESPONDENT	COLLEGE (%)	HIGH SCHOOL (%)	GRADE SCHOOL (%)
"Liberals" and "conservatives" correctly associating liberalism with an active role for federal government in the economy	Strong liberal	78	22	0
	Liberal	50	35	30
	Weak liberal	51	47	0
	Centrist	30	28	26
	Weak conservative	50	30	0
	Conservative	56	42	23
	Strong conservative	81	67	54

Note: Percentages reflect the proportion of respondents who associate liberalism with an active role for government and conservatism with individual self-help.

Source: Data from University of Michigan Survey Research Center.

"liberal" *should* know that a liberal position on this issue is to favor governmental guarantees, and a conservative position is to favor individual self-reliance. But the masses do not approach the issue in this way (see Table 8-2). Only among the college educated and among strong conservatives do more than half of respondents know that a liberal policy is one of federal intervention. The masses of non-college-educated voters have very little knowledge of the policy implications of the "liberal" and "conservative" labels.

In summary, ideology does not mean very much. Describing oneself as liberal or conservative does not mean that one advocates or even recognizes policies consistent with one's professed ideology.

Elites themselves frequently make the mistake of confusing the educated minority with the mass of uninformed voters. As Warren Miller concludes, "Levels of conceptualization have not altered much in recent years, but it remains difficult to convey to politically interested and active citizens the lack of complexity or sophistication in the ways most Americans talk and apparently think about politics."[2]

THE GROUP BASIS OF VOTING

The social group basis of voting is easily observed in presidential elections. Different social groups give disproportionate support to Republican and Democratic candidates. No group is *wholly* within one party or the other; and group differences are modest, with the exception of the strong Democratic loyalty shown by black voters over the years. If *no* group influences were involved in voter choices, we would expect that the percentage of each group's vote for Democratic and Republican candidates would be the same as the national percentages. But it is clear that Democratic presidential candidates have drawn disproportionate support from blacks, union members, less-educated manual workers, Catholics, and Jews; Republican presidential candidates, meanwhile, have drawn disproportionate support from whites, the college educated, professional and business people, and Protestants. And recently a significant "gender gap" has developed between the parties, with Democratic candidates doing better among women than men (see Table 8-3).

Pluralists argue that these social group differences in voting are evidence of a "responsible" electorate. Pluralists may acknowledge that most voters have no knowledge of specific policy issues, and some pluralists will even acknowledge that most voters do not consistently or accurately apply liberal or conservative policy dimensions to their electoral choice. However, pluralists argue that many voters use a *group benefits* standard in making their electoral choice. For example, many black voters may not follow specific arguments on civil rights legislation or study the candidates' records on the issue. But they have a general idea that the Democratic party, beginning with President Franklin D. Roosevelt and continuing through the administration of President Lyndon Johnson, took the lead in supporting the interests of black Americans. Thus, it is not irrational for black voters to give disproportionate support to Democratic candidates, even when particular Republican and Democratic candidates have similar records in support of civil rights. Likewise, voters in other social groups may employ a group benefits standard in evaluating parties and candidates. In short, group identification becomes the essential mediating device between the individual voter and electoral choice.

For many years the group basis of voter choice directed political campaign strategy. Candidates conscientiously solicited the support of identifiable social groups—union members, teachers, farmers, small business owners, Jews, the aged, ethnic groups, and so on—by appearing at rallies, securing the endorsement of group leaders, pledging to look after a group's interests, or citing their personal (sometimes manufactured) identification with the group they were addressing. And indeed, all candidates continue to be sensitive to group identifications among voters.

Group identifications in the electorate constitute the strongest arguments in support of pluralist political theory (see Chapter 1). However, there

| TABLE 8-3 | Vote in presidential elections, 1968–1992, by demographic factors |

DEMOGRAPHIC FACTORS	1972 McGOVERN	1972 NIXON	1976 CARTER	1976 FORD	1980 CARTER	1980 REAGAN	1980 ANDERSON	1984 MONDALE	1984 REAGAN	1988 DUKAKIS	1988 BUSH	1992 BUSH	1992 CLINTON	1992 PEROT	1996 CLINTON	1996 DOLE	1996 PEROT
National	38%	62%	50%	48%	41%	51%	7%	41%	59%	46%	54%	38%	43%	19%	49%	41%	8%
Sex																	
Male	37	63	53	45	38	53	7	37	61	41	57	38	41	21	43	44	10
Female	38	62	48	51	44	49	6	42	57	49	51	37	46	17	54	38	7
Race																	
Whites	32	68	46	52	36	56	7	34	66	40	59	41	39	20	43	46	9
Blacks	87	13	85	15	86	10	2	90	9	86	12	11	82	7	84	12	4
Education																	
College	37	63	42	55	35	53	10	40	59	31	62	41	40	19	44	45	8
High school	34	66	54	46	43	51	5	39	60	49	50	36	43	20	51	35	13
Grade school	49	51	58	41	54	42	3	49	50	56	43	28	56	17	59	21	11
Occupation																	
Prof. & business	31	69	42	56	33	55	10	37	62	40	59	48	36	16	43	45	9
White collar	36	64	50	48	40	51	9	40	59	42	57	38	42	20	46	31	7
Manual	43	57	58	41	48	46	5	46	53	50	49	23	59	18	53	26	19
Age																	
Under 30 years	48	52	53	45	47	41	11	41	58	47	52	34	44	22	53	44	10
30–49 years	33	67	48	49	38	52	8	40	59	45	54	38	42	20	48	41	9
50 years & older	36	64	52	48	41	54	4	37	62	46	54	40	45	15	47	49	8
Religion																	
Protestant	30	70	46	53	39	54	6	26	73	33	66	46	33	12	36	53	10
Catholic	48	52	57	42	46	47	6	44	55	47	52	36	44	20	53	37	9
Region																	
East	42	58	51	47	43	47	9	47	52	49	50	35	47	18	55	34	9
Midwest	40	60	48	50	41	51	7	38	61	47	52	37	42	21	48	41	10
South	29	71	54	45	44	52	3	36	63	41	58	43	42	16	45	46	7
West	41	59	46	51	35	54	9	40	49	46	52	34	44	22	48	40	8
Members of labor union families	46	54	63	36	50	43	5	53	45	57	42	24	55	21	59	30	3

Note: 1976 and 1980 results do not include vote for minor-party candidates.

Sources: Data from *Gallup Political Indexes*, 1968–1989; *New York Times* (November 5, 1992).

is evidence that these group identifications may be declining in importance in electoral politics.

THE ECONOMIC BASIS OF VOTING

Ever since the once-popular Republican incumbent Herbert Hoover was trounced by Franklin D. Roosevelt as the Great Depression of the 1930s deepened, politicians have understood that *voters tend to hold the incumbent party responsible for hard economic times.* Perhaps no other lesson has been as well learned by politicians: hard economic times hurt incumbents and favor challengers. The economy may not be the only important factor in presidential voting, but it is certainly a factor of great importance.

Fairly accurate predictions of voting outcomes in presidential elections can be made from models of the American economy. Economic conditions at election time—recent growth or decline in personal income, the unemployment rate, consumer confidence, and so on—are related to the vote given the incumbent versus the challenger. Economic recessions played a major role in the defeat of Presidents Herbert Hoover (1932), Jimmy Carter (1980), and George Bush (1992).

There is some evidence that it is not the voter's *own* personal economic well-being that affects his or her vote but rather the voter's perception of *general* economic conditions. People who perceive the economy as getting worse are likely to vote against the incumbent party, while people who think the economy is getting better support the incumbent. (See Table 8-4.) Thus, voters who thought the economy was getting *worse* in 1992 supported challenger Bill Clinton over President George Bush by a margin of 61 percent to 14 percent. And more than twice as many people thought the economy was getting worse in that year than getting better. But the reverse was true in 1996; more people thought the economy was *better,* and the people who thought so voted heavily for incumbent Bill Clinton.

CANDIDATE IMAGE VOTING

Today's media-oriented campaigning, emphasizing direct television communication with individual voters, reduces the mediating function of parties and groups. Media campaigning emphasizes *candidate image*—personal qualities such as leadership, compassion, character, humor, and charm. As party and group identifications have moderated and independent and

TABLE 8-4	Question: *Is the economy getting better, getting worse, or staying about the same?*		
		BETTER	WORSE	SAME

Views on the economy and recent presidential voting

	BETTER	WORSE	SAME
1996			
All	33%	20%	45%
Incumbent Clinton vote	66%	27%	46%
Challenger Dole vote	26%	57%	45%
1992			
All	24%	34%	41%
Incumbent Bush vote	62%	14%	62%
Challenger Dole vote	24%	61%	24%

middle-of-the-road identifications among voters have grown, the personal characteristics of candidates have become central to many voters. Indeed, the personal qualities of candidates are most important in the decision of less partisan, less ideological voters. Candidate image is more important in presidential than congressional contests, inasmuch as presidential candidates are personally more visible to the voter than candidates for lesser offices.

It is difficult to identify exactly what personal qualities appeal most to voters. Warmth, compassion, strength, confidence, honesty, sincerity, good humor, appearance, and "character" all seem important. "Character" has become a central feature of media coverage of candidates (see Chapter 6). Reports of extramarital affairs, experimentation with drugs, draft dodging, cheating in college, shady financial dealings, conflicts of interest, or lying or misrepresenting facts receive heavy media coverage because they attract large audiences. But it is difficult to estimate how many voters are swayed by "character" issues.

Attractive personal qualities can win support from opposition-party identifiers and people who disagree on the issues. John F. Kennedy's handsome and youthful appearance, charm, self-confidence, and disarming good humor defeated the heavy-jowled, shifty-eyed, defensive, and ill-humored Richard Nixon. Ronald Reagan's folksy mannerisms, warm humor, and comfortable rapport with television audiences justly earned him the title "The

FOCUS

Bill Clinton: Creating a Winning Image

For many years Democratic campaign strategists were painfully aware that Republicans were winning moderate as well as conservative voters in presidential elections. The strategic problem was diagnosed as follows: the Democratic party's liberal candidates enjoyed an advantage in primary elections, where low voter turnouts magnified the influence of the parties' core liberal constituencies—African-Americans, labor unionists, teachers, environmentalists, government employees. But in the general election, liberal candidates who won the parties' presidential nomination fared poorly among the moderate swing voters. Republicans Richard Nixon (1968 and 1972), Ronald Reagan (1980 and 1984), and George Bush (1988) had labeled their Democratic opponents, especially Hubert Humphrey, George McGovern, Walter Mondale, and Michael Dukakis, with the fatal "L-word"—*liberal.*

Becoming a "Moderate"   As early as 1982 in his comeback election as Arkansas governor, Bill Clinton began to shape his image as a youthful "New Democrat" and positioning himself to run for president as a "moderate." He avoided the "liberal" tag with tough talk about workfare, the death penalty, and personal responsibility. He emphasized economic growth over income redistribution. He referred to government spending as "investment." His "putting people first" theme emphasized help for the middle class and avoided direct references to core liberal Democratic groups.

Handling the Character Issue   But Bill Clinton almost lost the prize he had sought for a lifetime early in the 1992 Democratic primaries, when Gennifer Flowers held a nationally televised press conference to announce that she had had a long-term affair with him. Rumors of marital infidelity had shadowed Clinton for many years. The same problem had driven Gary Hart out of the presidential race in 1988. But a tenacious Clinton decided to confront the "bimbo issue" head-on. When Don Hewitt, producer of *60 Minutes,* offered Clinton a Sunday night prime-time interview just after the Super Bowl, the candidate accepted. With wife Hillary at his side, Clinton told a huge nationwide audience that his marriage had survived shaky moments but it was rock-solid now. He correctly calculated that the public was increasingly disgusted with the media's focus on sexual scandals.

Favoring "Change"   Clinton's 1992 campaign strategy was to hammer home, over and over again, a single theme: the economy is in bad shape, and the nation demands *change.* Yet in late spring, the most powerful voice for economic change in the nation was that of Ross Perot. Clinton was running third in the polls, trailing both President George Bush and the independent billionaire. But Perot's focus on the economy and the need for change was detaching millions of middle-class voters from Bush and sending the president's popularity rating into a nosedive.

With the prospect of a three-person race looming, some Clinton strategists urged their candidate to jettison his moderate image in favor of cultivating the core liberal constituencies of the Democratic party and thus eke out a plurality victory. But Clinton rejected this advice and insisted on sticking with the original game plan—change with moderation.

The Democratic convention was a celebration of Clinton's good fortune and sound political judgment. When the temperamental Perot unexpectedly withdrew from the race, millions of his disillusioned supporters were set adrift at precisely the moment that Clinton was broadcasting his message of change to national audiences. Perot's middle-class, independent supporters flocked to Clinton's banner. By the end of the Democratic convention, Clinton had soared to a twenty-point lead in the polls.

George Bush faced a challenging task—to focus the campaign on Clinton's character and somehow overcome the Democrat's lead in the polls. Bush tried to tag Clinton as a Vietnam War protester and draft-dodger who lacked the personal stature to be commander-in-chief. But in the first debate Clinton nimbly deflected Bush's attack: "Your father was right to stand up to Joe McCarthy. You were wrong to attack my patriotism." Bush was awkward and uncomfortable in the attack mode.

In the final days of the campaign, Bush finally hit his stride with a fierce attack on Clinton's character. Could "Slick Willie"—a taxer, a spender, a liberal, a draft-dodger, an antiwar demonstrator, and a liar—be trusted to run the country? But Bush's theme was negative and failed to give voters a reason to vote *for* the president.

While Clinton emerged only 5 percentage points ahead of Bush in the popular vote, the nation's desire for change was clearly evident in the combined votes for Clinton and Perot. Fully 62 percent of the voters chose to vote against President George Bush. Clinton prevailed in one of the toughest political campaigns in American history because he skillfully presented himself to the voters as an agent of change.

Creating a Presidential Image In his reelection campaign Bill Clinton reshaped his image into that of a responsible, centrist president—a president whose tireless efforts had improved the economy, reduced annual federal deficits, lowered the crime rate, and saved Medicare and Medicaid from mean-spirited Republicans in Congress. He shifted the public's attention away from his controversial early initiatives in office—his large tax increase, his confrontation with the military over homosexuals, and his unsuccessful national health care proposal. Instead, he focused on a series of modest but popular positions—for example, the family leave act, portable health insurance, minimum two-day hospital stays following childbirth, the V-chip, school uniforms, a ban on assault weapons—positions that appealed especially to female voters. As the incumbent, he sailed through the presidential primaries in 1996 with no opposition.

"Defining" Bob Dole General Colin Powell was the only potential opponent who led Clinton in presidential choice polls. When Powell removed himself from contention, a loud sigh of relief was heard in the White House. Bob Dole—an aging, dour, occasionally grumpy, long-time congressional leader—was a welcome opponent. Indeed, as polls consistently reported Clinton's twenty-plus percentage point lead over Dole, the only concern in the Clinton camp was overconfidence.

The Clinton campaign sought to "define" Bob Dole as "wrong in the past, wrong for the future." Indeed, from the beginning Dole seemed ill-suited as a presidential candidate: a Washington insider when the voters distrusted Washington; a congressional leader when Congress was the least-trusted branch of government; an aging World War II veteran out of touch with the baby boomer electorate. Clinton television ads showed Dole acknowledging that "I voted against Medicare," raising fears among Dole's own senior generation voters.

Building the Bridge The Clinton theme was an upbeat "bridge to the 21st century," suggesting his own forward-looking posture and subtly reminding voters of Dole's age. In the debates, Clinton remained cool, confident, unrattled, and "presidential" in the face of Dole's barbs. "No insult," he said at one point, "ever cleaned up a toxic waste dump." Dole's promise of a 15 percent tax cut went unheeded by voters more concerned with federal deficits. Polls reported that although Americans thought Dole was more "honest and trustworthy" than Clinton, they still preferred Clinton as president.

Clinton was judged the clear winner of the debates, but viewership was down. The campaign was the dullest in recent times, as reflected in a half-century-record low voter turnout (48 percent). An embarrassing last-minute flap over Democratic campaign contributions from foreign sources seemed to raise Perot's vote just enough to prevent the president from winning 50 percent of the electorate. The final vote was Clinton 49 percent, Dole 41 percent, Perot 8 percent, with 2 percent going to minor-party candidates.

Great Communicator." Reagan disarmed his critics by laughing at his own flubs—falling asleep at meetings, forgetting names—and by telling his own age jokes. His personal appeal won more Democratic voters than any other Republican candidate has won in modern history, and he won the votes of many people who disagreed with him on the issues.

An important reservation regarding image voting: While many voters cite favorable or unfavorable personal characteristics of the candidates as the reason for their vote, it turns out that Democratic voters usually perceive favorable attributes in Democratic candidates and unfavorable attributes in Republican candidates, while Republican voters see just the opposite. In other words, the voters' perceptions of the candidates' personal qualities are influenced by the voters' party identifications and perhaps by their group affiliations as well. Thus, evaluations of the candidates' personal characteristics may not be a significant independent determinant of voter choice, especially for people who identify themselves as strong Democrats or Republicans.

MONEY DRIVES ELECTIONS

The high costs of media campaigning add to the political influence of wealthy contributors, and thus add further to elitism in electoral politics. Campaign spending by *all* presidential and congressional candidates, the Democratic and Republican parties, and independent political organizations now exceeds *$2 billion* per election! The most important hurdle for any candidate for public office is raising the funds to meet campaign costs.

Politics grows more expensive each year (see Figure 8-1). All presidential candidates combined spent nearly $500 million in primary and general elections in 1996. Bill Clinton and Bob Dole each spent over $100 million in their official campaigns, but their respective parties poured in millions more in "soft money."

The average seat in the House of Representatives cost roughly $673,000 (in 1996). Ninety-four House candidates spent more than $1 million to get elected. The most expensive campaign was the reelection effort of House Speaker Newt Gingrich, which cost nearly $5.6 million.

The average U.S. Senate seat now costs $5 million or more. Averages mean less in the Senate, however, since there are comparatively few races (only one-third of Senate seats are up for election in any year) and since costs in any one year depend heavily on which states are holding elections.

FIGURE 8-1 The growth of campaign spending

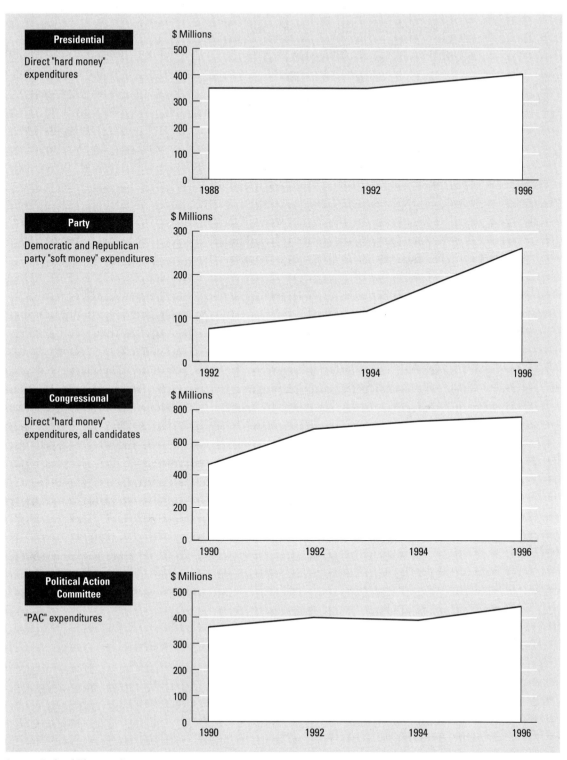

Finding and Feeding the "Fat Cats"

Most campaign funds are raised from individual contributions. In national surveys about 7 to 10 percent of the population claims to have contributed to candidates running for public office. Contributors are disproportionately high-income, well-educated, professional people with strong partisan views, or "fat cats." There are networks of contributors in every state, and campaign staffs use sophisticated computerized mailing lists and telephone directories of regular Democratic and Republican and liberal and conservative contributors to solicit funds. (See Table 8-5.)

Small donors (people who give less than $200 in a single contribution) account for the largest category of contributors. Under federal campaign finance laws, contributors of less than $200 are not required to provide their names and addresses to the Federal Elections Commission as part of the public record.

But "fat cats" (people who write checks to the candidates or parties for $500, $1,000, $5,000, or more) are the most valued of contributors. Despite their financial importance, these donors make up less than one-quarter of 1% of the nation's population. A thousand-dollar check is the preferred entry fee for fat-cat status, but many give substantially more. These are the donors whose names are on the candidates' Rolodexes. These are the ones in attendance when the president, the speaker of the House, or other top political dignitaries travel around the country for fund-raisers. They are also the ones who are wined, dined, prodded, and cajoled in a seemingly ceaseless effort by the parties and the candidates to raise funds for the next election.

Fund-raising occupies more of a candidate's time than any other campaign activity. Fund-raising dinners ($1,000 or more per plate), cocktail parties, barbecues, fish fries, and so on are scheduled nearly every day of a campaign. The candidates are expected to appear personally to "press the flesh" of big contributors. Movie and rock stars and other assorted celebrities may also be asked to appear at fund-raising affairs to generate attendance. Tickets may be "bundled" to well-heeled individual contributors or sold in blocks to organizations.

The Fat Cats: Top Campaign Contributors

The Center for Responsible Politics, a Washington-based reform organization, studied Federal Elections Commission campaign records in the 1995–1996 election cycle for all presidential and congressional

TABLE 8-5		$ MILLIONS	ALL CAMPAIGN %
Sources of campaign cash in 1996 elections	Public (Taxpayer) Financing	$211	8.8
	Small Donations	$734	30.6
	Large Individual Donors	$597	21.8
	Political Action Committees (PACs)	$243	10.1
	Soft money	$262	10.8
	Candidates	$161	6.7
	Other	$200	8.2
	TOTAL	$2,408	

Source: Center for Responsive Politics, from Federal Elections Commission data.

contributions. They included financial contributions to campaigns, such as political action committee contributions, individual gifts to campaigns, and "soft money" for political parties. The following table (Table 8-6) reflects the total contributions to candidates or political parties the top fifty givers, their PACs, employees, and members of their immediate families, according to a study by the Center for Responsive Politics. Not included are independent expenditures, money for issue advertisements, or other indirect expenses.

Milking the PACs

Interest groups generally channel their campaign contributions through political action committees. Corporations and unions are not allowed to contribute directly from corporate or union funds, but they may form PACs to seek contributions from managers and stockholders and their families, or union workers and their families. PACs are organized not only by corporations and unions but also by trade and professional associations, environmental groups, and liberal and conservative ideological groups. PAC contributions account for nearly 50 percent of all House campaign financing and about 25 percent of all Senate campaign financing.

PAC money goes overwhelmingly (80 percent or more) to incumbent officeholders. When the Democrats controlled Congress, business PACs split their dollars nearly evenly between Democrats and Republicans. In 1996,

| TABLE 8-6 | Top contributors in 1995–1996 election cycle |

CONTRIBUTOR	TOTAL CONTRIBUTION (DOLLARS)	PERCENTAGE TO DEMOCRATS	PERCENTAGE TO REPUBLICANS
Philip Morris Cos.*	4,208,505	21	79
American Federation of State, County and Municipal Employees*	4,017,553	99	1
Association of Trial Lawyers of America	3,513,588	85	14
National Education Association*	3,283,143	96	4
Teamsters Union*	3,164,297	96	3
Laborers Union*	3,076,378	93	7
United Auto Workers*	3,023,288	99	0
United Food and Commercial Workers Union	2,926,845	99	1
International Brotherhood of Electrical Workers*	2,820,528	98	2
American Medical Association*	2,794,894	23	77
Communications Workers of America*	2,745,264	100	0
AT&T Corp.*	2,715,101	41	58
Machinists/Aerospace Workers Union*	2,565,493	99	0
National Association of Realtors	2,558,358	34	66
Joseph E. Seagram and Sons*	2,555,836	67	33
American Federation of Teachers*	2,423,088	99	1
National Auto Dealers Association	2,421,575	19	81
RJR Nabisco*	2,300,336	20	80
United Parcel Service of America Inc.	2,176,700	35	65
AFL-CIO*	2,165,224	98	1
National Association of Letter Carriers*	2,151,219	80	10
Federal Express Corp.	2,113,200	46	54
Ernst & Young*	1,977,130	51	49
Carpenters Union*	1,888,472	96	4
American Institute of CPAs	1,853,000	34	66

*Contributions came from more than one affiliate or subsidiary.

(continued)

| TABLE 8-6 | Top contributors in 1995–1996 election cycle (continued) |

CONTRIBUTOR	TOTAL CONTRIBUTION (DOLLARS)	PERCENTAGE TO DEMOCRATS	PERCENTAGE TO REPUBLICANS
Marine Engineers Union*	1,837,115	50	50
United Steelworkers	1,828,665	100	0
American Bankers Association*	1,825,545	31	69
National Association of Home Builders*	1,807,574	22	78
National Rifle Association	1,694,746	15	84
American Dental Association*	1,683,420	37	63
Lockheed Martin Corp.*	1,662,268	34	66
Walt Disney Co.*	1,637,130	75	25
Goldman, Sachs & Co.	1,626,119	57	43
Merrill Lynch & Co.	1,587,291	27	73
National Association of Life Underwriters	1,583,350	32	68
Atlantic Richfield Co.*	1,530,182	35	65
BellSouth Corp.*	1,521,542	35	65
Emily's List	1,514,972	100	0
U.S. Tobacco Inc.*	1,461,215	17	83
National Beer Wholesalers Association	1,460,034	20	80
Blue Cross/Blue Shield*	1,440,137	35	65
United Transportation Union*	1,411,019	85	14
Time Warner Inc.*	1,400,163	54	46
Union Pacific Corp.*	1,380,676	14	89
Travelers Group Inc.*	1,377,527	36	64
American Hospital Association*	1,349,538	48	52
Sheet Metal Workers Union*	1,305,584	97	2
Service Employees International Union	1,294,330	100	0
General Motors Corp.*	1,286,312	26	74

*Contributions came from more than one affiliate or subsidiary.

Source: Center for Responsive Politics.

with Republicans newly in control of both houses of Congress, they shifted their dollars heavily to the GOP, giving $2 in contributions to Republicans for every $1 they gave to Democrats. Labor PACs, however, did not back down from their traditional support of Democrats, even though they too raised their allocation to Republicans.

The Soft Money Scam

Under federal election law, "hard money"—money that is subject to regulated limits—is used directly to benefit federal candidates such as the president and vice president. "Soft money," on the other hand, can be raised by the Democratic and Republican parties with no restrictions on amount or who can give. Technically, soft money is supposed to be used for party building, get out the vote drives, issue education, and general party participation. In reality, both parties undertook an all-out blitz to raise as much soft money as possible in the days before the election—an effort that had a lot more to do with electing the president than building the party.

Soft money is the fastest-growing source of campaign funds. Nearly all soft money is raised in large contributions—indeed, the reason soft money has been so popular with the parties is that it allows big donors to give without having to abide by the limits imposed on their contributions. Another advantage is that corporations, labor unions, and other groups can give directly from their organization's treasury—something they cannot do legally in contributions to candidates. For both the Democrats and Republicans, corporate donations were the biggest source.

Wealthy Candidates

Candidates for federal office also pump millions into their own campaign. Leading the field in 1996 was publishing magnate Steve Forbes, whose race for the Republican nomination for president was largely funded with $37 million of his personal fortune. But Ross Perot's independent presidential campaign in 1992 continues to own the record for personal campaign financing—nearly $70 million. In Congress, 54 Senate candidates and 91 House candidates put $100,000 or more of their own money into their campaigns, either through outright gifts or personal loans. (If a candidate lends himself or herself the money to run, he or she is able to pay the loan back later from outside contributions.)

Laws and Loopholes

Since 1974, the Federal Election Commission (FEC) has been responsible for enforcing limits on individual and organizational contributions to all federal elections, administering the public funding of presidential campaigns, and requiring full disclosure of all campaign financial activity in presidential and congressional elections. The FEC limits *individual* contributions to a candidate to $1,000 per election, and *organizational* contributions to $5,000 per election. These regulated campaign contributions are usually referred to as "hard money." There are many ways in which individuals and organizations can legally surmount even these hard money limits: contributors may give a candidate $1,000 for each member of their family in a primary election and then another $1,000 per member in the general election. Organizations may generate much more than the $5,000 limit by "bundling" (combining) $1,000 contributions from individual members.

The "soft money" loophole allows individuals and organizations to give money to the parties for "party building" or "voter registration" activity, as long as this *soft money* is not spent directly on the presidential campaign. Independent organizations can also spend money beyond the limits set by the FEC for a presidential candidate or party in order to promote their political views so long as these organizations do so "without cooperation or consultation with the candidate."

The Supreme Court opened another major loophole by declaring that, as an exercise of one's First Amendment right of free speech, individuals can spend as much of their personal wealth on their own campaigns as they wish. Specifically, in *Buckley* v. *Valeo* in 1976, the U.S. Supreme Court held that the government could not limit individuals' rights to spend money to publish or broadcast their own views on issues or elections. This means not only that candidates can spend unlimited amounts of their own money on their own campaigns, but also that private individuals can spend unlimited amounts to circulate their own views on an election (although their contributions to candidates and parties can still be limited).[3]

"Food Stamps for Politicians"

Federal funding is available to presidential candidates in both primary and general elections. Candidates seeking the nomination in presidential primary elections can qualify for federal funds by raising $5,000 from private contributions no greater than $250 each in each of twenty states. In the general election, the Democratic and Republican nominees are funded equally at levels determined by the FEC. Until 1992, all presidential candidates agreed to the FEC limits and accepted federal funding; but Independent Ross Perot funded his own campaign that year, rejecting federal funds. In 1996 Perot decided to accept federal funding.

Federal funding is financed by a $3 "checkoff" box on individual income tax returns. All taxpayers are asked whether they wish $3 of their tax

FOCUS

The Clinton Money Chase

President Clinton attended an unprecedented 237 fund-raising-related events—amassing $119.2 million in donations for the Democratic National Committee—during the 10 months leading up to his reelection in 1996. The schedule below reveals a typically frenetic—and lucrative—week:

Clinton's Fund-Raising Schedule
(One Week June 1996)

---

17 MON

9:15 AM/Arrive at White House from Camp David

9:30 AM/DNC coffee—Map room [raised $400,000]

12:45 PM/DBC lunch—Blue room [meetings with donors]

7:00 PM/Reception for Missouri Gov. Mel Carnahan [$80,000]

8:00 PM/DNC dinner—Ritz-Carlton Hotel [$500,000]

* * *

18 TUE

9:00 AM/DNC coffee—Map Room [$400,000]

12:45 PM/DNC coffee—Map Room [$150,000]

* * *

19 WED

9:00 AM/DNC coffee—Map Room [political supporters]

7:00 PM/Reception for Harvey Gantt at Va. residence [$340,000]

* * *

20 THU

9:00 AM/DNC coffee—Map Room [$102,000]

* * *

21 FRI

8:35 AM/Fly Air Force One to Chicago

1:00 PM/Travel to Houston

5:30 PM/DNC gala—Marriott Hotel [$1.5 million]

8:00 PM/Dinner at home of Marcia & Neil Strauss [$1.5 million]

10:00 PM/Sax Club at El Dorado Ranch [$90,000]

* * *

22 SAT

7:10 AM/Travel to Cleveland

1:30 PM/DNC lunch at Slam Jam Sports Grill [$500,000]

3:00 PM/Fly back to Washington, D.C.

7:00 PM/DNC White House barbecue & movie [meetings with donors]

Total Amount Raised This Week: $5,562,000

Source: *Los Angeles Times*, December 22, 1997.

All recent presidents have worked hard to raise money for their reelection campaigns, but probably none so much as Bill Clinton. Sleepovers in the payments to go into the federal presidential election campaign fund. But taxpayers have grown increasingly reluctant to have their tax dollars spent for political campaigning, even though the $3 contribution does not increase their taxes. Today only about 13 percent of taxpayers check off a dollar for presidential campaign funding.

It is sometimes argued that the way to reduce the influence of fat cat contributors in electoral politics is to provide government (taxpayer) financing of political campaigns. Both incumbents and challengers would

---

Lincoln Bedroom were only one of many access schemes developed in the Clinton White House and Democratic National Committee during the 1996 presidential campaign. Indeed, the money drive included an unwritten memo of perks for donors:

Saxophone Club	$250	Briefings by White House staff, lapel pins
Women's Leadership Club	$1,000	Coffee with Hillary Clinton, reception with Tipper Gore
White House Coffee	$5,000	Coffee with President Clinton, tour of Oval Office
White House Dinner	$25,000–50,000	Dinner with President Clinton in small groups of 10 or 20
Lincoln Bedroom White House sleepover	$50,000–100,000	Invitation to dinner, evening get-together, and White House overnight stay
President Golf Round	(Unknown)	Playing 9 to 18 holes of golf with the president at Congressional Country Club, Potomac, Maryland

President Clinton and the First Lady were reported to have invited more than one hundred guests for sleepovers in the White House and to have held hundreds of coffees, receptions, and tours for wealthy donors. The White House press secretary acknowledged, "It's clear that Mr. Clinton and the First Lady are social by nature. They enjoy entertaining in the White House."[a]

The intensity of the money drive occupied much of the Clintons' time during the election year. The Democratic National Committee raised "somewhere between $100 and $125 million" in soft money. These funds were *in addition to* taxpayer-funded presidential campaign spending of $62 million for each of the Democratic and Republican nominees in the general election.

For the donors, "Mostly it's ego. It's to be able to sit around in a room with the President and later be able to say they had dinner with the President."

But the intensity of the Democratic money drive in 1996 also led to some embarrassing disclosures and even the return of some contributions. Several major donors acknowledged before a Senate Judiciary Committee investigation that they made large contributions with the expectation of favorable review of their business ventures both at home and abroad. Evidence developed that foreign contributions (illegal under the federal campaign laws) were funneled through third persons (also an illegal practice) to the Clinton-Gore campaign and the Democratic National Committee. Republicans in Congress objected to the use of federal property (e.g., the White House, including the Oval Office, the Vice President's Office, etc.) to solicit campaign funds. An especially controversial luncheon was held at a Buddhist temple near Los Angeles featuring Vice President Al Gore; Senate testimony from the Buddhist nuns indicated they were illegally reimbursed for their political contributions.

[a]All quotations from *New York Times*, December 27, 1996.

have equal access to campaign dollars and they would no longer be obliged to solicit individual and PAC contributions. Some states have adopted variations of government financed campaigns, especially for gubernatorial races. However, many people resent the idea of politicians using taxpayers' money to finance their own office seeking. Opinion polls generally reflect popular opposition to "welfare payments" to politicians. Proposals to give vouchers to candidates to buy television time have been derisively labeled "food stamps for politicians."

THE UNLIKELY PROSPECTS FOR REFORM

Virtually all politicians in Washington have pledged their support for campaign finance reform. (Democratic President Bill Clinton and Republican House Speaker Newt Gingrich engaged in a much-publicized handshake endorsing campaign finance reform in 1996.) But few members of Congress are actually willing to vote for a reform bill that does not result in direct benefits to themselves. Reform proposals regularly fail to pass Congress.

Ideally, reform of campaign financing should minimize the opportunity for corruption, inspire voter confidence in the integrity of the political system, equalize influence between rich and poor, encourage competitive elections by giving challengers a fair chance against incumbents, and at the same time preserve free speech and the right of people to promote their views at election time. But it is not clear that any reform proposals could achieve all of these goals at once.

Eliminate PACs? Proposals to outlaw PACs and ban all contributions by corporations, unions, and interest groups raise constitutional questions about the right of groups to express their preferences and participate in the electoral process. The Supreme Court might strike down a congressional attempt to ban PACs as a violation of the First Amendment. Republicans might gain more from such a ban than Democrats; if PAC and union money were to be eliminated, individual contributions would become the only game in town, a situation that might favor Republicans.

Ban "Soft Money"? Current laws allow large contributions in "soft money" to political parties. Soft money allows big contributors ("fat cats") to exercise disproportionate influence in party affairs. But this soft money also gives the parties what little direct influence they have over members of Congress.

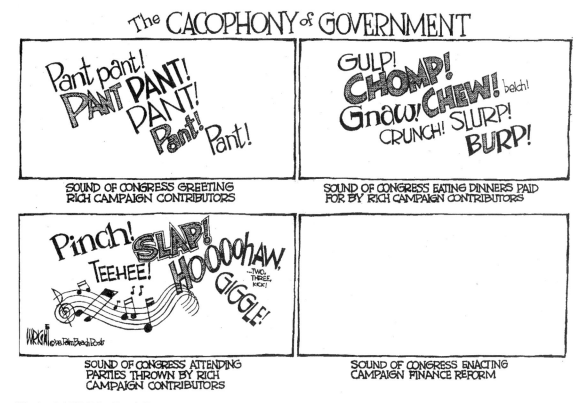

Wright © 1998 Palm Beach Post.

Cutting off party funding would further weaken the party system. A bill to ban soft money failed to pass Congress in 1997.

Curtail Independent Spending? Independent spending on "issue ads" by organizations are currently allowed by law, so long as the independent persons or groups doing so coordinate with the candidate. But curtailing independent spending on political communication is likely to be an unconstitutional infringement on First Amendment protected free speech. The Supreme Court ruled in *Buckley* v. *Valeo* (1976) that organizations and individuals may spend as much as they wish on political communications.

Public Funding and Limits on Spending? It is frequently argued that congressional elections should be publicly funded and limits placed on congressional campaign spending, just as they are in presidential elections. Most members of Congress dislike the constant chore of asking people for money. Presumably, freeing them from obligations to contributors would reduce the influence of well-heeled special interests in congressional decision making.

Members of Congress would no longer be obliged to give special consideration to the requests of wealthy individual contributors and big-spending PACs. Perhaps the general public would be less cynical about Congress and more confident of the fairness of the system.

But public funding would entail limits on campaign spending for the candidates. Equal limits for congressional incumbents and challengers would grant a strong advantage to incumbents, who already have name recognition and years of constituent contacts and services working on their behalf. Indeed, skeptics charge that public funding with campaign limits is really an "incumbent protection" plan. Finally, many taxpayers are offended by the very idea of politicians using tax dollars to run for public office.

Ignoring Mass Opinion American public opinion clearly favors campaign finance reform. Almost two-thirds (66 percent) believe excessive influence of political contributions on elections and government policy is a major problem with the political system. A similar number (65 percent) feel this way about the conflicts of interest created when elected officials solicit or accept political contributions while they are making policy decisions. An even greater number (71 percent) regard the high cost of campaigns discouraging good people from running for office as a major problem with the system. (See Table 8-7.)

A solid majority (63 percent) think elected officials in Washington spend too much time on political fund-raising. But many see money's effects as much more pernicious than simply reducing the efficiency of the federal government. More than half (55 percent) of Americans believe political contributions often buy influence in Washington for one group by denying another group its fair say; as many as half think money often determines who gets elected (52 percent) and appointed (50 percent) to federal office. Nearly half see the influence of money in politics seriously undermining democratic ideals by often leading elected officials to support policies they don't personally believe are best for the country (45 percent).

STAYING HOME ON ELECTION DAY

Another problem with the pluralist theory of popular control over public policy through elections is the fact that *half the adult population fails to vote*, even in presidential elections. Since the 1960 Kennedy–Nixon race, voter turnout steadily declined from 64 percent of eligible voters to a low of 48 percent in the 1996 Clinton–Dole election. (In 1992, voter turnout moved

TABLE 8-7		
Mass support for campaign finance reform	MAJOR PROBLEMS WITH POLITICAL SYSTEM	PERCENT SAYING
	Political contributions have too much influence on elections and government policy	66
	Elected officials seek or receive political contributions while making decisions about issues of concern to those giving money	65
	Elected officials spend too much of their time raising money for election campaigns	63
	Good people are being discouraged from becoming candidates because of the high costs of campaigns	71
	HOW FREQUENTLY DOES THE USE OF MONEY TO BUY POLITICAL INFLUENCE IN WASHINGTON . . .	PERCENT SAYING OFTEN
	Give one group more influence by keeping another from having its fair say	55
	Determine election outcomes	52
	Get someone appointed to office who would not otherwise be considered	50
	Keep important legislation from being passed	48
	Lead elected officials to support policies they don't think are best for the country	45

Source: Princeton Survey Research Associates for the Center for Responsive Politics, Money and Politics Survey, 1997.

upward for the first time in over three decades, owing, it seems, to the voter appeal of the well-financed Independent candidacy of Ross Perot.) Off-year (nonpresidential) elections bring out fewer than 40 percent of the eligible voters (see Figure 8-2), yet in these off-year contests the nation chooses all its U.S. representatives, one-third of its senators, and about half of its governors.

Participation is not uniform throughout all segments of the population (see Table 8-8). Voter turnout relates to such factors as age, race, education, and occupation. Although these figures pertain to voting, other forms of participation—running for office, becoming active in campaigns, contributing money, and so on—follow substantially the same pattern. Older, white, middle-class, college-educated Americans participate more in all forms of political activity than do younger, nonwhite, grade-school-educated Americans.

Election turnout figures in the United States are lower than those of most other democracies. The turnout in elections has been 74 percent in Japan, 77 percent in Great Britain, 83 percent in Israel, 88 percent in West

FIGURE 8-2	Participation in presidential and congressional elections, 1960–1996.

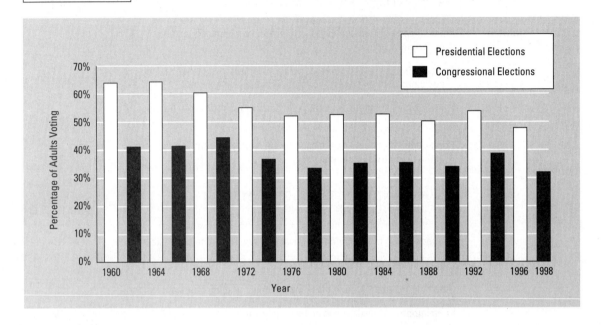

TABLE 8-8	**Age**		**Race**	
	18–25	38	White, non-Hispanic	64
Percent reported	26–40	53	Blacks	54
voter turnout in	41–54	64	Hispanics	29
presidential	55+	70		
elections by selected	**Education**		**Employment**	
groups, 1996	Eighth grade or less	35	Employed	64
	Some high school	41	Unemployed	46
	High school graduate	57		
	Some college	69		
	College graduate	81		

Source: *Statistical Abstract of the United States,* 1997.

Germany, and 93 percent in Italy. The lower U.S. turnouts may reflect stricter residence and registration requirements and greater frequency of elections. But Americans may also be less "political" than citizens of other democracies, less likely to care about the outcome of elections, and less likely to feel that government has much effect on their lives. Interest in politics may be lacking because differences are less significant between opposing parties and candidates, so that the electorate has less invested in which party or candidate wins.

ELECTIONS AS SYMBOLIC REASSURANCE

If elections do not enable voters to direct public policy, if they are largely money-driven, if most eligible voters stay home on election day, what are the purposes of elections? Elite theory views the principal function of elections to be the legitimization of government. Elections are a symbolic exercise to help tie the masses to the established order, to obligate the masses to recognize the legitimacy of government authority, and to obey the law. Political scientist Murray Edelman contends that elections are primarily "symbolic reassurance." According to Edelman, elections serve to "quiet resentments and doubts about particular political acts, reaffirm belief in the fundamental rationality and democratic character of the system, and thus fix conforming habits of future behavior."[4]

Elections Give Legitimacy to Government

Virtually all modern political systems—authoritarian and democratic, capitalist and communist—hold elections. Indeed, communist dictatorships took elections very seriously and strove to achieve 90 to 100 percent voter turnout rates, despite the fact that the Communist party offered only one candidate for each office. Why did these nations bother to hold elections when the outcome had already been determined? All political regimes seek to tie the masses to the system by holding symbolic exercises in political participation to give the ruling regime an aura of legitimacy. This is the first function of elections. Of course, democratic governments gain even greater legitimacy from elections; democratically elected officeholders can claim that the voters' participation legitimizes their activities and their laws.

Elections Choose Personnel, Not Policy

In democratic nations, elections serve a second function: choosing personnel to hold public office. In 1996 the American voters decided that Bill Clinton and not Bob Dole would occupy "the nation's highest office" for the next four years. (The vast majority of people in the world today have never had the opportunity to participate in such a choice.) However, this choice is one of personnel, not policy. Parties do not offer clear policy alternatives in election campaigns; voters do not choose the candidates' policy positions; and candidates are not bound by their campaign pledges anyway. Political scientist Gerald M. Pomper explains:

> *To choose a government is not to choose governmental policies. Whereas the voters largely do determine the players in the game of American politics, they have far less control over the signals the players will call, the strategies they will employ, or the final score. The popular will, as represented by a majority of voters, does not determine public policy.*[5]

Elections Allow for Retrospective Judgments

The third function of elections is to give the masses an opportunity to express themselves about the conduct of the public officials who have been in power. Elections do not permit the masses to direct *future* events, but they do permit the masses to render retrospective judgment about *past* political conduct.[6]

Elections give voters the opportunity to express their displeasure by ousting incumbents from office. But it is not always easy to decipher what the incumbents did wrong that aroused the voters' displeasure. Consider, for example, the crucial 1968 presidential election at the height of the Vietnam War. Democrat Lyndon Johnson, who had first committed U.S. ground combat troops to battle in 1965, announced that he would not be a candidate for reelection, and he halted bombing raids and opened peace talks with the North Vietnamese. In the general election that year, voters could choose between Republican Richard Nixon, Democrat Hubert Humphrey, and Independent George Wallace. All three promised to "end" the war, but none provided a specific program for doing so—whether surrender, all-out bombing, or anything in between. But the voters were able to express their discontent with Johnson's handling of the war by voting against a continuation of the Democratic administration.

Was Ronald Reagan's landslide reelection victory in 1984 over Democrat Walter Mondale a policy mandate for cutting taxes, reducing domestic spending, and a military buildup—the key policy directions in Reagan's first term? Or was it simply an expression of approval of Reagan's presidential style—his warmth, patriotism, good humor, and optimism about America? Throughout the eight years of Reagan's presidency, liberal academics and journalists argued strongly that Reagan's victories reflected his personal popularity, not support for his conservative message. In contrast, conservative commentators urged Reagan to use his voter "mandate" to advance a conservative policy agenda.

Perhaps the strongest support for the retrospective voting argument is found in the relationship between economic downturns and the vote for the incumbent party. In presidential elections, the candidate of the incumbent party (whether a president seeking reelection or the president's party nominee) tends to lose votes if the economy is experiencing a downturn during the election year. However, this message from the voters—keep the U.S. economy strong and growing—is hardly a policy directive.

In 1992 voters opted for *change!* Fully 62 percent of the voters cast their votes against incumbent President Bush—43 percent for Clinton and 19 percent for Perot. Voters cited the economy as the primary issue on their minds in polls taken as they exited the voting booth. But few voters knew what plans Clinton and Perot had offered to remedy the nation's economic ills. Clinton's stump speech offered everything to everybody: "We can be pro-growth and pro-environment, we can be pro-business and pro-labor, we can make government work again by making it more aggressive and leaner and more effective at the same time, and we can be pro-family and pro-choice." What kind of policy mandate could Clinton claim from such promises? What kind of policy mandate could he claim after winning only 43 percent of the vote?

Again in 1996 Clinton's principal theme was "Building a Bridge to the 21st Century." What policies are implied by this theme? Again Clinton won less than a majority of voters (49 percent), and only 48 percent of eligible voters showed up at the polls.

Elections are notoriously poor instruments for determining the policy preferences of the electorate. Even a staunch defender of the pluralist interpretation of American politics, political scientist Gerald Pomper, concedes that

> *Policy choices in elections are difficult to accomplish. They require, at least, that candidates take definable positions, that the voters correctly perceive these positions, and that the voters then cast their ballots on the basis of these positions. Even when all of these conditions are met, an election may still not be clearly the result of issue voting.*[7]

Although none of these conditions exists, and elections in the United States seldom serve as policy mandates, elites nevertheless *believe* that they can be held to account for their actions, and so they are more responsive than they otherwise would be. Elections, even if they are simple retrospective judgments on style, can still make elites more constrained in their behavior. Even if the electorate cannot issue policy mandates, voters can "throw the rascals out" and bring in new ones.

Elections Provide Protection against Official Abuse

Elections also serve to protect individuals and groups from official abuse. John Stuart Mill wrote, "Men, as well as women, do not need political rights in order that they might govern, but in order that they not be misgoverned."[8] He went on:

> *Rulers in ruling classes are under a necessity of considering the interests of those who have the suffrage; but of those who are excluded, it is in their option whether they will do so or not, and however honestly disposed, they are in general too fully occupied with things they must attend to, to have much room in their thoughts for anything which they can with impunity disregard.*[9]

Certainly the long history of efforts to ensure black voting rights in the South suggests that many concerned Americans believed that if blacks could secure access to the polls, they could better protect themselves from discrimination. In signing the Voting Rights Act of 1965, President Johnson said:

> *The right to vote is the most basic right, without which all others are meaningless. It gives people—people as individuals—control over their own destinies. . . . The vote is the most powerful instrument ever devised by man for breaking down injustice and destroying the terrible walls which imprison men because they are different from other men.*

But the high hopes stirred by the development of voting laws often deteriorated into frustration and disillusionment when blacks realized that the electoral process alone could not solve their problems. The vote is a symbol of full citizenship and equal rights that can contribute to black self-respect, but questions remain about how much blacks can gain through the exercise of their vote. It has proven much more difficult to resolve social and economic inequities through the electoral process than to eliminate directly discriminatory laws and regulations. (See Chapter 15).

Summary

Elite theory contends that the masses do not participate in policy making and that the elites who do are subject to little direct influence from apathetic masses. But many scholars who acknowledge that all societies are governed by elites seek to reaffirm democratic values by contending that voters can influence elite behavior in elections. In other words, modern pluralists sometimes challenge elitism on the ground that elections give the masses a voice in policy making by holding governing elites accountable to the people.

Our analysis suggests that elections are imperfect instruments of accountability. Even if the people can hold *government* elites accountable through elections, how can they hold accountable corporate elites, financial elites, union leaders, and other private leadership? The accountability argument usually ignores the realm of *private* decision making, to focus exclusively on public decision making by elected elites. But certainly our lives are vitally affected by the decisions of private institutions and organizations. So the first problem with the accountability thesis is that, at best, it applies only to elected government elites. However, our analysis of elections also suggests that it is difficult for the voters to hold even government elites accountable.

1. Competing candidates in elections do not usually offer clear policy alternatives; hence voters seldom can affect policy by selecting a particular candidate for public office.

2. Voters are not well informed about the policy stands of candidates, and relatively few voters are concerned with policy questions. The masses cast their votes in elections based on traditional party ties, candidates' personalities, group affiliations, and a host of other factors with little relation to public policy.

3. The only reasonably stable aspect of mass politics is party identification. But party identification in the mass electorate does not allow for significant policy choices.

4. Money, in the form of campaign contributions, drives elections. Elitism is strengthened by the ever-increasing role of "fat cat" corporate, PAC, and wealthy individual contributors.

5. Campaign finance laws have proven ineffective. Soft money contributions to parties, expenditures by independent organizations, including unions, and personal expenditures by wealthy candidates are largely unregulated. The prospects for reform are dim.

6. Elections are primarily symbolic exercises that help tie the masses to the established order. Elections offer the masses an opportunity to participate in the political system, but electoral participation does not enable them to determine public policy.

7. Elections are means of selecting personnel, not policy. Voters choose on the basis of a candidate's personal image, filtered through partisan commitment. A candidate's election does not imply a policy choice by the electorate.

8. At best, elections provide the masses with an opportunity to express themselves about the conduct of past administrations, but they do not help them direct the course of future events. A vote against the party or candidate in power does not identify the policy being censured. Moreover, voters have no guarantee that a newly elected official will pursue any specific policy alternatives.

9. Few individuals participate in any political activity other than voting. About half the adult population fails to vote even in presidential elections.

Notes

1. For an introduction to, and discussion of, the extensive political science literature on determinants of voter choice, see Richard G. Niemi and Herbert F. Weisberg, *Controversies in Voting Behavior,* 3rd ed. Washington, D.C.: CQ Press, 1993. Among the most important works: Angus Campbell et. al., *The American Voter* (New York: Wiley, 1960); Norman H. Nie, Sidney Verba, and John R. Petrocik, *The Changing American Voter* (Cambridge: Harvard University Press, 1976); Eric Smith, *The Unchanging American Voter.* See also Robert S. Erikson, Norman R. Luttbeg, and Kent L. Tedin, *American Public Opinion,* 3rd ed. (New York: Macmillan, 1988).

2. Warren E. Miller and Teresa E. Levitin, *Leadership and Change: The New Politics and the American Electorate* (Cambridge, Mass.: Winthrop Publishers, 1976), p. 15.

3. *Buckley* v. *Valeo,* 424 U.S. 1 (1976).

4. Murray Edelman, *The Symbolic Uses of Power* (Urbana: University of Illinois Press, 1964), p. 17.

5. Gerald M. Pomper, *Elections in America: Control and Influence in Democratic Politics* (New York: Dodd, Mead, 1980), p. 51.

6. See Morris P. Fiorina, *Retrospective Voting in American National Elections* (Princeton, N.J.: Princeton University Press, 1988).

7. Gerald M. Pomper, "The Presidential Election," in Gerald M. Pomper et al., *The Election of 1984* (Chatham, N.J.: Chatham House, 1985), p. 81.

8. John Stuart Mill, *Considerations on Representative Government* (Chicago: Henry Regnery, Gateway, 1962), p. 144.

9. Ibid., pp. 130–131.

Selected Readings

Campbell, Angus, Phillip Converse, Warren Miller, and Donald Stokes. *The American Voter: An Abridgement.* New York: Wiley, 1964. An abridged version of the classic study of voting behavior in the United States conducted by the Survey Research Center at the University of Michigan.

Conway, M. Margaret. *Political Participation in the U.S.,* 2nd ed. Washington, D.C.: CQ Press, 1991. The standard text on political participation in American politics, summarizing the research literature on who participates, how, and with what effects.

Flannagan, William H., and Nancy H. Zingale. *Political Behavior of the American Electorate,* 9th ed. Washington, D.C.: CQ Press, 1998. A text summary of the extensive research literature on the effects of party identification, opinion, ideology, the media, and candidate image on voter choice and election outcomes.

Sabato, Larry J., and Glenn R. Simpson. *Dirty Little Secrets: The Persistence of Corruption in American Politics.* New York: Random House Times Books, 1996. A political scientist and a journalist combine to produce a lurid report on unethical and corrupt practices in campaigns and elections.

Sorauf, Frank J. *Inside Campaign Finance.* New Haven, Conn.: Yale University Press, 1992. A comprehensive description of campaign financing in America, individual contributions, PACs, party funds, independent organizations, soft money, intermediaries and brokers, and so on, together with a balanced appraisal of the prospects and potential consequences of reform.

9

Organized Interests: Defenders of the Status Quo

There is overwhelming evidence that participation in voluntary organizations is related to upper social and economic status. . . . The flaw in the pluralist heaven is that the heavenly chorus sings with a strong upper class accent.

—E. E. SCHATTSCHNEIDER

Organized interest groups, not "the people," have the most direct day-to-day influence over government. The public interest is a fiction, but the organized interests are potent political realities, in Washington, state capitals, and city halls. Interest group activity, including lobbying, is generally protected by the First Amendment to the U.S. Constitution—"the right of the people peaceably to assemble and to petition the government for redress of grievances." But how democratic is the interest group system? Do interest groups represent "the people" fairly? Or is the interest group system another means of elite control over government?

INTEREST GROUPS: DEMOCRATIC OR ELITIST?

Pluralists contend that interest groups perform several important functions for their members and for a democratic society. First, the organized group links the individual and the government. Political scientists Gabriel Almond and Sidney Verba state:

> *Voluntary associations are the prime means by which the function of mediating between the individual and the state is performed.*

> *Through them the individual is able to relate himself effectively and*
> *meaningfully to the political system.*[1]

But is mediation by organized groups better than direct citizen–government interaction? Why do we need a middleman?

Pluralists also argue that interest groups enhance individual well-being. In a complex society, with primary associations (small groups, such as the family) diminishing in importance, secondary associations (less intimate but more goal-oriented) may help people overcome the sense of powerlessness characteristic of mass societies. Groups help integrate the individual with society.

Finally, the pluralists feel that interest groups help reduce potentially divisive conflicts. According to the theory of overlapping group memberships, all citizens are members of groups (some organized, some not).[2] Each person is a product of group affiliations. A person may be, for example, a lawyer, a southerner, a military veteran, and a Protestant, with each affiliation imposing its own values. No single group affiliation could claim the individual's total, undivided loyalty. Hence multiple group affiliations help modify the demands of any one group and reduce societal conflict.

In short, pluralists consider interest groups "good" because (1) they provide a more effective voice for citizens who are competing for resources, (2) they reduce the anxiety produced by feelings of powerlessness, and (3) they provide an element of stability.

However, the pluralist theory rests on several assumptions about interest groups that may or may not be correct:

★ Membership in organizations is widespread and thus broadly represents all individual interests.

★ Organized groups efficiently translate members' expectations into political demands; nothing is lost in the translation, and members gain a great deal by presenting demands through a representative association.

★ Although interest groups are not always and uniformly successful (some win and some lose), each group, whatever its demands, has equal access to the political resources necessary for success.

★ Organizations help bring about social change.

We shall refute all of these assumptions. We will argue that interest groups, rather than articulating the demands of masses, protect the values of established elites. Rather than advance social changes, they help maintain the status quo. Indeed, they contribute to political "gridlock"—the inability of the nation to deal effectively with its problems.

THE BUSINESS, PROFESSIONAL, AND CLASS BIAS OF INTEREST GROUPS

It is widely believed that Americans are joiners, and a majority of the population does in fact belong to at least one formal organization. Yet membership in organized interest groups is clearly linked to socioeconomic status. Membership is greatest among the professional and managerial, college-educated, and high-income people. The upper-middle and upper classes are the primary joiners of organized groups.

The Dominance of Business and Professional Organizations

Economic organizations dominate interest-group politics in Washington. Certainly in terms of the sheer number of organizations with offices and representatives in Washington, business and professional groups and occupational and trade associations predominate. More than half of the organizations with offices in Washington are business or trade associations, and another 15 percent are professional associations.

Business interests are represented, first of all, by large inclusive organizations, such as the U.S. Chamber of Commerce, representing thousands of local chambers of commerce across the nation; the National Association of Manufacturers; the Business Roundtable, representing the nation's largest corporations; and the National Federation of Independent Businesses, representing small business. Specific business interests are also represented by thousands of trade associations. These associations can closely monitor the interests of their specialized memberships. Among the most powerful of these associations are the American Bankers Association, the American Gas Association, the American Iron and Steel Institute, the National Association of Real Estate Boards, the American Petroleum Institute, and the National Association of Broadcasters.

Professional associations rival business and trade organizations in lobbying influence. The American Bar Association (ABA), the American Medical Association (AMA), and the National Education Association (NEA) are three of the most influential groups in Washington. For example, the American Bar Association, which includes virtually all of the nation's practicing

| FIGURE 9-1 | PACs by type |

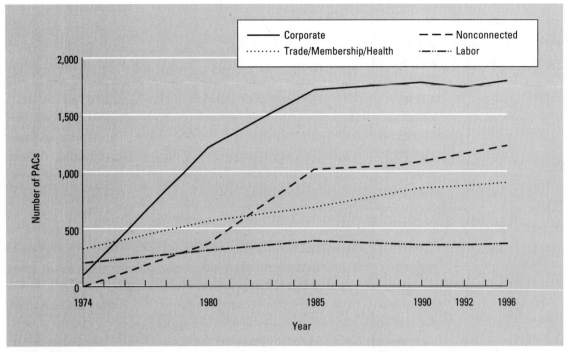

Source: Federal Election Commission.

attorneys, and its more specialized offspring, the American Association of Trial Lawyers, have successfully resisted efforts to reform the nation's tort laws.

Business and professional groups also dominate other types of organizations in the number of political action committees (PACs) reporting campaign contributions to the Federal Elections Commission (see Figure 9-1). Corporate, trade, and professional PACs vastly outnumber union PACs, as well as "unconnected" PACs. "Unconnected" is a term used by the Federal Elections Commission to lump together organizations devoted to single issues (e.g., abortion or gun control), or to ideologies (e.g., feminism, liberalism, or conservatism), or to public interest causes (e.g., environmentalism or consumerism).

The Influence of Organized Labor

Labor unions have declined in membership over the last several decades. (See Chapter 5.) Nevertheless, labor unions remain a major political influence in Congress and the Democratic party. The AFL-CIO is a federation of more than 100 separate unions with more than 14 million members. The AFL-CIO has long maintained a large and capable lobbying staff in Washington, and it provides both financial contributions and campaign services (registration, get-out-the-vote, information, endorsements) for members of Congress it favors. Many of the larger industrial unions (e.g., the International Brotherhood of Teamsters, United Auto Workers, and United Steel Workers) maintain effective lobbying staffs in Washington.

However, power within the labor movement has shifted dramatically in recent years to government employee unions, notably the American Federation of State, County and Municipal Employees, the National Education Association, and the American Federation of Teachers.

PIGs, Ideological, and Single Interest Groups

Public-interest groups (PIGs) claim to represent broad classes of people—consumers, voters, reformers, or the public as a whole. Groups with lofty-sounding names—such as Common Cause, Public Citizen, and the Consumer Federation of America—perceive themselves as balancing the narrow, "selfish" interests of business organizations, trade associations, unions, and other "special" interests. Public-interest groups generally lobby for greater government regulation of consumer products, public safety, campaign finance, and so on. Many PIGs were initially formed in the 1970s by "entrepreneurs" who saw an untapped "market" for the representation of these interests. Among the most influential public interest groups are Common Cause, a self-styled "citizens' lobby," and the sprawling network of organizations created by consumer advocate Ralph Nader. The Nader network of groups also includes Public Interest Research Groups (PIRGs) he established on college campuses throughout the nation, frequently by convincing idealistic students to vote to hand over student fees to his organizations.

Like public-interest groups, single-issue groups appeal to principle and belief. But as their name implies, these groups concentrate their attention on a single cause. They attract the support of individuals with a strong commitment to that cause. Among the most vocal single-issue groups in recent years have been the organizations on both sides of the abortion issue. The National Abortion Rights Action League (NARAL) describes itself as "pro-choice" and opposes any restrictions on a woman's right to obtain an abortion. The National Right-to-Life Committee describes itself as "pro-life" and opposes abortion for any reason other than to preserve the life of the mother. Other prominent single-issue groups include the National Rifle

Association (opposed to gun control) and Mothers Against Drunk Driving (MADD).

Ideological organizations pursue liberal, conservative, environmental, or feminist agendas, often with great passion and considerable financial resources derived from true-believing contributors. These groups rely heavily on computerized mailings to solicit funds from persons identified as sympathetic to their views. The oldest of the established ideological groups is the liberal Americans for Democratic Action (ADA), well-known for its annual liberalism ratings of members of the Congress according to their support for or rejection of programs of concern. Overall, Democrats do better on liberal lists and Republicans on conservative lists, though both parties include some members whose policies frequently put them on the opposite side of the fence from the majority of their fellow party members. Yet another prominent ideological group, People for the American Way, was formed by television producer Norman Lear to coordinate the efforts of liberals in the entertainment industry as well as the general public.

Women's organizations date back to the antislavery societies in pre–Civil War America. (See Chapter 15.) Today the largest women's group is the League of Women Voters, an organization that provides information to voters, backs registration and get-out-the-vote drives, and generally supports measures seeking to ensure honesty and integrity in government. But the most active feminist organization is the National Organization for Women (NOW), founded in 1966.

Environmental organizations have proliferated in recent decades. Among the largest and most prominent: the Environmental Defense Fund, Greenpeace, the National Wildlife Federation, the Natural Resources Defense Council, the Nature Conservancy, the Sierra Club, and the Wilderness Society.

Class Bias

The class bias of organized groups varies according to the organization. Unions (which frequently are not voluntary) recruit from the working class. But most other organizations have a strong middle- and upper-class bias. Upper-middle-class blacks lead civil rights organizations. Liberal causes, such as the women's movement and Common Cause, draw disproportionately from the university-educated and academically connected liberal establishment and rarely appeal to the lower classes. The social bias in association membership is complemented by the high social origins of lobbyists and the predominance of business and professional organizations in *effective* lobbying.

The business, professional, and class biases of interest groups challenge pluralist theories about representation in government. Whether or not interest groups are an effective link between the citizen and government, it is clear that many citizens do not avail themselves of this benefit. Even if the formal organization reduces anxiety or increases feelings of power, it does not serve the poor and the uneducated, whose alienation from the society is the greatest and whose need for such services is most extreme.[3]

Among members of organizations, active participation—and holding formal office—relates directly to social status. Whereas the majority of Americans are *members* of organizations, only a minority of members are *active* in them. Control typically rests with a small elite. The "iron law of oligarchy" states that even the most democratically inclined organizations gradually evolve into oligarchies. The oligarchs, who help shape the goals of the organizations, come disproportionately from the upper social classes.[4]

HOW WELL DO GROUPS REPRESENT MEMBERS?

The next test of pluralist group theory is how well interest groups translate members' demands into political action—or whether they do so at all.

Large versus Small Organizations

The size of the group is an important variable in its leadership's political effectiveness. Since elected officials are sensitive to numbers, a large membership enhances a group's access to legislators. However, large groups find it difficult to commit themselves to an explicit position since their membership is so heterogeneous. The policy positions of mass membership organizations are often vague and broad, devoid of specific content—and thus harmless. The U.S. Chamber of Commerce, for example, seeks to represent "businesspeople," without regard for the nature of the business. Since intrabusiness disputes are often as bitter as labor–management disputes, the chamber cannot take a position on many of the legislative and administrative details that affect the economic health of various segments of the business community. Narrowly focused organizations such as the American Petroleum Institute, which represents only the oil industry, are far more effective than the broad-based Chamber of Commerce.

In contrast to large groups, small and highly organized groups have attained very tangible benefits. Small groups with narrow interests can achieve cohesion more readily and can concentrate their resources on a limited, tangible objective. They can act decisively and persistently based on precise information. Such organizations are most frequently business, professional, or industrial; they are the major employers of lobbyists at the state and national level. Many businesspeople organize into trade associations representing many industrial and commercial activities. Because their membership represents a specific form of business activity—for example, the American Bankers Association—many trade associations are quite small, some with as few as twenty-five members. Their power to advocate specific issues is disproportionate, while the business community as a whole is less focused.

Leaders versus Followers

Leaders and followers differ. *All* groups are afflicted with the curse of oligarchy. For example, Linda Lichter discovered that civil rights organization leaders do not necessarily represent the views of black masses (see Table 9-1). Black leaders think black people are going backward, whereas followers think they are making progress. Leaders have experienced discrimination, whereas followers perceive they have not. Leaders support racial preferences but followers do not. Leaders think they have been abandoned by the Democrats but followers do not.

Black followers are *social* conservatives, but for leaders the opposite is true. Given this evidence, Lichter concludes:

> *Only about half of all blacks said that the leaders they see on television and read about in the newspapers represent a majority of black people. This split may be related to the small proportion of blacks, 14 percent, who said they belonged to any civil rights organization. Many blacks, therefore, may not be in close touch with the policies of some black leaders and civil rights groups.*[5]

Single-Interest versus Traditional Interest Groups

The leadership of single-interest groups may reflect the views of their members better than larger, traditional, better-financed organizations. Because

TABLE 9-1	Black leaders and followers: Do they agree?		
		BLACK LEADERS (%)	ALL BLACKS (%)
Are most blacks today making progress or going backward?			
Making progress		39	66
Going backward		61	34
Have you, personally, ever experienced racial discrimination against blacks in terms of applying for a job, or not?			
Have experienced racial discrimination		74	40
Have not		26	60
Some people say that to make up for past discrimination, members of minority groups should be given preferential treatment in getting jobs and places in college. Others say that ability, as determined by test scores, should be the main consideration. Which point of view comes closer to how you feel on this matter?			
Minorities should be given preference		77	23
Ability should be the main consideration		23	77
Would you say the Democratic party is now more interested, as interested, or less interested in helping solve the problems of black Americans as compared with four years ago?			
More interested		10	46
As interested		31	26
Less interested		59	28
Prayer in the public schools (percentage in favor)		40	83
The death penalty for murder (percentage in favor)		33	55
Allowing homosexuals to teach in the public schools (percentage in favor)		59	40

Source: Excerpted from *Public Opinion* (August/September 1985): 42–43.

single-issue groups focus on one narrow concern (abortion or gun control, for example), their leaders do not have much flexibility for bargaining or compromise. Their strength is almost solely the intensity of their beliefs. They offer no benefits to members other than political commitment that ranges from "merely strong" to "fanatical."[6]

The intense commitment of members to a particular issue has at least two important consequences. First, leaders have far less freedom of action than they would have with a membership recruited for nonissue reasons. The second consequence is that the clearer link between leaders and followers and the dedication of both to the cause hampers leaders from fully using the traditional processes of political compromise. Clearly, a person who sees abortion as a form of murder cannot compromise by saying, "I would agree to thirty thousand federally funded abortions and no more."

Why have single-issue groups proliferated in recent years? Much of the explanation lies in the decline of political parties (see Chapter 7). As political parties were reformed to increase their responsiveness, the strength of party organizations faded. More and more states turned to open primaries. Candidates came to rely more on personal organization and media exposure than on party organization support (see Chapter 6). Candidates turned to single-interest organizations, whose electoral influence grew in contrast to the decline of parties. Such groups, of course, represent minorities, but so do all other interest groups. The essential difference is that they are *more* representative of the views of their members—because they cannot compromise—than are the established groups. They are not the functional

---

FOCUS

Leaders and Followers—The American Association of Retired Persons

There is very little evidence to suggest that members know or care very much about what their leaders are doing in their name.[a] The larger the organization becomes, the more difficult is the task of speaking accurately for its members. Consider the largest interest group currently extant, the American Association of Retired Persons (AARP), which has nearly 40 million members. Since the membership is open to anyone over 50 who can pay the modest dues, it is easy to imagine the cross-cutting cleavages that characterize its membership. Other than age, what do they have in common, and how can an organization speak for them on issues of such complexity as increased funding

for mental health programs, home health care, coverage of prescription drugs, expansion of state Medicaid criteria, more extensive coverage of nursing home care and mental health programs, increased professional training for care givers, supplements to food stamps, a national senior service corps, housing supplements for the aged, rent vouchers, energy assistance, cleaning up the environment and—simultaneously—opposition to budget cuts designed to reduce national deficits? The AARP led the successful fight in Congress against the Balanced Budget Amendment to the Constitution. It is doubtful that all 40 million agree on even a portion of this expansive agenda.

Yet even though common sense tells them that such large groups cannot deliver a vote, Congress members are frequently intimidated by these groups. After each election, myriad organizations lay claim to having been the decisive bloc. More than the politicians of most democracies, American legislators feel that they are vulnerable, that they have no reliable defense against an organization's demands. During testimony at committee hearings, an annoyed legislator might ask for some evidence that an organization does indeed reflect the views of its members, but these outbursts are rare.

equivalent of political parties, for their causes are limited. They are, however, more responsive to issues than parties and traditional interest groups are.

LOBBYING: HOW ORGANIZED INTERESTS INFLUENCE GOVERNMENT

Lobbying is any communication directed at a government decision maker with the hope of influencing decisions. For organized interests, lobbying is a continuous activity—in congressional committees, in congressional staff offices, at the White House, at executive agencies, at Washington cocktail parties. If a group loses a round in Congress, it continues the fight in the agency in charge of executing the policy, or it challenges the policy in the courts.

The most widely followed example of a legislator calling an organization to task was Republican Senator Alan Simpson of Wyoming, who investigated the complex web of the AARP's varied and lucrative business enterprises. The organization earns more than $180 million annually from insurance, travel clubs, discount drugs, credit cards, and annuities. Simpson, troubled by the AARP's tax-exempt status, cut to the heart of big organization politics: "They're a huge cash flow operation, 33 million people paying $8 dues, bound together by a *common love of airline discounts and automobile discounts and pharmacy discounts,* and they haven't the slightest idea what the organization is asking for."[b] Simpson also alleged that AARP field representatives are subject to immediate dismissal if they disagree with its national board, and that those board members are chosen by the association's cadre of lobbyists.

He described the interests of the AARP members as "selective" economic advantages and "collective" advantages. The selective advantages are available only to those who join the organization. If the organization did not offer such benefits, a person would decline to join, because whatever policy advantages that the organization secures apply to

all, not just to the members. If the AARP and its allies persuade Congress to expand Medicaid, all people over 50 benefit. These benefits are "collective." The incentives are the "selective" benefits, and there is probably no organization that can match the AARP in providing them. For $8 a year, members have access to a mouth-watering list of economic opportunities: health and life insurances discounts; savings on mail-order drugs; low-interest-rate bank cards (the "geezer Visas"), discounted hotels, motels and rental cars; a newsletter, the AARP Bulletin, and a semimonthly magazine, *Modern Maturity.* Some members may, of course, develop a keen interest in the political aspirations of the organization, but most do not; they are there because it makes good economic sense.[c]

[a]Terry Moe, *The Organization of Interests* (Chicago: University of Chicago Press, 1980).

[b]These were Simpson's remarks of 1995, when he chaired a two-day hearing on the AARP. See Charles R. Morris, *The AARP: America's Most Powerful Lobby and The Clash of Generations* (New York: Times Books, 1996).

[c]Mancur Olson, *The Logic of Collective Action* (Cambridge: Harvard University Press, 1965).

"Trust me Mort—no electronic-communications superhighway, no matter how vast and sophisticated, will ever replace the art of the schmooze."

The following year it resumes the struggle in Congress: it fights for repeal of the offending legislation, for weakening amendments, or for budget reductions that would cripple enforcement efforts. The process can continue indefinitely.

We can classify lobbying techniques in four categories: (1) access, (2) information, (3) grass-roots mobilization, and (4) campaign support. In the real world of Washington power struggles, all these techniques may be applied simultaneously, or innovative techniques may be discovered and applied at any time.

One technique that most experienced lobbyists shun is the *threat*. Amateur lobbyists may threaten legislators by vowing to defeat them at the next election, a tactic guaranteed to produce a defensive reaction among members of Congress. Out of self-respect, legislators are likely to respond to crude pressures by demonstrating their independence and voting against the threatening lobbyist. Moreover, experienced members of Congress know that such threats are empty; lobbyists can seldom deliver enough votes to influence the outcome of an election.

Access

To communicate with decision makers, an organized interest first needs access to them. As a prominent Washington lobbyist explained: "Number 1 is the access—to get them in the door and get a hearing for your case . . . knowing the individuals personally, knowing their staffs and how they operate and the kind of information they want . . . that kind of personal knowledge can help you maximize the client's hearing."[7]

"Opening doors" is a major business in Washington. Individuals who have personal contacts with decision makers (or who say they do) sell their services at high prices. Washington law firms, public relations agencies, and consultants all offer their insider connections and their advice to potential clients. Many professional lobbyists are former members of Congress, former White House aides, or former congressional staff personnel who "know their way around." The personal prestige of the lobbyist, together with the group's perceived political influence, helps open doors in Washington.

Access is also the object of socializing. This too is becoming institutionalized. There are, of course, the usual dinners with lobbyists, but more often lobbyists are showing up at various fund-raising affairs. Lobbyists pay thousands of dollars a plate at the president's dinner, the Democratic congressional dinner, and fund-raisers for individual members of Congress. Few legislators can be bought for the price of an individual dinner, but how about a sixty-thousand-dollar dinner (the take in the average fund-raiser)?

Information

Once lobbyists gain access, their knowledge and information become their most valuable resources. A lobbyist may contribute such information as (1) knowledge of the legislative process, (2) expertise on the issue under debate, and (3) information about the group's position on the issue. Because legislators and their aides value all three types of knowledge, lobbyists can often trade their knowledge for congressional support.

Lobbyists must spend considerable time and effort tracking information about bills affecting their interests. They must be thoroughly familiar with the ins and outs of the legislative process—the relevant committees and subcommittees, their schedules of meetings and hearings, their key staff members, the best moments to act, the precise language for proposed bills and amendments, the witnesses for hearings, and the political strengths and weaknesses of the legislators themselves.

The lobbyist's policy information must be accurate as well as timely. A successful lobbyist never supplies faulty or inaccurate information; his or her success depends on maintaining the trust and confidence of the decision makers. A reputation for honesty is as important as a reputation for influence. Lobbyists provide the information and argumentation that members of Congress use in legislative debate and in speeches back home. In this role, the lobbyist complements the functions of congressional staff. Testimony at legislative hearings is a common form of information exchange between lobbyists and legislators. Lobbyists also provide the technical reports and analyses used by congressional staffs in their legislative research.

Grass-Roots Mobilization

Many organized interests also lobby Congress by mobilizing constituents to apply pressure on their behalf. Many lobbyists believe that legislators, especially insecure ones, pay close attention to letters, telegrams, and calls from "folks back home." The larger organized interests often have local chapters throughout the nation and can mobilize these local affiliates to apply pressure when necessary. Lobbyists encourage influential local elites to visit a Congress member's office personally or to make a personal phone call on behalf of the group's positions.

Of course, experienced lawmakers recognize attempts by lobby groups to orchestrate "spontaneous" grass-roots outpourings of cards and letters. Pressure mail is often identical in wording and content. Nevertheless, members of Congress dare not ignore a flood of letters and telegrams from home, for the mail shows that constituents are aware of the issue and care enough to sign their names.

Another grass-roots tactic is to mobilize the press in a Congress member's home district. Lobbyists may provide news, analyses, and editorials to local newspapers and then clip favorable articles to send to lawmakers. Lobby groups may also buy advertisements in hometown newspapers. And nearly every issue of the *Washington Post* carries full- or half-page ads placed by lobby groups.

Lobbying Expenditures

Lobbying is expensive. Influential lobbyists make more money than the Congress members they are lobbying. Indeed, many former Congress members, as well as former White House staff and cabinet members, pursue lucrative careers in Washington as lobbyists after leaving office. Direct lobbying expenditures are separate from PAC campaign contributions. It is not uncommon for a major interest group (e.g., the American Medical Association, the U.S. Chamber of Commerce, the Edison Electric Institute, or the American Association of Retired Persons) or a large corporation (e.g., Philip Morris, General Electric, United Technologies, AT&T, or Citicorp) to budget $5 million to $10 million per year for lobbying.[8]

Campaign Support

However, *the real key to success in lobbying is the campaign contribution.* Interest group contributions not only help lobbyists gain access and a favorable hearing but also help elect people friendly to the group's goals. As the costs of campaigning increase, legislators must depend more heavily on the contributions of organized interests.

It is illegal for a lobbyist to extract a specific vote pledge from a legislator in exchange for a campaign contribution. Crude "vote buying" is usually (but not always) avoided. Instead, organized interests contribute to the campaign fund of a member of Congress over a long period of time and leave it to the lawmaker to figure out how to retain their support. When a legislator consistently votes against an organized interest, that interest may then contribute to the opposition candidate in the next election.

Regulation of Lobbies

Although the First Amendment protects lobbying, government can regulate lobbying activities. The principal method is disclosure: the law requires lobbyists to register as lobbyists and to report how much they spend. But definitions of lobbying are unclear and enforcement is weak. Many of the larger lobby groups—for example, the National Association of Manufacturers, the National Bankers Association, and Americans for Constitutional Action—have never registered as lobbyists. These organizations claim that because lobbying is not their "principal" activity, they need not register under the law. Financial reports of lobbyists grossly underestimate the extent of lobbying in Congress because the law requires reports only on money spent on direct lobbying before Congress, not on money spent for public relations or for campaign contributions. Another weakness in the law is that it applies only to attempts to influence Congress and does not regulate lobbying activities in administrative agencies or the executive branch. However, restrictive legislation might violate the First Amendment freedom to "petition the government for a redress of grievances."

PAC POWER

Political parties are large, disorganized, and largely devoid of ideology. A contributor wishing to support a specific political cause gets more for his or her money by contributing to a PAC. A PAC, or political action committee, is a nonparty organization that solicits voluntary contributions to disburse to political candidates. PACs have been organized by labor unions, trade associations, and liberal and conservative groups: environmental groups, for example, all have organized PACs. However, the largest number of PACs is in the corporate sector. Contributions to PACs must be voluntary; corporations and labor unions cannot legally use corporate or union treasuries for political campaigns.

PACs have become a major force in Washington politics in recent years. An estimated one-third of all campaign contributions now originates with them. The increasing cost of television campaigning makes many legislators dependent on PAC contributions to run their campaigns.

PACs Prefer Incumbents

The PACs give most of their money to *incumbent* members of Congress (see Table 9-2). Not only does this practice strengthen incumbents against their opponents, but it also makes incumbents less likely to change the law governing PAC contributions. The object is *access*. Rarely will money be contributed to an explicit contract for a vote. Whereas some PACs are largely concerned with one set of policies, others are more interested in a long-term, institutionally structured relationship with the legislature. Thus, their preference for incumbents.

When Democrats controlled Congress prior to the 1994 election, PAC contributions tilted toward Democrats. After the GOP gained control of Congress, PACs shifted toward support of Republicans.

PACs even give money to officeholders not up for election in a particular year, in order to help them retire debts or prepare for a future election. Additionally, PACs spend money in "indirect" expenditures. Indirect expenditures include ads and endorsements that are not paid for directly by the candidates' campaign organizations.

TABLE 9-2	PERCENTAGE OF PAC CONTRIBUTIONS		
Distribution of PAC contributions in congressional elections	ALL CANDIDATES	1995–1996	1993–1994	1989–1990
	Incumbents	67%	72%	74%
	Challengers	15%	10%	12%
	Open Seats	18%	18%	14%
	SENATE			
	Democrats	35%	50%	57%
	Republicans	65%	50%	43%
	HOUSE			
	Democrats	50%	67%	67%
	Republicans	50%	33%	33%

Source: Federal Elections Commission, 1998.

The Big-Money PACs

PAC contributions come in larger lumps than most individual contributions. PACs are easier for Congress members to contact for contributions; only about 4,000 PACs regularly contribute to congressional campaigns. The largest distributor of PAC money in the 1996 election cycle was Emily's List—an organization that collects and distributes campaign funds for liberal, pro-choice female candidates. (See Table 9-3.)

CONSERVATIVE INFLUENCE OF ORGANIZATIONS

Organizations perform a conservative, stabilizing function for society. Formal organizations seldom cause social change. Of course, the goals of associations vary, but in general, organizations gradually become more moderate as the goal of perpetuating themselves takes priority over their original goals:

> *The day-to-day behavior of the permanent staff and active participants (a minority of the membership) becomes centered around proximate goals of primary internal importance, modifying or "displacing" the stated goals of the organization.*[9]

TABLE 9-3 The Big-Money PACs

CORPORATE PACs	LABOR PACs	TRADE AND PROFESSIONAL PACs	IDEOLOGICAL AND ISSUE PACs
American Telephone and Telegraph Co. (AT&T PAC)	American Federation of State, County & Municipal Employees (PEOPLE PAC)	Association of Trial Lawyers	Emily's List
Federal Express Corporation PAC (FEPAC)	United Auto Workers (V-CAP)	National Education Association	National Rifle Association
Team Ameritech (PAC)	Machinists Non-Partisan Political League	American Medical Association	Political Victory Fund
Philip Morris (PHIL-PAC)	Int'l Brotherhood of Electrical Workers	National Automobile Dealers	Women's Campaign Fund
United Parcel Service (UPSPAC)	United Food & Commercial Workers (Active Ballot Fund)	American Federation of Teachers	National Committee for an Effective Congress
Lockheed Martin Employees PAC	Communications Workers of America (CWA-COPE)	Realtors PAC	National Committee to Preserve Social Security and Welfare
Union Pacific Fund for Effective Government	United Steel Workers of America	American Bankers Association (BANKPAC)	National Right to Life PAC
	AFL-CIO Committee on Political Education (AFL-CIO COPE)	National Association of Life Underwriters	Hollywood Women's PAC
		National Association of Home Builders (BUILDPAC)	GOPAC
	Letter Carriers PAC		Black America's PAC

Source: Federal Elections Commission, 1998.

In other words, as organizations grow older, they shift from trying to implement their original values to maintaining their structure, even if they thereby sacrifice the organization's central mission. The people who have the greatest stake in the existing social system thus come to dominate the organization. Of course, organizations do not stop seeking change, increased benefits, but the extent of change they seek is minimal. Once they achieve even a few of their goals, they then have a stake in the ongoing system and a rational basis for pursuing more moderate politics. Social stability is a product of this organizational system.

Bias against Change

Since groups serve society by cementing their members to the established social system, those who seek to radically alter this system find organizations an unsatisfactory mechanism. True, some groups develop with radical change in mind, but the process of bureaucratization of leadership from "have-nots" to "haves" gradually reduces any organization's commitment to substantial change. Impoverished people and blacks have gained little from groups because the group structure is dominated by people with a favored position in society. For segments of society effectively barred from other forms of participation, violent protest may be the only method of entry into the political process. Ironically, if deprived people succeed in organizing themselves, violence will probably decline, to be replaced by organizational activity. But in time, the new organizations will develop their own commitment to the status quo, thus again leaving the truly deprived with little to show for their sacrifices.

Why Interest Groups Will Continue to Grow

A Congress of 535 people standing before a tidal wave of interest groups helps to produce what is commonly known as "gridlock." Each legislative proposal activates an array of powerful groups, both for and against any legislation, and so the easiest course for the legislature is to do nothing. In 1970, there were only half as many groups, (see Figure 9-2), but even then, cries of "gridlock" were often heard.

"Organization breeds counter-organization,"[10] wrote political scientist David Truman. This continuing proliferation of organizations has been said to create "demosclerosis":

> *More groups demand more benefits, more benefits spawn more*
> *groups. As the group formation process picks up speed, an invisible*

FIGURE 9-2   Groups listed in the *Encyclopedia of Associations*

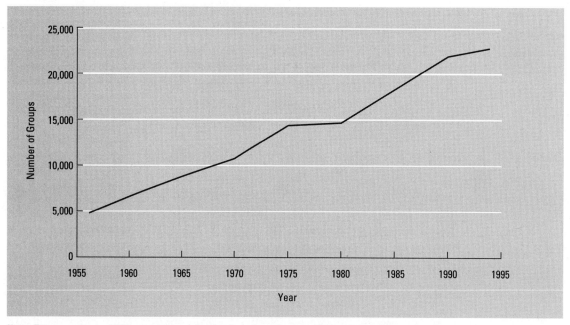

Note: Figures prior to 1975 are estimates by the American Society of Association Executives.

Sources: Gale Research, Inc.; American Society of Association Executives.

> *threshold may be crossed. At some point, there might be so many groups and so many more groups forming every year, that they would begin to choke the system that breeds them, to undermine confidence in politics, even to erode political stability.*[11]

The Case against Interest Groups

Pluralist theory rejects the notion of a "public interest." Regarding such an idea as naive, pluralist writers prefer to regard the public interest as the sum of the competing demands; a Darwinian notion that the strongest coalition will—and should—win.

But in the absence of a recognized public interest, governments become so ensnared in interest group squabbles that they cannot address broader, more distant goals. Political scientist Thomas Mann grieves that "when effective action on the country's most pressing problems requires the imposition of losses on organized interests, with benefits to all on the distant

FOCUS

The Business of the Business Roundtable

The Business Roundtable was established in 1972 "in the belief that business executives should take an increased role in the continuing debates about public policy." The organization is composed of the chief executives of the two hundred largest corporations in America and is financed through corporate membership fees. For many years, the U.S. Chamber of Commerce, the National Association of Manufacturers, the Business Council, and hundreds of industry associations such as the powerful American Petroleum Institute had represented business in traditional interest-group fashion. Why did business create this superorganization? The Business Roundtable itself says:

> *"The answer is that business leaders believed there was a need that was not being filled, and they invented the Roundtable to fill it. They wanted an organization in which the chief executive officers of leading enterprises take positions and advocate those positions."*[a]

In brief, traditional interest-group representation was inadequate for the nation's top corporate leadership. It wished to come together *itself* to decide upon public policy and press its views in Washington.

The power of the Business Roundtable stems in part from its "firm rule" that a corporate chief executive officer (CEO) cannot send a substitute to its meetings. Moreover, CEOs lobby the Congress in person rather than sending paid lobbyists. Members of Congress are impressed when the chairman of IBM appears at a congressional hearing on business regulation or when the chairman of GTE speaks to a congressional committee about taxation, or when the chairman of Prudential Insurance talks to Congress about Social Security. One congressional staff member explained: "If a corpora-

tion sends its Washington representative to our office, he's probably going to be shunted over to a legislative assistant. But the chairman of the board is going to get in to see the senator." Another aide echoed those sentiments: "Very few members of Congress would not meet with the president of a Business Roundtable corporation."[b]

Business Roundtable member corporations are a major source of campaign contributions. The table below lists those member corporations that contributed one-half million dollars or more in 1996. Most of this money went to Republican candidates.

[a]Business Roundtable, *What the Roundtable Is* January, 1988, Business Roundtable, 201 Park Ave, New York, NY, 10166.

[b]*Time*, April 13, 1981, p, 77.

Business Roundtable member campaign contributions, 1996

ORGANIZATION NAME	TOTAL AMOUNT CONTRIBUTED	% TO REPUBS	% TO DEMS
Philip Morris	$3,006,636	83%	17%
RJR Nabisco	$1,352,931	85%	15%
AT&T	$ 984,524	56%	44%
MCI Telecommunications Corp.	$ 934,514	36%	64%
Federal Express	$ 773,525	49%	51%
Anheuser-Busch	$ 736,057	46%	54%
Time Warner	$ 726,250	45%	55%
Chevron Corp.	$ 702,306	75%	25%
NYNEX Corp.	$ 651,602	63%	37%
Textron Inc.	$ 648,000	58%	42%
Eli Lilly & Co.	$ 627,835	70%	30%
Entergy Corp.	$ 580,975	49%	51%
WMX Technologies, Inc.	$ 551,200	66%	34%
Bank of America	$ 546,798	65%	35%
Bristol-Myers Squibb	$ 542,400	79%	21%
Coca-Cola Co.	$ 534,640	67%	33%
Travelers Group	$ 524,844	62%	38%
General Motors	$ 501,775	85%	15%

Source: Center for Responsive Politics.

(Continued)

FOCUS

Continued

The Business Roundtable has experienced both victories and defeats in Congress. During the Ford and Carter administrations, the Roundtable successfully opposed the creation of a new federal consumer protection agency comparable to the Environmental Protection Agency. During the Reagan years, the Roundtable was at the forefront of "deregulation" and tax cutting.

But in recent years the Roundtable seems to have lost some of its clout. Many CEOs are too busy restructuring, merging, acquiring new corporations, and globalizing their operations, to bother

with Washington politics. The Roundtable lost a lengthy battle over mandated family leaves in 1993 when Congress sent the Family Leave Act to President Bill Clinton to sign as his first major legislative victory. The Roundtable also was defeated in its opposition to the expansion of the Clean Air Act of 1990, which it believes imposes excessive compliance costs on industry and handicaps American corporations in global competition. And the Roundtable is regularly defeated in efforts to reform the nation's liability laws; its principal opponent in this struggle has been the American Association of Trial Lawyers, some of whose members sit in Congress itself. So even with all of its prestige and resources, the Business Roundtable does not win all of its battles.

horizon, the odds of success in the U.S. political system are not very high."[12] Only a government strong enough to impose costs on interest groups can truly serve the public interest. But the United States does not have that government. Mann therefore settles on a realistic if bleak prediction about the future of American politics: "a continuation of the escapism and deadlock of recent years."

Summary

Pluralism asserts that organized interest groups provide the individual with an effective way to participate in the political system. It contends that individuals can make their voices heard through membership in the organized groups that reflect their views on public affairs. Pluralists further believe that competition among organized interests provides a balance of power that protects the individual's interests. Interest groups divide power among themselves and hence protect the individual from rule by a single oppressive elite.

Earlier we pointed out that pluralism diverges from classical democratic theory. Even if the plural elite model accurately portrays the reality of American politics, it does not guarantee the implementation of democratic values. Our analysis of interest groups produces the following propositions:

1. Interest groups draw disproportionately from middle- and upper-class segments of the population. The pressure group system is not representative of the entire community.

2. Leadership of interest groups is recruited from the middle- and upper-class population.

3. Business and professional organizations predominate among organized interest groups.

4. Generally mass membership groups achieve only symbolic success, and smaller, more cohesive groups are able to achieve more tangible results.

5. Considerable inequality exists among organized interest groups. Business and producer groups with narrow membership but cohesive organization achieve their tangible goals at the expense of broad, unorganized groups seeking less tangible goals.

6. Organized interest groups are governed by small elites whose values do not necessarily reflect the values of most members.

7. Business groups and associations are the most highly organized and active lobbyists in Washington and in the state capitals. Their influence is especially evident in the growth of political action committees.

8. Organizations tend to become conservative as they acquire a stake in the existing social order. Therefore, pressures for substantial social change must generally come from forces outside the structure of organized interest groups.

Notes

1. Gabriel A. Almond and Sidney Verba, *The Civic Culture: Political Attitudes and Democracy in Five Nations* (Boston: Little, Brown, 1965), p. 245.

2. David B. Truman, *The Governmental Process* (New York: Knopf, 1951).

3. Sidney Verba and Norman H. Nie, *Participation in America* (New York: Harper & Row, 1972), p. 208.

4. Roberto Michels, *Political Parties: A Sociological Study of the Oligarchical Tendencies of Modern Democracy* (1915; reprint, New York: Dover, 1959), esp. p. 248.

5. Linda S. Lichter, "Who Speaks for Black America?" *Public Opinion* (August/ September 1985): 44.

6. Jeffrey M. Berry, *Lobbying for the People* (Princeton, N.J.: Princeton University Press, 1977), pp. 100, 109.

7. Congressional Quarterly, *The Washington Lobby*, 4th ed. (Washington, D.C.: Congressional Quarterly Press, 1982), p. 5.

8. Associated Press, March 6, 1998.

9. Harmon Zeigler and Wayne Peak, *Interest Groups in American Society*, 2nd ed. (Englewood Cliffs, N.J.: Prentice-Hall, 1972), p. 81.

10. David Truman, *The Governmental Process* (New York: Alfred A. Knopf, 1951), p. 65.

11. Jonathan Rauch, *Demosclerosis: The Silent Killer of American Government* (New York: Times Books, 1994), p. 61.

12. Thomas E. Mann, "Breaking the Political Impasse," in Henry J. Aaron, ed., *Setting National Priorities: Policy for the Nineties* (Washington, D.C.: The Brookings Institution, 1990), pp. 303, 313.

Selected Readings

Hrebenar, Ronald J. *Interest Group Politics in America,* 3rd ed. New York: M. E. Sharpe, 1996. A concise, readable, and timely introduction to the study of group power.

Lowi, Theodore J. *The End of Liberalism.* New York: Norton, 1969. A major critique of "interest group liberalism," describing how special interests contribute to the growth of government and the development of "clientism."

Mucciaroni, Gary. *Public Policy and Private Interests.* Washington: Brookings, 1995. Identifying the factors that contribute to the victory or defeat of producer groups—firms, industries, professional and trade associations—in the policy process.

Olson, Mancur. *The Rise and Decline of Nations.* New Haven, Conn.: Yale University Press, 1982. Argues that, over time, the development of powerful special interest lobbies has led to institutional sclerosis, inefficiency, and slowed economic growth.

Olson, Mancur. *The Logic of Collective Action.* Cambridge: Harvard University Press, 1965. The classic theoretical inquiry into the benefits and costs to individuals of joining groups and the obstacles (including the free rider problem) to forming organized interest groups.

Schlozman, Kay L., and John T. Tierney. *Organized Interests and American Democracy.* New York: Harper & Row, 1986. Comprehensive examination of interest groups in American politics, with original survey data from Washington lobbyists.

Truman, David B. *The Governmental Process.* New York: Knopf, 1951. The classic description and defense of interest group pluralism.

Walker, Jack L. *Mobilizing Interest Groups in America: Patrons, Professions, and Social Movements.* Ann Arbor: University of Michigan Press, 1991. A study of mobilization and maintenance of interest groups, based on large-scale mail surveys of Washington-based membership associations. It includes chapters on how and why organizations are formed, what inducements are offered to members, and what influences leaders' choices of strategy.

10

The Presidency

The Presidency is the focus for the most intense and persistent emotions. . . . The President is . . . the one figure who draws together the people's hopes and fears for the political future.

—JAMES DAVID BARBER

Governmental elites in the United States do not command; they seek consensus with other elites. Decision making by governmental elites is a process of bargaining, accommodation, and compromise among the dominant interests in American society. Governmental elites act essentially as go-betweens and mediators, seeking policies that are mutually beneficial to the major interests—industrial, financial, labor, farm, military, bureaucratic, and so on.

The presidency stands at the center of elite interaction in the American political system. For the *elite*, the president proposes policy initiatives, mobilizes influence within the political system, and supervises the management of government and the economy. For the *masses,* the president is a symbol of national unity, an outlet to express their emotions toward government, and a vicarious means of taking political action. For *both* elites and masses, the presidency provides a means of handling national crises—taking whatever actions are necessary in an emergency to stabilize the nation, protect its security, and calm its citizens.

THE PRESIDENT AS SYMBOLIC LEADER

More than any other political figure, the president attracts the attention and emotion of the American masses. The people look to the presidency for leadership and reassurance. They want a president who will personalize government, simplify political issues, and symbolize the "compassionate" and protective role of the state. They want someone who seems concerned with them.

The people also look for toughness, competence, and decisiveness in the presidency. They are prepared to support a president who is willing to *do something*, whether "something" is a good idea or not. National surveys regularly gauge presidential popularity by asking, "Do you approve or disapprove of the way (Clinton, Bush, or Reagan, for example) is handling his job as president?" (see Figure 10-1). Presidential popularity goes up when the president takes dramatic action or when the nation faces an external crisis or threat.

The people *want* to support the president. All presidents begin their terms with broad public support. Over time, however, support wanes as troubles pile up and the president is unable to cope with them. Indeed, the popular expectations of a president far exceed the president's powers to meet them. The result is an inevitable decline in public support until a new crisis occurs or dramatic action is necessary.

Variations in Presidential Approval Ratings

A brief overview of presidential popularity ratings over time confirms these notions: that a president takes office with broad public support, that support tends to decline over time, and that renewal of support can occur with dramatic action or crisis. Figure 10-1 compares approval ratings of seven presidents. Each took office, whether through election or assassination or resignation, with broad popular support. Over time this support declined. But dramatic action—peace in Vietnam for Nixon, the assassination attempt on Reagan, victory in the Persian Gulf War for Bush—produced dramatic increases in presidential support. The prolonged, stalemated war in Vietnam, economic recessions, and the major Watergate and Iran-Contra scandals eroded presidential popularity.

Nothing inspires elite support among the masses more than decisive military victory. President George Bush achieved the highest public approval ratings in history following victory in the Persian Gulf War. This unprecedented peak was followed by a rapid, disastrous slide, as the nation turned its attention to the economic recession at home.

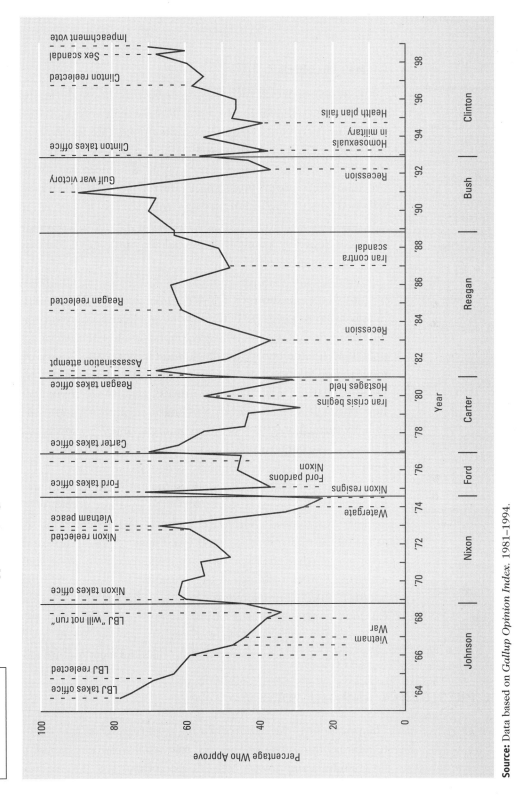

FIGURE 10-1

Presidential approval ratings

Source: Data based on *Gallup Opinion Index*, 1981–1994.

Clinton's Comeback

Bill Clinton's approval ratings were at best mediocre during his first term. His controversial decision to allow homosexuals to remain in the military ruined his early "honeymoon" with the public. (He was obliged to compromise with a "Don't ask, don't tell" policy, which allows homosexuals to remain in the military if they do not engage in homosexual activity or openly proclaim their sexual preference.) He recovered somewhat with a strong televised State of the Union message in January 1994, but when a Democratic-controlled Congress rejected the comprehensive national health care plan (developed by a commission headed by first lady Hillary Rodham Clinton), his popularity fell again.

Republicans captured control of Congress in November 1994 and promptly labeled Clinton a one-term president. But he gradually recovered in approval ratings as he battled the Republican Congress over the budget. To the surprise of the Republicans, public opinion blamed Congress, not the president, for the budget deadlock and temporary shutdown of the government in late 1995. Clinton cast himself as the protector of "Medicare, Medicaid, education, and the environment" against an unpopular antagonist, Republican House Speaker Newt Gingrich. Clinton's approval ratings rose steadily throughout 1996 as the economy boomed. He was reelected with 49 percent of the vote (to Dole's 43 percent and Perot's 8 percent), not really an enthusiastic endorsement of his presidency.

The sex scandals that surrounded the president early in his second term had exactly the opposite effect expected by most commentators. Clinton actually experienced an *upward* "bounce" in public opinion to 68 percent, as the public rallied to his support (see Focus: "Evaluating Presidential Character"). And when the Republican-controlled House of Representatives voted along party lines to impeach the president in December, 1998, his public approval rating skyrocketed to 73 percent, the highest of his career. Indeed, Clinton's continued strong public support among the masses became his most potent weapon in his fight to remain in office. Figure 10–2 traces Clinton's approval ratings from his first presidential election through 1998.

THE PRESIDENCY AND THE MASSES

The president is the nation's leading celebrity. When the president chooses to address the entire nation, the television networks cancel their regular programming and provide free television time.

FIGURE 10-2

President Clinton's approval ratings

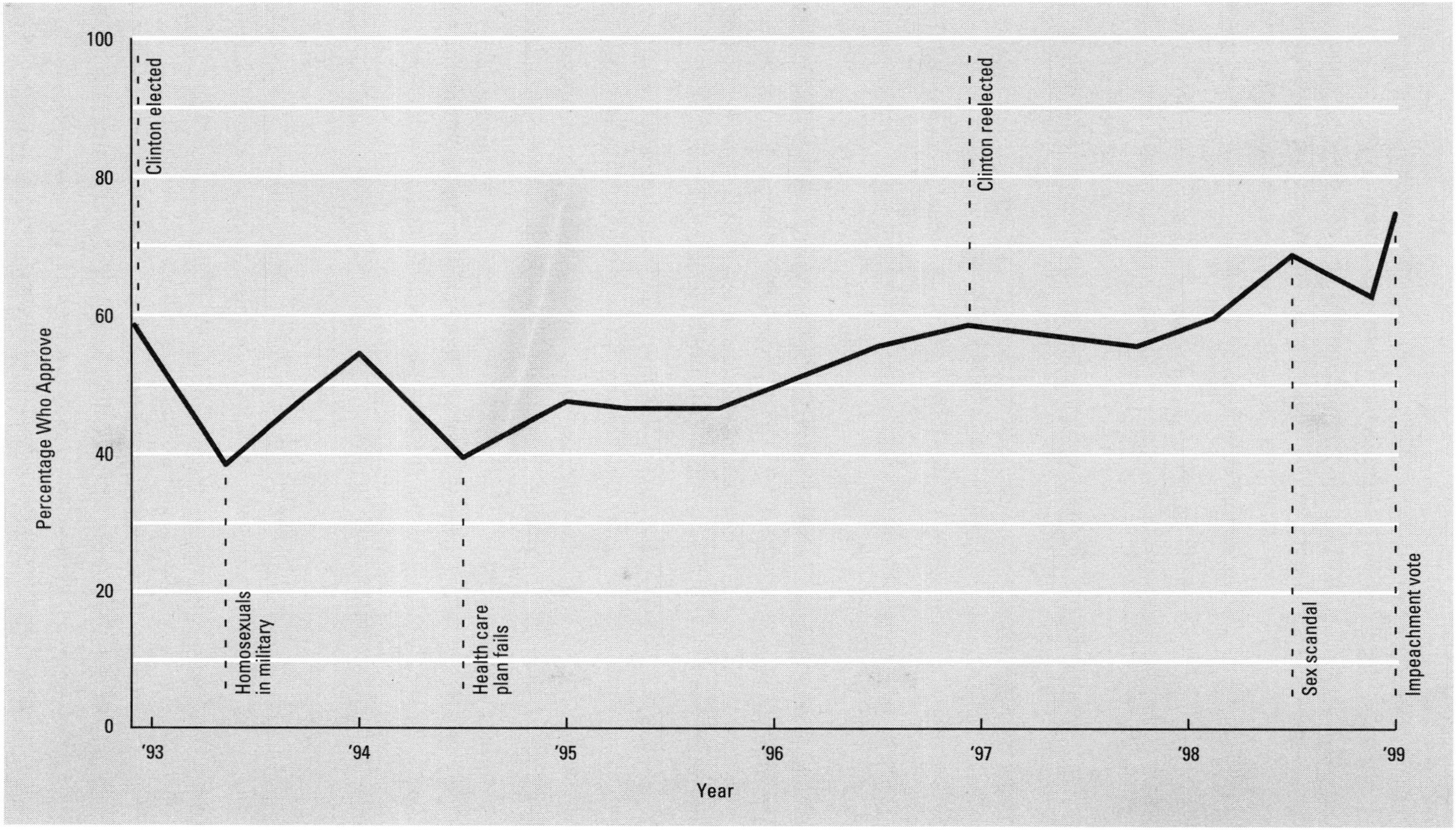

The presidency possesses enormous symbolic significance. The president affects popular images of authority, legitimacy, and confidence in the American political system. The president can arouse feelings of patriotism or cynicism, hope or despair, honor or dishonor. Political scientist James David Barber writes:

> The Presidency is the focus for the most intense and persistent emotions. . . .The President is . . . the one figure who draws together the people's hopes and fears for the political future. On top of all of his routine duties, he has to carry that off—or fail.[1]

The President and Mass Psychology

Political scientist Fred I. Greenstein has classified the "psychological functions of the presidency." The president:

1. "Simplifies perception of government and politics" by serving as "the main cognitive 'handle' for providing busy citizens with some sense of what their government is doing."

2. Provides "an outlet for emotional expression" through public interest in his and his family's private and public life.

3. Is a "symbol of unity" and of nationhood (as the national shock and grief over the death of a president clearly reveal).

4. Provides the masses with a "vicarious means of taking political action" in that the president can act decisively and effectively while they cannot do so.

5. Is a "symbol of social stability" in providing the masses with a feeling of security and guidance. Thus, for the masses, the president is the most visible elite member.[2]

Mass Popularity as a Power Base

Presidents are aware of their power as symbolic leader. Abraham Lincoln once declared, "Public sentiment is everything. With public sentiment nothing can fail, without it nothing can succeed."

A president's popularity with the masses in part determines presidential power in interactions with other elites. A president with high ratings in the polls for any reason can get better cooperation from other elites than when low in the polls. For example, Congress is more likely to support legislation proposed by the president when the president's popularity is high. Political scientist George C. Edwards reports overall positive correlations between presidential popularity and support in Congress for the president's proposals. Although these correlations are not perfect, popularity with the masses is certainly one basic component of the president's power in Congress.

Popularity has little to do with a president's position on the issues. In recent years, both Republican and Democratic and both liberal and conservative presidents have all at one time or other enjoyed high ratings and suffered low ratings in the polls. As Harvard political scientist Richard Neustadt has written, "Presidential standing outside of Washington is actually a jumble of imprecise impressions held by relatively inattentive men."[3]

Nonetheless, the president's popularity with the masses is immensely important. Indeed, President Clinton's continuing high approval ratings, despite highly publicized charges of misconduct, have prevented his removal from office by Congress. Each major setback for Clinton in Washington has been accompanied by a rally in mass support for his presidency throughout the country. In marked contrast to President Nixon's anemic 24 percent approval rating just prior to his resignation in the face of impeachment in 1974, Clinton's approval rating remained above 60 percent throughout 1998. Indeed, it jumped to an all-time high of 73 percent following the impeachment vote in the House of Representatives. (Although Clinton's bombing of Iraq at the same time as the House impeachment vote no doubt added to this exceptionally high rating.) Unquestionably, Clinton's support among the masses has become the key to his continuation in office.

The Character Issue

Traditionally Americans expected their presidents to be exemplary in their personal lives. Presidential scholar James David Barber, in his widely read book *Presidential Character,* once observed:

> *"The President is expected to personify our virtuousness in an inspiring way, to express in what he does and is (not just what he says) a moral idealism which, in the public mind, is the very opposite of politics."*

And traditionally the news media protected the president by not reporting on his private moral conduct. President John F. Kennedy's encounters with numbers of women, including movie star Marilyn Monroe and mobster girlfriend Judith Exner, were widely known during his term in office but not revealed until after his death. Subsequent writers have criticized the media for failing to report on Kennedy's "reckless" conduct:

> *Kennedy abused his high position for personal gratification. His reckless liaisons with women and mobsters were irresponsible, dangerous and demeaning to the office. . . . Had Kennedy lived to see a second term, the realities of his lechery and his dealings with [mobsters] might have leaked out while he was still in office, gravely damaging the presidency, debilitating his administration and severely disillusioning a populace which, no matter how jaded it seemed, looks to a president with hope for reassurance and leadership.*[4]

In contrast, the media today wallow in sexual scandal in high places, especially the White House (see Chapter 6). The "character issue" has long haunted Bill Clinton from Little Rock to the Oval Office. Indeed, no president has ever been confronted with so many allegations of sexual misconduct while in office. Yet public opinion polls indicate that most Americans believe that the president's private sexual conduct is irrelevant to the performance of his public duties.

Public versus Private Morality

Can private morality be divorced from public trust in the president? Even before President Clinton's admission of "inappropriate behavior" with Monica Lewinsky, the overwhelming majority of Americans believed he had engaged in a sexual affair with the 21-year-old White House intern. Yet most Americans continued to approve of the way that Clinton was performing his job as president. Clinton's job rating, already a healthy 60 percent at the beginning of 1998, even experienced a "Lewinsky bounce" following lurid news stories of the affair. Later, following the graphic report of the Independent Counsel Kenneth Starr, most Americans agreed that the president had "lied about having sex with Lewinsky" (86 percent), "lied under oath to the Starr grand jury" (78 percent), and tried to "conceal their relationship by concealing his gifts and getting her to lie under oath" (70 percent). Although the public held a negative opinion about Clinton "as a person" (58 percent), they continued to give him strong support in his handling of his job as president (68 percent).*

*Gallup poll, as reported in *USA Today,* Sept. 14, 1998.

How can we explain this apparent paradox—a mass public that believes the president had an affair in the White House and lied about it, yet gives the president the highest approval ratings of his career? Many Americans believe that private sexual conduct is irrelevant to the performance of public duties. Private morality is viewed as a "personal affair" about which Americans should be "nonjudgmental." Some people would emulate more "sophisticated" Europeans by ignoring the sex lives of political leaders. Others say, "If it's okay with Hillary, why should we worry?" Have we not had adulterous presidents before, from Thomas Jefferson to John F. Kennedy, presidents who were ranked high in history? And many Americans believe that "they all do it." Indeed, in response to the question "Do you think most presidents have or have not had extramarital affairs while they were president?" some 59 percent say "most have" while only 33 percent say "most have not."*

Yet others argue that private character should be considered in presidential performance, indeed that it is a prerequisite for public trust. The president performs a symbolic role—one that requires dignity, honesty, and respect. A president publicly embarrassed by sexual scandal, diminished by lunchroom jokes, laughed at by late-night television audiences, cannot perform a leadership role. Polls suggest that most Americans feel that the president does not "share their values" (56 percent no), does not "show good judgment" (56 percent no), nor is he "honest and trustworthy" (62 percent no). His motives, even in exercising his military duties as commander-in-chief of the armed forces, may be questioned. The acceptance of a president's adulterous behavior lowers societies standards of behavior. "The president's legacy . . . will be a further vulgarization and demoralization of society.**

THE PRESIDENT'S FORMAL POWERS

The president has many sources of formal power as chief administrator, chief legislator, party leader, chief diplomat, commander in chief, and chief of state and crisis manager (see Table 10-1, p. 280). But despite the great powers of the office, no president can monopolize policy making. The president functions within an established elite system and can exercise power only within the framework of that system. The choices available to the president are only those alternatives for which elite support can be mobilized. The president cannot act outside existing elite consensus—outside the

*Poll results reported in *The Polling Report,* February 9, 1998.
**Gertrude Himmelfarb, "Private Lives, Public Morality," *New York Times,* February 9, 1998.

"rules of the game"—and must be sensitive to the interests of major elites—business, agriculture, military, education, bureaucracy, and so on.

PRESIDENTIAL POWERS OF PERSUASION

The presidency's real power depends not on formal authority but on the president's abilities at persuasion. The president does not command American elites but stands in a central position in the elite structure. Responsibility for initiating public policy falls principally on the president and the presidential staff and executive departments. The president has a strong incentive to fulfill this responsibility, since a large segment of the American public holds the president responsible for everything that happens in the nation during that term of office, whether or not the president has the authority or capacity to do anything about it.

Through the power to initiate policy alone, the president's influence on the nation is considerable. The president sets the agenda for public decision

---

FOCUS

Up Close—
Sex, Lies and
Impeachment

Bill Clinton is the second president in the nation's history (following Andrew Johnson in 1867) to be impeached by the U.S. House of Representatives. (President Richard Nixon resigned just prior to an impeachment vote in 1974.) The 1998 House impeachment vote split along partisan lines (228 to 106, with all but five Republicans voting "yes" and all but five Democrats voting "no".) It followed a report to the House by Independent Counsel Kenneth Starr that recommended impeachment for perjury, obstruction of justice, witness tampering, and "abuse of power."

The Starr Report describes in graphic and lurid detail Clinton's sexual relationship with young White House intern Monica Lewinsky. It cites as impeachable offenses Clinton's lying about their re-

lationship to his staff, friends, and the nation; his misleading testimony in a sworn statement in the Paula Jones case; his conversations with close friend Vernon Jordan about finding Lewinsky a job; his attempts to impede Starr's investigation; and his evasive testimony before Starr's grand jury:

QUESTION: *"I have a question regarding your definition [of sexual relations] then. And my question is, is oral sex performed on you within that definition . . . ?"*
ANSWER: *"As I understood it, it was not, no."*

QUESTION: *"Well, the grand jury would like to know, Mr. President, why it is you think that oral sex performed on you does not fall within the definition of sexual relations?"*
ANSWER: *"Because that is—if the deponent is the person who has oral sex performed on him, then the contact is with—not with anything on that list, but with the lips of another person."*[a]

Does engaging in extramarital sex and lying about it meet the Constitution's standard for

[a]Congressional *Quarterly Weekly Report*, Sept. 26, 1998, pp. 2607–2613.

Mike Smith, *Las Vegas Sun,* for *USA Today.*

peachment—"treason, bribery, or other high crimes and misdemeanors." Perjury—knowingly giving false testimony in a sworn legal proceeding—is a criminal offense. But does the Constitution envision more serious misconduct—crimes that undermine the Constitution or abuse presidential power? Is sex and lying about it serious enough to warrant Congress' impeachment and removal of a president elected by the people? Alexander Hamilton in *The Federalist* 65 wrote that impeachment should deal with "the abuse or violation of some public trust." Is Clinton's acknowledged "inappropriate behavior" a private affair or a violation of the public trust?

The American people apparently do *not* believe that Clinton's misconduct should result in his impeachment and removal from office:

QUESTION: *Do you approve or disapprove of the House decision to vote in favor of impeaching Clinton and sending the case to the Senate for trial? Yes–35% No–63%*

QUESTION: *Do you think Bill Clinton should resign now and turn the presidency over to Al Gore? Yes–30% No–69%*

QUESTION: *Should the Senate vote in favor of convicting Clinton and removing him from office or vote against convicting? Vote to convict–29% Vote against convicting–68%*[b]

But the decision about what is impeachable is entirely in the hands of the House of Representatives, and the decision about whether or not to remove the president from office is entirely in the hands of the Senate. There is no appeal from the decisions of these chambers. The judgment of the House and the Senate is political as well as judicial, partisan as well as legal, and personal as well as public-opinion-driven.

Clinton's Senate impeachment trial ended in acquittal. Indeed, the strongest charge—that President Clinton tried to obstruct justice—failed to win even a majority of Senate votes, far less than the required two-thirds. All 45 Democrats were joined by 5 Republicans to create a 50-50 tie vote that left Clinton tarnished but still in office.

[b]Gallup poll reported in *USA Today,* December 21, 1998.

TABLE 10-1	**Chief Administrator** Implement policy—"Take care that laws be faithfully executed" (Art. II, Sec. 3). Supervise executive branch of government. Appoint and remove policy officials. Prepare executive budget.
Formal presidential powers	**Chief Legislator** Initiate policy—"give to the Congress information of the State of the Union and recommend to their consideration such measures as he shall judge necessary and expedient" (Art. II, Sec. 3). Veto legislation passed by Congress. Convene special session of Congress "on extraordinary occasions" (Art. II, Sec. 3).
	Party Leader Control national party organization. Control federal patronage. Influence (not control) state and local parties through prestige.
	Chief Diplomat Make treaties ("with the advice and consent of the Senate") (Art. II, Sec. 2). Make executive agreements. Exercise power of diplomatic recognition—"receive ambassadors and other public ministers" (Art. II, Sec. 3).
	Commander in Chief Command U.S. armed forces—"The President shall be Commander-in-Chief of the army and navy" (Art. II, Sec. 2). Appoint military officials. Initiate war. Exercise broad war powers.
	Crisis Manager and Chief of State Oversee formal national action—"The executive Power shall be vested in a President" (Art. II, Sec. 1). Represent the nation as chief of state.

making. The president presents programs to Congress in various presidential messages, including the annual State of the Union message, and in the annual Budget of the United State Government. The president thereby largely determines the business of Congress in any session. Few major undertakings ever get off the ground without presidential initiation, the president frames the issues, determines their context, and decides their timing.

Presidents: Active and Passive

The powers of the presidency and the importance of this office in the American political system vary with political circumstances and with the personalities of those who occupy the office. The contrasting views of Presidents William Howard Taft and Theodore Roosevelt often come up in debates about the true nature of executive power. Taft argued a somewhat *obsessive* view:

> *The true view of the executive function is, as I conceive it, that the president can exercise no power which cannot be fairly and reasonably traced to some specific grant of power or justly implied and included within such express grant as proper and necessary to its exercise. Such specific grants must be either in the federal constitution or in the pursuance thereof. There is no undefined residuum of power which can be exercised which seems to him to be in the public interest.*[5]

Theodore Roosevelt offered an alternative *activist* view:

> *I decline to adopt the view that what was imperatively necessary for the nation could not be one by the president unless he could find some specific authorization to do it. My belief was that it was not only his right but his duty to do anything that the needs of the nation demanded, unless such action was forbidden by the Constitution or by the laws.*[6]

Scholarly Ratings of Presidents

Historians may tend to rank activist presidents who led the nation through war or economic crisis higher than passivist presidents who guided the nation in peace and prosperity. Abraham Lincoln, George Washington, and Franklin Roosevelt are regularly ranked as the nation's greatest presidents. Initially Dwight Eisenhower, who presided in the relatively calm 1950s, was ranked low by historians. But later, after comparing his performance with those who came after him, his steadiness and avoidance of war raised his ranking. It is more difficult for historians to rate recent presidents; the views of historians are influenced by their own (generally liberal and reformist) political views. Richard Nixon once commented, "History will treat me fairly. historians probably won't."

Evaluations of presidents in mass opinion polls are more influenced by personal characteristics of presidents than their accomplishments in office. Among recent presidents, Ronald Reagan and John Kennedy rank high with the mass public.

| TABLE 10-2 | Scholarly ratings of the presidents |

SCHLESINGER (1962)	MURRAY (1982)	SCHLESINGER (1996)	W. J. RIDINGS S. B. McIVER (1997)
Great	**Presidential Rank**	**Great**	**Overall Ranking**
1. Lincoln	1. Lincoln	1. Lincoln	1. Lincoln
2. Washington	2. F. Roosevelt	2. Washington	2. F. Roosevelt
3. F. Roosevelt	3. Washington	3. F. Roosevelt	3. Washington
4. Wilson	4. Jefferson		4. Jefferson
5. Jefferson	5. T. Roosevelt	**Near Great**	5. T. Roosevelt
	6. Wilson	4. Jefferson	6. Wilson
Near Great	7. Jackson	5. Jackson	7. Truman
6. Jackson	8. Truman	6. T. Roosevelt	8. Jackson
7. T. Roosevelt	9. J. Adams	7. Wilson	9. Eisenhower
8. Polk	10. L. Johnson	8. Truman	10. Madison
Truman (tie)	11. Eisenhower	9. Polk	11. Polk
9. J. Adams	12. Polk		12. L. Johnson
10. Cleveland	13. Kennedy	**High Average**	13. Monroe
	14. Madison	10. Eisenhower	14. J. Adams
Average	15. Monroe	11. J. Adams	15. Kennedy
11. Madison	16. J. Q. Adams	12. Kennedy	16. Cleveland
12. J. Q. Adams	17. Cleveland	13. Cleveland	17. McKinley
13. Hayes	18. McKinley	14. L. Johnson	18. J. Q. Adams
14. McKinley	19. Taft	15. Monroe	19. Carter
15. Taft	20. Van Buren	16. McKinley	20. Taft
16. Van Buren	21. Hoover		21. Van Buren
17. Monroe	22. Hayes	**Average**	22. Bush
18. Hoover	23. Arthur	17. Madison	23. Clinton
19. B. Harrison	24. Ford	18. J. Q. Adams	24. Hoover
20. Arthur	25. Carter	19. B. Harrison	25. Hayes
Eisenhower (tie)	26. B. Harrison	20. Clinton	26. Reagan
21. A. Johnson	27. Taylor	21. Van Buren	27. Ford
	28. Tyler	22. Taft	28. Arthur
Below Average	29. Fillmore	23. Hayes	29. Taylor
22. Taylor	30. Coolidge	24. Bush	30. Garfield
23. Tyler	31. Pierce	25. Reagan	31. B. Harrison
24. Fillmore	32. A. Johnson	26. Arthur	32. Nixon
25. Coolidge	33. Buchanan	27. Carter	33. Coolidge
26. Pierce	34. Nixon	28. Ford	34. Tyler
27. Buchanan	35. Grant		35. W. Harrison
	36. Harding	**Below Average**	36. Fillmore
Failure		29. Taylor	37. Pierce
28. Grant		30. Coolidge	38. Grant
29. Harding		31. Fillmore	39. A. Johnson
		32. Tyler	40. Buchanan
			41. Harding
		Failure	
		33. Pierce	
		34. Grant	
		35. Hoover	
		36. Nixon	
		37. A. Johnson	
		38. Buchanan	
		39. Harding	

Sources: Arthur Murphy, "Evaluating the Presidents of the United States," *Presidential Studies Quarterly* 14 (1984): 117–126; Arthur M. Schlesinger, Jr., "Rating the Presidents: Washington to Clinton," *Political Science Quarterly* 112 (1997): 179–190; William J. Ridings and Stuart B. McIver, *Rating the Presidents* (Secaucus, N.J.: Citadel Press, 1997).

ISSUES IN PRESIDENTIAL POWER: THE WAR-MAKING CONTROVERSY

For decades, the liberal intellectuals in the United States praised the presidency and scorned Congress. Students were taught that the hope of the nation rested with a powerful president. Active presidents—Lincoln, Roosevelt, Truman—were eulogized; passive presidents—Coolidge, Hoover, Eisenhower—were ridiculed. Leading establishment scholars such as Harvard's Richard Neustadt taught that presidents should conduct themselves so as to maximize their power. These political analysts led Americans to believe that because the president is the only official elected by *all* the people, the presidential powers would be used to "do good."

But then came several presidents—Johnson, Nixon, and Reagan—whom the nation's liberal intellectuals distrusted. As a result, establishment views of the presidency did an about-face. The Vietnam War and Watergate convinced liberal intellectuals that the presidency was too powerful and that Congress must more actively check the actions of unruly presidents. What liberals had earlier praised as the *use* of presidential power became now the *abuse* of power—"the imperial presidency."[7] Many commentators, journalists, intellectuals, as well as Congress members, argued the importance of curtailing the president's war-making powers, overseeing White House activities, and protecting the nation from the abuses of presidential power.

War and the Constitution

The American colonists who declared their independence from Britain in 1776 were deeply suspicious of standing armies and of a king who would send British troops to the colonies. Their distrust carried over after independence, causing the Founding Fathers to make military affairs subject to civilian control. The Second Continental Congress had overseen the conduct of the military during the Revolutionary War. It commissioned George Washington to be Commander in Chief but instructed him "punctually to observe and follow such orders and directions . . . from this or a future Congress." Washington chaired the Constitutional Convention of 1787, and he recognized the need for a strong chief executive who could respond quickly to threats to the nation. Moreover, he was aware of the weaknesses of civilian militia and favored a national army and navy.

The Constitutional Convention of 1787 divided the war power between Congress and the president. Article I, Section 8, states, "The Congress shall have the power to . . . provide for the common defense . . . to declare war . . .

to raise and support armies . . . to provide and maintain a navy . . . to make rules for the government and regulation of the land and naval forces." But Article II, Section 2, states, "The President shall be Commander in Chief of the army and navy of the United States."

Historically the president has exercised the nation's war-making powers. Since 1789 U.S. forces have participated in military actions overseas on more than 150 occasions, but Congress has declared war only five times: the War of 1812, the Mexican War, the Spanish-American War, World War I, and World War II. Supreme Court Justice William H. Rehnquist wrote before he was elevated to the Court:

> *It has been recognized from the earliest days of the Republic, by the President, by Congress and by the Supreme Court, that the United States may lawfully engage in armed hostilities with a foreign power without Congressional declaration of war. Our history is replete with instances of "undeclared wars" from the war with France in 1789-1800 to the Vietnamese War.*[8]

The Supreme Court has generally refused to take jurisdiction in cases involving the war powers of the president and Congress.

Thus, whereas Congress retains the formal power to "declare war," in modern times wars are seldom "declared." Instead, they begin with direct military actions, and the president, as Commander in Chief of the armed forces, determines what those actions will be. Over the years Congress generally recognized the supremacy of the president in military affairs. Not until the Vietnam War was there serious congressional debate over who has or should have the power to commit the nation to war. In the past, Congress tended to accept the fact that under modern conditions of war only the president has the information-gathering facilities and the ability to act with the speed and secrecy required for military decisions during periods of crisis.

The War in Vietnam

The war in Vietnam was not an unprecedented use of the president's war-making powers. John Adams fought a war against the French without a congressional declaration; Thomas Jefferson fought the Barbary pirates; presidents throughout most of the nineteenth century fought the Indians; Abraham Lincoln carried presidential war-making powers further than any president before or since; Woodrow Wilson sent troops to Mexico and a dozen Latin American nations; Franklin D. Roosevelt sent U.S. destroyers to protect British convoys in the North Atlantic before Pearl Harbor; and Harry Truman committed American forces to a major war in Korea. So when President Johnson ordered bombing attacks on North Vietnam in 1965, and eventually committed more than half a million men to the battle, he was not really assuming any greater powers than those assumed by presidents before him (see the section "Vietnam: Elite Failure to Lead" in Chapter 3).

In the early days of the Vietnam War, the liberal leadership of the nation strongly supported the effort, and no one questioned the president's power to commit the nation to war. However, by 1969 most liberal Democratic congressional leaders who had supported the war in its early stages had rushed to become doves. Indeed, senators argued over who had been the first to change his mind about the war. Moreover, with a new, Republican president, Richard Nixon and a Democratic Congress, congressional attacks on presidential policy became much more partisan. As public opposition to the Vietnam War grew, and with the presidency and Congress now controlled by different parties, Congress sought to reassert its role in war-making decisions.

The War Powers Act

In 1973 the Congress passed the War Powers Act, designed to restrict presidential war-making powers. President Nixon vetoed the bill, but the Watergate affair appeared to undermine his support in this struggle with Congress, and Congress overrode his veto. The act is an interesting example of the continuing struggle over checks and balances in the U.S. government. The act has these provisions:

1. In the absence of a congressional declaration of war, the president can commit armed forces to hostilities or to "situations where imminent involvement in hostilities is clearly indicated by the circumstances" only:

   a. To repel an armed attack on the United States or to forestall the "direct and imminent threat of such an attack."

   b. To repel an armed attack against U.S. armed forces outside the United States or to forestall the threat of such attack.

   c. To protect and evacuate U.S. citizens and nationals in another country if their lives are threatened.

    d.   With specific statutory authorization by Congress, not to be inferred from any existing or future law or treaty unless Congress so specifies.

2. The president must report promptly to Congress the commitment of forces for such purposes.

3. Involvement of U.S. forces must be no longer than sixty days unless Congress authorizes their continued use by specific legislation.

4. Congress can end a presidential commitment by a concurrent resolution, an action that does not require the president's signature.

Presidential Noncompliance

The War Powers Act raises serious constitutional questions. Clearly any Commander in Chief can order military forces to go anywhere. Congress cannot constitutionally command troops, yet that is what the act attempts to do by specifying that troops must come home if Congress orders them to do so or if Congress simply fails to endorse the president's decision to commit them. No president—Democrat or Republican—can allow Congress to usurp this presidential authority.

President Ford ignored the act in sending U.S. forces to rescue the U.S. ship *Mayaguez* from the Cambodians in 1976. President Carter did not notify Congress prior to ordering U.S. military forces to attempt rescuing American embassy personnel held hostage in Iran, an effort that ended in disaster in the desert. After President Reagan had committed troops to Lebanon in 1983, Congress tried to invoke the War Powers Act by authorizing an eighteen-month stay for U.S. marines. The president proclaimed the act unconstitutional and Secretary of State George Shultz made it clear that the administration would keep the troops there as long as it desired. (The death of more than two hundred marines in a suicide act by an Islamic faction that October persuaded Reagan to withdraw U.S. troops from Lebanon). U.S. troops invaded the tiny Caribbean island of Grenada in 1983. Informing Congress *after* the act, Reagan made no mention of the sixty-day limitation imposed by the War Powers Act.

President George Bush ignored the War Powers Act in ordering the invasion of Panama in 1989 and in sending U.S. forces to Saudi Arabia in August 1990, following Saddam Hussein's invasion of Kuwait. Bush claimed he had the constitutional power to order U.S. military forces to liberate Kuwait from Iraqi occupation, whether or not Congress authorized the action. Bush ordered military preparations to begin, and despite its misgivings, Congress voted to authorize the use of force a few days before U.S. air attacks began. Rapid military victory in the ensuing Persian Gulf War silenced congressional critics.

President Clinton ordered U.S. troops into Bosnia as part of a "peace-keeping" operation in 1995. No mention was made of the War Powers Act even though Bosnia clearly presented a situation "where imminent involvement in hostilities is clearly indicated by the circumstances." But the fortunate absence of U.S. casualties in Bosnia silenced criticism in Congress. Clinton informed key members of Congress about "Operation Desert Fox"— an air bombardment targeted on Iraq's capabilities in weapons of mass destruction—only a few hours before the attack began.

Yet the War Powers Act reminds presidents that if the fighting goes badly, becomes protracted, or fails to produce decisive results, Congress is likely to desert the president.

WATERGATE AND THE LIMITS OF PRESIDENTIAL POWER

The president must govern the nation within the boundaries of elite consensus. Mass opinion can be manipulated, but elite opinion is a powerful restraint on executive action.

The forced resignation of President Nixon in 1973 is one of the most dramatic illustrations in American history of the president's dependence on elite support. A president reelected by an overwhelming majority had to resign his office less than two years after his landslide victory. We contend that Nixon's threatened impeachment and subsequent resignation were not a result of specific misdeeds or improprieties in office. Instead, Nixon's demise was a result of (1) his general isolation from established elites, (2) his failure to adopt an accommodating style of politics, and (3) his frequent disregard of traditional "rules of the game."

Isolation from Established Elites

Nixon's ouster was chiefly a result of his isolation from established elites and the suspicion, distrust, and hostility generated by his isolation. Established Eastern elites never fully accepted him. Despite his apprenticeship in a top Wall Street law firm, he was always regarded as opportunistic, uncultured, and middle class by the Eastern corporate and financial leaders he served, by influential segments of the news media, and by intellectuals in prestigious universities and foundations. Nixon was upwardly mobile, competitive, self-conscious, boorish; he stood in marked contrast to the wealthy, cool, self-assured, aristocratic John F. Kennedy. Nixon fought his way up—from rooms over his father's grocery store, through the local, unprestigious Whittier College (California), to Duke Law School (North Carolina)—by self-sacrifice and hard work, long hours of studying, and postponement of pleasures and luxuries.

Nixon's personality made it difficult for him to engage in the friendly, handshaking, backslapping politics that his predecessor Lyndon Johnson had developed into a fine art. As a consequence Nixon never fit comfortably into the accommodationist style of elite interaction. Nixon did not enjoy politics; he was by nature a loner.

Nixon's style was to confront crisis directly, to avoid surrender, to test his own strength of character against adversity. His instinct in a crisis was to "fight like hell" rather than to bargain, accommodate, and compromise.

Violating Rules of the Game

The Watergate bugging and burglary of Democratic national headquarters violated established "rules of the game." Elites and masses in the United States have generally condoned repressive acts against communists, subversives, and "radicals." But turning these tactics against established political opposition—Democrats, liberals, and assorted presidential critics—clearly violates elite consensus.

Yet despite all the media's revelations, Nixon would *not* have had to resign if he had publicly repented and cooperated with Congress, the news media, and representatives of the Eastern establishment in cleansing his administration.

But he did not. Instead, as the Nixon White House tapes later revealed, he authorized cash payments to the Watergate burglars to keep quiet about their connections to the White House and the president's reelection campaign.

The Irony of Richard Nixon

It is ironic that Richard Nixon saw himself as a tribune of the people—"the great silent majority," as he identified them—pitting himself against a liberal establishment that was not properly elected and did not reflect grass-roots sentiments. Nixon believed he understood "middle America," and he probably did, since he was middle American himself. But in the end, established elites turned middle America against him. Public opinion is unstable, changeable, and susceptible to manipulation by the mass media. In six months in 1973, Nixon suffered the steepest plunge in public opinion approval ratings ever recorded.

Richard Nixon failed to understand that without elite support, even landslide victories at the polls are meaningless. Popular majorities elect a president, but a president can govern only with the support of the nation's elite. Nixon learned this costly lesson in his "final crisis."[9]

GEORGE BUSH: THE DUAL PRESIDENCY

George Bush's presidency clearly illustrated the dual nature of the office—global leadership combined with domestic policy making. Bush succeeded in his global responsibilities but failed in his domestic ones.

George Bush spent most of his public life preparing for foreign policy leadership—as the U.S. representative to the United Nations, ambassador to China, director of Central Intelligence—even before his two terms as vice president. He became president at a turning point in world history—the collapse of communism in Eastern Europe, the end of the Soviet-led Warsaw Pact military alliance, and the disintegration of the Soviet Union itself. He was given the opportunity to declare Western victory in the decades-long Cold War, and to lay the foundation for a "new world order" in which the United States occupied the predominant global position.

Perhaps his finest hour was his resolute performance in the Persian Gulf War, during which he assembled a worldwide political coalition, including the former Soviet Union and the Arab nations, against Saddam Hussein's invasion and occupation of Kuwait. Bush wisely left the strategic planning and implementation of military operations to a capable team consisting of Defense Secretary Richard Cheney, Chairman of the Joint Chiefs of Staff Colin Powell, and field commander General Norman Schwarzkopf. He avoided the mistakes of Vietnam—gradual escalation of force, prolonged operations, accumulating casualties, muddled negotiations, moratoriums on bombings, and political interference in military operations. Instead, he sought a rapid, decisive military victory with the use of overwhelming force. He sought to limit casualties among American and coalition forces, and perhaps ended the war too soon. But his overall performance as commander in chief temporarily earned Bush the highest public approval ratings ever attained by an American president.

By contrast, in the domestic policy arena, George Bush was a failure. He came into office with no clear policy agenda, publicly referring to "the vision thing" as a public relations gimmick rather than as a guide for the nation. He lacked his predecessor Ronald Reagan's ideological commitments. On key issues he collapsed in the face of pressures from the Democratic Congress. He campaigned on as firm a promise as any candidate could make on taxes: "Read my lips! No new taxes!" Yet in his second year in office, he agreed to support an increase in the top income tax rate from 28 to 31 percent. And when recession struck the nation's economy, he responded with too little too late, leaving the impression that he was out of touch with the concerns of the American people.

George Bush's two presidencies were represented by *Time* magazine's presentation of its first and only "Men [plural] of the Year" award in 1991, and a double-exposure cover picture. "He seemed almost to be two presidents; turning to the world two faces that were not just different but also had few features in common. One was a foreign policy profile that was a study in resoluteness and courage, the other a domestic visage just as strongly marked by wavering and confusion."[10]

BILL CLINTON: AMBITION AND AMBIVALENCE

Bill Clinton has been "running for president all of his life."[11] As a teenage delegate to Boys Nation, he won a handshake from President John F. Kennedy in 1963. He chose to attend Georgetown University in Washington to be near the nation's centers of power. "By the time I was seventeen I knew I wanted to be what I'm doing now . . . and I knew that if I was in school in Washington I would have many opportunities to learn a lot."[12] As soon as he arrived in the capital he called on his state's U.S. senator, William J. Fulbright, chairman of the Senate Foreign Relations Committee, and won a part-time job as a legislative aide. Ambitious and competitive in the classroom (Phi Beta Kappa) and in student government (president of his freshman and sophomore classes), Clinton won a Rhodes scholarship to Oxford University with the help of Senator Fulbright, himself a former Rhodes scholar.

"Saved" from the Draft

Clinton never finished a degree at Oxford, but he cultivated friendships that would later enhance his public career. In London he helped organize anti–Vietnam War demonstrations, even while he worried that his antiwar activities might someday come back to haunt his political ambitions. When he received a draft notice, he promptly enrolled in the ROTC program at the University of Arkansas, making himself temporarily ineligible for the draft. Later, draft calls were cut back as President Richard Nixon deescalated the war, and a lottery system was instituted. Clinton drew a high number, making him unlikely to be drafted. Soon after he wrote to the ROTC, withdrawing his name, "Thank you for saving me from the draft . . .", and acknowledging that his real plans were to go to Yale Law School, which he entered in 1970. He continued to be active in the antiwar movement while in law school, and in 1972 he was George McGovern's Texas campaign manager. He met his future wife, Hillary Rodham, a classmate at Yale and a graduate of Wellesley.

Getting Started in Politics

Upon graduation from Yale Law School, Clinton turned down offers to return to Washington as a congressional staff aide. He was eager to launch his own political career and he knew that the road to elective office ran through his home state. He accepted a short-term post teaching law at the University of Arkansas, but within a year he was running for a seat in Congress. Trying to capitalize on the Watergate scandal, he challenged a veteran Republican congressman. As a young law professor with long sixties'-style hair, a Yale and Oxford background, and liberal friends such as Hillary Rodham coming from Washington to help in the campaign, he could have lost by a wide margin in conservative Arkansas. Instead, he came within a few votes of defeating a strong incumbent, in part as a result of the Watergate scandal which swept many Democrats into Congress in 1974, and in part as a result of his own tireless campaigning.

Clinton's strong showing in the 1974 congressional race against a well-entrenched incumbent won him political recognition statewide. When the state's elected attorney general vacated the post to run for Congress, Clinton mounted a successful campaign to replace him. He used the post to establish a reputation as a consumer advocate battling the big utility companies. In

1978, when Governor David Pryor left office to run for the U.S. Senate, Clinton jumped into the open gubernatorial contest and became the nation's youngest governor at age 32. Viewing himself as a vanguard of a new generation, he set about pushing a broad program of liberal reform for Arkansas, increasing taxes and expenditures. Nevertheless, as a Yale-educated Rhodes scholar, he appeared to be an arrogant, isolated, crusading, liberal politician, out of touch with his more conservative Arkansas constituency. He was defeated for reelection as governor in 1980.

Remolding His Image

Clinton's defeat "forever influenced the way he approached government and politics."[13] He proceeded to remold himself into a political moderate, calling for "workfare" to replace welfare, supporting the death penalty, and working to create a favorable business climate in Arkansas. He cut his hair and his wife began using her married name, so as not to offend social conservatives. He told his state's voters that he had been humbled by his earlier loss and he promised "to listen to the people." He was elected governor once again in 1982. By most accounts, Bill Clinton became a successful governor. He focused his energies on two areas: economic development and education. He raised taxes for education and forced both students and teachers to take competency tests. He declared himself an environmentalist but granted concessions to his state's giant chicken industry in the interest of the economy. His many compromises and accommodations led to his "slick Willie" label by the *Arkansas Democrat Gazette*.

Just as he had shaped his image to better fit his Arkansas constituents, he molded his national image as a "new" Democrat—concerned with economic growth, favoring workfare over welfare, tough on crime, and willing to stand up to traditional core Democratic interest groups such as labor unions, minorities, and government employees. He served for a while as chairman of the centrist Democratic Leadership Conference (DLC). He used the DLC as a platform to promote a winning Democratic presidential profile—a moderate, pro-business, pro-investment Democrat, capable of winning back the support of the white middle class. He espoused "neoliberal" ideas about government's role in promoting and "investing" in American industry, and he began winning constituents among Wall Street and business interests. In his winning campaign for the presidency in 1992, he promised everything to everybody: "We can be pro-growth and pro-environment, we can be pro-business and pro-labor, we can make government work again by making it more aggressive and leaner and more effective at the same time, and we can be pro-family and pro-choice."[14]

First-Term Ambivalence

The portrait of the Bill Clinton presidency that emerges is one of indefatigable activity in pursuit of no fixed goals other than "to crawl through to reelection."[15] No one doubts that Clinton is one of the most intelligent men ever to occupy the Oval Office, and that his knowledge of the details of government and public policy exceeds any other recent president. But with no firm sense of direction, no strong commitments other than reelection, no fixed ideological compass, the Clinton first-term presidency suffered "deep, near terminal ambivalence." Liberal and moderate factions continually warred with each other for Clinton's support. The moderates sought to pull the president to the center, that is, to curtail spending, moderate taxing, and reduce deficits. Liberals, including Hillary Rodham Clinton, sought the support of the president for big spending programs and heavy taxes on "the rich." But the real conflict was not so much between warring factions as it was within Clinton's mind. Each day brought wide swings in the president's pronouncements, flip-flops on his policy stances, and near paralysis in his decision making.

The sweeping Republican congressional victory in 1994 posed new conflicts for Clinton. Should he respond by moving back to the center, moderating his big spending plans, cooperating with Republicans in Congress on budget cutting and welfare reform? Or should he continue to fight for liberal policies and large-scale government programs, challenging the Republican Congress to reject his initiatives, and then campaign for reelection in the fashion of Harry Truman, by castigating a "do nothing" Congress?

Typically, Clinton followed *both* political strategies simultaneously. He encouraged Senate Democrats to defeat the balanced-budget amendment and he vetoed several Republican balanced-budget plans. When the government temporarily "shut down," Clinton uncharacteristically stood firm and shifted blame to the Republican Congress. He cast himself as the defender of "Medicare, Medicaid, education, and the environment"—against mean-spirited Republican budget cutters. Yet he signed the Republican welfare bill that he had vetoed twice. The Oklahoma City bombing seemed to warn the nation about the dangers of "extremism." Clinton's approval ratings began a long rise.

Second Term "Small Deal"

Following his reelection, Clinton announced—"The era of big government is over." Rather than champion large-scale change in the fashion of Roosevelt's New Deal, Clinton shifted to what might be labeled the "Small Deal"—an assembly of small changes easily understood by the American people and not costing very much. This shift toward minipolicies— V-chips, school uniforms, gun control, time off for family emergencies, longer stays in maternity wards—attracted female voters. (In 1996 men divided their vote almost equally between Clinton and Dole, but women voted for Clinton by a stunning 54 to 38 margin.)

Republicans and conservatives claimed that he won reelection as a deficit-cutting, welfare-reforming, more-cops-on-the beat president, that is, by "stealing" traditional Republican issues. Conservatives complained that Clinton ran from the right but governed from the left. Liberals complained that Clinton abandoned liberal principles when he thought it was to his political advantage to do so.

Clinton's "Place in History"

Second-term presidents often become highly attentive to their place in history, that is, to establishing a lasting legacy for which they will be forever remembered. But even before the Oval Office sex scandal revelations, critics of President Clinton described his second term as adrift and aimless. He spoke on a multitude of policy proposals, but he did not focus on any single issue as his overriding priority.

Clinton's second-term popular approval ratings were high—over 60 percent—an impressive level for any president. His popularity with the masses remained undiminished by sexual scandal. Most commentators attributed his high ratings to the nation's healthy economy—continued economic growth, low employment, low inflation. In "good times" there is no great demand by the people for major new program or policy directions, or great concern about the president's private sexual conduct.

The booming economy also provided a temporary solution to what had been the most vexing of all government problems—continuing deficit spending. Robust economic growth increased federal tax revenues enough to produce a projected balanced federal budget—a goal that had eluded presidents and Congresses for over a quarter century.

But Bill Clinton's presidency will be forever tainted by his personal moral lapses and the resulting House impeachment vote. The president's defenders argue that his misconduct, however objectionable, did not rise to the level of impeachable offenses as defined in the Constitution—"Treason,

FOCUS

Presidential Sex

Power itself may be an aphrodisiac, as Henry Kissinger once remarked. Or it may be that the media's current focus on the private life of public figures reveals flaws that affect many of us yet go unreported. Whatever the explanation, an unseemingly number of powerful men appear to have engaged in illicit sexual affairs.

★ George Washington wrote passionate letters professing his love to Sarah Cary Fairfax, known as "Sally," the wife of his best friend and neighbor at Mount Vernon. There is no evidence that they had intimate relations, but while he destroyed her correspondence to him, she kept his letters all her life, which is how their romance became known.

★ Thomas Jefferson is known or suspected to have had several extramarital partners, including Sally Hemmings, a slave at Monticello, his Virginia plantation.

★ In 1884, Republicans chided Democratic candidate Grover Cleveland for his relationship with Maria Crifts Halpin by pushing baby carriages through the streets and chanting, "Ma! Ma! Where's my Pa?" After Cleveland was elected, Democrats responded to the chant with one of their own—"Gone to the White House, Ha! Ha! Ha!"

★ Woodrow Wilson prepared a White House press release in case his relationship with Mary Peck, a young divorcée he had met while vacationing in Bermuda, became known. It was not published, but in the release, Wilson admitted to "a passage of folly and gross impertinence," and said he "had forgotten standards of honorable behavior."

★ Franklin D. Roosevelt reportedly had several extramarital affairs, including one over many years with Lucy Page Mercer, his wife Eleanor's social secretary. It was Mercer, not Eleanor, who was with him at his retreat in Warm Springs, Ga., on April 12, 1945, when he had a stroke and died.

★ Dwight Eisenhower's relationship with his World War II driver, Kay Summersby Morgan, became public when her biography was published in 1976, a year after her death. His wartime commander, Gen. George Marshall, and President Harry Truman had been aware of the relationship and squelched reports of it.

★ John F. Kennedy's encounters with numerous women, including movie star Marilyn Monroe and Judith Exner, a girlfriend of Chicago mobster Sam Giancana inspired books about "the dark side of Camelot."

★ Lyndon Johnson, upon hearing stories of JFK's sexual exploits, once boasted, "Hell, I've screwed more women by accident than he has on purpose!" Madeleine Brown, a radio advertising buyer for a Dallas ad agency, claimed in 1987 that she had been LBJ's mistress for twenty-one years and that he was the father of her son. Her son sued Johnson's widow, Lady Bird, seeking $10.5 million and claiming he had been deprived of his rightful inheritance. He died before the suit was resolved.

Bribery or other high Crimes and Misdemeanors." And indeed, it is unlikely that the Founders envisioned extramarital sex, or lying about it under oath, or lying to the American people about it, as impeachable offenses. Clinton's defenders argue that the removal of a popularly elected president from office should occur only for offenses that threaten the nation's security or its constitutional order. And his defenders also point to the polarized party-line impeachment vote in the House of Representatives as evidence of partisan vengeance at work.

Yet Clinton's mere survival in office is not likely to win him a high ranking among the nation's presidents. He may not have been the only president

FOCUS

Hillary "Stand by Your Man"

Hillary Rodham Clinton is not the first politically powerful first lady with strong ties to liberal interest groups. That distinction belongs to Eleanor Roosevelt; however, in her era the power of the first lady was exercised in a more subtle fashion.

Hillary Rodham grew up in suburban Chicago, the daughter of wealthy parents who sent her to the private, prestigious Wellesley College. A "Goldwater Girl" in high school, Hillary quickly reversed political directions to become a leader in radical and antiwar politics on campus. A 1969 honors graduate with a counterculture image—horn-rimmed glasses, long, straggling hair, no makeup—she was chosen by her classmates to give a commencement speech—a largely inarticulate rambling about "more immediate, ecstatic, and penetrating modes of living." (Years later her views would coalesce around the New Age writings of leftist Jewish thinker Michael Learner, who coined the phrase "the politics of meaning.")

At Yale Law School Hillary met a long-haired, bearded Rhodes scholar from Arkansas, Bill Clin-

ton, who was just as politically ambitious as she was. Both Hillary and Bill received their law degrees in 1973. Bill returned to Arkansas to build a career in state politics, while Hillary went to Washington as an attorney, first, for the liberal lobbying group, the Children's Defense Fund, and later, on the staff of the House Judiciary Committee seeking to impeach President Nixon. But Hillary and other Yale grads traveled to Arkansas to help Bill run unsuccessfully for Congress in 1974. Hillary decided to stay with Bill in Little Rock; they married before his next campaign, a successful run for state attorney general in 1976. Hillary remained Hillary Rodham, even as her husband went on to the governorship in 1978. She taught briefly at the University of Arkansas Law School and eventually joined Little Rock's influential Rose Law Firm. She kept her Washington ties with the Children's Defense Fund. She also became a director of Wal-Mart Stores, TCBY Enterprises, the LaFarge Corporation, and the federal government's Legal Services Corporation. Her husband's 1980 defeat for reelection as governor was blamed on his liberal leanings; therefore, in his 1982 comeback Bill repackaged himself as a moderate and centrist. Hillary cooperated by becoming Mrs. Bill Clinton, shedding her horn rims for contacts, blonding her hair, and echoing her husband's more moderate line. These tactics helped propel them back into the governor's mansion.

ever to engage in sexual misconduct (see Focus: "Presidential Sex"). But he brought greater public embarrassment to the office of the presidency than any of his predecessors, and the legacy of the impeachment vote in the House of Representatives will always tarnish his place in history.

OTHER EXECUTIVE ELITES

The presidency is not one person but more than five thousand permanent employees in the executive office of the president, which includes the White House Office, the Office of Management and Budget, the Council of

---

Hillary was far from the traditional governor's wife. She chaired the governor's task force on education and drew up his key educational reform package. She became a full partner in the Rose firm, regularly earning over $200,000 a year (while Bill earned only $35,000 as Arkansas governor). She won national recognition as one of the "100 most influential lawyers in the United States" according to the *American National Law Journal*. She chaired the American Bar Association's Commission on Women and the Profession.

Hillary's support for Bill's presidential ambitions was absolutely crucial to his success. Married life in the governor's mansion was at best "rocky," as Bill and Hillary would later acknowledge on national television. Rumors of Bill's "womanizing" had long circulated in Little Rock, and they broke into the national news early in the presidential race when Gennifer Flowers held a press conference, describing a long-term affair with the governor and playing tapes of their telephone conversations. Similar charges had destroyed the promising presidential candidacy of Gary Hart four years earlier. The focus was on Hillary when Don Hewitt, producer of *60 Minutes*, offered the Clintons prime time Sunday night following the Super Bowl to respond. In a very convincing performance, Bill and Hillary acknowledged that their marriage had been "shaky" but it was "rock solid" now. While never specifically acknowledging infi-

delity, Bill Clinton went further than any presidential candidate in describing his marital life. Hillary stood by her man.

In January 1993, newly elected President Bill Clinton named Hillary head of the President's Task Force on National Health Reform. Once installed as the "health czar," she moved expeditiously in the corridors of power. Her task force assembled a formidable array of staff, consultants, and committees. The *New York Times* dubbed her "St. Hillary" because of her unyielding commitment, a determination that did not stand her in good stead with powerful interest groups such as the American Medical Association and the American Association of Retired People, or with the members of Congress in whose hands the fate of Hillary's plans rested. The defeat of Hillary's health care plan caused her to temporarily assume a less public role in Washington politics.

It seems ironic that the most important contribution to the presidency of such an active, educated, and self-directed woman as Hillary eventually turned out to be her steadfast support of her husband in the face of charges of sexual misconduct. It was Hillary who counterattacked, alleging that "a vast right-wing conspiracy" was behind the charges. Hillary's "stand by your man" public posture appeared to be the central factor in Bill's continued popularity with the masses.

Economic Advisers, the National Security Council, the National Aeronautics and Space Council, the Office of Emergency Planning, and the Office of Science and Technology. In addition there is the presidential cabinet, consisting of heads of fourteen major executive departments. Finally, more than forty independent agencies function outside the regular departmental organization of the executive branch, including the Interstate Commerce Commission, the Federal Reserve Board, the Federal Trade Commission, the Federal Power Commission, the Federal Communications Commission, the Securities and Exchange Commission, the National Labor Relations Board, the Civil Aeronautics Board, and the Atomic Energy Commission (see Chapter 11).

Closest to the president is a group of aides and assistants who work with the chief executive in the White House Office, which the president can organize as he sees fit. These aides and assistants perform whatever duties the president assigns them. They usually include a chief of staff, a press secretary, an appointment secretary, and one or more special assistants for liaison with Congress. Some of the president's assistants have ad hoc assignments, while others have a specialty.

Staff Power

Increasingly White House staff members have come to exercise great power in the name of the president. They frequently direct affairs in the name of the president ("The president has asked me to tell you . . . "), but the president may have little direct oversight of their activities. Even more serious is the fact that staff members may come into power with little preparation or experience for elite membership. Often their training consists of nothing more than serving as "advance guard" in presidential election campaigns: scheduling presidential appearances, handling campaign advertising, and fetching coffee and doughnuts. These staff are valued not for their independent contributions to policy but rather for their personal loyalty to the president. Frequently in recent presidential administrations, staff members have embarrassed the president.

The Iran-Contra Scandal

Perhaps it was inevitable that the Reagan administration would fall prey to a major scandal. Reagan delegated more authority to the various executive staffs than any of his predecessors. The Iran-Contra scandal grew out of President Reagan's strong personal commitment to secure the release of hostages held by Iranian-backed terrorists in Lebanon, together with "a management style that put the principal responsibility for policy review and implementation on the shoulders of his advisors."[16] When Secretary of State George Shultz and Secretary of Defense Caspar Weinberger strongly recommended that the president *not* undertake trading arms for hostages, the president turned to his National Security Council staff to carry out the assignment. National Security Advisor John McFarlane and his staff assistant, marine Lieutenant Colonel Oliver North traveled secretly to Iran to negotiate the exchange. Although President Reagan denies that a trading arms for hostages deal was what he intended, investigators concluded that "whatever the intent, almost from the beginning the initiative became in fact a series of arms for hostages deals." To further complicate matters, Lieutenant Colonel North, with the knowledge and approval of National Security Advisor John Poindexter (who had replaced McFarlane), diverted money from the arms sales to support the Contra forces in Nicaragua in their fight against the communist Sandinista government. President Reagan claims to have had no knowledge of this use of the funds, and no evidence emerged in the many investigations on the matter to contradict his claim. But the president generally backed the Contras at a time when Congress by law had directed that no U.S. funds be spent for their military support. At the very least, President Reagan was guilty of loose supervision of his White House staff.

Clinton's White House

President Clinton's first chief of staff, boyhood friend Thomas F. McLarty, came to Washington from Little Rock with no experience in the nation's capital. He was soon washed overboard by the heavy seas of Washington politics, for which he was unprepared. He failed in the first responsibility of a chief of staff—to protect his boss from political damage. A more experienced chief of staff might have saved Clinton from various early political embarrassments—the dispute over homosexuals in the military, Clinton's $200 haircut, the firing of the White House travel staff, the strained relations with key Democratic Congress members, and the poor handling of reporters' questions regarding Bill and Hillary's Whitewater real estate investment. McLarty was replaced after the first year by the experienced former Congress member Leon Panetta, who brought somewhat more order to the White House.

Panetta resigned at the end of Clinton's first term. His replacement, Erskine Bowles, was a multimillionaire businessman from North Carolina and a major fund-raiser in Clinton's campaigns. He served sixteen months as deputy chief of staff under Panetta before assuming the top White House staff post. Indeed, Clinton's second-term staff appointments were generally older, wiser, and more experienced than the young faces who first came to the White House with Bill and Hillary.

Summary

The president is the popular symbol of governmental authority. However, presidents are substantially less able to control decisions than they would like.

1. Governmental elites in the United States do not command; they seek consensus. Governmental decision making involves bargaining, accommodation, and compromise among government and nongovernment elites. Our examination of the presidency provides clear evidence of the consensual nature of elite interaction and the heavy price a president must pay for failure to accommodate other elites.

2. Presidential power depends not on formal authority but on personal abilities of persuasion. Moreover, the president must still function within the established elite system. The choices available to presidents are limited to alternatives for which elite support can be mobilized. Despite access to mass opinion, the president can be effectively checked by other public and private elites.

3. For the masses, the president is the symbol of the government and the nation itself. Presidential popularity with the masses depends upon their perception of dynamic leadership in the face of crises. Prolonged stalemated wars erode presidential popularity, as do economic recessions.

4. Good economic times raise presidential popularity. Clinton's continued high ratings, despite widely publicized charges of sexual misconduct, suggest that the masses believe that private morality is unrelated to the evaluation of presidential performance in office.

5. The president can use his popularity with the masses to strengthen his position in dealings with other elites, notably Congress. Clinton's high ratings in the polls are his best defense against removal from office.

6. Controversies over presidential power are always linked to their political context. While liberal writers generally praise strong presidents in history, during the Vietnam War they turned against the presidency under Johnson and Nixon. Congress passed the War Powers Act in an unsuccessful effort to gain control over military interventions.

7. The forced resignation of President Nixon was a dramatic illustration of the president's dependence on elite support. A president must govern within the boundaries of elite consensus or face removal from office. The Constitution states that the president can be removed only for "treason, bribery, or other high crimes and misdemeanors." But in fact the president can also be removed for *political* offenses—violating elite consensus.

8. The president is expected to provide both global leadership and leadership in domestic policy making. George Bush's "dual presidency" illustrated these separate demands on the president. Bush was very successful in foreign policy leadership but failed to convince the nation that he could deal effectively with its domestic concerns.

9. The end of the Cold War refocused the nation on domestic issues. Bill Clinton may be more knowledgeable about public issues than any other person to occupy the Oval Office in modern times. Yet during his first term he failed to provide clear, consistent policy direction for the nation—alternately supporting moderate and liberal policy positions.

10. In his second term, Clinton shifted his attention toward "minipolicies"— modest policy initiatives clearly understood and easily supported by the American people. His mass popularity rose as the economy boomed. Yet his historic legacy as president will be forever tarnished by sexual scandal and the impeachment vote of the House of Representatives.

Notes

1. James David Barber, *The Presidential Character*, 3rd ed. (Englewood Cliffs, N.J.: Prentice-Hall, 1985), p. 2.

2. Fred I. Greenstein, "The Psychological Functions of the Presidency for Citizens," in Elmer E. Cornwell, ed., *The American Presidency: Vital Center* (Chicago: Scott, Foresman, 1966), pp. 30-36.

3. Richard Neustadt, *Presidential Power* (New York: New American Library, 1960), pp. 88-89.

4. Thomas Reeves, *John F. Kennedy* (New York: Kreiger, 1990), p. 190.

5. William Howard Taft, *Our Chief Magistrate and His Powers* (New York: Columbia University Press, 1938), p. 138. Reprinted in John P. Roche and L. W. Levy, eds., *The Presidency* (New York: Harcourt Brace Jovanovich, 1964), p. 23.

6. From Arthur B. Tourtellot, *President on the Presidency* (Garden City, N.Y.: Doubleday, 1964), pp. 55-56.

7. Authur M. Schlesinger, Jr., *The Imperial Presidency* (Boston: Houghton Mifflin, 1973).

8. Congressional Quarterly, *The Power of the Pentagon* (Washington, D.C.: Congressional Quarterly Press, 1972), p. 42.

9. For further information on Richard M. Nixon's career, see his political autobiography, *Six Crises* (Garden City, N.Y.: Doubleday, 1962).

10. *Time* (January 7, 1991): 20.

11. *U.S. News & World Report* (March 30, 1992): 28.

12. Robert E. Levin, *Bill Clinton: The Inside Story* (New York: S.P.I. Books, 1992), p. 35.

13. *New York Times* (July 16, 1992): A14.

14. *Time* (November 2, 1992): 33.

15. Bob Woodward, *The Agenda: Inside the Clinton White House* (New York: Simon & Schuster, 1994), p. 18.

16. *The Tower Commission Report* (New York: Times Books, 1987), p. 80.

Selected Readings

Barber, James David. *The Presidential Character: Predicting Performance in the White House*, 3rd ed. Englewood Cliffs, N.J.: Prentice-Hall, 1985. This extremely readable book seeks to classify presidents along two continua: an "active–passive" baseline, according to the amount of energy and enthusiasm displayed in the exercise of presidential duties, and a "positive–negative" baseline, dealing with the degree of happiness or "fun" each president displays in manipulating presidential power. Using these two baselines, Barber classifies the modern presidents into four types: active–positive (FDR, Truman, Kennedy), active-negative (Wilson, Hoover, Johnson), passive-positive (Taft, Harding), and passive–negative (Coolidge, Eisenhower).

Brody, Richard A. *Assessing Presidents: The Media, Elite Opinion, and Public Support.* Stanford, Calif.: Stanford University Press, 1991. Develops the thesis that media and elite interpretations of presidential actions shape public evaluations of the president; includes analysis of the president's "honeymoon," "rally around the president" events, and the rise and fall of public approval ratings.

Edwards, George C. III. *At the Margins: Presidential Leadership of Congress.* New Haven, Conn.: Yale University Press, 1989. A systematic examination of the factors affecting presidential success in Congress, including presidential popularity, party support, and lobbying efforts.

Lowi, Theodore. *The Personal President.* Ithaca, N.Y.: Cornell University Press, 1985. Lowi traces the process by which "the president" and "the government" become synonymous terms.

Milkus, Stanley, and Michael Nelson. *The American Presidency: Origin and Development, 1776–1990.* Washington, D.C.: Congressional Quarterly Press, 1990. A comprehensive history of the presidency that argues that the institution is best understood by examining its development over time; describes the significant presidential actions in the early days of the Republic that shaped the office, as well as the modern era in which the president has replaced Congress and the political parties as the leading instrument of popular rule.

Woodward, Bob. *The Agenda: Inside the Clinton White House.* New York: Simon & Schuster, 1994. An account of Clinton's first year in office, describing liberal and moderate warring factions in the White House and Clinton's indecision over the direction his presidency should take.

11

The Bureaucratic Elite

The problem is not conspiracy or corruption, but unchecked rule. And being unchecked, the rule reflects not the national need but the bureaucratic need.

—JOHN K. GALBRAITH

Power in the United States is gradually shifting from those who control economic and political resources to those who control technology, information, and expertise. The Washington bureaucracy has become a major base of power in American society—independent of Congress, the president, the courts, and the people. Government bureaucracies invade every aspect of modern life: the home, communications, transportation, the environment, the workplace, schools, the streets.

In theory, a *bureaucracy* is a form of social organization that the German sociologist Max Weber described as having (1) a chain of command (hierarchy); (2) a division of labor among subunits (specialization); (3) specification of authority for positions and units by rules and regulation (span of control); (4) impersonality in executing tasks (neutrality); (5) adaptation of structure, authority, and rules to the organization's goals (goal orientation); and (6) predictability of behavior based on maintenance of records and assurance of rules (standardization).[1] If we use Weber's definition, then both corporations and governments, and many other organizations in society, are bureaucracies.

In practice, *bureaucracy* has become a negative term. People have come to view bureaucracy as bringing with it red tape, paper shuffling, duplication of effort, waste and inefficiency, impersonality, insensitivity, and overregulation. More important, people have come to view governmental bureaucracy as unresponsive to the needs of the nation or the people.

Certainly "the people" have no direct means of altering bureaucratic decisions. Even the president, the White House staff, and cabinet officials have great difficulty establishing control over the bureaucracy. Congress and the courts can place only the broadest restrictions on bureaucratic power. The bureaucrats control information and technology, and they almost invariably outlast their political superiors in office. Very often, in fact, the bureaucrats feel a certain contempt for their superiors because political leaders do not have the information, technical expertise, and experience of the bureaucrats.

SOURCES OF BUREAUCRATIC POWER

The power of bureaucracies grows with advances in technology, increases in information, and growth in the size and complexity of society. Large, complex, technological societies cannot be governed by a single president and 535 members of Congress who lack the expertise, time, and energy to look after the myriad details involved in nuclear power or environmental protection or occupational safety or communications or aviation or trucking or fair employment or hundreds of other aspects of American life. So the president and Congress create bureaucracies, appropriate money for them, and authorize them to draw up detailed rules and regulations to govern us. The bureaucracies receive only vague and general directions from the president and Congress. Actual governance is in the hands of the Nuclear Regulatory Commission, the Environmental Protection Agency, the Occupational Safety and Health Administration, the Federal Communications Commission, the Federal Aviation Administration, the Interstate Commerce Commission, the Equal Employment Opportunity Commission, and hundreds of similar bureaucratic agencies. (There are approximately two thousand federal government agencies with rule-making powers.) One estimate suggests that the bureaucracies announce *twenty* rules or regulations for every *one* law of Congress. In this way, the power to make policy has passed from the president and Congress to the bureaucratic elite.

Organized Expertise

Why is policy making shifted to the bureaucracy? The standard explanation is that Congress and the president do not have the time, energy, or expertise to handle the details of policy making. A related explanation is that the increasing complexity and sophistication of technology require technical experts ("technocrats") to actually carry out the intent of Congress and the president. No single bureaucrat can master the complex activities of even a single large governmental agency—from budgeting, purchasing, personnel, accounting, planning, communication, and organization to the complexities of nuclear plants, energy transmission, the internal revenue (tax) code, or the computerized social security files. Each bureaucrat has relatively little knowledge of overall policy. But that person's narrow expertise, when combined with the narrow expertise of thousands of other bureaucrats, creates an organized base of power that political leaders find difficult to control.

Shifts in Responsibility

A second reason policy making is shifted to the bureaucracy is that Congress and the president deliberately pass vague and ambiguous laws, largely for symbolic reasons—to ensure nuclear safety, protect the environment, ensure occupational safety, allocate broadcasting channels, guarantee flight safety, prevent unfair interstate charges, guarantee "equal employment opportunity," and so on. The bureaucrats' role is to use the "authority" of these symbolic laws to decide what actually will be done. Thus bureaucrats must give meaning to symbolic measures. Frequently Congress and the president do not want to take public responsibility for unpopular policies. They find it easier to blame the bureaucrats and pretend that unpopular policies are a product of an ungovernable Washington bureaucracy. This explanation allows an elected president and an elected Congress to impose regulations without accepting responsibility for them.

Bureaucratic Expansionism

Finally, the bureaucracy itself is now sufficiently powerful to have its own laws passed—laws that allow agencies to expand in size, acquire more authority, and obtain more money. Bureaucracy has become its own source of power. Political scientist James Q. Wilson comments on "the great, almost overpowering, importance of the existing government and professional groups in shaping policy":

> *I am impressed by the extent to which policy making is dominated by the representatives of those bureaucracies and professions having a material stake in the management and funding of the*

> intended policy and by those political staffs who see in a new
> program a chance for publicity, advancement, and a good
> reputation for their superiors.[2]

FOCUS

Mass Attitudes toward Washington Bureaucracies

Opinion polls regularly report that Americans believe "the federal government in Washington" has "too much power." Among federal government agencies, the tax-collecting Internal Revenue Service (IRS) is clearly the most detested. The power of the Central Intelligence Agency (CIA) and the Bureau of Alcohol, Tobacco, and Firearms (ATF) also appear to raise concerns among Americans, no doubt in part because of adverse publicity in recent years. (The CIA was deeply embarrassed in 1994 by the revelation that a high officer, Aldrich Ames, had been paid millions of dollars by Russian agents to work secretly on their behalf; the ATF was strongly criticized for attacking the Branch Davidian compound near Waco, Texas, in 1993.)

In contrast, the U.S. military enjoys a favorable reputation among most Americans, 80 percent of whom believe it has "about the right amount of power" or "not enough." Local government in America and local police are also perceived as having about the right amount or not enough power.

QUESTION: *As I read off the following, please tell me whether you think it has too much power in the United States today, about the right amount of power, or not enough power.*

	TOO MUCH	ABOUT RIGHT	NOT ENOUGH
The federal government in Washington	60%	29%	8%
The Internal Revenue Service	63%	32%	3%
The Central Intelligence Agency	42%	37%	9%
The Federal Bureau of Alcohol, Tobacco, and Firearms	39%	34%	23%
The Federal Bureau of Investigation	32%	48%	16%
The military	17%	57%	23%
The local police in your community	13%	55%	31%

Source: Gallup Poll, 1995

"REMEMBER... NOW, HAGEDORN, YOU NO LONGER WORK FOR THE PRIVATE SECTOR. IN THE PUBLIC SECTOR, THE CUSTOMER IS NEVER RIGHT."

National Review/May 6, 1996.

ORGANIZATION OF THE WASHINGTON BUREAUCRACY

How big is big government? All governments in the United States—the federal government together with fifty state governments and over eighty thousand local governments, including cities, counties, and school and special districts—collectively spend about 35 percent of the gross national product (GNP), the sum of all goods and services produced in the nation. The federal government alone accounts for 23 percent of the GNP, and all other governments account for 12 percent. The "private sector" accounts for the remaining 65 percent of the GNP; however, most, if not all, of the private sector comes under governmental regulation.

The executive branch of the U.S. government includes fourteen departments, over sixty independent executive agencies operating outside these departments, and the large Executive Office of the President (see Figure 11-1).

Cabinet The cabinet rarely functions as a group. It consists of the secretaries of the fourteen executive departments, the vice president, the UN ambassador, the CIA director, and the special trade representative, with the president as its head. Cabinet officers in the United States are powerful because they head giant administrative organizations. The secretary of state, the secretary of defense, the secretary of the treasury, the attorney general, and to a lesser extent the other departmental secretaries are all people of power and prestige in America. But the cabinet, as a council, rarely makes policy.[3] Seldom does a strong president hold a cabinet meeting to decide important policy questions. More frequently, the president knows what he wants and holds cabinet meetings only to help him sell his views.

NSC The National Security Council (NSC) resembles a cabinet; the president is chairman and the vice president, secretary of state, secretary of defense, and director of the Office of Emergency Planning (a minor unit in the executive office) are participating members. The chairman of the Joint Chiefs of Staff and the director of the Central Intelligence Agency are advisors to the NSC. A special assistant to the president for national security affairs heads the NSC staff. The purposes of the council are to advise the president on security policy and to coordinate foreign, military, and domestic policies. However, in the Iran-Contra scandal a staff member of the NSC, Lieutenant Colonel Oliver North, undertook an operational role in security policy. As a result, various investigative committees strongly recommended that the NSC staff confine itself to an advisory role.

FIGURE 11-1 The organization of the U.S. government

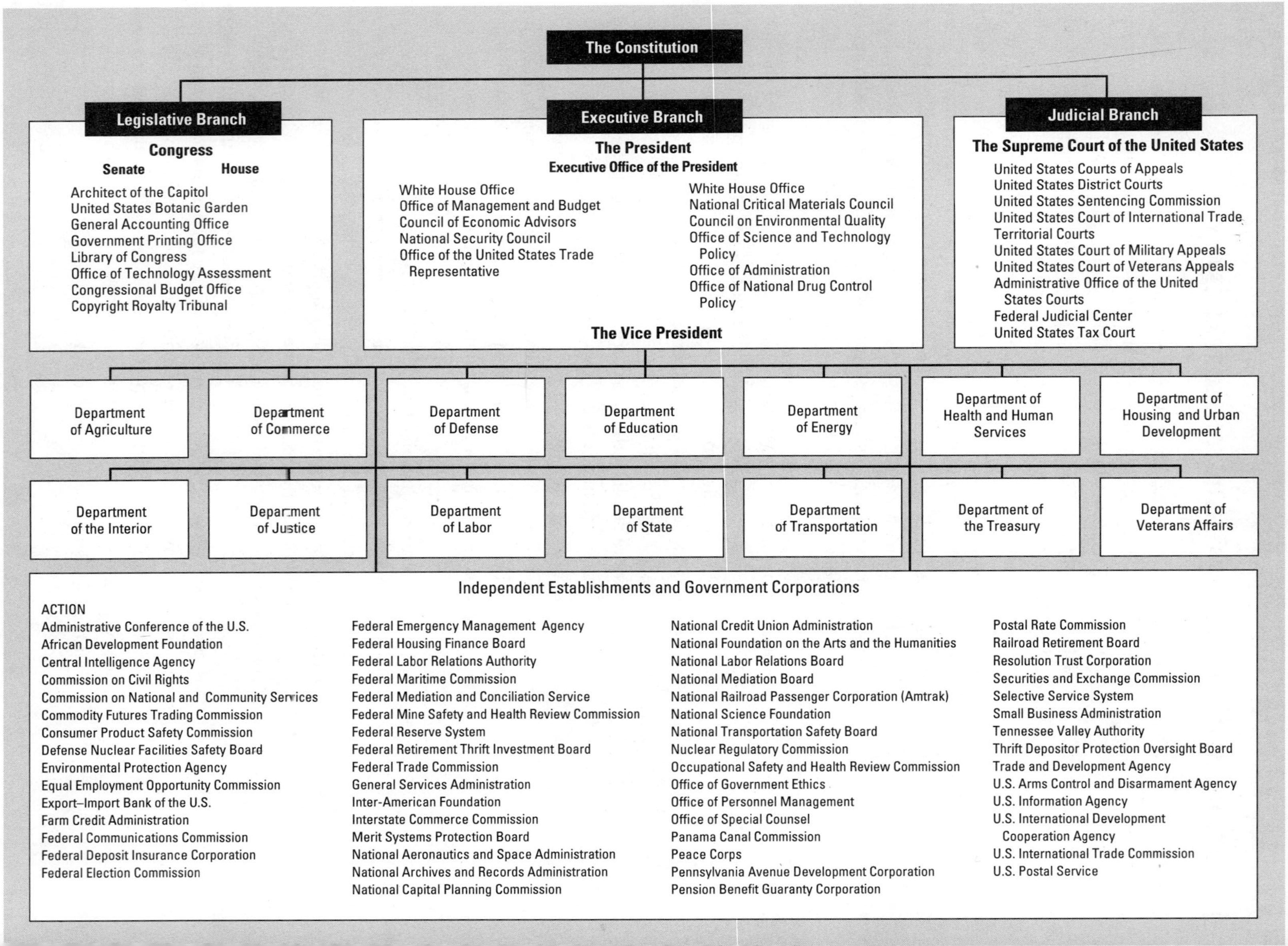

The Constitution

Legislative Branch

Congress

Senate | **House**

Architect of the Capitol
United States Botanic Garden
General Accounting Office
Government Printing Office
Library of Congress
Office of Technology Assessment
Congressional Budget Office
Copyright Royalty Tribunal

Executive Branch

The President

Executive Office of the President

White House Office
Office of Management and Budget
Council of Economic Advisors
National Security Council
Office of the United States Trade
  Representative
White House Office
National Critical Materials Council
Council on Environmental Quality
Office of Science and Technology
  Policy
Office of Administration
Office of National Drug Control
  Policy

The Vice President

Judicial Branch

The Supreme Court of the United States

United States Courts of Appeals
United States District Courts
United States Sentencing Commission
United States Court of International Trade
Territorial Courts
United States Court of Military Appeals
United States Court of Veterans Appeals
Administrative Office of the United
  States Courts
Federal Judicial Center
United States Tax Court

Department of Agriculture

Department of the Interior

Department of Commerce

Department of Justice

Department of Defense

Department of Labor

Department of Education

Department of State

Department of Energy

Department of Transportation

Department of Health and Human Services

Department of the Treasury

Department of Housing and Urban Development

Department of Veterans Affairs

Independent Establishments and Government Corporations

ACTION
Administrative Conference of the U.S.
African Development Foundation
Central Intelligence Agency
Commission on Civil Rights
Commission on National and Community Services
Commodity Futures Trading Commission
Consumer Product Safety Commission
Defense Nuclear Facilities Safety Board
Environmental Protection Agency
Equal Employment Opportunity Commission
Export-Import Bank of the U.S.
Farm Credit Administration
Federal Communications Commission
Federal Deposit Insurance Corporation
Federal Election Commission

Federal Emergency Management Agency
Federal Housing Finance Board
Federal Labor Relations Authority
Federal Maritime Commission
Federal Mediation and Conciliation Service
Federal Mine Safety and Health Review Commission
Federal Reserve System
Federal Retirement Thrift Investment Board
Federal Trade Commission
General Services Administration
Inter-American Foundation
Interstate Commerce Commission
Merit Systems Protection Board
National Aeronautics and Space Administration
National Archives and Records Administration
National Capital Planning Commission

National Credit Union Administration
National Foundation on the Arts and the Humanities
National Labor Relations Board
National Mediation Board
National Railroad Passenger Corporation (Amtrak)
National Science Foundation
National Transportation Safety Board
Nuclear Regulatory Commission
Occupational Safety and Health Review Commission
Office of Government Ethics
Office of Personnel Management
Office of Special Counsel
Panama Canal Commission
Peace Corps
Pennsylvania Avenue Development Corporation
Pension Benefit Guaranty Corporation

Postal Rate Commission
Railroad Retirement Board
Resolution Trust Corporation
Securities and Exchange Commission
Selective Service System
Small Business Administration
Tennessee Valley Authority
Thrift Depositor Protection Oversight Board
Trade and Development Agency
U.S. Arms Control and Disarmament Agency
U.S. Information Agency
U.S. International Development
  Cooperation Agency
U.S. International Trade Commission
U.S. Postal Service

OMB   The Office of Management and Budget (OMB) is the largest agency in the Executive Office of the President. Its function is to prepare the budget of the United States for the president to submit to Congress. The federal government cannot spend money without appropriations by Congress, and all requests for congressional appropriations must clear the OMB first, a requirement that gives the OMB great power over the executive branch. Since all agencies request more money than they can receive, the OMB has primary responsibility for reviewing, reducing, and approving estimates submitted by departments and agencies (subject, of course, to appeal to the president); it also continuously scrutinizes the organization and operations of executive agencies in order to recommend changes promoting efficiency and economy. Like members of the White House staff, the top officials of the OMB are responsible solely to the president; thus they must reflect the president's goals and priorities in their decision making.

CEA   The president, with Senate consent, appoints three professional economists of high standing to the Council of Economic Advisers (CEA). Created by the Employment Act of 1946, the CEA analyzes trends in the economy and recommends to the president the fiscal and monetary policies necessary to avoid depression and inflation. In addition, the CEA prepares the economic report that the act requires the president to submit to Congress each year. The economic report, together with the annual budget message to Congress, gives the president the opportunity to outline the administration's major policies.

PRESIDENTIAL CONTROL OF THE BUREAUCRACY

Constitutionally the president has authority over the federal bureaucracy. The president has formal power to appoint all secretaries, undersecretaries, and deputy secretaries and most bureau chiefs in the federal government. The president also has the power to reorganize the federal bureaucracy, subject to congressional veto. And, of course, the president exercises formal control over the budget. The OMB works directly under presidential supervision.

The president's formal powers over the bureaucracy center on appointments, reorganization, and the budget. We should, however, consider the *real* limitations on these three powers.

Appointments

Although the federal bureaucracy consists of nearly three million employees, the president actually appoints only about twenty-five hundred people. Approximately six hundred of those appointments are policy-making positions; the rest are subordinate positions often used for patronage. Many patronage positions go to professional bureaucrats by default because a president cannot find qualified political appointees. Many political appointees are baffled by the career bureaucrats in the agencies. The bureaucrats have the knowledge, skills, and experience to continue existing programs with little or no supervision from their nominal political chiefs. Many political heads "go native"; they yield to the pressures of the career bureaucrats. The president's appointee whose charge is to control a bureau ends up the bureau's captive instead.

Since a majority of career bureaucrats are Democrats, exercising policy control over the bureaucracy is particularly difficult for a Republican president. Richard Nixon attempted to deal with this problem by increasing the power of his immediate White House staff; he placed control of major programs in the White House staff at the expense of the cabinet departments. The unhappy result was that the White House staff itself became a powerful bureaucracy, frequently locked in conflict with executive departments and duplicating much of the departments' research and policy-planning activities. For example, Henry Kissinger, as Nixon's White House national security advisor, dominated foreign policy decision making to the virtual exclusion of the Department of State. When Secretary of State William P. Rogers resigned in frustration, Nixon appointed Kissinger to the post.

Ronald Reagan's approach was to appoint conservatives and Republicans to head many key agencies. But the bureaucracy fought back by isolating and undermining Reagan's appointees within the agencies. Lower-level bureaucrats often supplied damaging information to the press and to Congress, claiming that Reagan appointees did not enforce the laws properly. Then they sought to protect their jobs with special legislation preventing the president from firing "whistle blowers."

George Bush experienced less conflict with the bureaucracy because he did not pursue any clear domestic policy goals. Unlike his predecessor Ronald Reagan, Bush did not seek to slow the growth of government, to deregulate the economy, or to reduce taxing and spending—all policies that are strongly opposed by government bureaucrats. Bush himself held a variety of bureaucratic posts during his career—UN ambassador, CIA director, ambassador to the People's Republic of China. Because Bush did not seek to change bureaucratic ways in Washington, he did not encounter the vocal opposition of the bureaucracy.

The Washington bureaucracy is generally supportive of Bill Clinton's policy activism, with its promise of expanded governmental services and budgets. The only serious bureaucratic opposition Clinton encountered was the battle of the Department of Health and Human Services against welfare reform. Clinton's 1996 signing of the Republican-sponsored bill ending federal entitlements to welfare cash aid and shifting responsibility for cash assistance to the states was bitterly opposed by the Washington welfare bureaucracy.

Clinton's cabinet appointees are drawn heavily from Washington lawyers and lobbyists (see the Focus: "The Friends of Bill and Hillary" in Chapter 4). There are few "outsiders" in the Clinton administration; almost all of Clinton's top appointees have held previous governmental posts.

Reorganization

Presidents can choose to reorganize the bureaucracy to reflect their priorities. However, most presidents limit this practice to one or two key presidential programs (presidential reorganizations are subject to legislative veto). For example, in the 1960s President Kennedy created the National Aeronautics and Space Administration as an independent agency to carry out his commitment to a national space program. President Carter created the Department of Education to fulfill his campaign pledge to emphasize educational matters, even though the department's parent organization, the Department of Health, Education, and Welfare, bitterly opposed it. President Reagan promised in his 1980 campaign to eliminate the Department of Education as well as the Department of Energy. But reorganization is a difficult task. Nothing arouses the fighting instincts of bureaucrats as much as the rumor of reorganization. President Reagan was eventually forced to drop his plans to eliminate these two departments. Instead, Reagan ended his administration by creating a new cabinet-level department—the Department of Veterans Affairs—in response to demands for greater status and prestige by veterans' interests.

The Budget

The president exercises budgetary power over the bureaucracy through the OMB. Thus the OMB director must be a trusted ally of the president, and the OMB must support the president's programs and priorities if presidential

FOCUS

Bureaucratic Maneuvers

How can bureaucrats outmaneuver the president? One illustration of bureaucratic leeway and discretion in implementing presidential decisions has been widely quoted:

> *Half of a President's suggestions, which theoretically carry the weight of orders, can be safely forgotten by a cabinet member. And if the President asks about a suggestion the second time, he can be told that it is being investigated. If he asks a third time, the wise cabinet officer will give him at least part of what he suggests. But only occasionally do Presidents ever get around to asking three times.*[a]

Bureaucratic maneuvers can become even more complex. Morton Halperin, former staff member of the National Security Council under Henry Kissinger (Halperin later charged Kissinger and others with bugging his telephone), describes "ten commandments" of bureaucratic infighting.[b] These suggest the power of the bureaucracy and the frequently bitter nature of bureaucratic warfare:

1. Never play "politics" with security. But use your own notions of politics to screen out information from the president that conflicts with your own objectives.

2. Tell the president only what is necessary to persuade him of the correctness of your own position. Avoid giving him "confusing" information. Isolate the opposition by excluding them from deliberations.

3. Present your own policy option in the middle of two other obviously unworkable alternatives to give the president the illusion of choice.

4. If the president selects the "wrong" policy anyhow, demand "full authority" to deal with the undesirable consequences, which you say are sure to arise.

5. Always predict the consequences of not adopting your policy in terms of worst cases, making predictions of dire consequences that will follow.

6. If the president chooses your own policy, urge immediate action; if he selects another policy, you may agree in principle but argue that "now is not the time."

7. If the opposition view looks very strong, "leak" damaging information to your supporters in the press or Congress and count on "public opposition" to build.

8. Fully implement orders that result from the selection of your own policy recommendation; circumvent or delay those that do not.

9. Limit the issues that go to the president. Bring up only those favorable to your position or that he is likely to favor.

10. Never oppose the president's policy in such extreme terms that you lose his trust. Temper your disagreements so that you can live to argue another day.

Bureaucrats do not really consider these "commandments" cynical. Indeed, they may not realize when they are following them. They often sincerely believe that their own policies and projects are in the nation's best interest.

[a]Graham T. Allison, *Essence of Decision* (Boston: Little, Brown, 1971), p. 172.

[b]Leslie H. Gelb and Morton H. Halperin, "The Ten Commandments of the Foreign Policy Bureaucracy," *Harper's* (June 1972): 28–36.

control over the bureaucracy is to be effective. But even the OMB must accept the budgetary base of each department (the previous year's budget, adjusted for inflation) and engage in "incremental" budgeting. Despite its own expertise, the OMB rarely challenges the budgetary base of agencies but instead concentrates its attention on requested increases.

Any agency that feels shortchanged in the president's budget can leak the fact to its supporting interest groups and congressional subcommittee. Any resulting "public outcry" may force the president to restore the agency's funds. Or Congress can appropriate money not requested by the president. The president may go along with the increased expenditures simply to avoid another confrontation with Congress.

THE BUDGET MAZE

The budget is the most important policy statement of any government. The expenditure side of the budget shows "who gets what" from government, and the revenue side shows "who pays the costs." The budget lies at the heart of the policy-making process.

Presidential Budget

The president is responsible for submitting the annual federal budget, with estimates of revenue and recommendations for expenditures, to Congress. Congress controls the purse strings; no federal monies may be spent without congressional appropriation. The president relies on the Office of Management and Budget (OMB) to prepare a budget for Congress. The president's budget is usually submitted in late January of each year. The federal fiscal year (FY) begins October 1; this gives Congress about eight months to consider the president's budget and pass the appropriations acts for the coming fiscal year.

Preparation of the budget by the OMB starts more than a year before the beginning of the fiscal year for which it is intended. (Fiscal years are named for the year in which they *end*, so, for example, the OMB prepares FY 2000 in 1998 for presentation to Congress in January 1999 and passage before October 1, 1999; FY 2000 ends September 30, 2000.) The OMB considers budget requests by all executive departments and agencies, adjusting them to fit the president's overall policy goals. It prepares the *Budget of the United States Government* for the president to submit to Congress. Table 11-1 summarizes the steps in the overall schedule for budgetary preparation.

TABLE 11-1	The budget process

APPROXIMATE SCHEDULE	ACTORS	TASKS
Presidential Budget Making		
January–March	President and OMB	The Office of Management and Budget presents long-range forecasts for revenues and expenditures to the president. The president and the OMB develop general guidelines for all federal agencies. Agencies are sent guidelines and forms for their budget requests.
April–July	Executive agencies	Agencies prepare and submit budget requests to the OMB.
August–October	OMB and agencies	The OMB reviews agency requests and holds hearings with agency officials. The OMB usually tries to reduce agency requests.
November–December	OMB and president	The OMB presents revised budget to president. Occasionally agencies may appeal OMB decisions directly to the president. The president and the OMB write budget messages for Congress.
January	President	The president presents budget for the next fiscal year to Congress.
Congressional Budget Process		
February–May	CBO and congressional committees	Standing committees review taxing and spending proposals for reports to House and Senate budget committees. The Congressional Budget Office (CBO) also reviews entire presidential budget and reports to budget committees.
May–June	Congress; House and Senate budget committees	House and Senate budget committees present first concurrent resolution, which sets overall total for budget outlays in major categories. Full House and Senate vote on resolution. Committees are instructed to stay within budget committee's resolution.
July–September	Congress; House and Senate appropriations committees and budget committees	House and Senate appropriations committees and subcommittees draw up detailed appropriations bills. Bills are submitted to House and Senate budget committees for second concurrent resolution. Budget committees may force reductions through "reconciliation" provisions to limit spending. The full House and Senate vote on "reconciliations" and second (firm) concurrent resolution.

TABLE 11-1	The budget process (continued)	
APPROXIMATE SCHEDULE	**ACTORS**	**TASKS**
September–October	Congress and president	The House and Senate pass various appropriations bills (nine to sixteen bills, by major functional category, such as "defense"). Each is sent to president for signature. (If vetoed by the president, the appropriations bills go back to House and Senate, which must override veto with two-thirds vote in each body or revise bills to gain president's approval).
Executive Budget Implementation		
After October 1	Congress and president	Fiscal year for all federal agencies begins October 1. If no appropriations bill has been passed by Congress and signed by the president for an agency, Congress must pass and the president sign a continuing resolution to allow the agency to spend at last year's level until a new appropriations act is passed. If no continuing resolution is passed, the agency must officially cease spending government funds and must officially shut down.

Congressional Consideration

The Constitution gives Congress the authority to decide how the government should spend its money: "No money shall be drawn from the Treasury but in consequence of appropriations made by law" (Article I, Section 9). The president's budget is sent initially to the House and Senate budget committees, whose job it is to draft a *budget resolution* for Congress, setting future target goals for appropriations in various areas. The House and Senate budget committees rely on their own bureaucracy, the Congressional Budget Office (CBO), to review the recommendations made by the president and the OMB. Congress is supposed to pass a budget resolution by late spring. The resolution should guide the House and Senate appropriations committees and their subcommittees in writing the appropriations acts.

There are usually thirteen separate *appropriations acts* each year. Each one covers a broad area of government; for example, defense, labor, human services and education, commerce, justice, state, and judiciary. These appropriations bills must pass both House and Senate in identical form, just as any other legislation must. All the acts are supposed to be passed before the start of the fiscal year, October 1. These procedures were mandated in the Congressional Budget and Impoundment Control Act of 1974. However, Congress rarely follows its own timetable or procedures.

The common goal of the congressional budget procedures, the House and Senate budget committees, and the Congressional Budget Office is to allow Congress to consider the budget in its entirety rather than in separate segments. But after the budget resolution is passed, the thirteen separate appropriations bills begin their tortuous journeys through specialized appropriations subcommittees. Agency and department leaders from the administration are frequently called to testify before these subcommittees to defend the president's request. Lobbying activity is very heavy in these subcommittees.

If the appropriations committees report bills that exceed the ceilings established by the budget resolution, Congress must prepare a *reconciliation bill* to reconcile the amounts set by the budget resolution and the amounts set by the appropriations committees. This procedure tends to match the power of the House and Senate budget committees against the House and Senate appropriations committees. When passed, the reconciliation bill binds the appropriations committees and the Congress to ceilings in each area. However, all this congressional infighting generally runs beyond the October 1 deadline for the start of the fiscal year.

Continuing Resolutions and Government Shutdowns

All appropriations acts *should* be passed by both houses and signed by the president into law before October 1, but Congress rarely meets this deadline. Government agencies frequently find themselves beginning a new fiscal year without a budget. Constitutionally, any U.S. government agency for which Congress does not pass an appropriations act may not draw money from the Treasury and thus is obliged to shut down. To get around this problem, Congress usually adopts a *continuing resolution* that authorizes government agencies to keep spending money for a specified period at the same level as in the previous fiscal year.

A continuing resolution is supposed to grant additional time for Congress to pass, and the president to sign, appropriations acts. But occasionally this process has broken down in the heat of political combat over the budget: the time period specified in a continuing resolution has expired without agreement on appropriations acts or even on a new continuing resolution. Shutdowns occurred during the bitter battle between President Bill Clinton and the Republican-controlled Congress over the Fiscal Year 1996 budget. In theory, the absence of either appropriations acts or a continuing resolution should cause the federal government to shut down, that is, to cease all operations and expenditures for lack of funds. But in practice, such shutdowns have been only partial, affecting only "nonessential" government employees and causing relatively little disruption.

The Line-Item Veto Controversy

Presidents, both Democratic and Republican, have long struggled to obtain the *line-item veto*—the ability to veto some provisions of a bill while accepting other provisions. The lack of presidential line-item veto power was especially frustrating when dealing with appropriations bills because the president could not veto specific pork-barrel provisions from major spending bills for defense, education, housing, welfare, and so on. In 1996 Congress granted the president authority to "cancel" spending items in any appropriation act, any new entitlements, or any limited tax benefits. Such cancellation would take effect immediately unless blocked by a special "disapproval bill" passed by Congress. The president could veto the disapproval bill, and a two-thirds vote of both houses would be required to override the veto.

But opponents of the line-item veto challenged its constitutionality, arguing that it transferred legislative power—granted by the Constitution only to Congress—to the president. The U.S. Supreme Court agreed, holding that the line-item veto was unconstitutional because it allowed the president to amend legislation by repealing specific spending provisions: "The Line Item Veto Act authorizes the president himself to elect the repeal of laws, for his own policy reasons, without observing procedures set forth in Article I. The fact that Congress intended such a result is of no moment. . . . The Congress cannot alter the procedures set out in Article I without amending the Constitution."[4]

ELITE FISCAL RESPONSIBILITY?

Over the years, total federal spending has gown dramatically. In 1962, federal spending amounted to only $92 billion; in 1998, this figure had grown to $1,733 billion (see Figure 11-2). The growth of federal spending is being driven by "entitlement" programs, notably Social Security, which is now the single largest item in the budget, and Medicare and Medicaid, the

| FIGURE 11-2 | Federal spending |

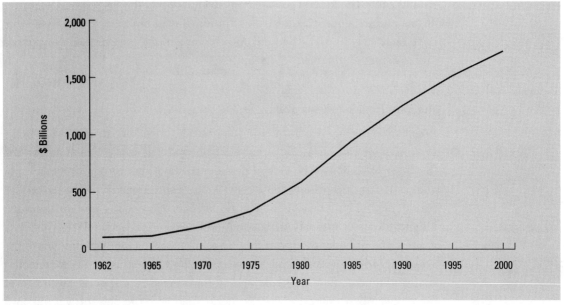

Source: Data from *Budget of the United States Government, 1999.*

fastest-growing items in the budget. National defense, which in 1960 constituted 56 percent of all federal spending, has declined to 15 percent. As annual deficits continued to add to the national debt, interest payments rose to 14 percent of federal spending.

Overall Federal Spending

The enormous growth of federal spending in billions of dollars, however, is in part offset by America's dynamic economy. Expressed as a percentage of the gross domestic product (GDP)—the sum of all of the goods and services produced in the U.S. in a year—federal spending rose only modestly from 18.8 percent in 1962 to a high of 23.1 percent in 1998. Since then federal spending as a percent of the GDP has actually declined to about 20 percent. In other words, while total dollar spending by Washington grew by over 1,800 percent, this spending remained relatively stable in relation to the nation's overall economy.

However, *within* these overall figures, national priorities changed considerable over the last forty years.

FIGURE 11-3 | Federal budget priorities

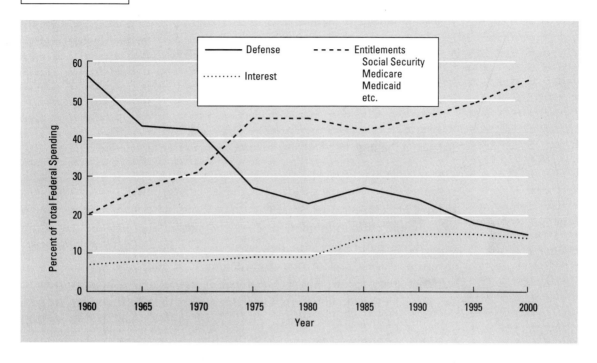

Source: *Budget of the United States Government, 1997.*

Changing National Priorities

It was in the decade of the 1970s that the United States changed its "national priorities," and for the first time in history social-welfare ("entitlement") spending took precedence over national defense. As Figure 11-3 shows, it was during the end of Nixon's administration (1973) that entitlement spending began to outrun defense spending in the federal budget. Note that the general direction of trend lines changed somewhat in the early Reagan administration (1980). Defense spending rose temporarily in the early 1980s and then steeply declined following the end of the Cold War. Entitlement spending continued its upward direction.

Today "entitlement" spending, primarily for Social Security, Medicare, and Medicaid, consumes over 55 percent of all federal spending. Note that *this spending goes primarily to the aged, not the poor.* As the large "baby boom" generation begins to retire early in the next century, entitlement payments to the aged, if unchanged, will consume an ever-increasing share of federal spending as well as push up overall federal spending to unprecedented levels.

"Capping entitlements" is widely recognized by economists as the only way to rein in future federal spending. But no one in Washington—president, Congress members, bureaucrats, Republicans or Democrats—is willing to challenge the powerful senior citizen lobby (see Focus: "Leaders and Follows: The AARP" in Chapter 9).

Balancing the Budget

For thirty years, prior to 1998, Washington spent more than it received in revenue. These annual deficits put the U.S. government over *five trillion dollars in debt,* a figure equal to twenty thousand dollars for every man, woman, and child in the nation. The debt is more than half the size of the gross domestic product. The debt is owed to banks, insurance companies, investment firms, and anyone else who buys U.S. government bonds. International investors own about 20 percent of the national debt. Government interest payments to holders of the debt amounts to about 14 percent of governmental expenditures. The debt need not ever be paid off, but future generations of American taxpayers must continue to pay the annual interest on it as long as it is not paid. Democrats and Republicans, liberals and conservatives, all contributed to government deficits, but they differ only in placing blame. Conservatives blame runaway government entitlement programs such as Social Security and Medicare, as well as large-scale spending programs in welfare, education, job training and agriculture. Liberals blame defense spending and tax cuts during the Reagan administration.

The booming national economy of the 1990s enabled the federal government to reduce and finally end its annual deficits in 1998. But the painful legacy of these deficits will linger for generations in the form of a huge national debt. (*Deficits* refer to annual excess of expenditures over revenues; the national *debt* refers to the total accumulation of deficits over the years on which the government must continue to pay interest.)

The Burden of Debt

Interest payments on the national debt divert money away from *all* other government programs. Even if the federal government were to continue to balance its budget and eliminate current annual deficits, interest payment on the accumulated debt from past years will remain obligations of the children and grandchildren of the nation's current generation.

There is no guarantee that politicians and bureaucrats will not return to deficit spending. Deficit spending remains attractive to politicians who know that they can spend money on current voters and keep their taxes low by shifting costs to future generations. Politicians know that they will be long gone before these generations become voters.

BUREAUCRATIC POWER, IRON TRIANGLES, AND REVOLVING DOORS

Traditionally it was assumed that when Congress passed a law and then created a bureaucracy and appropriated money to carry out the intent of the law, that was the end of the political process. It was assumed that the intent of Congress would be carried out—the political battle having been resolved—and government would get on with the job of "administering" the law.

It turns out, however, that political battles do not end with victory or defeat in Congress. Organized interests do not abandon the fight and return home simply because the site of the battle shifts from the political arena to an administrative one. We tend to think that "political" questions are the province of the president and Congress, and "administrative" questions the province of the bureaucracy. Actually "political" and "administrative" questions do not differ in content; they differ only in who decides them.

Implementation, Regulation, Adjudication

Bureaucracies are not *constitutionally* empowered to decide policy questions. But they do so, nevertheless, as they perform their tasks of implementation, regulation, and adjudication.

Implementation is the development of procedures and activities to carry out policies legislated by Congress. It requires bureaucracies to translate laws into operational rules and regulations and to allocate resources—money, personnel, offices, supplies—to functions. All of these tasks involve decisions by bureaucrats—decisions that drive how the law will actually affect society. In some cases, bureaucrats delay the development of regulations based on a new law, assign enforcement responsibility to existing offices with other higher-priority tasks, and allocate few people with limited resources to the task. In other cases, bureaucrats act forcefully in making new regulations, insist on strict enforcement, assign responsibilities to newly created aggressive offices with no other assignments, and allocate a great deal of staff time and agency resources to the task. Interested groups have a strong stake in these decisions, and they actively seek to influence the bureaucracy.

Regulation involves the development of formal rules for implementing legislation. The federal bureaucracy publishes about sixty thousand pages of rules in the *Federal Register* each year. Regulatory battles are important because regulations that appear in the *Federal Register* have the effect of law. Congress can amend or repeal a regulation only by passing new legislation and obtaining the president's signature. Controversial bureaucratic regulations often remain in place because Congress is slow to act, because key committee members block corrective legislation, or because the president refuses to sign bills overturning the regulation.

Adjudication involves bureaucratic decisions about individual cases. In adjudication, bureaucrats decide whether a person or firm is failing to comply with laws or regulations and, if so, what penalties or corrective actions are to be applied. Regulatory agencies and commissions—for example, the National Labor Relations Board, the Federal Communications Commission, the Equal Employment Opportunity Commission, the Federal Trade Commission, the Securities and Exchange Commission—are heavily engaged in adjudication. Their elaborate procedures and body of previous decisions closely resemble the court system. Some agencies authorize specific hearing officers, administrative judges, or appellate divisions to accept evidence, hear arguments, and decide cases. Individuals and firms involved in these proceedings usually hire lawyers specializing in the field of regulation. Administrative hearings are somewhat less formal than a court trial, and the "judges" are employees of the agency itself. Losers may appeal to the federal courts, but the record of agency success in the federal courts discourages many appeals.

Bureaucratic Goals

Bureaucrats generally believe strongly in the value of their programs and the importance of their tasks. Senior military officers and civilian officials of the Department of Defense believe in the importance of a strong national defense, and top officials in the Social Security Administration are committed to maintaining the integrity of the retirement system and serving the nation's senior citizens. Beyond these public-spirited motives, bureaucrats, like everyone else, seek higher pay, greater job security, and added power and prestige for themselves.

These public and private motives converge to inspire bureaucrats to seek to expand the powers, functions, and budgets of their departments and agencies. Rarely do bureaucrats request a reduction in authority, the elimination of a program, or a decrease in their agency's budget. Rather, bureaucracies strive to add new functions, acquire more authority and responsibility, and increase their budgets and personnel.

"Iron Triangles"

Once the bureaucracy takes over an issue, three major power bases—the "iron triangles"—come together to decide its outcome: the executive agency administering the program; the congressional subcommittee charged with overseeing it; and the most interested groups, generally those directly affected by the agency. The interest groups develop close relationships with the bureaucratic policy makers. And both the interest groups and the bureaucrats develop close relationships with the congressional subcommittees that oversee their activities. Agency–subcommittee–interest group relationships become established; even the individuals involved remain the same over fairly long periods of time, as senior members of Congress retain their subcommittee memberships.

Note that the parts of this triumvirate do *not* compete (as pluralist ideology suggests). Instead, bureaucratic agency, congressional subcommittee, and organized interest come together to "scratch each other's back" in bureaucratic policy making. Bureaucrats get political support from interest groups in their requests for expanded power and authority and increased budgetary allocations. Interest groups get favorable treatment of their members by the bureaucracy. Congressional committee members get political and financial support from interest groups, as well as favorable treatment for their constituents and contributors who are served or regulated by the bureaucracy.

Revolving Doors

Washington "insiders"—bureaucrats, lobbyists, former members of Congress, White House and congressional staffers—frequently change jobs. They may move from a government post (where they acquired experience, knowledge, and personal contacts) to a job in the private sector as a consultant, lobbyist, or salesperson. Defense contractors may recruit high-ranking military officers or Defense Department officials to help sell weapons to their former employers. Trade associations may recruit congressional staffers, White House staffers, or high-ranking agency heads as lobbyists, or these people may leave government service to start their own lobbying firms. Attorneys from the Justice Department, the Internal Revenue Service, and federal regulatory agencies may be recruited by Washington law firms to represent clients in dealings with their former employees. Following retirement, many members of Congress turn to lobbying their former colleagues.

Concern about *revolving doors* centers not only on individuals cashing in on their knowledge, experience, and contacts obtained through government employment but also on the possibility that some government officials will be tempted to tilt their decisions in favor of corporations, law firms, or interest groups that promise these officials well-paid jobs after they leave government employment. (The Ethics in Government Act limits postgovernment employment: former members of Congress are not permitted to lobby Congress for one year after leaving that body; former employees of executive agencies are not permitted to lobby their agency for one year after leaving government service, and they are not permitted to lobby their agency for two years on any matter over which they had any responsibility while employed by the government.)

THE BUREAUCRATIC ELITE

What kind of person inhabits the Washington bureaucracy? In a study of more than a thousand people who occupied top federal positions during five presidential administrations, the prestigious Brookings Institution reported that 36 percent rose through the ranks of government, 26 percent came from law firms, 24 percent from business, and 7 percent from a variety of other fields.[5] A plurality of top federal executives are career bureaucrats. Most top federal executives (63 percent) were federal bureaucrats at the time of their appointment to a top post; only 37 percent had no prior experience as federal bureaucrats. Thus the federal bureaucracy is producing its own leadership, with some limited recruitment from business and law.

Like other sectors of the elite, the bureaucracy recruits its top federal executives primarily from the middle- and upper-middle-class segments of the population. More than 99 percent of top federal executives are college educated, and 68 percent have advanced degrees (44 percent in law, 17 percent with earned master's degrees, and 11 percent with earned doctorates). The Brookings Institution reports that the Ivy League schools plus Stanford, Chicago, Michigan, and Berkeley educated more than 40 percent of the top federal executives, with Yale, Harvard, and Princeton leading the list.[6]

Little difference exists between Republican and Democratic administrators. Of course, Democratic presidents tend to appoint Democrats to top posts and Republican presidents tend to appoint Republicans. However, few discernible differences are evident in the class backgrounds, educational levels, occupational experiences, or previous public service of Democratic and Republican appointees.

One troublesome problem at the top of the federal bureaucracy is federal executives' short tenures. The median tenure in office of top federal executives is only two years. Only the regulatory commissions have significantly longer tenure. Such a short tenure at the top has obvious disadvantages. The head of a large department or agency needs a year or more to become fully productive by learning the issues, programs, procedures, technical problems, and personalities involved in the work. If such a person resigns after two years, the federal bureaucracy is not getting continuous, knowledgeable direction from its top officials.

THE REGULATORY QUAGMIRE

The Washington bureaucracy has become the regulator of the national economy, the protector of business against its rivals, and the guardian of the American people against everything from tainted foods to rickety stepladders. Federal regulatory bureaucracies began in 1887 with the creation of the Interstate Commerce Commission to regulate railroad rates. Since then thousands of laws, amendments, court rulings, and executive orders have expanded the powers of the regulatory commissions over every aspect of our lives (see Figure 11-1 for a list of independent commissions and agencies).

Federal regulatory bureaucracies are legislatures, investigators, prosecutors, judges, and juries—all wrapped into one. They issue thousands of pages of rules and regulations each year; they investigate thousands of complaints and conduct thousands of inspections; they require businesses to submit hundreds of thousands of forms each year; they hold hearings, determine "compliance" and "noncompliance," issue corrective orders, and levy fines and penalties. Most economists agree that overregulation adds greatly to the cost of living (perhaps one to two hundred billion dollars a year), that it is an obstacle to innovation and productivity, and that it hinders economic competition. Most regulatory commissions are *independent;* they are not under an executive department, and their members are appointed for long terms by a president who has little control over their activities.

The Captured Regulators

Over the years, the reform movements that led to the establishment of the older regulatory agencies have diminished in influence. Many regulatory agencies have become closely identified with regulated industry. The capture theory of regulation describes how regulated industries come to benefit from government regulation and how regulatory commissions come to represent the industries they are supposed to regulate rather than "the people." From time to time, various regulatory commissions have behaved as if "captured" by their industry. These have included the Interstate Commerce Commission (ICC) with railroads and trucking, the Federal Reserve Board (FRB) with banking, the Federal Communications Commission (FCC) with television and radio, the Securities and Exchange Commission (SEC) with the stock market, and the Federal Power Commission (FPC) with the natural gas industry.

Historically, regulatory commissions have acted against only the most wayward members of an industry. By attacking the businesses giving the industry bad publicity, the commissions actually helped improve the public's opinion of the industry as a whole. Regulatory commissions provided symbolic reassurance to the public that the behavior of the industry was proper.

By limiting entry into an industry by smaller firms (either directly, by denying them routes or broadcast channels, for example; or indirectly, by making the requirements for entry very costly), the regulatory commissions reduce competition. This function is an important asset to larger, established businesses; they no longer fear new, cut-rate competitors.

The close relationships between the regulatory bureaucracies and their client industries stem from a common resource: expertise. Not only do the regulatory commissions frequently turn to the regulated industries for information but they also recruit bureaucrats from industry leaders. Commission members usually come from the industry they are supposed to regulate. And after a few years in government, the "regulators" return to high-paying jobs in the industry. This practice is known as the "revolving door" problem.

Many federal regulatory commissions attract young attorneys, fresh from law school, to their staffs. When the attorneys are successful, they frequently are offered much higher-paying jobs in the industries they are regulating. So industry siphons off "the best and the brightest" to become defenders against government regulation. And of course these people have already learned the intricacies of government regulation, with taxpayers paying for their training. People see jobs in federal regulatory agencies as stepping stones to lucrative careers in private (regulated) industry.

Over the years, then, industry came to *support* the regulatory bureaucracies. Industry often strongly opposes proposals to reduce government control—deregulation. Proposals to deregulate railroads, interstate trucking, and airlines have met with substantial opposition from both the regulating bureaucracies and the regulated industries, working together.

The Activist Regulators

Congress has created several regulatory agencies to cover areas in which members of Congress have little or no expertise. To make matters worse, their jurisdiction extends to all industries rather than specific ones. Prime examples are the Equal Employment Opportunity Commission (EEOC), the Occupational Safety and Health Administration (OSHA), and the Environmental Protection Agency (EPA). The business community widely resents regulations by these agencies. Rules developed by the EEOC to prevent discrimination in employment and promotion (affirmative action guidelines) have been awkward, and the EEOC enforcement of these rules has been nearly chaotic. Many businesses do not believe that the EEOC has the expertise to understand their industry or their labor market. The same is true of the much-despised OSHA, which has issued thousands of safety regulations that appear costly and ridiculous to those in the industry. The complaint about the EPA is that it seldom considers the *costs* of its rulings to business or the consumer. Industry representatives contend that the EPA should weigh the costs of its regulations against the benefits to the environment.

The EEOC, OSHA, and EPA have general responsibilities across all business and industry. Thus these agencies are unlikely to develop expertise in the fashion of the FCC, SEC, or other single-industry regulators. They are unlikely to be captured by industry. Rather, they are bureaucratic extensions of civil rights (EEOC), consumer (OSHA), and environmental (EPA) lobbies, to whom they owe their existence.

Deregulation

The demand for deregulation has echoed in Washington for many years. Complaints about excessive regulation include the following:

1. The increased costs to businesses and consumers of complying with many separate regulations, issued by separate regulatory agencies, are excessive. Environmental regulation alone may be costing Americans one to two hundred billion dollars a year, but the costs never appear in a federal budget because businesses and consumers absorb them.

2. Overregulation hampers innovation and productivity. For example, the United States lags behind all other advanced nations in the introduction of new drugs because of lengthy testing by the Food and Drug Administration (FDA). Most observers feel that the FDA would

not approve aspirin if it were proposed for marketing today. The costs and delays in winning permission for a new product tend to discourage invention.

3. Regulatory bureaucracies' involvement in licensing and business start-up reduces competition. The red tape involved—the cost of complying with federal reporting requirements—is in itself an obstacle to small businesses.

4. Regulatory agencies do not weigh the costs of complying with their regulations against the benefits to society. Regulators generally introduce controls with little regard for the cost–benefit trade-offs.

In 1978 Congress acted for the first time to significantly reduce the burden of regulation. Acting against the objections of the airline industry, which wanted continued regulation, Congress stripped the Civil Aeronautics Board (CAB) of its power to allocate airline routes to various companies and to set rates. The CAB went out of existence in 1985. The airlines were "set free" (against their will) to choose where to fly and what to charge and to compete openly with one another.

Airline deregulation brought about a huge increase in airline travel. The airlines doubled their seating capacity and made more efficient use of their aircraft through the development of hub-and-spoke networks. Air safety continued to improve. Fatalities per millions of miles flown declined, and, because travelers were diverted from far more dangerous highway travel, overall transportation safety was improved. But these favorable outcomes were overshadowed by complaints about congestion at major airports and increased flight delays, especially at peak hours. (The major airports are publicly owned, and governments have been very slow in responding to increased air traffic.) Congestion, delays, and accidents are widely reported in the media, usually accompanied by demands for reregulation.

Reregulation

Deregulation threatens to diminish politicians' power and eliminate bureaucrats' jobs. It forces industries to become competitive and diminishes the role of interest group lobbyists. Thus in the absence of strong popular support for continued deregulation, pressures for *reregulation* remain strong in Washington.

Reregulation gained impetus from the financial disaster in the savings and loan industry. During the 1970s, deregulation of the financial industry allowed savings and loans to expand well beyond their traditional function of providing home mortgage loans and encouraged them to make riskier loans for commercial development. Removal of limits on interest rates savings and loans could pay on deposits forced them to compete for

FOCUS

Regulation— Hiding the Costs of Government

The costs of government regulations do not appear in the federal budget. Rather, they are paid for by businesses, employees, and consumers. Indeed, politicians prefer a regulatory approach to the environment, health, and safety precisely because it forces costs on the private sector—costs that are largely invisible to voters and taxpayers.

How large is the regulatory bill? Proponents of a regulatory activity usually object to estimating its cost. Politicians who wish to develop an image as protectors of the environment, of consumers, of the disabled, and so on do not want to call attention to the costs of their legislation. Only recently has the Office of Management and Budget even attempted to estimate the costs of federal regulatory activity. Overall, regulatory activity costs Americans between $300 billion and $500 billion a year, an amount equal to about one-quarter of the total federal budget. This means that each of America's 100 million households pays about $4,000 per year in the hidden costs of regulation. Paperwork requirements consume more than five billion hours of people's time, mostly to comply with the administration by the Internal Revenue Service of the tax laws. However, the costs of environmental controls, including the Environmental Protection Agency's enforcement of clean air and water and hazardous waste disposal regulations, are the fastest-growing regulatory costs.

The real question is whether the *benefits* of this regulatory activity—for example, cleaner air and water, safer disposal of toxic wastes, safer consumer products, fewer workplace injuries, fewer highway deaths, protections against discrimination, improved access for the disabled, and so on—are greater or less than the costs. But assessing the value of benefits is extraordinarily difficult. Many people object on ethical grounds to economic estimates of the value of a human life saved.

Regulation places a heavy burden on innovations and productivity. The costs and delays in winning permission for a new product tend to discourage invention and to drive up prices. For example, new drugs are difficult to introduce in the United States because the Food and Drug Administration (FDA) typically requires up to ten years of testing. Western European nations are many years ahead in their number of life-saving drugs available; they speak of the "drug lag" in the United States. Recently activists have succeeded in speeding up FDA approval of drugs to treat AIDS, but the agency has continued to delay the introduction of drugs to treat other diseases.

Competition declines when regulatory bureaucracies license and limit entry into a field. The cost of complying with federal reporting requirements is an obstacle to the survival of small businesses. And larger businesses must cope with reams of reports on employee relations, taxes, Social Security, affirmative action, occupational safety and health, environmental impact, and so on. Only the largest corporations have high-priced legal staffs prepared to do battle with the regulators, and only the largest corporations can afford the expensive delays involved in obtaining governmental approval. But all of these costs and delays hurt American business in global competition with foreign firms that do not confront these obstacles.

depositors, which encouraged them to make riskier loans to recover their higher costs. But because the federal government guaranteed deposits (up to one hundred thousand dollars) through the Federal Deposit Insurance Corporation (FDIC), the savings and loans were really risking money guaranteed by American taxpayers. Fraud and mismanagement played a role in the disaster in the 1980s, but the real problem was the moral hazard created by allowing these companies free rein with government-guaranteed funds. If the U.S. government is going to guarantee deposits, then it must regulate their use. Alternatively, if the financial industry is deregulated, then the government should stop insuring deposits. The savings and loan disaster has resulted in tightened federal regulation of banking and savings institutions.

CONTROLLING THE BUREAUCRACY: CONGRESS AND COURTS

Congress or the courts can overturn the decisions of bureaucracies if sufficient opposition develops to bureaucratic policies. But such opposition is unlikely if bureaucracies work closely with their congressional subcommittees and their interest groups.

Congressional Constraints

Congress can restrain the bureaucracy by:

1. Passing direct legislation changing rules or regulations or limiting bureaucratic activity.

2. Altering or threatening to alter the bureau's budget.

3. Retaining specific veto powers over certain bureaucratic actions (agencies must submit some proposed rules to Congress; if Congress does not act within a specified time, the rules take effect).

4. Conducting investigations, usually during legislative or appropriations hearings, that publicize unpopular decisions, rules, or expenditures by bureaus.

5. Making direct complaints to the bureaucracy through formal contacts.

Yet it is difficult for Congress to use these powers as a truly effective check on the bureaucracy.

Judicial Constraints

The federal courts exercise more direct control over the bureaucracy than Congress does. Decisions by executive agencies usually can be appealed to federal courts. Moreover, federal courts can issue injunctions (orders) to executive agencies before they institute their rules, regulations, projects, or programs.

Judicial control of the bureaucracy has its limitations, however:

1. Judicial oversight usually emphasizes *procedural* fairness rather than policy content.

2. Bureaucracies have set up elaborate administrative processes to protect their decisions from challenge on procedural grounds.

3. Lawsuits against bureaucracies are very expensive; the bureaucracies have armies of attorneys paid for out of tax monies to oppose anyone who attempts to challenge them in court.

4. Excessive delays in federal courts add to the time and expense of challenging bureaucratic decisions.

In fact, citizens have not had much success in court cases against bureaucracies. Political scientists Bradley Cannon and Michael Giles report that the courts rarely reverse the decisions of federal regulatory commissions. For example, the Federal Power Commission and the Federal Trade Commission win 91 percent of the cases they argue before the Supreme Court; the National Labor Relations Board wins 75 percent; and the Internal Revenue Service wins 73 percent. Only the Immigration and Naturalization Service has a mediocre record of 56 percent.[7]

Summary

The federal bureaucracy is a major base of power in the United States, largely independent of the other branches of government and not very responsive to the American people. Governmental bureaucracies invade every aspect of modern life, and their power is growing each year. A bureaucratic elite that both formulates and implements public policy is emerging. Elitism in bureaucracy takes several forms:

1. Bureaucratic power increases with the size and technological complexity of modern society. Official lawmaking bodies—Congress and the president—set forth only general policy statements. Bureaucracies write tens of thousands of rules and regulations and actually undertake the tasks of government.

2. Bureaucratic power increases because (a) Congress and the president do not have the time or expertise to master policy details; (b) Congress and the president deliberately pass vague laws for symbolic reasons, then turn over actual governance to bureaucracies; and (c) the bureaucracy has now amassed sufficient power to influence the president and Congress.

3. Although the president is officially in charge of the executive branch of government, presidential control is limited by (a) the relatively small number of policy-making patronage positions appointed by the president versus the large numbers of professional civil service bureaucrats, (b) the difficulty of achieving meaningful reorganization, and (c) the large number of "uncontrollable" items in the budget.

4. The budget is the most important policy statement of a government. The president, through the Office of Management and Budget, is responsible for the preparation of the *Budget of the United States Government* each year for submission to Congress. But only Congress can authorize the expenditure of federal funds; it does so through annual appropriations acts for major areas of government spending.

5. Federal spending has grown dramatically over the years, driven largely by "entitlement" spending, notably Social Security and Medicare. A booming economy in the 1990s produced the first balanced budget in thirty years, but future generations are still burdened with an accumulated national debt of over five trillion dollars.

6. Once a political question shifts to the bureaucracy, an "iron triangle" of power bases comes together to decide its outcome: the executive bureaucracy, the congressional subcommittee, and the organized interest groups.

7. The federal regulatory commissions are investigators, prosecutors, judges, and juries—all wrapped into one. Members of these commissions serve long, overlapping terms, and they do not report to executive departments. They are relatively free from mass influence.

8. In theory, Congress restrains the bureaucracy directly by ordering changes in rules, altering the budget, retaining veto powers over bureaucratic action, conducting investigations, and registering complaints. In practice, however, Congress rarely reverses bureaucratic decisions and seldom tampers with "uncontrollable" budget items. In theory, the courts can also restrain the bureaucracy. But rarely do they actually reverse administrative decisions.

9. Regulations hide the true costs of government by shifting them from the government itself to businesses, employees, and consumers. Bureaucrats seldom weigh the costs of their actions against whatever benefits are produced.

Notes

1. Max Weber, *The Theory of Social and Economic Organization*, A. M. Henderson and Talcott Parsons, trans. (New York: Oxford University Press, 1947). Summary by Robert C. Fried, *Performance in American Bureaucracy* (Boston: Little, Brown, 1976).

2. James Q. Wilson, "Social Science: The Public Disenchantment, A Symposium," *American Scholar* (Summer 1976): 358; also cited by Aaron Wildavsky, *Speaking Truth to Power* (Boston: Little, Brown, 1979), p. 69.

3. See Richard F. Fenno, Jr., *The President's Cabinet* (Cambridge, Mass.: Harvard University Press, 1959).

4. *Clinton* v. *City of New York* (June 25, 1998).

5. David T. Stanley, Dean E. Mann, and Jameson W. Doig, *Men Who Govern* (Washington, D.C.: Brookings Institution, 1967).

6. Ibid., p. 21.

7. Bradley Cannon and Michael Giles, "Recurring Litigants: Federal Agencies before the Supreme Court," *Western Political Quarterly* 15 (September 1972): 183–191.

Selected Readings

Gore, Al. *The Best Kept Secrets in Government.* New York: Random House, 1996. Gore's own evaluation of progress in "reinventing the way Washington works."

Gore, Al. *Creating a Government That Works Better and Costs Less.* Washington, D.C.: Government Printing Office, 1993. Specific recommendations for "reinventing" government by making citizens "customers," introducing competition, cutting red tape, and privatizing government services.

Henry, Nicholas. *Public Administration and Public Affairs,* 6th ed. Upper Saddle River, N.J.: Prentice-Hall, 1995. Authoritative introductory textbook on public organizations (bureaucracies), public management, and policy implementation.

Howard, Philip K. *The Death of Common Sense: How Law Is Suffocating America.* New York: Random House, 1995. Outrageous stories of bureaucratic senselessness coupled with a plea to allow bureaucrats flexibility in achieving the purposes of laws and holding them accountable for outcomes.

Osbourne, David, and Ted Gaebler. *Reinventing Government.* New York: Addison-Wesley, 1992. The respected manual of the "reinventing government" movement with recommendations to overcome the routine tendencies of bureaucracies and inject "the entrepreneurial spirit" in them.

Rourke, Francis E. *Bureaucracy, Politics and Public Policy,* 4th ed. Boston: Little, Brown, 1988. A classic examination of the power of the bureaucracy in policy making: its sources of power in expertise, advice, and discretion, and its ability to mobilize clientele groups and the public to influence the president and Congress. Updated with discussions of "antibureaucratic ferment" and the resiliency of bureaucracies.

Schick, Allen. *The Federal Budget: Politics, Policy, Process.* Washington, D.C.: Brookings Institution, 1995. A comprehensive explanation of the federal budgetary process.

Wildavsky, Aaron. *The New Politics of the Budgetary Process.* Boston: Scott Foresman, 1988. The revised version of the classic work on politics and incrementalism in budgeting, including strategies by bureaucrats, the OMB, the president, and Congress, with emphasis on the collapse of political consensus, the entitlements problem, and the failure of budget-balancing efforts.

Wilson, James W. *Bureaucracy: What Bureaucrats Do and Why They Do It.* New York: Basic Books, 1989. In the author's words, "an effort to depict the essential features of bureaucratic life in the government agencies of the United States." An examination of what really motivates middle-level public servants. Wilson argues that congressional attempts to "micromanage" government activities hamper the ability of bureaucrats to do their jobs.

12

Congress: The Legislative Elite

Your representative owes you, not his industry only, but his judgement; and he betrays instead of serving you, if he sacrifices it to your opinion.

— **EDMUND BURKE**

The Founders intended that Congress be the first and most powerful branch of government. Article I of the Constitution describes the *national government's powers*, for example, "to lay and collect Taxes Duties Imposts and Excises and provide for the common Defense and general Welfare of the United States," *as powers given to Congress.* The Founders also intended that the House of Representatives represent "the people" in government. Among the governmental bodies created by the Constitution of 1878, *only the House of Representatives was to be directly elected by the people.* The Senate was to be elected by state legislatures (until the Seventeenth Amendment in 1913 provided for their direct election); the president was to be chosen by the Electoral College; and the Supreme Court was to be appointed for life. House members were to be elected every two years to ensure their responsiveness to the people. Indeed, even today House members fondly refer to their chamber as "the people's House."

But who are "the people" that Congress really represents? It is our argument that Congress members principally represent themselves. We contend that they are recruited from local elite structures; that the masses are largely inattentive to congressional affairs and elections; that the overriding interest of Congress members is their own reelection; that in pursuit of that goal they depend heavily upon large campaign contributors; that Congress has structured itself as "an incumbent protection society," that is, to assist its members to remain in office; that even *within* Congress a leadership "establishment" controls legislation; and finally that Congress has largely ceded policy initiation to the president, the bureaucracy, the courts, and organized interest groups.

THE ELITE BIAS OF CONGRESSIONAL RECRUITMENT

The elite bias of Congress begins with the recruitment of its members. Senators and House members are seldom recruited from the masses; they are drawn from the well-educated, prestigiously employed, affluent, upper and upper-middle classes of their home constituencies. They are drawn from the most ambitious, politically motivated, skilled communicators in their communities. Their social ties are mainly to state and community elite structures; they retain their local contacts, club memberships, business ties, and contributor networks. Members who sacrifice local ties and succumb to the attractions of Washington's "inside the beltway" social life do so at some risk.

Political Entrepreneurship

"Who sent these people to Washington? They sent themselves."[1] The most important qualification for Congress is political entrepreneurship—the ability and desire to sell oneself to others as a candidate, to raise money from political contributors, to organize and motivate others to work on one's campaign, and to communicate to others personally, in small groups and large audiences, and, most importantly, through the media.

For most members of Congress politics has become their career. They are professional public officeholders. "Citizen officeholders"—people with business or professional or commercial careers who get into politics part-time—have largely been driven out of political life in America by people who enter politics early in life and become career professionals in it. Both holding office and campaigning for it demand the full-time attention of politicians.

Increasingly political careers are begun early in life. Politically ambitious young people, fresh out of college or law school, seek out internships or staff positions with members of Congress, or congressional committees, or in state capitols or city halls. Others volunteer to work in political campaigns. They find political mentors to guide them in learning to organize campaigns, contact financial contributors, and deal with the media. They prudently wait for "open seats" in their state legislatures, city councils, or perhaps Congress itself, to launch their own initial campaigns for elective office.

Political parties seldom recruit candidates any more; candidates recruit themselves. Nor do interest groups recruit candidates, rather, candidates seek out interest groups in the hope of winning their support. Once elected to office, most successful members of Congress devote full time to staying there.

Professionalism

Professional and business backgrounds dominate the halls of Congress. Congress members are almost always of higher social standing than their average constituent. Candidates for Congress have a better chance at election if their occupations are socially "respectable" and provide opportunities for extensive public contacts. Lawyers, bankers, insurance brokers, and real estate brokers establish in their businesses the wide circle of friends necessary for political success.

The overrepresentation of lawyers in Congress and other public offices is particularly marked (see Table 12-1), since lawyers constitute no more than two-tenths of 1 percent of the labor force. Lawyers have always played a prominent role in the American political system. Twenty-five of the fifty-two signers of the Declaration of Independence and thirty-one of the fifty-five members of the Continental Congress were lawyers. The legal profession has also provided 70 percent of the presidents, vice presidents, and cabinet officers of the United States and more than 50 percent of the U.S. senators and House members. Lawyers are in a reasonably high-prestige occupation, but so are physicians, business executives, and scientists. Why, then, do lawyers dominate Congress?

It is sometimes argued that lawyers bring a special kind of skill to Congress. They represent clients in their work; therefore they can use the same skill to represent constituents in Congress. Also, lawyers deal with public policy as it is reflected in the statute books, so they may be reasonably familiar with public policy before entering Congress. But professional skills alone cannot explain the dominance of lawyers in public office. Of all the high-prestige occupations, only lawyers can really enhance their careers through political activities. Physicians, corporate managers, and scientists

TABLE 12-1		HOUSE			SENATE			CONGRESS
Congressional occupations		D	R	TOTAL	D	R	TOTAL	TOTAL
Actor/Entertainer		0	1	1	0	1	1	2
Aeronautics		0	1	1	1	0	1	2
Agriculture		8	14	22	2	6	8	30
Artistic/Creative		1	1	2	0	0	0	2
Business or Banking		55	126	181	8	25	33	214
Clergy		1	0	1	0	1	1	2
Education		40	33	74*	5	8	13	87*
Engineering		1	7	8	0	0	0	8
Health Care		1	1	2	0	0	0	2
Journalism		4	7	12*	2	7	9	21*
Labor Officials		1	0	1	0	0	0	1
Law		87	85	172	26	27	53	225
Law Enforcement		8	2	10	0	0	0	10
Medicine		3	9	12	0	2	2	14
Military		0	1	1	0	1	1	2
Miscellaneous		0	5	5	0	0	0	5
Professional Sports		0	3	3	0	0	0	3
Public Service		54	46	100	9	17	26	126
Real Estate		3	20	23	2	3	5	28
Technical/Trade		0	1	1	0	0	0	1

*Because some members have more than one occupation, the total is higher than congressional membership.

Source: Figures from 105th Congress, 1997–1999.

pay a high cost if they neglect their vocations for politics. But political activity can help boost lawyers' careers; free public advertising and contacts with potential clients are two important benefits. Moreover, lawyers have a monopoly on public offices in law enforcement and the court system, and the offices of judge or prosecuting attorney often provide lawyers with stepping stones to higher public office, including Congress.

Thus information on the occupational background of congressional members indicates that more than high social status is necessary for election to Congress. Experience in personal relations and public contacts, easy access to politics, and a great deal of time to devote to political activity are also helpful.

Education

Congressional members are among the most highly educated occupational groups in the United States. Their educational level is considerably higher

TABLE 12-2		WOMEN	AFRICAN-AMERICANS
Race and gender in Congress	*House Members (435)*		
	1985–1987	20	20
	1987–1989	23	23
	1989–1991	25	24
	1991–1993	28	26
	1993–1995	47	38
	1995–1997	48	38
	1997–1999	54	39
	1999–2001	58	39
	Senators (100)		
	1985–1987	2	0
	1987–1989	2	0
	1989–1991	2	0
	1991–1993	2	0
	1993–1995	6	1
	1995–1997	8	1
	1997–1999	9	1
	1999–2001	9	0

than that of the populations they represent. Their education reflects their occupational background and their middle- and upper-class origins.

Race and Gender

African-Americans make up just over 12 percent of the nation's population. Beginning in 1993, their membership in the House of Representatives reached 9 percent for the first time. The leap in black membership was a product of judicial interpretations of the Voting Rights Act, which requires that minorities be given maximum opportunity to elect minorities to Congress through redistricting. Hispanic membership also rose in the House (to eighteen members) as a result of redistricting. African-American and Hispanic membership in the House has remained steady in recent years.

It was not until 1966 that the first African-American, Republican Edward Brooke of Massachusetts, was popularly elected to the Senate; he served until 1979. Carol Moseley Braun was the first black woman to be elected to the Senate in 1992; she was defeated for reelection in 1998.

A record number of women won House and Senate seats in 1992. Women have continued to add to their numbers in both the House and the Senate since then, with Republican women members gaining seats. (See Table 12-2.)

WHOM DOES CONGRESS REALLY REPRESENT?

The relevant political constituencies of members of Congress are the elites of their districts rather than their districts' mass populations. In reality, their constituencies are small groups of political activists with the time, interest, and skill to communicate about political events.

Mass Inattention

For the great mass of people, Congress is an institution with very low visibility. Opinion polls consistently report grim facts about the public's lack of awareness of Congress. Only 59 percent of Americans can identify one U.S. senator from their state; only 25 percent can name both of their state's senators. Members of the House of Representatives fare even worse. Only 29 percent of the general public can identify their representative.[2]

Even when constituents know a congressional member's name, few know the member's specific policy positions or, for that matter, the member's overall political position. One study found that among those who offered a reason for candidate choice, only 7 percent indicated that their choice had any "discernible issue content." If one asks for detailed information about policy stands, only a "chemical trace" of the population qualifies as attentive to their congressional candidate's policy positions.[3]

Only about 15 percent of the population has *ever* written a letter to a senator or House representative, and 3 percent of the population accounts for more than two-thirds of congressional mail. During periods of turmoil the flow of letters becomes more urgent. However, even in critical national situations, the flow of communication is unrepresentative.

Elites as the Relevant Constituents

A legislator's relevant constituents, then, are the home district's active, interested, and resourceful elites. In an agricultural district, they are the leaders of the American Farm Bureau Federation and the major agricultural producers—cotton producers, wheat growers, and so on; in the Southwest, oil producers or ranchers; in the mountain states, the copper, lead, and silver mining interests; in upper New England, the lumber, granite, and fishing interests; in central Pennsylvania and West Virginia, the coal interests and leaders of the United Mine Workers. More heterogeneous urban constituencies may contain a variety of influential constituents—bankers and financial leaders, real estate owners and developers, owners and managers of large

Congressional theory of representation? © Reprinted courtesy of the *Boston Globe*.
All Rights Reserved.

industrial and commercial enterprises, top labor leaders, and the owners
and editors of newspapers and radio and television facilities. In certain big-
city districts with strong, disciplined party organizations, the key congressional constituents may be the city's political and governmental elites—the
city or county party chairpersons or the mayor. And, of course, anyone who
makes major financial contributions to a congressional candidate's campaign becomes a very important constituent.

Sending Messages to Legislators

The elite of a constituency tends to transmit messages to its representatives
that are in *agreement* with the representative's known policy preferences.
Representatives, like most other people, tend to associate with people with
whom they agree. Thus they will maintain contact with the constituency
primarily through existing acquaintances. Representatives gain most of their
information about constituency preferences through such personal contact.
They may also monitor mail and telephone calls, assigning their staff to

count pro and con messages. But representatives hear largely what they want to hear. Their selective perception may help explain why conflicting reports of public opinion are so common.

Legislators spend a great deal of time in their districts listening to local *elites.* When elites and masses do not share the same opinion, it is not surprising that legislators' actions do not fit mass preferences. However, on a few particularly visible issues, those on which the masses have strong opinions, the agreement between legislative performance and constituency demand can be relatively high. On civil rights issues, for instance, the correlation between congressional voting and constituency opinion is high. On most other issues, however, the correlation is nonexistent.

Although we cannot say with assurance what the representative process *is,* we certainly know what it is *not.* It is not the representation of the will of the people. At best, representation is intraelite communication.

CONGRESS IN DISREPUTE

Congress is the least popular branch of government. Polls reveal that a large majority of Americans believe (perhaps accurately) that members of Congress "spend more time thinking about their own political futures than they do in passing legislation."[4]

Throw the Rascals Out?

If Congress is so unpopular, we should reasonably expect voters to "throw the rascals out." The theory of representative democracy implies that dissatisfied voters will defeat incumbents running for reelection. But just the opposite occurs in congressional elections. Over 90 percent of House members and over 70 percent of senators seeking reelection succeed in doing so (see Table 12-3). Even during the sweeping Republican victories in 1994, when Republicans gained control of both the House and the Senate, 91 percent of House incumbents running for reelection won, as well as 92 percent of Senate incumbents. The failure of voters to throw the rascals out, despite mass disapproval of the performance of Congress, is more consistent with elite theory than with democratic theory.

Popular Members, Unpopular Congress

In an apparent paradox, most voters approve of their own representative, yet disapprove of the Congress as a whole. Individual members of Congress

TABLE 12-3	YEAR	PERCENTAGE OF SENATE INCUMBENTS REELECTED	PERCENTAGE OF HOUSE INCUMBENTS REELECTED
Congressional incumbent reelection rates	1966	96	90
	1968	83	96
	1970	88	95
	1972	84	93
	1974	92	90
	1976	61	96
	1978	68	95
	1980	59	92
	1982	93	90
	1984	90	96
	1986	75	98
	1988	77	98
	1990	96	97
	1992	86	87
	1994	92	91
	1996	95	94
	1998	91	98

Source: *Congressional Quarterly Weekly Report.*

are generally popular in their districts, even while Congress itself is an object of distrust and even ridicule. (See Table 12-4.) Obviously, if most incumbents are popular in their home districts, incumbents will continue to be reelected. The real question is, how do they maintain their popularity?

Incumbent Advantages

Why do incumbents win? First of all, name familiarity—in the absence of any knowledge of issues—can be a powerful advantage. The average voter, even if only vaguely aware of the incumbents, is likely to recognize their names on the ballot and vote for them. Even during a political campaign an incumbent enjoys much higher name recognition than a challenger (see Table 12-5).

More importantly, incumbents use the resources of their office—staff time, travel funds, perks, and privileges—to tend to the needs of their constituents. Over time, incumbents are likely to have developed an effective political organization and a stable network of communication with local elites. They use their franking privilege for mailing newsletters, polls, and other information; they appear at various public events, call news conferences, address organizational meetings, and, in general, make themselves as visible as possible, largely at taxpayers' expense.

TABLE 12-4		APPROVAL OF CONGRESS	APPROVAL OF "MY REPRESENTATIVES"
Mass attitudes toward Congress versus "my representatives"	1978	31	62
	1980	34	57
	1982	34	52
	1984	43	69
	1986	44	59
	1988	52	66
	1990	36	64
	1992	28	62
	1994	30	59
	1996	22	54

QUESTION: *In general do you approve or disapprove of the way [Congress/your representative] has been handling [its/his/her] job?*

Source: National election studies.

TABLE 12-5		PERCENT HAD CONTACT WITH	
Congressional candidate recognition: incumbents versus challengers		INCUMBENT	CHALLENGER
	1978	75	36
	1980	77	37
	1982	78	45
	1984	76	37
	1986	77	33
	1988	78	34
	1990	77	23
	1992	77	40
	1994	76	40
	1996	76	39

QUESTION: *Have you come into contact with or learned anything about [candidate/representative] through any of these ways? [met with, heard speak, talked to staff; received mail from, read about in newspaper, heard on radio, saw on TV]?*

Source: National election studies.

Finally, incumbents attract heavy campaign contributions. Because the "smart money" backs a winner, incumbents have more to spend in their campaigns. Indeed, incumbents usually raise and spend twice as much money as their challengers (see Table 12-6).

Mass Reaction: Term Limits

Mass distrust of politicians has fueled a national grass-roots movement to limit the terms of public officials—notably members of Congress and state

TABLE 12-6		HOUSE	SENATE
Congressional campaign spending: incumbents versus challengers	Average incumbent	$628,064	$5,015,685
	Average challenger	$301,289	$2,418,075
	Average open-seat candidate	$638,571	$2,970,011

Source: Federal Election Commission, 1998.

legislators. Term limits are very popular with voters; national surveys regularly show overwhelming support for limiting the terms of senators and representatives.

Proponents of term limits rely on antielitist arguments: Citizen-legislators have largely been replaced by career professional politicians. Over time, professional officeholders become isolated from the lives and concerns of average citizens; they acquire an "inside the beltway" mentality (a reference to the circle of interstate highways that surrounds Washington, D.C.). They respond to the media, to polls, to interest groups, but have no direct feeling for how their constituents live. Term limits would force politicians to return home and live under the laws that they make. Term limits would increase competition in the electoral system. Creating "open-seat" races on a regular basis would encourage more people to seek public office. Incumbents continually win reelection not because they are the most qualified people in their districts, but rather because of the many electoral advantages granted by incumbency itself.

Elite Opposition to Term Limits

However, the enthusiasm of the mass public for term limits is more than matched by the intense opposition the proposal meets on Capitol Hill. It is not likely that members of Congress will ever vote to limit their own terms of office, especially since a constitutional amendment to do so would require two-thirds of the members of both houses to vote to limit their own legislative careers.

Elites argue that term limits infringe on the voters' freedom of choice. If voters are upset with the performance of Congress or their state legislature, they can always "throw the rascals out." If they want to limit the terms of their own members of Congress, they can do so by not reelecting them. But if voters wish to keep popular, able, experienced, and hard-working legislators in office, they should be permitted to do so.

Deciding on Term Limits

If the question were left to voters in the states, Congress would certainly confront term limits. Congressional term limits have won by landslide margins almost every time they have appeared on statewide referenda ballots. (The only state whose electorate appeared ambivalent about term limits was Washington. In 1991, when Speaker of the House Tom Foley returned to his state to lead a fight against a retroactive measure that threatened to oust him, voters rejected it by a narrow margin. The following year they approved a term limit measure that would allow Foley and his other House colleagues an additional six years only. Then in 1994, Foley himself was defeated for reelection in his home district—the only House speaker in modern history to lose a reelection bid.)

However, the U.S. Supreme Court held in 1995 that the voters in state referenda cannot limit terms of Congress members. In a controversial 5–4 decision, the Court argued that the Founders intended that age, citizenship, and residency be the *only* qualifications for membership in Congress, inasmuch as these are the only qualifications mentioned in Article I of the Constitution.[5] The effect of this decision, together with Congress' steadfast opposition to term limits, is to largely destroy the hopes of the congressional term-limit movement.

THE ELABORATE PROCEDURES OF LEGISLATIVE ELITES

The rules and procedures of Congress are elaborate but important to the functioning of legislative elites. Legislative procedures and rules make the legislative process fair and orderly. Without established customs, rules, and procedures, 535 men and women could not arrive at collective decisions about the thousands of items submitted to them during a congressional session. Yet the same rules also delay or obstruct proposed changes in the status quo; they strengthen Congress's conservative role in policy making. In congressional procedures, legislation faces many opportunities for defeat and many obstacles to passage.

The elaborate procedures of Congress ensure that very few of the bills introduced are ever passed. In a two-year congressional session, more than 10,000 bills will be introduced, but fewer than 800 bills will be enacted. In other words, fewer than 10 percent of the measures introduced will ever find their way through the lawmaking process.

The Lawmaking Process

Congress follows a fairly standard pattern in the formal process of making laws; Figure 12-1 describes briefly some of the most important procedural steps. Bills generally originate in the president's office, in executive departments, or in the offices of interested elites, but a member of the House or Senate must formally introduce them into Congress. Except for bills raising revenue, which must begin in the House of Representatives according to the Constitution, bills can be introduced in either house. Upon introduction, a bill moves to one of the standing committees of the House or Senate, which may (1) recommend it for adoption with only minor changes, (2) virtually rewrite it into a new policy proposal, (3) ignore it and prevent its passage through inaction, or (4) kill it by majority vote. The full House or Senate *may* overrule a committee decision but does so rarely. Most members of Congress are reluctant to upset the prerogatives of the committees and the desires of recognized leaders. Therefore committees have virtual power of life or death over every legislative measure.

Standing Congressional Committees

Committee work is essential to the legislative process; Congress as a body could never hope to review all the measures put before it. As early as 1885 Woodrow Wilson described the American political process as "government by the standing committees of Congress."[6] But while reducing legislative work to manageable proportions, the committee system allows a minority of the legislators, sometimes a single committee chairman, to delay and obstruct the legislative process.

In the Senate, the most prestigious committees are Foreign Relations, Appropriations, and Finance; in the House, the most powerful are the Rules Committee, Appropriations, and Ways and Means. (Table 12-7 lists the twenty standing committees of the House and the twenty of the Senate.) To expedite business, most standing committees create subcommittees to handle particular matters falling within their jurisdiction. This practice further concentrates power over particular subject matter in the hands of a very few congressional members. Considerable power lies in the hands of subcommittee members, especially the chairpersons; interested elites cultivate the favor of powerful subcommittee and committee chairpersons.

FIGURE 12-1 | How a bill becomes a law

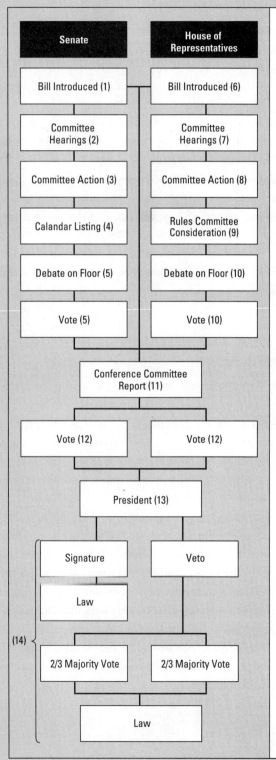

1. **Introduction.** Most bills can be introduced in either house. (In this example, the bill is first introduced in the Senate.) It is given a number and referred to the proper committee.

2. **Hearings.** The committee may hold public hearings on the bill.

3. **Committee action.** The full committee meets in executive (closed) session. It may kill the bill, approve it with or without amendments, or draft a new bill.

4. **Calendar.** If the committee recommends the bill for passage, it is listed on the calendar.

5. **Debate, amendment, vote.** The bill goes to the floor for debate. Amendments may be added. The bill is voted on.

6. **Introduction to the second house.** If the bill passes, it goes to the House of Representatives, where it is referred to the proper committee.

7. **Hearings.** Hearings may be held again.

8. **Committee action.** The committee rejects the bill, prepares a new one, or accepts the bill with or without amendments.

9. **Rules Committee consideration.** If the committee recommends the bill, it is listed on the calendar and sent to the Rules Committee. The Rules Committee can block a bill or clear it for debate before the entire House.

10. **Debate, amendment, vote.** The bill goes before the entire body and is debated and voted upon.

11. **Conference Committee.** If the bill as passed by the second house contains major changes, either house may request a conference committee. The conference—five persons from each house, representing both parties—meets and tries to reconcile its differences.

12. **Vote on conference report.** When committee members reach an agreement, they report back to their respective houses. Their report is either accepted or rejected.

13. **Submission to the president.** If the report is accepted by both houses, the bill is signed by the speaker of the House and the president of the Senate and is sent to the president of the United States.

14. **Presidential action.** The president may sign or veto the bill within ten days. If the president does not sign and Congress is still in session, the bill automatically becomes law. If Congress adjourns before the ten days have elapsed, it does not become law. (This is called the "pocket veto.") If the president returns the bill with a veto message, it may still become a law if passed by a two-thirds majority in each house.

TABLE 12-7	SENATE	HOUSE OF REPRESENTATIVES
The standing committees of Congress	Agriculture, Nutrition, and Forestry Appropriations Armed Services Banking, Housing, and Urban Affairs Budget Commerce, Science, and Transportation Energy and Natural Resources Environment and Public Works Finance Foreign Relations Governmental Affairs Indian Affairs Judiciary Labor and Human Resources Rules and Administration Select Ethics Small Business Special Aging Veterans' Affairs	Agriculture Appropriations Banking and Financial Services Budget Commerce Economic and Educational Opportunities Government Reform and Oversight House Oversight International Relations Judiciary National Security Resources Rules Science Select Intelligence Small Business Transportation and Infrastructure Veterans' Affairs Ways and Means

Public Hearings   In examining legislation, a committee or subcommittee generally holds public hearings on bills deemed worthy by the chairperson or, in some cases, by the majority of the committee. Influenced by the legal profession, represented by a majority of legislators, the committees tend to look upon public hearings as trials in which contestants present their sides of the argument to the committee members, who act as judges. Presumably, during this trial the skillful judges will sift facts on which to base their decisions. In practice, however, committees use public hearings primarily to influence public opinion or executive action or, occasionally, to discover the position of major elite groups on the measure under consideration. Major decisions take place in secret executive session.

Committee Membership   The membership of the standing committees on agriculture, labor, interior and insular affairs, and the judiciary generally reflects the interest of particular elite groups in the nation. Legislators representing farm interests sit on the agricultural committees; representatives of land, water, and natural resource interests serve on interior and insular affairs committees; members of Congress with labor ties and urban industrial constituencies gravitate toward the labor committee; and lawyers dominate the judicial committees of both houses.

Given the power of congressional committees, the assignment of members to committees is one of the most significant activities of Congress. In the House of Representatives, the Republicans assign their members to committees through the Committee on Committees, which consists of one representative from each state that sends a Republican to Congress. Each representative votes with the strength of his or her state delegation. But the real business of this committee is conducted by a subcommittee appointed by the Republican party leader. The subcommittee fills committee vacancies with freshman members and those who request transfer from other committees. The Committee on Committees considers the career backgrounds of members, their seniority, and their reputation for soundness, which usually means support for the party leadership. Often the chairperson of a standing committee tells the Committee on Committees his or her preferences for committee members. Democrats in the House make committee assignments through the Steering and Policy Committee. This committee is composed of the party leadership; the caucus elects twelve members to represent geographic regions, and the speaker appoints the additional nine members.

In the Senate, the Committee on Committees fills Republican committee positions, and a steering committee appointed by the Democratic leader selects Democratic committee members. Usually only senators with seniority are eligible for positions on the major Senate committees, such as the foreign relations, armed services, and appropriations committees.

The Power of the Chair   Committee and subcommittee chairpersons are very powerful. They usually determine the bills the committee will consider, select issues for public hearings, and establish the agenda of the committee. Governmental and nongovernmental interests officially must consult the chairperson on all questions relating to his or her committee; this procedure confers status on the chairperson with the executive branch and with interested nongovernmental elites. Only occasionally does a majority within the committee-subcommittee "baronage" overrule a chairperson's decision on a committee matter.

The Seniority System

The practice of appointing chairpersons according to seniority guarantees conservatism in the legislative process. The member of the majority party with the longest continuous service on the committee becomes chairperson; the member of the minority party with the longest continuous service on the committee is the ranking minority member. Therefore chairpersons are not chosen by their own committees, by their own party, or by the House and Senate as a whole. They are chosen by the voters of noncompetitive congressional districts whose representatives are likely to stay in office the longest. The major decisions in Congress rest with those members from areas where party competition and voter participation are low. In both houses, the seniority system works against the politically competitive districts.

As their influence within Congress grows, high-seniority legislators tend to identify with Congress as an institution, to the detriment of possible influence of their constituencies. Two factors are at work here. Legislators get to know each other well (they see one another more regularly than they see constituents), and older legislators probably have learned from experience that a perceived unpopular vote will not bring the vigorous constituency response they once thought was inevitable. Thus the experienced legislator tends to develop a more realistic view of the electorate, expressed well in one senator's remarks: "After several terms, I don't give a damn anymore. I'm pretty safe now and I don't have to worry about reaction in the district."[7] Legislators also specialize in certain kinds of legislation, thus developing expertise that draws their colleagues to them as credible sources of information. As one put it, "That's the beauty of the seniority system—there are informed, experienced people on each Committee you can consult."[8] When members of Congress need advice, they usually turn to someone of higher seniority.

Decentralization: Subcommittees and "Iron Triangles"

Over time, the specialized subcommittees of Congress have gained power. At present the House has about 150 subcommittees and the Senate about 90 subcommittees. Each subcommittee develops its own specialized policy network. These policy networks are the "iron triangles" of interest groups, executive bureaucracies, and subcommittee members and staff. These "subgovernments" develop to the benefit of all participants: legislators benefit from campaign contributions by interest groups; lobbyists benefit from personal working relationships with committees and their staffs; administrative agencies benefit from interest groups' and congressional committees' support of their budget requests. Gradually, legislators, lobbyists, and bureaucrats develop a common bond whose strength frequently exceeds that of loyalty to the party.

There is a subcommittee chair for virtually every majority party legislator; there is also at least one subcommittee, and frequently no more than three, to attract the attention of a particular interest group. Each subcommittee is theoretically answerable to the full committee and to the membership of the Senate and House. In practice, the centrifugal force tugging them away from the center is very powerful. A fragmented, disjointed decision-making process is not easily controlled by party leaders and the president. Such a process is easily accommodated to the needs of the political action committees, whose financial generosity toward members of "their" subcommittees exceeds the contribution of political parties by a ratio of 5 to 1.

The House Rules Committee

After a standing committee reports a bill in the House (step 8 in Figure 12-1), the Rules Committee must issue a special rule or order before the bill can go before the House membership for consideration. Consequently each bill must go through two committees. (The only exceptions are bills reported by the House Appropriations and the Ways and Means committees; the House may consider their bills at any time as privileged motions.) The Rules Committee can kill a bill by shelving it indefinitely. It can insist that the bill be amended as the price of permitting it on the floor and can even substitute a new bill for the one framed by another committee. The Rules Committee determines how much debate will be permitted on any bill and the number and kind of amendments that may be offered from the floor. The only formal limits on Rules Committee authority are the *discharge petition* (which is rarely used and hardly ever successful) and *calendar Wednesday*, a cumbersome procedure that permits standing committees to call up bills the Rules Committee has blocked. The Rules Committee, clearly the most powerful committee in Congress, is dominated by senior members elected from noncompetitive districts.

Senate Filibusters

In the Senate, control of floor debate rests with the majority leader. But the majority leader does not have the power to limit debate; a senator who has the floor may talk without limit and may choose to whom he or she yields the floor. If enough senators wish to talk a bill to death, they may do so in what is known as a *filibuster*. This device permits a minority to tie up the business of the Senate and prevent it from voting on a bill. Debate can be limited only by a process called *cloture*. Sixteen members' signatures on a petition will bring cloture to a vote; a three-fifths vote of the full Senate is required to end debate. This means that forty-one senators can, if they choose, block legislation by voting against cloture. The filibuster is a means by which a minority can defend itself against majority preferences.

The Floor Vote

Of the ten thousand bills introduced into Congress every year, only about a thousand, or one in ten, become law. After approval of a bill by the standing committee in the Senate or by the standing committee and the Rules Committee in the House, the bill moves to the floor for a vote. Usually the most crucial votes come on the amendments to the bill that are offered to the floor (however, the Rules Committee may prevent amendments in the House). Once the membership defeats major amendments or incorporates them into the bill, the bill usually picks up broad support, and the final vote is usually heavily in favor of it.

Conference Committees

One of the most conservative features of American government is its *bicameralism;* after following a complicated path in one house, a bill must repeat the process in the other. A bill must pass both branches of Congress in identical form before it goes to the president for signature. However, the Senate often amends a House bill, and the House usually amends Senate bills. And every time a house amends a bill, it must resubmit the bill to the originating house for concurrence with the changes. If either house declines to accept changes in the bill, an ad hoc joint committee, called a *conference committee*, must iron out specific differences. Disagreements between the houses are so frequent that from one-third to one-half of all public bills, including virtually all important ones, must go to conference committees after passage by both houses.

Conference committee members, appointed by the presiding officers of each house, usually come from the two standing committees that handled the bills in each house. Since the final bill produced by the conference committee is generally accepted by both houses, these committees have tremendous power in determining the final form of legislation. Both houses must accept or reject conference committee reports as a whole; they cannot further amend them. Most conference committee meetings are closed and unrecorded; the committees hold no hearings and listen to no outside testimony. The bill that emerges from their deliberations may not represent the view of either house and may even contain items never considered by either one. Some people have dubbed conference committees a "third house" of Congress, whose members are not elected by the people, keep no record of their work, and usually operate behind closed doors—with no debate about their products allowed.

ELITES WITHIN ELITES: THE CONGRESSIONAL ESTABLISHMENT

A power hierarchy exists among federal government elites that is supported by protocol, by the distribution of formal constitutional powers, by the powers associated with party office, by the committee and seniority systems of Congress, and by the "informal folkways" of Washington. According to the protocol of Washington society, the president holds the highest social rank, followed by former presidents and their widows, the vice president, the Speaker of the House, members of the Supreme Court, foreign ambassadors and ministers, cabinet members, U.S. senators, governors of states, former vice presidents, and, finally, House members.

Senatorial Power

The Constitution grants greater formal powers to senators than to House members. There being only one hundred senators, individual senators are more visible than House members in the social and political life of Washington, as well as in their home states. Senators also have special authority in foreign affairs not accorded to House members, for the Senate must advise and consent by a two-thirds vote to all treaties entered into by the United States. The threat of Senate repudiation of a treaty makes it desirable for the president to solicit Senate views on foreign affairs; generally the secretary of state works closely with the Senate Foreign Relations Committee on such matters. Influential senators undertake personal missions abroad and serve on delegations to international bodies. Another constitutional power afforded senators is to advise and consent on executive appointments, including Supreme Court justices, cabinet members, federal judges, ambassadors, and other high executive officials. Although the Senate generally approves the presidential nominations, the added potential for power contributes to the difference between the influence of senators and of House members. Finally, senators serve six-year terms and represent broader and more heterogeneous constituencies. Thus they have a longer guaranteed tenure in

TABLE 12-8	SENATE	SENATOR	STATE
Party leadership in the 106th Congress	Majority Leader	Trent Lott (R)	Mississippi
	Majority Whip	Don Nickles (R)	Oklahoma
	Minority Leader	Tom Daschle (D)	North Dakota
	Minority Whip	Harvey Reid (D)	Nevada
	President Pro Tempore	Strom Thurmond (R)	South Carolina
	HOUSE	REPRESENTATIVE	STATE
	Speaker	Dennis Hastert (R)	Illinois
	Majority Leader	Dick Armey (R)	Texas
	Majority Whip	Tom DeLay (R)	Texas
	Minority Leader	Richard Gephardt (D)	Missouri
	Minority Whip	David Bonior (D)	Michigan

Washington, more prestige, and greater freedom from minor shifts in opinion among nongovernmental elites in their home states.

Senators can enhance their power through their political roles; they often wield great power in state parties and can usually control federal patronage dispensed in their state. The power of the Senate to confirm nominations has given rise to the important political custom of "senatorial courtesy": senators of the same party as the president have virtual veto power over major appointments—federal judges, postmasters, customs collectors, and so on—in their states. Presidential nominations that go to the Senate are referred to the senator or senators from the state involved. If the senator declares the nominee personally obnoxious to him or her, the Senate usually respects this declaration and rejects the appointment. Thus before the president submits a nomination to the Senate, he usually makes sure that the nominee will be acceptable to his party's senator or senators from the state involved.

The Speaker of the House

Party leadership roles in the House and the Senate are major sources of power in Washington. (See Table 12-8 for a list of Senate and House leaders for the 106th Congress.) The speaker of the House of Representatives, elected by the majority party of the House, exercises more power over public policy than any other member of either house. Before 1910 the speaker appointed all standing committees and their chairs, possessed unlimited discretion to recognize members on the floor, and served as chair of the

Rules Committee. But in 1910, progressives severely curtailed the speaker's authority. Today the speaker shares power over committee appointments with the Committee on Committees; committee chairs are selected by seniority, not by the speaker; and the speaker no longer serves as chair of the Rules Committee. However, the speaker retains considerable authority: referring bills to committees, appointing all conference committees, ruling on

FOCUS

The Troubled Speakership

Recent Speakers have faced turmoil and trouble in trying to lead the House of Representatives. Their troubles have included ethics investigations, votes of censure by their colleagues, ouster by voters in their home district, and resignation under fire from their own party members.

The last Speaker of the House to leave the post voluntarily was the crafty Boston Irish politician Thomas P. ("Tip") O'Neill, who became a media celebrity in the 1980s as the Democratic counterpoint to Republican President Ronald Reagan. O'Neill's replacement, Democrat Jim Wright from Texas, was renowned for his legislative skills. But he lasted only two years in the job (1987–1989). He was forced to resign following an ethics investigation of his outside income. Wright's most vociferous critic was a Georgia Republican, Newt Gingrich, who was quickly gaining a reputation in the House for his hardball politics.

Wright's successor was the genial Democrat Thomas S. Foley of Washington. Foley was well liked by House members of both parties. But Foley apparently fell victim to the "inside the Beltway" mentality—focusing almost exclusive attention on affairs in the nation's capital while ignoring the opinions of the voters at home. In 1994, Foley became the first Speaker in modern history to be thrown out of Congress by the voters in his home district.

Enter "Speaker Newt" Newt Gingrich was a young professor of history at West Georgia College when he first ran for Congress in 1974. Twice he ran and lost in a traditionally Democratic district, but on his third try in 1978 he won election to the House by projecting a strong conservative image. Upon his arrival in Washington, Gingrich rejected the traditional apprentice role for freshman members and chose instead to organize his fellow Republican conservatives. He quickly acquired a reputation as a "bomb thrower"—a pugnacious guerrilla fighter—even within his own party. In 1986 he took control of a political action committee, GOPAC, dedicated to helping Republicans get elected. In this role he won the loyalty of many House Republicans to whom he directed money. Although the media despised Gingrich's politics, his aggressive style made news, and soon Gingrich became the spokesman for House Republicans. When the soft-spoken moderate Republican leader, Bob Michel, decided to retire, Newt assumed the GOP leadership post.

The political earthquake that shook Washington in the 1994 midterm congressional elections was largely due to Gingrich's efforts. The GOP not only captured control of the U.S. Senate, but also control of the House of Representatives, for the first time in forty years. This dramatic power shift enabled Gingrich to assume the office of Speaker of the House. Indeed, Gingrich saw himself as the architect of the stunning GOP victory. He sought to revive the traditional responsible party (see Chapter 7) by setting forth clear party all matters of House procedure, recognizing those who wish to speak, and generally directing the business of the floor. More important, the speaker is the principal figure in House policy formulation, leadership, and responsibility; although sharing these tasks with standing committee chairs, the speaker is generally "first among equals" in relation to them. (See Focus: "The Troubled Speakership.")

positions on key issues in the Republican "Contract with America."

Newt's Downfall   But the "Contract with America" soon fell apart in Congress, despite GOP control of both the House and Senate. The contract's keystone, the Balanced Budget Amendment, passed the House but failed to win the necessary two-thirds vote in the Senate by a single vote. Speaker Gingrich failed to get the House to approve term-limits amendment to the Constitution, and it was never even considered in the Senate. Lawyers in Congress defeated meaningful tort reform, and the promised tax cuts became mired in lengthy budget battles with the president. In these battles, Speaker Newt's budget cuts appeared mean-spirited; while the president polished his image as a defender of "Medicare, Medicaid, education and the environment." When President Clinton vetoed congressional budgets, the resulting temporary government "shutdown" was widely blamed on Newt and the congressional Republicans, rather than the president.

Speaker Newt's public image nosedived. He had failed to deliver on key items in the "Contract with America," and his aggressive and sometime abrasive style contrasted poorly with Clinton's smooth rhetoric.

Newt Gingrich—Favorability Rating

	1998	1996	1995
Favorable	24%	31%	34%
Unfavorable	62%	57%	37%
No opinion	14%	12%	29%

As a player of "hardball politics," Gingrich often found himself on the receiving end of personal attacks by enraged Democrats. Ethics complaints were filed against the speaker over the use of funds from his political action committee, GOPAC, over a $2 million book deal (which he was forced to forgo), and over funding and use of his videotaped college course "Renewing American Civilization." The House Ethics Committee fined Gingrich $300,000; former GOP presidential candidate Bob Dole offered to lend Gingrich the money to pay the fine.

Leadership Turmoil   The Republican party managed to retain control of the House in 1996 and 1998, but they lost seats in both elections. Newt succeeded in quelling a mini-revolt among House Republicans against his leadership following the 1996 election, but the unexpected loss of seats in 1998 undermined Newt's support even among his fellow conservatives. He was forced to resign shortly after the election.

Robert Livingston, Louisiana Republican and chairman of the powerful House Appropriations Committee, was selected to become Speaker when the new Congress convened in 1999. But he shocked his colleagues in the House with a dramatic speech acknowledging an extramarital sexual affair, resigning as Speaker-designate, and calling on President Clinton to follow his example. House Democratic Leader, Richard Gephardt, responded by denouncing "the politics of personal destruction" and pledging continued Democratic support for Clinton. House Republicans chose little-known but well-liked Illinois Representative Dennis Hastert to assume the troubled role of Speaker of the House.

Floor Leaders and Whips

Next to the speaker, the most influential party leaders in the House are the majority and minority floor leaders and the party whips. These party leaders are chosen by their respective party caucuses at the beginning of each congressional session. The party caucus, composed of all the party's members in the House, usually does little more than elect these officers; it makes no major policy decisions. The floor leaders and whips have little formal authority; their role is to influence legislation through persuasion. Party floor leaders must combine parliamentary skill with persuasion, maintain good personal relationships with party members, and cultivate close ties with the president and administration. They cannot deny party renomination to members who are disloyal to the party, but because they can control committee assignments and many small favors in Washington, they can prevent a maverick from becoming an effective legislator.

The whips, or assistant floor leaders, keep members informed about legislative business, see that members are present for important floor votes, and communicate party strategy and position on particular issues. They also serve as the eyes and ears of the leadership, counting noses before important votes. Party whips should know how many votes a particular measure has, and they should be able to get the votes to the floor when the roll is called.

The Vice President

The vice president of the United States, who serves as president of the Senate, has less control over Senate affairs then the speaker has over House affairs. The vice president votes only in case of a tie and must recognize senators in the order in which they rise. The majority party in the Senate also elects from its membership a president pro tempore, who presides in the absence of the vice president.

Majority and Minority Leaders

The key power figures in the Senate are the majority and minority leaders, who are chosen by their respective parties. The majority leader usually has great personal influence within the Senate and is a power figure in national affairs. The majority leader, when of the same party as the president, is in charge of getting the president's legislative program through the Senate. Although having somewhat less formal authority than the Speaker of the House, the majority leader has the right to be the first senator to be heard on the floor and, with the minority floor leader, determines the Senate's agenda. But on the whole, the majority leader's influence rests on powers of persuasion.

Committee Chairs

The committee system and the seniority rule also create powerful congressional figures: the chairs of the most powerful standing committees, particularly the Senate Foreign Relations, Appropriations, and Finance committees and the House Rules, Appropriations, and Ways and Means committees. The chairs of the standing committees in both houses have become powerful through members' respect for the authority of their committees. The standing committee system is self-sustaining because an attack on the authority of one committee or committee chairperson is much like a threat to all; members know that if they allow one committee or committee chairperson to be bypassed on a particular measure, they open the door to other similar infringements of power. Hence committee chairs and ranking committee members tend to stand by one another and support one another's authority over legislation assigned to their respective committees. Committee chairs and ranking committee members also earn respect because of their seniority and experience in the legislative process. They are often experts in parliamentary process as well as in the substantive area covered by their committees. Finally, and perhaps most important, committee chairs and ranking committee members acquire power through their close relationships with the bureaucratic and interest group elites within their committee's jurisdiction.

CONFLICT AND CONSENSUS: VOTING IN CONGRESS

Party Voting

Studies of roll-call voting in Congress show that the role of party influence in legislative conflict varies according to the issue.[9] Party votes, those roll-call votes in which a majority of voting Democrats oppose a majority of voting Republicans, occur on more than half the roll-call votes in Congress. Indeed, roll-call voting follows party lines more often than it follows sectional, urban–rural, or any other divisions that have been studied.

How much cohesion exists within the parties? Table 12-9 shows the percentage of party votes in Congress in recent years, and the average support Democratic and Republican members of Congress have given to their

		PARTY VOTES AS PERCENTAGE	PERCENTAGE OF PARTY SUPPORT:	PERCENTAGE OF PARTY SUPPORT:
TABLE 12-9	YEAR	OF TOTAL VOTES	DEMOCRATS*	REPUBLICANS*
Party voting in Congress	1986			
	Senate	52	72	76
	House	57	79	70
	1988			
	Senate	42	78	68
	House	47	80	74
	1990			
	Senate	54	82	77
	House	49	86	78
	1992			
	Senate	64	82	83
	House	53	86	84
	1994			
	Senate	52	84	79
	House	62	83	84
	1996			
	Senate	62	84	89
	House	56	80	87
	1997			
	Senate	53	85	87
	House	54	82	88

*Average percentage of times a member voted with majority of party of affiliation in disagreement with the other party's majority.

Source: *Congressional Quarterly Weekly Report,* various years.

parties. Members of both parties vote with their party majority more than two-thirds of the time. Party voting appears more frequent in the House than in the Senate.

However, party-line votes are the result more of members' personal predispositions than of explicitly formulated party policy. Political scientist Theodore Lowi makes the distinction between party "regularity," which is strong, and party organization and discipline, of which there is very little.[10]

Conflict

Conflict between parties occurs most frequently over social-welfare programs, housing and urban development, economic opportunity, medical care, antipoverty programs, health and welfare, and the regulation of

| FIGURE 12-2 | Presidential success on votes in Congress |

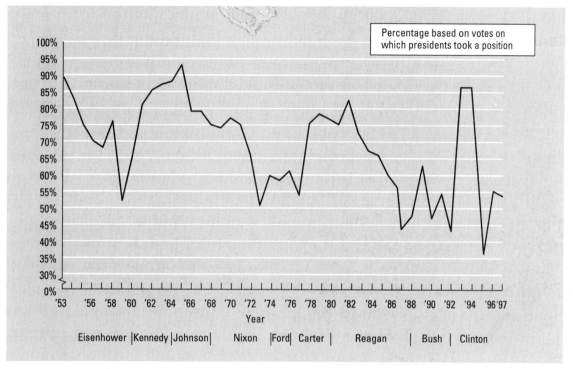

Source: *Congressional Quarterly Weekly Report,* January 3, 1998.

business and labor. Party conflict is particularly apparent on spending and taxing proposals in the budget. The budget is the president's product and carries the label of the president's party. On some issues, voting generally follows party lines during roll calls on preliminary motions and amendments, but swings to a bipartisan vote on the final legislation. In such situations the parties disagree on certain aspects of the bill but compromise on its final passage. Bipartisan votes, those roll calls in which divisions do *not* fall along party lines, occur more frequently on foreign policy and defense issues.

Presidential Support

The president generally receives greater support from his own party than from the opposition party in Congress. Thus, the presidents who have run up the highest legislative "box scores"—victories for bills that they publicly supported—are those whose party controlled the Congress (see Figure 12-2). Since Democrats controlled the House of Representatives for forty years prior to 1995, and the Senate for all but eight of those years, Democratic presidents (Kennedy, Johnson, Carter, and Clinton, 1993–1994) generally achieved higher box scores than Republican presidents. Indeed, Eisenhower and Reagan in their first years in office were uncommonly successful in pushing their legislation through a House of Representatives controlled by Democrats. But during Reagan's second term and throughout Bush's presidency, policy "gridlock" developed between these Republican administrations and the Democratically controlled House and Senate.

President Clinton was extraordinarily successful during his first two years in office in getting his legislative proposals enacted by a Democratically controlled Congress. Despite a few well-publicized defeats such as his health-care bill, Clinton posted the highest "box scores" since Lyndon

FOCUS

Is "Congressional Ethics" an Oxymoron?

Bribery is a criminal act: it is illegal to offer, to solicit, or to receive anything of value in exchange for the performance of a government duty. However, performing a service for a constituent, including a constituent who contributes generously to a Congress member's campaign, is not illegal. Drawing an ethical line between bribery and services to campaign contributors has proven difficult.

The case of the Keating Five dates back to 1985, when Charles H. Keating, owner of California-based Lincoln Savings and Loan, ran into difficulties with the Federal Home Loan Bank Board, which regulates the savings and loan industry. Keating invested Lincoln's government-insured funds in a wide variety of risky stocks, bonds, and commercial real estate ventures. When the bank board regulators charged that he had violated savings and loan regulations, Keating began to line up prominent politicians to pressure the board to

drop their "vendetta" against him, among them U.S. Senators Alan Cranston (D-California), John Glenn (D-Ohio), Donald W. Riegle (D-Michigan), Dennis DeConcini (D-Arizona), and John McCain (R-Arizona).

Most of the senators' work on behalf of Keating consisted of contacting regulators and urging speedy and favorable consideration of his case. Regulators appeared ready to close down the shaky Lincoln S&L in early 1987 in order to save its remaining assets and limit the taxpayers' responsibility for additional losses. But Keating arranged to have his senators meet with top regulators and pressure them to postpone for two years the government's decision to close down the bankrupt S&L, a decision that eventually cost U.S. taxpayers *$2 billion.*

How did Keating win the active support of five U.S. senators in his fight against the bank board? Keating contributed a total of $1.5 million to their campaign chests and political causes. Nearly $1 million of these contributions went to Senator Alan Cranston; specific contributions of $250,000, $250,000, and $500,000 were made within days of Cranston's calls and meetings with bank board officials. Senator John Glenn received a total of $242,000 from Keating and John McCain received $110,000. Dennis DeConcini and Donald Riegle,

Johnson. However, Clinton's scores tumbled dramatically after the Republicans captured control of the Congress after 1994.

The Conservative Coalition

On some issues, a "conservative coalition" emerges. This coalition is said to appear when a majority of southern Democrats joins a majority of Republicans to oppose a majority of northern Democrats. Historically this coalition has reflected conservative Republican and southern Democratic opposition to the liberal agenda and has generally resisted new federal interventions in the economy and supported tax cuts and a strong national defense. Although the conservative coalition has appeared less frequently in recent years, it has been very successful in votes in which it did appear.

who received $85,000 and $78,250, respectively, later returned those monies.

The key question in the subsequent Senate Ethics Committee investigation in 1991 was whether there was any direct connection between Keating's payments and the actions of the five senators on behalf of their benefactor. (Remember: bribery is an exchange of payment for official actions.) When Keating himself was asked whether his large campaign contributions brought him political influence, he replied, "I certainly hope so." Keating was later tried and convicted on fraud charges stemming from his S&L operations.

But Senator Cranston contended that he was just performing a service for a constituent. His "everyone does it" defense cited his own and other senators' efforts on behalf of defense contractors, automobile manufacturers, and others seeking specific government benefits and subsidies. "Nothing I did violated any law or specific Senate rule . . . there is no evidence that I agreed to help Charles Keating in return for a contribution."[a]

But the Ethics Committee found that Cranston's "impermissible pattern of conduct violated established norms of behavior in the Senate . . . [and] was improper and repugnant." The committee "strongly and severely reprimanded" Cranston, but took no further action due to "exten-

© Tribune Media Services, Inc. All Right Reserved. Reprinted with permission.

uating circumstances . . . Senator Cranston is in poor health . . . [and] has announced his intention not to seek reelection to the Senate." The Senate Ethics Committee also determined that the other four senators—DeConcini, Glenn, McCain, and Riegle—were guilty of "poor judgment" in conduct that gave "the appearance of impropriety." But the Ethics Committee offered little in the way of future guidance in handling constituent services and campaign contributions.

[a]U.S. Senator Alan Cranston, statement in the U.S. Senate, reported in *Congressional Quarterly Weekly Report* (November 23, 1991): 3437.

CONGRESS AND THE PRESIDENT: AN UNSTABLE BALANCE OF POWER

The President Initiates, Congress Deliberates

How do the roles of Congress and the other governmental elites differ? Policy proposals are usually initiated outside of Congress. The role of Congress primarily is to respond to proposals from the president, bureaucratic elites, and interested nongovernmental elites. Congress does not merely ratify or rubber-stamp decisions; it plays an independent role in the policy-making process. But the role is essentially deliberative; Congress accepts, modifies, or rejects the policies initiated by others. For example, the annual federal budget, perhaps the most important policy document of the national government, is written by executive elites and modified by the president before Congress receives it. Congress may modify it further but does not formulate its own budget. Of course, Congress is the critical conduit through which appropriations and revenue measures must pass. But sophisticated lawmakers are aware that they function largely as arbiters rather than initiators of public policy.

However, the relationship between Congress and other policy-making elites is not necessarily stable. Whether Congress merely ratifies the decisions of others or asserts its voice independently depends on many factors, such as the aggressiveness and political skills of the president, the strength of congressional leadership, and whether there is divided party control of the White House and Capitol Hill. A politically weakened president, combined with opposition party control of the Congress, provides the environment for congressional assertions of power. A Democratic Congress flexed its muscles in the years immediately following the downfall of Republican President Nixon in the Watergate scandal. Today a Republican Congress vies for power with a Democratic president, Bill Clinton.

The Power of the Purse

Theoretically, Congress can control the president through its power over government spending. The Constitution (Article 1, Section 9) states that "No money shall be drawn from the Treasury, but in consequence of appropriations made by law." Congress can withhold funds or place elaborate restrictions on the use of funds in order to work its will over the president. But even through the use of budgetary power, its most effective tool, Congress has *not* been able to dominate the presidency. More often than not, the president's budget recommendations are accepted by the Congress with relatively minor changes (see Chapter 11).

Occasionally, Congress and the president have engaged in highly publicized budgetary battles. President Clinton twice vetoed budget resolutions passed by the Republican-controlled Congress in late 1995. The federal government temporarily shut down because appropriations acts had not been passed. But when opinion polls showed that more Americans blamed Congress rather than the president for the gridlock, Congress relented and sent the president a budget that more closely reflected his preferences.

Congressional Investigations

The Congress retains the power to embarrass a presidential administration and occasionally even to force it to change course through congressional investigations. Such investigations, with the cooperation of the television media, can compel presidents to abandon unpopular actions. In the Iran-Contra hearings in 1987, a Democratic-controlled Congress exposed President Reagan's arms-for-hostages dealings with Iran and forced the administration to curtail all negotiations with terrorist regimes. A Republican-controlled Congress held lengthy hearings on Clinton's campaign finances (see Focus: "The Clinton Money Chase" in Chapter 8), but failed to pass any reform legislation or reduce the influence of money in elections.

Impeachment

The ultimate congressional power over the president is impeachment. Despite the Constitution's admonition that impeachment can only be voted for "Treason, Bribery, and other high Crimes and Misdemeanors" (Article II, Section 4), all impeachment movements in U.S. history have developed on political grounds (see Chapter 10).

Despite pious rhetoric in Congress about the "search for truth," "impartial investigation," and "unbiased constitutional judgment," the impeachment process, whatever the merits of the charges against a president, is political, not judicial. The House vote to impeach President Clinton (228 to 106) followed partisan lines with all but five Republicans voting "yes" and all but five Democrats voting "no."*

---

*The only precedent for a presidential impeachment—the impeachment and trial of Andrew Johnson in 1868—was also political. No evidence proved President Johnson's personal involvement in a crime for which he could be indicted and found guilty in a court of law. Johnson was

The Founders anticipated that impeachment would be a raucous, messy, and partisan process. Impeachable offenses, wrote Hamilton,

> *are of a nature which may with peculiar propriety be denominated POLITICAL, as they relate chiefly to injuries done immediately to the society itself. The prosecution of them, for this reason, will seldom fail to agitate the passions of the whole community and to divide it into parties more or less friendly or inimical to the accused. In many cases it will connect itself with the pre-existing factions, and will enlist all their animosities, partialities, influence, and interest on one side or the other; and in such cases there will always be the greatest danger that the decision will be regulated more by the comparative strength of parties, than by the real demonstrations of innocence or guilt.*[11]

Why then, is the impeachment of a president so rare, even during periods of divided government? Because in a democracy, the ultimate jury is the people—through elections—and Congress knows that.

Opinion polls clearly indicated that most Americans did not believe that Clinton's misconduct should result in his removal from office. (See Chapter 10 Focus: "Up Close—Sex, Lies, and Impeachment.") Backlash against the House impeachment process may have contributed to the Republicans' loss of five seats in the 1998 elections. But a president's popularity can fade. President Nixon's public support had plummeted to a meager 24 percent be-

---

a southern Democrat, a U.S. senator from a seceding state (Tennessee) who had remained loyal to the Union. Lincoln chose him as vice president in 1864 as a gesture of national unity. When Johnson acceded to the presidency after Lincoln's assassination, he resisted attempts by "radical" Republicans in Congress to restructure southern society by force. When Johnson dismissed some federal officials who opposed his conciliatory policies, Congress passed the Tenure of Office Act over Johnson's veto, forbidding executive removals without Senate consent. Johnson contended that the act was an unconstitutional infringement of his powers as chief executive. (Years later the Supreme Court agreed, holding that the power of removal is an executive power and specifically declaring that the Tenure of Office Act had been unconstitutional.) When Johnson dismissed his "radical" Republican secretary of war, Edwin M. Stanton, Congress was enraged. The House impeached Johnson on a party-line vote, charging that Johnson had violated the Tenure of Office Act. The Civil War had left a legacy of bitterness against Johnson as a southerner and a Democrat. But following a month-long trial in the Senate, the result was thirty-five "guilty" votes and nineteen "not guilty" votes—one vote short of the necessary two-thirds vote for removal. Seven Republicans joined the twelve Democrats in supporting the president. John F. Kennedy, in his book *Profiles in Courage,* praised the strength and courage of those senators who resisted popular emotions and prevented the president's removal. See Michael Les Benedict, *The Impeachment and Trial of Andrew Johnson* (New York: Norton, 1973).

fore the 1974 vote of the House Judiciary Committee to recommend his impeachment. In contrast, Clinton's high popular approval ratings appeared to be the key to his acquittal by the Senate. House Republicans who had voted for impeachment failed to convince even a majority of Senators to vote for Clinton's removal from office. By placing the power of impeachment and removal in the hands of Congress, the Founders ensured that ultimately this power would be held accountable to the people.

Summary

The Founders intended that Congress be the first and most powerful branch of government, and that the House of Representatives represent "the people." But the Founders' intentions are not an accurate description of Congress today. Rather, elite theory suggests several contrary propositions regarding Congress.

1. Congress tends to represent locally organized elites, who inject a strong parochial influence into national decision making. Members of Congress are responsible to national interests that have a strong base of support in their home constituencies.

2. A member's relevant political constituency is not the general population of the home district but its elite. Less than half the general population of a district knows its legislator's name; fewer still have any idea of how their representative voted on any major issue. Only a tiny fraction ever express their views to their legislators.

3. Congress seldom initiates changes in public policy. Instead, it responds to policy proposals initiated by the president and by executive, military, and interested nongovernmental elites. The congressional role in national decision making is usually deliberative: Congress responds to policies initiated by others.

4. Congressional committees are important to communication between governmental and nongovernmental elites. "Iron triangles" (or "policy clusters") consisting of alliances of leaders from executive agencies, congressional committees, and private business and industry tend to develop in Washington. Committee chairs are key members of the policy clusters because of their control over legislation in Congress.

5. The elaborate rules and procedures of Congress delay and obstruct proposed changes in the status quo, thus strengthening Congress' conservative role in policy making. Transforming a bill into law is a difficult process; congressional procedures offer many opportunities for defeat and many obstacles to passage.

6. An elite system within Congress places effective control over legislation in the hands of relatively few members. Most of these congressional "establishment"

members are conservatives from both parties who have acquired seniority and therefore control key committee chairs.

7. Most bills that do not die before the floor vote pass unanimously. The greatest portion of the national budget passes without debate. The conflict that exists in Congress tends to follow party lines more often than any other factional division. Conflict centers on the details of domestic and foreign policy but seldom on its major directions.

Notes

1. See Alan Ehrenhalt, *The United States of Ambition* (New York: Random House, 1991).

2. Michael X. DelliCarpini and Scott Keeter, "The U.S. Public's Knowledge of Politics," *Public Opinion Quarterly* vol. 55 (May, 1991), 583–612.

3. Warren Miller and Donald Stokes, "Constituency Influence in Congress," *American Political Science Review* 57 (March 1963).

4. Survey by Louis Harris, reported in *American Enterprise* (May/June 1992): 103.

5. *U.S. Term Limits* v. *Thornton* (1995).

6. Woodrow Wilson, *Congressional Government* (1885; reprint, New York: Meridian Books, 1956), p. 178.

7. John W. Kingdon, *Congressmen's Voting Decisions* (New York: Harper & Row, 1973), p. 62.

8. Ibid., p. 88.

9. See Malcolm E. Jewell and Samuel C. Patterson, *The Legislative Process in the United States* (New York: Random House, 1966); William J. Keefe and Morris Ogul, *The American Legislative Process* (Englewood Cliffs, N.J.: Prentice-Hall, 1964).

10. Theodore Lowi, *The Personal President* (Ithaca, N.Y.: Cornell University Press, 1985), p. 127.

11. *The Federalist,* Number 65.

Selected Readings

Fenno, Richard F. *Home Style.* Boston: Little Brown. 1978 The classic description of how attention to constituency by members of Congress enhances their reelection prospects. Home-style activities, including casework, pork-barreling. travel and appearances back home, newsletters, and surveys, are described in detail.

Fiorina, Morris P. *Congress: Keystone to the Washington Establishment,* 2d ed. New Haven, Conn.: Yale University Press, 1989. A lively description of members of Congress as independent political entrepreneurs serving themselves by serving local constituencies and ensuring their own reelection, often at the expense of the national interest.

Gingrich, Newt. *To Renew America.* New York: HarperCollins, 1995. The Republican speaker of the House describes the "third wave information age" that will "empower and enhance" the lives of Americans and the "liberals, lawyers, and bureaucrats" who will try to block it to maintain their own power.

Kaptor, Marcy. *Women of Congress.* Washington: Congressional Quarterly Press. 1996. An account of the progress of women toward longer tenure, greater seniority, and more influential committee appointments and how women in Congress still differ from men on these factors.

Oleszek, Walter J. *Congressional Procedures and the Policy Process,* 4th ed. Washington, D.C.: Congressional Quarterly Press, 1995. An explanation of the interaction between congressional rules and policy making that includes a description of committee and floor procedures and an explanation of the role of the leadership.

Sinclair, Barbara. *Unorthodox Lawmaking.* Washington. D.C.: *Congressional Quarterly Press,* 1997. A description of the various detours and shortcuts a major bill is likely to take in Congress, including five recent case studies.

Swain, Carol M. *Black Faces, Black Interests.* Cambridge: Harvard University Press, 1993. An examination of African-American Congress members, their districts, and strategies for their election.

13

Courts: Elites in Black Robes

Scarcely any political question arises in the United States that is not resolved, sooner or later, into a judicial question.

—ALEXIS DE TOCQUEVILLE

The Supreme Court of the United States and the federal court system compose the most elitist institution in American government. Nine justices—none of whom is elected and all of whom serve for life—possess ultimate authority over all the other institutions of American government. These people have the power to declare void the acts of popularly elected presidents, Congresses, governors, state legislators, school boards, and city councils. No appeal is possible from their determination of what is the "supreme law of the land," short of undertaking the difficult task of amending the Constitution itself.

The Supreme Court, rather than the president or Congress, has made many of the nation's most important domestic policy decisions. The Supreme Court took the lead in eliminating segregation from public life, ensuring separation of church and state, defining rights of criminal defendants and the powers of law enforcement officials, ensuring voters equality in representation, defining the limits of free speech and a free press, and declaring abortion a fundamental right of women. Sooner or later in American politics, most important policy questions come before these justices—who are not elected to office and cannot be removed for anything other than "treason, bribery, or high crimes and misdemeanors." As de Tocqueville observed as early as 1835, "Scarcely any political question arises in the United States that is not resolved, sooner or later, into a judicial question."[1]

JUDICIAL REVIEW AS AN ELITIST PRINCIPLE

Recognition of the undemocratic character of judicial power in the United States is not new. The Founders viewed the federal courts as the final bulwark against mass threats to principle and property:

> *Limited government . . . can be preserved in practice no other way than through the medium of courts of justice, whose duty it is to declare all acts contrary to the manifest tenor of the Constitution void.*[2]

In *Marbury* v. *Madison* (1803), the historic decision establishing the power of judicial review, John Marshall argued persuasively that (1) the Constitution is "the supreme law of the land" and U.S. and state laws must be congruent with it; (2) Article III of the Constitution gives to the Supreme Court the judicial power, which includes the power to interpret the meaning of laws and, in case of conflict between laws, to decide which law shall prevail; and (3) the courts are sworn to uphold the Constitution, so they must declare void a law that conflicts with the Constitution.

Since 1803 the federal courts have struck down more than one hundred laws of Congress and uncounted state laws that they believed conflicted with the Constitution. Judicial review and the power to interpret the meaning and decide the application of law are judges' major sources of power.

The Founders' decision to grant federal courts the power of judicial review over *state* court decisions and *state* laws is easy to understand. Article VI states that the Constitution and national laws and treaties are the supreme law of the land, "anything in the Constitution or laws of any state to the contrary notwithstanding." Federal court power over state decisions is probably essential in maintaining national unity, for fifty different state interpretations of the meaning of the Constitution or of the laws and treaties of Congress would create unimaginable confusion. Thus the power of federal judicial review over state constitutions, laws, and court decisions is seldom questioned.

However, at the *national* level, why should an appointed court's interpretation of the Constitution prevail over the views of an elected Congress and an elected president? Members of Congress and presidents swear to uphold the Constitution, and we can assume that they do not pass laws they believe to be unconstitutional. Since both houses of Congress and the president must approve laws before they become effective, why should federal courts be allowed to set aside these decisions?

The answer is that the Founders distrusted popular majorities and the elected officials subject to their influence. They believed government should be prevented from attacking principle and property, whether to do so was the will of the majority or not. So the Founders deliberately insulated the courts from popular majorities; by appointing judges for life terms, they sought to ensure their independence. The Founders originally intended that a president—who is not directly elected—would appoint judges and that a Senate—also not directly elected—would confirm the president's appointments. Only in this way, the writers of the Constitution believed, would judges be sufficiently protected from the masses to permit them to judge courageously and responsibly.

THE MAKING OF A SUPREME COURT JUSTICE

All federal judges are appointed by the president and confirmed by a majority vote of the Senate. The recruitment process is highly political. The attorney general's office assists the president in screening candidates for all federal judgeships. For positions on the Supreme Court, presidents usually nominate judges who share their political philosophy. One might assume that this practice is a democratizing influence on the Court, assuming that the people elect a president because they agree with his political philosophy. But Supreme Court justices frequently become independent once they reach the Court. Former Chief Justice Earl Warren, as Republican governor of California, had swung critical delegate votes to Eisenhower in the 1952 Republican convention. When the grateful president rewarded him with the chief justiceship, little in Warren's background suggested that he would lead the most liberal era in the Court's history. Later Eisenhower complained that the Warren appointment was "the biggest damn mistake I ever made."[3]

Social Background

Justices' social backgrounds generally reflect close ties with the upper social strata. More than 90 percent of the Supreme Court justices have been from socially prominent, politically influential, upper-class families. More than two-thirds of the justices ever serving on the Court attended Ivy League or other prestigious law schools (see Tables 13-1 and 13-2).

Of course, social background does not necessarily determine judicial philosophy. However, "if . . . the Supreme Court is the keeper of the American conscience, it is essentially the conscience of the American

| TABLE 13-1 | Backgrounds of current U.S. Supreme Court justices |

JUSTICE	YEAR OF BIRTH	LAW SCHOOL	POSITION AT TIME OF APPOINTMENT	APPOINTED BY (YEAR)
William H. Rehnquist	1924	Stanford	Associate Supreme Court justice (Assistant U.S. attorney general prior to initial Supreme Court appointment)	Chief Justice— Reagan (1986) Associate justice— Nixon (1972)
John Paul Stevens	1920	Northwestern	Judge, U.S. Court of Appeals	Ford (1975)
Sandra Day O'Connor	1930	Stanford	Judge, Arizona	Reagan (1981)
Antonin Scalia	1936	Harvard	Judge, U.S. Court of Appeals	Reagan (1986)
Anthony M. Kennedy	1936	Harvard	Judge, U.S. Court of Appeals	Reagan (1987)
David Souter	1939	Harvard	Judge, New Hampshire	Bush (1990)
Clarence Thomas	1948	Yale	Judge, U.S. Court of Appeals	Bush (1991)
Ruth Bader Ginsberg	1933	Columbia	Judge, U.S. Court of Appeals	Clinton (1993)
Stephen G. Breyer	1938	Yale	Judge, U.S. Court of Appeals	Clinton (1994)

upper-middle class, sharpened by the imperative of individual social responsibility and political activism, and conditioned by the conservative impact of legal training and professional legal attitudes and associations."[4]

Politicizing the Confirmation Process

Historically, the Senate Judiciary Committee, which holds hearings and recommends confirmation to the full Senate, consented to nominations by the president with a minimum of dissent; the Senate has rejected only 29 of the 132 Supreme Court nominations ever sent to it. The prevailing ethos had been that a popularly elected president deserves the opportunity to appoint judges; that the opposition party will have its own opportunity to appoint judges when it captures the presidency; and that partisan bickering over judicial appointments is undesirable. But the U.S. Senate's rejection of President Reagan's nomination of Judge Robert H. Bork in 1987 ended the traditional confirmation ethos. Securing the Senate's confirmation of a Supreme Court nominee is now a televised political campaign.

No appointee to the Supreme Court was ever more qualified in terms of scholarship, judicial experience, and knowledge of the law than Judge Bork.

TABLE 13-2	ALL U.S. SUPREME COURT JUSTICES, 1789 TO PRESENT	NUMBER OF JUSTICES (109 TOTAL)

Backgrounds of all U.S. Supreme Court justices

Occupational Position Before Appointment

Private legal practice	25
State judgeship	22
Federal judgeship	27
U.S. attorney general	7
Deputy or assistant U.S. attorney general	2
U.S. solicitor general	2
U.S. senator	6
U.S. representative	2
State governor	3
Federal executive posts	10
Other	3

Religious Background

Protestant	85
Roman Catholic	9
Jewish	7
Unitarian	7
No religious affiliation	1

Age on Appointment

Under 40	4
41–50	30
51–60	59
61–70	15

Political Party Affiliation

Federalist (to 1835)	13
Democrat-Republican (to 1828)	7
Whig (to 1861)	2
Democrat	45
Republican	42

Sex

Male	107
Female	2

Race

White	107
Black	2

Sources: Elder Witt, *Congressional Quarterly's Guide to the U.S. Supreme Court,* 2d ed. (Washington, D.C.: Congressional Quarterly, 1990). Updated by authors.

As a law school professor at the University of Chicago and Yale University, Bork had written many scholarly volumes and articles on constitutional law; he had served as solicitor general of the United States and as a judge of the prestigious U.S. Court of Appeals for the District of Columbia, where he had written hundreds of opinions. But Bork had a reputation for "conservative activism"—a desire to better reflect the "original intent" of the Constitution's framers by rolling back some of the Supreme Court's broad interpretations of privacy rights, free speech, and equal protection of the law. Perhaps most controversial were his views of *Roe* v. *Wade;* he had labeled the Court's striking down of state laws prohibiting abortion as a "wholly unjustifiable judicial usurpation of state legislative authority." Historically, judicial nominees were not asked to tell the Senate how they will vote on pending cases; to do so before considering evidence and hearing arguments would presumably impair the nominees' ability to render impartial judgments. But, unlike previous nominees, Bork was subjected by the Senate Judiciary Committee to extensive case-by-case questioning in nationally televised confirmation hearings. The bearded, scholarly Bork presented a poor TV image, and liberal interest groups conducted an unprecedented political campaign to derail his nomination. His public and private life was extensively investigated, and he was obliged to defend himself from a wide variety of charges. When overnight opinion polls showed the prickly professor to be losing ground, the Democratic-controlled Judiciary Committee and U.S. Senate rejected his nomination. A second unfortunate nominee, Douglas H. Ginsberg, withdrew in the face of press reports that he had smoked marijuana. Finally, when President Reagan submitted the name of a relatively unknown and ideologically bland nominee, Anthony M. Kennedy, who solemnly testified that he had "no overarching theory of [constitutional] interpretation" and "no fixed or immutable ideas," the Senate relented and confirmed the appointment. (See also Focus: "Senate Confirmation as Sleazy Spectacle".)

THE SPECIAL STYLE OF JUDICIAL POLICY MAKING

An *appearance of objectivity* cloaks the power of the courts to shape American life. Because judges serve for life and are legally accountable to no one, they maintain the fiction that they are not engaged in policy making but merely "applying" the law to specific cases.[5] To admit otherwise would spotlight the conflict between judicial power and the democratic myth of policy making by elected representatives.

"*Since you have already been convicted by the media,
I imagine we can wrap this up pretty quickly.*"

Many of the nation's best judicial thinkers question this mechanistic theory of judicial objectivity, however. For example, former Justice Felix Frankfurter once observed:

> *The meaning of "due process" and the content of the terms like "liberty" are not revealed by the Constitution. It is the Justices who make the meaning. They read into the neutral language of the Constitution their own economic and social views. . . . Let us face the fact that five Justices of the Supreme Court are the molders of policy rather than the impersonal vehicles of revealed truth.*[6]

The courts also maintain the *fiction of nonpartisanship.* Judges must not appear as if political considerations affected their decisions. Once appointed to the federal bench, they are expected to have fewer direct ties to

FOCUS

Senate Confirmation as Sleazy Spectacle

If the Bork battle signaled the Senate's descent into bitter partisanship in the confirmation process, the battle over the nomination of Clarence Thomas to the U.S. Supreme Court marked the Senate's collapse into disgraceful spectacle. Indeed, the Senate Judiciary Committee's sleazy performance in the Thomas confirmation established a new low in public ethics.

Clarence Thomas, as President Bush's nominee to replace Thurgood Marshall, the first African-American Supreme Court justice, reflected the generally conservative judicial philosophy of earlier Reagan appointees. Born to a teenage mother who earned $10 a week as a maid, Clarence Thomas and his brother lived in a dirt-floor shack in Pin Point, Georgia, where they were raised by strict, hard-working grandparents. They taught young Clarence the value of education and sacrificed to send him to a Catholic school. He excelled academically and went on to mostly white Immaculate Conception Seminary College in Missouri to study for the Catholic priesthood. But when he overheard a fellow seminarian express satisfaction at the assassination of Dr. Martin Luther King, Jr., Thomas left the seminary in anger and enrolled at Holy Cross College in Washington, D.C., where he helped found the college's Black Student Union. He graduated with honors and went on to Yale Law School.

Thomas began his legal career as an assistant Missouri attorney general under John C. Danforth, before Danforth became a popular Republican U.S. senator. Thomas came to Washington with Danforth, and was appointed assistant secretary for civil rights in the U.S. Department of Education and later chairman of the U.S. Equal Employment Opportunity Commission. In the latter role, Thomas spoke out against racial quotas in favor of individual rights and against welfare programs that create permanent dependency. Although Thomas had not directly spoken out on the Court's *Roe* v. *Wade* abortion decision, it was widely believed that Thomas would join the Court's abortion opponents and modify or reverse the decision. Thus, Thomas's Republicanism and conservatism challenged the prevailing stereotype of black political leaders.

The Bush White House strategists believed that Thomas provided them with an opportunity to push a strong conservative past the liberal, Democratic-controlled Senate Judiciary Committee and win confirmation by the full Senate. They reasoned that liberal groups who had blocked the earlier nomination of conservative Robert Bork would be reluctant to launch personal attacks on an African-American.

In the early proceedings, the Thomas nomination progressed fairly well. The Judiciary Committee, led by Chairman Joseph Biden, initially treated Thomas with respect, even while boring in on his views on affirmative action and abortion. Thomas's cautious testimony gave his liberal opponents no real openings; at the end of a week of testimony the Judiciary Committee forwarded the confirmation to the full Senate, where at least sixty senators were prepared to vote for the nominee.

Behind the scenes, liberal interest groups, including the National Abortion Rights League, People for the American Way, and the National Organization for Women, were searching for evidence to discredit Thomas. On the third day of the hearings, a University of Oklahoma law professor, Anita Hill, a former legal assistant to Thomas both at the Department of Education and later at the Equal Employment Opportunity Commission, contacted the staff of the Judiciary Committee with charges that Thomas had sexually harassed her in both jobs. Initially, Hill declined to make her charges public, but when Chairman Biden refused to circulate anonymous charges, she agreed to be interviewed by the FBI and went on to give a nationally televised press conference, elaborating on her charges against Thomas. Her bombshell became a media extravaganza and sent the Senate into an uproar.

Thomas's Senate supporters were outraged at what they believed to be a sleazy last-minute ploy to destroy Thomas. But sensing a possible defeat in the full Senate, Republicans agreed to reopen the hearings. In a powerful opening statement, with his wife sitting behind him, Thomas heatedly denied the charges and appealed to the huge national television audience watching the proceedings live.

Anita Hill was a convincing witness on her own behalf. She began by saying that only three months after coming to the civil rights office in the Department of Education, Thomas, who was then single, asked her to go out with him. She testified that he initiated sexual conversations with her that included references to pubic hair, penis size, and sex with animals. Chairman Biden and other Democrats on the committee treated Hill with great deference, asking her to talk about her feelings and provide even more explicit details of Thomas's alleged misconduct.

In contrast, Senator Arlen Specter, a Republican moderate with a history of strong support for abortion rights, was not convinced that Hill was telling the truth. Why, he asked, with her legal education and knowledge of civil rights, had she failed to report this harassment? Why did she accept another job at the EEOC from Thomas if she had been harassed by him earlier at the Department of Education? Why had she made many calls to Thomas over the years, leaving friendly messages with his secretary? Senator Orin Hatch, a conservative Republican, was more hostile, suggesting that

Hill was either fantasizing her charges or making them up for political reasons.

The confirmation process exploded into a sleazy soap opera. The only restraint was Chairman Biden's rule that no questions could be asked about either Clarence Thomas's or Anita Hill's sex life. The damage was done, anyway, not only to Clarence Thomas and Anita Hill, but also to the Senate confirmation process and the Senate as an institution.

The televised hearings captured the nation's attention, touching directly on emotional issues of race and sex. Feminist groups cast the issue as one of sexual harassment and male insensitivity to women's concerns. But Clarence Thomas fought back hard, denying all charges and accusing the committee of conducting a "high-tech lynching" of an "uppity" black man who dares to have conservative opinions.

The mass public may not know or care much about judicial philosophy. Yet race and sex elicit strong opinions. And the "truth" in Washington is all too often determined by opinion polls. An astonishing 86 percent of the general public said they had watched the televised hearings. A majority of blacks as well as whites, and a majority of women as well as men, sided with the nominee. (In response to the question "Who do you believe more—Anita Hill or Clarence Thomas?" 54 percent said Thomas and 27 percent said Hill. Black opinion was even more heavily weighted in Thomas's direction, 61 to 19.[a])

In a fitting close to the most bitter and sleazy conflict over a Supreme Court nominee in congressional history, the final Senate confirmation vote was 52 to 48, the closest vote in the history of Supreme Court confirmations.

[a]*Gallup Opinion Reports* (October 15, 1991): 209. A year later these percentages would shift in Hill's favor, following widespread attention in the media to the issue of sexual harassment.

political organizations than members of Congress do. Federal judges must not appear to base their decision on partisan considerations or party platforms or to bargain in the fashion of legislators. Perhaps as a result of their nonpartisan appearance, courts enjoy a measure of prestige that other government institutions lack. Judicial decisions are more acceptable to the public if the public believes that the courts dispense unbiased justice.

Courts function under *special rules of access.* The Constitution gives jurisdiction to federal courts only in "cases and controversies." Courts do not issue policy pronouncements, rules, or orders on their own initiative. For example, courts do not declare a law of Congress or an action of the president unconstitutional immediately upon its passage or occurrence. Nor do the federal courts render advisory opinions prior to congressional or executive action. The courts assume a passive role and wait until a case comes before them that directly challenges a law of Congress or an action of the president.

To gain access to the federal courts, one must present a *case* in which the federal courts have *jurisdiction.* A case must involve two disputing parties, one of which must have incurred some real damages as a result of the action or inaction of the other. The federal courts will accept jurisdiction based on (1) the nature of the parties—a case in which the U.S. government is a party; or a controversy between two or more states, or between a state and a citizen of another state, or between citizens of different states; or a case involving a foreign nation or citizen; or (2) the nature of the controversy—a case that arises under the Constitution (a "constitutional question") or under the laws and treaties of the United States. Congress has further limited the jurisdiction of federal courts in cases between citizens of different states by requiring that the dispute involve more than fifty thousand dollars. State courts hear all other cases.

Judicial policy making follows a *legalistic style.* Plaintiffs and defendants present facts and arguments to the courts in formal testimony, cross-examination, legal briefs, and oral arguments, all of them highly ritualized. Legal skills are generally necessary to make presentations that meet the technical specifications of the courts. Decorum in court proceedings is highly valued because it conveys a sense of dignity; legislative or executive offices rarely function with as much decorum.

These distinctive features of judicial policy making—the appearance of objectivity, the fiction of nonpartisanship, special rules of access, limited jurisdiction, and legalistic style—all contribute to the power of the courts. They help to legitimize court decisions, to win essential support for them, and thus to contribute to the influence of judges in the political system.

THE STRUCTURE OF THE FEDERAL COURT SYSTEM

The federal court system consists of three levels of courts with general jurisdiction, together with various special courts (the Court of Claims, Customs Court, Patent Court, and Court of Military Appeals). The Constitution establishes only the Supreme Court, although Congress determines the number of Supreme Court justices—traditionally nine. Article III authorizes Congress to establish "such inferior courts" as it deems appropriate. Congress has designed a hierarchical court system consisting of nearly one hundred U.S. federal district courts and eleven U.S. circuit courts of appeals, in addition to the Supreme Court of the United States (see Figure 13-1).

Federal District Courts

Federal district courts are the trial courts of the federal system. Each state has at least one district court, and larger states have more. (New York, for example, has four.) More than six hundred judges, appointed for life by the president and confirmed by the Senate, preside in these courts. The president also appoint U.S. marshals for each district court to carry out orders of the court and maintain order in the courtroom. Federal district courts hear criminal cases prosecuted by the U.S. Department of Justice, as well as civil cases. As trial courts, the district courts use both grand juries (juries composed to hear evidence and, if warranted, to indict a defendant by bringing formal criminal charges against that person) and petit, or regular, juries (juries that determine guilt or innocence). District courts may hear as many as three hundred thousand cases in a year.

Circuit Courts of Appeals

Circuit courts of appeals are *appellate courts.* They do not hold trials or accept new evidence but consider only the record of the trial courts and oral or written arguments (briefs) submitted by attorneys. Federal law provides that every individual has a right to appeal his or her case, so courts of appeals have little discretion in hearing appeals. Appellate judges themselves estimate that more than 80 percent of all appeals are "frivolous"—that is, they are without any real basis at all. These courts require nearly one hundred circuit court judges, appointed for life by the president and confirmed by the Senate. Normally three judges serve together on a panel to hear

FIGURE 13-1   The U.S. court system

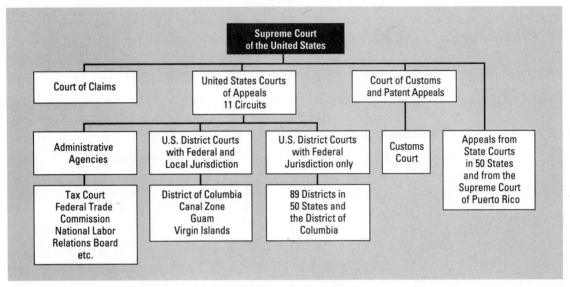

Source: U.S. House of Representatives, Committee on the Judiciary, *The United States Courts: Their Jurisdiction and Work* (Washington, D.C.: U.S. Government Printing Office, 1969), p. 3.

appeals. More than 90 percent of the cases decided by circuit courts of appeals end at this level. Further appeal to the Supreme Court is not automatic; the Supreme Court itself decides what appeals it will consider. Hence, for most cases, the decision of the circuit court of appeals is final.

U.S. Supreme Court

The Supreme Court of the United States is the final interpreter of all matters involving the U.S. Constitution and federal laws and treaties, whether the case began in a federal district court or in a state court. In some cases the Supreme Court has original jurisdiction (authority to serve as a trial court), but it seldom uses this jurisdiction. Appellate jurisdiction is the Supreme Court's major function. Appeals may come from a state court of last resort (usually a state supreme court) or from lower federal courts. The Supreme Court determines for itself whether to accept an appeal and consider a case. It may do so if a "substantial federal question" is at issue in the case, or if "special and important reasons" apply. Any four justices can grant an appeal. However, the Supreme Court denies most cases submitted to it on *writs of appeal* and *writs of certiorari;* the Court need not give any reason for denying appeal or certiorari.*

In the early days of the republic, the size of the U.S. Supreme Court fluctuated, but since 1869 its membership has remained at nine: the chief justice and eight associate justices. The Supreme Court is in session each year from October through June, hearing oral arguments, accepting written briefs, conferring, and rendering opinions.

THE JURISDICTION OF THE FEDERAL COURT SYSTEM

In the U.S. federal system, each state maintains its own court system. The federal courts are not necessarily superior to state courts; both state and federal courts operate independently. But since the U.S. Supreme Court has appellate jurisdiction over state supreme courts, as well as over lower federal courts, the Supreme Court oversees the nation's entire judicial system.

State courts have general jurisdiction in all criminal and civil cases. According to Article III of the U.S. Constitution, federal court jurisdiction extends to:

★ Cases arising under the Constitution, federal laws, or treaties.

★ Cases involving ambassadors, public ministers or counsels, or maritime and admiralty laws.

★ Cases in which the U.S. government is a party.

★ Cases between two or more states.

★ Cases between a state and a citizen of another state.

★ Cases between citizens of different states.

★ Cases between a state or a citizen and a foreign government or citizen of another nation.

Obviously, it is not difficult "to make a federal case out of it," regardless of what "it" might be. The Constitution contains many vaguely worded guarantees—"due process of law," "equal protection of the laws," protection from "cruel and unusual punishment" and "unreasonable searches and seizures,"

---

*The Court technically must hear writs of appeal, but only a few matters qualify; among them are cases involving clear constitutional issues (for example, a finding that a federal law is unconstitutional, that a state law is in conflict with federal law, or that a state law is in violation of the U.S. Constitution). Writs of certiorari are granted when four members agree that an issue involves a "substantial federal question" (as decided by the Supreme Court).

and so forth—which allow nearly every party to any case to claim that a federal question is involved and that a federal court is the proper forum.

The great bulk of the national caseload begins and ends in state court systems. The federal courts do not intervene once a state court has started hearing a case, except in very rare circumstances. And Congress has stipulated that legal disputes between citizens of different states must involve fifty thousand dollars or more in order to be heard in federal court. Moreover, parties to cases in state courts must "exhaust their remedies"—that is, appeal their case all the way through the state courts—before the federal courts will hear their appeal. Appeals from state supreme courts go directly to the U.S. Supreme Court and not to federal district or circuit courts. Usually appeals from state supreme courts to the U.S. Supreme Court are made on the grounds that the case raises "a federal question"—that is, a question on the application of the U.S. Constitution or federal law. The U.S. Supreme Court reviews only a very small fraction of appeals from state court decisions.

Of the ten million civil and criminal cases begun in the nation's courts each year, less than 3 percent (250,000) are filed in federal district courts. State and local courts hear the great bulk of legal cases. The U.S. Constitution "reserves" general police powers to the states so that crimes and civil disputes are generally matters of state and local concern. Murder, robbery, assault, and rape are normally state offenses rather than federal crimes. Federal crimes generally center on offenses (1) against the U.S. government or its property; (2) against U.S. government officials or employees while they are on duty; (3) that involve crossing state lines (such as nationally organized crime, unlawful escape across state lines, taking kidnapping victims across state lines); (4) that interfere with interstate commerce; and (5) that occur on federal territories or on the seas.

Majority opinions of the Supreme Court are usually written by a single justice who summarizes majority sentiment. Concurring opinions are written by justices who vote with the majority but who feel that the majority opinion does not fully explain their reasons. A dissenting opinion is written by a justice who is in the minority; such opinions have no impact on the outcome of the case. Written opinions are printed, distributed to the press, and published in *U.S. Reports* and other legal reporting services.

JUDICIAL POWER: ACTIVISM VERSUS SELF-RESTRAINT

Great legal scholars have argued the merits of activism versus self-restraint in judicial decision making for more than a century.[7] Proponents of judicial *self-restraint* argue that since justices are not popularly elected, the Supreme Court should move cautiously and avoid direct confrontation with legislative and executive authority. Justice Felix Frankfurter wrote, "The only check upon our own exercise of power is our own sense of self-restraint. For the removal of unwise laws from the statute books, appeal lies not to the courts but to the ballot and to the processes of democratic government."[8]

But Frankfurter was arguing a minority position on the Court. The dominant philosophy of the Supreme Court under Chief Justice Earl Warren (1953–1969) was one of *judicial activism.* The Warren Court believed it should shape constitutional meaning to fit its estimate of the needs of contemporary society. By viewing the Constitution as a deliberately broad and flexible document, one can avoid dozens of new constitutional amendments to accommodate a changing society. The strength of the U.S. Constitution lies in its flexibility—its relevance to contemporary society.[9]

The Supreme Court's posture of judicial activism, combined with its lifetime appointments, greatly strengthens its elitist character. If a nonelective institution such as the federal judiciary assumes a strong, activist role in national policy making, the result is an even more elitist political system. This is true whether the Supreme Court is active on behalf of liberal or conservative policies. Liberals who praise the virtues of judicial activism, who urge the Court to stand against the misguided policies of an elected president and Congress, must recognize the elitist nature of their argument.

Rules of Restraint

Even an activist Supreme Court adheres to some general rules of judicial self-restraint. These rules include the following:

★ The Court will not pass upon the constitutionality of legislation in a nonadversary proceeding but only in an actual case. Thus the Court will not advise the president or Congress on constitutional questions.

★ The Court will not anticipate a question on constitutional law; it does not decide hypothetical cases.

★ The Court will not formulate a rule of constitutional law broader than required by the precise facts to which it must be applied.

★ The Court will not pass upon a constitutional question if some other ground exists upon which it may dispose of the case.

★ When doubt exists about the constitutionality of a law, the Court will try to interpret the meaning of a law so as to give it a constitutional meaning and avoid the necessity of declaring it unconstitutional.

★ A complainant must have exhausted all remedies available in lower federal courts or state courts before the Supreme Court accepts review.

★ Occasionally the Court defers to Congress and the president and classifies an issue as a political question, and refuses to decide it. The Court has stayed out of foreign and military policy areas.

★ If the Court holds a law unconstitutional, it will confine its decision to the particular section of the law that is unconstitutional; the rest of the statute stays intact.[10]

Stare Decisis

Courts are also limited by the principle of *stare decisis,* which means that the issue has already been decided in earlier cases. Reliance upon precedent is a fundamental notion in law. Indeed, the underlying common law of England and the United States is composed simply of past decisions. Students of the law learn through the case-study method: the study of previous decisions. Reliance on precedent gives stability to the law; if every decision were new law, then no one would know what the law is from day to day. Yet judicial activists are frequently willing to discard precedent. Former Justice William O. Douglas, who seldom felt restrained by legal precedent, justified disregard of precedent as follows:

> *The decisions of yesterday or of the last century are only the starting points. . . . A judge looking at a constitutional decision may have compulsions to revere the past history and accept what was once written. But he remembers above all else that it is the Constitution which he swore to support and defend, not the gloss which his predecessors may have put on it. So he comes to formulate his own laws, rejecting some earlier ones as false and embracing others. He cannot do otherwise unless he lets men long dead and unaware of the problems of the age in which he lives do his thinking for him.*[11]

Original Intent

Should the Constitution be interpreted in terms of the intentions of its original writers or according to the morality of society today? Most jurists agree that the Constitution is a living document, that it must be interpreted by each generation in the light of current conditions, and that to do otherwise would soon render the document obsolete. But in interpreting the document, whose values should prevail—the values of the judges or the values of its writers? The doctrine of original intent takes the values of the Founders as expressed in the text of the Constitution and applies these values to current conditions. Defenders of original intent argue that the words in the document must be given their historical meaning and that meaning must restrain courts as well as the legislative and executive branches of government. The Supreme Court should not set aside laws made by elected representatives unless they conflict with the original intent of the Founders. A Supreme Court that sets aside laws because they do not accord with today's moral standards is simply substituting its own morality for that of elected bodies. Such decisions lack democratic legitimacy, because there is no reason why judges' moral views should prevail over those of elected representatives. But this original intent doctrine has had little influence among the activists on the Supreme Court.

Wisdom versus Constitutionality

Distinguished jurists have long urged the Supreme Court to exercise self-restraint. A law may be unwise, unjust, unfair, or even stupid and yet still be constitutional. One cannot equate the wisdom of the law with its constitutionality, and the Court should decide only the constitutionality and not the wisdom of a law. Justice Oliver Wendell Holmes once lectured his colleague, sixty-one-year-old Justice Harlan Stone, on this point:

> *Young man, about 75 years ago I learned that I was not God. And so, when the people . . . want to do something I can't find anything in the Constitution expressly forbidding them to do, I say, whether I like it or not, "Goddamn it, let 'em do it."*[12]

However, the actual role of the Supreme Court in the nation's power struggles suggests that the Court indeed equates wisdom with constitutionality. People frequently cite broad phrases in the Fifth and Fourteenth Amendments establishing constitutional standards of "due process of law" and "equal protection of the laws" when attacking laws they believe are unfair or unjust. Most Americans have come to believe that laws that are simply unwise must also be unconstitutional and that the courts have become the final arbiters of fairness and justice.

The Supreme Court and Abortion

It is ironic indeed that a nation that thinks of itself as a democracy must call upon a nonelective, lifetime elite to decide its most contentious issues.

Historically, abortions for any purpose other than saving the life of the mother were criminal offenses under most state laws. A few states permitted abortions in cases of rape or incest or to protect the health of the woman. Then in 1970, New York, Alaska, Hawaii, and Washington enacted laws that in effect permitted abortion at the request of the woman involved and the concurrence of her physician. A growing pro-abortion coalition formed, including the American Civil Liberties Union, a new National Association for the Repeal of Abortion Laws, Planned Parenthood, and women's organizations, including the National Organization for Women.

At about the same time, the Supreme Court was developing a new constitutional right—the right of privacy—partly in response to a case brought to it by Planned Parenthood in 1965. When Estelle Griswold opened a birth control clinic on behalf of the Planned Parenthood League of Connecticut, the state found her in violation of a Connecticut law prohibiting the use of contraceptives. She challenged the constitutionality of the statute, and in its ruling in *Griswold* v. *Connecticut* the Supreme Court struck down the law by a vote of 7 to 2.[a] Voting for the majority were Brennan, Clark, Douglas, Goldberg, Harlan, Warren, and White. Dissenting were Black and Stewart.

The right to privacy is nowhere specifically stated in the Constitution. But Justice Douglas found it in "the penumbras formed by emanations from" the First, Third, Fourth, Ninth, and Fifteenth Amendments. Justices Goldberg, Warren, and Brennan found it in the Ninth Amendment: "The enumeration of the Constitution of certain rights, shall not be contrived to deny or disparage others retained by the people." Justice Harlan found the right in the word *liberty* in the Fourteenth Amendment. The fact that *Griswold* dealt with reproduction gave encouragement to groups advocating abortion rights.

When Norma McCorvey sought an abortion in Texas in 1969, her doctor refused, citing a state law prohibiting abortion except to save a woman's life. McCorvey bore the child and gave it up for adoption, but then enlisted the aid of two young attorneys, Linda Coffee and Sarah Weddington, who challenged the Texas law in federal courts on a variety of constitutional grounds, including the right to privacy. *Amicus curiae* briefs were filed by a wide assortment of groups on both sides of the issue. McCorvey became "Jane Roe," and *Roe* v. *Wade* became one of the most controversial cases in the Court's history.[b]

The Supreme Court ruled in 1973 that the constitutional right to privacy as well as the Fourteenth Amendment's guarantee of "liberty" included a woman's decision to bear or not to bear a child. The Court ruled that the word *person* in the Constitution did *not* include the unborn child; therefore, the Fifth and Fourteenth Amendments' guarantee of "life, liberty and property" did not protect the "life" of the fetus. The Court also ruled that a state's power to protect the health and safety of the mother could not justify *any* restriction on abortion in the first three months of pregnancy. Between the third and sixth months of pregnancy, a state could set standards for abortion procedures in order to protect the health of women, but a state could not prohibit abortions. Only in the final three months could a state prohibit or regulate abortion to protect the unborn. Voting with the majority were Blackmun, Brennan, Burger, Douglas, Marshall, Powell, and Stewart. Dissenting were Rehnquist and White.

Roe v. *Wade* set off a political conflagration. A new movement was mobilized to restrict the scope of the decision and if possible to bring about its overturn. Congress defeated efforts to pass a constitutional amendment restricting abortion or declaring that life begins at conception. However, Congress banned the use of federal funds under Medicaid (medical care for the poor) for abortions except to protect the life of a woman. The Supreme Court upheld the ban, holding that there was no constitutional obligation for governments to pay for abortions.[c]

Initial efforts by some states to restrict abortion ran into Supreme Court opposition.[d] But opponents of abortion won a victory in *Webster* v. *Reproductive Health Services* in 1989.[e] In this case, the Supreme Court upheld a Missouri law denying public funds for abortions that were not necessary to preserve the life of the woman, and denying the use of public facilities or employees in performing or assisting in abortions. More importantly, the justices recognized the state's "interest in the protection of human life when viability is possible," and they upheld Missouri's requirement for a test of "viability" after twenty weeks and prohibition on abortions of a viable fetus except to save a woman's life.

Webster gave hope to pro-life groups that the Supreme Court might eventually overturn *Roe* v. *Wade*. Justices Rehnquist and White had dissented in the original *Roe* v. *Wade* case; they were now joined in upholding restrictions on abortion by three new Reagan appointees, O'Connor, Kennedy, and Scalia. Dissenting were Blackmun, Brennan, Marshall, and Stevens.

However, the current Supreme Court appears to have chosen a policy of affirming a woman's right to abortion while upholding modest restrictions, as evidenced by its ruling in *Planned Parenthood of Pennsylvania* v. *Casey* in 1992.[f] In this case, the Supreme Court considered a series of restrictions on abortion enacted by Pennsylvania: that physicians must inform women of risks and alternatives; that women must wait twenty-four hours after requesting one before having an abortion; and that minors must have the consent of parents or a judge. It struck down the requirement that spouses be notified.

Justice Sandra Day O'Connor took the lead in forming a moderate swing bloc on the Court, consisting of herself, Kennedy, and Souter. (Blackmun and Stevens voted to uphold *Roe* v. *Wade* with *no* restrictions, making the vote 5 to 4.) O'Connor's majority opinion strongly reaffirmed the fundamental right of abortion, both on the basis of the Fourteenth Amendment and on the principle of *stare decisis*. But the majority also upheld a state's right to protect any fetus that reached the point of "viability." The Court went on to establish a new standard for constitutionally evaluating restrictions: they must not impose an "undue burden" on women seeking abortion, or place "substantial obstacles" in her path. All of Pennsylvania's restrictions met this standard and were upheld, except spousal notification.

[a]*Griswold* v. *Connecticut*, 381 U.S. 479 (1965).

[b]*Roe* v. *Wade*, 400 U.S. 113 (1973).

[c]*Harris* v. *McRae*, 448 U.S. 297 (1980).

[d]*Planned Parenthood of Missouri* v. *Danforth*, 418 U.S. 52 (1976); *Belloti* v. *Baird*, 443 U.S. 662 (1979); *Akron* v. *Akron Center for Reproductive Health*, 103 S. Ct. 2481 (1983).

[e]*Webster* v. *Reproductive Health Services*, 492 U.S. 111 (1989).

[f]*Planned Parenthood of Pennsylvania* v. *Casey*, 505 U.S. 110 (1992).

DO THE COURTS RULE THE NATION?

George C. Wallace once put the argument bluntly: "Thugs and federal judges have just about taken charge of this country."[13] Others have also worried about the increasing role of the judiciary—the ability of courts to intrude into people's lives in ways unprecedented in history. One need not be a "conservative" in politics to be concerned about the extent to which we now rely upon a nonelected judiciary to solve our problems, rather than upon democratically elected executives and legislators.

Growing Reliance on the Courts

Harvard Law School professor Archibald Cox, who became famous as the first Watergate prosecutor, warned that "excessive reliance upon courts instead of self-government through democratic processes, may deaden the people's sense of moral and political responsibility for their own future, especially in matters of liberty, and may stunt the growth of political capacity that results from the exercise of the ultimate powers of decision."[14] For good or for ill, Americans have come to rely on courts to solve problems once handled by legislatures, local officials, school boards, teachers, parents, or other social organizations.

Court Congestion

Nearly one million lawyers practice in the United States. Each year the nation's courts try more than 10 million cases, most of them in state and local courts. Over 250,000 cases begin in federal courts each year. Most of these cases will be settled before trial, but about 25,000 (10 percent) go to trial. People appeal more than 50,000 cases to U.S. courts of appeal each year. And the U.S. Supreme Court receives about 7,500 cases each year, although it gives serious attention to only about 200 of them.

The growing number of legal cases not only raises questions about the increasing power of a nonelected, lifetime judicial elite, but it also overburdens the court system and creates many injustices. As more and more cases get into the judicial system, congestion and costs mount. Cases may be backed up on court dockets for years. As a result, injured parties in civil cases must suffer long delays before receiving compensation. Defendants in criminal cases who are free on bail may deliberately delay the trial, hoping that witnesses will move away or forget important details or that victims will grow frustrated and give up trying to prosecute. Most lawsuits require attorneys on both sides, and attorneys are expensive. The longer a case drags on, the more expensive it is likely to be.

Plea Bargaining

Congestion forces prosecuting attorneys in criminal cases to *plea bargain* with defendants—that is, to make special arrangements for criminal defendants to plead guilty in exchange for reduced charges. For example, a prosecutor may reduce the charge of rape to sexual assault, which usually carries a lighter penalty. The prosecutor enters into such a bargain in order to avoid the delays and costs of a trial; the defendant makes such a bargain to escape serious penalty for the crime. Estimates suggest that 90 percent of all criminal cases are now plea bargained.

Judicial Reforms

Federal courts are so well insulated from popular pressure and from congressional and presidential pressures that we will probably have to wait for them to "reform" themselves. If federal judges are slow in handling cases, if their decisions are arbitrary, if congestion and confusion reign in their courtrooms, if they bog themselves down in details of managing school districts or prisons or hospitals, if they are lazy or poorly trained in the law, if they are in poor health or senile, no one can do much about it. Only five federal court judges have *ever* been impeached and convicted by Congress. In 1989, Federal District Court Judge L. C. Hastings became the first sitting judge in more than fifty years to be impeached, tried, and found guilty by the Congress. (Ironically, the politically popular and flamboyant Hastings won election to Congress from a reapportioned majority black south Florida district in 1992.) Other judges have resigned under fire: Federal Judge Otto Kerner (former governor of Illinois) resigned his judicial post only five days before he was scheduled to enter prison for income tax evasion, perjury, bribery, and mail fraud.[15] In short, the U.S. citizenry has little control over the judiciary, despite the control it exercises over all of us.

Summary

The Supreme Court determines many of the nation's most important policies. Indeed, most political questions sooner or later end up in the courts. Any fair examination of the court system in the United States will reveal the elitist character of judicial decision making.

1. The Supreme Court is the elitist branch of the national government. Nine justices—none of whom is elected and all of whom serve for life—can void the acts of popularly elected presidents, Congresses, governors, legislatures, school boards, and city councils.

2. The principle of judicial review of congressional acts grew out of the Founders' distrust of popularly elected officials subject to influence by popular majorities. Judicial review enables the courts to protect constitutional principles against attacks by elected bodies.

3. The social backgrounds of judges reflect close ties to upper-class segments of society. Presidents may attempt to influence court decisions through their selection of judges, but life terms make judges independent of presidential or congressional influence once they are appointed.

4. Judicial decision making takes on an appearance of objectivity, maintains the fiction of nonpartisanship, employs special rules of access, and reflects a legalistic style. These features help legitimize the decisions of people who have no electoral mandate.

5. Since justices are not popularly elected, some scholars and jurists have urged self-restraint in judicial policy making. They argue that the Supreme Court should decide only the constitutionality of a law, not its wisdom; the Court should not substitute its own judgment for the judgment of elected representatives. But over the years judicial activism has augmented the power of judges. Justices have used broad phrases in the Constitution such as "due process of law" and "equal protection of the law" to strike down laws they believe are unfair or unjust.

6. Even an activist Supreme Court adheres to some rules of restraint. It does not give advisory opinions, or decide hypothetical cases, or decide upon the constitutionality of a law until an actual case directly involving the law comes before it.

7. Americans have come to rely on courts to resolve key conflicts in society. There are more lawyers and more court cases in the United States than any other nation in the world.

Notes

1. Alexis de Tocqueville, *Democracy in America* (New York: Mentor Books, 1956), p. 73.

2. James Madison, Alexander Hamilton, and John Jay, *The Federalist* (New York: Modern Library, 1937), p. 505.

3. Joseph W. Bishop, "The Warren Court Is Not Likely to Be Overruled," *New York Times Magazine* (September 7, 1969): 31.

4. John R. Schmidhauser, *The Supreme Court* (New York: Holt, Rinehart & Winston, 1960), p. 59.

5. *U.S.* v. *Butler,* 297 U.S. 1 (1936); Carl Brent Swisher, "The Supreme Court and the Moment of Truth," *American Political Science Review* 54 (December 1960): 879.

6. Felix Frankfurter, "The Supreme Court and the Public," *Forum* 83 (June 1930): 332-334.

7. Frank Jerone, *Law and the Modern Mind* (New York: Coward-McCann, 1930); Benjamin N. Cardozo, *The Nature of the Judicial Process* (New Haven, Conn.: Yale University Press, 1921); Roscoe Pound, *Justice According to Law* (New Haven, Conn.: Yale University Press, 1951).

8. *West Virginia State Board of Education* v. *Barnette,* 319 U.S. 624 (1943).

9. Archibald Cox, *The Warren Court* (Cambridge: Harvard University Press, 1968), p. 2.

10. Henry Abraham, *The Judicial Process* (New York: Oxford University Press, 1968), pp. 310–326.

11. Justice William O. Douglas, "Stare Decisis," *Record* (April 1947).

12. Quoted by Charles P. Curtis, *Lions Under the Throne* (Boston: Houghton Mifflin, 1947), p. 281.

13. *Newsweek* (January 10, 1977): 42.

14. Archibald Cox, *The Role of the Supreme Court in American Government* (New York: Oxford University Press, 1976), p. 103.

15. *Time* (August 20, 1979): 54.

Selected Readings

Abraham, Henry J. *The Judicial Process,* 6th ed. New York: Oxford University Press, 1993. This book is one of the most comprehensive introductions to the basics of the judicial process. It provides both a sound theoretical introduction to the nature, sources, and types of law and a thorough nuts-and-bolts knowledge of the staffing, organization, and technical processes involved in the judicial process. The book provides four extensive bibliographies dealing with U.S. constitutional law, biographies and autobiographies of and by justices of the Supreme Court, a discussion of comparative constitutional law, and analysis of civil liberties.

Baum, Lawrence. *The Supreme Court,* 6th ed. Washington, D.C.: Congressional Quarterly Press, 1997. A readable introduction to the Supreme Court as a political institution, the book covers the selection of justices, the nature of cases decided, the process of decision making, and the impact of the Supreme Court's decisions.

Carp, Robert A., and Ronald Aidham. *The Federal Courts,* 3rd ed. Washington, D.C.: Congressional Quarterly Press, 1998. An overview of the federal judicial system, arguing that federal judges and Supreme Court justices function as part of the political system and engage in policy making that influences all our lives.

Epstein, Lee, and Jack Knight. *The Choices Justices Make.* Washington, D.C.: Congressional Quarterly Press, 1998. An account of the U.S. Supreme Court's strategic political decision making based on both public records and the private papers of justices.

Schwartz, Bernard. *A History of the Supreme Court.* New York: Oxford University Press, 1995. A comprehensive one-volume history of the nation's highest court and the influence the Court has had on American politics and society.

14

American Federalism: Elites in States and Communities

The importance of denationalizing conflicts can hardly be over-estimated, particularly in a large country like the United States where there is great diversity in resources and local problems.

—ROBERT A. DAHL

Elites are themselves stratified with national elites supported by subelites in states and communities. Decentralization—decision making by subelites—reduces strain on the national political system and on national elites by keeping many issues out of the national arena. National conflict is reduced by allowing subelites to pursue their own policies within the separate states and communities; they need not battle for a single national policy to be applied uniformly throughout the land. For example, subelites who wish to raise taxes and spend more money for public schools can do so in their own states and communities, and those who wish to reduce taxes and eliminate what some consider to be educational "frills" can also do so within their own states and communities.

But the masses play an even less influential role in state and local politics than they do in national politics. The news media emphasize national politics rather than state or community politics. Very few citizens know who their state senator or state representative is or who their city council members or county commissioners are. We can expect about 50 percent of the nation's eligible voters to cast ballots in presidential elections, but turnout in state gubernatorial elections in nonpresidential years is generally less than

40 percent. Municipal elections often attract fewer than 20 to 30 percent of the eligible voters.

Americans have more confidence in state and local government than the federal government (see Table 14-1). Moreover, the masses would prefer that governmental power be concentrated at the state rather than the federal level and they believe that local and state governments do the best job. Yet, as we shall see in this chapter, *power in America has shifted over time to Washington and away from states and communities.*

FEDERALISM: THE ORIGINAL DIVISION OF POWER BETWEEN NATION AND STATES

The U.S. Constitution divides power between two separate authorities, the nation and the states, each of which can directly enforce its own laws on individuals through its own courts. There are more than 86,000 separate governments in the United States, of which more than 60,000 have the power to levy their own taxes. The Constitution endows *states* with all governmental powers not vested specifically in the national government or reserved to the people. All other governmental jurisdictions are subdivisions of states. States may create, alter, or abolish these other units of government by amending state laws or constitutions.

American federalism differs from a "unitary" political system in that the central government has no constitutional authority to determine, alter, or abolish the power of the states. At the same time, American federalism differs from a confederation of states, in which the national government depends on its states for power. The American system shares authority and power constitutionally and practically.

The U.S. Constitution originally defined federalism in terms of (1) the powers exercised by the national government (delegated powers) and the national supremacy clause; (2) the powers reserved to the states; (3) the powers denied by the Constitution to both the national government and the states; and (4) the constitutional provisions giving the states a role in the composition of the national government.

Delegated Powers

The U.S. Constitution lists eighteen grants of power to Congress, including authority over war and foreign affairs, authority over the economy ("interstate commerce"), control over the money supply, and power to tax and

TABLE 14-1	CONFIDENCE

Mass attitudes toward federal, state and local governments

How much confidence do you have in these institutions?

YOUR LOCAL GOVERNMENT

Great deal	11%
Quite a lot	20
Some	46
Very little	21

YOUR STATE GOVERNMENT

Great deal	6%
Quite a lot	17
Some	53
Very little	23

THE FEDERAL GOVERNMENT

Great deal	4%
Quite a lot	11
Some	47
Very little	37

POWER

Where should power be concentrated?

State government	64%
Federal government	26

BEST JOB

Which level of government does the best job of dealing with the problems it faces?

Federal	14%
State	34
Local	41

Note: All figures are percentages of the U.S. public in national opinion surveys. "No opinion" and "Don't know" are not shown.

Source: Gallup/CNN/*USA Today* polls reported in *The Polling Report,* February 10, 1997.

spend "to pay the debts and provide for the common defense and general welfare." Finally, after seventeen specific grants of power comes the power "to make all laws which shall be necessary and proper for carrying into execution the foregoing powers and all other powers vested by this Constitution in the government of the United States or in any department or officer thereof." This statement is generally known as the "necessary and proper" clause.

These delegated powers, when coupled with the assertion of "national supremacy" in Article VI, ensure a powerful national government. The national supremacy clause is very specific in asserting the supremacy of federal laws:

> The Constitution, and the laws of the United States which shall be made in pursuance thereof; and all treaties made or which shall be made under the authority of the United States, shall be the supreme law of the land; and the judges in every state shall be bound thereby, anything in the constitution or laws of any state to the contrary notwithstanding.

Reserved Powers

Despite these broad grants of power to the national government, the states retained considerable governing power from the beginning of the republic. The Tenth Amendment reassured the states that "the powers not delegated to the United States . . . are reserved to the states respectively, or to the people." The states generally retain control over property and contract law, criminal law, marriage and divorce, the provision of education, highways, and social-welfare activities. The states control the organization and powers of their own local governments. Finally, the states, like the federal government, retain the power to tax and spend for the general welfare.

Powers Denied to the States

The Constitution denies some powers to both national and state government, namely the powers to abridge individual rights. The first eight amendments to the U.S. Constitution originally applied only to the national government, but the Fourteenth Amendment, passed by Congress in 1866, provided that the states must also adhere to fundamental guarantees of individual liberty.

The Constitution denies the states some powers in order to safeguard national unity: the powers to coin money, enter into treaties with foreign nations, interfere with the "obligations of contracts," levy taxes on imports and exports, and engage in war, along with some others.

The States' Role in National Government

The states are also basic units in the organizational scheme of the national government. The House of Representatives apportions members to the states by population, and state legislatures draw up their districts. Every state has one House representative regardless of population. Each state elects two U.S. senators regardless of population. The president is chosen by the electoral votes of the states; each state has as many electoral votes as it has senators and House representatives. Finally, three-fourths of the states must ratify amendments to the U.S. Constitution.

POWER FLOWS TO THE NATIONAL ELITE

Over time governmental power has centralized in Washington. While the formal constitutional arrangements of federalism remain in place, power has flowed relentlessly toward the national government since the earliest days of the nation. Perhaps the most important developments over time have been (1) the broad interpretation of the "necessary and proper" clause to obscure the notion of "delegated powers" and allow the national government to do anything not specifically prohibited by the Constitution; (2) the victory of the national government in the Civil War, demonstrating that states could not successfully resist federal power by force of arms; (3) the establishment of a national system of civil rights based upon the Fourteenth Amendment, which brought federal government into the definition and enforcement of civil rights; (4) the growth of federal power under the interstate commerce clause as a national industrial economy emerged; and (5) the growth of federal grants-in-aid to state and local governments as a major source of revenues for these governments and a major source of federal intervention into state and local affairs.

The "Necessary and Proper" Clause

Chief Justice John Marshall added immeasurably to national power in *McCullough v. Maryland* (1819) when he broadly interpreted the "necessary and proper" clause of Article I, Section 8, of the Constitution. In

approving the establishment of a national bank (a power not specifically delegated to the national government in the Constitution), Marshall wrote:

> *Let the end be legitimate, let it be within the scope of the*
> *Constitution, and all means which are appropriate, which are*
> *plainly adopted to that end, which are not prohibited but consistent*
> *with the letter and the spirit of the Constitution, are constitutional.*

Since then, the "necessary and proper" clause has been called the "implied powers" clause or even the "elastic" clause, suggesting that the national government can do anything not specifically prohibited by the
Constitution. Given this tradition, the courts are unlikely to hold an act of
Congress unconstitutional solely because no formal constitutional grant of
power gives Congress the power to act.

The Civil War

The Civil War was the nation's greatest crisis in federalism. Did a state have
the right to oppose federal action by force of arms? The issue was decided in
the nation's bloodiest war. (Combined casualties in the Civil War, military
and civilian, exceeded U.S. casualties in the Second World War, even though
the U.S. population in 1860 was only one-quarter of the population in 1940.)
The same issue was at stake when the federal government sent troops to
Little Rock, Arkansas, in 1957 and Oxford, Mississippi, in 1962 to enforce
desegregation; however, in those confrontations it was clear which side held
the military advantage.

Civil Rights

Over the years, the U.S. Supreme Court has built a national system of civil
rights based on the Fourteenth Amendment. This amendment rose out of
the Civil War: "No *state* shall . . . deprive any person of life, liberty, or property, without due process of law; nor deny to any person within its jurisdiction the equal protection of the laws." In early cases, the Supreme Court
held that the general guarantee of "liberty" in the first phrase (the "due
process" clause) prevents states from interfering with free speech, press, religion, and other personal liberties. Later, particularly after *Brown* v. *Board
of Education of Topeka* in 1954, the Supreme Court also used the "equal
protection" clause to ensure fairness and equality of opportunity throughout
the nation.

The Interstate Commerce Clause

The growth of national power under the interstate commerce clause is also an important development in American federalism. The Industrial Revolution created a national economy governable only by a national government. Yet until the 1930s the Supreme Court placed many obstacles in the way of government regulation of the economy. Finally in *National Labor Relations Board* v. *Jones & Laughlin Steel Corporation* (1937), the Supreme Court recognized the principle that Congress could regulate production and distribution of goods and services for a national market under the interstate commerce clause. As a result, the national government gained control over wages, prices, production, marketing, labor relations, and all other important aspects of the national economy.

MONEY AND POWER

Money and power go together. In 1913, when the Sixteenth Amendment gave the national government the power to tax incomes, financial power shifted from the states to Washington. The income tax gave the federal government the authority to raise large sums of money, which it spent for the "general welfare," as well as for defense. Of course, federal *land* grants to the states began as far back as the famous Northwest Ordinance in 1787, when Congress gave federal land to the states to assist in building public schools. Again, by the Morrill Land Grant Act in 1862, Congress made land grants to the states to promote higher education. But the first major federal *money* grants to the states began shortly after enactment of the federal income tax. Grant programs began in agricultural extension (1914), highways (1916), vocational education (1917), and public health (1918).

Gradually the federal government expanded its power in states and communities by use of grants-in-aid. During the Great Depression of the 1930s, the national government used its taxing and spending powers in a number of areas formerly "reserved" to states and communities. Congress began grants-in-aid programs to states and communities for public assistance, unemployment compensation, employment services, child welfare, public housing, urban renewal, highway construction, and vocational education and rehabilitation. The inadequacy of state and local revenue systems contributed significantly to the increase of national power in states and communities. Federal grants-in-aid to state and local governments expanded

| **FIGURE 14-1** | Washington's money in state and local government finance |

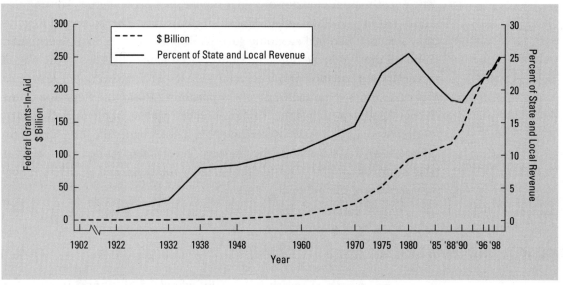

Sources: *Statistical Abstract of the United States, 1997,* p. 302, and *Budget of the United States Government, 1999.*

over the years in both dollar amounts and the percentage of the total revenue of states and communities that comes from the federal government (see Figure 14-1). For a time, the Reagan administration was successful in slowing the growth of federal grants and reducing state and local dependence on federal money. Nonetheless, today state and local governments rely on the federal government for over 20 percent of their total revenues.

THE EVOLUTION OF AMERICAN FEDERALISM

American federalism has undergone many changes during the more than two hundred years that it has been in existence. And it continues to change over time.

Dual Federalism

The pattern of federal–state relations during the nation's first hundred years has been described as *dual federalism.* The states and the nation divided most governmental functions. The national government concentrated its attention on the delegated powers—national defense, foreign affairs, tariffs, commerce across state lines, coining money, establishing standard weights and measures, maintaining a post office and building post roads, and admitting new states. State governments decided the important domestic policy issues—slavery (until the Civil War), education, welfare, health, and criminal justice. This separation of policy responsibilities was once compared to a layer cake, with local governments at the base, state governments in the middle, and the national government at the top.

Cooperative Federalism

The Industrial Revolution, bringing the development of a national economy; the income tax, which shifted financial resources to the national government; and the challenges of two world wars and the Great Depression all combined to end the strict distinction between national and state concerns. The new pattern of federal–state relations was labeled *cooperative federalism*. Both the nation and the states exercised responsibilities for welfare, health, highways, education, and criminal justice. This merging of policy responsibilities was compared to a marble cake. "As the colors are mixed in a marble cake, so functions are mixed in the American federal system."[1]

The Great Depression of the 1930s forced states to ask for federal financial assistance in dealing with poverty, unemployment, and old age. Governors welcomed massive federal public-works projects. In addition, the federal government intervened directly in economic affairs, labor relations, business practices, and agriculture. Through the grant-in-aid device, the national government cooperated with the states in public assistance, employment services, child welfare, public housing, urban renewal, highway building, and vocational education.

Yet even during this period when the nation and the states shared responsibility, the national government emphasized cooperation in achieving common national and state goals. Congress generally acknowledged that it had no direct constitutional authority to regulate public health, safety, or welfare. Congress relied primarily on its powers to tax and spend for the general welfare in providing financial assistance to state and local governments to achieve shared goals. Congress did not usually legislate directly on local matters.

Centralized Federalism

Over the years it became increasingly difficult to maintain the fiction that the national government was merely assisting the states in performing their domestic responsibility. By the time President Lyndon B. Johnson launched the Great Society in 1964, the federal government clearly set forth its own national goals. Virtually all problems confronting American society—from solid-waste disposal and water and air pollution to consumer safety, home insulation, noise abatement, and even metric conversion—were declared to be national problems. Congress legislated directly on any matter it chose. The Supreme Court no longer concerned itself with the reserved powers of the states; the Tenth Amendment lost most of its meaning. The pattern of federal–state relations became centralized.

New Federalism

The term *new federalism* has been applied to efforts to return power and responsibility to states and communities. Actually, the term was first used by President Nixon in the early 1970s to describe his general-revenue-sharing proposal: the direct allocation of federal tax revenues to state and local governments to use for general purposes with no strings attached. Later the term referred to a series of proposals by President Reagan to reduce state and local dependency on federal revenues and return powers to states and communities.

To implement the new federalism, Reagan consolidated many *categorical grants* (by which the federal government specifies individual projects or programs in cities and states) into a few large *block grant* programs (by which the federal government provides funds for use by states and cities for broad purposes, such as law enforcement and community development, with state and local officials deciding about specific projects or programs). These block grants provide greater flexibility in the use of federal funds and allow state and local officials to exercise more power over projects and programs within their jurisdictions. Reagan also ended the federal government's general-revenue-sharing program, which had funneled billions of dollars annually to states and cities. These efforts succeeded for a time in slowing the growth of federal grant money to the states and even reducing state and local reliance on federal funds (see Figure 14-1).

Coercive Federalism

Despite the attempts at the new federalism, the flow of power toward national elites continued. In 1985 the U.S. Supreme Court ended all pretense of constitutional protection of state power in its *Garcia* decision.[2] Prior to this case it was generally believed that the states were constitutionally protected from direct congressional coercion in matters traditionally "reserved" to the states. The Congress could bribe states with grant-in-aid money to enact federal programs—or threaten them with the loss of such aid if they failed to conform to federal rules—but Congress was careful to avoid direct orders to state and local governments. However, in the *Garcia* case, the Supreme Court upheld a federal law requiring state and local governments to obey federal wage and hour rules. The Court dismissed the argument that the nature of American federalism and the reserved powers clause of the Tenth Amendment prevented Congress from legislating directly in state and local affairs. The Court declared that there were no constitutionally protected state powers, that the only protection given the states is in congressional and presidential elections.

This weakened view of American federalism—that there is no constitutional protection for state power other than the states' role in electing the members of Congress and the president—has been labeled *representational federalism*.

ELITE STRUCTURES IN THE STATES

Elite structures vary among the fifty states. To understand elite patterns in state politics, we can identify several categories of elite systems.

Unified Elite System

In states with a dominant single industry and weak, noncompetitive parties, a cohesive group of economic interests can dominate state politics. Historically, the states of the Deep South displayed such a structure, called a "unified elite system." "Populist" candidates sometimes briefly challenged the dominance of the planting, landowning, and financial elites in southern states. Once in power, the demagogues seldom implemented populist programs; more frequently, they became instruments of the established elites whom they had castigated in campaign oratory. But as these states industrialized, their economies became somewhat more diversified. Agricultural landowning elites had to make way for newer elites with interests in oil, textiles, food processing, furniture making, and other labor-intensive industries that moved south in increasing numbers after World War II.

Dominant Elites Among Lesser Elites

Today rural states with a relatively nondiversified economy are more likely to harbor an elite structure we call "dominant elites among lesser elites." This structure features a few major industrial corporations, banks, and insurance companies that dominate decision making with occasional input from lesser elites. Political and governmental leaders are heavily dependent upon a relatively small group of economic interests. Political history accounts describing the power of DuPont in Delaware, the oil companies in Texas and Louisiana, the coal companies in West Virginia, and similar companies are abundant. Doubtless their reputations for absolute control of a state far exceeded their actual control over public policy. The oil industry's reputation for control of Texas politics was often exaggerated. The chairman of the Texas Democratic Executive Committee once said, "It may not be a wholesome thing to say, but the oil industry today is in complete control of state politics and state government."[3] This type of overstatement is common in political circles; in fact, many issues in state politics are of little concern to the oil interests. However, Texas politicians are unlikely to oppose the oil industry on issues that directly affect it. The same is true of the dominant interests in other states: although they may not control all aspects of state politics, they control those matters that directly affect their interests.

Increasingly Diversified Elite Structures

Yet Texas, as well as Florida, Georgia, and North Carolina among southern states, has grown much more diversified as the "Sun Belt" economies have strengthened over the past few decades. New industries and new concentrations of wealth have developed to challenge the traditional power structures of these states. For example, citrus and agriculture and forestry in Florida now share power with Winn-Dixie and Publix stores, Republic industries, W. R. Grace, Office Depot, and Walt Disney World. Today oil in Texas shares powers with high-tech industries, represented by such companies as SBC Communications, Compaq Computers, Texas Instruments, Electronic Data Systems, Dell Computer, Tandy, and others. Georgia is more than just the home of Coca-Cola; it is also home to Home Depot, United Parcel Service, BellSouth, Delta Air Lines, and several other billion-dollar corporations. Moreover, in some midwestern states, notably Michigan, Wisconsin, and Minnesota, elites have been somewhat diversified over the years. The automobile industry, Michigan's largest employer, has faced an organized labor movement since the 1930s. Dairy farmers remain important in Wisconsin, but not everyone in the state is a "cheesehead"; Northwestern Mutual Life, Johnson Controls, and Manpower Inc. are headquartered today in Milwaukee. Minnesota Mining & Mfg. (3M) shares power with Dayton Hudson and Honeywell in Minnesota.

FOCUS

Corporate Elite Structures in the States

Cohesive elite structures are more likely to emerge in states in which relatively few major industrial corporations are located. The following table lists the number of corporations with more than two billion dollars in revenue in each state. Some states have no large corporation located in them: Alaska, Hawaii, Montana, Nevada, New Mexico, North

Dakota, Vermont, and Wyoming. This indicates that no large national corporation locates its home office there. Nonetheless, these states, because of their mostly rural, nondiversified economies are likely to have fairly cohesive elite structures. Likewise, the states with only a few major corporations (Arkansas, for instance, with Wal-Mart and Dillard's retail store headquarters and Tyson's chicken-processing) are also likely to have relatively unified elite structures.

In contrast, states with large numbers of corporations engaged in a wide variety of industrial activities are likely to have plural elite structures. California and New York, for example, are too large and diversified, and house too many top-ranked corporations, to be dominated by a unified elite.

Types of Elite Structure in Various States

Likely Plural Elite Structures (number of major corporations)

New York	61	Texas	36	Pennsylvania	29	Connecticut	18
California	52	Ohio	30	New Jersey	26	Massachusetts	17
Illinois	41						

Likely Increasingly Diversified Elite Structures

Virginia	18	Missouri	15	Washington	9	Indiana	6
Florida	15	Georgia	14	Wisconsin	8	Maryland	6
Minnesota	15	Michigan	13	North Carolina	7	Nebraska	6

Likely Dominant Elite Among Lesser Elite Structures

Alabama	5	Tennessee	5	Oregon	4	Idaho	3
Arkansas	5	Kentucky	4	Delaware	3	Rhode Island	3
Colorado	5	Oklahoma	4				

Likely Unified Elite Structures

Arizona	2	Mississippi	1	Alaska	0	New Mexico	0
Iowa	2	New Hampshire	1	Hawaii	0	North Dakota	0
Kansas	2	South Carolina	1	Montana	0	Vermont	0
Maine	2	South Dakota	1	Nevada	0	Wyoming	0
Louisiana	1	Utah	1				

Plural Elite Structure

A state with an already highly diversified economy is likely to produce a "plural elite structure." California may have the most diversified economy of any state in the nation, with thriving agricultural interests, timber and mining resources, and manufacturing enterprises that run the gamut from cement to motion pictures. Railroads, brewers, racetracks, motion pictures, citrus growers, airplane manufacturers, insurance companies, utilities, defense contractors, and a host of other economic interests coexist in this state. No one economic interest or combination of interests dominates California politics. Instead, a variety of elites govern within specific issue areas; each elite concentrates its attention on matters directly affecting its own economic interest. Occasionally, the economic interests of elites may clash, but on the whole elites coexist rather than compete. Political parties are somewhat less cohesive and disciplined in the plural elite system. Economic elites, hesitating to identify too closely with a single party, even make financial contributions to opposing candidates to ensure protection of their interest no matter which party or candidate wins.

THE OLD COMMUNITY ECONOMIC ELITES

Most of the nation's economic resources are controlled by *national* institutions—industrial corporations, banks, utilities, insurance companies, investment firms, and the national government. Most of the forces shaping life in American communities arise outside of these communities; community leaders cannot make war or peace, or cause inflation or recession or determine interest rates or the money supply. But there is one economic resource—land—that is controlled by *community* elites. Land is a valuable resource: capital investment, labor and management, and production must be placed somewhere.

Traditionally, community power structures were composed primarily of landed interests whose goal was to intensify the use of their land and add to its value. These community elites sought to maximize land values, real estate commissions, builders' profits, rent payments, and mortgage interest and to increase revenues to commercial enterprises serving the community. Communities were traditionally dominated by mortgage lending banks, real estate developers, builders, and landowners. They were joined by owners or managers of local utilities, department stores, attorneys and title companies, and others whose wealth is affected by land use. Local bankers who financed the real estate developers and builders were often at the center of the elite structure. Unquestionably these community elites competed among themselves for wealth, profit, power, and preeminence. But they shared a consensus about intensifying the use of land.

Growth was the shared elite value. The old community elite was indeed a "growth machine."[4] The old community elite believed that capital investment in the community would raise land values, expand the labor force, generate demand for housing as well as commercial services, and enhance the local tax base. Attracting investors required the provision of good transportation facilities—highways, streets, rail access, and water and airport facilities. It required the provision of utilities—water, gas and electrical power, solid waste disposal, and sewage treatment. It required the provision of good municipal services, especially fire and police protection; the elimination of harassing business regulations and the reduction of taxes on new investments to the lowest feasible levels; the provision of a capable and cooperative labor force, educated for the needs of productive capital and motivated to work; and finally, the provision of sufficient amenities—cultural, recreational, aesthetic—to provide the corporate managers with a desirable lifestyle.

Traditional community elites strove for consensus. They believed that community economic growth—increased capital investment, more jobs, and improved business conditions—benefited the entire community. According to Paul E. Peterson, community residents share a common interest in the economic well-being of the city: "Policies and programs can be said to be in the interest of cities whenever the policies maintain or enhance the economic position, social prestige, or political power of the city as a whole."[5] Economic elites themselves would have agreed with Peterson.

Local government officials were expected to share in the elite consensus. Economic prosperity was necessary for protecting the fiscal base of local government. Growth in local budgets and public employment, as well as governmental services, depends upon growth in the local economy. Governmental growth expanded the power, prestige, and status of government officials. Moreover, economic growth was usually good politics. Growth-oriented candidates for public office usually had larger campaign treasuries than antigrowth candidates. Finally, according to Peterson, most local politicians had "a sense of community responsibility." They knew that if the economy of the community declines, "local business will suffer, workers will lose employment opportunities, cultural life will decline, and city land values will fall."[6]

THE NEW COMMUNITY POLITICAL ELITES

Today, in most American communities, the old economic elites have been replaced by new political elites. Many of the old economic elites sold their businesses to national corporations and vacated their positions of community leadership. Locally owned stores and factories became manager-directed plants and chain stores. The result was a weakening of community loyalties in the business sector. The new corporate managers could easily decide, in response to national economic conditions, to close the local plant or store with minimal concern for the impact on the community. Local banks were merged into national banking corporations and local bankers were replaced by banking executives with few community ties. City newspapers that were once independently owned by families who lived in the communities were bought up by giant newspaper and publication chains. Instead of editors and reporters who expected to live the lives of their communities, city newspapers came to be staffed with people who hope to move up in the corporate hierarchy—people who strive primarily to advance their own careers, not the interests of the local community.

The nationalization of the American economy and the resulting demise of locally owned enterprises created a vacuum of leadership in community affairs. Professional politicians moved into this vacuum in city after city, largely replacing the local bankers, real estate developers, chambers of commerce, and old-style newspaper editors who had dominated community politics for generations. The earlier economic elites were only part-time politicians who used local government to promote their economic interests. The new professional political elites work full time at local politics. They are drawn primarily by personal ambition, not so much for the wealth as for the power and celebrity that accompany running for and winning public office. They are not "screened" by economic elites or political parties, but rather they nominate themselves, raise their own funds, organize their own campaigns, and create their own publicity.

The political elites are independent entrepreneurs. They win office "by selling themselves to the voters, in person, one at a time, day after day. People who do not like to do this, people who do not like to knock on strangers' doors or who find it tedious to repeat the same thirty-second personal introduction thousands of times, are at a severe disadvantage."[7] Thus, over time these full-time political elites drive out the part-time economic elites.

The new political elites seldom have a large financial stake in the community, aside from their homes. They are *not* corporate leaders, or bankers, or developers. They may be lawyers, but they are not highly successful lawyers from prestigious law firms; rather, they are "political activists with law degrees."[8] They are not strongly committed to the community's economic growth or well-being. They do not necessarily seek community consensus on behalf of prosperity.

On the contrary, it's fashionable among new political elites to complain loudly about the problems created by growth—congestion, pollution, noise, unsightly development, or the replacement of green spaces with concrete slabs. No-growth movements appeal to people who already own their houses and do not intend to sell them, people whose jobs are secure in government bureaucracies or tenured professorships, people who may be displaced from their homes and neighborhoods by new facilities, and people who see no direct benefit to themselves from growth. These no-growth movements (or, to use the current euphemism, "growth-management" movements) are *not* mass movements. They do *not* express the aspirations of workers for jobs or renters for their own homes. Instead, they reflect upper-middle-class lifestyle preferences of educated, affluent, articulate homeowners. Growth brings ugly factories, cheap commercial outlets, hamburger stands, fried chicken franchises, and "undesirable" residents. Even if new business or industry would help hold down local taxes, these affluent citizens would still oppose it, preferring to retain the appearance or lifestyle of their community.

New political elites waving the no-growth banner challenge traditional economic elites in many large and growing cities in the West and South. The no-growth leaders may themselves have been beneficiaries of community growth only five or ten years ago, but they quickly perceive their own political interest in slowing or halting additional growth.

Halting or curtailing growth serves the financial interest of homeowners, apartment owners, and owners of already-developed commercial property. Curtailing growth serves to freeze out competition from new homes, apartment complexes, and commercial centers. It allows owners of existing homes and properties to raise prices and rents to new residents. It is no surprise that "neighborhood associations" led by upper- and upper-middle-class homeowners are at the forefront of no-growth politics.

Municipal government offers the tools to challenge the old growth elites. Communities may restrict growth through zoning laws, subdivision control restrictions, utility regulations, building permits, and environmental regulations. Opposition to street widening, road building, or tree cutting can slow or halt development. Public utilities needed for development—water lines, sewage disposal facilities, fire houses, and so on—can be postponed indefinitely. High development fees, "impact fees," utility hookup charges, and building permit fees can all be used to discourage growth. Environmental laws and even historic preservation laws can be employed aggressively to halt development.

Summary

The existence of political subelites within the larger American political system permits some decentralization of decision making. Decentralization, or decision making by subelites, reduces potential strain on the consensus of national elites. Each subelite sets its own policies in its own state and community, without battling over a single national policy to be applied uniformly throughout the land. The following propositions summarize our consideration of American federalism and our comparative analysis of elites in states and communities.

1. American federalism divides power constitutionally between national and state governments, each of which can directly enforce its own laws on individuals through its own courts. The Constitution itself cannot be amended without the consent of the national government (two-thirds of both houses of Congress) and the states (three-fourths of the legislatures).

2. Over time, however, power has centralized in Washington owing to (a) a broad interpretation of the "necessary and proper" clause granting the national government the power to do anything not specifically prohibited by the Constitution, (b) the victory of the national government in the Civil War, (c) the establishment of a national system of civil rights, (d) the growth of national power under the interstate commerce clause, and (e) the growth of federal grants-in-aid to state and local governments.

3. The principal instrument of national power in states and communities is the federal "grant-in-aid." Federal grants now provide over 20 percent of all state and local government revenue. Federal rules, regulations, and guidelines accompanying the grants give the federal government great power over the activity of local governments. The "new federalism" proposed to reverse the flow of power to Washington and return responsibility to states and cities. The Reagan administration consolidated many categorical grant programs into block grants, ended general-revenue sharing, and temporarily reversed the growing dependence of state and local governments on federal revenue.

4. Despite efforts to implement the new federalism, power continues to flow toward national elites. The Supreme Court in its *Garcia* decision removed all constitutional protections for state power, other than the states' role in electing the members of Congress and the president.

5. Cohesive elite structures such as the "unified elite system" and "dominants among lesser elites" are more likely to be found in states in which relatively

few major industrial corporations are located. These are the more rural states with nondiversified economies. States with larger numbers of national corporations engaged in a wide variety of economic activities are more likely to have plural elite structures.

6. Traditional community power structures concern themselves with economic growth. These community power structures are dominated by banks, real estate developers, builders, and landowners, all of whom benefit directly from increasing the value of land. These power structures mobilize mass support for local growth policies by promising more jobs.

7. New community political elites have arisen in many cities to replace old community economic elites. As the economy nationalized, locally owned businesses, banks, and newspapers were replaced by national corporations and chains, whose managers have fewer ties to community affairs. Local political elites moved into the vacuum of power. These new elites are self-nominated, full-time, professional politicians.

8. The new political elites are not necessarily committed to economic growth. They frequently endorse "growth management" proposals designed to halt or curtail growth. These new elites do *not* reflect mass interests but rather the preferences of upper-middle-class, educated, articulate homeowners for avoiding noise and pollution, ugly factories, cheap commercials, and "undesirable" residents.

Notes

1. Morton Grodzins, *The American System* (Chicago: Rand McNally, 1966), p. 265.

2. *Garcia* v. *San Antonio Metropolitan Authority,* 469 U.S. 528 (1985).

3. Robert Engler, *The Politics of Oil* (New York: Macmillan, 1981), p. 354.

4. See Harvy Molotch, "The City as Growth Machine," *American Journal of Sociology* 82 (September 1976): 309–330; and "Capital and Neighborhood in the United States," *Urban Affairs Quarterly* 14 (March 1979): 289–312.

5. Paul E. Peterson, *City Limits* (Chicago: University of Chicago Press, 1981), p. 20.

6. Ibid., p. 29.

7. Alan Ehrenhalt, *The United States of Ambition* (New York: Time Books, 1991), p. 15.

8. Ibid., p. 16.

Selected Readings

Dahl, Robert A. *Who Governs?* New Haven, Conn.: Yale University Press, 1961. This classic study is perhaps the most important pluralist community power book. Using a decisional approach, Dahl finds that a variety of separate elites make decisions in different issue areas.

Ehrenhalt, Alan. *The United States of Ambition.* New York: Time Books, 1991. A description of fundamental changes in community, state, and national politics over the last thirty years, illustrated with a series of case studies. Ehrenhalt argues that in communities across the country new professional political elites have grabbed power from the old economic elites. The new political elites nominate themselves and win elections through hard work and self-promotion. They are not committed to community prosperity so much as to their own careers.

Hunter, Floyd. *Community Power Structure*. Chapel Hill: University of North Carolina Press, 1953. Although classical elitism has its origins in European sociological theory, much of the current American controversy over elitism has resulted from community power research. This book was one of the first community power studies reporting elitist results.

Ricci, David M. *Community Power and Democratic Theory: The Logic of Political Analysis*. New York: Random House, 1981. This book is an excellent review of both past and current philosophical, ideological, and methodological differences between elitists and pluralists of each theory, including the contributions of Joseph Schumpeter ("process" theory of democracy), David Truman ("group" theory of democracy), Floyd Hunter ("reputational" theory of elitism), C. Wright Mills ("positional" theory of elitism), and Robert Dahl ("pluralist" theory of democracy). The text also includes an excellent discussion of "the present scholarly impasse" between advocates of each point of view, as well as an annotated bibliography of relevant literature.

15

Elite Response to Mass Protest

The social origins of protest leaders are rather similar to, instead of strikingly different from, the social origins of leaders of established parties with whom they clash.

—ANTHONY OBERSCHALL

People without access to the resources of interest group politics, and people whose values are substantially at odds with the prevailing public policy, occasionally enter mass protest movements. These protest *movements* sometimes lead to the establishment of protest *organizations* designed to represent and shape mass movements. This shaping and organizing is where protest movements and the protest organizations either succeed or fail.

Established elites do not ignore protests. Rather they may (1) make symbolic gestures to pacify the active protesters (co-opting them through programs that bring protest leaders into the "system"), (2) limit protests through repression (increased law enforcement), or (3) do both simultaneously. Often elite response is a combination of accommodation and repression, with heavier doses of accommodation handed out to movements whose goals are within the general framework of elite consensus.[1]

As organizations arise to direct the aspirations of protest movements, the advantages of accommodation increase. Protest leaders find that by moderating their demands they can gain a portion of their original goals and also achieve for themselves and the organization a stake in the elite system. Thus protest movements that become protest organizations eventually come to share the elite consensus.

Protest movements tend to be cyclical. Many fail to achieve organizational stability and soon fade from memory. Others successfully travel the road from protest to organization to accommodation, but the price is high. Movement toward political success not only requires accommodation to the acceptable norms of established elites, but also requires organizational leadership by people with negotiating skills and willingness to sustain activity for long periods of time. Protest leaders, irrespective of the movements they represent, do *not* come from the lower strata of society.[2]

From the variety of movements that have risen and fallen during the history of the United States, the civil rights movement and the feminist movement offer interesting and contemporary examples for discussion.

THE HISTORY OF BLACK SUBJUGATION

The place of blacks in American society has been a central issue of domestic politics in the United States since the first black slaves stepped onto these shores in 1619. The American nation as a whole, with its democratic tradition, has felt strong conflicting sentiments about slavery, segregation, and discrimination. White America has harbored an ambivalence toward blacks—a recognition of the evils of inequality but a reluctance to take steps to eliminate it. This "American dilemma" reflects the larger issue of the American masses' attitudes toward democracy: commitment to abstract ideals with substantially less commitment to their practice.[3] To a large extent, we can view the struggle of African-Americans for full citizenship as a dialogue—sometimes violent, sometimes peaceful—between the demands of black counterelites and the response of dominant white elites.

Abolition

In 1865 the Thirteenth Amendment abolished slavery everywhere in the United States. The Fourteenth Amendment, passed in 1867 by a Republican Congress that intended to reconstruct southern society after the Civil War, made "equal protection of the laws" a command for every state to obey. The Fifteenth Amendment, passed in 1869, prohibited federal and state governments from abridging the right to vote "on account of race, color, or previous condition of servitude." In addition, Congress passed a series of civil rights statutes in the 1860s and 1870s guaranteeing newly freed African-Americans protection in the exercise of their constitutional rights. The Civil

Rights Act of 1875 specifically outlawed segregation by privately owned businesses offering to serve the public. Between 1865 and the early 1880s the success of the civil rights movement was evident in widespread black voting throughout the South, the presence of many blacks in federal and state offices, and the almost equal treatment afforded blacks in theaters, restaurants, hotels, and public transportation.

The Rise of White Supremacy

But by 1877 support for Reconstruction policies began to crumble. In what was labeled the "Compromise of 1877," the national government agreed to end military occupation of the South, give up its efforts to rearrange southern society, and lend tacit approval to white supremacy in that region. In return, the southern states pledged their support to the Union, accepted national supremacy, and agreed to permit the Republican presidential candidate, Rutherford B. Hayes, to assume the presidency, although the Democratic candidate, Samuel Tilden, had received a majority of the popular vote in the disputed election of 1876. The Supreme Court adhered to the terms of this compromise. In the famous Civil Rights Cases of 1883, the Supreme Court declared unconstitutional those federal civil rights laws preventing discrimination by private individuals. By denying Congress the power to protect blacks from discrimination, the Court paved the way for the imposition of segregation as the prevailing social system of the South. In the 1880s and 1890s, white southerners imposed segregation in public accommodations, housing, education, employment, and almost every other sector of private and public life. By 1895 most southern states had passed laws *requiring* racial segregation in education and in public accommodations.

In 1896, in the famous case of *Plessy* v. *Ferguson*, the Supreme Court upheld state laws requiring segregation.[4] Although segregation laws involved state action, the Court held that segregating the races did not violate the equal protection clause of the Fourteenth Amendment so long as people in each race received equal treatment. Schools and other public facilities that were "separate but equal" won constitutional approval.

The violence that occurred during that period was almost entirely one-sided: whites attacked blacks.[5] The pattern of race relations at the turn of the century was clearly one of violent repression, exclusion of blacks from jobs and labor unions, and rigid segregation. African-Americans lost most of what they had gained during Reconstruction.

TWENTIETH-CENTURY BLACK RESPONSES

The Black Response: Initial Developments

The NAACP and National Urban League   The first African-American organizations emerged in response to the repressive pattern of the late nineteenth century; notably the National Association for the Advancement of Colored People (NAACP) and the National Urban League in 1909 and 1910, respectively. Both organizations reacted against Booker T. Washington's acceptance of the inferior status of blacks, and both worked closely with white liberals. These organizations sought black equality through court action and other legal means. They were (and still are) dominated by middle-class blacks and upper-class whites. They accepted the premise that they could effect meaningful change within the American legal system. They were (and are) conservative in that their techniques require commitment to the institutional status quo. They disavowed attempts to change or overthrow the basic political and economic structure of the society; they simply sought to integrate blacks into the existing society. In other words, they took literally the ideology and premises of the American democratic system that "all men are created equal."

The Development of Counterelites   The concentration of African-Americans in northern cities early in the twentieth century increased the potential for mass action. First, the black community began to *express* its grievances. As grievances such as discrimination in housing and transportation built up and expression became more aggressive, a precipitating incident would occur, and blacks responded by attacking whites or their property. The northern-style riot differed substantially from southern-style violence; blacks no longer remained passive victims but became active participants. The northern-style riot made its first appearance in Springfield, Illinois, in 1908.

Perhaps the first important African-American counterelite was Marcus Garvey. Since the NAACP was an elitist organization in both membership and appeal, Garvey, a West Indian, organized the Universal Negro Improvement Association to articulate the latent feelings of black nationalism. Garvey's programs for a separate black nation in Africa appealed to impoverished blacks, especially as white bigotry in the form of the Ku Klux Klan spread north in the wake of black economic advance. Garvey was essentially a forerunner of the Black Muslims of the 1950s and 1960s and the more radical black nationalists of the late 1960s. Like the Muslims, Garvey urged his followers to practice personal frugality and establish a high level of morality. Like the nationalists, he sought to teach blacks that their color could be a source of pride rather than shame. At one time, Garvey had a following estimated at three million, but his movement collapsed in the mid-1920s. His appeal to the black masses, nevertheless, was very important, for Garvey asserted that blacks would never gain what the NAACP insisted that they could achieve: an equal share in the American economic system. As sociologist Gunnar Myrdal observed, the Garvey movement "tells of the dissatisfaction so deep that it mounts to hopelessness of ever enjoying a full life in America."[6]

Court Declaration of Equality   The period following the Korean War, marked by enormous legal and symbolic victories, was crucial in the development of the relationship between blacks and whites. The long labors of the NAACP paid off in the historic *Brown* v. *Board of Education of Topeka, Kansas* decision, in which the Court reversed the *Plessy* v. *Ferguson* doctrine of "separate but equal."[7] This decision symbolized the beginning of a new era of high expectations among blacks. Whereas *elected* elites had remained largely silent on civil rights, an *appointed* elite, the Supreme Court, declared that blacks and whites were equal in the eyes of the law.

However, *Brown* v. *Board of Education of Topeka* was only the beginning of the political battle over segregation. Segregation did not disappear simply because the Supreme Court declared it unconstitutional. Segregation was widespread and deeply ingrained. Seventeen states required segregation by law, and the U.S. Congress required segregation in Washington, D.C. Four other states (Arizona, Kansas, New Mexico, and Wyoming) authorized segregation at local option. Unless the national political elite directly challenged the political power of the white majority in the South, the pattern of segregation was unlikely to change.

Initially the Supreme Court placed primary responsibility for enforcing its decision on *local* officials and school boards, in effect returning power to the white subelites in the South. As a result, during the 1950s the white South developed many schemes to resist integration. Ten years after *Brown*, only about 2 percent of the blacks in the South attended integrated schools; the other 98 percent remained in segregated schools. In short, for a decade the decision meant little to the overwhelming majority of blacks, whose frustrations intensified as they saw the discrepancy between the Supreme Court's intent and the behavior of local officials. Blacks had gained a legal victory, but they were impotent politically. As a result, the civil rights movement changed its focus from legal restrictions to de facto segregation and unequal socioeconomic institutions.

***Symbolic Importance of* Brown**   The symbolic importance of the *Brown* decision is great, and despite the paucity of tangible benefits, the decision undoubtedly increased blacks' expectations and demands. African-American sociologist Kenneth Clark assesses the importance of official sanction as follows:

> *This [civil rights] movement would probably not have existed at all were it not for the 1954 Supreme Court school desegregation decision which provided a tremendous boost to the morale of Negroes by its clear affirmation that color is irrelevant to the rights of American citizens. Until this time the Southern Negro generally had accommodated to the separation of the black from the white society.*[8]

Creative Disorder

Bus Boycotts   In 1955 an African-American woman, Rosa Parks, refused to ride in the back of a bus in Montgomery, Alabama, lending dramatic support to Clark's hypothesis. Her act brought about the Montgomery boycott, in which blacks refused to use the public transportation system until they could sit wherever they preferred; this action was the first significant step away from the NAACP's legalism. The Montgomery bus boycott required mass-oriented leadership. Martin Luther King, Jr., who gained instant national prominence through the bus boycott, initially filled this need. His Southern Christian Leadership Conference (SCLC) emerged in 1957 as the first southern-originated civil rights group. Although substantially more militant than the older black organizations, it was nevertheless explicitly nonviolent. The purposes of mass demonstrations were to challenge the legality of both legal and de facto segregation and to prick the consciences of white elites.

Direct-Action Tactics   The tactics of the SCLC were extended by the Student Nonviolent Co-ordinating Committee (SNCC), which developed in the next phase of direct action—the sit-in demonstrations and freedom rides of the 1960s. In February 1960, at Greensboro, North Carolina, students of the

North Carolina Agricultural and Technical College conducted the first sit-ins. As other sit-ins followed, SNCC organized to coordinate the new student protest. SNCC, unlike the SCLC, encouraged blacks to feel proud of being black. The Congress on Racial Equality (CORE), which had begun in the 1940s, emerged from quiescence to lead the freedom rides, which challenged the Jim Crow laws of transportation facilities. Many thousands of students participated in these extremely dangerous rides, refusing to obey the segregation laws.

The vigor with which blacks pursued the freedom rides and sit-ins was a clear sign that the civil rights movement was committing itself to direct action. However, even this new phase of the civil rights movement was not really a mass movement; the participants were still relatively privileged in comparison with the black masses. The most frequent participants in the confrontations of the early 1960s were urban students. These relatively privileged youths were disappointed in the white society's unwillingness to recognize their merits.

Birmingham Demonstrations   In 1963, in Birmingham, Alabama, blacks conducted prolonged demonstrations on the broadest front yet conceived by civil rights leaders. Blacks presented demands to end discrimination in public accommodations, employment, and housing to the white elite of Birmingham. Under the leadership of Martin Luther King, Jr., these demonstrations were committed to nonviolence. Probably because of the broad nature of the demands, the grass roots of the black community began to participate for the first time. All strata of the black community became active.

The Civil Rights Act of 1964

The Birmingham demonstrations were another landmark in the civil rights movement. Partly because of the southern elites' repressive behavior toward these peaceful demonstrations, the Kennedy administration proposed significant civil rights legislation. Thus the Birmingham demonstrations of 1963 stimulated what was to become the Civil Rights Act of 1964, Congress's first significant entry into civil rights. The act passed both houses of Congress by more than a two-thirds vote, winning the overwhelming support of both Republicans and Democrats. It ranks with the Emancipation Proclamation, the Fourteenth Amendment, and *Brown* v. *Board of Education of*

Topeka as one of the most important steps toward full equality for blacks in the United States. Among its more important provisions are the following:

★ It is unlawful to apply unequal standards in voter registration procedures or to deny registration for irrelevant errors or omissions on records or applications.

★ It is unlawful to discriminate against or segregate people on the grounds of race, color, religion, or national origin in any place of public accommodation, including hotels, motels, restaurants, movies, theaters, sports arenas, entertainment houses, and other places that offer to serve the public. This prohibition extends to all establishments whose operations affect interstate commerce or whose discriminatory practices are supported by state action.

★ Each federal department and agency must act to end discrimination in all programs or activities receiving federal financial assistance in any form. This action will include termination of financial assistance.

★ It is unlawful for any employer or labor union to discriminate against any individual in any fashion in employment because of race, color, religion, sex, or national origin; an equal Employment Opportunity Commission will enforce this provision through investigation, conference, conciliation, persuasion, and, if necessary, civil action in federal court.

The Civil Rights Act of 1964 brought about tangible gains for southern blacks. The withdrawal of federal grant-in-aid money as a sanction was a re-markable innovation in federal enforcement of civil rights. When the U.S. Office of Education began to apply pressure in the South, its progress was impressive compared with that of the preceding ten years.

CONTINUING INEQUALITIES BETWEEN BLACKS AND WHITES

Blacks' economic position has improved substantially in recent years, but this improvement still leaves the black masses well below the white stan-dards of living (see Table 15-1). Examining black income as a percentage of white income allows a comparison of the condition of blacks *relative* to that of whites. Between 1947 and 1970 the gap gradually narrowed, but this nar-rowing did not continue. To date, black per capita income remains at 62 per-cent or less of white per capita income.

TABLE 15-1				
Black income per capita as a percentage of white income per capita	1947	51%	1977	57%
	1964	54	1978	57
	1965	54	1980	56
	1966	58	1982	56
	1967	59	1984	56
	1968	60	1986	57
	1969	61	1988	57
	1970	64	1990	60
	1971	60	1991	59
	1972	59	1992	58
	1973	58	1993	59
	1974	58	1994	60
	1975	58	1995	60
	1976	59	1996	62

Source: U.S. Bureau of the Census, *Statistical Abstract of the United States 1997,* p. 472; www.census.gov/hhes/income.

Compared to white children, black children are:

Five times more likely to

★　Be dependent on welfare

★　Become pregnant as teenagers

Four times more likely to

★　Live with neither parent and be supervised by a child-welfare agency

★　Be murdered

★　Be incarcerated between 15 and 19 years of age

Three times more likely to

★　Be poor

★　Have their mothers die in childbirth

★　Live with a parent who has separated from his or her spouse

★　Live in a female-headed household

★　Be placed in an educable, mentally retarded class

★　Be in foster care

★　Die of known child abuse

★　Score below average on scholastic aptitude tests

Twice as likely to

★　Die in the first year of life

★　Be born prematurely

TABLE 15-2	MEDIAN INCOME OF FAMILIES				
Minority life chances	1970	1975	1980	1985	1995
White	$10,236	$14,268	$21,904	$29,152	$42,646
Black	6,279	8,779	12,674	16,786	25,970
Hispanic	—	9,551	14,716	19,027	24,570

PERCENTAGE OF PERSONS BELOW POVERTY LEVEL

	1975	1980	1985	1995
White	9.7%	10.2%	11.4%	11.2%
Black	31.3	32.5	31.3	29.3
Hispanic	26.9	25.7	29.0	30.3

UNEMPLOYMENT RATE

	1980	1985	1996
White	6.3%	6.2%	4.7%
Black	14.3	15.1	10.5
Hispanic	10.1	10.5	8.9

EDUCATION: PERCENTAGE OF PERSONS OVER TWENTY-FIVE COMPLETING

	HIGH SCHOOL	COLLEGE
White	83%	24%
Black	74	14
Hispanic	53	9

Source: *Statistical Abstract of the United States, 1997*, pp. 159, 398, 469.

★ Suffer from low birthweight

★ Have a mother who received late or no prenatal care

★ Be born to a teenager or single-parent family

★ See a parent die

★ Live in substandard housing

★ Be suspended from school or suffer corporal punishment

★ Live in institutions

TABLE 15-3		NUMBER	PERCENTAGE OF POPULATION
Minorities in America—2000	African-Americans	35,456,000	12.9%
	Hispanic Americans	31,366,000	11.4
	Asian or Pacific Islander Americans	11,246,000	4.1
	Native Americans, Eskimos, Aleuts	2,402,000	0.9
	Total Population	274,634,000	100.0

Source: *Statistical Abstract of the United States, 1997*, p. 35.

BATTLES OVER AFFIRMATIVE ACTION

What public policies should be pursued to achieve equality? Is it sufficient that government eliminate discrimination, guarantee equality of opportunity to blacks and whites, and apply color-blind standards to both groups? Or should government take action to overcome the results of past unequal treatment of blacks: preferential or compensatory treatment that will favor black applicants for university admission and scholarships, job hiring and promotion, and other opportunities for advancement in life?

Increasingly, the goal of the civil rights movement has shifted from the traditional goal of *equality of opportunity* to one of affirmative action to establish goals and timetables to achieve *equality of results*. Although usually avoiding the term *quota*, affirmative action tests the success of equal employment opportunity by observing whether certain groups achieve admissions, jobs, and promotions in proportion to their numbers in the population, and it allows for preferential or compensatory treatment to overcome the results of past discrimination.

The constitutional question posed by affirmative action programs is whether they discriminate against whites in violation of the equal protection clause of the Fourteenth Amendment. Clearly, this is a question for the Supreme Court to resolve, but unfortunately the Court has failed to develop a clear-cut answer.

The Bakke Case

In an early, controversial case, *Regents of the University of California* v. *Bakke* (1978), the Supreme Court struck down a special admissions program for minorities at a state medical school on the grounds that it excluded a white applicant because of his race and violated his rights under the equal protection clause.[9] Allan Bakke had applied to the University of California Davis Medical School two consecutive years and was rejected; in both years black applicants with significantly lower grade point averages and medical aptitude test scores were accepted through a special admissions program that reserved sixteen minority places in a class of one hundred. The University of California did not deny that its admissions decisions were based on race. Instead, it argued that the objective of its racial classification was "benign," that is, designed to assist minorities, not to hinder them. The Supreme Court held that this objective was legitimate and that race and ethnic origin may be considered in reviewing applications to a state school without violating the equal protection clause. However, the Court also held that a separate admissions program for minorities with a specified quota of openings that were unavailable to white applicants did violate the equal protection clause. The Court ordered Bakke admitted to medical school and the elimination of the special admissions program. It recommended that California consider developing an admissions program that considered disadvantaged racial or ethnic background as a "plus" in an overall evaluation of an application but did not set numerical quotas or exclude any persons from competing for all positions.

Affirmative Action as a Remedy for Past Discrimination

However, the Supreme Court appears willing to approve affirmative action programs where there is evidence of past discriminatory actions. In *United States* v. *Paradise* (1987), the Court upheld a rigid 50 percent black quota system for promotions in the Alabama Department of Safety, which had excluded blacks from the ranks of state troopers before 1972 and had not promoted any blacks higher than corporal before 1984. In a 5-to-4 decision, the majority stressed the long history of discrimination in the agency as a reason for upholding the quota system. Whatever burdens were imposed on innocent parties were outweighed by the need to correct the effects of past discrimination.[10]

Limits on Affirmative Action

Yet in the absence of past discrimination, the Supreme Court has expressed concern about whites who are directly and adversely affected by government action solely because of their race. In *Firefighters Local Union* v.

"I think I preferred it before he became an equal-opportunity employer."

Stotts (1984), the Court ruled that a city could not lay off white firefighters in favor of black firefighters with less seniority.[11] In *Richmond v. Crosen* (1989), the Court held that a minority set-aside program in Richmond, Virginia, which mandates that 30 percent of all city construction contracts must go to "blacks, Spanish-speaking, Orientals, Indians, Eskimos, or Aleuts," violates the equal protection clause of the Fourteenth Amendment.[12]

It is important to note that the Supreme Court has never adopted the color-blind doctrine, first espoused by Justice Harlan in his dissent from *Plessy* v. *Ferguson,* that "Our Constitution is colorblind, and neither knows nor tolerates classes among citizens." If the Equal Protection Clause required that the laws of the United States and the states be truly colorblind, then no racial guidelines, goals, or quota would be tolerated. Occasionally this view has been expressed in recent minority dissents.[13]

However, the Court has held that racial classifications in law must be subject to "strict scrutiny." This means that race-based actions by government—any disparate treatment of the races by federal, state, or local public agencies—must be found necessary to remedy past proven discrimination, or to further clearly identified, compelling, and legitimate government objectives. Moreover, race-based actions must be "narrowly tailored" so as not to adversely affect the rights of individuals. In striking down a federal construction contract "set-aside" program for small businesses owned by racial minorities, the Court expressed skepticism about governmental racial classifications: "There is simply no way of determining what classifications are 'benign' and 'remedial' and what classifications are in fact motivated by illegitimate notions of racial inferiority or simple racial politics."[14]

General Tendencies in Supreme Court Policy

The Supreme Court has failed to provide a clear rule of law, legal test, or constitutional principle to tell us what is permissible and what is prohibited in the way of racially conscious laws and practices. Each affirmative action program must be judged separately. One circuit court of appeals has held that the use of race as a university admission factor violates the equal protection clause of the Fourteenth Amendment. This decision in *Hopwood* v. *Texas* requires the University of Texas system to end racial preferences in admission. The U.S. Supreme Court affirmed this Court of Appeals decision, yet even while doing so warned that it may not fully agree with the circuit court opinion.[15] Thus, the constitutionality of affirmative action programs remains unclear.

Nonetheless, some general tendencies in Supreme Court policy can be identified. Affirmative action programs are more likely to be found constitutional when:

★ They are adopted in response to past history of discrimination.

★ They are narrowly tailored to remedy the effects of previous discrimination.

★ They do not absolutely bar whites or men from competing or participating.

★ They serve an important social or educational objective.

The Civil Rights and Women's Equity Act of 1991

In 1989 the Supreme Court, in *Wards Cove Packing Company* v. *Antonio*, denied relief to low-paid Asian-American employees of an Alaska cannery who contended that they had been the victims of racial discrimination in the workplace.[16] The Court said that the burden of proof in such lawsuits was on the plaintiff to show actual discrimination, as opposed to showing merely that certain employment practices had a disparate impact upon racial minorities or women. Statistical imbalances in race or gender in the workplace were not sufficient evidence by themselves to prove discrimination.

Civil rights groups were highly critical of what they regarded as the Supreme Court's "narrowing" of the Civil Rights Act protections in employment. They turned to Congress to rewrite portions of the Civil Rights Act to restore these protections. Business lobbies, however, believed that accepting statistical imbalances as evidence of discrimination or shifting the burden of proof to employers would result in hiring by "quotas" simply to avoid lawsuits. After nearly two years of negotiations on Capitol Hill and a reversal of President Bush's initial opposition, Congress crafted a policy.

In its Civil Rights and Women's Equity Act of 1991, Congress legislated that

★ The mere existence of statistical imbalance in an employer's work force is not, by itself, sufficient evidence to prove discrimination. However, statistical imbalances may be evidence of employment practices (rules, requirements, academic qualifications, tests) that have a "disparate impact" on minorities or women.

★ Employers bear the burden of proof that any practice that has a "disparate impact" is necessary and has "a significant and manifest relationship to the requirements for effective job performance."

ELITE VERSUS MASS RESPONSE TO CIVIL RIGHTS

Progress in civil rights policy—from *Brown* v. *Board of Education of Topeka,* through the Civil Rights Act of 1964, to affirmative action programs today—has been a response of a national *elite* to conditions affecting a minority of Americans. Advances in civil rights have *not* come about because of demands by the white majority of citizens. On the contrary, the civil rights policies of the national elite have met with varying degrees of resistance from white masses in states and communities.

Mass Opinion about Discrimination

The attitudes of white masses toward blacks in the United States are ambivalent. Most whites believe that blacks face little discrimination in jobs, housing, or education and that any differences between whites and blacks in society is a result of blacks' lack of education and motivation. In contrast, most blacks believe that differences between blacks and whites in standards of living are "mainly due to discrimination."[17] Whites constitute a large majority of the nation's population. If public policy reflected the views of this majority, there would be very little civil rights legislation.

Mass Opinion about Affirmative Action

Affirmative action is more popular among elites than masses. Overall, the American public opposes racial preferences in hiring and promotion, even when asked to consider "past discrimination."

QUESTION: *"In order to make up for past discrimination, do you favor or oppose programs which impose quotas for racial minorities?"*

	ALL	WHITES	BLACKS
Favor	19	15	48
Oppose	72	78	37

Source: CBS News/*New York Times* Poll, reported in *The Polling Report,* December 22, 1997.

According to one scholar:

> *Americans' response to pollsters' questions leave little doubt that they believe that equality of access and opportunity rather than of condition or result should be the defining principle of our commitment to egalitarianism. . . . They disapprove of making race or ethnicity a legitimate or predominant ground for awarding jobs, social benefits, or opportunities.*[18]

Affirmative Action in Mass Referenda

White masses have turned to citizens' initiatives to battle racial preferences. We have already suggested that elites generally consider popular referenda votes to be a threat to democratic values as well as elite governance (see Chapter 5 "The Masses in America"). Such votes are clearly a threat to affirmative action.

The California Civil Rights Initiative, "Prop 209," was placed on that state's ballot by citizens' initiative in 1996. The initiative added the following phrase to the state's constitution:

> *Neither the state of California nor any of its political subdivisions or agents shall use race, sex, color, ethnicity or national origin as a criterion for either discriminating against,* or granting preferential treatment to, *any individual or group in the operation of the State's system of public employment, public education or public contracting.*

The key words are "or granting preferential treatment to." Opponents challenged the California Civil Rights Initiative in federal courts arguing that by preventing minorities and women from seeking preferential treatment under law, the initiative violated the equal protection clause of the Fourteenth Amendment. But a circuit court of appeals held, and the U.S. Supreme Court affirmed, that:

> *"[A] ban on race or gender preferences, as a matter of law or logic, does not violate the Equal Protection Clause in any conventional sense. . . . Impediments to preferential treatment do not deny equal protection."*[19]

The success of the California Initiative has inspired similar mass movements in other states; Washington adopted a similar state constitutional amendment in 1998.

FEMINISM IN AMERICA

Feminism in America is nearly as old as the nation itself. In 1776, Abigail Adams wrote to her husband, John Adams, at the Second Continental Congress while it was debating whether to declare American independence:

> *I long to hear that you have declared an independency. And in the new code of laws which I suppose it will be necessary for you to make, I desire you would remember the ladies, and be more generous and favorable to them than your ancestors. . . . If particular care and attention is not paid to the ladies, we are determined to foment a rebellion and will not hold*

> *ourselves bound by any laws in which we have no voice or*
> *representation.*[20]

The political movement forecast by Abigail Adams did not really emerge until a generation later.

The First Wave

The "first wave" of active feminist politics grew out of the pre–Civil War antislavery movement. The first generation of feminists, including Lucretia Mott, Elizabeth Cady Stanton, Lucy Stone, and Susan B. Anthony, learned to organize, hold public meetings, and conduct petition campaigns as abolitionists. After the Civil War, women were successful in changing many state laws that abridged the property rights of married women and treated them as chattel (property) of their husbands. Activists were also successful in winning some protection for women in the workplace, including state laws limiting women's hours of work, working conditions, and physical demands. At that time, these laws were regarded as progressive.

The most successful feminist efforts of the 1800s centered on protections of women in families. The perceived threats to women's well-being were their husbands' drinking, gambling, and consorting with prostitutes. Women led the Anti-Saloon League and succeeded in outlawing gambling and prostitution in every state except Nevada and provided the major source of moral support for the Eighteenth Amendment (Prohibition).

In the early twentieth century, the feminist movement concentrated on women's suffrage—the drive to guarantee women the right to vote. The early suffragettes employed mass demonstrations, parades, picketing, and occasional disruption and civil disobedience, tactics similar to those of the civil rights movement of the 1960s. The culmination of their efforts was the 1920 passage of the Nineteenth Amendment to the Constitution: "The right of citizens of the United States to vote shall not be denied or abridged by the United States or by any state on account of sex." The suffrage movement spawned the League of Women Voters. In addition, the league has provided more information to voters and more honest election practices.

The goal of this first wave of feminist activity was *equality*. When a delegation of American women was excluded from the World Anti-Slavery Convention in London in 1840, they realized that the cause of emancipation affected them as well as slaves. On July 19, 1848, they met in Seneca Falls, across the New York border in Canada, to draw up "The Seneca Falls

Declaration of Sentiments and Resolutions." The Resolution parallels the Declaration of Independence and reads in part:

> *We hold these truths to be self-evident: that all men and women are created equal; that they are endowed by their Creator with certain inalienable rights; that among these are life, liberty, and the pursuit of happiness.*

Equity Feminism

Today equality remains the goal of what might be labeled *equity feminism.* Equity feminism continues in the classic liberal tradition of seeking equal opportunity for women and men, equal treatment for every individual, equal justice for all. It builds upon the earlier feminist efforts to gain for women the rights that men had taken for granted. The principles of equity feminism remain the vision of the vast majority of women in the United States. A majority of women say that there continues to be a need for a strong women's movement in America to guarantee equality. Yet, paradoxically perhaps, a majority of women also decline to call themselves "feminists."[21] This reluctance to identify with the term may derive from views currently expressed by the elites of national women's organizations.

Gender Feminism

A "second wave" of feminism, which we have labeled *gender feminism,* currently prevails in leadership circles in leading feminist organizations such as the National Organization for Women (NOW) and the National Women's Studies Association (representing university-based women's studies programs). Gender feminism goes beyond a demand for equality and becomes "a call for liberation."[22] Women must not look to men to grant their freedom, rather they must choose their own freedom. They must liberate themselves from the patriarchal family and the male-dominated society. This requires, first of all, that women become aware of their oppression; "consciousness-raising" exposes the oppression of women that is inherent in sex roles, family structure, education, religion, the economy, and many other aspects of society. The next imperative is for women to transform themselves personally and collectively from powerlessness to power and in so doing to reform and restructure society's institutions to reflect feminine values.[23]

Variations of Gender Feminism

Gender feminism includes a number of camps with diverse views of both the source of women's oppression and strategies for its elimination. "Radical feminism" perceives male dominance in virtually all of society's institutions and seeks revolutionary restructuring of these institutions. Rape, pornography, sexual harassment, and domestic violence are visible products of a deeper, "phallocentric" culture. Men are largely unaware of the devaluation and repression in women's experience—they "just don't get it." "Socialist feminism," following the doctrine of Marx, sees male oppression arising from capitalism, which gives men control of "the means of reproduction" as well as "the means of production." "Liberal feminism" focuses on the early socialization of children into clearly differentiated sex roles, and seeks reform measures including nonsexist education. "Post-modern feminists" perceive sexism in ways of thinking and speaking and seeks to reconstruct philosophy, history, and language to liberate them from "masculinist modes and patriarchal ideology" of "dead white European males."

Victim Feminism

A "third wave" of feminism, sometimes labeled *victim feminism*, is frequently reflected in sexual harassment codes. While equity feminism emphasized equal rights and the sameness between the sexes, the new victim feminism portrays women as in need of special legal help (much like the nineteenth-century laws limiting the working hours of women, which were later abandoned at the demand of the equity feminists). Without special protective legislation (such as the Violence Against Women Act of 1994), women will be harassed, raped, and abused. Victim feminism offers a new orthodoxy: "I was surprised at how many things there were not to say, at the arguments and assertions that could not be made, lines that could not be crossed, taboos that could not be broken. The feminists around me had created their own rigid orthodoxy."[24] Victim feminism politicizes women's pain and frustration and propels women toward special legislative protections that equity feminism would deny.

WOMEN AND WORK

Modern feminism has been driven by the changing role of women in America's workforce. As late as 1960 fewer than one-third of married women

| FIGURE 15-1 | Women in the workforce |

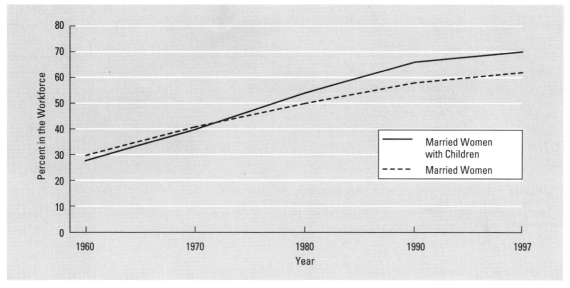

Source: *Statistical Abstract of the United States 1998,* p. 404.

worked. Today nearly two-thirds of married women work. Indeed, economic pressures on family budgets today have sent over *70 percent of married women into the workforce* (see Figure 15-1).

The Dual Labor Market

Despite increases in the number and proportion of working women, the nation's occupational fields are still divided between traditionally male and female jobs. Women continue to dominate the traditional "pink-collar" jobs (see Table 15-4). Women have made important inroads in traditionally male white-collar occupations—doctors, lawyers, and engineers, for example—although men still remain in the majority in these professions. However, women have only begun to break into the "blue-collar" occupations usually dominated by men. Blue-collar jobs usually pay more than pink-collar jobs.

The Earnings Gap

The existence of this "dual" labor market, with male-dominated "blue-collar" jobs distinguishable from female-dominated "pink-collar" jobs,

| TABLE 15-4 | The dual labor market |

		PERCENTAGE FEMALE	
		1960	1997
"White collar"	Women are increasingly entering white-collar occupational fields traditionally dominated by men:		
	Architects	3	17
	Computer analysts	11	28
	College and university teachers	28	44
	Engineers	1	20
	Lawyers and judges	4	29
	Physicians	10	26
"Pink collar"	Women continue to be concentrated in occupational fields traditionally dominated by women:		
	Nurses	97	93
	Elementary school teachers	89	83
	Secretaries	98	98
	Receptionists	97	97
	Waitress/Waiter	91	98
"Blue collar"	Women continue to be largely shut out of blue-collar occupational fields traditionally dominated by men:		
	Carpenters	1	1
	Mechanics	1	1
	Firefighters	0	2
	Police officers	1	16
	Truck drivers	1	5
	Bartenders	21	54

Source: U.S. Bureau of the Census, *Statistical Abstract of the United States 1998* (Washington, D.C.: U.S. Government Printing Office, 1998), pp. 410–412.

continues to be a major obstacle to economic equality between men and women.

Despite protections under federal laws, women continue to earn substantially less than men do. Today women, on average, earn only about 72 percent of what men do (see Table 15-5). This earnings gap is not primarily a product of *direct discrimination*; women in the same job with the same skills, qualifications, experience, and work record are not generally paid less than men. Such direct discrimination has been illegal since the Civil Rights Act of 1964. Rather, the earnings gap is primarily a product of a division in the labor market between traditionally male and female jobs, with lower salaries paid in traditionally female occupations

TABLE 15-5	MEDIAN ANNUAL EARNINGS OF WOMEN AS A PERCENTAGE OF MEDIAN ANNUAL EARNINGS OF MEN.

The earnings gap

1972	59%
1978	59%
1983	62%
1985	67%
1987	70%
1996	72%

Source: *Statistical Abstract of the United States 1997*, p. 432.

Gender Equality in Civil Rights Laws

Title VII of the Civil Rights Act of 1964 prevents sexual (as well as racial) discrimination in hiring, pay, and promotions. The Equal Employment Opportunity Commission, the federal agency charged with eliminating discrimination in employment, has established guidelines barring stereotyped classifications of "men's jobs" and "women's jobs." The courts have repeatedly struck down state laws and employer practices that differentiate between men and women in hours, pay, retirement age, and so forth.

The federal Equal Credit Opportunity Act of 1974 prohibits sex discrimination in credit transactions. Federal law prevents banks, credit unions, savings and loan associations, retail stores, and credit card companies from denying credit because of sex or marital status. However, these businesses may still deny credit for a poor or nonexistent credit rating, and some women who have always maintained accounts in their husband's name may still face credit problems if they apply in their own name.

Title IX of the Education Act Amendment of 1972 deals with sex discrimination in education. This federal law bars discrimination in admissions, housing, rules, financial aid, faculty and staff recruitment and pay, and—most troublesome of all—athletics. The latter problem has proven difficult because men's football and basketball programs have traditionally brought in the money to finance all other sports, and men's football and basketball have received the largest share of school athletic budgets.

Cultural Divisions of Labor

Working women face obstacles not encountered by men. Women who work are still likely to do more housework than men. Most women are still expected to follow their husbands wherever their jobs take them. Working outside the home *is* a tough decision, and some women who have made this decision later reverse it. Studying a group of women who became adults in the 1970s, sociologist Kathleen Gerson describes two types of women, domestic and nondomestic:

> *Those who developed non-domestic orientations sought to restructure the sexual division of labor at home and at work and also to redefine traditional ideologies of child rearing. They met opposition from domestically oriented women who found it in their interest to preserve traditional arrangements and beliefs. The study found emerging divisions among women that promise to add to the social turmoil generated by women's changing position.*[25]

Like all other groups that strive to build consensus among disparate elements (such as consumers, businesspeople, and the working class), the size of the potential clientele for women's movements, creates both the raw material of political power and the discord that diminishes political power.

FEMINISM AND ELITISM

It is our argument that feminist ideology and political activists are concentrated among women elites—politically active, often university-based, highly educated women. "They hold the keys to many bureaucratic fiefdoms, research centers, women's studies programs, tenure committees, and para-academic organizations.[26] They claim to speak for all women, but not all women, or even all feminists, share the view that women's oppression is a product of a male culture that exalts individualism, competition, and violence. Yet, as elite theory predicts, the more moderate female majority is "not temperamentally suited to activism. . . . They do not network. They do not ally. They do not threaten their opponents with loss of jobs or loss of patronage. They are not especially litigious."[27]

Working Women, Educated Women, and Feminism

Employed women and housewives* differ in their attitudes toward feminist issues. Support for feminist ideology is greater among employed women than housewives. In recent opinion polls, *unmarried* women with college

*The U.S. Census Bureau defines "working [employed] women" as women who are employed outside the home, "housewives" as women who, regardless of marital status, work solely in the home. This text uses the same convention in categorizing women.

educations and jobs are most likely to identify themselves as feminists (48 percent). *Married* women with college educations and jobs are somewhat less likely to identify themselves as feminists (34 percent). And relatively few married noncollege graduates not in the workforce identify themselves as feminists (18 percent).[28]

"There has always been questions about whether a movement led by white, college-educated women could represent the interests of the Latina waitress from Arizona, the black textile worker from South Carolina, for the white secretary from Ohio."[29] America's high-income women are three times more likely to call themselves feminists than the country's lowest earners.

The women's movement suffers from a perception that it is more upper-class, more liberal, and indeed more elitist, than the mainstream. To combat this elitist image, feminist organizations in recent years have tried to become more "family-friendly." Feminist organizations were strong supporters of the Family and Medical Leave Act of 1993. Yet even so, the leading women's lobbying groups in Washington—NOW, the Women's Legal Defense Fund, the American Nurses Association, the National Federation of Business and Professional Women, the American Association of University Women—tend to emphasize the concerns of well-educated, professionally employed women.

Social Class and Feminist Ideology

The inability of the women's movement to attract lower-class recruits reflects not only the lower political participation of such classes in general but also the more conservative views of the lower classes toward changing familial and social relationships. In a similar vein, the relative absence of black women from the feminist movement probably reflects their lower socioeconomic status as well as the reluctance of blacks (both female and male) to associate with a white-dominated movement for fear of being co-opted. Black women approve of feminist goals more than white working-class women do, but consider racial discriminations a more serious problem.

The "Glass Ceiling"

Relatively few women have climbed the ladder to become president or chief executive officer or director of the nation's largest industrial corporations, banks, utilities, newspapers, or television networks. Large numbers of

FOCUS

Elites, Masses, and Sexual Harassment

What is "sexual harassment"? Various surveys report that up to one-third of female workers say they have experienced sexual harassment on the job.[a] But it is not always clear exactly what kind of behavior constitutes "sexual harassment."

Elite Definition

The U.S. Supreme Court has provided some guidance in the development of sexual harassment definitions and prohibitions. Title VII of the Civil Rights Act of 1964 makes it "an unlawful employment practice to discriminate against any individual with respect to his [sic] compensation, terms, conditions or privileges of employment because of such individual's race, color, religion, sex, or national origin." In the employment context, the U.S. Supreme Court has approved the following definition of sexual harassment:

> *"Unwelcome sexual advances, requests for sexual favors, and other verbal or physical conduct of a sexual nature constitute sexual harassment when (1) submission to such conduct is made either explicitly or implicitly a term or condition of an individual's employment; (2) submission to or rejection of such conduct by an individual, is used as the basis for employment decisions affecting such individual; or (3) such conduct has the*

> *purpose or effect of unreasonably interfering with an individual's work performance or creating an intimidating, hostile, or offensive working environment."[b]*

There are no great difficulties in defining sexual harassment when jobs or promotions are conditioned on the granting of sexual favors. But several problems arise in defining a "hostile working environment." This phrase may include offensive utterances, sexual innuendoes, dirty jokes, the display of pornographic material, and unwanted proposals for dates. First, it would appear to include speech and hence raise First Amendment questions regarding how far speech may be curtailed by law in the workplace. Second, the definition depends more on the subjective feelings of the individual employee about what is "offensive" and "unwanted" than on an objective standard of behavior that is easily understood by all. Justice Sandra Day O'Connor wrestled with the definition of a "hostile work environment" in *Harris* v. *Forklift Systems* in 1993. She held that a plaintiff need not show that the utterances caused psychological injury but that a "reasonable person," not just the plaintiff, must perceive the work environment to be hostile or abusive. Presumably a single incident would not constitute harassment; rather, courts should consider "the frequency of the discriminatory conduct," "its severity," and whether it "unreasonably interferes with an employee's work performance."[c]

Mass Definitions

Masses appear to be divided on what they think constitutes sexual harassment. Surveys indicate that women are somewhat more likely to perceive sexual harassment in various behaviors than men (see table). But neither women nor men are likely to perceive it to include repeated requests for a date, the telling of dirty jokes, or comments on attractiveness—even though these behaviors often inspire formal complaints.

QUESTION: *Here is a list of some different situations. We're interested in knowing whether you think they are forms of sexual harassment—not just inappropriate or in bad taste, but sexual.*

DEFINITELY IS SEXUAL HARASSMENT

	MEN	WOMEN
If a male boss makes it clear to a female employee that she must go to bed with him for a promotion	91%	92%
If a male boss asks very direct questions of a female employee about her personal sexual practices and preferences	59%	68%
If a female boss asks very direct questions of a male employee about his personal sexual practices and preferences	47%	57%
If a man once in a while asks a female employee of his to go out on dates, even though she has said no in the past	15%	21%
If a man once in a while tells dirty jokes in the presence of female employees	15%	16%
If a male boss tells a female employee that she looks very attractive today	3%	5%

Source: Roper Organization as reported in *American Enterprise,* September/October 1993, p. 93.

University Policies

Students and professors beware! Most university policies go well beyond both Supreme Court rulings and opinion polls in defining what constitutes sexual harassment, including:[d]

★ "Remarks about a person's clothing."

★ "Suggestive or insulting sounds."

★ "Leering at or ogling of a person's body."

★ "Nonsexual slurs about one's gender."

★ "Remarks that degrade another person or group on the basis of gender."

The National Association of Scholars worries that overly broad and vague definitions of sexual harassment can undermine academic freedom and inhibit classroom discussions of important yet sensitive topics, including human sexuality, gender differences, sexual roles, and gender politics. Teaching and research on such topics, in their view, must not be constrained by the threat that the views expressed will be labeled "insensitive," "uncomfortable," or "incorrect"; faculty members must feel free to provide their best academic and professional advice to students, collectively and individually, without fear that their comments will be officially labeled "offensive" or "unwelcome"; and students must feet free to express themselves on matters of gender, whether or not their ideas are biased, immature, or crudely expressed.

[a]*Washington Post* National Weekly Edition, March 7, 1993.

[b]*Meritor Savings Bank* v. *Vinson,* 477 U.S. 57 (1986).

[c]*Harris* v. *Forklift Systems,* 126 L. Ed. 2d 295 (1993).

[d]Statements in student and faculty handbooks, State University System of Florida.

women are entering the legal profession, but as yet few are senior partners in the largest and most prestigious law firms.

The barriers to women's advancement to elite positions are often subtle, giving rise to the term "glass ceiling." There are many explanations for the glass ceiling, but all are controversial or questionable: Women choose staff assignments rather than fast-track, operating-head assignments. Women are cautious and unaggressive in corporate politics. Women have lower expectations about peak earnings and positions, and these expectations become self-fulfilling. Women bear children, and even during relatively short maternity absences they fall behind their male counterparts. Women are less likely to want to change locations than men, and immobile executives are worth less to a corporation than mobile ones. Female executives in sensitive positions come under even more pressure than men in similar posts. Female executives believe that they get much more scrutiny than men and must work harder to succeed. And at all levels, increasing attention has been paid to sexual harassment (see Focus: "Elites, Masses and Sexual Harassment"). Finally, it is important to note that affirmative action efforts by governments—notably the Equal Employment Opportunity Commission—are directed primarily at entry-level positions rather than senior management posts.

Summary

Elite theory helps us to understand the development of protest movements and organizations, their accommodation by governing elites, and their eventual moderation and incorporation into the elite structure. Elites modify public policy to defuse protest movements; they grant symbolic victories and elite status to protest leaders in exchange for the moderation of their demands and their support for the system. Masses frequently resist even these accommodationist policies. Progress in civil rights is an elite response to minority appeals, not to mass demands.

1. The first governmental institution to act for equality of opportunity for blacks in the twentieth century was the Supreme Court. The Court, structurally the furthest removed from the influence of white masses, was the first to apply liberal public-regarding policies to blacks. Elected elites who are more accessible to white masses were slower to act on black rights than were appointed elites.

2. Elected white elites did not respond to black requests until faced with a prolonged campaign of nonviolent civil disobedience, public demonstrations, and creative disorder and crises. Generally elites have responded by making modest changes in the system in order to maintain stability. Often these changes are only symbolic.

3. Elimination of legal discrimination and guaranteed equality of opportunity have largely resulted from the efforts of black middle-class groups who share a dominant elite consensus and who appeal to the conscience of white elites to extend that consensus to include blacks.

4. Elites have not responded to demands that go beyond accepted elite consensus, for example, demands for absolute equality that have replaced demands for equality of opportunity. New mass-oriented black counterelites have emerged to contend with established middle-class black elites. Mass counterelites have less respect for the rules of the game than do either white elites or established middle-class black leaders.

5. Affirmative action—defined as preferential treatment for minorities and women in employment and education—is more likely to be supported by elites than by masses. Mass opposition to such preferential treatment is widespread and growing over time.

6. Protest movements have a spillover effect; they ripple from group to group. Groups only recently beginning to protest, such as modern feminists, have not developed the group consciousness of more severely repressed groups.

7. Leaders of the women's movement are professional, educated, upper-middle-class women, whose views are not universally shared by the masses of women in the United States. Yet it is difficult to mobilize masses of women on behalf of feminist goals.

8. Differences prevail even among feminist elites regarding both the nature of the obstacles to women's advancement and the remedial strategies to be pursued. Should the women's movement focus primarily on achieving equality, or securing special protections, or radically restructuring male-dominated society?

Notes

1. See more on accommodation and repression in Francis Fox Piven and Richard A. Cloward, *Regulating the Poor* (New York: Vintage Books, 1971).

2. Anthony Oberschall, *Social Conflict and Social Movements* (Englewood Cliffs, N.J.: Prentice-Hall, 1973), p. 155.

3. Gunnar Myrdal, *An American Dilemma* (New York: McGraw-Hill, 1964), vol. I, p. xxi.

4. *Plessy v. Ferguson*, 163 U.S. 537 (1896).

5. Allen D. Grimshaw, "Lawlessness and Violence in America and Their Special Manifestations in Changing Negro-White Relationships," *Journal of Negro History* 44 (January 1959): 67.

6. Myrdal, op. cit., vol. II, p. 749.

7. *Brown* v. *Board of Education of Topeka*, 347 U.S. 483 (1954).

8. Kenneth B. Clark, "The Civil Rights Movement: Momentum and Organization," in Talcott Parsons and Kenneth B. Clark, eds., *The Negro American* (Boston: Beacon Press, 1966), p. 610.

9. *Regents of the University of California* v. *Bakke*, 438 U.S. 265 (1978).

10. *United States* v. *Paradise,* 480 U.S. 149 (1987).

11. *Firefighters Local Union* v. *Stotts,* 467 U.S. 561 (1984).

12. *Richmond* v. *Crosen,* 109 S. Ct. 706 (1989).

13. See Justice Antonin Scalia's dissenting opinion in *Johnson* v. *Transportation Agency of Santa Clara County,* 480 U.S. 616 (1987).

14. *Adarand Construction* v. *Pena,* 132 L Ed 2d 158 (1995).

15. *Hopwood* v. *Texas,* 135 L Ed 1095 (1996).

16. *Wards Cove Packing Co., Inc.* v. *Antonio,* 490 U.S. 642 (1989).

17. *The American Enterprise* (January/February 1990): 96–103.

18. John H. Bunzel, "Affirmative Reactions," *Public Opinion* (February/March 1986): 49.

19. *Coalition for Economic Equity* v. *Pete Wilson,* Ninth Circuit Court of Appeals, April 1997.

20. Reprinted in Alice Rossi, ed., *The Feminist Papers From Adams to deBeauvoir* (New York: Columbia University Press, 1993).

21. *Time*/CNN poll reported in *Time* (March 9, 1992): 54.

22. Marilyn Pearsall, *Women and Values,* 2nd ed. (Belmont, Calif.: Wadsworth, 1993), p. xi.

23. Alison M. Jaggar, *Feminist Politics and Human Nature* (Totowa, N.J.: Rowman & Littlefield, 1988). See also Maggie Homm, ed., *Modern Feminism* (New York: Columbia University Press, 1992).

24. Katie Roiphe, *The Morning After* (Boston: Little, Brown, 1993), p. 6.

25. Kathleen Gerson, *Hard Choices* (Berkeley: University of California Press, 1985), pp. 216–217.

26. Christina Hoff Sommers, *Who Stole Feminism?* (New York: Simon & Schuster, 1994), p. 273.

27. Ibid., p. 274.

28. Gallup poll reported in *Los Angeles Times Magazine,* February 2, 1992.

29. *Los Angeles Times Magazine,* February 2, 1992.

Selected Readings

Barker, Lucius J. and Mack H. Jones. *African Americans and the American Political System.* 3d ed. Upper Saddle River, N.J.: Prentice-Hall, 1994. A comprehensive analysis of African-American politics, examining access to the judicial arena, the interest-group process, political parties, Congress, and the White House.

Clark, Kenneth B. *Dark Ghetto: Dilemmas of Social Power.* New York: Harper & Row, Harper Torchbook, 1967. A classic analysis of the life of American blacks in urban ghetto areas and of the pathologies this life produces, written by a black sociologist.

Conway, M. Margaret. *Women and Public Policy: A Revolution in Progress.* Washington, D.C.: Congressional Quarterly Press, 1994. Coverage of a broad range of policy areas that affect women, including education, employment, health, marriage and family law, and child care.

Fox-Genovese, Elizabeth. *Feminism Is Not the Story of My Life.* New York: Doubleday. 1995. A critique of radical feminism for failing to understand the central importance of marriage and motherhood in women's lives, and a discussion of how public policy could ease the clashing demands of work and family on women.

Kirkpatrick, Jeane. *Political Women.* New York: Basic Books, 1978. This early book explores the conditions leading to women's seeking political office, written by the former UN ambassador.

McGlen, Nancy E., and Karen O'Conner. *Women, Politics, and American Society.* Upper Saddle River. N.J.: Prentice-Hall, 1996. A comprehensive text contrasting women's rights and realities in politics, employment, education, reproduction, and family.

Myrdal, Gunnar. *An American Dilemma,* 2nd ed. Vol. I: *The Negro in a White Nation.* Vol. II: *The Negro Social Structure.* New York: McGraw-Hill, 1964. Originally published in 1944, Myrdal's classic study is one of the most comprehensive analyses of the situation of blacks in the United States. It draws broadly from many disciplines.

Pearsall, Marilyn. *Women and Values,* 2nd ed. Belmont, Calif.: Wadsworth, 1993. Essays describing variations in feminist thought.

Sommers, Christina Hoff. *Who Stole Feminism?* New York: Simon & Schuster, 1994. A controversial critique of gender feminism by an equity feminist.

Thernstrom, Stephen, and Abigail Thernstrom. *America in Black and White.* New York: Simon & Schuster, 1997. An information-rich analysis tracing social and economic progress of African-Americans and arguing that gains in education and employment were greater *before* the introduction of affirmative action programs.

16

Public Policy: How and What Elites Decide

In making policy in a highly participatory system, officials will have no incentive to say that the government shouldn't tackle a problem or doesn't know how to solve it and every incentive to claim that government must "do something" and that they know just what to do. As a result, we have crime bills that don't reduce crime, drug abuse bills that don't curb drug abuse, education bills that don't improve learning and disability insurance that can't define "disability."

—JAMES Q. WILSON

Public policy does not reflect demands of "the people," but rather the preferences, interests, and values of the very few who participate in the policy-making process. Changes or innovations in public policy come about when elites redefine their own interests or modify their own values. Policies decided by elites need not be oppressive or exploitative of the masses. Elites may be very public-regarding, and the welfare of the masses may be an important consideration in elite decision making. Yet it is *elites* that make policy, not the *masses*.

PUBLIC POLICY AS ELITE PREFERENCE

Our elite model contends that the major directions of public policy in America are determined by a relatively small group of like-minded individuals interacting among themselves and reflecting their own values and preferences in policy making. By contrast, the pluralist model of the policy process portrays public policy as the product of competition, bargaining, and compromise among many diverse *groups* in society. Interest groups are viewed as the principal actors in the policy-making process—the essential bridges between individuals and government. Public policy, according to the pluralists, reflects an equilibrium of the relative influence of interest groups.

The Elite Model

A portrait of the elite model of the public policy-making process is presented in Figure 16-1. The model suggests that the initial resources for research, study, planning, and formulation of national policy are derived from corporate and personal wealth. This wealth is channeled into foundations, universities, and policy-planning groups in the form of endowments, grants, and contracts. Moreover, corporate presidents, directors, and top wealthholders also sit on the governing boards of the foundations, universities, and policy-planning groups to oversee the spending of their funds. In short, corporate and personal wealth provides both the financial resources and the overall direction of policy research, planning, and development.

The Foundations

The foundations provide a linkage between wealth and the intellectual community. They provide the initial "seed money" to identify social problems, to determine national priorities, and to investigate new policy directions. Universities must respond to the policy interests of foundations, and of course they also try to convince foundations of new and promising policy directions. But research proposals originating from universities that do not fit the previously defined "emphasis" of foundations are usually lost in the shuffle of papers. Although university intellectuals working independently occasionally have an impact on the policy-making process, on the whole, intellectuals respond to policy directions set by the foundations, corporations, and government agencies that underwrite the costs of research.

The Think Tanks

The *policy-planning groups* or "think tanks" are the central coordinating points in the policy-making process. They review the relevant university- and foundation-supported research on topics of interest, with the goal of

FIGURE 16-1   The elitist model of the public policy-making process

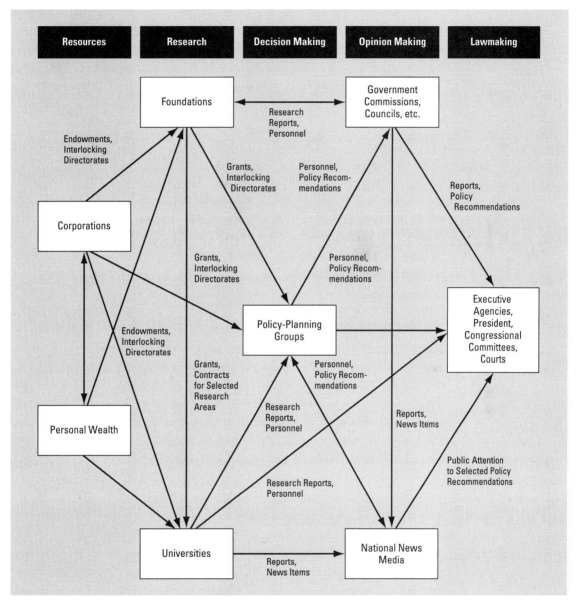

Source: Thomas R. Dye, *Who's Running America? The Clinton Years* (Englewood Cliffs, N.J.: Prentice-Hall, 1994), p. 221.

developing *policy recommendations*—explicit programs designed to resolve or ameliorate national problems. At the same time, they endeavor to build consensus among corporate, financial, media, civic, intellectual, and government leaders around major policy directions. Certain policy-planning groups—notably the Council on Foreign Relations, the American Enterprise Institute, the Heritage Foundation, and the Brookings Institution—are influential in a wide range of key policy areas.

The Media

Policy recommendations of the leading policy-planning groups are distributed to the mass media, federal executive agencies, and Congress. The mass media play a vital role in preparing public opinion for policy change. The media define the "problem" as a problem and thus set the agenda for policy making. They also encourage politicians to assume new policy stances by allocating valuable network broadcast time to those who will speak out in favor of new policy directions.

The Washington Insiders

The White House staff, congressional committee staffs, and top executive administrators usually maintain close contact with policy-planning groups. Often these groups help prepare legislation for Congress to implement policy decisions. Particular versions of bills will pass between executive agencies, the White House, policy-planning groups, and the professional staffs of the congressional committees that eventually will consider the bills. This groundwork is laid for making policy into law.

AGENDA SETTING AND "NONDECISIONS"

Agenda setting is deciding what will be decided. It includes defining the problems of society and suggesting solutions. Conditions in society that are not defined as problems, and for which alternatives are never proposed, never become policy issues. They never get on the "agenda" of decision makers. Government does nothing and conditions remain the same. On the other hand, if certain conditions in society are defined as problems and alternative solutions put forward, the conditions become policy issues. Governments are forced to decide what to do.

Deciding What Will Be Decided

The power to decide what will be a policy issue is crucial to the policy-making process. Deciding what will be the problems is even more important than deciding what will be the solutions. Pluralists often imply that agenda setting just "happens." They argue that in an open plural society such as ours, channels of access and communication to government are always open, so that any problem can be discussed and placed on the agenda of national decision making. Individuals and groups, it is said, can organize themselves to assume the tasks of defining problems and suggesting solutions. People can define their own interests, organize themselves, persuade others to support their cause, gain access to government officials, influence decision making, and watch over the implementation of government policies and programs.

In reality, however, policy issues do not just "happen." Creating an issue, dramatizing it, calling attention to it, and pressuring government to do something about it are important political tactics. These tactics are employed by influential individuals, organized interest groups, policy-planning organizations, political candidates and officeholders, and perhaps most importantly, the mass media. These are the tactics of "agenda setting."

Deciding What Will *Not* Be Decided

"Nondecision making" occurs when influential individuals, organizations, or the structure of the political system itself prevent the emergence of challenges to the dominant values and interests in society. Keeping issues *out* of politics is an important aspect of power, one that is just as important as deciding the issues that *are* presented to public officials—perhaps more important. So power really has two manifestations: decisions and nondecisions.

Nondecisions can occur (1) when influential elites act directly to exclude an issue from the political arena; (2) when subordinates anticipate the negative reaction of elites and ignore proposals or suggestions that would "cause trouble"; or (3) when the underlying values of society and its institutional structure prevent serious consideration of alternative programs and policies.

In nondecision making, those at the top of institutional structures need not exercise their power overtly; the subordinates who carry on the day-to-day business of industry, finance, government, and the media know the values of their bosses. These subordinates obtained their jobs in part because they exhibited elite values in their thinking and actions. Whether consciously or unconsciously, their decisions reflect the values of those at the top.

Suppressing "Factious Issues"

The institutional structure of society also exercises power when it limits the scope of public decision making to issues that are relatively harmless to the elite. Institutions support the achievement of some values while obstructing the achievement of others. For example, we already know that the nation's Founders deliberately constructed the American government system to suppress certain values and issues. James Madison, in *The Federalist,* Number 10, defended the structure of the new American government, particularly its republican and federal features, on the grounds that it would suppress "factious issues." Madison even named some of these issues that must be avoided: "a rage for paper money, for an abolition of debts, for an equal division of property, or any other improper or wicked project." Note that all the issues Madison wished to avoid involved challenges to the dominant economic interests.

ECONOMIC POLICY

Government taxing and spending has an enormous effect on the economy. The expenditures of all governments in the United States—federal, state, and local governments combined—amount to about 35 percent of the GNP. The federal government itself spends over $1.7 *trillion* each year—over 22 percent of the GNP.

Uncontrollable Spending

Much of the growth of federal government spending over the years is attributed to "uncontrollables" in the federal budget. "Uncontrollables" are items that are determined by past policies of Congress and represent commitments in future federal budgets. Most federal spending is said to be "uncontrollable," that is, based on previous decisions of Congress and not easily changed in annual budget making. Sources of uncontrollable spending include

★ *"Entitlement" programs.* Federal programs that provide classes of people with a legally enforceable right to benefits are called

FIGURE 16-2

Entitlements in the
federal budget

Source: *Budget of the
United States
Government, Fiscal
Year 1999.*

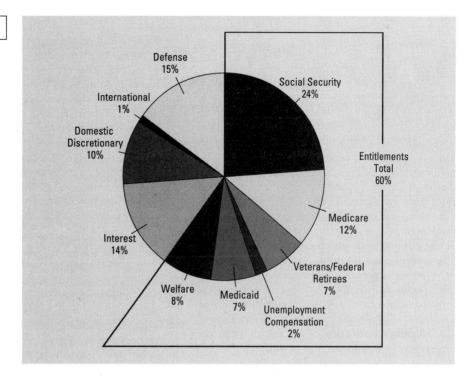

entitlement programs. Entitlement programs—including Social
Security, welfare and food stamps, Medicare and Medicaid, federal
employees' retirement, veterans' benefits, and unemployment
compensation—now account for 60 percent of all federal spending.
Entitlements are not really uncontrollable: Congress can always amend
the basic laws that established them, but doing so is politically very
difficult. Entitlements now constitute well over half of the federal
government's budget (see Figure 16-2).

★ *Indexing of benefits.* Another reason that spending increases each year
is that Congress has authorized "indexing" of benefits—automatic
increases each year based on increases in the cost of living. Benefits
under such programs as Social Security, Supplemental Security
Income, food stamps, and veterans' pensions are tied to the Consumer
Price Index. This indexing pushes up the cost of entitlement programs
each year, as do increases in the number of recipients.

★ *Increasing costs of in-kind benefits.* Rises in the costs of major in-kind
(noncash) benefits, particularly the medical costs of Medicaid and

FOCUS

The Elite Think Tanks

The nation's private policy-planning organizations, popularly referred to as "think tanks," compose the center of our elitist model of national policy making. There are a host of think tanks in Washington, but among the generally recognized elite organizations are the Brookings Institution, the American Enterprise Institute, and the Heritage Foundation. The leading think tank in the fields of foreign affairs, national security, and international trade is the Council on Foreign Relations, together with its multinational arm, the Trilateral Commission.[a]

The Brookings Institution This organization has long been the dominant policy-planning group for American domestic policy, despite the growth of other think tanks over the years. Brookings has been described as the central locus of the Washington "policy network."[b] The Brookings Institution was started early in the twentieth century with grants from Robert Brookings, a wealthy St. Louis merchant; Andrew Carnegie, head of U.S. Steel (now USX); John D. Rockefeller, founder of the Standard Oil Company (now Exxon); and Robert Eastman, founder of Kodak Corporation. Its early recommendations for economy and efficiency in government led to the Budget and Accounting Act of 1921, which established the annual unified federal budget. (Before 1921, each department submitted separate budget requests to Congress.) In the 1960s, the Brookings Institution, with grants from the Ford Foundation, helped design the War on Poverty. Today Brookings continues to influence federal tax and spending policies and social programs. It led the way in preparing President Bill Clinton's "deficit reduction" plan in 1993. Brookings staffers were influential in developing Clinton's comprehensive health-care package, and Brookings economists long pushed for the North American Free Trade Agreement.

The American Enterprise Institute For many years, Republicans dreamed of a "Brookings Institution for Republicans" that would help offset the liberal bias of Brookings. In the late 1970s, that role was assumed by the American Enterprise Institute (AEI). AEI attracted many distinguished "neoconservative" scholars who were beginning to have doubts about big government. Their work was influential in shaping Reagan administration efforts in deregulation, tax reduction, and anti-inflationary monetary policy. Today AEI harbors both moderate Republicans and pro-growth "new" Democrats.

The Heritage Foundation Conservatives gradually came to understand that without an institutional base in the capital they could never establish a strong and continuing influence in the policy network. The result of their efforts to build a "solid institutional base" and establish "a reputation for reliable scholarship and creative problem solving" is the Heritage Foundation. The initial funding came from Colorado businessman-brewer Joseph Coors, who was later joined by two drugstore magnates, Jack Eckerd of Florida and Lewis I. Lehrman of New York. Heritage boasts that it accepts no government grants or contracts and that it has a larger number of individual contributors than any other think tank. Heritage is "unabashedly conservative," but there are no specific policy initiatives that can be traced to Heritage. President Ronald Reagan once hailed the foundation as changing "the intellectual history of the West" and testified to its "enormous influence on Capitol Hill and—believe me, I know—at the White House."[c] George Bush was even more extravagant, telling Heritage, "You have been real world movers." But these plaudits were designed more to polish the conservative images of Reagan and Bush than to describe the real influence of Heritage in their administrations.

The Council on Foreign Relations The influence of the CFR throughout government is so pervasive that it is difficult to distinguish the CFR from government programs. "The Council on Foreign Relations, while not financed by government, works so closely with it that it is difficult to distinguish Council actions stimulated by government from autonomous actions."[d] Of course, the CFR denies that it exercises any control over U.S. foreign policy. Indeed, its by-laws declare that "the Council shall not take any position on questions of foreign policy and no person is authorized to speak or purport to speak for the Council on such matters."[e] But policy initiation and consensus building do not require the CFR to officially adopt policy positions.

The history of CFR policy accomplishments is dazzling. It developed the Kellogg Peace Pact in the 1920s, stiffened U.S. opposition to Japanese Pacific expansion in the 1930s, designed major portions of the United Nations' charter, and devised the "containment" policy to halt Soviet expansion in Europe after World War II. It also laid the groundwork for the NATO agreement and devised the Marshall Plan for European recovery. In the Kennedy and Johnson administrations, the Council took the lead in formulating U.S. policy in Southeast Asia—including both the initial decision to intervene militarily in Vietnam and the later decision to withdraw. Secretary of State Henry Kissinger avoided directly attributing U.S. policy to the CFR peace plan, but the plan itself eventually became the basis of the January 1973 Paris Peace Agreement.

Following Vietnam, the CFR, under David Rockefeller's tenure as chairman, developed an international campaign on behalf of "human rights" with money from the Ford, Lilly, Mellon, and Rockefeller foundations. The campaign became the centerpiece of the Carter administration's foreign policy.

Today the Council takes pride in the success of the Cold War containment policy, which was first outlined by CFR member George Kennan in his 1947 "X" article in CFR's leading publication, *Foreign Affairs.* But it recognizes that the end of the Cold War necessitates another restructuring of fundamental policy goals. Above all, the Council seeks to keep the United States actively involved in international politics; that is, to avoid isolationism, trade barriers, and "xenophobia." Its members actively support U.S. aid to Russia and other former Soviet republics, the North American Free Trade Agreement, GATT, and other efforts to stimulate global trade, an active U.S. role in peace efforts in the Middle East and in Bosnia and other republics of the former Yugoslavia, and the development of a strategy for dealing with the Islamic world.

The Trilateral Commission The Trilateral Commission was established by CFR Board Chairman David Rockefeller in 1972, with the backing of the Council and the Rockefeller Foundation. The Trilateral Commission is a small group of top officials of multinational corporations and governmental leaders of industrialized nations who meet periodically to coordinate economic policy between the United States, Western Europe, and Japan. According to David Rockefeller, a small, private group of international bankers, business leaders, and political figures—about 290 in all—can assist governments in a wide variety of decisions. "Governments don't have time to think about the broader longer-range issues," said Rockefeller, in typically elitist fashion.[f]

---

[a]Serious students of public policy are advised to read the books and journals published by these leading policy-planning organizations, especially *The Brookings Review* (published quarterly by the Brookings Institution, 1775 Massachusetts Avenue NW, Washington, DC, 20036); *The American Enterprise* (published bimonthly by the American Enterprise Institute, 1150 17th St. NW, Washington, DC, 20036); *Policy Review* (published quarterly by the Heritage Foundation, 214 Massachusetts Avenue NE, Washington, DC, 20002); and *Foreign Affairs* (published five times annually by the Council on Foreign Relations, J8 East 68th St., New York, NY 10021).

[b]Leonard Silk and Mark Silk, *The American Establishment* (New York: Basic Books, 1980), p. 160.

[c]Heritage Foundation, *Annual Report* (1985): 1.

[d]Lester Milbraith, "Interest Groups in Foreign Policy," in *Domestic Sources of Foreign Policy*, ed. James Rosenau (New York: Free Press, 1967), p. 247.

[e]Council on Foreign Relations, *Annual Report* (1992): 174.

[f]*Newsweek* (March 24, 1980): 38.

Medicare, also guarantee growth in federal spending. These in-kind benefit programs have risen faster in cost than cash benefit programs.

★ *Interest on the national debt.* The federal government has a long history of spending more each year than it receives in revenue. In 1998 the president sent the first balanced budget to Congress in thirty years. But the accumulated annual deficits over the years still leave the federal government with over $5.5 *trillion* of national debt. Interest payments on this debt make up 14 percent of federal spending.

Despite all of the pious rhetoric in Washington about the need to "balance the budget," for decades neither presidents nor Congress, Democrats nor Republicans, were willing to reduce expenditures or raise taxes to balance the budget (see "Elite Fiscal Responsibility?" in Chapter 11). Currently the federal budget is officially in balance. But it is likely that deficit spending will return. Deficit financing appeals to political elites. It allows them to provide high levels of government benefits, while avoiding the onerous task of raising taxes. To be sure, the burden of future interest payments is shifted to young people and future generations. But today's elected politicians know they will be long gone before these burdens are fully realized; their time frame is the next election.

Tax Politics

The *personal income* tax is the federal government's largest source of revenue; it accounts for 43 percent of the federal government's income (see Figure 16-3). Individual income is now taxed at five rates: 15, 28, 31, 36, and 39.6 percent, with these rising rates geared to increasing income "brackets." These are *marginal* rates, a term that economists use to mean *additional.* That is, income up to the top of the lowest bracket is taxed at 15 percent; additional income in the next bracket is taxed at 28 percent; up to the top marginal rate of 39.6 percent on income over $250,000. A personal exemption for each taxpayer and dependent together with a standard deduction for married couples and a refundable earned income tax credit ensure that the poorest families pay no income tax. (However, they still must pay Social Security taxes on wages.) Tax brackets, as well as the personal exemption and standard deduction, are indexed annually to protect against inflation.

Americans are often surprised to learn that half of all personal income is *not* taxed. The tax code is filled with exemptions, deductions, and special

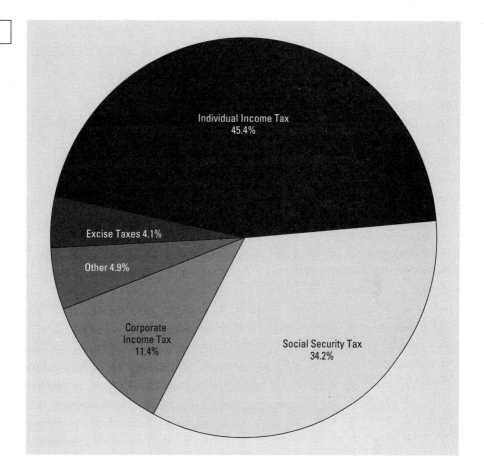

FIGURE 16-3

Sources of federal revenue

Source: *Budget of the United States Government, Fiscal Year 1999.*

treatments that allow individual taxpayers and corporations to exclude vast amounts of income from taxation. The major "tax expenditures" are

★ Personal exemption.

★ Deductibility of mortgage interest on homes.

★ Deductibility of property taxes on first and second homes.

★ Deferral of capital gains on home sales.

★ Deductibility of charitable contributions.

★ Credit for child-care expenses.

★ Exclusion of employer contributions to pension plans and medical insurance.

★ Partial exclusion of Social Security benefits.

★ Exclusion of interest on public-purpose state and local bonds.

★ Deductibility of state and local income taxes.

★ Exclusion of income earned abroad.

★ Accelerated depreciation of machinery, equipment, and structures.

★ Medical expenses over 7.5 percent of income.

Although each of these loopholes supposedly has a larger social goal behind it (for example, the deductibility of mortgage interest is supposed to stimulate the purchases and construction of homes, keeping up the value of those assets for current homeowners and keeping the construction industry employed), many of these loopholes cost far more than they are worth to society. Much of the political infighting in Washington involves interest groups trying to obtain exemptions, exclusions, deductions, and special treatment in tax laws. Former Representative Dan Rostenkowski of Chicago, once chairman of the powerful House Ways and Means Committee, before he was convicted of fraudulent use of government funds, admitted:

> *We gave oil companies breaks to fuel our oil industry. We gave real estate incentives to build more housing. We sharpened our technology with research and development credits. We gave tax breaks to encourage people to save. We pile one tax benefit on top of another—each one backed with good intention.*
>
> *Unfortunately it didn't take too long before those with the best accountants and lawyers figured out how to beat the system . . . and the cost of government was shifted to families like those in my neighborhood who don't have the guile to play the game of hide-and-seek with the IRS. . . .*
>
> *In the end tax reform comes down to a struggle between the narrow interests of the few—and the broad interests of working American families.*

Who Pays?

Tax politics also center on the issue of who actually bears the heaviest burden of a tax—especially which income groups must devote the largest proportion of their income to taxes. "Progressive" taxation requires high-income groups to pay a larger percentage of their incomes in taxes than low-income groups. "Regressive" taxation takes a larger share of the income of low-income groups. "Proportional" (flat) taxation requires all income groups to pay the same percentage of their income in taxes.

Progressive taxation is generally defended on the principle of ability to pay; the assumption is that high-income groups can afford to pay a larger percentage of their incomes into taxes at no more of a sacrifice than that required of lower-income groups to devote a smaller proportion of their income to taxation. Hence, *added* dollars of income can be taxed at higher *rates* without violating equity principles. Opponents of progressive taxation generally assert that equity can be achieved only by taxing everyone at the *same* percentage of their income, regardless of the size of their income. Progressivity penalizes initiative, enterprise, and the risk taking necessary to create new products and businesses. It reduces incentives to expand and develop the nation's economy. Highly progressive taxes curtail growth and make everyone poorer.

Reagan Tax Cuts

Certainly the most dramatic change in federal tax policy during the Reagan years was the reduction in the progressivity of individual income tax rates. The top marginal tax rate fell from 70 percent when President Reagan took office to 28 percent by the end of his administration. This reduction in progressivity in the rate structure occurred in two major tax enactments: the Economic Recovery Tax Cut Act of 1981 reduced the rate structure from 14–70 percent to 11–50 percent, and the Tax Reform Act of 1986 reduced the fourteen rate brackets varying from 11 to 50 percent to only two rate brackets, 15 and 28 percent. When the Reagan tax cuts took effect, the nation began a long economic recovery and expansion—indeed, the longest continuous period of GNP growth in the century, lasting nine years. Reagan had promised a balanced budget, but it proved impossible to cut taxes, increase defense spending, and maintain Social Security and other entitlement programs, without incurring large deficits. Indeed, during the Reagan–Bush years, the federal government ran *the largest peacetime deficits in history.*

Bush-Clinton Tax Increases

At the Republican National Convention in 1988, presidential nominee George Bush made a firm pledge to American voters that he would veto any tax increases passed by the Democratic-controlled Congress. "Read my lips!

No new taxes." Yet in a 1990 budget "summit" with Democratic congressional leaders, President Bush agreed to add a top rate of 31 percent to the personal income tax. Breaking his solemn pledge on taxes contributed heavily to Bush's defeat in the 1992 presidential election.

Clinton's 1993 "deficit reduction" plan centered on major tax increases on upper-income Americans, combined with a small increase in the corporate income tax and major cuts in defense spending. His campaign promise for a

---

FOCUS

Sneaking Preferential Treatment into the Tax Laws

All income is *not* equal under federal tax laws. Income earned from wages is taxed at *higher* top rates than income derived from the sale of investments. The tax code distinguishes between "earned income" and "capital gains"—profits from the buying and selling of property, including stocks, bonds, and real estate. Currently the top marginal rate on capital gains is 20 percent, compared to 39.6 percent on earned income.

Why should income earned from working be taxed at a higher rate than income earned from investments? The real estate industry, together with the powerful investment and securities firms, argue that high tax rates on capital gains discourage investment and economic growth. (But if it is true that high taxes discourage investment, high taxes must also discourage work, and both capital and labor are required for economic growth.) These interests had long supported preferential treatment for capital gains.[a]

A major reform in the Tax Reform Act of 1986 was the elimination of special tax preferences for capital gains. All income was to be taxed at the same rates. But George Bush was never an enthusiastic supporter of tax reform. As vice president he had tried to retain special tax breaks for the oil and gas industry, and after becoming president he pushed hard to restore preferential treatment of capital gains income.

Many Congress members are reluctant to go on record voting in favor of a tax break that clearly favors the rich. In 1990 President Bush publicly supported preferential treatment for capital gains, but many congressional Democrats sought to restore this favor to the special interests without attracting too much public attention. So the 1990 tax increase to a top rate of 31 percent was quietly made applicable *only to earned income;* capital gains would continue to be taxed at a top rate of 28 percent. The same ploy was used in 1993 when President Bill Clinton won congressional approval for additional top marginal rates of 36 and 39.6 percent: the tax on capital gains remained at 28 percent. Few Americans took notice of how a major goal of tax reform—treating all income equally—had been undone.

In 1997 a Republican Congress went even further, cutting the capital gains tax rate to 20 percent. Apparently the Republicans no longer saw any need to hide this preferential treatment in the nation's tax laws.

[a]A reasonable argument might be made that the definition of a capital gain should exclude inflationary price increases over time. That is, if the increase in the price of an asset at sale is attributable to inflation and not a true gain in value, then there should be no capital "gain" to tax. Thus, capital gains should be indexed for inflation. But federal tax laws have never done so.

"middle-class tax cut" was shelved, and Congress rejected his proposal for a broad energy tax. Clinton succeeded in getting Congress to raise taxes on:

★ *The affluent.* The tax rate for families with incomes above $140,000 a year rose from 31 percent to 36 percent, while those with incomes above $250,000 rose to 39.6 percent; estate taxes rose from 37 to 55 percent, and the affluent must pay more in Medicare taxes.

★ *The elderly.* Retired couples with incomes over $44,000 a year and singles with incomes over $34,000 must now pay income tax on 85 percent of their Social Security benefits. Premiums for Medicare also rose.

★ *Corporations.* The tax rate for corporations rose from 34 to 35 percent, and lobbying costs are no longer deductible business expenses.

A Budget Surplus?

Thirty years of deficit spending have left Americans skeptical that the federal government can really balance its budget, let alone produce a surplus. Despite President Clinton's presentation to Congress of a balanced *Budget of the United States Government* for both fiscal year 1999 and 2000, Americans in national opinion polls doubt that the federal government can continue to balance its budget.

QUESTION: *If the budget is balanced in 1999, do you think that it will stay balanced for the next several years?*

Yes	26%
No	63%

Source: Reported in *USA Today,* February 6, 1998, based on *USA Today*/CNN/Gallup poll.

Washington politicians are already arguing over what to do with projected surpluses over the next five years. Liberals have long chafed under the constraints that deficits have placed on the possibility of enacting new social welfare spending programs. They welcome projected surpluses as an opportunity to make new "investments" in children, health care, education, and the environment.

Conservatives argue that projected surpluses should be used to reduce taxes, or to pay off part of the national debt, or some combination of both.

They contend that surplus tax dollars should be returned to the American people so they can decide for themselves how to spend them. If any surplus is retained in Washington, they want it to be used to pay down the nation's $5.5 trillion debt, which would further reduce interest rates and spur additional economic growth.

Most Americans are aware that the Social Security and Medicare programs face enormous financial problems in the years ahead as more and more "baby boomers" retire. A majority of Americans appear to agree with President Clinton's announced priority for the use of budget surpluses; "Save Social Security first!"

Finally, it is interesting to note that more Americans credit "good economic conditions" (77 percent) for reducing deficits than they do either President Clinton (63 percent) or Republicans in Congress (54 percent).

SOCIAL-WELFARE POLICY

When most Americans think of social-welfare programs, they think of the poor. An estimated 36 million people in the United States (13.7 percent of the population) have incomes below the official poverty line (that is, their annual cash income falls below what is required to maintain a decent standard of living). If the approximately $1 trillion spent per year for social welfare were directly distributed to the nation's 36 million poor people, each poor person—man, woman, and child—would receive nearly $28,000 per year!

Why does poverty persist in a nation where total social-welfare spending is more than four times the amount needed to eliminate poverty? Because the poor are *not* the principal beneficiaries of social-welfare spending. Most such spending, including the largest programs—Social Security and Medicare—goes to the *non*poor. Only about one-sixth of federal social-welfare spending is "means-tested"—that is, distributed on the basis of the recipient's income. The middle class, not the poor, is the major beneficiary of the nation's social-welfare system.

Poverty in America

Poverty occurs in many kinds of families and in all races and ethnic groups. However, some groups experience poverty (low income) in greater proportions than the national average (see Table 16-1).

TABLE 16-1	

Percent living below the poverty level

Total population	13.7%
Husband-wife families	5.6
Families with female heads	32.6
White	11.2
Black	28.4
Hispanic	29.4
Over age 65	10.8
Under age 18	20.5

Source: U.S. Bureau of the Census, 1998.

Poverty is most common among families headed by women, a fact called the "feminization of poverty." (In 1996 the incidence of poverty among these families was 32.6 percent, compared with only 5.6 percent for married couples. These women and their children constitute over two-thirds of all the persons living in poverty in the United States. About one of every five children in the United States lives in poverty. Clearly, poverty is closely related to family structure. Today the disintegration of the traditional husband–wife family is the single most influential factor contributing to poverty.

Blacks also experience poverty in much greater proportions than whites. Over the years, the poverty rate among blacks in the United States has been almost three times higher than the poverty rate among whites. Poverty among Hispanics is also significantly greater than among whites.

In contrast, the aged in America experience *less* poverty than the nonaged. The aged are not poor, despite the popularity of the phrase "the poor and the aged." The percentage of persons over 65 years of age with low incomes is *below* the national average. Moreover, the aged are generally much wealthier in terms of assets and have fewer expenses than the nonaged. They are more likely than younger people to own homes with paid-off mortgages. Medicare pays a large portion of their medical expenses. With fewer expenses, the aged, even with relatively smaller cash incomes, experience poverty in a different fashion than younger mothers with children.

Entitlements

Entitlements are government benefits for which Congress has set eligibility criteria—age, income, disability, unemployment, and so on—and granted a legal entitlement to the benefits to everyone who meets the criteria. Today nearly one-third of the U.S. population receives some form of government benefits: Social Security, Medicare or Medicaid, disability insurance, unemployment compensation, government employee retirement, veterans' benefits, food stamps, school lunches, job training, public housing, and cash public-assistance benefits (see Table 16-2). The "welfare state" now encompasses a very large part of our society.

Social Security   With payments of over $400 billion to 43 million beneficiaries, Social Security is the single largest spending program in the federal budget. The Old Age and Survivors Insurance program provides monthly cash benefits to retired workers and their dependents and to survivors of insured workers. The Disability Insurance program provides monthly cash benefits for disabled workers and their dependents. An automatic, annual cost-of-living adjustment (COLA) for both programs matches any increase in the annual inflation rate. About 96 percent of the nation's paid workforce is covered by the program, which is funded by a payroll tax on employers and employees. Retirees can begin receiving full benefits at age 65, regardless of their personal wealth or income.

Unemployment compensation   Unemployment compensation temporarily replaces part of the wages of workers who lose their jobs involuntarily and helps stabilize the economy during recessions. The U.S. Department of Labor oversees the system, but states administer their own programs, with latitude within federal guidelines to define weekly benefits and other program features. Benefits are funded by a combination of federal and state unemployment taxes on employers.

Supplemental Security Income   Supplemental Security Income (SSI) is a means-tested, federally administered income assistance program that provides monthly cash payments to the needy elderly (65 or older), blind, or disabled. Benefits are indexed to (rise with) inflation; they amount to about 75 percent of the poverty line for individuals and about 89 percent for couples.

Temporary Assistance to Needy Families   Cash assistance to needy families is a means-tested, cash grant program to enable the states to assist needy children. It replaced a federal entitlement program (Aid to Families with Dependent Children) in welfare reform legislation passed by Congress in

TABLE 16-2	SOCIAL-INSURANCE PROGRAM (NO MEANS TEST)	BENEFICIARIES (MILLIONS)

Major federal social-welfare programs

SOCIAL-INSURANCE PROGRAM (NO MEANS TEST)	BENEFICIARIES (MILLIONS)
Social Security	
Total	43.4
Retirement	30.1
Survivors	7.4
Disabled	5.8
Unemployment Compensation	
Total	8.0
Government retirement and veterans	
Veterans	3.4
Federal employees	2.8
State and local	4.9
Medicare	
Total	37.5
PUBLIC ASSISTANCE PROGRAMS (MEANS TESTED)	
Cash Aid	
Assistance to Families (formerly AFDC)	13.9
Supplement Security Income (SSI)	6.5
General assistance	0.9
Medical Care	
Medicaid	36.3
Veterans	1.5
Indians	1.3
Maternal and child health	4.6
Food Benefits	
Food stamps	28.9
School lunches	14.0
Women, Infants Children (WIC)	6.5
Child and adult care food	5.2
Elderly nutrition	1.1
Housing Benefits	
Total	4.3
Education Aid	
Pell Grants	3.8
Stafford Loans	4.5
Head Start	0.5
Job Training	
Total	1.8
Energy Assistance	
Total	6.1

Source: U.S. Bureau of the Census, *Statistical Abstract of the United States,* 1997, pp. 115, 118, 375.

1996. States operate the program and define "need," they set their own benefit levels.

Medicare   Medicare is a two-part program that helps the elderly and disabled pay acute-care (as opposed to long-term-care) health costs. Hospital Insurance (Part A) helps pay the cost of hospital inpatient and skilled nursing care. Anyone 65 or older who is eligible for Social Security is automatically eligible for Part A benefits. Also eligible are people under 65 who receive Social Security disability or railroad retirement disability, and people with end-stage kidney disease. Part A is financed primarily by the 1.45 percent payroll tax collected with Social Security (FICA) withholding.

Supplemental Medical Insurance (Part B) is an optional add-on taken by virtually all those covered by Part A. It pays 80 percent of covered doctor and outpatient charges. Monthly premiums deducted from Social Security benefit checks finance about 25 percent of the cost of Part B, while most of the rest comes from general taxpayer revenues.

Medicaid   Medicaid is a federal–state program providing health services to low-income Americans. Most Medicaid spending goes to the elderly and the nonelderly disabled. However, women and children receiving cash welfare benefits automatically qualify for Medicaid, as does anyone who gets cash assistance under SSI. States can also offer Medicaid to the "medically needy"—those who face crushing medical costs but whose income or assets are too high to qualify for welfare benefits. Medicaid also pays for long-term nursing home care, but only after beneficiaries have used up all of their savings and income. The federal government pays about 57 percent of Medicaid costs, while states pick up 43 percent, both out of general taxpayer revenues.

Food stamps   The food stamp program provides low-income households with coupons that they can redeem for enough food to provide a minimal, nutritious diet. The program is overseen by the federal government but administered by the states.

Social Security Reform

Social Security benefits are paid to all eligible retirees, regardless of any other income they may receive. There is no means test for Social Security benefits. As a result, large numbers of affluent Americans receive government checks each month. Of course, they paid into Social Security during their working years and they can claim these checks as an "entitlement" under the social-insurance principle. But their prior payments amount to less than 15 percent of the benefits they currently receive.

The aged experience *less* poverty than today's workers (see Table 16-1) and possess considerably more wealth. The elderly are generally better off than the people supporting them. Moreover, they get annual cost-of-living increases (COLAs) based upon the Consumer Price Index, which estimates the cost of all consumer items each year. These costs include home buying, mortgage interest, child rearing, and other costs that most retirees do not confront. Most *workers* do not have the protection against inflation that retirees have.

Social Security is financed on a pay-as-you-go system; payments by individuals are *not* held in "reserve" by the federal government. Instead, the income from all social-insurance premiums (taxes) pays for current Social Security benefits. This generation of workers is paying for the benefits of the last generation, and this generation must hope that its future benefits will be financed by the next generation of workers. Thus, the "dependency ratio"—the number of recipients in relation to the number of contributing workers—is an important component of evaluating the future of Social Security. Americans are living longer and increasing the dependency ratio. In the early years of Social Security, there were ten workers supporting each retiree—a dependency ratio of 10 to 1. But today, as the U.S. population grows older—due to lower birth rates and longer life spans—there are only three workers for each retiree, and by 2010 the dependency ratio will rise to two workers for each retiree. In other words, the burden of Social Security may become too heavy for future workers to carry.

But Social Security is politically sacrosanct. Politicians regularly call it the "third rail of American politics"—touch it and die. As entitlement programs, Social Security and Medicare spending grow automatically each year as numbers of beneficiaries increase and COLAs raise benefit levels. As entitlement programs with strong political support, spending on them is sometimes called "uncontrollable."

But Congress can change or repeal any law it passes. Lawmakers can reduce entitlements, including Social Security and Medicare, in a variety of ways. They could legislate reductions in benefits levels; limit eligibility (for example, by increasing the age at which Social Security benefits begin); limit COLAs; or introduce means tests to deny benefits to high-income retirees.

Yet another proposed reform is to allow the Social Security trust fund to invest in the private stock market with the expectation that stock values will increase over time. This would mean shifting funds away from federal government bonds. It would mean that a government agency, presumably the Social Security Administration, would be making private stock market investment decisions for Americans. Perhaps the nation's workers would prefer a plan that allows them to deposit part of their payroll tax into an individual retirement account to buy securities of their own choosing. But such a plan would expose individuals to the risk of bad investment decisions.

Despite near universal agreement that some reforms must be undertaken to preserve social security, partisan political differences in Washington have so far prevented the enactment of any solution.

Welfare Reform

Can the government itself create poverty by fashioning social welfare programs and policies that destroy incentives to work, encourage families to break up, and condemn the poor to social dependency? Can the social welfare system sentence many people to a life of poverty who would otherwise form families, take low-paying jobs, and perhaps with hard work and perseverance gradually pull themselves and their children into the mainstream of American life?[1]

The effect of generous welfare benefits and relaxed eligibility requirements on employment has been argued for centuries. Surveys show that the poor prefer work over welfare, but welfare payments may produce subtle effects on the behavior of the poor. People unwilling to take minimum-wage jobs may never acquire the work habits required to move into better-paying jobs later in their lives. Welfare may even help to create a dependent and defeatist subculture, lowering personal self-esteem and contributing to joblessness, illegitimacy, and broken families. There is little doubt that social dependency and family structure are closely related. As noted earlier, poverty is much more frequent among female-headed households with no husband present than among husband–wife households.

Over the years, there emerged a political consensus that welfare policies were contributing to long-term social dependency. The fact that most non-poor mothers work convinced many *liberals* that welfare mothers had no special claim to stay at home with their children. And many *conservatives* acknowledged that some transitional assistance—education, job training, continued health care, and day care for children—might be necessary to move welfare mothers into the workforce.

Although President Clinton had once promised "to end welfare as we know it," it was a Republican-controlled Congress that proceeded to do so in 1996. The Republican-sponsored welfare reform legislation ended the 60-year-old federal "entitlement" of cash aid for low-income families with children—the venerable AFDC program. In its place the Republicans devised a "devolution" of responsibility to the states through federal block grants—Temporary Assistance to Needy Families—lump sum allocations to the states for cash welfare payments with benefits and eligibility requirements decided by the states. Conservatives in Congress imposed tough-minded "strings" to state aid, including a two-year limit on continuing cash benefits and a five-year lifetime limit. States were authorized to impose a "family cap" that would deny additional cash benefits to women already on welfare who bear more children; to deny cash welfare to unwed parents under 18 years of age unless they live with an adult and attend school; and to deny federally funded public assistance to illegal immigrants as well as legal immigrants who have not become citizens. Food stamps, SSI, and Medicaid were continued as federal "entitlements." President Clinton promised to "improve" welfare reform by eliminating restrictions on immigrant aid, making community service an alternative to work requirements, and so on. But continuing GOP control of Congress promises strong opposition to any efforts to "undo" welfare reform.

HEALTH-CARE POLICY

America spends more of its resources on health care than any other nation. Nearly 14 percent of the United States' GNP is devoted to health care, versus 6 to 8 percent in most other advanced nations. Nonetheless, the United States ranks well *below* other advanced nations in key measures of the health of its people, such as average life expectancy and infant death rate. Moreover, unlike most other democracies, which make provision for health care for all citizens, Americans have no guarantee of access to medical care. In short, the American health-care system is the most expensive and least universal in its coverage in the world.

Access to Care

A major challenge in health care is extending coverage to all Americans. Today about 85 percent of the nation's population is covered by either government or private health insurance. Government pays nearly half of all health-care costs—through Medicare for the aged, Medicaid for the poor, and other government programs, including military and veterans' care. Private insurance and direct payments by patients account for the remainder.

But about 15 percent of the U.S. population—an estimated 40 million Americans—have *no* medical insurance. These include (1) workers and their dependents whose employers do not offer a health insurance plan; (2) unemployed people who are not eligible for Medicare or Medicaid; and (3) self-employed people who cannot afford individual health insurance policies or who chose not to purchase them. Another 30 million Americans suffer gaps in insurance coverage in any year owing to temporary unemployment or shifts in jobs. People who lack health insurance may postpone or go without needed medical care, or be denied medical care by hospitals and physicians in all but emergency situations. Confronted with serious illness, they may be obliged to impoverish themselves in order to become eligible for Medicaid. Any unpaid medical bills must be absorbed by hospitals or shifted to paying patients and their insurance companies.

Health-Care Inflation

The costs of health care in the United States have risen much faster than prices in general. Medical costs quadrupled between 1980 and 1990. There is little cost constraint on patients and physicians when they know "third-party payers" will foot the bill. Payment by government and private insurance has contributed to health-care inflation, but there are other causes as well. Advances in medical technology have produced elaborate and expensive equipment. Hospitals that have made heavy financial investments in this equipment must use it as often as possible. Physicians trained in highly specialized techniques and procedures wish to use this equipment. The threat of malpractice suits forces doctors to practice "defensive medicine"— or order multiple tests and consultations to guard against even the most remote medical possibilities. The system encourages the provision of unnecessary tests and services.

Health-Care Reform

Health-care reform centers on two central problems: controlling costs and expanding access. These problems are related: expanding access to

Americans who are currently uninsured and closing gaps in coverage require increases in costs, even while the central thrust of reform is to bring down overall health-care costs.

Clinton's Failed Plan

President Bill Clinton campaigned on the promise to reform the nation's health-care system, both by expanding access and containing costs. Months of study by a committee headed by first lady Hillary Rodham Clinton resulted in 1993 in a 1,342-page bill to restructure completely the nation's health-care system. Its key elements included

★ Mandated employer-paid health insurance for workers and their dependents (80 percent of costs with a cap of 7.9 percent of payroll).

★ Mandated "comprehensive" benefits, including prescription drugs, mental health and substance abuse treatment, childhood immunization, dental coverage, eyeglasses for children, and all pregnancy related services, including abortion.

★ Government sponsored "health alliances" throughout the country to pool the mandated insurance premiums of firms and individuals to purchase health care from HMOs, hospitals, physicians' groups, nursing homes, and so on.

★ That all citizens and legal residents would be offered health insurance. Government subsidies would be provided for small employers and persons not covered by employer-mandated insurance.

★ Cost containment by a national health board that would set an overall health-care budget and allocate totals to health alliances around the country.

Political Opposition

The Clinton plan failed to pass Congress for a variety of reasons. The choice of a rational-comprehensive plan that would have restructured one-sixth of the economy, as opposed to more modest incremental reforms, may have been the initial mistake. The complex plan caused a great deal of public confusion and enabled opponents—notably the health insurance industry with its effective "Harry and Louise" television ads—to raise fears about the effects of the plan on consumers. Indeed, for the 85 percent of Americans already covered by public and private health insurance, the plan raised more questions than it resolved. The thrust of Clinton's proposal was "universal coverage"; the plan's major benefits went to the minority 15 percent of Americans who were uninsured. Cost containment, the greatest concern of the middle class, was largely ignored. Liberals in Congress, who favored a Canadian-style government health-care system paid for by tax increases, were only lukewarm supporters of the president's plan. Republicans and some conservative Democrats opposed employer mandates, preferring instead incremental insurance reforms—requiring companies to accept persons with "preexisting conditions" and making insurance coverage "portable," that is carryable by employees from job to job. Republicans were able to brand the president's bill as a "government takeover" of health care. The president was unwilling to consider more modest reforms. After months of debate, public opinion polls showed a majority of Americans opposing Clinton's plan.

Kennedy-Kassebaum Act

Some modest reforms were enacted in 1996 in the Kennedy-Kassebaum Act, named for its bipartisan sponsorship by liberal Democratic Senator Edward M. Kennedy of Massachusetts and moderate Republican Senator Nancy Kassebaum of Kansas. This act guarantees the "portability" of health insurance—allowing workers to maintain their insurance coverage if they lose or change jobs. Their new employer's health insurance company cannot deny them insurance for "preexisting conditions."

Health Insurance for Children and the "Near Elderly"

In his second term, President Clinton shifted his health-care strategy from his earlier comprehensive plan to more modest, incremental proposals to expand government health insurance. He advocated the expansion of Medicaid to cover children who would not otherwise qualify as poor but who are not covered by private insurance. And he proposed to extend Medicare to the "near elderly," persons between the ages of 55 and 65, who have no health insurance. But partisan differences between Congress and the White House as well as the impeachment battle stalemated virtually all major social legislation.

Summary

Public policy reflects the preferences and values of elites. Elites may consider the welfare of the masses in policy making, but it is elites, not masses, that make policy.

1. The elite model of national policy making suggests that the initial resources for policy planning are derived from corporations and personal wealth. These resources are channeled through foundations and universities in the form of grants, contracts, and endowments. The elite policy-planning organizations, such as the Brookings Institution, the American Enterprise Institute, and the Council on Foreign Relations play a central role in preparing policy recommendations and developing policy consensus among corporate, governmental, and media elites.

2. Agenda setting is deciding what will be decided, defining what conditions in society will be viewed as problems, and determining what issues will be addressed by policy makers. The pluralist model implies that agenda setting just "happens," but the elite model portrays agenda setting as the key to the policy process.

3. "Nondecisions" occur when influential individuals, organizations, or the political system prevent the emergence of challenges to the dominant values and interests in society. Keeping issues out of the political arena is an important aspect of elite power.

4. Policy formulation is the development of policy alternatives for dealing with issues on the agenda of decision makers. Policy formulation takes place in policy-planning organizations ("think tanks"), interest group offices, the White House and executive offices, and congressional committee chambers and staff offices.

5. Policy legitimation is the development of political support for policy proposals and their enactment into law. These are the activities of the president and White House staff, party and congressional leaders, and bureaucrats and interest groups. But the agenda for policy making has already been established before these "proximate policy makers" begin their work.

6. Economic policy revolves around government taxing and spending. The nation's spending is driven by entitlements, but most entitlements go to the *non*poor. Half of the nation's personal income is *not* taxed, owing to a host of exemptions, deductions, and special treatments in the tax code. Income earned from wages is taxed at *higher* top rates than income derived from capital gains.

7. American social-welfare policy benefits the nation's middle classes, not the poor. Social Security, together with Medicare, is the largest item in the federal government; it is *not* means-tested, that is, distributed on the basis of the recipient's income. Only about one-sixth of the nation's social-welfare spending is directed toward the poor.

8. America spends more on health care than any other nation, yet ranks below many advanced nations in measures of the health of its citizens. About 15 percent of Americans have no health insurance, and health-care costs have risen faster than the rate of inflation. Health-care reform centers on the problems of expanding access and controlling costs.

Notes

1. See Charles Murray, *Losing Ground* (New York: Basic Books, 1984), p. 165.

Selected Readings

Aaron, Henry J., and Charles E. Schultze, eds. *Setting Domestic Priorities.* Washington, D.C.: Brookings Institution, 1992. The nation's policy agenda as set forth by the influential policy-planning organization, the Brookings Institution.

Clinton, Bill, and Al Gore. *Putting People First.* New York: Times Books, 1992. Policy directions for the Clinton administration set forth during the presidential campaign.

Mead, Lawrence M. *The New Politics of Poverty.* New York: Basic Books, 1992. A persuasive argument that the underlying problem of poverty today is one of social values—resocializing the dependent poor—rather than the provision of jobs.

Murray, Charles. *Losing Ground.* New York: Basic Books, 1984. A well-argued, yet controversial, thesis that government social-welfare programs, by encouraging social dependency, have had the unintended and perverse effect of slowing and even reversing earlier progress in reducing poverty, crime, ignorance, and discrimination.

Wilson, William J. *The Truly Disadvantaged.* Chicago: University of Chicago Press, 1987. The thesis here is that the growth of the "underclass" is primarily a result of the decline of manufacturing jobs and their shift to the suburbs, and the resulting concentration of poor, jobless, isolated people in the inner city.

Epilogue

What Can Students Do?

The kind of elitists I admire are those who ruthlessly seek out and encourage intelligence and who believe that competition—and, inevitably, some measure of failure—will do more for character than coddling ever can. My kind of elitist does not grade on a curve and is willing to flunk the whole class.

—WILLIAM A. HENRY III

Regardless of what students are told by high school graduation speakers about their ability to reshape the world, elites—not students—govern the nation. It will be a long while before anyone in college today occupies a position of power allowing him or her to shape American society. In the meantime, what can students really do to help preserve democratic values?

1. *Avoid being exploited or used by demagogues of the left or right.* It is wise to lower your expectations about short-term possibilities for change. Excessive idealism, coupled with impatience to change society now, leads only to bitterness and disillusionment. In the long run, these feelings may reduce rather than increase your political effectiveness. Excessive idealism can also expose you to the demagogic appeals of those politicians who exploit others' idealism for their own advantage. Understanding your personal limits in shaping the world and resolving society's problems is important. It is time to reexamine adolescent optimism about "changing the world."

2. *Develop your powers to think critically.* You will benefit from reexamining the "truths" taught in the public schools—looking beyond the slogans of democracy (and of Marxism) to the realities of power in contemporary

"Résumés over there."

society. Just as this book has tried to reexamine traditional teachings about American government, concerned students should also critically reexamine the economic system, the social system, the communications system, and even the accepted "truths" of the physical and biological sciences. Developing your independent powers of social and political analysis can help you resist the flood tide of popular rhetoric, the symbolic posturing of politicians, the pseudoscience of the bureaucratic social engineers. You can learn to be wary of the politician or bureaucrat who promises to solve society's problems with a stroke of the pen: to end racism, eliminate poverty, cure the sick, prevent crime, clean the air and water, provide new energy, all without imposing any new taxes or further restricting individual freedom. You will learn that society's problems have no simple solutions.

3. *Master the technological revolution rather than letting it master you.* For example, you should endeavor to learn about one or more aspects of technology in the pursuit of your education. If computers are going to direct your life, why not learn some computer technology yourself? The same applies to social institutions. If laws regulate your life, why not master some aspects of the law yourself, even as an undergraduate? If you are going to be

the object of the administrative, managerial, and budgetary practices of large bureaucracies, why not learn something about these subjects, for self-defense if nothing else? If you are not majoring in any of the physical or biological sciences, why not explore some of these courses—perhaps on a pass-fail basis if your school permits it? The more you know about today's technology, the less impressed you will be when someone tells you that certain policies are "technological requirements."

4. *Become familiar with the meaning of individual freedom and dignity throughout the ages.* Read about and understand the human quest for freedom in many times and cultures—from St. Thomas More to Aleksandr Solzhenitsyn, from Antigone to Galileo. You should also learn to view American democracy from a world perspective, comparing the personal freedoms we enjoy with those existing in other nations. It is one thing to struggle against mindless corporate and governmental bureaucracies in this country but quite another to conclude that the United States is "not worth saving"— especially when viewing the personal liberties of Americans in the context of the personal restrictions in many other nations.

5. *Maintain a healthy distrust of government and assume responsibility for your own life.* Personal freedom is most endangered when we place too much trust in government, see great idealism in its actions, and have unquestioning faith in our public leaders. Democratic values—individual dignity, freedom of speech and press, rights of dissent, personal liberty—are safer when we are suspicious of government and its power and worry about its size and complexity. Perhaps the most important danger to a free people is that they "politicize" all the problems confronting them as individuals, they blame government and "society" for the problems that beset them, and they therefore excuse themselves from personal efforts to confront these problems. If we look to government to resolve all our problems, our social dependency will increase, and we will assume less responsibility for our lives. The traditional democratic value is to encourage individuals to shape their own destinies.

Appendix

The Constitution of the United States of America

We the People of the United States, in Order to form a more perfect Union, establish Justice, insure domestic Tranquility, provide for the common defense, promote the general Welfare, and secure the Blessings of Liberty to ourselves and our Posterity, do ordain and establish this Constitution for the United States of America.

—**PREAMBLE TO THE CONSTITUTION OF THE UNITED STATES OF AMERICA**

ARTICLE 1

Section 1 All legislative Powers herein granted shall be vested in a Congress of the United States, which shall consist of a Senate and House of Representatives.

Section 2 The House of Representatives shall be composed of Members chosen every second Year by the People of the several States, and the Electors in each State shall have the Qualifications requisite for Electors of the most numerous Branch of the State Legislature.

No Person shall be a Representative who shall not have attained to the age of twenty five Years, and been seven Years a Citizen of the United States, and who shall not, when elected, be an Inhabitant of that State in which he shall be chosen.

Representatives and direct Taxes shall be apportioned among the several States which may be included within this Union, according to their respective Numbers, *which shall be determined by adding to the whole Number of free Persons, including those bound to Service for a Term of Years, and excluding Indians not taxed, three fifths of all other persons.* *

The actual Enumeration shall be made within three Years after the first Meeting of the Congress of the United States, and within every subsequent Term of ten Years, in such Manner as they shall by Law direct. The Number of Representatives shall not exceed one for every thirty Thousand, but each State shall have at Least one Representative, and until such enumeration shall be made, the State of New Hampshire shall be entitled to chuse three, Massachusetts eight, Rhode-Island and Providence Plantations one, Connecticut five, New York six, New Jersey four, Pennsylvania eight, Delaware one, Maryland six, Virginia ten, North Carolina five, South Carolina five, and Georgia three.

When vacancies happen in the Representation from any State, the Executive Authority thereof shall issue Writs of Election to fill such Vacancies.

The House of Representatives shall chuse their Speaker and other Officers; and shall have the sole Power of Impeachment.

Section 3   The Senate of the United States shall be composed of two Senators from each State, *chosen by the Legislature thereof,*† for six Years; and each Senator shall have one Vote.

Immediately after they shall be assembled in Consequence of the first Election, they shall be divided as equally as may be into three Classes. The Seats of the Senators of the first Class shall be vacated at the Expiration of the second Year, of the second Class at the Expiration of the fourth Year, and of the third Class at the Expiration of the sixth Year, so that one third may be chosen every second Year; *and if Vacancies happen by Resignation, or otherwise, during the Recess of the Legislature of any State, the Executive thereof may make temporary Appointments until the next Meeting of the Legislature, which shall then fill such Vacancies.* **

No Person shall be a Senator who shall not have attained to the Age of thirty Years, and been nine Years a Citizen of the United States, and who shall not, when elected, be an Inhabitant of the State for which he shall be chosen.

---

*Superseded by the Fourteenth Amendment. Throughout, italics indicate passages altered by subsequent amendments.
†See Seventeenth Amendment.
**See Seventeenth Amendment.

The Vice President of the United States shall be President of the Senate, but shall have no Vote, unless they be equally divided.

The Senate shall chuse their other Officers, and also a President pro tempore, in the Absence of the Vice President, or when he shall exercise the Office of President of the United States.

The Senate shall have the sole Power to try all Impeachments. When sitting for that Purpose, they shall be on Oath or Affirmation. When the President of the United States is tried, the Chief Justice shall preside: And no Person shall be convicted without the Concurrence of two thirds of the Members present.

Judgment in Cases of Impeachment shall not extend further than to removal from Office, and disqualification to hold and enjoy any Office of Honor, Trust or Profit under the United States: but the party convicted shall nevertheless be liable and subject to Indictment, Trial, Judgment and Punishment, according to Law.

Section 4   The Times, Places and Manner of holding Elections for Senators and Representatives, shall be prescribed in each State by the Legislature thereof; but the Congress may at any time by Law make or alter such Regulations, except as to the Places of chusing Senators.

The congress shall assemble at least once in every Year, and such Meeting shall be on the first Monday in December, unless they shall by Law appoint a different Day. *

Section 5   Each House shall be the Judge of the Elections, Returns and Qualifications of its own Members, and a Majority of each shall constitute a Quorum to do Business; but a smaller Number may adjourn from day to day, and may be authorized to compel the Attendance of absent Members, in such Manner, and under such Penalties as each House may provide.

Each House may determine the Rules of its Proceedings, punish its Members for disorderly Behaviour, and, with the Concurrence of two thirds, expel a Member.

Each House shall keep a Journal of its Proceedings, and from time to time publish the same, excepting such Parts as may in their Judgment require Secrecy; and the Yeas and Nays of the Members of either House on any question shall, at the Desire of one fifth of those Present, be entered on the Journal.

*See Twentieth Amendment.

Neither House, during the Session of Congress, shall, without the Consent of the other, adjourn for more than three days, nor to any other Place than that in which the two Houses shall be sitting.

Section 6 The Senators and Representatives shall receive a Compensation for their Services, to be ascertained by law, and paid out of the Treasury of the United States. They shall in all Cases, except Treason, Felony and Breach of the Peace, be privileged from Arrest during their Attendance at the Session of their respective Houses, and in going to and returning from the same; and for any Speech or Debate in either House, they shall not be questioned in any other Place.

No Senator or Representative shall, during the Time for which he was elected, be appointed to any civil Office under the Authority of the United States, which shall have been created, or the Emoluments whereof shall have been increased during such time; and no Person holding any Office under the United States, shall be a Member of either House during his Continuance in Office.

Section 7 All Bills for raising Revenue shall originate in the House of Representatives; but the Senate may propose or concur with Amendments as on other Bills.

Every Bill which shall have passed the House of Representatives and the Senate, shall, before it become a Law, be presented to the President of the United States; If he approves he shall sign it, but if not he shall return it, with his Objections to that House in which it shall have originated, who shall enter the Objections at large on their Journal, and proceed to reconsider it. If after such Reconsideration two thirds of that House shall agree to pass the Bill, it shall be sent, together with the Objections, to the other House, by which it shall likewise be reconsidered, and if approved by two thirds of that House, it shall become a Law. But in all such Cases the Votes of both Houses shall be determined by Yeas and Nays, and the Names of the Persons voting for and against the Bill shall be entered on the Journal of each House respectively. If any Bill shall not be returned by the President within ten Days (Sundays excepted) after it shall have been presented to him, the Same shall be a Law, in like Manner as if he had signed it, unless the Congress by their Adjournment prevent its Return, in which Case it shall not be a Law.

Every Order, Resolution, or Vote to which the concurrence of the Senate and House of Representatives may be necessary (except on a question of Adjournment) shall be presented to the President of the United States; and before the Same shall take Effect, shall be approved by him, or being disapproved by him, shall be repassed by two thirds of the Senate and House of Representatives, according to the Rules and Limitations prescribed in the Case of a Bill.

Section 8 The Congress shall have Power To lay and collect Taxes, Duties, Imposts and Excises, to pay the Debts and provide for the common Defense and general Welfare of the United States; but all Duties, Imposts and Excises shall be uniform throughout the United States;

To borrow Money on the credit of the United States;

To regulate Commerce with foreign Nations, and among the several States, and with the Indian Tribes;

To establish a uniform Rule of Naturalization, and uniform Laws on the subject of Bankruptcies throughout the United States;

To coin Money, regulate the Value thereof, and of foreign Coin, and fix the Standard of Weights and Measures;

To provide for the Punishment of counterfeiting the Securities and current Coin of the United States;

To establish Post Offices and post Roads;

To promote the Progress of Science and useful Arts, by securing for limited times to Authors and Inventors the exclusive Right to their respective Writings and Discoveries;

To constitute Tribunals inferior to the Supreme Court;

To define and punish Piracies and Felonies committed on the high Seas, and Offences against the Law of Nations;

To declare War, grant Letters of Marque and Reprisal, and make Rules concerning Captures on Land and Water;

To raise and support Armies, but no Appropriation of Money to that Use shall be for a longer Term than two Years;

To provide and maintain a Navy;

To make Rules for the Government and Regulation of the land and naval Forces;

To provide for calling forth the Militia to execute the Laws of the Union, suppress Insurrections and repel Invasions;

To provide for organizing, arming, and disciplining the Militia, and for governing such Part of them as may be employed in the Service of the United States, reserving to the States respectively, the Appointment of the Officers, and the Authority of training the Militia according to the discipline prescribed by Congress;

To exercise exclusive Legislation in all Cases whatsoever, over such District (not exceeding ten Miles square) as may, by Cession of particular States, and the Acceptance of Congress, become the Seat of the Government of the United States, and to exercise like Authority over all Places purchased by the Consent of the Legislature of the State in which the Same shall be, for the Erection of Forts, Magazines, Arsenals, dock-Yards, and other needful Buildings;—And

To make all Laws which shall be necessary and proper for carrying into Execution the foregoing Powers, and all other Powers vested by this Constitution in the Government of the United States, or in any Department or Officer thereof.

Section 9 The Migration or Importation of such Persons as any of the States now existing shall think proper to admit, shall not be prohibited by the Congress prior to the Year one thousand eight hundred and eight, but a Tax or duty may be imposed on such Importation, not exceeding ten dollars for each Person.

The Privilege of the Writ of Habeas Corpus shall not be suspended, unless when in Cases of Rebellion or Invasion the public Safety may require it.

No Bill of Attainder or ex post facto Law shall be passed.

No Capitation, or other direct, Tax shall be laid, unless in Proportion to the Census or Enumeration herein before directed to be taken.

No Tax or Duty shall be laid on Articles exported from any State.

No Preference shall be given by any Regulation of Commerce or Revenue to the Ports of one State over those of another: nor shall Vessels bound to, or from, one State be obliged to enter, clear, or pay Duties in another.

No Money shall be drawn from the Treasury, but in Consequence of Appropriations made by Law; and a regular Statement and Account of the Receipts and Expenditures of all public Money shall be published from time to time.

No Title of Nobility shall be granted by the United States: And no Person holding any Office or Profit or Trust under them, shall, without the Consent of the Congress, accept of any present, Emolument, Office, or Title, of any kind whatever, from any King, Prince, or foreign State.

Section 10 No State shall enter into any Treaty, Alliance, or Confederation; grant Letters of Marque and Reprisal; coin Money; emit Bills of Credit; make any Thing but gold and silver Coin a Tender in Payment of Debts; pass any Bill of Attainder, ex post facto Law, or Law impairing the Obligation of Contracts, or grant any Title of Nobility.

No State shall, without the Consent of the Congress, lay any Imposts or Duties on Imports or Exports, except what may be absolutely necessary for executing its inspection Laws: and the net Produce of all Duties and Imposts, laid by any State on Imports or Exports, shall be for the Use of the Treasury of the United States; and all such Laws shall be subject to the Revision and Control of the Congress.

No State shall, without the Consent of Congress, lay any Duty of Tonnage, keep Troops, or Ships of War in time of Peace, enter into any Agreement or Compact with another State, or with a foreign Power, or engage in War, unless actually invaded, or in such imminent Danger as will not admit of delay.

ARTICLE II

Section 1 The executive Power shall be vested in a President of the United States of America. He shall hold Office during the Term of four Years, and, together with the Vice President, chosen for the same Term, be elected, as follows:

Each State shall appoint, in such Manner as the Legislature thereof may direct, a Number of Electors, equal to the whole Number of Senators and Representatives to which the State may be entitled in the Congress: but no Senator or Representative, or Person holding an Office of Trust or Profit under the United States, shall be appointed an Elector.

The Electors shall meet in their respective States, and vote by Ballot for two Persons, of whom one at least shall not be an Inhabitant of the same State with themselves. And they shall make a List of all the Persons voted for, and of the Number of Votes for each; which List they shall sign and certify, and transmit sealed to the Seat of the Government of the United States, directed to the President of the Senate. The President of the Senate shall, in the Presence of the Senate and House of Representatives, open all the Certificates, and the Votes shall then be counted. The Person having the greatest Number of Votes shall be the President, if such Number be a Majority of the whole Number of Electors appointed; and if there be more than one who have such Majority, and have an equal Number of Votes, then the House of Representatives shall immediately chuse by Ballot one of them for President, and if no Person have a Majority, then from the five highest on the List the said House shall in like Manner chuse the President. But in chusing the President, Votes shall be taken by States, the Representation from each State having one Vote: A quorum for this Purpose shall consist of a Member or Members from two thirds of the States, and a Majority of all the States shall be necessary to a Choice. In every Case, after the Choice of the President, the Person having the greatest Number of Votes of the Electors shall be the Vice President. But if there should remain two or more who have equal Votes, the Senate shall chuse from them by Ballot the Vice President. *

The Congress may determine the Time of chusing the Electors, and the Day on which they shall give their Votes; which Day shall be the same throughout the United States.

No Person except a natural born Citizen, or a Citizen of the United States, at the time of the Adoption of this Constitution, shall be eligible to the Office of President; neither shall any Person be eligible to that Office who shall not have attained to the Age of thirty five Years, and been fourteen Years a Resident within the United States.

In Case of the Removal of the President from Office, or of his Death, Resignation, or Inability to discharge the Powers and Duties of the said Office, the Same shall devolve on the Vice President, and the Congress may by Law provide for the Case of Removal, Death, Resignation or Inability, both of the President and Vice President, declaring what Officer shall then act as President, and such Officer shall act accordingly, until the Disability be removed, or a President shall be elected. †

The President shall, at stated Times, receive for his Services, a Compensation which shall neither be encreased nor diminished during the Period for which he shall have been elected, and he shall not receive within the Period any other Emolument from the United States, or any of them.

Before he enter on the Execution of his Office, he shall take the following Oath or Affirmation:—"I do solemnly swear (or affirm) that I will faithfully execute the Office of President of the United States, and will to the best of my Ability, preserve, protect and defend the Constitution of the United States."

Section 2 The President shall be the Commander in Chief of the Army and Navy of the United States, and of the Militia of the several States, when called into the actual Service of the United States; he may require the Opinion, in writing, of the principal Officer in each of the executive Departments, upon any Subject relating to the Duties of their respective Offices, and he shall have Power to grant Reprieves and Pardons for Offences against the United States, except in Cases of Impeachment.

*Superseded by the Twelfth Amendment.
†See Twenty-Fifth Amendment.

He shall have Power, by and with the Advice and Consent of the Senate, to make Treaties, provided two thirds of the Senators present concur; and he shall nominate, and by and with the Advice and consent of the Senate, shall appoint Ambassadors, other public Ministers and Consuls, Judges of the Supreme Court, and all other Officers of the United States, whose Appointments are not herein otherwise provided for, and which shall be established by Law: but the Congress may by Law vest the Appointment of such inferior officers, as they think proper, in the President alone, in the Courts of Law, or in the Heads of Departments.

The President shall have Power to fill up all Vacancies that may happen during the Recess of the Senate, by granting Commissions which shall expire at the End of their next Session.

Section 3 He shall from time to time give to the Congress Information of the State of the Union, and recommend to their Consideration such Measures as he shall judge necessary and expedient; he may, on extraordinary Occasions, convene both Houses, or either of them, and in Case of Disagreement between them, with Respect to the Time of Adjournment, he may adjourn them to such Time as he shall think proper; he shall receive Ambassadors and other public Ministers; he shall take Care that the Laws be faithfully executed, and shall Commission all the Officers of the United States.

Section 4 The President, Vice President, and all civil Officers of the United States, shall be removed from Office on Impeachment for, and Conviction of, Treason, Bribery, or other high Crimes and Misdemeanors.

ARTICLE III

Section 1 The judicial Power of the United States, shall be vested in one supreme Court and in such inferior Courts as the Congress may from time to time ordain and establish. The Judges, both of the supreme and inferior Courts, shall hold their Offices during good Behaviour, and shall, at stated times, receive for their Services, a Compensation, which shall not be diminished during their Continuance in Office.

Section 2 The judicial Power shall extend to all Cases, in Law and Equity, arising under this Constitution, the Laws of the United States, and Treaties made, or which shall be made, under their Authority;—to all Cases affecting Ambassadors, other public Ministers and Consuls;—to all Cases of admiralty and maritime Jurisdiction;—to Controversies to which the United States shall be a Party;—to Controversies between two or more States;—*between a State and Citizens of another State*;*—between Citizens of different States;—between Citizens of the same State claiming Lands under Grants of different States, and *between a State or the Citizens thereof, and foreign States, Citizens, or Subjects.*†

In all Cases affecting Ambassadors, other public Ministers and Consuls, and those in which a State shall be Party, the supreme Court shall have original Jurisdiction. In all the other Cases before mentioned, the supreme Court shall have appellate Jurisdiction, both as to Law and Fact, with such Exceptions, and under such Regulations as the Congress shall make.

The Trial of all Crimes, except in Cases of Impeachment, shall be by Jury; and such Trial shall be held in the State where the said Crimes shall have been committed; but when not committed within any State, the Trial shall be at such Place or Places as the Congress may by Law have directed.

Section 3   Treason against the United States, shall consist only in levying War against them, or in adhering to their Enemies, giving them Aid and Comfort. No Person shall be convicted of Treason unless on the Testimony of two Witnesses to the same overt Act, or on Confession in open Court.

The Congress shall have Power to declare the Punishment of Treason, but no Attainder of Treason shall work Corruption of Blood, or Forfeiture except during the Life of the Person attained.

ARTICLE IV

Section 1   Full Faith and Credit shall be given in each State to the public Acts, Records, and judicial Proceedings of every other State. And the Congress may by general Laws prescribe the Manner in which such Acts, Records, and Proceedings shall be proved, and the Effect thereof.

Section 2   The Citizens of each State shall be entitled to all Privileges and Immunities of Citizens in the several States.

A Person charged in any State with Treason, Felony, or other Crime, who shall flee from Justice, and be found in another State, shall on Demand

*See Eleventh Amendment.
†See Eleventh Amendment.

of the executive Authority of the State from which he fled, be delivered up, to be removed to the State having Jurisdiction of the Crime.

No Person held to Service of Labour in one State, under the Laws thereof, escaping into another, shall, in Consequence of any Law or Regulation therein, be discharged from such Service or Labour, but shall be delivered up on Claim of the Party to whom such Service of Labour may be due. *

Section 3   New States may be admitted by the Congress into this Union; but no new State shall be formed or erected within the Jurisdiction of any other State; nor any State be formed by the Junction of two or more States, or Parts of States, without the Consent of the Legislatures of the States concerned as well as of the Congress.

The Congress shall have Power to dispose of and make all needful Rules and Regulations respecting the Territory or other Property belonging to the United States; and nothing in this Constitution shall be so construed as to Prejudice any claims of the United States, or of any particular State.

Section 4   The United States shall guarantee to every State in this Union a Republican Form of Government, and shall protect each of them against Invasion; and on Application of the Legislature, or of the Executive (when the Legislature cannot be convened) against domestic Violence.

ARTICLE V

The Congress, whenever two thirds of both Houses shall deem it necessary, shall propose Amendments to this Constitution, or, on the Application of the Legislatures of two thirds of the several States, shall call a Convention for proposing Amendments, which, in either Case, shall be valid to all Intents and Purposes, as Part of this Constitution, when ratified by the Legislatures of three fourths of the several States, or by Conventions in three fourths thereof, as the one or the other Mode of Ratification may be proposed by the Congress; Provided that no Amendment which may be made prior to the Year One thousand eight hundred and eight shall in any Manner affect the first and fourth clauses in the Ninth Section of the first Article; and that no State, without its Consent, shall be deprived of its equal Suffrage in the Senate.

*See Thirteenth Amendment.

ARTICLE VI

All debts contracted and Engagements entered into, before the Adoption of this Constitution, shall be as valid against the United States under this Constitution, as under the Confederation.

This Constitution, and the Laws of the United States which shall be made in Pursuance thereof; and all Treaties made, or which shall be made, under the Authority of the United States, shall be the supreme Law of the Land; and the Judges in every State shall be bound thereby, any Thing in the Constitution or Laws of any State to the Contrary notwithstanding.

The Senators and Representatives before mentioned, and the Members of the several State Legislatures, and all executive and judicial Officers, both of the United States and of the several States, shall be bound by Oath or Affirmation, to support this Constitution; but no religious Test shall ever be required as a Qualification to any Office or public Trust under the United States.

ARTICLE VII

The Ratification of the Conventions of nine States, shall be sufficient for the Establishment of this Constitution between the States so ratifying the Same.

Done in Contention by the Unanimous Consent of the States present the Seventeenth Day of September in the Year of our Lord one thousand seven hundred and eighty seven and of the Independence of the United States of America the Twelfth. In witness whereof We have hereunto subscribed our Names.

Articles in Addition to, and Amendment of, the Constitution of the United States of America, Proposed by Congress, and Ratified by the Several States, Pursuant to the Fifth Article of the Original Constitution:

AMENDMENT I

(Ratification of the first ten amendments was completed December 15, 1791.)

Congress shall make no law respecting an establishment of religion, or prohibiting the free exercise thereof; or abridging the freedom of speech, or of the press; or the right of the people peaceably to assemble, and to petition the Government for a redress of grievances.

AMENDMENT II

A well regulated Militia, being necessary to the security of a free State, the right of the people to keep and bear Arms, shall not be infringed.

AMENDMENT III

No Soldier shall, in time of peace be quartered in any house, without the consent of the Owner, nor in time of war, but in a manner to be prescribed by law.

AMENDMENT IV

The right of the people to be secure in their persons, houses, papers, and effects, against unreasonable searches and seizures, shall not be violated, and no Warrants shall issue, but upon probable cause, supported by Oath or affirmation, and particularly describing the place to be searched, and the persons or things to be seized.

AMENDMENT V

No person shall be held to answer for a capital, or otherwise infamous crime, unless on a presentment or indictment of a Grand Jury, except in cases arising in the land or naval forces, or in the Militia, when in actual service in time of War or public danger; nor shall any person be subject for the same offence to be twice put in jeopardy of life or limb; nor shall be compelled in any criminal case to be a witness against himself, nor be deprived of life, liberty, or property, without due process of law; nor shall private property be taken for public use, without just compensation.

AMENDMENT VI

In all criminal prosecutions, the accused shall enjoy the right to a speedy and public trial, by an impartial jury of the State and district wherein the crime shall have been committed, which district shall have been previously ascertained by law, and to be informed of the nature and cause of the accusation; to be confronted with the witnesses against him; to have compulsory process for obtaining witnesses in his favor, and to have the Assistance of Counsel for his defense.

AMENDMENT VII

In Suits at common law, where the value in controversy shall exceed twenty dollars, the right of trial by jury shall be preserved, and no fact tried by a jury, shall be otherwise reexamined in any Court of the United States, than according to the rules of the common law.

AMENDMENT VIII

Excessive bail shall not be required, nor excessive fines imposed, nor cruel and unusual punishments inflicted.

AMENDMENT IX

The enumeration in the Constitution, of certain rights, shall not be construed to deny or disparage others retained by the people.

AMENDMENT X

The powers not delegated to the United States by the Constitution, nor prohibited by it to the States, are reserved to the States respectively, or to the people.

AMENDMENT XI (1795)

The Judicial power of the United States shall not be construed to extend to any suit in law or equity, commenced or prosecuted against one of the United States by Citizens of another State, or by Citizens or Subjects of any Foreign State.

AMENDMENT XII (1804)

The Electors shall meet in their respective states and vote by ballot for President and Vice President, one of whom, at least, shall not be an inhabitant of the same state with themselves; they shall name in their ballots the person voted for as President, and in distinct ballots the person voted for as Vice President, and they shall make distinct lists of all persons voted for as President, and of all persons voted for as Vice President, and of the number of votes for each, which lists they shall sign and certify, and transmit sealed to the seat of the government of the United States, directed to the President of the Senate;—The President of the Senate shall, in the presence of the Senate and House of Representatives, open all the certificates and the votes shall then be counted;—the person having the greatest number of votes for President, shall be the President, if such number be a majority of the whole number of Electors appointed; and if no person have such majority, then from the persons having the highest numbers not exceeding three on the list of those voted for as President, the House of Representatives shall choose immediately, by ballot, the President. But in choosing the President, the votes shall be taken by states, the representation from each state having one vote; a quorum for this purpose shall consist of a member or members from two-thirds of the states, and a majority of all the states shall be necessary to a choice. And if the House of Representatives shall not choose a President whenever the right of choice shall devolve upon them, *before the fourth day of March next following,* * then the Vice President shall act as President, as in the case of the death or other constitutional disability of the President.— The person having the greatest number of votes as Vice President shall be the Vice President, if such number be a majority of the whole number of Electors appointed, and if no person have a majority, then from the two highest numbers on the list, the Senate shall choose the Vice President; a quorum for the purpose shall consist of two-thirds of the whole number of Senators, and a majority of the whole number shall be necessary to a choice. But no person constitutionally ineligible to the office of President shall be eligible to that of Vice President of the United States.

AMENDMENT XIII (1865)

Section 1   Neither slavery nor involuntary servitude, except as a punishment for crime whereof the party shall have been duly convicted, shall exist within the United States, or any place subject to their jurisdiction.

Section 2   Congress shall have the power to enforce this article by appropriate legislation.

*Altered by the Twentieth Amendment.

AMENDMENT XIV (1868)

Section 1   All persons born or naturalized in the United States, and subject to the jurisdiction thereof, are citizens of the United States and the State wherein they reside. No State shall make or enforce any law which shall abridge the privileges or immunities of citizens of the United States; nor shall any State deprive any person of life, liberty, or property, without due process of law; nor deny to any person within its jurisdiction the equal protection of the laws.

Section 2   Representatives shall be apportioned among the several States according to their respective numbers, counting the whole number of persons in each State, excluding Indians not taxed. But when the right to vote at any election for the choice of electors for President and Vice President of the United States, Representatives in Congress, the Executive and Judicial officers of a State, or the members of the Legislature thereof, is denied to any of the male inhabitants of such State, being twenty-one years of age, and citizens of the United States, or in any way abridged, except for participation in rebellion, or other crime, the basis of representation therein shall be reduced in the proportion which the number of such male citizens shall bear to the whole number of male citizens twenty-one years of age in such State.

Section 3   No person shall be a Senator or Representative in Congress, or elector of President and Vice President, or hold any office, civil or military, under the United States, or under any State, who, having previously taken an oath, as a member of Congress, or as an officer of the United States, or as a member of any State legislature, or as an executive or judicial officer of any State, to support the Constitution of the United States, shall have engaged in insurrection or rebellion against the same, or given aid or comfort to the enemies thereof. But Congress may by a vote of two-thirds of each House, remove such disability.

Section 4   The validity of the public debt of the United States, authorized by law, including debts incurred for payment of pensions and bounties for services in suppressing insurrection or rebellion, shall not be questioned. But neither the United States nor any State shall assume or pay any debt or obligation incurred in aid of insurrection or rebellion against the United States, or any claim for the loss or emancipation of any slave; but all debts, obligations, and claims shall be held illegal and void.

Section 5   The Congress shall have power to enforce, by appropriate legislation, the provisions of this article.

AMENDMENT XV (1870)

Section 1   The right of citizens of the United States to vote shall not be denied or abridged by the United States or by any State on account of race, color, or previous condition of servitude.

Section 2   The Congress shall have power to enforce this article by appropriate legislation.

AMENDMENT XVI (1913)

The Congress shall have power to lay and collect taxes on incomes, from whatever source derived, without apportionment among the several States, and without regard to any census or enumeration.

AMENDMENT XVII (1913)

The Senate of the United States shall be composed of two Senators from each State, elected by the people thereof, for six years; and each Senator shall have one vote. The electors in each State shall have the qualifications requisite for electors of the most numerous branch of the State legislature.

When vacancies happen in the representation of any State in the Senate, the executive authority of such State shall issue writs of election to fill such vacancies: *Provided*, That the legislature of any State may empower the executive thereof to make temporary appointments until the people fill the vacancies by election as the legislature may direct.

This amendment shall not be so construed as to affect the election or term of any Senator chosen before it becomes valid as part of the Constitution.

AMENDMENT XVIII (1919)

Section 1   After one year from the ratification of this article the manufacture, sale, or transportation of intoxicating liquors within, the importation thereof into, or the exportation thereof from the United States and all territory subject to the jurisdiction thereof for beverage purposes is hereby prohibited.

Section 2 The Congress and the several States shall have concurrent power to enforce this article by appropriate legislation.

Section 3 This article shall be inoperative unless it shall have been ratified as an amendment to the Constitution by the legislatures of the several States, as provided in the Constitution, within seven years from the date of submission hereof to the States by the Congress.*

AMENDMENT XIX (1920)

The right of citizens of the United States to vote shall not be denied or abridged by the United States or by any State on account of sex.

Congress shall have power to enforce this article by appropriate legislation.

AMENDMENT XX (1933)

Section 1 The terms of the President and Vice President shall end at noon on the 20th day of January, and the terms of Senators and Representatives at noon on the 3rd day of January, of the years in which such terms would have ended if this article had not been ratified; and the terms of their successors shall then begin.

Section 2 The Congress shall assemble at least once in every year, and such meeting shall begin at noon on the 3rd day of January, unless they shall by law appoint a different day.

Section 3 If, at the time fixed for the beginning of the term of the President, the President elect shall have died, the Vice President elect shall become President. If a President shall not have been chosen before the time fixed for the beginning of his term, or if the President elect shall have failed to qualify, then the Vice President elect shall act as President until a President shall have qualified; and the Congress may by law provide for the case wherein

*Repealed by the Twenty-First Amendment.

neither a President elect nor a Vice President elect shall have qualified, declaring who shall then act as President, or the manner in which one who is to act shall be selected, and such person shall act accordingly until a President or Vice President shall have qualified.

Section 4 The Congress may by law provide for the case of the death of any of the persons from whom the House of Representatives may choose a President whenever the right of choice shall have devolved upon them, and for the case of the death of any of the persons from whom the Senate may choose a Vice President whenever the right of choice shall have devolved upon them.

Section 5 Sections 1 and 2 shall take effect on the 15th day of October following ratification of this article.

Section 6 This article shall be inoperative unless it shall have been ratified as an amendment to the Constitution by the legislatures of three-fourths of the several States within seven years from the date of its submission.

AMENDMENT XXI (1933)

Section 1 The eighteenth article of amendment to the Constitution of the United States is hereby repealed.

Section 2 The transportation or importation into any State, Territory, or possession of the United States for delivery or use therein of intoxicating liquors, in violation of the laws thereof, is hereby prohibited.

Section 3 This article shall be inoperative unless it shall have been ratified as an amendment to the Constitution by conventions in the several States, as provided in the Constitution, within seven years from the date of submission thereof to the States by the Congress.

AMENDMENT XXII (1951)

Section 1 No person shall be elected to the office of the President more than twice, and no person who has held the office of President, or acted as President for more than two years of a term to which some other person was elected President shall be elected to the office of President more than once. But this Article shall not apply to any person holding the office of President when this Article was proposed by the Congress, and shall not prevent any person who may be holding the office of President, or acting as President, during the term within which this Article becomes operative from holding the office of President or acting as President during the remainder of such term.

Section 3 This article shall be inoperative unless it shall have been ratified as an amendment to the Constitution by the legislatures of three-fourths of the several States within seven years from the date of its submission to the States by the Congress.

AMENDMENT XXIII (1961)

Section 1 The District constituting the seat of Government of the United States shall appoint in such manner as the Congress may direct:

A number of electors of President and Vice President equal to the whole number of Senators and Representatives in Congress to which the District would be entitled if it were a State, but in no event more than the least populous State; they shall be in addition to those appointed by the States, but they shall be considered, for the purposes of the election of President and Vice President, to be electors appointed by a State; and they shall meet in the District and perform such duties as provided by the twelfth article of amendment.

Section 2 The Congress shall have power to enforce this article by appropriate legislation.

AMENDMENT XXIV (1964)

Section 1 The right of citizens of the United States to vote in any primary or other election for President or Vice President, for electors for President or Vice President, or for Senator or Representative in Congress, shall not be denied or abridged by the United States or any state by reason of failure to pay any poll tax or other tax.

Section 2 The Congress shall have the power to enforce this article by appropriate legislation.

AMENDMENT XXV (1967)

Section 1   In case of the removal of the President from office or of his death or resignation, the Vice President shall become President.

Section 2   Whenever there is a vacancy in the office of the Vice President, the President shall nominate a Vice President who shall take office upon confirmation by a majority vote of both Houses of Congress.

Section 3   Whenever the President transmits to the President pro tempore of the Senate and the Speaker of the House of Representatives his written declaration that he is unable to discharge the powers and duties of his office, and until he transmits to them a written declaration to the contrary, such powers and duties shall be discharged by the Vice President as Acting President.

Section 4   Whenever the Vice President and a majority of either the principal officers of the executive departments or of such other body as Congress may by law provide, transmit to the President pro tempore of the Senate and the Speaker of the House of Representatives their written declaration that the President is unable to discharge the powers and duties of his office, the Vice President shall immediately assume the powers and duties of the office as Acting President.

Thereafter, when the President transmits to the President pro tempore of the Senate and the Speaker of the House of Representatives his written declaration that no inability exists, he shall resume the powers and duties of his office unless the Vice President and a majority of either the principal officers of the executive departments or of such other body as Congress may by law provide, transmit within four days to the President pro tempore of the Senate and the Speaker of the House of Representatives their written declaration that the President is unable to discharge the powers and duties of his office. Thereupon Congress shall decide the issue, assembling within forty-eight hours for that purpose if not in session. If the Congress, within twenty-one days after the receipt of the latter written declaration, or, if Congress is not in session, within twenty-one days after Congress is required to assemble, determines by two-thirds vote of both Houses that the President is unable to discharge the powers and duties of his office, the Vice President shall continue to discharge the same as Acting President; otherwise, the President shall resume the powers and duties of his office.

AMENDMENT XXVI (1971)

Section 1   The right of citizens of the United States, who are eighteen years of age or older, to vote shall not be denied or abridged by the United States or any state on account of age.

Section 2   The Congress shall have the power to enforce this article by appropriate legislation.

AMENDMENT XXVII (1992)

No law, varying the compensation for the service of the Senators and Representatives shall take effect, until an election of Representatives shall have intervened.*

*The 27th Amendment (1992), proposed in 1789 by James Madison, became law more than two centuries later when ratified by the Michigan legislature on May 7, 1992.

Index